BASIC CONCEPTS IN DATA PROCESSING

BASIC CONCEPTS
IN DATA PROCESSING

MARJORIE LEESON

Delta College / University Center, Michigan

WM. C. BROWN COMPANY PUBLISHERS
Dubuque, Iowa

To my family
Glen, Bruce, and Gary

CONTENTS

PREFACE

This book is written for the introductory study of data processing. It is equally well suited for schools with or without data processing equipment, since actual examples and lucid graphic illustrations are provided. Many realistic, accurate, and easy-to-comprehend examples are used which assume no prior knowledge of either data processing or *any other field*. Entire systems are presented in depth in order to provide a comprehensive understanding of data flow, systems design, software development, documentation, operations, data entry, and control. Computer systems are presented as a method of processing, retrieving, and utilizing all types of data.

Flexibility in content and organization of an individual course is provided through the use of a *modular* approach. Each module contains the following features: A quick overview of what should be gained from studying the module is shown by a listing of topics and questions. Another preview of the module's contents is provided by the written introduction. Questions which both challenge thinking and reinforce concepts, as they are presented, are found throughout the module. These questions can also be used as a method of self-evaluation since complete and comprehensive answers are available at the end of the module. The unique, and sometimes strange, vocabulary of data processing often provides an unnecessary hurdle. To prevent this from occurring, clear, concise definitions are provided for all of the "key" terms used within the module. Each module is concluded with a brief summary.

By the use of a case study, along with the modular approach, most data processing concepts are introduced, covered in more depth, and then reinforced. Lou, founder of the rapidly expanding L. C. Smith Corporation, and his need for an improved data processing system are introduced in module 1. The case study is used to bring in the "human element" and to *again* reinforce data processing concepts in a realistic and practical setting. A simplified sales order system illustrates data flow, editing and checking techniques, control totals, processing of the data, and documentation. By providing continuity in the examples used, the systems can be contrasted. Entire systems—the CPU, peripherals, and the software—are presented. As Smith's data processing needs become more complex, so do their hardware and software.

Module 1 provides an overview of the evolution of electronic data processing and its importance in today's society. Many of the typical examples found in data processing texts have been omitted in order to make the introductory module more relevant, timely, and interesting. As Lou's story unfolds, the need for better data processing methods is made more meaningful, and much of the basic terminology to be used throughout the case study is effectively explained.

Module 2 highlights the principles of punched card data processing utilizing unit record equipment. The concepts stressed in the module are the ones which are relevant to computerized data processing.

"Systems and Options for the Small Company," module 3, presents the choices which are now available such as the utilization of a service bureau, a time-sharing service, or a small computer system. The study of three small computer systems, and how they can be expanded, introduces many computer concepts. The potential of a system is presented by studying the characteristics of the CPU, the peripherals, and the software. Application packages and IBM's customizer services are presented as possible alternatives to the development by a company of its own software.

Module 4, "Basic Computer and Programming Concepts," not only reinforces many of the ideas presented in module 3, but also covers in depth the computer's functional units, methods of storing data, numbering systems, validity checks, and types of languages used to develop software. Common programming tasks and techniques are explained in order to stress the importance of software as it relates to both the computer's potential and the integrity of the data. The discussion of the hardware and software of a medium-size system relates and reinforces the many new concepts presented in the module. The medium-size system is also used to introduce, in an almost casual manner, the more detailed study of I/O devices, multiprogramming, operating systems, and the expansion of a batch system to a large-scale online, real-time system.

Input/output devices are covered in module 5. The data flow of the sales invoicing system is illustrated by the use of card-, tape-, and disk-oriented systems. The advantages and disadvantages of the more conventional card punch, card reader, printer, magnetic tape, and disk are contrasted to different types

Mary Beth Hughes
Mary Morrissey

Art Work

Marcia Compton and Sharlene Smeage

The assistance that Debbie Schroeder provided cannot be put into one single category. Debbie, who is now a Programmer/Analyst with Michigan Bell, was a very valuable consultant, programmer, secretary, typist, keypunch operator, and friend. Without Deb's help the book and project manual would not have been written.

Vendors

Richard A. French, Cincinnati Milacron
A. Guy Simmons, Control Data Corporation
Charleston W. Stephens, General Automation Inc.
Charles Donegan, Hewlett-Packard
Travis Henry, Honeywell
Buck Morrison, IBM Corporation
David W. Storey, Kodak
Gary Warner, Mohawk Data Sciences
George Willett, National Cash Register
Brent Braddock, Teletype Corporation
John Humphrey, Texas Instruments
M. Katzman, Bendix Corporation

Case Studies and Examples

Mr. Charles Scott, Blue Cross of Florida, Inc.
Mr. William Dana, Bay City Samaritan Hospital
Mr. Lloyd Smith and G. A. Momany, Dow Chemical
Mr. Presley Williams, First Savings & Loan
Mr. Rodger Gach, Sperry Univac Computer Systems
Mr. Roger Mikusek, Wesley's Data Processing, Inc.

The book could have been dedicated to either the students or administration of Delta College. Many very fine Delta students provided suggestions and encouragement. The administration of the college provided counsel, support, and assistance throughout the project.

of optical character recognition equipment, terminals, computer output to microfilm and offline printers.

"Designing Systems and Procedures," module 6, uses the case study to provide a realistic illustration which starts with the receipt of a request for systems work and is concluded with the testing, documentation, and evaluation of the procedure. Used in the documentation are forms, computer printouts, flowcharts, and decision tables.

Each language module, RPG, COBOL, and FORTRAN, contains a brief overview of the characteristics and unique features of the language. The same example is used in all three modules which makes it easy to contrast the detail required, power, and syntax of the three languages. A sufficient number of commands are illustrated, and explained, to enable the student to write programs which utilize sequential files and printed reports.

The role of the operating system, as well as some of its typical features, is covered in module 10. Although the concepts presented, such as interrupts, messages to the operator, multiprogramming, job priorities, SPOOLing, data base management, and virtual storage, are complex, they are clearly stated, well illustrated, and will be easily understood. Whenever possible, actual examples are used in order to make the concepts less abstract.

The three actual case studies used in module 11, Blue Cross of Florida, Inc., The First Savings and Loan Association, and the Dow Chemical Company, explain how each company's time-sharing system was developed. The material presented in each case study provides reinforcement and review of systems development, operating systems, accuracy control, protection of files, and illustrates the necessary hardware, software, and personnel requirements.

Module 12 provides a brief review of both the case study and the development of computer technology. Not only are the characteristics of the minicomputer and how they are used in industry, business, and education covered, but in direct contrast a "super" system, the Burroughs 7700, is covered in some depth. The potential of the microcomputer in industrial application is also covered in the review of the "state of the art."

As the book is reviewed, the following features should be observed by the reader:

- The ease with which most of the illustrations can be comprehended.
- The presentation of entire systems which range from "mini" systems to extremely sophisticated large-scale systems.
- The emphasis placed on software and the individual's role in data processing.
- The emphasis placed on the need for adequate controls and documentation for all systems to insure the integrity and security of the data.

- The manner in which a topic is introduced, covered in more depth, and then referred to in the case studies or in other illustrations to provide reinforcement of learning.
- Familiar examples and terms are used, whenever possible, in presenting new data processing concepts.
- The major emphasis is placed on data entry, control, and documentation.

The Project Manual provides realistic projects which vary in complexity and are designed to illustrate the activities performed by individuals engaged in data processing. Study guides are also available which will help to reinforce the concepts presented in the textbook.

The Teacher's Guide includes many items which will make the use of *Basic Concepts in Data Processing* easier. The suggested performance objectives, for each module, show the anticipated learning level. Since the objectives are measurable, tests are provided which will determine if the objectives have been met. Also included in the Teacher's Guide are the solutions to all problems, exercises, tests, and materials from which to make overhead transparencies. Computer printouts which show the source code, input, and output are provided for all programming problems.

ACKNOWLEDGMENTS

Each book published is made possible by combining ability, talent, and help of a great many people. A very sincere thank-you is given to all of the people listed who were so gracious in providing much needed assistance.

Advisory Committee

The advisory committee reviewed the performance objectives and the outline from which the book was developed.

Mr. Lloyd Smith, Dow Chemical Company
Mr. Robert Huskins, Frankenmuth Mutual Life Insurance Company
Mr. James Hatch, General Motors
Mr. A. James Devers, First Savings and Loan
Mr. Stan Rowe, Dow Corning Corporation
Mr. Dennis McNeal, Delta College
Mr. Richard Niemann, Delta College
Mr. Ben Paulson, Systems Analyst, Delta College
Mr. Gene Phillips, Averill Career Center

Student Reviewers

Although many students have used a large percentage of the material which appears in the text, the following former students patiently and carefully reviewed and critiqued the manuscript.

Russell Rousseau
Theresa Kroll

BASIC DATA 1
PROCESSING
CONCEPTS

Who are the data processors riding around on the cloud and what do they do? The systems analyst and the programmer still appear to many people to live in a world apart. With whom can they communicate? As you listen to them talk, strange words and phrases float down, such as "bits" and "bytes," "hardware" and "software," "shall we go with CRTs or COM," "will it be COBOL or FORTRAN," "how much of the CPU does your supervisor get when he resides in the CPU," and so forth. At last, you have found something that you have in common, as you know what a supervisor is. But wait, where is the CPU that he lives in? A supervisor stays in his office. Maybe the supervisor isn't really a person?

As you explore data processing you will find that the language really isn't all that strange, and what the programmer and analyst do is very logical and understandable. The analyst determines the best way, perhaps with the computer's help, to get a job done. If the computer is to be used, the programmer tells it what to do.

For many of you learning about what programmers and analysts do and how they communicate with their computers can be enjoyable, beneficial, and fun. Since data processing is usually logical, you can, after studying the information that is available, apply reasoning to a given situation and come up with some solutions to problems.

You may be thinking, "so it's going to be fun? How about letting us in on what data processing is?"

A WORKABLE DEFINITION

Data processing is capturing data and putting it in a form which can be easily utilized and retrieved.

Although many definitions are available for data processing, it is not as important that you memorize a precise definition as it is for you to understand the concepts that are involved in the processing of data. What should be done and how it can be done most effectively are the two prime considerations. *A definition, as such, is of no value unless an understanding of why data processing is vitally important today, and what all it encompasses, is achieved.*

Since to many people the data processing terminology seems almost a foreign language, definitions of the terms will be given so that we may effectively communicate. Once you learn the terms associated with data processing, you will find that the concepts are logical and relatively simple.

Data processing starts whenever an event takes place. The data is then worked with in a variety of ways and finally emerges in a form that can be easily retrieved and effectively utilized. The event that takes place can be almost anything—an increase in pressure in a manufacturing process or the winning of the Kentucky Derby.

In the case of the manufacturing process, an analysis can take place at the source as to what caused the increase in pressure, how often it has happened in the past, and corrective action may be automatically set into motion as the result of the information obtained by processing the data. The data is also stored so it can be retrieved easily and used again. This example could well represent one of the ultimate goals in data processing: to capture, or record, in machine processing form, the data, as the event, in this case a manufacturing process, takes place. The data is then analyzed and used in a decision-making process. *What occurs is an endless cycling of the recording of the event, the analysis of the data, and, when necessary, corrective action.*

Why is this concept a goal of data processing? In the case of a manufacturing process, if the corrective action can take place almost at the same moment in time as when the problem occurs, there will be fewer spoiled products. The consumer, you and I, will get better products and production costs will be lower. Can this "feedback" occur in the more traditional data processing involving business transactions? The answer is obviously "yes,"

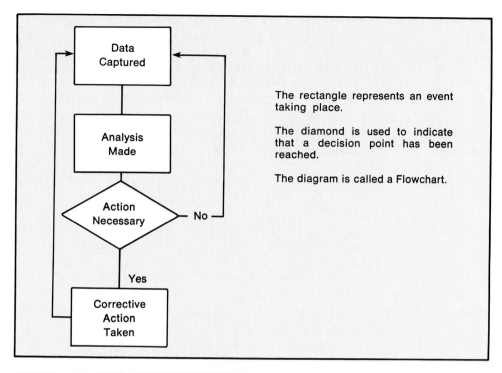

The rectangle represents an event taking place.

The diamond is used to indicate that a decision point has been reached.

The diagram is called a Flowchart.

FIGURE 1–1. A GOAL OF DATA PROCESSING

as it is also important in business applications that corrective decisions be made rapidly. For example, a salesman enters an order for ten tires but unfortunately uses the product description for tires and the part number for tractors. What happens if corrective action is not taken and the order is processed? Ten tractors may be shipped and it will be costly to get the tractors back. In addition, the customer is unhappy because he did not receive the tires which he ordered.

If the firm can prevent an error from occurring by utilizing data processing more effectively, many problems such as shipping the wrong merchandise can be avoided. There are basic concepts involved in data processing that will help lessen the chance of such a situation occurring. There is also equipment available and people who can effectively tell it what to do and provide the corrective action necessary before the mistake is implemented. You will learn about the concepts involved, the *hardware* (machines), and the *men*.

The concept of data being processed so that it is available for the decision-making process is important. The second event mentioned earlier, the horse race, has a different pattern than the manufacturing process because the race is won and done with, and the data pertaining to it becomes a part of a vast amount of information which will be used in many different ways. It is vital that information be stored in such a way that it can be quickly retrieved, when needed, and processed. Selection of the right equipment, methods, and personnel to achieve the desired goals in both types of situations is critical.

It may be some time before you will realize the full impact of the simple definition for data processing that was given: **data processing is capturing data and putting it in a form which can be easily utilized and retrieved.** How *is* it captured, utilized, and retrieved? These are the questions that the text will cover.

The term *captured* may seem a strange one to use in the definition, but it implies that data needs to be contained and held on to! It has been said that the amount of data is doubling every eight years. How can this vast amount of new data be kept in a form readily usable? For example, a recent medical study was made at a tremendous cost, both in terms of dollars and in time, and when the data was analyzed and the results ready for publication it was found that the same exact research had been done many years before. The identical conclusions had been reached! The results of the first study had been available— if you knew where to find them! Had some of the *now available* techniques of data processing been employed, with the results of the first study easily accessible, the costly duplication of effort could have been avoided.

Many people associate the term data processing with higher mathematics. The level and amount of mathematics involved, however, depends entirely upon the application for which the computer is being used. The problems and examples associated with this text involve only the use of very simple arithmetic, *but will require you to think.*

Data processing need not involve the use of computers. Does this statement surprise you? If a poll were taken on Main Street today, many, or perhaps most people, would define data processing by stating, "It is using computers." Although computers play an increasingly important part in data processing, *the concepts and definition also apply to methods that do not involve their use.*

It is also true that in the past (the far distant computer past—say 15 years ago) management was more concerned with the processing, which is the manipulation of the data, than with how data could be successfully captured in a machine-readable form. Now, many managers, especially those who have been involved in data processing for a decade or more, are looking for better ways to record the data *at the source* where the transaction occurs. In the case of the manufacturing process, "capturing the data at the source" was illustrated because as the event took place, the data was entered into the analysis and decision-making process.

A transaction, or event, in a business application is defined as an exchange of one value for another. In the case of the customer who finally got his ten tires, wouldn't it have been tremendous if his order could have gone directly into processing, within seconds after it was placed, with any necessary corrective action being taken automatically? His correct order would have been quickly started on its way, he would have been much happier, and the company selling the tires would have saved both time and money. The illustration may sound simple, but rather complex concepts are involved. For this reason, throughout the text basic concepts will be developed using simple illustrations and methods. When an automated order system, with corrective actions built in for many common occurrences, is presented in detail, you will understand what must be done to achieve such a system.

UP TO THIS POINT

1–1. In simple terms, what is a programmer?
1–2. A bowler gets a strike while bowling. Is data processing involved?
1–3. Corrective action is taken after data is analyzed. Is this important in business data processing?
1–4. There are really four different concepts in the definition of data processing. Capturing the data, manipulating the data, and storing the data are three of the concepts. What is the fourth?
1–5. Is a computer always used in data processing?
1–6. What is a flowchart?
1–7. On a flowchart what is the diamond used for?
1–8. Why is learning terms so important in data processing?

IS DATA PROCESSING NEW?

Man has been processing data since the beginning of time. Perhaps the early cliff dweller made a mark on the wall each time large game was killed. Each year he compared the number of marks with the total from the previous year. He may not have known that he was doing data processing but the results were used in determining if he, along with his fellow cave dwellers, should move to a new location where the hunting would be better. He had recorded the data, calculated the data, and made his decision based upon the results of processing the data.

THE DATA PROCESSING CYCLE

As time passed and life became more complex, improved and more sophisticated methods of processing data were, of necessity, developed. But even in the simplest example of a data processing cycle, there is always: *input*, *processing*, and *output*. Since data is processed and then made available for future uses, the *output* from one operation may become the input for the next procedure.

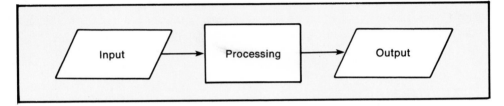

FIGURE 1-2. THE DATA PROCESSING CYCLE

The new terms should be explained in understandable definitions:

Input—information to be processed
Processing—the manipulation of the input which may involve one simple operation or a series of activities
Output—the end result of processing

In using electronic data processing (EDP) many forms of input are available to the user. The term *electronic data processing* indicates that the computer, which is an electronic device capable of extremely fast calculations, will be utilized in the processing of the data. The kind of *input* devices that a firm uses depends upon the type of jobs it has, the costs of the different devices, the volume of work that is to be done, and the funds available for data processing.

Processing can involve one or more of the four basic processing functions:

1. Sequencing—putting the information in a predetermined order
2. Merging—combining the new information with existing information
3. Calculating—anywhere from one very basic arithmetic operation to thousands of complex operations using higher mathematics may be performed
4. Summarizing—condensing the information so that it can be utilized more effectively by management

Output, which is the result of processing, can also utilize many different devices. There are now a wide range of devices available and the decision of which to use depends upon the needs of the company processing the data and the funds available.

JUST CHECKING

1–9. What are the three elements in the data processing cycle?
1–10. What is the information to be processed?
1–11. What is the end result of processing?
1–12. Three of the four processing functions are sequencing, merging, and calculating. What is the fourth processing function?
1–13. In any one job must all four processing functions be present?

SYSTEMS AND PROCEDURES

Is data processing really so hard? You already know a definition for data processing, what a programmer and a systems analyst do, and the three steps in the data processing cycle. In addition, you should be able to define input, processing, and output. The utopia, or ultimate goal, is to have the data entered directly into the SYSTEM as the transaction, or event, takes place. A data processing system is defined as an orderly means of accomplishing one or more procedures or tasks. Simple uncomplicated tasks make up procedures which in turn make up the more complex data processing systems.

Figure 1–3 is oversimplified but illustrates the concept. An entire payroll system might involve 50 or 60 individual procedures. The payroll system is part of the company's overall information processing system.

Each task in figure 1–3 represents a data processing cycle. Figure 1–4 shows what is involved in task 3, the time card procedure.

DECISION MAKING

Data can originate from many different sources. Regardless of the source, it must be processed if it is to be used effectively. One of the most important uses of output is its utilization by management in the decision-making process.

A patient recovering from surgery is monitored and data is both created and processed pertaining to his heart rate, respiratory rate, and other vital

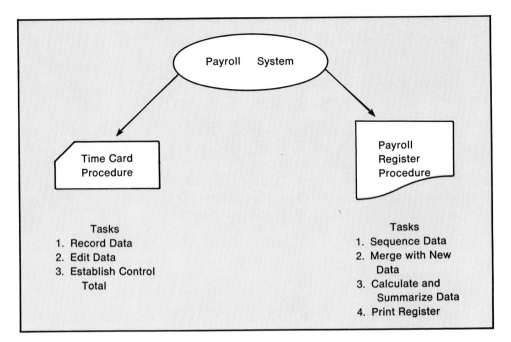

FIGURE 1–3. THE SYSTEMS CONCEPT

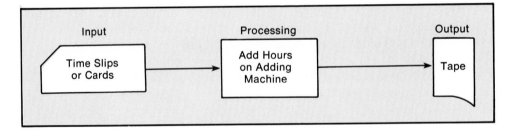

FIGURE 1–4. ESTABLISHING CONTROL TOTAL

life processes. Management, or doctors, in this case, use the processed data in making decisions pertaining to the treatment that the patient will receive.

The football coach has his assistants record the statistics of Saturday's football game. The data is processed and becomes part of the information that the coach must use in determining his strategy for next Saturday's game. Not only is the data that he processed used but other variables such as the statistics of the other team, on whose field the game will be played, and the anticipated weather must all be considered.

A marketing research department is responsible for determining how much advertising should be conducted in each section of the country for their company's many products. They must also advise the production department as to how much of each product should be manufactured. The current sales information, historical information pertaining to past sales of both their company and their competitors, and many other factors must be utilized to make a reasonably intelligent decision. Data processing can provide the information that is used and assist management in many other ways in making the decisions that are required.

Data is fed back to earth as space missions are carried out. As the flight is in progress the data is instantaneously processed, and if corrective action is necessary, a revised plan can be put into effect immediately. After the flight is over the data is also utilized to determine if changes should be made in the basic design of the spacecraft. All of the planning for future flights is based upon the analysis of the vast amount of information that has been collected during the many flights in space.

As our society becomes more complex the need for more information on which to base complex decisions becomes increasingly apparent. How can the need be met? Did technology respond to the need?

BEFORE YOU CONTINUE

1–14. What is an organized method of accomplishing a given task?
1–15. Systems are made up of procedures. What makes up procedures?
1–16. Why is it essential that management has relevant timely information?

DATA PROCESSING METHODS

Data may be processed in one of four ways:

> Manually
> Mechanically
> Electromechanically
> Electronically

The four methods are sequenced not only from the earliest means available to the newest methods but also in what might be termed the levels of sophistication. For each situation the best method, depending upon the factors involved, must be selected. Computers, or electronic data processing, may not always be the best solution.

Manual Data Processing

When the total length of time is considered in which man has inhabited the earth, it was only yesterday that any method, other than manual, was available. There are still many tasks that are part of the total system that are accomplished manually, and in studying how to improve present systems, improvement of manual operations should not be overlooked.

Regardless of the "computer power" that might be available there may be certain tasks that should be done manually, because it is the most economical and practical way of performing the task. Consider the following example:

A special seminar on drug education is conducted. Since the Department of State wants an alphabetic listing of the name and address of each individual who attended the seminar, each person as he registers for the conference fills out a card which will supply the required data.

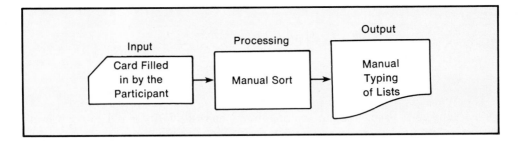

FIGURE 1–5. REGISTERING FOR THE CONFERENCE

In a sense the concept of *source data automation* is present. Processable input is prepared by each individual as he registers for the conference. The manual sort for the 20 cards is accomplished in approximately one minute, while a good typist should complete the job in less than ten minutes. Since the information pertaining to the people attending the conference is not available in the school's data processing system, any other method would be both more costly and time consuming. Some manual methods will always be employed, even by firms who have very sophisticated electronic equipment, because the task to be performed can be accomplished more economically manually.

Manual methods alone were enough for the small amount of data that had to be processed when we were a young nation and 90% of our population was self-employed, primarily in agriculture. The few small businesses which were operated to provide products and services had little data to process. *Today it would be impossible to process all of the data available if only manual methods were available.*

Mechanical Data Processing

As a need developed new methods were devised. The term *mechanical data processing* implies that mechanical (not electronic) equipment such as adding machines, cash registers, and calculators are utilized.

The way in which the development of the early calculating machines occurred reflects the fact that until recently a need for fast calculation, analysis, and retrieval of information was not felt.

The first adding machine was developed by Pascal in 1642 and not until 50 years later was a calculator, which could do all four arithmetic functions, invented. The early calculator had one basic problem: it wasn't always correct. Not much additional progress was made until 1834 when Babbage, a professor of mathematics, partially built the "analytical engine" which would have been the first completely automatic mechanical general purpose digital computer. Babbage, however, did not live to complete his analytical engine. In 1872, Baldwin and Thomas, who had an idea similar to Babbage's, designed and developed the first calculator that was considered successful. They also founded the first calculating machine company in the United States. It took 250 years from the time the first adding machine was developed until a reliable, workable calculator that could perform all four arithmetic functions was developed. Since a need for fast data processing equipment was not yet felt, people were not as motivated to work in this direction. As computers are discussed, contrast their history and how rapidly developments were made with the progression from a crude adding machine to a similarly crude calculator.

Other Alternatives

Many businesses today still use only simple mechanical machines for all of their data processing. The difference between now and 50 years ago is that there are many feasible alternatives from which the best method for data processing can be selected. Some of the alternatives from which to choose are:

1. Continue using only simple office equipment such as typewriters, calculators, cash registers, and perhaps duplicating equipment.
2. Update the present office equipment by replacing it with some of the smaller, more efficient, electronic models which are available. You have all seen

the electronic calculators and adding machines that are now on the market. If not, visit almost any department store or office equipment company.

3. Use electromechanical equipment to process the punched card.
4. Use the facilities of a service bureau that specializes in doing data processing for other businesses.
5. Join with others engaged in similar business operations to purchase or rent more sophisticated computers and related equipment and share the costs.

How should the choice be made? The selection of the right method for each individual or business is never an easy decision. There are techniques that can be utilized in making the decision which can prove to be very helpful. After a study is made to determine what action should be taken, the conclusion may be that mechanical methods will most effectively meet the needs of the individual company. Perhaps a portion of the work will be sent to a service bureau that utilizes a computer. The study may also recommend basic improvements in some of the manual methods that are being used. Creativity and ingenuity, usually associated with computer applications, can be equally as important in the design of either mechanical or manual systems. The word "system" used in this manner merely means the way in which a firm organizes and processes its data.

An Improved Manual Method

A rather imaginative and creative office employee was responsible for doing a small payroll every two weeks. Since the information regarding the employees' earnings had to be entered *manually* in four different places the procedure took approximately two days to complete. After the procedure was redesigned, using only very simple mechanical equipment, the time spent in producing the payroll was cut to ½ day. The records were also less likely to have errors as the information had to be entered only one time. Figure 1–6 illustrates the procedure.

Although the system is purely mechanical, some very basic concepts are illustrated.

1. *The time sheets are both edited and calculated.* The editing or checking is done to make certain that the information is correct; because once it enters the system, it will be utilized on all four forms.
2. *Batch totals* are utilized. Batch totals, which are totals taken on a given quantity of data, are used to establish *controls*. If the total hours added from the time sheets is 1,592 hours and the total obtained by adding the hours from the current earnings report is 1,602, there obviously is a problem.

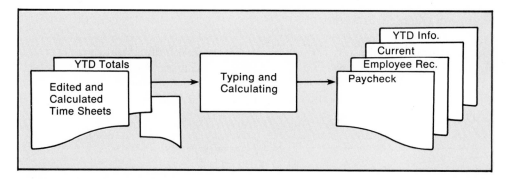

FIGURE 1–6. MECHANICAL METHOD

When procedures are run which have batch totals or control totals the job is not released until the error is found. In the illustration, the checks would not be released, nor would the job be considered finished, until the error was found and corrected. If the totals had balanced, it would have *indicated* that the time sheets for all employees had been processed and that the hours had been correctly entered on all of the forms.

Careful planning and good forms design were the two key factors which in the illustration made it possible to do the job in one-fourth of the time that it took under the former manual method. Many small companies still use systems which are designed around a "write it once principle" that utilize pre-designed forms and simple office machines. Today some of these systems are really unique and well designed.

The entry of valid, complete, and timely data into the system and then making it available for many different procedures is the key to successful applications that use the next two methods: electromechanical and electronic.

REVIEW QUESTIONS

1–17. Based upon the total history of man, why weren't fast accurate computer devices developed until recently?

1–18. Does an individual, who has little data to be processed, have any option other than to process the data manually or mechanically?

1–19. What does editing mean when it is used as a term in explaining a data processing task or procedure?

1–20. The employee's hours are added from both the time card and the report listing his current earnings. What term is used to refer to the total hours?

Electromechanical Methods

A simple term that is often used for electromechanical data processing is unit-record. The terms *tab, unit-record, tabulating,* or *electromechanical* are all used to identify the equipment that is used to process the punched card. Figure 1–7 shows the card that is often called the IBM card or the "standard" punched card.

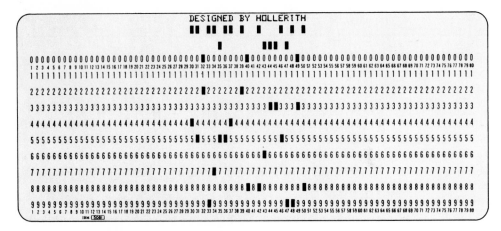

FIGURE 1–7. STANDARD PUNCHED CARD

The Standard Punched Card

How long has the card illustrated, which has 80 columns, been in existence? Again the man on Main Street will usually answer 10 or 20 years. The card was actually designed, in its present form, in 1888. The story behind its design and usage illustrates the point that when a need develops new technology usually emerges.

Dr. Herman Hollerith, who was a statistician, was employed by the U.S. Census Bureau in 1880 to design a system that would speed up the processing of the census data. Today he would have been called a *systems analyst.* The 1880 census, using the old method, took 7½ years just to process the data. With an increase in population expected, due to the large numbers of people who were still immigrating to the United States, it was anticipated that the 1890 census would take 11 years. Two key words exist in determining if processed information is useful: *reliable* and *timely.* Would the information from 1890 census be useful if not available until 1901?

Dr. Hollerith came up with a new system in time for the 1890 census, which used the card, a punch, electromagnetic counters, and a sorting box.

The equipment first was designed for punching paper strips but the card soon replaced the strips. The 1890 census data was tabulated in 2½ years! For that period of time, this achievement was considered fantastic.

The punched card can be used to activate hundreds of different kinds of machines. It is interesting to observe that the card has remained almost totally unchanged in design. When the card was about 70 years old, International Business Machines (IBM) announced the new innovation—round corners—that you see on figure 1–7; prior to that time the card had square corners. Why hasn't the standard card changed? Since it is utilized by many different pieces of equipment made by many different manufacturers, and distributed throughout the entire world, can you visualize the problem that would develop if a larger 85-column card was designed to take its place? All *existing* equipment would need to be redesigned to be able to process the new card and this would become extremely costly.

Processing the Punched Card. The basic principle behind the use of the punched card is simple. *Record one unit of information on each card so that multiple usage may be obtained from the card.* Record the data *once* in the card, *verify the accuracy* of the data in the card, and then let electromechanical equipment process the card in a number of different applications. Machines were developed that could

1. *sort* the cards (sequencing),
2. *merge* cards containing the current or new data with other cards containing additional information needed,
3. *calculate* the numeric information,
4. *summarize* the data.

Does the list look familiar? It should; one or more machines were made available to do each of the four basic data processing functions.

Figure 1–8 illustrates the concept of multiple card usage as four applications are shown which use a card punched with the student's name and address. The card becomes part of the student's *record.* Information pertaining to *one* student is called a *record.* The entire collection of cards for all students is referred to as a *file.* In the case of a card system, several cards, each containing different information, might be required for each student.

In procedure 1, the name and address card is used to produce a master listing of all students. In procedure 2, the name card is merged with the student grade cards to print grade reports. Procedure 3 indicates that the cumulative credit cards are sorted by student number, merged with the master name and address card, and then used to print a report of all students and their grade-point averages. Since the grades must be mailed to the student, procedure 4 uses the card to print an address sticker.

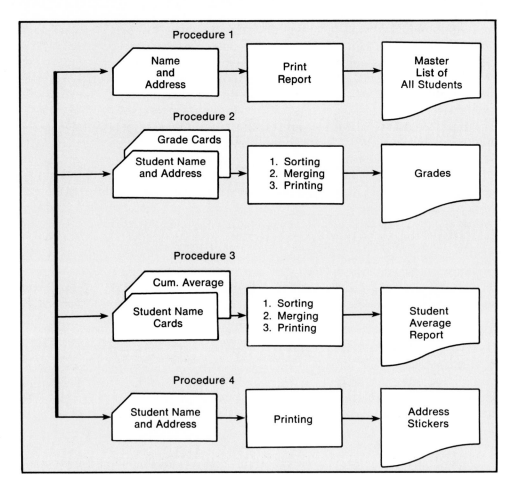

FIGURE 1–8. TYPICAL STUDENT ACCOUNTING REPORTS USING PUNCHED CARDS

A number of different machines would be required to actually do the various tasks. The important concept at this time, however, is that you are aware that when information is punched into *master* cards which are processed many times to produce different reports there is generally a saving in time, effort, and cost. A *master* card is one that contains mostly *constant* information. Unless the student moves, the same card may be used for the entire time that he is in college. A *detail card* is one that has a limited useful life and contains mostly variable data. In procedure 3, would you use the *same* cumulative average card each semester? Since the average changes from semester to semester, the card would be referred to as a detail card as it contains mostly *variable* information.

Procedures, such as the one illustrated in figure 1–8, were well suited to the use of unit-record equipment as all four procedures represent *routine repetitive* jobs. Once the information is captured on the master card, the data can be utilized many times.

Would the registration procedure illustrated in figure 1–9 be well suited to the use of this kind of equipment? Could time, and money, be saved by using punched cards for that application? Study the illustration in figure 1–9 and see what you think.

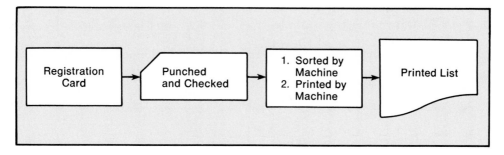

FIGURE 1–9. PUNCHED CARD REGISTRATION PROCEDURE

If anything, the job has become more complex, time consuming, and costly. Since the name cards contain variable data and will not be used again, it would have been better to type the list. In addition, how does the "machine" used to process the card know what to do? Unit-record, or tab equipment, is told what to do by physically placing wires in what is called a *control panel*. A control panel is pictured on page 98.

Each wire is manually inserted into the panel by the operator and serves as a means of communication with the machine. In the job illustrated, the wires communicate two things to the machine: (1) where the data is on the input cards which must be read by the machines; and (2) where the data is to be printed on the list.

It is not a complex job to wire the panel. The entire procedure took approximately 10 minutes when done manually. If the procedure is processed according to figure 1–9, it will probably take a minimum of 30 minutes. As illustrated, the registration cards are used as the *source document* from which to punch and verify the card. The cards will then be sorted alphabetically by a machine called the *sorter*. Still another machine will then be used to print the list of names and addresses. If *multiple usage* of the card can be obtained or if the job involves many *calculations*, punched card processing using unit-record equipment would probably *save time* and *effort*. *Routine repetitive jobs are well suited to this concept.*

DO YOU KNOW?

1–21. Who designed the punched card and the first equipment used to process the card?
1–22. Why was the punched card first used?
1–23. Did Dr. Hollerith achieve his goal?
1–24. If all of the 80-column cards were taken off the market and a new 85-column card took its place, what problem would this create?
1–25. A record of information pertains to how many students?
1–26. What would a payroll record contain?
1–27. What term is used to refer to a collection of individual records?
1–28. What is the name of the card which contains constant information? Generally this type of file is used in many different applications.
1–29. What is the name of the card, or file, which contains mostly variable information and is usually used over a rather short period of time?
1–30. What term is used to indicate that two files are combined for one application?
1–31. What does a control panel do?
1–32. A source document contains data that was entered on the document when the transaction first took place. Can a time card used by an employee as he enters the plant be considered a source document?

Electronic Data Processing

Electronic data processing involves the use of computers. While tab or unit-record equipment was instructed by the operator by means of a wired control panel, computers are given instructions by a *programmer* who writes a series of instructions called a *program*. Eventually his program is stored in the *memory* of the computer. The computer never becomes tired or bored with executing the commands given to him by the programmer and will perform the task rapidly and accurately until told to do something else.

You will learn that programming is not difficult. There are a number of *languages* that may be used in writing the instructions. A *computer language* may be thought of in much the same sense as a foreign language. Nevertheless, a computer language is usually limited to a very few basic commands and words and the programmer must learn what each command or phrase means.

You might think of the computer as a fantastic new employee that can perform countless calculations per second, has a printer that can print at a remarkable rate of speed, and can access information rapidly from a variety of different storage devices. Yet, you must tell him *everything* that is to be done. In communicating with an employee, you may say "get me my pencil." The computer would have to be told:

Stand up; take ten steps, turn; take five steps, reach out your hand; pick up the red pencil, turn; take five steps, turn; take ten steps; put out your hand; give me the pencil; sit down.

Of course, computers are not generally used to pick up pencils! The point is, when working with computers *exact, explicit* instructions must be given in the limited vocabulary that it understands, and each language, such as COBOL, FORTRAN, and RPG, has its own set of rules.

As the wheel increased man's physical power and made it possible for him to increase his physical productivity, the computer has extended man's mind. Dr. Carl Hammer, who was selected by the Data Processing Management Association as the Computer Science Man of the Year, when interviewed regarding the potential of the computer, stated:

> . . . We already have built into our society a mind amplifying factor of 2,000 to one. Behind every man, woman and child in this country, there stands the power of 2,000 human beings. The responsibility of any data processing manager of today, of the computer scientist, and of anyone in electronics today is so enormous that even I cannot envision it. I can touch it sometimes, but I cannot grasp it fully, because we are dealing here with a power that is inconceivable to the human mind. I think it is the greatest challenge that has ever faced mankind.[1]

Dr. Hammer also stated that if the 80,000 computers in use today were no longer available, it would take 400 *billion* people to do the work that they now accomplish. Progress in computer technology has increased at a fantastic rate, and the developments were in a direct response to needs, which were expressed by many different segments of the population.

COMPUTER HISTORY

In 1946, Dr. John W. Mauchly and J. Presper Eckert used the facilities of the Moore School of Electrical Engineering to design and build ENIAC (Electronic Numerical Integrator and Calculator). It was programmed by means of a series of switches and plug-in connections and ENIACs abilities were limited to very few applications. Several years later in England the first computer capable of storing data and instructions was designed and built. Neither computer was available for commercial use because they were used exclusively for the government or for research projects.

It was not until 1951 that UNIVAC I, the world's first electronic commercial computer, which utilized a stored-program, was available. The 16,000

---

[1] Helen M. Milecki, "DPMA'S 1973 Computer Science Man of the Year," *Data Management,* June 1973, pp. 14–20.

pound computer had over 5,000 vacuum tubes and could perform approximately 1,000 calculations per second.

First Generation

The development of what was termed first-generation computers continued until 1959. They were characterized by the use of vacuum tubes which stored both the instructions and the data. Because of the bulkiness, heat problems, and unreliability of the vacuum tubes, the first-generation computers were never considered to be totally successful. Their storage capability was usually limited to a few thousand characters. Programming had to be done in *machine language*. To do so, the programmer had to understand exactly how each command would be executed by the computer, and he was responsible for determining where within the computer the data and the instructions would be stored.

Second Generation

The second-generation computers, introduced in 1959, used transistors. The use of transistors made it possible for computers to process instructions in millionths of a second. The IBM 1401, which was one of the more popular second-generation computers, could perform 193,300 additions or 25,000 multiplications in one minute.

The second-generation computers became more powerful, contained larger memories, yet were substantially smaller in size than the first-generation computers. Programming was made easier as it could be done in *symbolic* or *assembler language*. Generally, a symbolic language relieves the programmer of the responsibility of assigning the locations in the memory of the computer for either the storage of data or instructions. The programmer can also use symbols in programming, rather than the actual digital instructions that the computer understands, which makes the logic of the program much easier to follow.

Third Generation

The computers that were placed on the market after 1965 were labeled third-generation computers and were characterized by monolithic integrated circuits. The amount of memory available became almost unlimited and a wider range of I/O (input/output) devices were also available. Programming was also made far easier by the development of more powerful languages.

Third-generation computers made the nanosecond (1/1,000,000,000 second) a reality in computer processing speeds. They were again proportionately smaller due to the microminiaturized integrated circuits which had components so small that they were barely visible to the naked eye. Their accomplishments were, and are, almost unbelievable. For example, the UNIVAC 1108 outperforms human beings at the rate of ten million to one. The third-generation computers were again truly revolutionary.

Fourth Generation

Fourth-generation computers promise to offer even greater input/output, storage, and processing capabilities than ever before. Lazer and holographic storage may make disk and tape obsolete for the large system user. The fourth is now predicted to be more revolutionary, when contrasted to the third, than the third was in contrast to the second-generation computer. It is predicted that by 1985 a large computer system will occupy no more space than that occupied by a shoe box.

While the capabilities, in terms of data storage, computational speed, and input/output device availability, have continued to shoot upward, the price per unit of data processed has decreased downward. The mini computer appeared during the reign of the third-generation computer. The term *mini* is used to denote small-scale computers with a rather limited amount of memory. The mini made electronic data processing a feasible reality for many smaller companies and caused entirely new and unique applications to be developed.

Business and industry first used computers almost exclusively for financial applications. Today, in a company which has only one computer, its utilization between financial and nonfinancial applications may be about equal.

ABOUT COMPUTERS

1–33. What does a programmer do?

1–34. What is used in writing the series of commands necessary to instruct a computer?

1–35. Instructions given to the computer can be rather vague and only implied, because computers can think. Why is this statement either true or false?

1–36. How does Dr. Hammer view computers?

1–37. Why would it create a problem if tomorrow all computers were to stop?

1–38. The UNIVAC I was the first commercial computer. Computers developed up to that time were used only by governments or for research. When was the UNIVAC I first available for commercial use?

1–39. What device was used for the storage of data by first-generation computers? What type of language was used to program first-generation computers?

1–40. Why were second-generation computers so much smaller? Why was programming the second-generation computers so much easier?

1–41. What additional improvements were made in third-generation computers?

WHEN CAN THE COMPUTER HELP?

What concepts carry over from other methods which were illustrated to computerized methods? Can a computer be effectively utilized for creating the list of names and addresses of those attending the drug conference? Unless the names and addresses were already in the system's files, the answer is "no." Perhaps if a very sophisticated method were employed it might cut the work, but based upon the fact that only 20 people attended the conference, the cost could not be justified.

Could an improvement be made upon the payroll system that was illustrated in figure 1–6 (p. 13). Yes, this is a natural for the computer as it is a routine task involving many calculations. Figure 1–10 illustrates how the job would be revised. From the payroll master file a great deal of other useful information is available to serve the needs of management.

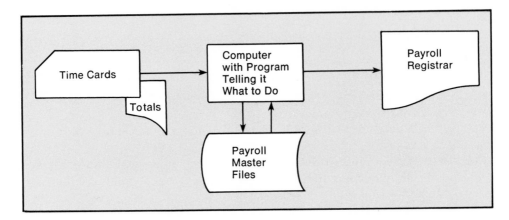

FIGURE 1–10. COMPUTERIZED PAYROLL SYSTEM

What information should be in the master file? How does it get there? Should only payroll data be available in the master file or should personnel information such as job promotions, employee's educational background, and awards received also be available? Questions such as these are answered by the systems analyst working with management.

What concepts carry over using mechanical methods to a computerized system?

1. The time cards *must* still be edited. Nevertheless, some of the editing or checking can be done by the computer if the programmer provides the necessary instructions.
2. Control totals are still used. In fact, the more automated the job becomes the more important it is that controls be used. Control totals are established in an effort to determine if the procedure is providing valid results.

You will observe from comparing figure 1–6 (p. 13) with 1–10 that the calculations are now done by the computer. The time cards would contain only the employee's number and the hours he worked which would mean a saving in time in preparing the weekly input. All other data that is needed is on the payroll master file that is used along with the cards. The register, or listing of the employee's current earnings, is produced on the first computer run. If the control totals check, the payroll checks are then printed. The final step would be to print the year-to-date information. Although three computer "runs" are needed, the computerized method would take from one to five minutes of actual "run" time depending upon the type of computer being used, the speed of the card reader, the speed of the printer, and numerous other facts. To process the payroll for the same number of employees, using the unit-record method would take several hours.

Can the computer be used more effectively in producing student reports than using electromechanical equipment? The concepts illustrated in the unit-record method stressed the value of automating jobs which make multiple use of machine processable data.

In contrasting the punched card and computerized methods, you will observe how much less detail is shown on figure 1–11. The punched card method involved a great deal of card handling and merging of the master cards with the detail cards. Figure 1–11 illustrates how it is possible to combine all data, both *constant* and *variable,* into one large file where each student has a record pertaining to his student history. How this is done is not important at this time. You should see how helpful a computerized method becomes when large amounts of information in machine processable form are available. From the student master file 40 or 50 different reports may be produced, each taking only a few minutes of computer time.

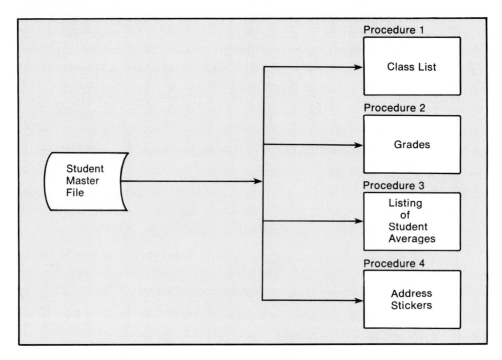

FIGURE 1–11. STUDENT REPORTS USING A COMPUTERIZED SYSTEM

QUESTIONS ON CONCEPTS

1–42. Are concepts utilized when a computerized method is used different from those employed by a well-designed method which uses less sophisticated equipment?

1–43. Is using a computer always the most effective way of processing data?

1–44. Computers are best suited for handling tasks which involve many calculations, routine processing of large amounts of data, and problems that can be clearly defined. In what other situations do you feel that a computer should be used?

THE EVOLUTION TO COMPUTERS

In many areas if it were not for computers, many things that we now accept, without thinking of how they are accomplished, would no longer be possible.

The space program would certainly be ended. Other research would either be ended or would continue at a pace so slow that it would seem almost unproductive. The design of new products would be much slower as more actual testing would be required to replace the simulated testing now done by the computer. The massive data banks which contain a vast array of useful information would become worthless as the data could not be retrieved and utilized. The convenience of making airline reservations with immediate confirmation would no longer be available to the traveler. The diagnostic services of the computer, which range from determining an individual's medical problem to a locomotive's maintenance needs, would become only history. Your Sara Lee Bakery products or Coors Beer might not be as tasty, as both companies use computers to monitor and control the quality of their products.

The list of services provided by computers to business, industry, and to individuals is endless. One recent publication listed 1,400 different computer applications. Commercial applications, which were mostly financial, were the first major use of computers by private enterprise. Many companies followed an evolutionary process that proceeded from manual to mechanical, to electromechanical, and, ultimately, to a computerized system. Some of the more common reasons why business found it necessary to change to more automated procedures are provided in the next section of the module.

Common Reasons for Changing Data Processing Methods

Labor

In 1900 one office worker was employed for each ten employees who worked on production. By 1950 the ratio had changed from 1:10 to 1:3. Using the technology available at that time it was difficult to make the factory worker much more productive. It was still predicted, however, that the ratio of office workers to factory workers would continue to increase as the volume of data to be processed was increasing. Management was concerned about the increasing number of employees involved, of necessity, in the handling and processing of data. These people are termed "unproductive" because they do not actually produce a marketable product. The cost of their services, however, has to be included in the cost of producing the firm's product or service.

Management was also concerned with increasing the productivity of those involved in data handling since a shortage of trained personnel existed in many sections of the country. The shortage was due, in part, to the increase in the amount of data that had to be processed. A short time ago in Detroit, Michigan, the shortage of *trained* office personnel was severe enough that "crash" training programs were implemented and it was rumored that anyone who knew the difference between a sewing machine and a typewriter would probably be able to secure an office job.

Both the shortage of trained personnel and the need to increase the office worker's productivity, in much the same way that automation in the factory had increased the factory worker's productivity, caused management to start looking for ways to improve information processing.

Cost

As competition increases, costs are looked at more closely. The price that a product is sold for must be competitive with similar products from which the consumer makes his choice. Since there is a direct relationship between the cost of producing the product and the selling price, all cost factors must be considered. The more intense the competition among firms who sell like products becomes, the more important it is that all costs are evaluated. One element of "cost" is the amount of labor and supplies that it takes to process data. What does it actually cost to produce a paycheck or a purchase order? Industry found that the costs per unit of work, such as the cost involved to prepare one paycheck, were continuing to increase. It was found that if unit-record equipment or computers could be economically justified the cost of *each* paycheck or purchase order decreased. The key word in the statement is *justified*, for if a company rents or buys a computer which is idle a large percentage of the time, their unit cost will not decrease and total costs will increase.

In the past many cases could be cited to illustrate that a cost reduction from using electronic data processing did not develop as anticipated. When challenged by management, the data processing manager could always point to the "extras" that they now had for which a tangible savings could not be calculated. What dollar value do you associate with a *daily* sales analysis or quality control report that would have been impossible to have without the utilization of a computerized system? As firms gain more experience in computer usage, they can more accurately determine both the costs and savings that will result from a new system. Many companies feel that a return of from 10 to 15% should be realized on the dollars that they have invested in computers. One way that this is possible is if the cost per unit of work is decreased and the employee's productivity is increased.

Speed

It was illustrated that by using better manual methods, the time needed to produce a payroll could be decreased from two days to one-half day. When the same quantity of work was done on the computer, the time ranged from one to five minutes depending upon a number of factors. Another very specific example that can be comprehended easily is an illustration regarding a student payroll application. When a printing calculator was used by a clerk to perform the calculation, it took 1 ½ days to do just the calculations. When the job of calculating the student's pay was assigned to a second-generation computer, the task was accomplished in 55 seconds. When the job was reassigned to a third-generation computer, it took only 20 seconds to compute the same volume of calculations. A "bonus" factor also resulted as the payroll report was printed as fast as the calculations were made. It would have taken far less time if faster I/O devices had been used as the calculation speeds of some computers are measured in a trillionth of a second. Second- and third-generation computers were generally said to be "I/O bound." The term was used to explain the fact that in almost all cases the computational speed of the computer was many times faster than its ability to read the input into its memory or output the results of its calculations. The full potential of the computer's ability was seldom, if ever, used. Still the speed and accuracy that was obtained was remarkable. *We will see how improvements have been made which make it possible to process data almost before it happens.* Why is this speed so important?

In the past, inventory reports, cost analysis, and other information vital to good management lagged well behind actual production. It was not uncommon to find out in March or April that the cost of production in January had increased to such an extent that either the problem had to be corrected immediately or the price of the product would have to be increased to maintain the anticipated profit level. How *immediate* is it if the information is already ten weeks old? To give an actual example, a firm found out when they employed better methods of cost determination that the price they were selling their product for was just one cent *less* than what it cost to manufacture the product.

By using computers, management can have their inventory reports and cost analysis on a day-to-day basis and adjustments can be made when they are needed. Other information, needed in the decision-making process, is equally as timely.

Errors

What may happen when routine tasks, especially the ones that are rather dull and uninteresting, are assigned to employees? Errors begin to occur as the employee becomes bored with the job and loses interest. A computer, or unit-record equipment, if given proper instructions and *valid* data will produce accurate output, as it will not get tired, bored, or careless in doing routine jobs.

As you begin to study how computers and other related equipment work you will understand why they are so reliable. When people state "the computer made a mistake" in almost all cases what should have been said is either, "the programmer who instructed the computer failed to test all possible variations of the program" or "the input was invalid." *The basic design of most equipment provides many ways of checking against the computer actually making an error without the computer operator knowing that an error occurred.*

Errors should be substantially decreased when electronic data processing equipment is used. You will learn that if this statement is to be true, the systems analyst, who designs the procedure, and the programmer, who instructs the computer on what it is to do, are responsible for building in additional "checks."

Data Storage

Information storage may seem a minor problem; yet unless the data is condensed for storage, the cost can be excessively high. It presently costs anywhere from $50 to $120 per year to rent space occupied by one file cabinet. In addition, it costs $150 to $160 a year to maintain the file. At $6 per square foot per month for office space, data storage becomes a problem. Using electronic data processing, improved and less costly methods of storing information can be utilized. The information is not only more effectively stored but can be retrieved much faster.

MANAGEMENT'S USE OF THE COMPUTER

There has been a far greater emphasis on management as a science rather than as an "art." In the past, many managers made their decisions by intuition or what was often referred to as the "seat of the pants" method. This may work fine when there are relatively few decisions to be made. But in our complex society today when decisions require consideration of many different internal and external factors, the decisions made must be based upon an analysis of information. Management must consider not only their firm's historical information, but must also consider the general economy of the entire world, the probable action of competitors, the technical changes that *may occur,* what legislation is pending that will have an effect upon their situation, and many other factors. Management's functions are to plan, organize, and control. In all three areas the computer can assist management.

What Is Planning?

A company is faced with a decision to make. Should the new plant be in San Jose, California, or in Denver, Colorado? Perhaps a better location can be determined after all of the necessary factors are carefully considered. From their data base, the computer can extract and summarize information useful to management in making the decision. *Data base* is a term used to imply that a great deal of information is stored in a manner that makes it directly accessable, or reachable, by the computer.

In addition, mathematical formulas, called *models,* can be used to help with decisions. The actual decision must be made by management, but employing techniques that use the computer to secure, condense, and help analyze information can be extremely beneficial.

Earlier we saw how the football coach needed data to *plan* his strategy for Saturday's game. The same concepts apply to either situation: where to build a new plant or what plays are best for Saturday's football game. In both cases good planning requires the use of *reliable, timely information.* The university coach is not concerned with what Yale did in 1910. But if they play Yale this week, he must know what Yale did last week!

What Is Organizing?

A plan must be established, as firms increase in size, as to how decisions are to be made and who is responsible for making the decision. Each manager is given an area of responsibility. The information that flows from one individual to another in the firm is the communication link that makes it possible for each person to perform his part in the total managerial network. The organizational pattern today is *dependent upon the informational flow* because electronic data processing has resulted in changes in the entire managerial structure.

Here is a simple example that pertains to organizing. The salesman reports to the sales manager who is responsible to the vice-president in charge of sales. The salesman creates data as he sells the company's products and communicates with his immediate boss, the sales manager, by submitting sales reports. Of course, these reports may have been produced for him by a computerized system. The sales manager takes the reports, combines them with the reports of the other salesmen, correlates information pertaining to previous financial periods, condenses and summarizes the data, and submits the information to the vice-president. Again this may be done for him by the computer whom he affectionately calls "Friendly Ben." The vice-president is primarily interested in the sales trends and the possibility that a problem might be developing in either a given area of the country or for a given type of product. Each individual in the organization has different informational needs which can be effectively met by using a well-designed computerized system.

The exchange of game statistics between the head coach and his assistants is vital in the organizing function of good football management. The head coach is interested in the total picture whereas the line coach is more concerned with the performance of each individual lineman. So that each may function and carry out his responsibility, information must be transmitted from the head coach to the assistant, and from the assistant to the head coach. The more complex the management structure becomes, the more important it becomes to have a *good communication network*. This is possible only if *accurate information* is available *when needed* in a form which can be easily utilized.

What Is Controlling?

Actual summarized information pertaining to events that occurred is compared against what was expected and planned for. A company based its

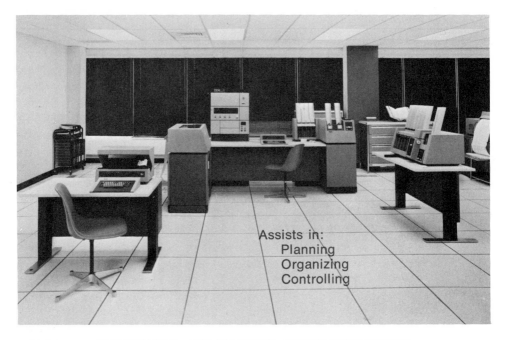

FIGURE 1–12. "FRIENDLY BEN"—THE COMPUTER ASSISTS MANAGEMENT

production of goods on information that made them believe that they could sell 100 products per day. If only 80 products were sold, is there an answer as to "why?" Was the planning poor? Did the organization fail? Were there external factors such as a flood in the eastern section of the country or a General Motors strike that caused a decrease in sales? Perhaps a study of the types and numbers of complaints will show that the quality of the product is not as good as what it should be. The computer can help with *control—contrasting actual results with the expected results.*

The football coach anticipated completing ten passes and making 235 yards rushing. If only two passes were completed and 100 yards were gained by rushing, not only will the coach demand answers but so will the university officials, board of directors, and important people like the fans and the "downtown quarterbacks."

A computer can assist in all three vital areas—*planning, organizing,* and *controlling.* How much the computer helps depends on how effectively man utilizes its abilities. One factor must always be remembered: good utilization of a computer system which provides more timely information can make good management even better. It cannot solve the problems created by poor management. A good coach can do a better job if given more information and video tape replays. It isn't possible, however, to solve the problems of a poor coach who cannot effectively relate to his players and assistants by merely giving him more information to work with. Management must be able to effectively utilize the information that can be provided for them as well as to have a certain amount of basic managerial "skill."

AVAILABILITY OF DATA

Data has been processed in one form or another for centuries. Today with technology increasing rapidly each year, more scientific experimentation being carried on, and better communication systems available, there is far more data available. As stated earlier, the amount of data available has been doubling every eight years. Computer systems are needed to keep track of the increased volume of data in order that it can be retrieved and utilized.

The Internal Revenue Service, for example, is responsible for maintaining records pertaining to tax information for millions of corporations, partnerships, and individuals. The income that each individual states he received must be matched against what is reported as being paid to that same individual. Could this vast amount of information be processed manually? Think of the sorting, merging, calculating, and summarization that must be done for millions of people pertaining to their many different tax transactions.

When computerized systems are used, pertinent, timely information can be extracted and summarized from the massive amount of data available in data bases. An actual sales analysis report, which was printed by a large chemical company, required approximately 40 cartons of paper. Is the president or board of directors interested in reading a report transmitted in a truck? A summarization of the report, with the unusual items highlighted, can be quickly prepared by the computer.

It is also possible for the corporate executive to "inquire" into the data base and get an immediate answer to such questions as, "How much of product "X" did we sell yesterday in comparison to what we sold on the same day last year?" "If we increase our price for "Y" by 10%, what probable effect will it have on sales?" Another question might be, "Who in our personnel file can speak German, has some knowledge of Russian, has a good background in statistics, and is between the ages 35 and 40, male and unmarried?" *Inquiries such as these are possible and are being made directly into the data base.* These systems are expensive, require vast amounts of stored information to be available, and must be cost justified.

LEGISLATIVE ACTION

A great many laws have been enacted which make it necessary to maintain far more information now than in the past. The federal income tax laws require that a clear audit trail is available so that the tax people may check, if they so desire, to see that the income and expenses were accurately reported by an individual, partnership, or corporation. The term *audit trail* is used to indicate that they must be able to see when the transaction first occurred and then be able to follow it through the processing to its completion by studying available records.

Other legislation pertaining to social security and fair labor standards requires that payroll data be maintained, and available, for a given number of years. A corporation is required to provide a summarization of their yearly income and expenses to all of their stockholders. In addition, their records must be accurately maintained and checked by individuals, other than their own employees, to protect the stockholder's interests. Prior to the enactment of legislation pertaining to the pricing and sales of products, income tax laws, labor laws, and other such regulatory laws, it was optional if records were to be maintained or not. This is no longer true, because understandable, accurate records must be maintained and available. The requirements that must be met for more information to be processed to comply with the current laws is still another reason that many companies have turned to computers and other more automated methods to provide the required information.

MANAGEMENT REVIEW QUESTIONS

1–45. Will the use of a computer make poor management look good?

1–46. Can a computer system be utilized in all three areas of management: planning, organizing, and controlling?

1–47. What is a data base?

1–48. Is the cost of processing information always decreased when a computer is used?

1–49. You have received your grades and find that you have a "D" in Basic Science. When you check with your instructor, he states that the computer really made a mistake as the grade was to have been a "B." What would be, in all probability, a more accurate explanation of the mistake?

1–50. Why is this statement false? "After a computer does a routine task for a long period of time (such as computing payroll), it becomes less accurate than when it started the procedure."

1–51. Is a listing of names and addresses or a statistical report concerning grade distribution more costly if produced by a computerized system than a manual system?

1–52. Can a company always decide for themselves how much data and what data will be processed?

1–53. Does top management (e.g., the president of a company) usually want a full report with none of the details of the transactions omitted?

1–54. Why did many companies feel they should make the office worker who processed information more productive?

SUMMARIZE YOUR THINKING

Some basic data processing terms and information pertaining to data processing methods have been presented. The vocabulary and functions of the data processors will become even more understandable as you progress through the course. A few simple illustrations have been given as to how data is captured, processed, retrieved, and utilized. It should be apparent that valid information is essential to the successful management of any venture—from raising cattle to producing electronic components for a satellite. Since management has become so dependent upon having relevant, timely information, controls must be built into the system to make certain that the output is accurate.

A quick overview of the evolution of the data processing technology and methods was presented. Some of the reasons why firms found it necessary to use methods, other than manual or mechanical, for processing data were briefly explored.

As our society becomes even more complex, computer technology will be utilized to even a greater extent in attempting to solve some of the critical and fundamental social problems. To solve a problem, you must first understand the problem. The fundamental issues can be better understood if all pertinent information is available in a usable form. Electronic data processing can assist in providing the relevant information.

Many people view data processing and computer usage in many different ways. Dr. Hammer, when discussing the mind amplifying factor of the computer, was quoted as saying, "it is the greatest challenge that ever faced mankind."

Art Buchwald had a somewhat lighter viewpoint regarding data processing and computers when he editorialized on "The Great Data Famine" of the 1970s. According to Buchwald's expert source, by January 12, 1976, ". . . every last bit of data in the world will have been fed into a machine and an information famine will follow. To cope with this impending disaster, a crash program is urged in which (1) no computer can be plugged in more than three hours a day, (2) the government will spend $50 billion to set up data manufacturing plants and their output will be mixed with soy bean production, and finally, (3) a birth control program will be advocated for all computers—provided 'the Vatican's computer gives us its blessing.' "[2]

As you begin to understand some of the fundamental concepts involved in data processing, you will see how the computer can be utilized as an extension of man's mind. As with anything, simple basic concepts and understanding must be developed before some of the complex illustrations, such as inquiry into a data base, can be fully appreciated. For now, it is sufficient that you understand that the applications presented were not only possible but also practical.

The following case study about Lou and how and why he became involved in data processing will emphasize many of the basic concepts which have already been presented.

A CASE HISTORY

Let me introduce to you a friend of mine from Saginaw. As you can see from the 1888 picture of Lou, he was self-employed and engaged in a business which at that time required only a few very simple tools. Since he had homesteaded the land and built his own home, using primarily the materials that were available, he had no debts. Since the federal income tax laws had not

[2] Copyrighted by Art Buchwald, 1971, from *"I Never Danced at the White House."*

yet been enacted, he was really only accountable to himself, and it was not necessary that he maintain any records or files. When he did cut logs for others, he just remembered how much each person owed him and eventually they either paid cash or helped him with his farming or logging.

1888—A START OF A CORPORATION!

Like many of his friends, who were also self-employed in either lumbering or farming, Lou felt that if at the end of the year he owed no one and had been able to provide adequate food, clothing, and shelter for his family, he had been successful. He had had a good year. If at the end of the year, he found that he was in debt for a small amount for the necessities of life, it had not been such a good year. Lou was an intelligent and ambitious individual and it was his nature to want to provide more for his family, so he began to work a little harder to achieve his goal.

By 1900 he decided that perhaps more of his time should be devoted to logging as there seemed to be a ready market for all of the logs he could cut. Each year he spent more of his time filling the requests for logs, and often his neighbors helped him when he got behind with the orders. Lou decided if he could secure better equipment, he would become far more productive. At the same time that he made his decision to concentrate more of his efforts on logging, a paper mill was established in a nearby town which gave him an additional market for his product. If only he could cut more logs, he would have more to sell!

A bank was well-established in the rapidly growing community of Saginaw and Lou had heard his friends talk about borrowing money for farming equipment. He thought that if he went in and talked to Mr. Stone, the bank president, that he too could secure a loan. He could then purchase the necessary equipment which would enable him to cut logs faster and handle them easier. When he went into the bank to talk to Mr. Stone, he felt that he would easily get a loan since everyone in Saginaw knew that he was honest. In addition he had never borrowed money, as the only debts he had ever had were during those few bad years when he owed a small amount to Mr. Blake at the general store. Mr. Blake was certainly nice about not pushing him for the money until his crop of beans was harvested.

In 1900 bankers really weren't much different than they are today. The first thing Mr. Stone asked Lou was how much profit had he made during the past five years and what method would he use to repay the loan? Lou, of course, didn't have the answers. His entire data processing system had consisted of little squares of paper, very neatly cut, and two nails. When someone placed an order for logs, he wrote it down and put the slip on the first nail—his "unfilled order file." After he cut and delivered the logs, the square of paper was transferred to the second nail which was his "they owe me file." When the logs were paid for the square of paper was destroyed, since the transaction was completed.

It was essentially a good system because Lou knew exactly how many logs he needed to cut to fill the orders in his "unfilled order file." He knew also if he added the slips on the second nail together he could determine what was owed to him. He also knew having been in business for 12 years about how many logs he would need to cut each year.

The banker was not satisfied and said that Lou must provide him with some records to show how many logs he had actually cut and sold, how many orders he had yet to fill, and how much money was owed to him. He asked Lou to establish a simple system that would provide the necessary information. After a year or so, based upon the information that Lou would be able to provide, he would reconsider the question of the loan.

Mr. Stone suggested that a record be maintained for each of the customers. The record could start with a written order on which Lou would enter the customer's name, date, number of logs ordered, and when they were to be delivered. Mr. Stone also suggested that Lou have each person indicate *when* and *how* the order would be paid for. This would help Lou in planning so he would know when to expect payment.

The orders would be placed in a file, by customer name, for "unprocessed orders." After the orders were filled, they would be moved to the "orders filled file." In the front of that file would be the orders which had not yet been paid for.

This would provide the basis of the information that Mr. Stone would want: the total of all orders received, the total amount of logs which were actually delivered, and the amount that was due on the delivered orders. Lou thought that his system had worked well but was willing to try Mr. Stone's method if it would enable him to secure the funds needed for new equipment.

At the end of the year Lou totaled all of the orders that were in both the filled and unfilled order file and added the two amounts together to determine how many logs had been ordered during the year. He also totaled the amount of the orders that were filled but not yet paid for which Mr. Stone referred to as *accounts receivables.* When he added the unpaid orders it reminded him that many of the individuals to whom he had delivered logs still owed him money. Perhaps it had just slipped their minds. He would have to talk to some of the people on the list and see if they would pay for their logs. He took the totals, the list of accounts receivables, and his files and went to see Mr. Stone about the loan.

Mr. Stone was impressed with the volume of work that Lou had been able to do with his simple tools and the help of his neighbors. Surely with the expanding market and better tools to work with he could do even better. Mr. Stone was a little concerned about the number of people who owed Lou money, for if he was not paid on time, how would he make his payments when they became due? The banker agreed to loan him enough money to buy the needed equipment.

By 1913 Lou was really in the lumbering business and doing very well. He not only made his payments to Mr. Stone on time but also sent reminders to people who were a little late in paying for their logs.

Lou's life was made a little more complex by the passing of the Sixteenth Amendment which stated:

> . . . The Congress shall have the power to lay and collect taxes on the incomes from whatever source derived, without apportionment among these several States, and without regard to any census of enumeration.

He did check with Mr. Stone, who he considered by this time to be one of his friends, to find out what it all meant. Mr. Stone explained to him that the law required him to pay an income tax of 1% on all that he earned above $4,000, which was the exemption for a married man. In addition, a percentage surtax was imposed which increased as his earnings increased. Lou still did not know how much he really had earned because sometimes he failed to write down his expenses. Mr. Stone and Lou both felt that an improved data processing system was needed that would tell him not only how much he had sold but how much he had actually earned. Mr. Stone stressed that all of his business expenses would be deducted before he would have to pay any tax. To Lou this all seemed very complex. The simple way of life that he had experienced in 1888 certainly seemed to be changing.

During 1914, 1915, and 1916 his business really expanded. Lou also found out that a furniture factory was coming into the area and if he had more equipment he could sell additional lumber to the new company. With the amount of building that was going on in the nearby community of Saginaw, his sales were bound to increase. This time when he went into the bank he was prepared. He took with him the summarized reports of all of his transactions which showed both the income received and the expenses incurred during the year. It was a good thing that he had followed Mr. Stone's suggestion and written down all of his expenses, because the bank now had something called a board of directors that wanted a written statement pertaining to both his income and expenditures. They also wanted to know how much he owed to other people. The board of directors called these his *accounts payable*. In addition, they wanted to know how much inventory (logs cut but not sold) that he had on hand. Integrity, hard work, and intuition on how to manage a business seemingly paid off as he was able to expand his logging operation to a lumbering operation. The government, as well as the bank, was interested in information pertaining to his business operations. Sometimes his customers called and wanted information about how much they had purchased from him during the past few years. He had long ago found out that he didn't have time to work in the actual logging and lumbering operations because he was too busy managing the business.

1928—BUSINESS IS EXPANDING

You can see from the 1928 picture that he really did progress a great deal. He had employees working for him on a regular basis and had a substantial amount of equipment. He seemed to be spending a great deal more of his time recording data about his business, as he had to maintain records for the employees working for him, record expenses, and keep track of an increasing number of orders.

Lou's son, who had attended college, suggested that they should hire someone to take over the recording and processing of all of the data. Orders would get filled faster if they didn't have to wait for Lou to find time to check to see if the lumber was available and if the customer who wanted the lumber had been paying his bills on time. Lou had found out the hard way that it was better not to let people charge an excessive amount of lumber without making payments on a regular basis. To him, not being able to sell to people with overdue bills was one of the more disagreeable tasks of managing his business. Often he just could not say "no" to an individual.

If they hired someone to help with the routine checking and processing of the orders, Lou could work with the summarized information and spend more time on actual *planning*. Lou thought that his son's idea to hire someone to take care of the many routine recording functions and to process the sales orders was a good one. If questions arose about the availability of unusual items or the overextension of credit, Lou could handle these few exceptions. Today, using electronic data processing equipment, this would be called *management by exception*. As you can see, some of the concepts that were stressed as advantages of the new computer technology were things that had been going on for a long time.

At the suggestion of his son, Lou had also expanded his product line to include far more than just lumber. The mere keeping track of how many of each item he had on hand was a chore and often he lost a sale as he was out of the item a customer wanted. Sometimes he was sure that he had the item on hand but *just couldn't seem to find it*. Maybe the person hired to handle sales could also establish some better inventory records.

Lou's son thought that perhaps his accounting professor, Floyd L. Feusse, whose opinions he respected and judgment he trusted, might have some ideas as to what they should do to improve the paper flow. He might even know of a sharp young college student that could be hired to help implement a new system.

Consulting with Professor Feusse really helped because he made some very positive recommendations for change. He explained to Lou that he wasn't just recording data to find out how much money he made. The summarized information should help to make some of the decisions required to manage the business. Lou should be able to determine from studying the information for the last several years the rate that his business had been growing and what items had been in demand. He would then be able to determine how many employees would be needed, how much merchandise to order, and what items to delete from stock. Items that just remained on the shelf and were not in demand were actually costing him money. Professor Feusse said that it must be possible to trace each transaction through the entire system from the time the sale was made until the goods had been delivered and paid for.

Professor Feusse did know a really sharp student who was graduating in the spring. John Krawczyk, an accounting student, felt that he would want some of the forms redesigned and that additional "checks" should be built into the system to make certain that the data was recorded and processed correctly. He pointed out that by using some additional basic forms for recording the transactions more complete information could be obtained. Working with Professor Feusse they redesigned the system taking into consideration that the firm would probably continue to expand. After they finished redesigning the system, they had provided a better way of accounting for both inventory and accounts receivable.

Lou implemented the recommended changes, and perhaps because of some of the techniques that he had learned about from talking with Professor Feusse, he survived the depression of the 1930s. This may have been because he had neither overextended his credit nor permitted his customers to overextend theirs. He had learned the value of making his decision on an accumulation of information and not just by using intuition. Usually when his friends had failed in their business ventures, they had been told that it was because they had inadequate information available to help them effectively manage their firms.

The thirties brought a lot of changes which made it necessary for Lou to maintain even more information regarding his employees. He can still remember all of the employers in Saginaw complaining about the records and reports that were required for the Workman's Compensation, Social Security, and the Fair Labor Standards acts.

By this time Lou had turned over even more of the management of the firm to young Lou, who really wasn't so young as he also had a son working in the business.

1938—BRANCH OPERATIONS

As you can see from the picture taken in 1938, they had established branch lumberyards in other cities. Again they began to wonder if they shouldn't find a better way of processing their data. The branch operation required an increasing amount of paper work to keep the branch managers informed about new products and price changes. In addition, the payroll and inventory records for all of the lumberyards were maintained in the central office which was located in Saginaw.

Just as Lou had realized earlier that good reliable information was absolutely essential in both the *planning* for and the *controlling* of his operation, he now realized that data was the *communication link* between the home office and the increasing number of branches. He could only evaluate how successful each operation was by the information that was submitted to him.

In 1950, John Krawczyk thought perhaps it was time to reassess their total data processing system as he was beginning to hear a great deal about unit-record equipment. The punched card method appealed to John since the accuracy of the information in the card is usually carefully verified. If they could justify the use of the equipment, it might help solve some of their problems.

In checking, John found that two companies were making most of the unit-record equipment. One company, International Business Machines, had initiated a new concept that permitted companies to rent their equipment. What risk was there if you didn't have to spend your money for the equipment? Of course, their entire system would have to be redesigned.

An outside consulting firm was hired to work with John to determine if it would be wise to change his manual system over to a unit-record system. They studied how the data was being processed at that time and how costly it was to process it under the manual method. They gave special attention to the problem areas and worked on some ideas that would help the office workers to become more productive.

The work resulted in a much improved system which still used only mechanical equipment such as calculators, cash registers, and other relatively simple machines. They did get some new posting equipment that enabled them in one machine operation to update the customer's record, prepare his bill, and do a register or listing of the transaction. The same machine could be used in a similar manner to help process payroll information. Although John's ideas pertaining to the use of unit-record equipment could not be justified at that time, a much improved system did result from the study.

Also in the 1950s, Lou's Lumber changed its name and became the L. C. Smith Corporation which enabled them to sell stock to secure more capital. Their tax consultant also felt that for many other reasons it would be beneficial to become a corporation. This again increased their data processing requirements as stockholders' records had to be maintained and an annual report prepared. It also meant that the L. C. Smith Corporation's records must be checked (audited) at least once a year to better protect the stockholders' interests. After the depression and the resulting stock market crash, the government was interested that every precaution be taken to protect the interests of the stockholders.

During that decade they continued to expand, add new products, and acquire companies that were closely related to the lumbering merchandising business. Some new concepts were developed in marketing their products that accounted for their unusual growth.

During the late 1950s they again reassessed their data processing needs. If they didn't do something soon, there would't be enough people for them to hire in Saginaw to keep up with their data processing needs! John was beginning to read in his professional magazines a lot about the computer, but as yet it did not impress him. Perhaps at this time unit-record equipment and the punched card were the answer to their data processing problems. Certainly, unless you were Ford, General Motors, or Dow Chemical, you could not begin to think of a computer.

Another alternative that they considered for the 1960s was the use of a service bureau for a portion of their work. This would mean that they would have the benefit of the more sophisticated data processing methods without the problems associated with trying to find personnel, or retrain some of their own people, to implement a completely new system. The bulk of the routine repetitive jobs, such as accounts receivable, inventory, and payroll, could be processed by the service bureau.

During 1959 and 1960 these were the alternatives that seemed best for the L. C. Smith Corporation: (1) develop their own data processing department and hire or train the personnel necessary; (2) utilize the data processing capabilities of an outside firm.

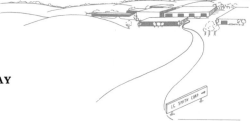

THE L. C. SMITH CORPORATION—TODAY

Bringing you completely up-to-date on the L. C. Smith Corporation in the 1970s will be done a little later after you learn the details of the 1960s.

As you can see, all their predictions of growth were inaccurate as the company developed far faster than what had been optimistically planned for. By the time third-generation computers appeared on the market, there was no choice that was realistic in terms of their increased need for better, faster, more reliable information than to utilize a computerized system.

In meeting Lou and his son you have seen how one man created a company which expanded into a vast corporation. Lou saw his life change from a simple, uncomplicated existence, where he was accountable only to himself, to an existence where he was responsible for the well-being of many people who worked for him. Lou was quick to realize how vital it was to have relevant reliable information available. The younger men he employed in management depended even more on the availability of data when they worked with their mathematical formulas.

When Lou's son thought back to his father's simple system of 1888—two nails and neat squares of paper—and contrasted it to the sophisticated system he must utilize today, it caused moments of reflection as to what else the future would bring.

The success stories of people like Lou are always interesting to reflect upon. What would have happened if he had not heeded the advice of Mr. Stone and Professor Feusse? What if people like John had not insisted that the information be timely, reliable, and relevant? Now that you understand some of the background of the L. C. Smith Corporation and some of their early developmental history, we will look at some of the details of their sales and payroll systems as they advance through the various stages from relatively simple automated systems to the ultimate—capturing data pertaining to sales and payroll at the source in machine processable form and having it available for all of their informational needs.

GLOSSARY OF TERMS TO CHECK YOUR KNOWLEDGE

Analyst. An individual who studies a given situation and determines the best method to use in the solution of the problem.

Batch Total. A total usually taken before processing starts which is used in determining if the data is being accurately processed. Control total is another term that is often used in place of batch total.

Computer Language. A set of rules, symbols, and commands which are used to write a program, or series of instructions, for a computer.

Control. Provides a means of making certain that a procedure or task is done accurately. The term is also used to refer to the management technique of contrasting the actual results with the expected results.

Control Panel. A device in which wires are placed. Each wire represents an instruction given to direct or control the function of unit-record equipment. Very early computers also had control panels which told the computer where in the card the information to be processed was punched.

Data. The results of a transaction or event that is still in its original state. For example, the time recorded on a time card as an employee "punches in."

Data Base. Large files of data directly accessible by the computer. The trend is to combine files, such as the payroll and personnel file, into one large data base.

Data Processing. Data processing is capturing data and putting it in a form which can be easily utilized and retrieved.

Detail Card or *Record.* One that contains primarily variable data. Its useful life is generally limited to the current fiscal period.

Electromechanical Data Processing. Electromechanical data processing uses equipment, which is primarily mechanical in nature, to process punched cards. It is commonly referred to as *unit-record, tabulating,* or *tab equipment.*

File. A collection of records generally pertaining to one topic.

Hollerith, Dr. Herman. Dr. Herman Hollerith is credited with designing both the standard punched card and the early tabulating equipment which processed the card.

Information. The results of processing data and putting it into a more usable form.

Input. Information, or data, to be processed.

I/O. Input/Output.

Machine Language. The language that is used and understood by the computer without translation. Numbers are used for both the commands and the locations within the memory of the computer. It was the only way that the early first-generation computers could be programmed.

Management. The individuals responsible for planning, organizing, and controlling a function or organization.

Master Card or Record. Contains constant, or fixed, information. It is generally used over a long period of time and for many different uses.

Mechanical Data Processing. A method of data processing which involves the use of relatively small and simple, usually non-programmable, mechanical machines. Some of the machines are the adding machine, calculator, cash register, billing machines, and duplicating machines. Some of the "new generation" of smaller office machines today, however, are electronic and may perform a series of commands in a given sequence.

Merge. Combining two files (both must be in the same sequence) into one file.

Output. The results of processing data. The output from one procedure may be input for the next procedure.

Procedure. A precise step-by-step method for effecting a solution to a problem. Complex systems are subdivided into procedures.

Program. A series of instructions tell the computer what it is to do and the sequence in which the commands must be executed.

Service Bureau. A professional organization that provides data processing service for other individuals or organizations.

Source Data Automation. The data which is created due to an event taking place is entered directly into the system in a machine processable form.

Symbolic Language. A type of language that permits the use of symbols in writing computer commands, rather than using only numbers. It must be translated to machine language before it is understood by the computer. It is somewhat easier to use than machine language.

System. An orderly means of accomplishing one or more tasks. It generally refers to a more complex method which is composed of many procedures each of which may be divided into specific tasks.

ANSWERS

UP TO THIS POINT (p. 5)

1–1. One who writes a series of instructions telling the computer what it is to do.

1–2. Yes. The strike is the event. Recording it is the first actual phase of data processing.

1–3. Yes. Even in a manual system data must be processed and available for management's use in making decisions.

1–4. The fourth concept is retrieval of the data.

1–5. No, not all data processing is computerized.

1–6. A graphic representation of a data processing cycle.

1–7. To represent a decision-point in the data processing cycle.

1–8. Data processing has a somewhat strange vocabulary all of its own. To communicate effectively its terminology must be defined.

JUST CHECKING (p. 7)

1–9. Input
   Processing
   Output

1–10. Input

1–11. Output

1–12. Summarizing

1–13. No. A given job might involve only one of the four processing functions.

BEFORE YOU CONTINUE (p. 9)

1–14. System

1–15. Tasks

1–16. Decisions made by management must be based on relevant timely information.

REVIEW QUESTIONS (p. 13)

1–17. Until our society became more complex and other technology had advanced to the point that a need was felt there did not seem to be much interest in the computing equipment field.

1–18. Yes. Several options were pointed out in the text and there are many more such as use of a "mini" and time-sharing.

1–19. Editing, either by using the computer or manual methods, is done to determine if the data on either the source document or input is valid.

1–20. The total taken by adding the hours from the time cards can be called either a *batch* or *control* total.

DO YOU KNOW? (p. 18)

1–21. Dr. Herman Hollerith in the 1880s.
1–22. To speed up the processing of the census data. As the volume increased, it was impossible to get the job done fast enough so that the information was relevant.
1–23. Yes. The time to process the 1890 census data was decreased to 2½ years.
1–24. Thousands of machines now use the standard card. Each would have to be changed to accept the new card as input.
1–25. One
1–26. A payroll record contains information pertaining to one employee
1–27. File
1–28. Master
1–29. Detail
1–30. Merged
1–31. A control panel is wired for each job instructing the machine what is to be done. In the illustration the control panel was wired to tell the machine (the accounting machine) where the data was in the input card and where the output was to be printed.
1–32. Yes

ABOUT COMPUTERS (p. 21)

1–33. A programmer writes a series of instructions which makes it possible for a computer to process data.
1–34. A programming *language* is used in writing programs.
1–35. The statement is false as computers can't think; they must be given exact explicit instructions.
1–36. Dr. Hammer views computers as one of the greatest challenges that has ever faced mankind.
1–37. It would, according to Dr. Hammer, take 400 billion people to do the work that is now assigned to computers. Since computers are used to process data of every conceivable type and used to control many scientific projects, manufacturing operations, etc., there would be complete chaos.

1–38. 1951

1–39. Vacuum tubes were used for the storage of data. Machine language was used in programming.

1–40. The use of transistors made second-generation computers much smaller and the use of symbolic and assembler languages made programming easier.

1–41. Third-generation computers were characterized by monolithic integrated circuits, more memory, faster calculation, more and faster I/O devices to select from, and easier methods of programming.

QUESTIONS ON CONCEPTS (p. 24)

1–42. No. The basic concepts of editing, establishing controls, and recording the data at the source in processable form apply to any method.

1–43. No. There are certain types of tasks where a computer cannot be effectively utilized. Problems which cannot be clearly defined by the user can never be assigned to a computer.

1–44. Computers should also be used when instantaneous or immediate "feedback" is necessary in order for management to make decisions or to take corrective action.

MANAGEMENT REVIEW QUESTIONS (p. 33)

1–45. No. As was pointed out in the text a computer can assist management in a variety of ways but is not a "cure" for poor management.

1–46. Yes. Examples were cited in the text of not only what each term means but how a computer can be utilized for each of the basic functions of management.

1–47. The term usually implies that a large amount of data is in files which are directly accessible by the computer.

1–48. Generally, it is if the application can be justified and is well designed. For a small company that secures a computer and cannot really justify its use, the cost per unit of work may increase.

1–49. The mistake was probably due to the faculty member sending in the wrong grade, or a programming error caused the problem. It is unlikely that a malfunction on the part of the computer occurred.

1–50. One of the very basic advantages to using a computer is that it can do routine repetitive tasks and *still retain its accuracy*.

1–51. No. If automated methods can be cost justified, the work per unit is generally substantially reduced.

1–52. No. In many cases it is required by legislative action that certain kinds of information be available when, or if, requested.

1–53. No. It would be impossible for the president to effectively use such a vast amount of information. The information pertaining to trends and problems that he should be made aware of must be extracted and summarized for his use.

1–54. Increased competition made it necessary for companies to be more cost conscious. One way to keep costs lower is to increase the office worker's productivity. The overhead associated with information processing had increased in a far greater proportion than the labor costs of actually manufacturing or producing the product.

PUNCHED CARD 2
DATA PROCESSING

SMITH'S DECISION

In 1960 the L. C. Smith Corporation made a decision to use unit-record equipment to process their data. The unit-record equipment, which is controlled by means of a wired panel, seemed far less complicated than did the available second-generation computers.

Management had carefully considered many alternatives and had decided to formulate a data processing department which would be responsible to the controller, John R. Krawczyk. Since unit-record equipment was used primarily to process financial data such as payroll, inventory, and accounts receivable, most data processing departments were originally under the chief financial officer of the corporation. The personnel department was contacted to see if anyone within the company might be interested in the position of data processing manager.

Dale K. Keyser, a young accountant with the firm, indicated that he was very interested in the position. Since he seemed to have an aptitude for the position, he was appointed manager of the newly established department.

Job Title	Description

Data Processing Manager	The data processing manager is directly responsible to the controller. He is responsible for
	
	1. designing, testing, and implementing all new applications which include
	
	  a. designing forms,
	
	  b. developing the processing procedures,
	
	  c. providing accuracy checks whenever possible,
	
	  d. wiring panels,
	
	  e. documenting the procedure and providing detailed operator instructions;
	
	2. scheduling all jobs, a priority will be both established and adhered to;
	
	3. training all data processing employees;
	
	4. supervising all data processing employees;
	
	5. operating the equipment in the event that the regular operator is not available.

Machine Operator	The machine operator will follow the posted schedule and is responsible for completing work according to schedule. In addition, he is responsible for 1. following the directions in the operator's guide for the processing of all data, 2. checking the validity of control totals before releasing reports, 3. maintaining a neat and orderly work area, 4. maintaining a daily log of all procedures.
Keypunch Operator	The keypunch operators are responsible for 1. punching and verifying the data from the source documents received from the other departments, 2. stamping all documents with the date and time they were processed, 3. keeping all source documents in the same sequence in which they were received, 4. explicitly following the directions for each job which are given on an operator's instruction sheet.

FIGURE 2–1. JOB DESCRIPTIONS

IBM, whose equipment Smith's was renting, helped train Keyser by sending him to their school to learn to wire and operate the equipment. An IBM systems analyst also helped Keyser design the applications which would be implemented on the new equipment.

Because other employees in the company were concerned about how their jobs might be affected, IBM suggested that information regarding the status of the systems development should be made available to all employees. As part of the effort to keep everyone informed, the job descriptions illustrated in figure 2–1 were made available to all employees. Interested employees were encouraged to apply for the new positions within the data processing department.

The Sales Invoicing Procedure

In addition to expanding their product line, Smith's had established a wholesale business. The sales order submitted by salesmen on standard order forms took at least five days to process. For this reason management felt that the sales invoicing procedure should be implemented on the new equipment as soon as possible.

When the order is received by Smith's, it is opened and dated in the mail room and then routed to the credit department where both the customer's number and credit are checked. The order is then sent to the sales department to determine if the items ordered are available for shipment.

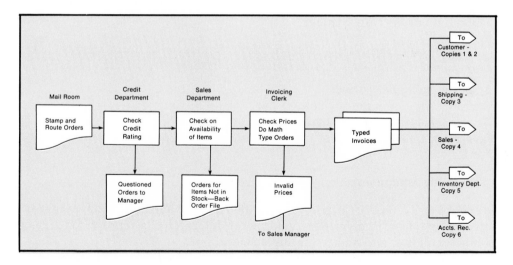

FIGURE 2–2. THE SALES INVOICING PROCEDURE

An inventory system is maintained on cards by subtracting the quantity sold of any given item from the quantity on hand. A delay in processing orders often results from the lack of *timely* information because the purchase department is slow in notifying the sales department that new shipments of merchandise have arrived. The purchase department is not totally to blame for the delay as they seem unable, with the number of employees available, to keep up with their work load.

If a customer's order cannot be filled, it is placed on backorder until a new shipment of merchandise is received by the L. C. Smith Corporation. Orders which can be processed are given to a second clerk who checks the unit price, multiplies the price times the quantity, and totals the order.

The orders are then typed on six-part *sales invoices* which have been pre-numbered as a means of establishing a control over the use of the forms. All forms must be accounted for! The time-consuming and tedious credit and inventory checks cause most of the delay in processing the orders. During the "peak" sales seasons, the time required to process the sales orders may be as long as eight or nine days.

The design and implementation of a new sales order system was given top priority for three major reasons.

1. There had been an increase in the number of customer complaints regarding the time that it takes to process orders.
2. Two percent of the time the customer received the wrong merchandise.
3. An increasing number of customers had overextended their credit limit.

Objectives of the New System

After studying the problems of the previous sales order system, it was determined that the new design must provide for

1. better customer service,
2. faster processing of the sales order,
3. more accurate processing of orders,
4. a more timely method of checking the customer's credit balance.

Tabulating Equipment

The L. C. Smith Corporation decided to rent the following equipment: two keypunches, two verifiers, a sorter, an interpreter, a reproducer, a calculator, a collator, and an accounting machine.

Although the equipment is available with many different options, and at different speeds and prices, only the basic functions of the equipment will be presented. The discussion on wiring the interpreter panel is intended only to show the basic principles of control panel wiring.

REVIEW QUESTIONS

2–1. Why were the data processing departments usually placed under the controller?

2–2. Are jobs usually executed on a first-come, first-serve basis in the data processing department?

2–3. Why did the company decide to automate the sales order procedure first?

2–4. Were the customers happy with the old system?

THE STANDARD 80-COLUMN CARD

The 80-column card, designed in 1888, has served the data processing industry well and is still referred to as a *common language media* because it can communicate effectively with so many different machines. As late as 1973, the card was still used for 80% of all original input into electronic data processing systems (fig. 2–3).

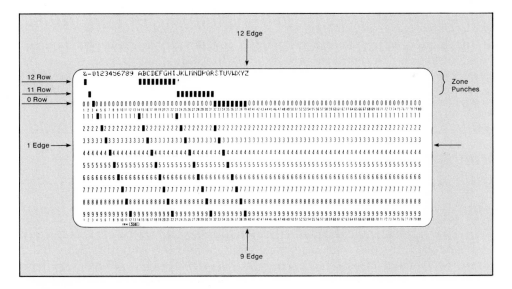

FIGURE 2–3. THE 80-COLUMN CARD

Card Punching Positions

Figure 2–3 illustrates the various punching positions of the card. The top three punching positions, which are labeled as the 12, 11, and 0 rows, are referred to as the *zone punching positions*. If a number becomes negative while it is being processed, it is not uncommon for an 11 punch to be punched above the last digit of the number. The 11 punch is often referred to as an "X" punch and is used frequently for a *control punch*. Control punches are used to tell a machine to process the card in a different manner when the punch exists than when it is not present in the card. For example, an 11 punch in card column 49 might tell a machine to subtract while the amount fields in an "NX" (no 11 punch) card will be added.

Hollerith Code

The 0, 11, and 12 rows are referred to as the *zone punching positions*, while the 0 through 9 rows are called the *digit* punching positions. Keep this in mind as you look at figure 2–3 again. Do you see the pattern that is made by the alphabet as it is punched into the card? What is required for each letter of the alphabet? The code which uses *1 zone* and *1 digit* punch in the same card column for representing the letters of the alphabet is called the *Hollerith code*. Looking at the code, where is there a "skip" in the pattern? The pattern is broken when the zone of a 0 and the digit of a 1 is not used to represent the letter *S*. No one really knows why Hollerith chose not to use the 0–1 for the letter *S* but most people feel that he was concerned that the early equipment used to process the card might not treat the 0–1 as a letter since the digit punch is so close to the 0 zone punch. The easy way to remember the Hollerith code is that *J–R* is in the middle.

LETTER	ZONE	DIGITS FROM	EXAMPLES
A–I	12	1–9	A = 12 & 1, B = 12 & 2 . . .
J–R	11	1–9	J = 11 & 1, K = 11 & 2 . . .
S–Z	0	2–9	S = 0 & 2, T = 0 & 3 . . .

Why is the Hollerith code important? As you see from looking at figure 2–3, what is punched in the card is printed directly above the column in which it is punched. If this is the case, why worry about the Hollerith code? There are a few isolated cases when the operator may wish to know what is punched in a given card column that has not been interpreted. The operator would then need to know the code to find out what was punched in the card. A more valid reason for learning the Hollerith code is that so many other codes used to store data in the computer, on magnetic tape, or on disk, are based on a variation of the code.

CARD FORMATS

When a given card *format* or design is used frequently, the cards are printed and ruled so that both the keypunch operators and the machine operator can more easily identify the area of the card in which the data is punched. The "drop" and "add" cards in figure 2–4 illustrate the use of printed cards. Each *field* is ruled and labeled so there is no question where the student's name, number, or other data should be punched in the card. A *field* is one or more columns reserved for a particular purpose. If the data is not punched in the exact card columns that are reserved for it, the machine processing the card would have no idea of what data it is actually processing. Information must also be *justified* correctly in the card. Justification is a term used to indicate if the field of data is to be aligned to the right or left. The rules for justification are simple and logical.

Justify alphabetic fields to the left.
Justify numeric fields to the right.

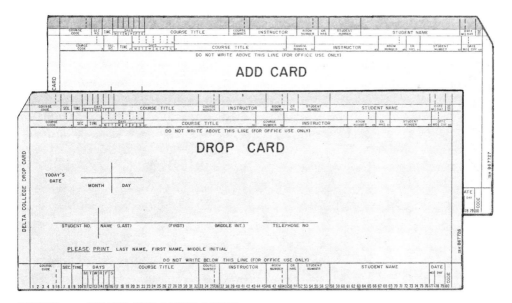

FIGURE 2–4. "DROP" AND "ADD" CARDS

Isn't this what you always do when you process information manually? If you want to add 9,417, 813, and 12, how would you list the fields?

RIGHT WAY TO JUSTIFY	WRONG WAY	WHY WRONG?
9	9	Would be added as 900
417	417	
813	813	
12	12	Would be added as 120

You can see that if the numeric information is not justified in the field correctly the results will be wrong. You as an individual have an edge over both the unit-record equipment or the computer because when you look at the figures which are listed incorrectly you immediately think, "I can't add them like that because the answer would be incorrect." You would then list them correctly, add, and get a correct total. *Machines only know what man tells them.* If the machine is told that the field has three digits in it, it has no way of recognizing that the 9 should really have been represented by 009. If alphabetic fields are justified incorrectly, the results will not print out as we have become accustomed to seeing printed material. For example, there are three fields of alphabetic information in the card. The first field is from 1–20, the second from 21–40, and the third from 41–60.

		HOW PRINTED IF:	
CARD COLUMNS	CONTENTS	JUSTIFIED CORRECTLY	JUSTIFIED INCORRECTLY
1–20	Joe Smith	Joe Smith	Joe Smith
21–40	2113 Park Street	2113 Park Street	2113 Park Street
41–60	Bay City, Michigan	Bay City, Michigan	Bay City, Michigan

How the fields are justified when the card is punched may seem a minor point yet so much depends on it. Machines must know exactly where the information will be in the card, and the simple rules pertaining to justification of the data must be followed in preparing the input if the desired results are to be achieved.

Card Identification

There are a number of things that can be done to make it easier to handle cards and prevent errors from occurring. The "drop" card in figure 2–4 has a green stripe at the top while the "add" card has a pink stripe. If payroll cards have a pink edge and a green card appears in the deck, the operator should immediately question why that card is in the deck. Corner cuts, color, stripes, marking the first card with the word "first" and the last card in the deck with the word "last," and labeling decks are all simple ways of making sure that the right cards are used in the right way in the procedure being processed. Simple techniques used to make certain that the cards are processed correctly result in valid output.

ABOUT MR. HOLLERITH'S CODE

2–5. Why is the standard punched card limited to 80 characters of data?

2–6. What term is used to identify one or more card columns that are reserved for a specific purpose?

2–7. Can the machines that process the cards distinguish color and know, by the color, when a wrong card is being processed?

2–8. Card columns 11–16 are reserved for the amount field. The amount of 1414 (fourteen dollars and fourteen cents) is to be punched in the card. How must it be punched?

2–9. Why would the name CHARLIE be punched in card columns 21 through 27 if the first name field is in 21 through 30?

2–10. When you manually record a column of numbers for processing how are they justified?

2–11. The Hollerith code requires that a zone punch and a digit punch be used in the same card column to represent each letter of the alphabet. Give the zone and digit punches required for each of the following letters: A, K, D, and T.

2–12. What punches in the card are referred to as the zone punches?

2–13. What is punched in the card if the operator is told to use the "X" control punch?

CARD PUNCH MACHINES

The card punch machines, or keypunches, can vary a great deal depending upon which model is selected. It is possible to buy or rent keypunches which punch only numeric data, can punch both numeric and alphabetic data but have no printing capabilities, or keypunches that both print and punch each character as the operator strikes the key. The full keyboard machines with the printing capability are by far more popular than the other two types of keypunches. These machines are referred to as *serial* punching machines because the data is punched into the card, column by column, as the operator depresses the appropriate key. If the operator senses that a mistake has been made, it is necessary to release the card which has the mistake, duplicate the data into a new card up to the point where the error occurred, make the necessary correction, and then continue keying the rest of the data into the card.

UNIVAC was the first company to develop a storage *buffer* which makes it possible for the operator to backspace and correct the wrong column of information. After all of the data is keyed in and at the request of the operator, the entire contents of the buffer are punched into the card. The simple backspace and rekeying operation needed to correct errors can be accomplished much faster than releasing the card with the error, duplicating up to the point of the error, correcting the error, and then continuing on with the keying in of the rest of the data. IBM also has available a data recorder which allows the operator to key in the entire contents of the card and then, upon the operator's request, all of the data is punched into the card.

The IBM Data Recorder has additional capabilities as it can store statistical data pertaining to the punching operation. The number of cards punched, the number of strokes, and the number of mistakes can be punched, from a memory buffer, into a card at the end of the job. This information can be used to determine the efficiency of the operator. In addition, it is also possible to store the totals from up to three numeric fields and punch them into a card at the end of the job. For example, a batch total was established for the time cards by adding both the regular hours and the overtime hours on an adding machine or by using a printing calculator. The keypunch is *programmed* so that the totals for both the regular hours and overtime hours are available at the end of the job. As the operator keys in the hours, the totals are accumulated and at the end of the job are punched into a card and compared with the batch totals that were established earlier. If the two totals do not agree, the operator must determine the cause of the discrepancy in the two totals.

Operating the Keypunch

The keyboard illustrated in figure 2–5 is the one used on the IBM 129 Data Recorder. Not all keyboards have the same special characters, and care must be taken when a keypunch is ordered that it is compatible with the equipment that will be used to process the card. In a large installation, with perhaps several different kinds of equipment, conversion charts must be used to determine what key should be used to punch a special character, depending upon which piece of equipment will be used to process the card. This lack of uniformity, as to what is actually punched into the card for a given symbol on the keyboard, applies only to the special characters and not the numeric or alphabetic characters.

FIGURE 2–5. 129 DATA RECORDER KEYBOARD. (Courtesy International Business Machines Corporation)

The Keyboard

The major difference between the typewriter and the keypunch keyboard is the location of numbers. The keyboard of the keypunch is by far the more efficient arrangement for recording numeric data. In contrast the numbers on a typewriter are harder to reach, and generally even a good typist is far slower on numeric data than on alphabetic data. In keypunching far more numeric data is punched than alphabetic so the efficiency of punching numeric data becomes important. Another advantage to the numeric keyboard arrangement of the keypunch is that only the right hand is needed to punch numbers which leaves the left hand free to handle documents. Rather than shifting for upper or lower case letters as you do on the typewriter, the shift on a keypunch is to numeric or alphabetic *mode*.

Looking at the keyboard you will see that the "J" key appears as the Ⓙ.
If the keypunch is in *numeric shift* and the key is depressed, a single punch
will be made in the 4 row of the card. If the keypunch is in alphabetic shift,
two punches will be made in the same column of the card. A punch will be
made in both the 11 row and the 1 row of the same card column which is the
representation, or Hollerith code, for the letter J. There are a few special keys
on the keyboard with which you should be familiar.

KEY	IN NUMERIC SHIFT WILL PUNCH	WILL PRINT ON THE CARD
(SKIP)	11 punch	—
(& P)	12 punch	& (or +)
(0 /)	0 punch	0

The Program Card

The keypunch can be programmed to skip card columns which are to be
left blank, duplicate constant data from one card to another, and to automatically shift from one mode to another. If the keypunch *is not* under program control, *it is in alphabetic shift.* If the keyboard is under program control, it is automatically in numeric shift unless the field is designated on the
program card as alphabetic.

No program card ⟶ Alphabetic shift
Under program control → Numeric shift unless coded to shift
    to alphabetic

Skip, dup, and *shift* are the three functions that can be programmed for
by punching the correct codes into the program card which will go on the
drum in the program control unit. Figures 2–6 and 2–7 illustrate both the program control unit and the program drum.

Figure 2–8 illustrates a simple card format which contains four fields of
information. Since the card contains both constant and variable information,
as well as an area to be skipped, it is far easier to punch the data into the card
if the keypunch is under *program control.* The program control card which
would be punched to control the keypunching operation is illustrated in figure
2–9.

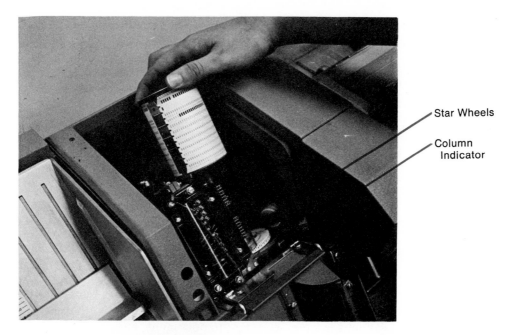

Star Wheels

Column
Indicator

FIGURE 2–6. PROGRAM CONTROL UNIT.

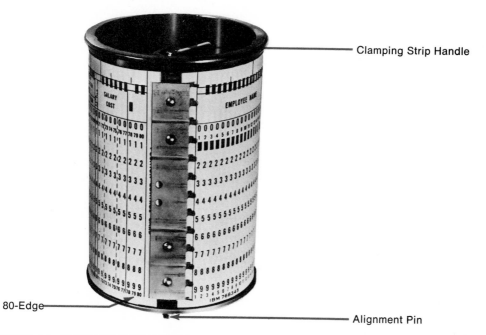

Clamping Strip Handle

80-Edge

Alignment Pin

FIGURE 2–7. PROGRAM DRUM. (Courtesy
International Business Machines Corporation)

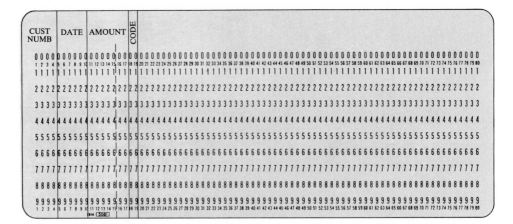

FIGURE 2–8. CARD FORMAT

In the card format illustrated, the customer's number is in card columns 1–4. The field must be keyed in by the operator as it contains *variable numeric information* which changes from document to document. The date field, which is in card columns 5–10, is *constant* information, as it is the same on all documents and may therefore be duplicated into the cards. The next field, in card columns 11–17, is *variable* information, as the amount differs on each source document. Since the code field contains alphabetic data, the keypunch must be told that it is to shift from numeric to alphabetic mode. The rest of the card, from card columns 20–80, may be treated as one large field to be "skipped."

The card codes that will be needed to instruct the keypunch to skip, duplicate, or to shift from numeric to alphabetic mode are:

IN THE FIRST CARD COLUMN OF THE FIELD, PUNCH A:	FUNCTION
11	To initiate a skip.
0	To initiate a duplicate field.
1	To initiate a shift from numeric mode to alphabetic mode.
(blank)	First card column of a variable numeric field. Nothing is punched in the card column. The space bar is used to leave a blank column in the card.
12	Field definition.

To initiate a skip, duplication, or shift, a punch is used in row 11, 0, or 1 of the first card column of the field in which the function takes place. The rest of the field is defined with a punch in the 12 row to tell the keypunch how long it is to skip or duplicate. The 1 code for alphabetic shifting is continued throughout the entire field. In coding the program card for the card format in figure 2–8 the following codes would be punched in each of the card columns designated.

CARD COLUMNS	FIELD	PUNCH	FUNCTION
1	CUSTOMER	blank	First card column of variable numeric data.
2–4	NUMBER	12	Tell how long the field is.
5	DATE	0	Duplicate date as it is constant data.
6–10		12	Define length of duplicated field.
11	AMOUNT	blank	First card column of variable numeric data.
12–17		12	Define the length of the field.
18	CODE	1	Shift to alphabetic.
19		A	Define field and continue in alphabetic mode.
20	Blank card	11	Start a skip.
21–80	columns	12	Define length of field that is skipped.

The drum card that was punched according to the codes indicated for the card format illustrated in figure 2–8 is shown in figure 2–9.

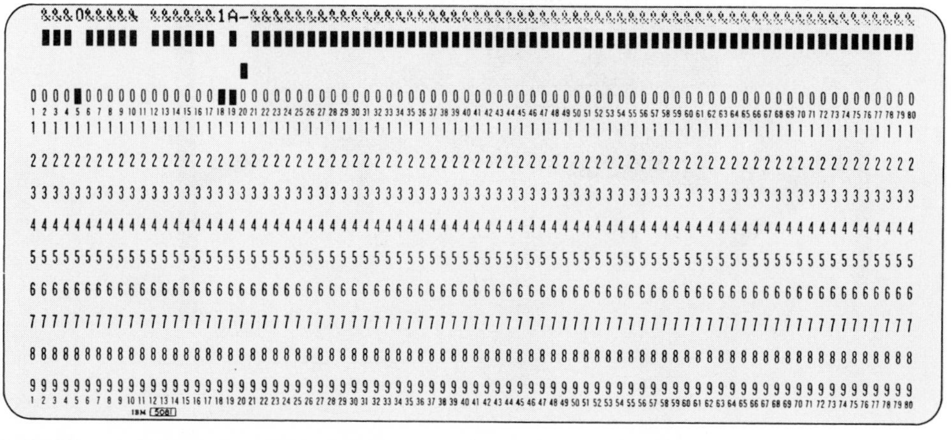

FIGURE 2–9. PROGRAM DRUM CARD

Advantages of Punching under Program Control

Why make a program drum card? The functions desired will be performed automatically and save the keypunch operator a great deal of time and effort. In addition there are some "bonus" factors. If the field is defined as a numeric field and the operator depresses the "A" key, the machine will lock. Having the keyboard lock will prevent the operator from making a mistake. The keyboard is unlocked by using the error correction key or backspace key. If the operator wishes to skip an entire field that had been defined for either

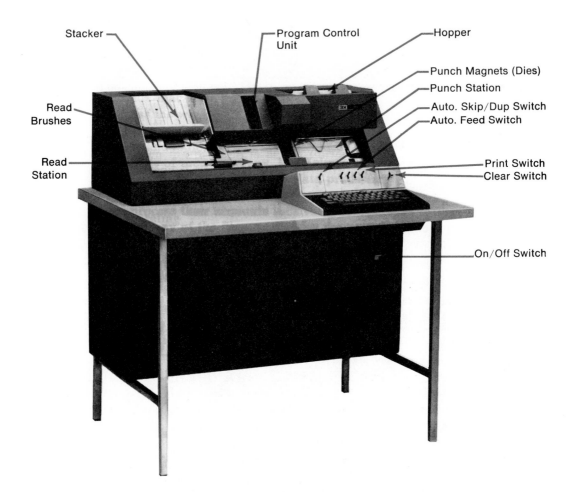

FIGURE 2–10. 029 KEYPUNCH

variable alphabetic or numeric information, the *skip* key is depressed and the card is positioned automatically at the first card column of the next field that is to be punched. It is also easier to justify fields correctly when the keypunch is under program control rather than manual control.

The program card is placed on the drum of the keypunch and the star wheels, which are small "star-shaped" devices that read the code, are lowered. When a punch is detected in a given row, by a star wheel coming in contact with the drum, an impulse is transmitted to the keypunch control device to instruct the machine what it is to do—skip, shift, or duplicate.

Starting the Job

The machine is turned on by using the mainline switch. At the same time the operator usually turns on both the automatic feed and the print switch. Cards are placed in the hopper and the feed key is depressed which causes a card to be positioned at the punch station. The feed key is again depressed which *registers* the first card under the *punch dies* and causes the second card to be positioned in the punch station.

Since card column 1 is defined on the program card as the first column of variable numeric data, the machine waits for the operator to key in four digits of data. The next field, the date, is to be duplicated. Until there is a card with the date punched in it under the *read brushes,* the keypunch has no way of duplicating the information into the date field. The operator keys the date into the first card and *then turns on the automatic skip-dup key.* The amount field, which is keypunched next, may be recorded on the source document as 42.13. The operator would key in 0004213 so that the field would be *justified correctly. The decimal is not punched in the card.*

The keypunch shifts automatically to alphabetic mode and the operator keys in the code. After the second character of the code is entered, the card "skips" out, another card is fed, and the card which was waiting in the punch station is automatically registered. The operator keys in the second customer's number, the date is automatically duplicated from the first card (now under the reading brushes) into the second card, the amount is keyed in, and then the code. The first card goes into the *stacker.* The second card advances to under the reading brushes, and a third card is registered under the punch dies.

Other Ways to Increase Productivity

Using a program drum card and keypunching under program control is one way to increase productivity. Productivity can also be increased if:

1. The flow of information on the card is the same as the flow of information on the source document. If this is done, production will be increased and the error rate will decrease.
2. The card is designed so that the fields to be keyed in are all adjacent to one another. An exception to this rule would be made if the card were to be handled a great deal and the fields read visually. Blank spaces between fields would then increase the readability of the data.

Other Special Features of Card Punch Machines

The IBM Data Recorder has the ability of having up to six different formats available to the user simultaneously. This is a convenient feature as often one document will require that two or three different formats be used when punching the data into the appropriate cards. The operator codes the desired formats in much the same manner, but an actual drum card is not used. Other machines have an alternate program feature which permits the desired codes for the second format to be punched in the 3–9 rows of the drum card. The operator, when punching a job that requires two different card formats, can easily switch from one format to another by using the alternate program switch.

Another feature which helps to increase productivity and decrease errors is the lead zero insertion feature. If a field is seven digits long, the appropriate code is used to define the numeric field in the program control card. When keypunching, if the amount of 14.13 is to be punched into the card, the operator only keys in 1413, and then use the left zero key. The number, which was stored in a buffer, is automatically punched into the card with the correct number of lead zeroes inserted so that 0001413 is actually punched into the card. This feature not only justifies the data correctly but also permits the operator to rekey a field which is recorded incorrectly if the error is sensed before the left zero key is used. The entire field of data, stored in the buffer, can be erased by using the error correction key which then permits the operator to key in the right amount.

The keypunch can also be used to duplicate a card which is damaged to such an extent that it cannot be processed in other machines. This can be done since the critical area of the card, as far as the keypunch is concerned, is *not* the 9 or 12 edge. In most other machines which process the card, if the 9 or 12 edge is even slightly "nicked" the card will not be read into the machine.

An interpreting feature also is available on the keypunch which will cause what is punched in the card to be printed on the top edge of the card. This is a useful feature as computer output is generally not interpreted and it is sometimes desirable to be able to read what is punched in the card.

2–14. When the keyed data first goes into a buffer rather than being punched directly into the card, what advantage is achieved?

2–15. The 129 Data Recorder can accumulate statistics regarding the keypunching operation such as the number of cards punched, the number of keystrokes. What else can it record?

2–16. In addition, how many fields of information can a data recorder total? It might, for example, total all of the amounts keypunched from the cash receipts forms. What could the total punched at the end of the keypunching operation be compared with?

2–17. Why is it so essential that the input which is keypunched be correct? Perhaps, it is even more important when punched cards are used than when the data is processed manually.

2–18. If you punch the key with the + on the top of the key, will it always, regardless of the keypunch used, cause a punch to occur in the 12 row?

2–19. What is the major difference between the typewriter keyboard and that of the keypunch?

2–20. What key is used for the 11 punch, the 12 punch, and the 0 punch?

2–21. The "K" key has a 5 above the K. What must the operator do, if there is no program card on the drum, to get a 5 punch rather than the "K"?

2–22. A numeric field is to be punched in card columns 11–16. How would 3.33 be keyed in the card?

2–23. Why is it so important to justify numeric information?

2–24. What are the three automatic features that can be programmed for by using the correct codes in the drum card?

2–25. What punches are used in the control card for the following purposes:
A. to initiate a skip,
B. to initiate a duplication,
C. to initiate a shift, or
D. to tell the keypunch how long to skip, duplicate, or to remain shifted?

2–26. Identify the card path through the keypunch:
A. Where are the blank cards placed?
B. What is card column one under after the card is registered?
C. Where does the card go immediately after it is punched?
D. Where does the card go after it is read by the reading brushes?

2–27. Why can a card which is damaged and cannot be read by the computer's card reader or other card processing equipment still be manually duplicated on the keypunch?

2–28. What does the interpreting feature of the keypunch do?

CARD VERIFICATION

After the card is keypunched it is usually verified by a machine which looks like the keypunch except that it has sensing devices rather than punch magnets. The verifier operator begins the verification process by putting the same control card on the verifier as the one used during the keypunching operation. The source documents must be in their original sequence as the operator must use them in the verification process. If the documents are out of sequence, it would be very difficult to know which card corresponds to which document. Usually there is a way of relating the card to the document, such as having the order number which is on the document punched in the card, but the whole process is much easier if the documents are kept in sequence.

Figure 2–11 illustrates a correctly verified card, which is notched on the right edge of the card, and an invalid card, which is notched above card column 17. In card column 17 a 4 had been incorrectly punched. When the verifier operator depressed the 3, which is correct, the sensing mechanism could not make contact as it should since there was not a punch in row 3. A red light comes on which notifies the operator that the same key was not used for the card column being verified, as the key used by the keypunch operator who originally recorded the data. The verifier operator uses the error correction key and tries again. Once again the light comes on because the verifier operator is correct. The operator is given the third chance. This time, however, the

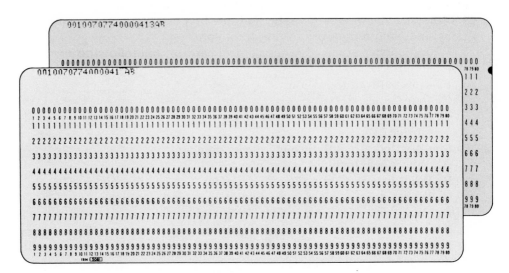

FIGURE 2–11. INVALID CARD AND VERIFIED CARD

machine says "I have given you three chances—three and out!" The card is notched above the column that contains the error. The operator does finish verifying the rest of the card to make certain that there are no additional errors.

The notched card must be keypunched over again and then reverified. In correcting the mistake, the card can be duplicated up to the point of error, card column 17 is rekeyed with a 3, and the balance of the card is duplicated. After the corrected card is verified and found to be correct, a notch is punched automatically by the verifier on the 80 edge of the card.

Some data recorders can serve as both a keypunch and a verifier. The IBM 129, for example, can be used to

1. serially (one card column at a time) punch data into the card,
2. store the entire contents of the card into a buffer from which it is punched into the card all at one time,
3. verify the card.

WHY VERIFY CARDS?

The more automated a job becomes the more vital it is that the data is entered into the system correctly. Each installation must decide for itself what fields in the card should be verified. As much more sophisticated methods are studied regarding entering data into the system, you will discover that even more emphasis is placed upon making certain that the data is valid.

One installation does no verification other than visually checking the cards. They have an extremely low error rate as the keypunching is decentralized and each department does its own punching. No longer can the sales department say "the data processing department did not use valid input." The problem, if there is one, is all theirs! The concept of decentralization is a good one except that the utilization of the equipment is not as high as when the operation is centralized. Most data processing managers and analysts, who make the decision as to what should be verified or not, are of the "old school" and tend to insist that all fields be verified. Therefore, if it takes four hours to punch the cards it will take four hours to verify the cards.

Who should verify the cards? It is generally considered good practice to have your more experienced operators verify the cards. The person who punches the cards should not be the same person as the one who verifies the cards. One of the reasons that the card has continued to be popular is that the verification method, although expensive, is a good one. The recording of data from the source document is divided into two operations: recording the data and checking the data. *It is much cheaper to correct the error at the re-*

cording stage rather than letting the error get into the system. Once invalid data enters the system, several reports may be invalid, wrong merchandise may be shipped, the wrong customer billed, or any number of costly errors can result.

REGARDING VERIFICATION

2–29. If a 5 is punched in a given card column, what will happen if the person verifying the cards depresses the 6 rather than the 5?

2–30. How many additional chances is the operator given before the card will notch as an error card?

2–31. When a card is noted as an error card, what must be done?

2–32. Why is it so important that the information be recorded in the card correctly?

SEQUENCING THE CARDS

If multiple usage is to be obtained from cards, each use may require that the input be arranged in a different order. The cards that are keypunched from the sales order will eventually have the following fields of data:

Customer Number   Salesman's Number
Order Number   Item or Part Number
Date   Selling Price
Quantity   Description

There are many potential uses for the information once it is correctly recorded in the card.

SEQUENCED BY	USE OR REPORT GENERATED FROM CARD
Customer Number	Credit check Printing of actual sales invoice Summary card for accounts receivable statement
Item or Part Number	Check to determine if the items are on hand to fill the order Updating the inventory Sales analysis by part number Report on inactive or slow moving items
Salesman's Number	Commission report Sales analysis by salesman

CARD SORTER

Many other possible uses for the sales order cards do exist. The sequence the cards are in determines to a large extent the type of report that can be prepared from the cards. Figure 2–12 illustrates the IBM 083 Sorter which can sort cards at the rate of 1,000 cards per minute. The basic functions that the sorter is used for are

1. sequencing cards either numerically or alphabetically,
2. selection of cards,
3. card count,
4. under certain conditions the merging of two or more decks of cards.

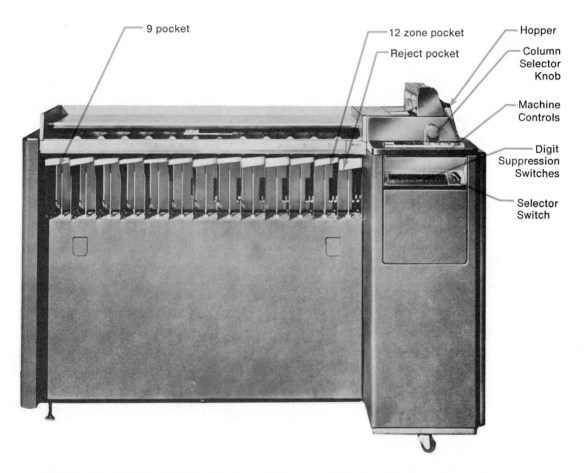

9 pocket   12 zone pocket   Hopper

Reject pocket   Column Selector Knob

Machine Controls

Digit Suppression Switches

Selector Switch

FIGURE 2–12. IBM 083 SORTER (Courtesy of International Business Machines Corporation)

Since the sorter only has one brush, only one column of information is sequenced at a time. If the account number is in card columns 1–4, four passes would be required to sequence the deck. The cards are first sorted on 4, then 3, 2, and finally card column 1. The sorter uses a very simple mechanical principle which makes it possible for the card to go into the pocket corresponding to the punch in the card. Figure 2–13 illustrates a situation where a 5 was punched in the card. The impulse created activates the metal coils and the chute blades are pulled down, and since the card cannot go under the blades it will be channeled, in this case, into the 5 chute which leads to the 5 pocket. If a blank card column is detected, the blades remain up for the entire duration of processing that particular card. The card will then go into the reject pocket. Although the principle is simple, it is remarkable when you consider that the various sorters available sequence *a given column of information* at the rate of from 400 to 2,000 cards per minute.

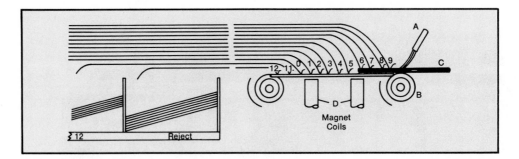

FIGURE 2–13. BASIC PRINCIPLE OF THE 082 SORTER

In the illustration, *A* is the brush which must be positioned over the card column which is being sorted. The brush consists of many fine wires which will create an impulse when they come in contact with *B* which is the metal contact roller. The only way an impulse can be created is to have a hole punched in the card being processed. The magnetic coils are utilized to pull the metal chute blades down so that the card may no longer pass underneath the blades. Once this happens, the card must go into a chute which carries it into the corresponding pocket.

Numeric Sorting

The simplest sort is merely to arrange records, with one control field, in a given sequence. If the field sorted on is the part number, which is in card columns 11–15, the brush is first placed over card column 15, which is called the *unit position* of the field, and the cards are sorted. They are removed from the stackers, joggled, and placed back in the hopper. The brush is moved to column 14 and the process repeated until all five card columns are sorted. *Cards are sorted from unit position to high order position.* The terms unit position and high order position are important as a way of referencing where the data is within the field. When the computer is studied, these terms will also be used.

The sort operation takes the constant attention of the operator, as there is a good deal of card handling which must be done. If a given pocket becomes full, a lever is tripped due to the weight of the cards and the sorter will stop. The operator then puts the cards into the storage rack and continues the sort procedure.

Most card processing equipment has a way of notifying the operator that the stacker is full and that operator intervention is required. The operator learns to listen for "what stopped?" without being aware that he is doing so.

Block Sorting

The cards are sorted on the high order position which divides the deck into ten parts. In the zero pocket will be the cards ranging from 00000–09999, which is the first $\frac{1}{10}$ of the deck. Each *block* must be sorted in the conventional manner which is from card column 15 through 12. As soon as the first block is sorted, those cards may go to the next processing step.

Block sorting is used for three basic purposes.

1. It permits some of the cards to go to the next processing step before the entire sort operation is complete.
2. It permits two or three sorters to be used for the one job.
3. It divides the deck into more manageable segments.

If *today* the L. C. Smith Corporation had a very large sorting job, they would first convert the cards to tape or disk and then sort the tape or disk records. For a small job involving only two or three hundred cards, the sorter would still be used.

Relationship between Sorting and the Report

A report is desired which will give the total sales by year, by month, and by day, plus providing a final total of all sales made over a ten-year period of time. The only way to get such a report is to sort on the smallest unit first (days), then the next smallest unit (months), and finally on the year. The date field which is recorded as month, day, and then year is punched in card columns 11–16. The cards would therefore be sorted in the following manner:

FIELD NAME	CARD COLUMNS	SORTED BY	FIELD REFERENCED AS
Day	13–14	14,13	Minor
Month	11–12	12,11	Intermediate
Year	15–16	16,15	Major

The former rule of sorting from unit position to high order position still holds true for each individual field. Regardless of the equipment being used to sort the data, the operator must know the relationship between the various fields and know exactly where each field is within the record that is being processed.

Alphabetic Sorting

Alphabetic sorting is rarely done on a sorter because it becomes extremely time-consuming if a large number of cards are involved. On the 082 Sorter for each card column in the field, the cards must be sorted first on digit and then on zone. Figure 2–14 illustrates the first pass which sorts the cards by digit. Since the card enters the sorter face down, 9 edge first, the digit is

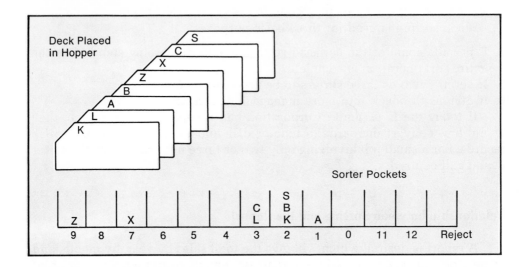

FIGURE 2–14. 082 SORT PASS ONE

encountered before the zone. For the first pass nothing is suppressed and the cards will go into their appropriate digit pocket. Figure 2–14 illustrates how the cards went into the sorter and how they were arranged in the pockets after the first pass.

The operator picks the cards up from right to left, joggles the cards, and places the cards in the hopper of the sorter for pass two. He uses the *suppression switch which when depressed makes it impossible for the card to get into a digit pocket.* The card will therefore continue on its way and end up in one of the three zone pockets. Figure 2–15 illustrates how the cards would have been placed in the hopper for the second pass and how they will appear in the pockets after completion of the pass.

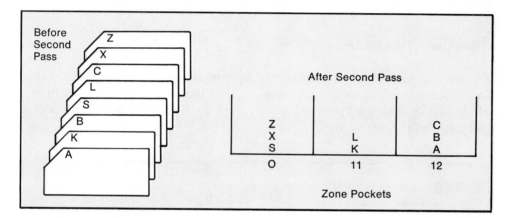

FIGURE 2–15. 082 SECOND PASS

Are the cards correct? Students sometimes feel that they would like to reverse the process and sort first on zone and then on digit. You might try this using the same eight cards, but unfortunately it will not arrange the cards in alphabetic sequence. You will find the cards must be sorted first on digit and then on zone if they are to be alphabetized correctly.

If an 083 Sorter is used, not all of the cards for any given card column must be sorted a second time. The operator has an option of having one group, by zone, sorted completely on the first pass. By using the A–I switch, that group of cards is completely sorted after the first pass as the A cards will be in pocket 1, the B cards in pocket 2, and so on. On the second pass the cards in the 11 pocket, the J–R cards, are sorted on digit with the results that the J cards will be in pocket 1, the K cards in pocket 2, and so on. The third pass, which involves only the S–Z cards, completes the sort.

Alternatives for Alphabetic Sorting

One alternative for sorting the cards alphabetically is to assign an alphanumerical code which can be used in sorting the cards. For example, each customer is given a number which when arranged in sequence will correctly alphabetize the cards.

Another solution is to sort only part of the field. Cards from which a mailing list is printed have the last name punched in 1–16, the first name in 17–26, and the middle initial in card column 27. The cards could be sorted first on 27, the middle initial, then the first two characters of the first name, 18 and 17, and then finally on the first four letters of the last name, 4, 3, 2, and 1. If the cards are listed on a printer, they will be in nearly perfect alphabetical sequence.

Other Uses of the Sorter

Two or more decks of cards may be merged on the sorter if the *control field,* such as student or account number, is in the same card columns in each of the decks that are to be merged. Figure 2–16 illustrates the concept of merging on the sorter.

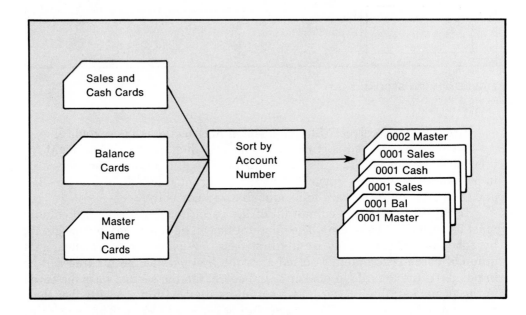

FIGURE 2–16. MERGING WHILE SORTING

The sorter may also be used to select out cards of any given number. The dean, for example, wants a report listing all students in data processing, which is curriculum 18. From the deck, which is in random sequence, all curriculum code 18 cards may be quickly selected by using the sorter. Experienced operators may also select out cards between a range of numbers. After decks are merged, the sorter is frequently used to separate the "X" cards from the "NX" cards. For example, the name and address master card has an 11 punch in card column 80 while the detail card does not have the "X" punch in 80. After the cards are passed through the sorter, the master cards will be in the 11 pocket and the "NX" cards in the reject pocket.

A counter is also available on most sorters which will keep track of the number of cards which are sorted. The card count can be used as another control device because each subsequent processing of the cards should provide a count showing the same number of cards as were sorted. There are also statistical sorters that count the cards that are in each pocket.

ABOUT SORTING

2-33. In producing reports from cards, does the card sequence make any difference?

2-34. In doing a numeric sort on a field located in card columns 15-20:
   A. What is the first card column the cards are sorted on?
   B. After they have been fanned and joggled, where are the cards placed for the second pass?
   C. Over what card column is the brush placed for the second pass?

2-35. Why does a blank card always end up in the reject pocket?

2-36. Why are cards seldom sorted on long alphabetic fields?

2-37. What alternatives are available if the firm feels it cannot justify the time and expense of sorting on a long alphabetic field, yet it wants a report which is listed alphabetically?

2-38. What sorting technique can be used which will permit part of the cards to go to the next task before an entire sort is completed?

2-39. Exactly how are the cards sequenced on the sorter if a report is to be printed which provides a total for *each* salesman, department, and store?

2-40. In 2-39 how is each individual field sorted?

2-41. A card has numeric data in 25-29. How are card columns 29 and 25 referenced?

2-42. Discuss the following statement. A firm has very limited funds. The newly hired data processing manager decides that a sorter is not all that important and eliminates the sorter from the rental agreement. They do not have a computer.

THE INTERPRETER

The interpreter, illustrated in figure 2–17, has only one function and that is to print what is punched in the card on the top of the card. The upper printing position is above the 12 row while the lower printing position is between the 11 and 12 rows of the card. Since the interpreter has only 60 typebars, the

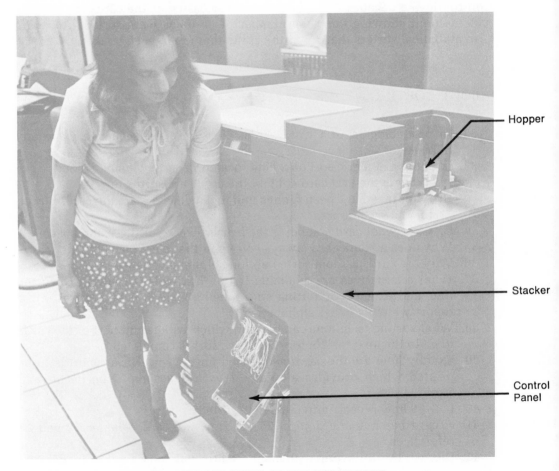

Hopper

Stacker

Control Panel

FIGURE 2–17. PLACING THE CONTROL PANEL IN THE INTERPRETER

card is interpreted twice if more printing is desired. Using the first panel, the printing would be done on either the upper or lower printing position of the card; then, using a second panel, the interpreter is adjusted by the operator to print on the opposite printing position and the cards are again interpreted.

The interpreter is used to explain the basic concept of control panel wiring since it has the simplest panel. All IBM unit-record equipment discussed in the text (other than the sorter, keypunch, and verifier) is instructed on how to perform its assigned tasks by means of a wired control panel which is found on the exterior of the machine.

Interpreter Control Panel

A basic understanding of how a control panel functions should be acquired as this will help in developing an understanding of why one machine can perform several basic tasks. To illustrate the flexibility of the interpreter the following example is provided.

The card illustrated in figure 2–18 has been prepunched on the reproducer or computer's card punch, with the employee number, name, department, cost center, and rate. The hours, job, and total fields will be keypunched into the card later. Each foreman in the plant has cards for the employees in his department which he uses to record the hours they work on each job. The card will serve as both a source document and input for a report that is run each day to show the labor cost which is to be added to each job under production. The report which will be run from the cards will give the total cost by job and by department.

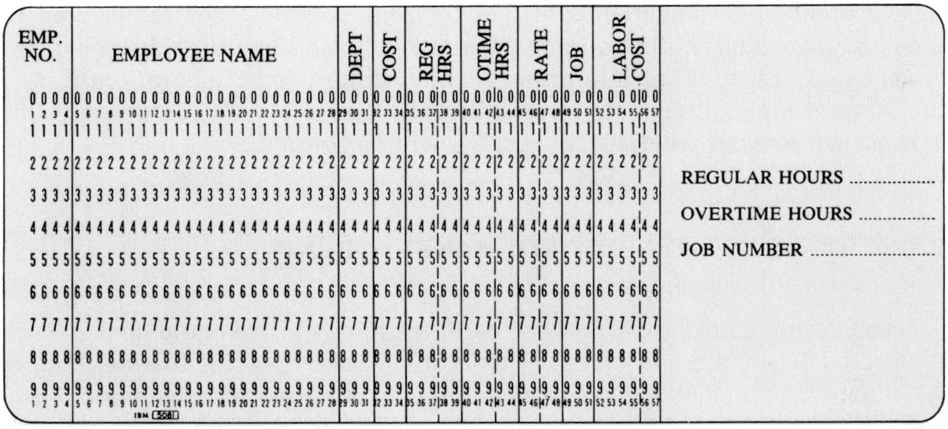

FIGURE 2–18. PREPUNCHED CARD USED AS SOURCE DOCUMENT

The analyst must determine what information he wants to interpret on the prepunched card, for he can, of course, interpret all of the fields. Perhaps the only really pertinent information that the foreman would be concerned with is the employee's number and name. In this case he might ask to have the employee's number printed on each end of the card. What is to be interpreted and where it will be printed are determined by how the control panel is wired. Figure 2–19 shows how the panel would be wired to print the employee number on both ends of the card. Note that the name is centered in the middle of the card rather than being printed on the left where it is punched.

Four wires are inserted in the hubs (holes in the control panel) marked "reading brushes" and then connected to the hubs marked "print entry." Since the print hubs are common, the impulse is available out of the hubs labeled as row N. They are then connected, by four more wires, to the hubs for print entries 57–60. The name field which is also to be interpreted is wired from reading brushes to print entries. As illustrated in figure 2–17 (p. 78), the panel is inserted in the exterior of the interpreter after it is wired to instruct it in what to read and where to print.

The card inset at the bottom of the diagram shows how the information would be printed on the card. You should also observe that the printing is larger than when the printing is added during the keypunching operation. Each character requires $1\frac{1}{3}$ card columns in which to print.

Straight Interpreting

Figure 2–20 illustrates how the panel would be wired if the analyst had decided that all fields would be interpreted. The card would be far easier to read if blank spaces had been left between the fields as they are printed on the card. The inset at the bottom of figure 2–20 also illustrates the use of the lower print positions for interpreting while the previous illustration utilized the upper print position. You can see that the user can easily determine what is to be printed and where on the card it will be printed.

BASIC CONCEPTS OF CONTROL PANEL WIRING

In figure 2–21 the basic concept behind all unit-record equipment is again illustrated. The entire card is ready by a full set of 80 reading brushes labeled A. If there is a punch in a given card column, an impulse is created which skips merrily along to the exterior of the machine which is labeled B on the diagram. The impulse can either be ignored or wired by the operator to activate a given

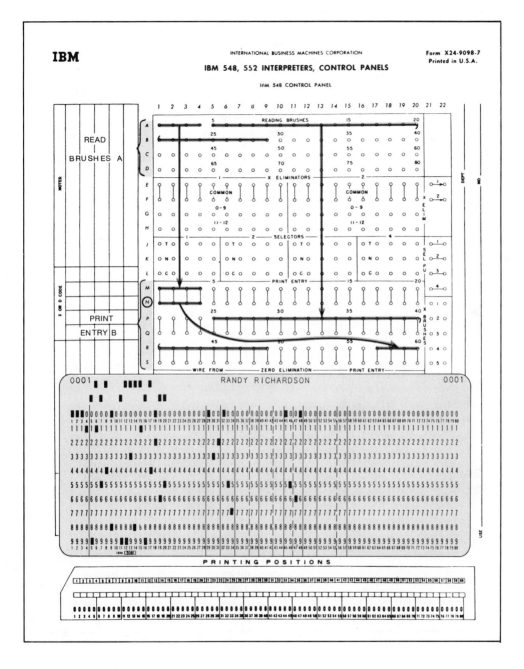

FIGURE 2-19. OFFSET INTERPRETING

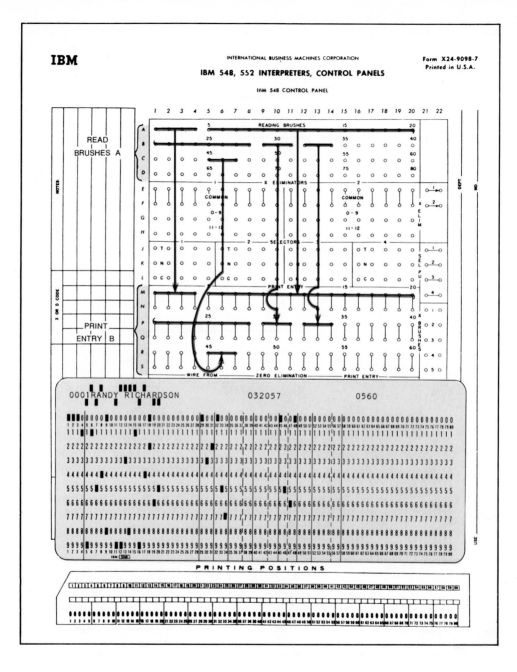

FIGURE 2-20. STRAIGHT INTERPRETING

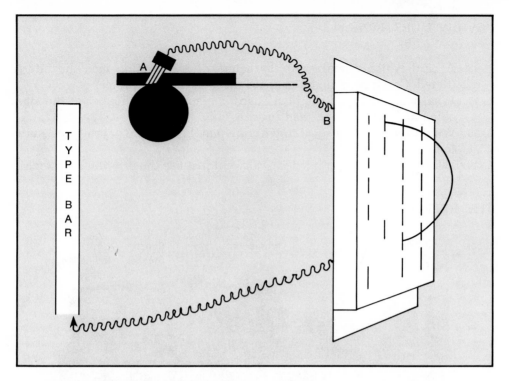

FIGURE 2–21. ACTIVATING THE TYPE BARS

typebar. The wires are manually inserted into the control panel by the operator. By referring back to figure 2–19 (p. 81), you can see that the 80 reading brushes are numbered and are at the top of the panel at the point labeled *A*. Each reading brush reads the corresponding column in the card. The operator can select which card columns he wishes to read and where he wants to print the data.

SUMMARY

1. The interpreter can only read punches and print what it reads on the card.
2. Each character printed requires 1⅓ card columns in which to print.
3. When the panel is wired, the machine is instructed as to what to read and where it is to be printed.
4. Usually the panels which are used for frequently run jobs are labeled and the same panel is used each time the job is run.

REVIEW QUESTIONS

2–43. A card which contains 70 characters of information must be inter-preted. Can it be done in one pass through the interpreter?

2–44. What would happen if a blank card is placed in the hopper of the ma-chine and read by the read brushes?

2–45. Would the operator need to wire the panel each time payroll cards are to be interpreted?

2–46. Why is an interpreter needed? Why not just use the printing keypunch?

THE REPRODUCER

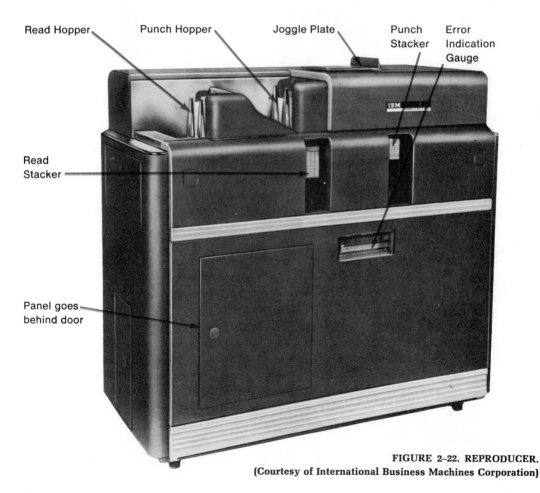

FIGURE 2–22. REPRODUCER.
(Courtesy of International Business Machines Corporation)

The reproducer can almost be thought of as two distinct machines. The read side has two sets of brushes and the punch side has one set of punch dies and one set of punch brushes.

The reproducer is again controlled by a wired panel. The importance of the panel is illustrated even better with this machine because the reproducer can perform four basic functions depending upon how the panel is wired.

1. *Reproducing*—A new deck is made either exactly like the old deck or with minor revisions such as dropping a field, enlarging another field, or re-arranging the fields into a different format. In reproducing, there is a one to one ratio because for each old card one new card is punched.
2. *Gangpunching*—Constant information is duplicated into one or more cards which follow the master card.
3. *Mark Sensing*—Information shaded on the card by using an electromagnetic pencil is converted to punches.
4. *Summary Punching*—Totals accumulated in the *counters* of the accounting machine can be punched into a new card. The two machines, the accounting machine and the reproducer, are connected with a large cable during summary punching.

Reproducing

A few illustrations are given as to why the reproducer is used to make a new deck of cards.

A keypunch operator has incorrectly punched the date into an entire deck of cards. The easiest and least expensive solution to the problem is to use the reproducer to punch all of the correct information into new cards. While this is being done, the date can be gangpunched into the new cards which are being reproduced from the invalid deck. Figure 2–23 illustrates the correction process which results in a valid deck of cards.

Because business has grown, the number of accounts receivable have increased to the point where the account number field, which is in card columns 1–4, is no longer large enough. By doing *offset reproducing*, the master deck may be duplicated, and any fields that are too small can be expanded. It is much less expensive to duplicate the information in this manner than to rekeypunch the master deck.

Straight reproduction may be done to replace a master deck which has become nicked or warped. When this happens, card jams will occur or the cards may not read into the machines, and time must be spent in replacing the master cards. At this point it is better to reproduce and interpret the entire master deck. A special panel called the 80–80 board may be used which has each reproducing brush wired to its corresponding punch magnet.

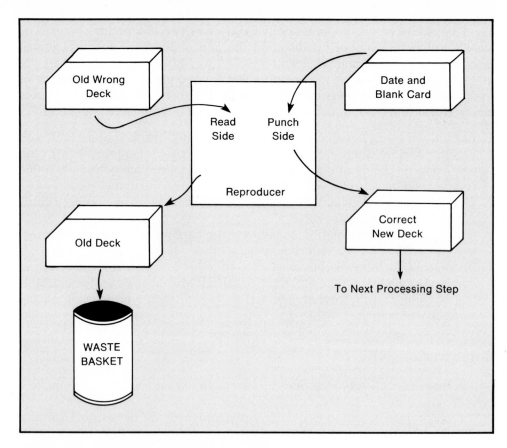

FIGURE 2–23. CORRECTION OF INVALID CARDS

The reproducer is often used to make a "backup" deck, which is an identical reproduction of the original master deck. *Throughout the entire text, the subject of how a backup for a master file is created will be referenced as it is an extremely important data processing function.*

Comparing

Are the cards accurately reproduced on the reproducer or not? The reproducer has a comparing feature which will check the original data against what is punched in the new card to determine if the two sets of information are the same. If not, an indicator appears on the card gauge which shows the operator where an unequal comparison exists. When this happens, the reproducer stops and the red error light is turned on. The comparing function is actually providing verification that the information punched into the cards by the reproducer is correct. If the reproducer malfunctions, this may also cause the compare light to be turned on.

Gangpunching

A master card contains the cost price, selling price, and description of the product. Rather than keypunching this data into each detail card, the reproducer can be used to gangpunch the data into the detail cards. By using the comparing feature of the reproducer, the accuracy of the gangpunching operation can be checked. Figure 2–24 illustrates the function which is called *master interspersed gangpunching*. When the reproducer is used for master interspersed gangpunching, the two sides of the machine are not functioning as one machine but as two separate units—one side for punching and the other side for comparing.

In *single gangpunching* one master card followed by the detail deck is placed in the punch hopper of the reproducer. The information is duplicated from the master card into all of the detail cards. In gangpunching the data from the master is punched into the first detail card, then from the first detail card into the second detail card, and so on, until the data has been added to the entire deck.

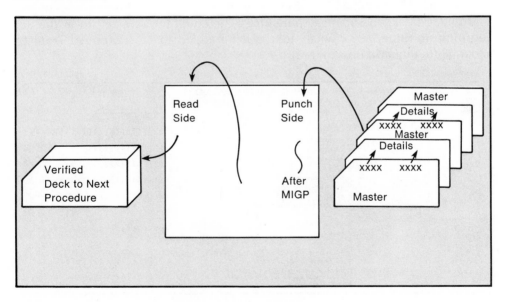

FIGURE 2–24. MASTER INTERSPERSED GANGPUNCHING

Mark Sensing

The area on the left of the card illustrated in figure 2–25 shows an area reserved for mark sensing. The number of finished pieces, in this case 005, is recorded on the card by using an electromagnetic pencil (like the one many of you have used in taking tests). Since each mark sensing area extends across three card columns, a maximum of 27 digits of information can be recorded on one card. The mark sensed deck is then placed in the punch hopper of the reproducer where the data is converted to punches.

What is good about mark sensing? *The information can be recorded at the source where the transaction occurred in a machine processable form by using a pencil.* If each individual records only a limited amount of information the technique works well. Since it is a dull repetitive job, however, if one employee is required to do mark sensing over a long period of time there would probably be an excessively high error rate. Much of the emphasis of data processing today is concerned with the concept which mark sensing illustrates—*let the individual at the point where the transaction is occurring record the data in machine processable form.*

Summary Punching

When the accounting machine, which is used as a printer, is connected to the reproducer the information stored in the *counters* of the accounting machine may be punched into a card by the reproducer. This function of the reproducer is called *summary punching*. The counters, referred to in the accounting machine, are devices that can be added to or subtracted from to accumulate numeric information.

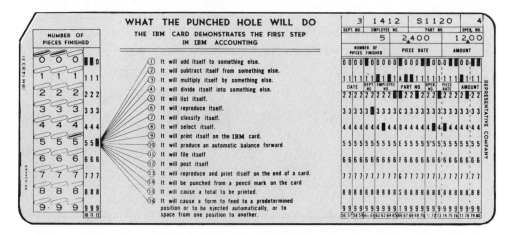

FIGURE 2–25. MARK SENSING. (Courtesy of International Business Machines Corporation)

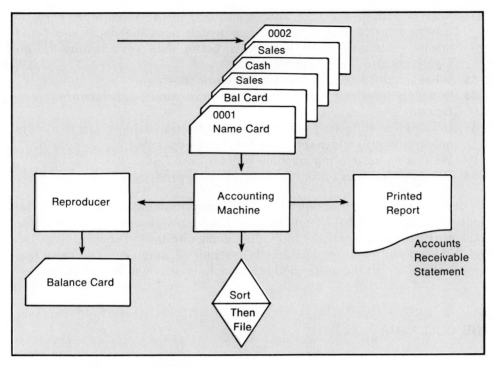

FIGURE 2–26. SUMMARY PUNCHING

Figure 2–26 illustrates the summary punching of a new balance card. For each customer there is a master card followed by the transaction cards which are then processed by the accounting machine to produce both a statement and a new balance card.

REVIEW THE REPRODUCER

2–47. What two kinds of reproducing jobs can be done on the reproducer?

2–48. In reproducing operations there is always a ratio of one to one. What does this mean?

2–49. In reproducing operations why are both sides of the machine used?

2–50. Is it common to gangpunch data into the new cards during a reproducing operation?

2–51. What are the two types of gangpunching?

2–52. In master interspersed gangpunching the punching is done on the punch side of the machine. What is the read side used for?

2–53. Why is adding the price and description to the sales order card by master interspersed gangpunching, which uses the detail cards and master price and description cards, better than keypunching the information into the cards?

2–54. What is the basic principle behind mark sensing?

2–55. Summary punching is a good illustration of what basic data processing function?

2–56. Discuss the following statement: In data processing there is always only one way in which the procedure can be executed.

2–57. What is an accounting machine *counter* used for?

2–58. What are the four basic functions of the reproducer?

It should be noted that reproducers, like any other data processing equipment, are available with different options. Some reproducers may not have the mark sensing capability if the individual designing the procedures does not feel there are sufficient applications to warrant its inclusion. The more features that are added the more costly the machine becomes to rent or buy.

THE COLLATOR

The collator is very versatile and can perform a wide range of assignments. Usually one of its two hoppers contains master cards while the other hopper contains the detail cards which are to be used in the application. The collator may compare in a given field to determine if the number in the one card is higher than, equal to, or lower than the same field in the second card. This is the same logical ability that the computer has. *Two values can be compared to determine if one is higher than, equal to, or lower than the other.*

Depending upon which model collator is being used, it will have either four or five pockets. Figure 2–27 shows a four-pocket collator. The following illustrations will be for a collator with five pockets. Figure 2–28 shows the restrictions placed on the master and detail cards in terms of to which pocket they may actually be sent. The master cards were placed in the primary hopper and the detail cards in the secondary hopper (see fig. 2–28).

Based on the comparison of the two numbers, the collator decides into which pocket the cards are to go. The master card can physically go into only the 1, 2, or 3 pocket. The detail cards are restricted to pockets 3, 4, and 5. Which feed will be activated, the primary or the secondary, is also determined by the results of the comparison. In some operations, however, no comparisions are made, so by control panel wiring the collator is instructed to continuously feed either masters, details, or both.

Stacker One

Hoppers
One for
masters,
one for
details.

Control Panel
behind door

FIGURE 2–27. 085 COLLATOR. (Courtesy of International Business Machines Corporation)

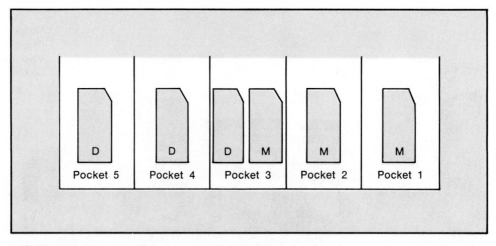

FIGURE 2-28. DETAILS IN 3, 4, 5—MASTERS IN 1, 2, 3

Most functions require that the *cards be sequenced in either ascending or descending* order before the collator can be used. Unless a sorter is available, the use that can be made of a collator is limited. The basic functions of the collator are:

1. *Merging*—two files, both in the same sequence, can be combined into one file.
2. *Merging with Selection*—two files, both in the same sequence, are combined into one file. If either file has a card that is unmatched in the other file, the card is put into a pocket other than the one being used for the merged deck. This form of merging is also referred to as match-merging.
3. *Matching*—the cards in the two files are compared to determine if there is both a master and a detail card for the number being compared. Both decks must be sequenced first on the sorter.
4. *Sequence checking*—Either one or both files may be checked to determine if the cards are in the correct sequence. Any time that merging, matching, or match-merging is being done, the sequence check is a "bonus" operation, as only two additional wires need be inserted on the control panel to have the additional check made on the validity of the job. Some collators can sequence only the primary or master file.
5. *Selection*—the collator can select out zero balance cards, the first card of a group, the last card of a group, the "X" cards, the "NX" cards, cards containing a given number such as 1213, or cards between a range of numbers. The examples given are only a few of the many different kinds of selection that can be done by the collator.

Match-merging

Figure 2–29 illustrates a match-merge operation. One card file contains the master cards while the second file which was already merged without selection contains the balance, cash, and sales cards for the customers. Both decks are in sequence by the customer number. Management has decided that if the customer has no detail cards that a statement should not be sent as the customer's sales account has been inactive for at least one month. Therefore, unmatched masters must be selected out of the operation.

In this operation would having selected masters be normal? Certainly, and perhaps one half or more of the inactive customer's master cards may select out. Should there be selected details? If a detail card does select out, a master name and address card must be prepared in order that the customer may be sent a statement. The most likely case where it might occur is when a new customer has been granted credit but the data processing department has not been notified to punch master cards. A special form should be used to transmit the information pertaining to new customers to the data processing department in order that master records can be established for new customers.

Can you see any possible use for the unmatched masters in pocket 1? A mailing could be sent out to all of the inactive customers. If this is to be done,

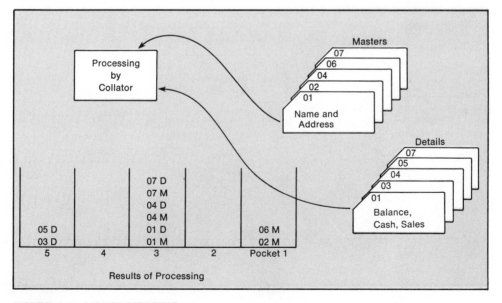

FIGURE 2–29. MATCH-MERGING

the selected masters can be used to produce a mailing label for the letter and other promotional materials that will be sent to the customer.

After the processing of the accounts receivable statements, the master deck *must be returned to the file as one complete deck.* An operator is always responsible for returning the decks to the file in the same way in which he found them. Figure 2–30 illustrates a simple merge operation that is required before the master cards can be refiled.

If the operator wishes, he may place two extra wires on the panel that will check the sequence of both decks as the merge operation takes place. This is usually done as it "costs" nothing and might detect sequence errors that occurred due to improper or poor card handling.

Matching and Selection

The academic dean would like a listing of all the students with a grade point average of 3.5 or above. The selected master cards will also be used to print mailing labels that are to be used in sending out a letter of congratulation to each student.

There are three different collator functions that will take place in completing the procedure. The job is complicated by the fact that the detail card

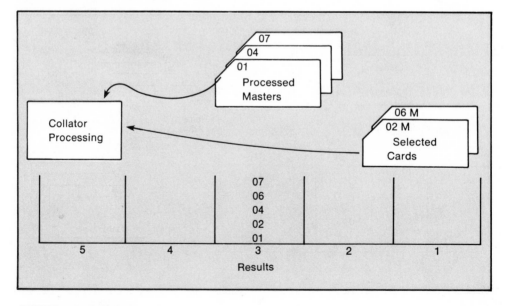

FIGURE 2–30. MERGING

contains the student's average while the master card contains the student's name and address.

1. The collator is used to select the detail cards for all students who have a grade point average of 3.5 or above (see fig. 2–31).

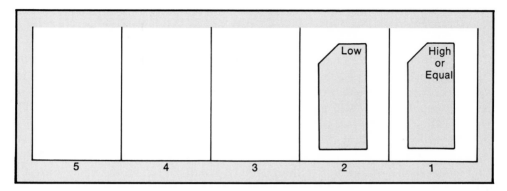

FIGURE 2–31. SELECTING HIGH OR EQUAL DETAIL CARDS

2. The "high" or "equal" detail cards are used in a matching operation with the student's master cards. The master cards for the students who do not have the required average will be unmatched and will therefore be selected into pocket 5 (see fig. 2–32).
3. The unmatched masters, or "low" cards are placed in a temporary file until they can be remerged with the matched masters. The detail cards that were used may be returned to the file along with the detail cards of those stu-

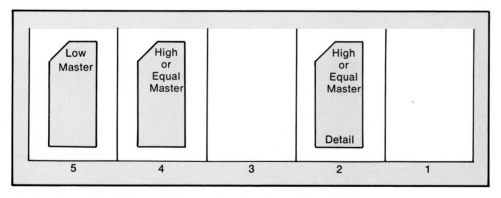

FIGURE 2–32. MATCHING MASTERS TO SELECTED DETAIL CARDS

dents who have less than a 3.5 grade point average. Since the detail file was maintained in no specific order, the cards are placed behind the ones already in the file.

4. The matched masters are used to produce the report and the mailing stickers that the dean wanted. The accounting machine would be used to produce both the report and the stickers.

5. The unmatched masters are taken from the temporary file and merged with the matched masters that were used to produce the desired report.

Another example of selection is the extraction of all records from a file that are between a range of numbers. The data processing department is instructed to pay bills (accounts payable) twice a week. A payment due on April 6 would have 0406 punched in the field reserved for the due date. On April 4 they wish to pay all bills that will become due on April 5, 6, or 7. A finder card is read first that contains the low date (0404) and the high date (0408). The cards to be removed from the file by the collator must be higher than 0404 (April 4) and lower than 0408 (April 8). Between the ranges are the cards that are desired for April 5, 6, and 7. Again, because the collator can compare and do a little simple logic, it will select those cards that meet the compound condition of being higher than April 4 and also lower than April 8.

ABOUT THE COLLATOR

2–59. List the five basic functions of the collator.

2–60. What must be done before two decks of cards can be merged, matched or match-merged on the collator?

2–61. Is there any relationship or similarity between the collator and a computer?

2–62. What function would you use for the following situations?
A. Combining two decks of cards, both of which are in sequence by student number.
B. The dean wants a report of all accounting students. They are identified with an 18 punched in card column 43–44 of the detail deck. What is the process for identifying the accounting student's detail cards?
C. We have 1,000 master cards for employees. However, only 900 of of the employees worked. The master cards are to be combined with the detail (time cards) in order that the payroll may be processed. What operation of the collator should be used to combine the master and detail cards?

D. New balance cards were punched on the reproducer or computer's card punch. Zero balance cards are to be removed from the deck before the cards are interpreted. If the collator is used, what operation would it be doing?

CALCULATORS

Sorters, reproducers, and collators can be found in many installations that have computers. In the small card oriented data processing installation they still serve many useful functions.

The calculator, however, is rarely found in a computer center. As the computer came in the front door, the calculator went out the back door. Or it did as soon as the jobs it had been doing were reassigned to the computer.

The calculator actually had two units, both of which had control panels. One unit read the information from the card and transmitted the data to the second unit. The second unit could store a limited amount of data and could do all four basic mathematical functions. The way in which the calculator was given the instructions is similar to programming a computer, because the problem had to be broken down into steps. One step might be to read a card, the second to add A and B, the third to store the answer, and so on. A step-by-step analysis of the problem had to be done before the calculator could perform the desired tasks. After the answer, or answers, were calculated, they were punched in the input card that had been read by the first unit.

The calculators were "programmed" to do up to 20, 40, or 60 steps in a given sequence. The maximum number of steps was determined by which model calculator was used. If a job had too many steps, the problem was broken into two parts and run as separate jobs. When first- and second-generation computers were more widely used than the third-generation computers, the same problem of exceeding the machine's capacity existed and computer programs had to be run in segments.

ACCOUNTING MACHINES

The accounting machine is also referred to as a tabulator or printer. Depending upon the model of the machine being used, it is possible to accumulate sixteen or more totals simultaneously in individual *counters*. The accounting machine, because of its ability to compare two numbers and determine if they are the same, can detect when the first card of a new group has

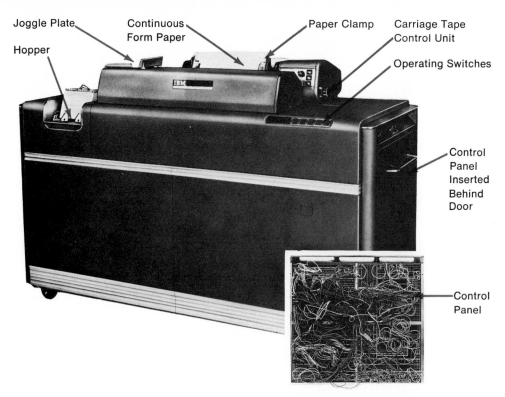

Joggle Plate Continuous Paper Clamp Carriage Tape
Form Paper Control Unit

Hopper Operating Switches

Control
Panel
Inserted
Behind
Door

Control
Panel

FIGURE 2–33. 407 ACCOUNTING
AND CONTROL PANEL. (Courtesy of International Business Machines Corporation)

been read. When the comparison of the two numbers is unequal a *level break occurs* which can be used to instruct the accounting machine to print totals, summary punch a card, and so on.

The concept of *level breaks* is important because it is used not only in the accounting machine to produce minor, intermediate, and major totals, but also in programming languages such as Report Program Generator and COBOL.

If the accounting machine is comparing on the man number, department number, and store number, which are punched in the input cards, the following results could occur:

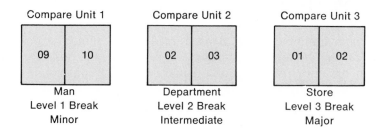

Compare Unit 1	Compare Unit 2	Compare Unit 3
09 10	02 03	01 02
Man	Department	Store
Level 1 Break	Level 2 Break	Level 3 Break
Minor	Intermediate	Major

Through control panel wiring the accounting machine is provided with the following information:

1. What to add or subtract
2. When to add or subtract
3. When to print out the answer
4. Where to print the answer
5. When to single space, double space, or skip to a new section of a report
6. What fields of information are to be accumulated for a new balance
7. When to summary punch a new balance card
8. When the report is to be *listed* and when it is to be *group printed*

Printing Reports

The *continuous form paper* used in the accounting machine has pin feed holes along both edges which insert over metal prongs prior to clamping the paper into position (see fig. 2–34). The vertical movement of the paper is controlled by a carriage tape and the control panel. The tape is matched against the special form, such as the student grade report, that is to be used in the printing application. Each vertical printing position is indicated by using a separate channel on the tape.

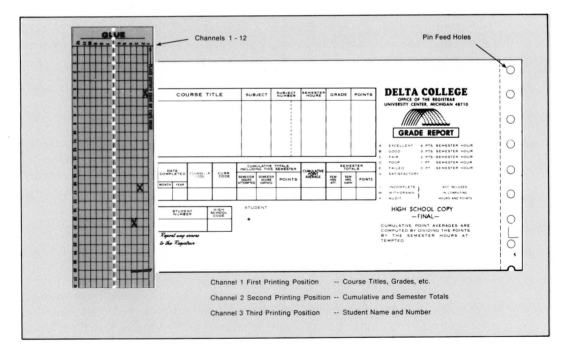

Channel 1 First Printing Position -- Course Titles, Grades, etc.

Channel 2 Second Printing Position -- Cumulative and Semester Totals

Channel 3 Third Printing Position -- Student Name and Number

FIGURE 2–34. CONTINUOUS FORM PAPER AND GRADE REPORT

Debate Club Report

The procedure used to produce the debate club report not only illustrates some of the features of the accounting machine but also shows what other unit-record equipment is needed for the application.

A college has a number of different organizations which all channel their funds through the college's accounting office. The college uses unit-record equipment to process the receipts and expenditures for each club. The illustration shows the card design used and the procedure which must be followed to produce the report. The input card contains:

CARD COLUMNS	DATA PUNCHED IN CARD
1–2	The club number.
3	An "X" punch is used for an expense item—to be subtracted from the balance. NX cards are added to the balance.
4–5	Account number—each different income or expense item has a different number.
6–11	Amount of money.
12–30	The account title.

Machines must know exactly where the data will be in the card. The card format dictates both how the input is punched in the card as well as where the machine will read each field of data for processing.

Group Printed Reports

The output, a printed report, will look something like the report shown in figure 2–35. Each club will have its report printed on a separate section of paper so that when the forms are decollated they will receive only their report. The report is printed on three-part paper; one copy is sent to the club treasurer and two copies are retained in the college's accounting office.

There are many different factors that are illustrated by the report.

1. It is a *group printed report,* which means that only one line is printed for each type of expenditure. A *detailed report* would list each individual expenditure.
2. The control punch in card column 3 is used to tell the accounting machine if it should add to or subtract from the balance that is being accumulated in a counter. The amount in the card is subtracted from the counter if there is an "X" in card column 3, while "NX" cards are added to the counter.

01	Debate			
	Beginning Balance			1100.00
01	Income From Dues		500.00*	
02	Postage Expenses	10.00*		
07	Misc. Office Supplies	18.00*		
09	Speakers	60.00*		
11	Refreshments	62.00*	150.00**	
				1450.00***

FIGURE 2–35. GROUP PRINTED REPORT—*MINOR, **INTERMEDIATE, ***MAJOR

3. The three levels of totals that are accumulated are referred to as *minor, intermediate,* and *major.* Each level of total requires the use of its own individual counter.

    a. When the account number changes, the minor total is printed on the report, after which the counter is cleared back to zero in order to be able to accumulate a balance for the second item number, "postage expense." *The total of all expenses is an intermediate total.*

    b. When the club number changes an *intermediate and major* total is available and the following steps will occur.

        (1) The total for refreshments *and the total of all expenses* will print on the report.

        (2) A card will be summary punched and contain the club's number and new balance.

        (3) The club's balance in the counter reserved for the major total will print on the report. In this case 1450.00 is printed.

        (4) The counter used to accumulate the total for each club is then cleared back to zero. This same counter will be used to accumulate the balance for the second club.

        (5) The paper is advanced so that it is positioned at the top of a new page. Printing will then start again for the second club's report.

4. The control punch is also used to tell the accounting machine where it should print. Observe that the balance is at the extreme right, *and the income items, as well as the total expenses,* in the next column. The *individual* expense items *are* in the extreme left column. In the balance card

there is a control punch in column 31 which is used to determine where the amount will print on the report.

A Graphic Representation

The narration of the club's report tells only part of the story. How were the cards sequenced? What added steps are needed to print the report? Using standard flowcharting symbols recommended by the American National Standards Institute (ANSI), the complete procedure is illustrated in figure 2–36.

The cards were already keypunched and verified from the source documents submitted by the clubs. In file 1 is a heading card followed by the balance card for each club. The cards in file 1 are already sequenced and merged by club number. File 2 contains the income and expense cards which are in random order for each club.

1. The detail cards, income and expense cards, must be *sorted* first by account number and then by club number. Since account number is the minor field, it *must* be sorted before the major field is sorted.
2. Use the collator to *match-merge* the two decks of cards. The details just sorted are merged with the deck containing both the heading card and the balance card.
3. The combined deck is placed in the hopper of the accounting machine. The report is printed, and at the same time a new balance card is *summary punched.*
4. The combined deck is taken from the stacker of the accounting machine and placed in the hopper of the sorter to split the deck into its various parts. The old balance cards are no longer of value. The income and expense cards are kept for utilization in other reports.
5. The report is decollated and distributed.
6. The new balance cards are interpreted and filed.

The flowchart is referred to as *procedure flowchart* because it shows the movement of the cards in and out of the various files, illustrates the machines that are used, and shows the output which is produced. The concept of the entire job can be quickly visualized by referring to a flowchart once the symbol becomes familiar to the reader.

Level Breaks

Since so much of the success of the operation depends upon the level breaks that are detected by the accounting machines comparing on both the

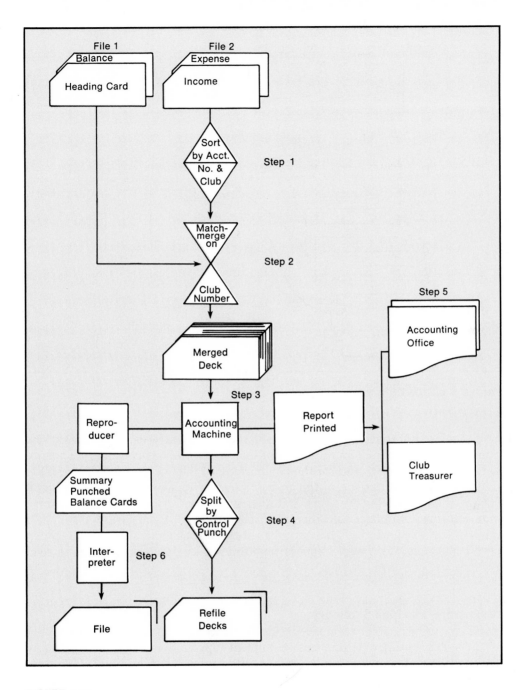

FIGURE 2–36

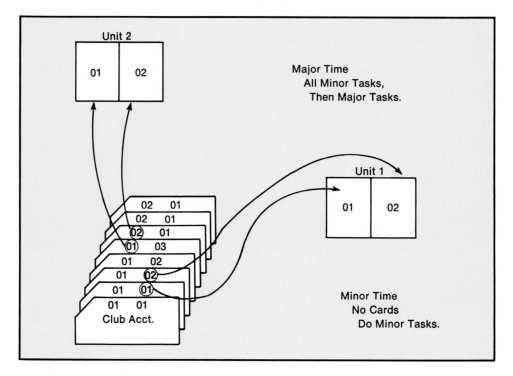

FIGURE 2–37. CONTROL TIME

club number and the account number, figure 2–37 illustrates level breaks. The number of cards is kept small so as not to confuse the basic issues. Two compare units are needed: one for the comparison of the account number and the second for the comparison of the club number. Whenever a major level break occurs, the accounting machine first does any tasks assigned for minor time, then intermediate tasks, and then proceeds with the items assigned to major time. The entire period of time may be referred to as *control time* rather than *card cycle time*. Card cycle time is the duration of time that it takes to read and process one card.

Accounting Machine Summary

The accounting machine is used to print reports that might have as many as four different levels of totals—minor, intermediate, major, plus a final total for the report. Its ability to compare two numbers and determine if they are equal makes it possible to detect the "level breaks." Mathematically, it can only add or subtract unless a special feature is added to the machine which makes it possible for the accounting machine to also multiply. It has a number of both unique and *limiting features*. For example, the 402 can print both alphabetic and numeric data on the left side of the page while only numeric information can be printed on the right. When working with unit-record equipment or computers, an analyst or programmer must learn to work with the features that are available.

LET'S REVIEW THE ACCOUNTING MACHINE

2–63. What is another name for the accounting machine?

2–64. What mathematical operations can be done on the accounting machine?

2–65. By comparing control numbers, such as account number or club number, the accounting machine can maintain up to three levels of totals. What are these three levels called?

2–66. When a major level break occurs, what takes place before any tasks assigned to "major time" can be accomplished?

2–67. Are cards read by the accounting machine during total time?

2–68. What is a report called that prints out the contents of each card read by the accounting machine?

2–69. What would a report be called that prints only the total sales for each salesman rather than each man's individual sales?

2–70. What controls the vertical movement of the paper in the accounting machine?

2–71. Does the concept of control level breaks carry over to some programming languages?

2–72. Why are uniform symbols used on a flowchart?

A SALES INVOICING PROCEDURE

The L. C. Smith Corporation had decided that the first job that would be assigned to the new equipment was the sales invoicing procedure. The method that had been used under the manual system was described and the following weaknesses were cited:

1. Too long a delay between the time the order was received and the invoice was prepared.
2. Too many customers were complaining about receiving the wrong merchandise.

3. Too many customers were permitted to overextend their credit.
4. Too often items had to be placed on backorder because the merchandise was not available.

Sales orders are received on the newly-designed order form, which is illustrated in figure 2–38. The order when it is received is sent directly to the credit department where each customer's credit is checked against a master list printed by the data processing department. The list, however, is not timely because it is printed at the end of each month when the accounts receivable statements are prepared. The customer's number is either added to the sales order or, if it is on the form already, it is checked against the master listing to make certain it is correct. Since the credit check had been one of the "bottle-necks," an additional employee was hired to assist with the task.

The order is then routed to the sales department. The check previously made to determine if the item is available for shipment is eliminated, as this procedure is done by the unit-record equipment after the cards are punched from the sales order. The sales department checks the completeness of the order. Prices are not checked because a master deck is maintained for use in adding the prices to the sales invoice cards. The arithmetic is not checked since it will no longer be done manually but by the unit-record equipment.

The sales order is then sent to the keypunching department. The key-punch operators have been given a keypunching instruction sheet, shown in figure 2–39, that contains both the card format and the special instructions. The card is designed so that the fields, except for the customer's number, are in the same sequence as the data appearing on the source document. Since customer master cards will be needed, a decision was made that the customer number would be punched in all cards related to the sales invoicing procedure in columns 1–4, as this makes the cards much easier to handle. The multiple card layout form, figure 2–40, shows the other cards that will be needed in the invoice procedure.

The decision was made that only the customer number, order number, date, salesman's number, item number, and quantity would be keypunched and verified. The order number is punched in the card because it provides a way of relating the source document to the card. Management must be able to trace any procedure through the various steps, from input to output, to make certain all processing was accurate.

All 24 card columns that are keypunched must be verified. The order in figure 2–38 is for three different items, which means that *three cards* must be punched. If alternate programming is available on the keypunch being used, the operator can punch the first card for the sink units under program control 1, then switch to alternate programming. Under alternate programming the customer number, order number, date, and salesman's number would all du-

L. C. SMITH CORPORATION

Saginaw, Michigan 48603

1314 Larch Street

ORDER NUMBER   00987   DATE: July 13, 1960

SOLD TO: James H. Henderlong
1413 North Bay Road
Green Bay, Wisconsin
0127

SOLD BY: J. Green 18   TERMS: 2/10, N/30

ITEM NUMBER	QUANTITY	DESCRIPTION	UNIT COST		TOTAL COST	
00149	10	Sink Unit – Walnut	156	93	1569	30
00177	20	Wall Unit – Walnut	53	50	1070	00
00179	2	Corner Unit – Walnut	47	32	94	64
TOTAL AMOUNT:					2733	94

FIGURE 2–38. SALES ORDER—PREPARED BY SALESMEN

DATE ACCEPTED July 10, 1960

BY _____

JOB NUMBER S 012

JOB NAME Sales Order

CARD FORMAT

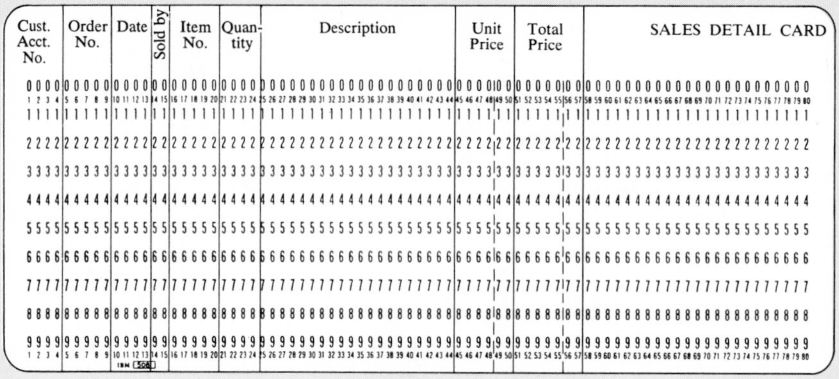

Cust. Acct. No.	Order No.	Date	Sold by	Item No.	Quan-tity	Description	Unit Price	Total Price	SALES DETAIL CARD

FIELD NAME	FROM	THRU	A/N	REMARKS
Customer Number	1	4	N	All fields are to be verified.
Order Number	5	9	N	
Date	10	13	N	Use month and day only—duplicate field.
Salesman's Number	14	15	N	
Item Number	16	20	N	
Quantity	21	24	N	

FIGURE 2–39. CARD DESIGN AND PUNCHING INSTRUCTIONS

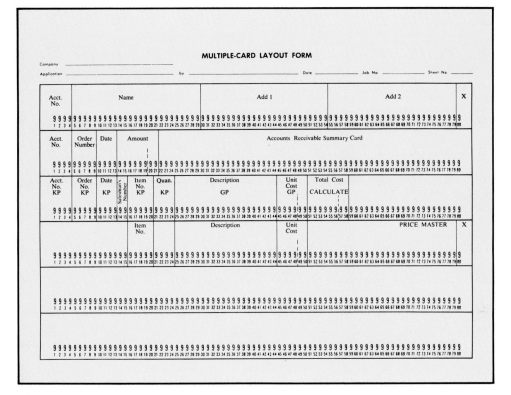

FIGURE 2-40

plicate from the first card into the second card. If alternate programming is not available, the operator can depress the duplicate key once for each field and achieve the same results.

Printing the Sales Invoice

The sales invoice shown in figure 2–41 is very similar in appearance to the sales order. Since one of the final steps in the procedure will be to compare the sales order with the invoice to determine if there are discrepancies in prices, descriptions, or quantities, it is very helpful to have the two forms nearly identical.

The method used to print the invoice can be broken down into five different steps or tasks which make the procedure more understandable. The steps involved in preparing the invoice are listed on page 113.

INVOICE NUMBER: 00987

L. C. SMITH CORPORATION

1314 Larch Street

Saginaw, Michigan 48603

DATE: July 16, 1960

SOLD TO: James H. Henderlong
1413 North Bay Road
Green Bay, Wisconsin

TERMS: 2/10,N/30

ITEM NUMBER	QUANTITY	DESCRIPTION	UNIT COST		TOTAL COST	
00149	10	Sink unit—walnut	156	93	1569	30
00177	20	Wall unit—walnut	53	50	1070	00
00179	2	Corner unit—walnut	47	32	94	64
TOTAL AMOUNT:					2733	94

FIGURE 2–41. PRINTED SALES INVOICE

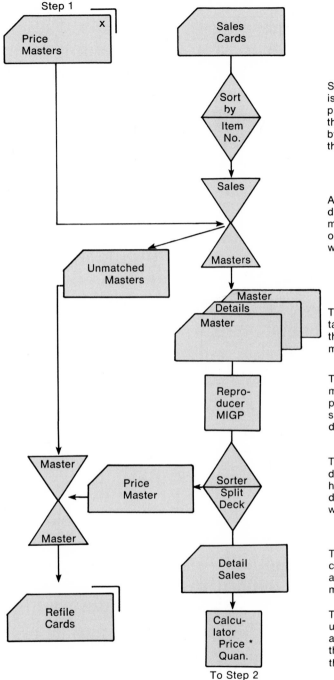

Step 1

Price Masters   x

Sales Cards

Sort by Item No.

Since the common characteristic in the sales card and the price master is item number, the cards must be sequenced by item number in order to then combine the two decks.

Sales / Masters

A match-merge operation is done on the collator. The unmatched masters are selected out. This is normal. No orders were placed for that product.

Unmatched Masters

Master Details Master

The deck is merged and contains price masters for item 1, the sales detail cards, price master for item 2, details, etc.

Reproducer MIGP

The reproducer is used for master interspersed gang-punching. The price and description are punched into the detail card.

Master

Price Master

Sorter Split Deck

The sorter is used to split the deck. Since the master card has an "X" in 80 and the detail does not, this is the logical way to split the deck.

Master

Detail Sales

The detail cards are ready for calculating. The price masters are merged with the unused masters and refiled.

Refile Cards

Calculator Price * Quan.

The calculator multiplies the unit price times the quantity and punches the answer into the sales detail card. Finally the card is complete!

To Step 2

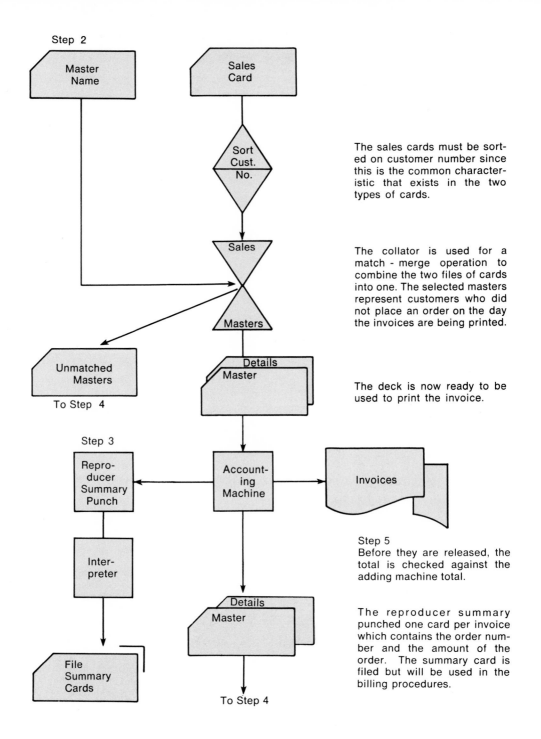

Step 2

Master Name

Sales Card

Sort Cust. No.

The sales cards must be sorted on customer number since this is the common characteristic that exists in the two types of cards.

Sales

Masters

The collator is used for a match - merge operation to combine the two files of cards into one. The selected masters represent customers who did not place an order on the day the invoices are being printed.

Unmatched Masters

To Step 4

Details
Master

The deck is now ready to be used to print the invoice.

Step 3

Reproducer Summary Punch

Accounting Machine

Invoices

Inter-preter

Step 5
Before they are released, the total is checked against the adding machine total.

Details
Master

File Summary Cards

To Step 4

The reproducer summary punched one card per invoice which contains the order number and the amount of the order. The summary card is filed but will be used in the billing procedures.

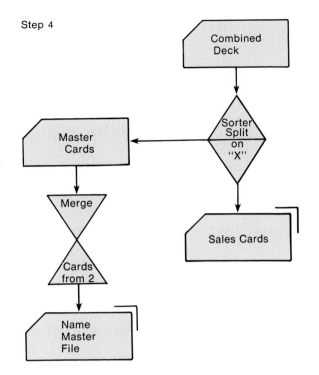

Step 4

Combined Deck

Sorter Split on "X"

Master Cards

Sales Cards

Merge

Cards from 2

Name Master File

1. *Completion of the Sales Order Card*—the price and description will be added to the sales card from a master card by using the reproducer in a master interspersed gangpunching operation. The unit price is then multiplied times the quantity and the resulting extension is punched into the card by the calculator.
2. *Assembling the Deck*—to print the invoices, both a master name and address card and the sales detail cards are needed for each customer.
3. *Printing the Invoices and Summary Punching a Balance Card*—the balance card will be used when the customer's statement is prepared at the end of the month. Using the summary card condenses the information, and fewer cards and time will be needed in the billing process.
4. *Refiling Cards*—the cards must all be returned to their files in the same manner in which they were found.
5. *Decollating and Distributing the Report*—often controls are established that must be checked *before the report is released*. In the case of the sales invoice procedure, the batch total taken on quantity is checked in the data processing department before the invoices are sent to the sales department.

Evaluation—Was the Procedure Successful?

How well did the new system meet the basic requirements? Did the number of customer complaints decrease? Did the amount of time that it took to process the sales order decrease?

After any new procedure is implemented, a post-evaluation must be made. After the new system was implemented, the invoices were produced more accurately and in less time than was possible under the former method. If the wrong merchandise was shipped, the error could generally be traced back to the salesman who had submitted the order incorrectly. Salesmen were also held more accountable for making certain that their prices were correct. The final check made in the procedure of comparing the sales order against the sales invoice proved to be well worth the time involved.

The problem of overextension of credit by customers was not corrected; nor was the problem of stock shortages. The area of inventory control and management is the second system that is scheduled to be studied.

Under the new system it now takes an average of 2.5 days to prepare the sales invoices from the sales orders. Both Krawczyk and Keyser were well pleased with their new system, but they did feel that it would improve even more as they gained experience in working with the new equipment.

Regarding Unit-record Equipment

The basic principle of recording data on a card, then being able to make multiple usage of the card, is an excellent concept. The equipment was versatile and met the needs of many businesses as they found it necessary to utilize more automated methods.

Today many installations that utilize computers will still use sorters, reproducers, collators, and interpreters. Unless an installation has only unit-record equipment, accounting machines and calculators are seldom used.

Module one stated that the data processing cycle consists of input, processing, and output. The examples used in this module illustrate how unit-record equipment can be used for the processing phase of the cycle: the sequencing, merging, summarizing, and calculating of the data.

DISCUSSION REVIEW QUESTIONS

2–73. In the case study, what were the basic problems that the L. C. Smith Corporation wanted to solve in regard to the sales invoice procedure? Were they successful? What is meant by a post-evaluation?

2-74. When the company was considering getting new equipment, why did IBM suggest that the company keep their employees informed on the progress of the study?

2-75. Referring back to figure 2-2 (p. 51) which illustrated the manual methods that were used in the sales invoicing procedure, which of the functions was taken over by the unit-record equipment?

2-76. If you were to determine what kind of unit-record equipment should be ordered for a very small business and could select only three pieces of equipment, which three would you select that would give you the widest range of functions and permit you to do many of your routine jobs?

2-77. Discuss the use of the punched card and how it should be handled.

2-78. What is the Hollerith code and why is it necessary to use a code to punch alphabetic information into the cards?

2-79. Discuss the major difference between operating a keypunch and a typewriter.

2-80. Why is it so essential that the data be verified after it is punched into the cards?

2-81. What advantages are provided by using a program card while keypunching?

2-82. Describe briefly the basic functions of the following machines.

A. Sorter	C. Calculator	E. Reproducer
B. Collator	D. Accounting machine	F. Interpreter

2-83. What are some of the alternatives to long alphabetic sorting operations?

2-84. Why is it necessary to interpret cards?

2-85. Why are decks reproduced?

2-86. What machine or machines can be used to perform each of the four basic data processing functions?

A. Sequencing	C. Merging
B. Calculating	D. Summarizing

2-87. What advantage is there in having a machine controlled by a wired panel? Refer back to the discussion on the interpreter (p. 78) before you answer the question.

GLOSSARY OF NEW AND OLD TERMS TO CHECK YOUR KNOWLEDGE

Accounting Machine. The accounting machine is also called the tabulator or printer. It reads punched cards, adds and subtracts, and prints. Its most outstanding feature is that it can compare two numbers, such as a salesman's number, and if the numbers from the two cards are not the same, cause the machine to go into *level break* or *control time*.

Accounts Receivable. An account showing the money owed to your firm by another firm or individual.

Backorder File. A listing of actual files or orders that cannot be processed due generally to a shortage of the item that is requested on the purchase order submitted by the customer.

Buffer. A storage device that temporarily holds data.

Calculator. The calculators, which were controlled by wired panels, had some of the characteristics of computers as they could store a *very limited* amount of data and perform a series of mathematical operations. They were "programmed" by the operator who wired each step that was to be performed.

Card Columns. A point of reference. The standard card has 80 columns.

Carriage Tape. A paper tape that controls the vertical movement of the form in either a high-speed printer or the accounting machine. Each special form usually has its own carriage tape that is used when the forms are in the printer.

Collator. A machine which can merge, match-merge, or match two decks of cards. In addition, it can sequence check the decks or do a variety of different types of selection.

Comparing Unit. A device used on the reproducer, accounting machine, and collator to compare data from two different cards. The reproducer and the accounting machine can only detect if the cards contain the same data. The collator can determine if the data from one card is equal to, less than, or higher than the data from the second card. A unit can compare either a single card column or an entire field of data.

Control Punch. A control punch may be any digit or character that can be recognized by the equipment processing the card. It serves a variety of purposes such as enabling the equipment to tell a master card from a detail card, to add rather than subtract, or to print using locations 51–60 rather than 71–80.

Counters. A device within an accounting machine that is used to accumulate numeric values. The data in the counter may be added to or subtracted from during the processing of the cards.

Field. One or more card columns set aside for a specific purpose, such as the date, a control punch, or the account number.

Gangpunching. Punching constant data from one card into one or more cards which follow the master card. Punching is suspended each time a master card is under the punch dies.

High Order. The extreme left position of a field.

Interpreter. A machine that reads the punches in the card and prints what is punched in the card on the card.

Justified. Refers to how the data is to be punched, or printed from, a given field. Numeric data is justified to the right while alphabetic data is justified to the left.

Keypunch. A machine similar in operation to a typewriter which is used to punch the data recorded on a source document into the card.

Level Break. When a change occurs in the control number, the events scheduled for "control time" will take place. In the accounting machine totals may be printed, counters are cleared to zero, or the form advanced in order to start printing a new page. The control number may be account number, part number, or invoice number.

Mark Sensing. Data in the form of pencil marks are put on a card with an electro-magnetic pencil, which is then machine processable. The reproducer converts the marks to punches.

Mode. Denotes if the keypunch is in numeric shift or alphabetic shift.

Offset Reproducing. A reproducing operation in which the card format of the new card differs from the format of the original card.

Program Card. A card in which special codes have been punched which provide for automatic skipping, duplicating, and shifting during a keypunch operation.

Reproducer. A machine, controlled by a wired panel, which can be used to make new decks of cards, gangpunch, summary punch, or convert mark sensed data to punches.

Rows. A point of reference. Each standard 80 column card has 12 rows designated from 12–9.

Sales Invoice. A form printed by the vendor showing the merchandise that was shipped to the customer who placed the order.

Sales Order. An order for merchandise placed by a customer with the vendor.

Sorter. A machine used to sequence decks of cards. Under certain conditions it is used for selection of cards and merging of two or more card files.

Straight Reproducing. Making a new deck exactly like the old deck.

Unit Position. The extreme right position of a field.

Verifier. A machine used to check the accuracy of the keypunching operation. Some keypunches may be put in a VERIFY MODE and function as a verifier.

ANSWERS

REVIEW QUESTIONS (p. 53)

2–1. The controller is responsible for processing the financial information; the early equipment was used almost exclusively for this purpose.

2–2. Usually priorities are established for all jobs that are to be run. A schedule is made up and it is considered important that it be followed.

2–3. The answers should be obvious: customers were unhappy, wrong merchandise was shipped, it took too long to process the orders, customers were often extended too much credit. All of these problems relate directly to the sales ordering system. A sales system is far more than just typing an invoice.

2–4. No. One of the most important criteria of any system is that the system must be designed in such a way as to ensure customer satisfaction.

ABOUT MR. HOLLERITH'S CODE (p. 57)

2–5. Since each card column can contain only one character, it is limited to 80 characters of information per card.

2–6. Field

2–7. No. Different colored cards are used for *operator,* not machine identification.

2–8. 001414

2–9. The name CHARLIE would be punched in card columns 21 through 27 if the first name field is in 21 through 30. This is because alphabetic information is justified to the left while numeric information is justified to the right.

2–10. When numbers are recorded manually, they are justified to the *right.* This is the same way they are justified when punched in a card.

2–11.

Letter	Punches Needed Zone	Digit
A	12	1
K	11	2
D	12	4
T	0	3

2–12. The zone punches are the 12, 11, and 0 punches.

2–13. The "X" punch used as a control punch is really the 11 punch.

REGARDING THE KEYPUNCH (p. 67)

2–14. The operator can backspace and rekey the data if an error is sensed during the punching operation.

2–15. The 129 Data Recorder can also accumulate statistics regarding *the number of corrections (or errors) made.*

2–16. In addition, a data recorder can total up to three (3) fields of information. It might, for example, total all of the amounts that were keypunched from the cash receipts forms. At the end of the job, when the total is punched, it could be compared with *a batch total taken from the source documents.*

2–17. The basic concept of using punched cards is to get multiple usage from the cards. If the input is incorrect, several reports could be in error. Machines also do not have logical ability and will not "catch" errors that an individual might notice.

2–18. No. In the 026 it will normally cause a single punch in the 12 row. But using the 029 will provide a different punch configuration. It should be noted that regardless of what is printed on the key, if the "P" key is used in numeric shift a punch will occur in just the 12 row.

2–19. The major difference is the arrangement of the numbers. Most people feel that the keypunch arrangement for numbers is far better than that found on the typewriter.

2–20. The (SKIP) key is used for the 11 punch; the ($&/P$) key is used for the 12 punch; and the ($0/$) key is used for the 0 punch.

2–21. Hold the numeric shift and use the "K" key.

2–22. 000333

2–23. If the numeric information is not justified correctly, the machine processing will handle it incorrectly. Working with machines demands that standards and rules be followed exactly. One such rule is to justify numeric data to the right of the field.

2–24. Skip
Dup
Shift

2–25. A. To initiate a skip use the 11 punch.
B. To initiate a duplication use the 0 punch.
C. To initiate a shift use the 1 punch.
D. The 12 punch is used to tell the keypunch how long to skip, duplicate, or to remain shifted. It is referred to as the field definition code.

2–26. A. The blank cards are placed in the hopper. This term is generally used to denote where the cards to be processed are placed.
B. After the card is registered, it is underneath the *punch dies.*
C. After the card is punched, it is positioned under the *read brushes.*
D. From there it goes into the *stacker.*

2–27. The critical area of the keypunch is not the 9 or 12 edge of the card as it is in most of the other pieces of equipment.

2–28. The interpreting feature reads the punches and prints what is punched in the card on the top of the card.

REGARDING VERIFICATION (p. 70)

2–29. The machine locks and a red light comes on.

2–30. Two.

2–31. The card is keypunched over again and then reverified.

2–32. If the error gets into the system, it is far more costly to correct.

ABOUT SORTING (p. 77)

2–33. The type of report available from any kind of records is directly related to the *sequence the records (cards) are in.*

2–34. A. The cards are first sorted on card column 20.
B. After they are fanned and joggled, they are placed in the hopper.
C. The brush is moved to card column 19 for the second pass.

2–35. Since there are no holes in the card, no impulses are created. The card will, therefore, pass under all of the chute blades and drop into the reject pocket.

2–36. Depending upon the sorter that is being used, each card may be required to pass through the sorter twice for each card column in the alphabetic field. A large deck would therefore take a considerable amount of time.

2–37. They can assign an alphanumerical code. They could sort only a portion of the alphabetic field. The few names out of sequence will be close enough to where they should be listed and can be easily found.

2–38. A large job can be block sorted. This will permit part of the cards to go to the next task before the entire job is completed.

2–39. First, man number; then, department number; and finally, store number.

2–40. Each field is sorted from unit position to high order position.

2–41. A card has numeric data in 25–29. Card column 29 is called the unit position, while card column 25 is called the high order position.

2–42. If the manager can secure only part of the basic tabulating equipment, the sorter should not be eliminated. The relationship between the sequencing of the cards and the reports that can be produced make it essential to sort records. The collator or reproducer could be eliminated but not the sorter.

REVIEW QUESTIONS (p. 84)

2–43. No. The interpreter has only 60 typebars. It would therefore require two passes through the machine.

2–44. Nothing would happen as no impulses are created. It simply would pass through the machine and end up in the stacker.

2–45. No. Generally, the control panels for jobs that are run frequently are labeled and stored in a special cabinet.

2–46. Not all cards are punched by using the keypunch. Both computer output and cards punched on the reproducer are unprinted. If a large amount of handling of the cards is required, they should probably be interpreted for easier card handling.

REVIEW THE REPRODUCER (p. 89)

2–47. Reproducing jobs can be either straight reproducing or offset reproducing.

2–48. For each old card in the original deck, one new card is punched.

2–49. The read side is used to read the old card and the punch side is used to punch the new card.

2–50. Yes. The two operations are very often combined.

2–51. Gangpunching may be single or master interspersed gangpunching.

2–52. In master interspersed gangpunching the punching is done on the punch side of the machine. The read side acts independently to compare the results of the gangpunching operation. The cards are moved from the stacker of the reproducer to the hopper of the read unit by the operator.

2–53. Several reasons could be given. Some of the possible answers are faster, cheaper, less likely to have pricing errors if one master deck is used. Using this method may also serve as a means of detecting errors.

2–54. The basic principle behind mark sensing is to provide an economical means of capturing data in machine processable form at the source— where the transaction occurs.

2–55. Summary punching is a good illustration of one of the basic data processing functions which is to summarize information or to condense information.

2–56. False. A point was made in the text that there are many solutions to a problem. The solution that is used depends upon the resources that are available.

2–57. A counter is a device used to store numeric data.

2–58. A. Reproducing   C. Mark sensing
      B. Gangpunching   D. Summary punching

ABOUT THE COLLATOR (p. 96)

2–59. Merge
      Match
      Match-merge
      Sequence check
      Card selection.

2–60. Both decks must be sorted into the same sequence.

2–61. The computer's logic is derived from the fact that it can compare two numbers and see if the first is equal to, lower than, or higher than the first. The collator can make the same comparisons. The determination of which pocket the card will go in and which feed will be activated is determined by the results of the comparison.

2–62. A. Merging
B. Selection
C. Match-merge
D. Selection

LET'S REVIEW THE ACCOUNTING MACHINE (p. 105)

2–63. Another name for the accounting machine is the tabulator or printer.

2–64. Mathematically, it can only add or subtract.

2–65. Minor
Intermediate
Major

2–66. Minor, then intermediate tasks will be performed.

2–67. No. During total time the reading of cards is suspended.

2–68. The report is called a listed or detail report.

2–69. If only the totals are printed, it is called a group printed report.

2–70. The vertical movement of the paper is controlled by a carriage tape. The control panel wiring really starts the skipping process and the punch in the tape tells it where to stop skipping.

2–71. Yes. The concept of control level breaks carries over to several programming languages.

2–72. Uniform symbols are used in flowcharting in order that more people can understand the system or procedure being illustrated.

DISCUSSION REVIEW QUESTIONS (p. 114)

2–73. The company wanted to solve the problems of the delay in producing the sales invoice, the number of complaints received from customers, and the shortages that existed in merchandise with which to fill orders. Yes. For the first job automated it would have to be judged as successful. Post-evaluation implies that statistics will be maintained on the types of problems and errors that exist in a given system in order that corrective action may be taken.

2–74. Before the new equipment arrives, a complete study should be made of how procedures are now implemented. If the employees are not apprehensive and are aware of likely changes, they will be far more co-operative and better results may be obtained.

2–75. A. The credit department check is approximately the same.

B. In the sales department the check on the availability and the back-ordering procedure were both automated by using a punched card inventory system. The details were not provided but reference was made to such a system.

C. The price check, mathematics check, and typing of the invoices were all eliminated by the new method.

2–76. The system would be very limited but many small installations do work with just these three pieces of equipment: keypunch, sorter, and accounting machine.

2–77. The standard 80-column card is widely used to activate many different pieces of equipment. It should be stored under pressure in a humidity controlled room. If properly stored, it is durable.

2–78. Dr. Herman Hollerith designed the code that permitted a letter of the alphabet or special character to be punched in the card and occupy only one card column.

2–79. The location of the numeric keys is probably the biggest difference. At first a typist may find it strange to shift for numbers, not upper case letters.

2–80. The basic principle of unit-record, or tabulating, equipment is that once the data is punched in the card, multiple usage may be made of the information. An error which gets into the system is far more costly to correct at some future date.

2–81. The shifting from numeric to alphabetic mode is done automatically. It is also possible to skip fields automatically and to duplicate information from the card under the read station into the card at the punch station.

2–82. A. Sorter—Sequence cards, count cards, and under certain conditions merge and select cards

B. Collator—Merge, match, match-merge, sequence checks, and selection

C. Calculator—The machine can do all four mathematical functions and be "programmed" to do calculations in a series of steps

D. Accounting Machine—Functions as a printer, can carry three levels of totals plus the final total, and can add and subtract

E. Reproducer—Straight and offset reproducing, gangpunching, mark sensing, and summary punching (when connected to the accounting machine)

F. Interpreter—Prints what is punched in the card on the card

2–83. Use an alphanumerical code or sort on only part of the field. This would put the deck in nearly perfect alphabetic sequence. For many jobs this type of alphabetic arrangement may meet the needs of the user.

2–84. Many cards are punched either on the reproducer or by the punch unit of the computer. If the cards are to be visually referred to or handled a lot, they should be interpreted.

2–85. Several examples were cited, such as to correct errors by reproducing the good data and gangpunching in the corrections, replacing worn out decks, and rearranging the fields of information on the cards.

2–86. A. Sequencing—sorter
B. Calculating—calculator
C. Merging—collator—and in some cases the sorter
D. Summarizing—the reproducer connected to the accounting machine. The accounting machine would produce only a printed summary.

2–87. Using the interpreter as an example, the panel provides a good deal of flexibility. If a panel were not used, the choice would be to interpret a field or not to interpret it. With a panel, the information could be printed in two locations; the information can be rearranged to make it more readable. Although not discussed in the text, lead zeroes can be suppressed. In addition, it is possible to have two different types of cards in the procedure and treat each differently.

SYSTEMS AND OPTIONS 3
FOR THE
SMALL COMPANY

CHOICES AVAILABLE TO THE L. C. SMITH CORPORATION

Data processing is capturing data and putting it in a form that can be easily utilized and retrieved. The method used—manual, mechanical, electro-mechanical, or electronic—depends today upon the choice made by the company. It has been illustrated how a company's need for better methods of processing data increases as the company expands. Because data processing serves the company in so many different ways, its data processing needs generally increase more than its actual growth. External forces, such as legislative action and competition, make it essential that a company has valid, timely information which can be rapidly retrieved for use in reports and decision-making.

In module 2, the L. C. Smith Corporation chose to utilize unit-record equipment as a means of solving their immediate problem. Initially, the transaction was *recorded* on the source document, *transcribed* into the machine-processable punched card, and *verified*. The input was then *transmitted* to the data processing center where it was *processed*. When unit-record equipment, or a small computer card system, is utilized a number of steps are necessary in order to secure the desired output. Equipment is necessary to sort, merge, calculate, and summarize the data. Many companies did elect to first utilize unit-record equipment and then convert, when it was feasible to do so, to a computerized system. Other companies have solved the growth in their data processing needs in other ways. You will see that there are choices available that can eliminate some of the steps between the occurrence of the event, the transaction, and the entry of the data into the system.

Let's assume that the L. C. Smith Corporation had not elected to utilize their own unit-record equipment. What other choices did they have at that time? What additional choices are available today?

MAKING A DECISION

Early in 1960 when Lou and his entire management staff were determining what action they should take in regard to data processing, there were not the options for a company that was small, yet expanding very rapidly, that exist today. The L. C. Smith Corporation considered the following options.

Unit-record equipment could be secured for the amount of funds which had been budgeted for their data processing expansion. If this was done, should they have someone trained from their own staff to design and implement the new automated procedures? Or should someone be hired who already understood data processing concepts? Could that individual study their existing system, learn the objectives of the L. C. Smith Corporation, and design a new system that would be effective all at the same time? Would this solution only meet their needs for a short time before another major change would be required? Would computer technology continue to improve so that perhaps a small computer system, which would meet their needs, might become available soon?

Another option would be to invest in a 1401 system. The local users were very enthusiastic about the results that they were obtaining. Since rental of a 1401 would overextend the budgeted amount for data processing, the more they analyzed the problem the more unrealistic the acquisition of a 1401 became. Although it would solve their data processing problems, the unit cost of the work produced on the system would be exceedingly high because the system would be idle a large percentage of the time. In addition, they would have to hire programmers and operators since no one on their staff was trained in electronic data processing. Even if the board of directors approved the acquisition of a 1401, where would the additional staff come from that would be needed to handle a conversion? With no experience in the use of computers, the procedures would certainly have to be run both the old and new way until complete testing of the new system had been accomplished. Lack of trained personnel, one of the problems they were trying to solve, would be increased rather than decreased.

Another alternative was to increase their staff and continue using the same manual methods. This would not solve the problem, but only postpone a decision as to its solution. If more people were hired the same problem—a shortage of competent personnel—would soon recur as their business expanded unless some of their methods were automated. Problems such as the dissatisfaction of customers over the delay in their order processing and the lack of timely information for management must be solved. The solution of hiring more help and not changing any of the existing methods would be only a temporary solution. Management felt what was really needed was time to study the problem in depth in order to determine a permanent solution.

There was one more possibility. John Krawczyk had been studying the services offered by several local data processing service bureaus. Some of the service bureaus had already established a reputation for providing *good service*. Their clients were satisfied with the quality of the work, which was accomplished according to schedule, and also felt they had received a great deal of assistance in solving many of their basic data processing problems.

Today there would be far more possibilities to explore than the four mentioned because time-sharing, or a small computer system which could be justified, might be utilized.

Let's examine the decision that was made in 1961, as most of the factors are still relevant. After this is done, the various solutions to the problem that are available today will be presented. The last module in the text will deal with tomorrow. *In the rapidly changing technology, the hardware changes but the problems and concepts remain the same.* What the L. C. Smith Corporation wanted was an improved method of handling its data so that the results obtained would be accurate and timely. This must be done while achieving the corporate objectives of providing better customer service and maintaining cost at a reasonable level so a given profit level can be achieved.

USING A SERVICE BUREAU

John and two of his assistants were assigned the task of investigating the service bureaus which were available in the local area. It had been decided that the bureau selected should be a local one because it would be easier to communicate with the individual assigned to work with the personnel of the L. C. Smith Corporation. They felt that they would get faster service as the input, and resulting output, would not have to be mailed. Lou felt a little uneasy about taking the company's data outside of the firm. He probably never would have agreed that it was a good plan except that the firm which was selected processed data for several of his friends who assured him that their data was not lost and was always returned in good condition. Lou may have had the same feeling of apprehension that many people have when they mail an important letter. Will it get there? How do you know when it does get there? Data is *valuable*. If some documents were lost, they would be very difficult, if not impossible, to replace.

Gateway Processing Service

The L. C. Smith Corporation selected Gateway Processing Service to do some of their data processing. Mr. Keim, the manager, explained that there were many different options available to clients. Gateway, like most of the service bureaus that were established at that time, used unit-record equipment to process the work of their clients.

Mr. Keim gave John and his assistants a demonstration of a complete payroll system and indicated that modifications would be made to better meet the payroll needs of their company. Mr. Keim said that 95% of their applications were adjusted to the individual data processing requirements of customers. In addition to payroll, the bureau would maintain their inventory records and process their accounts receivable and payable. Since the bureau would not keep any of the files, except for the payroll master files, the sales order processing would still be done at Smith's. It was felt that it was better not to automate their invoice procedures until a complete study could be made. The delay in processing orders was more directly concerned with the *conditioning* and *editing* of the data rather than with the mechanics of producing the invoice. The delay was actually caused by the credit and item checking methods used by Smith's. When they had tried to eliminate those steps, they found it was far more costly to correct the resulting errors than to do the checking prior to the completion of the sales invoice. The sales invoice procedure will be one of the first areas studied, but for the present time they will continue processing the sales order by the method illustrated in module 2.

Service Bureau Charges

John had also made a study of how service bureaus charge for their services and found that the following rate structures were usually available.

1. A flat rate per month is charged for the service rendered. This type of

charge is generally made if the company has very little fluctuation in the amount of data that is to be processed.

2. A per document charge is assessed. In the case of payroll, a fixed amount is charged per employee record. This includes maintaining the files and printing all of the reports.

3. A charge is made for the amount of time that the job takes to run on the equipment at a set rate per hour. In addition, an hourly charge is made for designing and implementing the procedure.

The first method would not be applicable to the L. C. Smith Corporation because the amount of data they process varies a great deal. As a general pattern, the volume of data processed is continually increasing. The third method did not appeal to John as there would be no way of accurately determining exactly how much a particular job would cost until after it had been executed. Remember, John believes in planning for an event by establishing it in the budget, and then controlling the activity by checking to make certain the expenditures do not exceed what was budgeted. The "time and materials" method would make budgeting, as a means of achieving control, difficult. The bureau and the L. C. Smith Corporation mutually agreed that the per document charge method should be used.

An Analyst Is Assigned to L. C. Smith

Keim indicated that he would assign one of his systems analysts, Ben J. Paulson, to the Smith account. Paulson would work directly with the employees of the L. C. Smith Corporation in redesigning payroll, accounts receivable, and accounts payable. Not only would he work with the company during the planning stage but he would also help design the input forms that are necessary to transmit the data to the service bureau. Well-designed forms, with clear, concise instructions, are *essential* to the success of any application. It would be part of Paulson's responsibility to make certain that *controls* were established to check the validity of output.

After the forms are designed, Paulson will help train the employees who will be required to use the new documents. He will go through the procedure of filling out the forms with Smith's employees. After any questions are answered, Smith's employees will write up the procedures (document each task).

The Gateway Company stresses to all clients the importance of good documentation. Documentation in this case means nothing more than writing down the details of (1) how each form is to be filled out; (2) what the various codes used mean; and (3) the controls that are established. Paulson could do the documentation, but he feels that when each employee does his own it is more useful to the employee. When each task is clearly documented, in simple understandable terms, there will be far less errors at the point where the data enters the system. *A system can be designed brilliantly, but it will never be any more successful than the entry of the data into the system.*

The success of any system depends upon the person who fills in the form or originates the data. Methods can be devised for editing, checking, and verifying the data. If account number 13 was recorded rather than 12, the editing procedures will not detect the error. The invalid information may go throughout the entire system before the error is detected. It is far more time-consuming to make all of the changes necessary to correct the wrong entry than it is to process many orders in the usual manner. This is more evident as faster, more sophisticated equipment is used to achieve a higher level of "source" data automation.

"A Simple Little Error"

Since the concept of what can happen when a "simple litle error" gets into the system is so important, an illustration is provided that also stresses the importance of good documentation.

The payroll was being processed on an IBM 360 Model 40 computer system, and the "edit" program, which looks for errors on the time cards, printed a message which read: "Check employee code for Sally Blake." Since it was a new message, based upon some changes that had been made which were not clearly documented, the operator and the payroll clerk made the decision that the card was correct. Three days later a different procedure, which used a file created from the edited cards, terminated due to invalid input.

It took a programmer and an analyst an hour to trace the error back to the cause of the problem—"the case of the ignored message!" It took two more hours to correct the error in the system itself. Five people in five different departments had reports that had to be adjusted. How costly was the error? The cost can be accurately determined, but more important is what caused the error? The answer—the documentation was not complete and easy to understand.

A New Department

Mr. Keim, manager of Gateway, also suggested that it would be beneficial to both of the companies if a coordinator were selected from the L. C. Smith Corporation to work with Paulson. L. C. Smith's management had been given the objective of improving their data processing techniques and developing some long-range plans. Therefore, a data processing department was formed and Mr. Keyser, a young accountant with the firm, was appointed its manager. He was still responsible to John Krawczyk who expected him to continue with some of his previously assigned accounting duties. He was asked to begin working with Ben Paulson to determine how the applications should be implemented. More important perhaps was his assignment to organize a task force made up of representatives from each major area, to develop recommendations for (a) in-service training for both top and middle management in the use of electronic data processing techniques, and (b) long-range objectives for data processing.

REVIEW QUESTIONS

3–1. Identify at least three reasons why the L. C. Smith Corporation did not feel they should secure a computer at this time.

3–2. Besides having their applications automated by using unit-record equipment, what other benefits did they receive from Gateway?

3–3. Why didn't Gateway's analyst, who was assigned to Smith's, document the procedures that the employees were to perform?

3–4. Comment upon the approach taken in establishing the task force and the new department.

THE ACCOUNTS RECEIVABLE APPLICATION

Keyser and Paulson recommended that the first application to be converted to punched card data processing would be accounts receivable. Their recommendation was accepted and they began to design the required procedures. What is needed for any application?

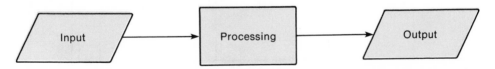

Although it may seem backwards, the design is started by first considering output. This was easy as management was satisfied with their present accounts receivable statements (see fig. 3–1). It was somewhat modified to adjust for the limitations of the equipment that would be used to print the statements.

L. C. SMITH CORPORATION

1314 LARCH STREET

SAGINAW, MICHIGAN, 48603

Mr. Charles Brown
4327 Rosemont Drive
Kalamazoo, MI 48635

DATE: October 31, 1975

ACCOUNT NUMBER 529

$...
AMOUNT PAID

PLEASE DETACH THE TOP PORTION OF THE STATEMENT AND REMIT WITH YOUR PAYMENT

DATE	INVOICE NO.		CHARGES		PAYMENTS		BALANCE	
0831		Balance					1000	00
0910					1000	00		
0915	124678		499	99				
0916	134678		500	00				
0920		Cr Adjustment			99	99		

BALANCE DUE:			900	00

FIGURE 3–1. ACCOUNTS RECEIVABLE STATEMENT

What input cards are needed to produce the desired output? The multiple-card layout form in figure 3–2 illustrates the cards that are needed in the application. The identification code in the first column makes it easier to process the cards. Fields, such as the account number, which are used in more than one card should be in the same card columns in all cards. This will make both the card handling and programming much easier. The "Pd. on Acct" card and the "Cr. Adjustment" card will have an 11 punch, or "X" punch, in column 25, which will tell the accounting machine, or computer, to subtract the amount from the balance.

The same cards would be used in a computerized system if only a card reader, card punch, and printer were available. The sales invoice cards would usually contain more data because the data would be used in other applications also. To keep the example simple, only the data relevant to the illustration is considered.

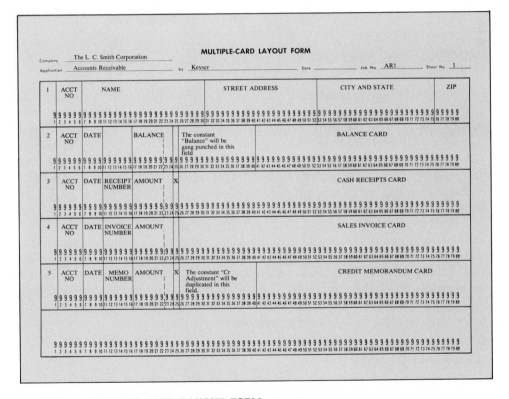

FIGURE 3–2. MULTIPLE CARD LAYOUT FORM

How is the data punched in each of the different cards? What is the source document that is used for each different card? What "controls" are exercised to make certain that the input cards are valid? A table is provided to show each card type, its source document, and how the card is prepared.

CARD TYPE	SOURCE DOCUMENT	CARD PREPARED BY
Beginning Balance	None	Card is summary punched while preparing the statements the previous month.
Paid on Account	Top Half of Accounts Receivable Statement	Keypunch and verified from statement.
Charges	Sales Invoices	Keypunched and verified from the sales invoices. The amount represents the total amount of the invoices.
Credit Adjustment	Credit Memorandum	Keypunched and verified from the credit memorandum issued to the customer.

PRINTING THE STATEMENT

The flowchart is illustrated in figure 3–3. Except for the calculator, all of the service bureau's equipment is utilized in the accounts receivable application. There is more information printed on the flowchart than what is normally provided in order that you may more easily follow the illustration. The symbols used are the uniform flowcharting symbols which were standardized by ANSI. The flowchart should provide a clear picture of what is occurring as the cards are processed even to someone who is totally unfamiliar with data processing.

If a computer, such as an 1130 or 1401, is used for processing the cards, the flowchart would be essentially the same. Instead of using the accounting machine to accumulate and print the balances, the computer would be used. The balances would be accumulated mathematically within the central processing unit of the computer. The statements would be printed by the on-line printer which is controlled by the computer. The card punch, also controlled by the computer, would punch the new balance cards.

What About Controls?

How does the service bureau and L. C. Smith know that the processing was done accurately? The cards were keypunched and then verified on the

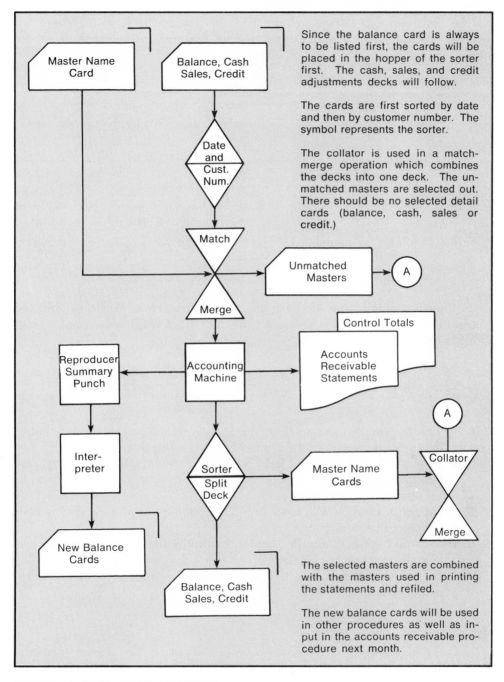

Master Name Card

Balance, Cash Sales, Credit

Since the balance card is always to be listed first, the cards will be placed in the hopper of the sorter first. The cash, sales, and credit adjustments decks will follow.

The cards are first sorted by date and then by customer number. The symbol represents the sorter.

The collator is used in a match-merge operation which combines the decks into one deck. The un-matched masters are selected out. There should be no selected detail cards (balance, cash, sales or credit.)

Date and Cust. Num.

Match

Merge

Unmatched Masters

A

Reproducer Summary Punch

Accounting Machine

Control Totals

Accounts Receivable Statements

Inter-preter

New Balance Cards

Sorter Split Deck

Master Name Cards

A

Collator

Merge

Balance, Cash Sales, Credit

The selected masters are combined with the masters used in printing the statements and refiled.

The new balance cards will be used in other procedures as well as in-put in the accounts receivable procedure next month.

FIGURE 3–3. PRINTING THE INVOICES

verifier, but still *this doesn't ensure that the processing is valid.* There are several "control" totals that are printed on the accounting machine at the end of the job.

TOTAL PRINTED	CHECKED WITH
Total of All Customers' Balance	Accounts receivable control accounts balance as shown by the accounting department.
Total Cash Received	Total of all deposits made during the period for cash or checks received on account.
Total Sales	An adding machine total was taken of each day's total. The totals are added.
Total Credit Memorandum	Total taken from the credit memorandums.
Total of Beginning Balances	Total from last month's report.

What happens if one of the totals does not agree with the established control total? The answer is a very simple one. *It has to!* If it does not, everything is checked until it does.

QUESTIONS ON THE ACCOUNTS RECEIVABLE APPLICATION

3–5. Which do you determine first: the input needed or the output that is going to be produced as the results of processing the data?

3–6. Why is the location of the field within the record of such importance when the input is read by either unit-record equipment or some form of input device for the computer?

3–7. What control punch was used to tell the equipment processing the card to subtract rather than add?

3–8. How would the L. C. Smith Corporation know that the accounts receivable statements were correct?

3–9. Name all of the machines that were used to produce the accounts receivable statements.

When Will They Change?

How long the L. C. Smith Corporation will continue to have their data processed by a service bureau depends upon a number of different factors.

If management *at all levels* does get involved in data processing, they will be able to accurately determine when they can justify the utilization of their own equipment.

Advantages of In-House Equipment

There are both advantages and disadvantages of having the equipment in-house. The company has complete control of their data at all times. Since more flexibility is permitted as to when reports are run, management can ask that a desired report be run *now* and usually get it. No matter how elaborate the system, man does have the final word as to *what* will be processed and *when* it will be processed. A company's own programmers and analysts provide for, and understand, the peculiarities of their particular business. The greatest benefit may come from greater utilization of the computer in the intangible areas. The contribution made by the computer in these areas cannot be measured in terms of dollars saved. How can you calculate the value of its use in the allocation of a company's resources, or in planning future sales strategies which are based on past history and present economic trends and movements? When a company uses a service bureau, they may be utilizing the computer only as a "superclerk" and not taking advantage of all of its other capabilities.

Disadvantages of an In-House Small System

The disadvantage of having the in-house availability of a computer system may still be *cost*. If a company is utilizing its own system for only a few hours a day, even if it is a small system, they may have made a wrong decision. A wrong decision in the utilization of computer hardware can be a very costly one! Even if the equipment is rented, the *conversion cost may be greater than the actual cost of the equipment*. Conversion costs include redesigning the system, converting files to a new media, writing and testing programs, and physically preparing a location for the new equipment.

The company may also be disappointed because the desired "intangibles" may *not* be possible on their own small system. A small or medium-sized system may not be able to provide management with all of the information it needs. Forecasting and using the computer in other decision-making processes usually requires a large amount of computer memory, sophisticated high-level programming languages, and large data bases that are under the direct control of the computer.

When should a company leave the service bureau and process their own data? Probably the answer is a two-part answer. First, the company must have the expertise (ability) to design and implement new procedures and systems. Secondly, they should be able to show mathematically that they can process the information as well as the service bureau, and at a reduction in cost.

Other Factors Pertaining to Service Bureaus

Not all companies give the kind of service that the Gateway Company[1] provided for the L. C. Smith Corporation. Many bureaus do not tailor programs to the needs of the individual customer. They have standardized programs which require each company to follow the same basic procedures and they discourage anyone from wanting unique features or services. If modifications are required by a client, the changes made may be rather costly.

In many of the larger cities service bureaus have started, been in business for a short period of time, and then either completely ceased to exist or have closed their local office. This is one of the reasons why a service bureau must be carefully selected. It is not implied that the companies did not have experienced personnel or the ability to perform the tasks. In some cases, they became committed to the rental of equipment that they could not maintain on the volume of business which they were able to obtain. If the service bureau goes out of business, regardless of the reason, the client will find switching to another company both time-consuming and expensive.

In selecting a company, it is also important that they have adequate capacity to process the data of their clients. If their equipment is "down" for a period of time, there should be a "safety-margin," in terms of available machine time, that still makes it possible for them to meet their schedules. Who has priority when the run schedule is delayed due to down time? Employees of a company whose payroll is not available because the bureau's system is "down" would not on that particular day be among the more satisfied employees in town.

It is wise to determine what type of equipment is used by the bureau. If it is the only equipment of its kind in the area, it may be "down" far more than would otherwise be the case as their maintenance service may be unusually slow. Travel time may have to be considered in the time that it takes to get a response to a request for service.

Service Bureaus that have been successful have built their business on a foundation of providing dependable "Service." For example, the Gateway Company has an excellent reputation in the area where it is located. They provide service for more than 80 different clients including banks, credit unions, school systems, governmental agencies, construction companies, drug

---

[1] Although the L. C. Smith Corporation is not an actual company, all of the material referring to the Gateway Company is based upon the actual philosophy, practices, and growth of Westley's Data Processing, Inc., Midland, Michigan.

stores, food processors, printers, hospitals and clinics, certified public accountants, insurance companies, manufacturing companies, wholesale distributors, and physicians. Some clients pay as little as $100 a month while others are billed as much as $14,000 per month.

The company helps new clients in determining which applications can be most effectively processed by their company. An analyst is assigned to work with the personnel of the client's company to help decide how existing procedures should be modified to utilize more effectively the equipment that will process their data.

The analyst also assists the client in designing the necessary forms that will be used to transmit the data to the bureau. When "conversion day" arrives, they will make certain that the forms are filled out correctly and completely. When the first output is available, the analyst will go over it with the client to be sure that the necessary controls are provided and that the output is correctly interpreted.

The small client is receiving the services of a large staff of highly skilled people who are working for him at a very nominal charge. Gateway's 37 employees who work indirectly for the clients are utilized as follows: a general manager, 2 in marketing, 5 programmer/analysts who work directly with the clients, 10 equipment operators, 3 employees in distribution and delivery, and 16 input preparation clerks who do primarily keypunching and verifying.

In the 12 years that Gateway has been in existence they have phased out some of their unit-record equipment and have acquired two computers and the necessary input/output devices to support the computers. They have the capacity to provide one-day service for their regular clients plus doing additional work for a user who wants a "one-time only" job. Just as a client, or user, might expand and change their hardware, so did Gateway. They are now considering the acquisition of a much larger system which would permit their larger clients to input data directly into the system. This would eliminate the *transcription* from the source document to the punched card, the *verification* using the verifier, and the physical *transmittal* of the actual documents to the service bureau. The service provided to the customers on that basis would be called *time-sharing*. Currently, the bureau is operating only in a "batch mode" which means each job is processed as a separate procedure.

Service bureaus today process 5 to 6% of all of the commercial data. They do perform an important function for the small client who cannot meet his needs. Large corporations contract with service bureaus to do special one-time jobs for which they do not have the computer capacity. Another reason that the large company may elect to use a bureau for a particular job is that the software (program) is already developed and available. Developing their own programs to produce the desired results may be far more costly than paying the bureau's fee.

QUESTIONS FOR THOUGHT

3–10. What do you feel is the major advantage of having a computer in-house rather than using the services of a bureau?

3–11. What may be the major disadvantage of having an in-house computer rather than utilizing the services of a bureau?

3–12. Why is it important that the service bureau selected be fairly well established in an area?

3–13. Does the Gateway Processing Service process data for only very small companies?

3–14. Gateway processes only one client's job at a time. What "mode" of processing are they using?

3–15. What percentage of business data processing is done by service bureaus?

3–16. In the future, what kind of service would Gateway like to be able to offer their clients?

OTHER ALTERNATIVES CURRENTLY AVAILABLE

Time-sharing

Time-sharing places the capability of the computer at the immediate service of a number of independent, remotely located users who each feel they have exclusive use of the system.

Time-sharing was developed through research and experimentation at the Massachusetts Institute of Technology in the late 1950s and the early 1960s. The concept was initially developed as a means of making it possible for universities to work together on research projects of mutual interest. It now gives people at different locations the ability to "converse" with the ultra-powerful computer and enlist its assistance in problem solving. The applications, markets, and sales revenues from time-sharing are rapidly expanding, and today it is the fastest growing segment of the computer industry. For example,

YEAR	APPROXIMATE REVENUE FROM TIME-SHARING
1965	10 Million
1968	70 Million
1969	125 Million
1971	250 Million
1975	2 Billion (Estimated)

As users gain more experience in time-sharing they progress from easier to more difficult problems. As more programs are developed in the question/response mode (conversational mode) the interaction of man and the computer will increase and the need for complicated computer languages will decrease.

Conversational Mode

When a conversational mode is used, the terminal, *which is the device used to communicate with the computer,* is used to both receive and transmit messages. A typical terminal is illustrated in figure 3–4. When the terminal is dedicated to a particular business application, the messages printed may tell the operator exactly, step-by-step, what is to be done. When the terminal is used for instruction, the student types his responses and the computers are printed. The student/computer conversation may be something like this:

Computer: Good morning. Please enter your name.
Student: Mark Willard
Computer: Are you ready to begin your history lesson for today? I hope you read assignment ten yesterday. Let's begin with today's lesson. Who was the first president of the United States?

FIGURE 3–4. TIME-SHARING TERMINAL (Courtesy of Teletype Corporation)

Student:	Lincoln
Computer:	Please go back and review page 12 of your study guide and then try again.
Student:	Washinton
Computer:	Much better, but you should check the spelling of his name. Now let's continue.

The extent that the student or business employee can actually converse with the computer depends upon how the software, or program, is written. Not all programs would permit a deviation in the spelling of the response. For example, at a demonstration at the University of Michigan the computer asked: What were the names of the Nelsons' two boys that appeared in the television series? The response was given as "David and Rick." The computer deducted ten points for a wrong answer as it was looking for Dave and Ricky.

Conversational mode also implies that the user may ask for information from the files that are under the control of the computer. Special languages were developed, which can be learned very quickly, to assist the user in obtaining the desired information. One of the more popular languages, BASIC, will be introduced in a later module.

Why Time-sharing?

Both large and small companies, even entire industries and cities, will find it to their advantage to operate in-house time-sharing systems. They may wish to rely on time-sharing suppliers for both equipment and *expertise*. With the capacity available in present generation computers, idle computer time is simply too expensive to be permitted. For example, if an application program, such as an accounts receivable update, calls for a computer search of a disk file to find a customer's record, this may take as much time as it would take for the computer to perform hundreds of thousands of mathematical calculations. The computer's output can be increased if time-sharing is used as it is possible for the computer to "swap" a number of different users' jobs back and forth within its memory and data storage facilities. Therefore, while the computer searches for the record, it can "compute" for another user.

In a time-sharing system the input may be processed on a first-in/first-out basis without priority ranking. Unless it can be completed sooner, each input is processed for a predetermined period of time. This period is known as a *time slice*. The time slice is usually long enough to permit one man/machine interaction. A typical time slice may be only 150 milliseconds (.15 seconds) in duration. What can be done in that period of time? It depends upon the computer being used, but a medium scale computer could secure 50,000 answers on 1,000 exams and evaluate the effectiveness of the question, debit 1,300 checks in 1,000 different bank accounts, or do the salary calculations necessary to compute the payroll for 350 employees.

One user is usually unaware of the fact that others are also using the computer. This is true because of the vast difference between the user's response time and the system's processing time. When studying the response time needed by the user, it was found that depressing a key takes about three seconds, while typing a single instruction, at a maximum rate, takes about seven seconds. During a three second response time, a time-sharing system with a 150 millisecond time slice would be able to serve 20 users. The major portion of the time-sharing market today consists of
1. university-based problem solving,
2. computer program testing,
3. scientific and engineering applications,
4. business applications.

Problem solving by the universities was the first major use of time-sharing. The *biggest potential* user, however, *is business for business applications*. The time-sharing service must be economically sound which means that the same, or better, performance must be available for no more than the cost of the method which is now utilized.

Types of Time-sharing Services

The three general types of time-sharing services offered are (1) hardware utilization; (2) hardware and software utilization; and (3) hardware, software, and data utilization.

The first type of service is not too widely used because the customers must provide their own programs. They must be stored so that in the customer's time slice they can be retrieved from *online files,* brought into the memory of the computer, and executed. The customer's master files are usually stored on disk in order that data may be accessed by the computer when it is needed. The required variable information is entered through a terminal. The user may generally select the type of terminal that best meets his needs. When the L. C. Smith Corporation was considering using time-sharing, they lacked the experienced personnel to design and program their applications. Therefore, this type of service, hardware utilization only, would not meet their particular need. Since this is also true of many companies who use time-sharing, it is the type of service that is least likely to be utilized.

When the second type of service is offered, the user can communicate directly with the computer system and call in the program that he wishes to execute because they are supplied by the time-sharing service. This is by far the more common type of service that is contracted for because the user supplies only the data. The choice of programs may be somewhat limited and usually the user is discouraged from asking to have any changes made to better meet his particular needs. A company may start by utilizing only the programs of the time-sharing service and then add their own software as their personnel develop both the interest and the ability to write and test the needed programs.

When the third type of service is offered, the user not only uses the programs but also has access to a *common data base*. This type of service is not utilized too frequently if the users are a number of individual companies who just happen to subscribe to the same time-sharing service.

Charges are usually made in a time-sharing system for the amount of computer time used plus an additional charge for storing the user's data and programs. In addition, the user must pay for both the terminal time and a communication charge, which may be a set amount per month or it may vary with the actual amount of time that is used.

Cost Justification

How is the *cost justification* done to determine if it is feasible to utilize time-sharing? First, it must be determined which applications are going to be considered and what the present data processing costs are for those systems. Let's assume that the L. C. Smith Corporation has decided to investigate time-sharing for their accounts receivable, inventory, and sales invoicing procedures.

Their present system is primarily a manual one which uses some old, and very simple, mechanical accounting machines for preparing the accounts receivable statements. The inventory is maintained manually on a card system and the sales invoices are typed. Since the accounting machines are fully depreciated no charge is made for their use. The total cost of the present system, excluding materials and supplies, is the labor involved in maintaining the accounts receivable balances, updating the inventory, and typing the sales invoices. The present cost was therefore determined as follows:

1 Supervisor	@ $8,500.00	$ 8,500.00
6 Clerks	@ 7,000.00	42,000.00
		$50,500.00

To determine accurately the cost of the proposed time-sharing system, it must be determined how much activity will take place in each of the files. In the manual method it took the employee's time to record the transactions pertaining to inventory, accounts receivable, and sales. Employee's time, communication time, and computer time are all involved in entering transactions into the time-sharing system.

All variable data will be entered into the system by means of a terminal such as the one shown in figure 3–4 (p. 141). It must be determined how many entries will be required to record the cash, sales, and purchase transactions in addition to doing the required file maintenance. File maintenance will include the corrections, changes, additions to, and deletions from the master files.

How many items are sold and received each month? How many different stock items will be maintained in the inventory file? How many active customers does the firm have? How many invoices are written each month and how many lines, on an average, does each invoice contain? All of this data, and much more, must be determined in order to predict: the amount of storage space needed for the files, the number of required terminals and operators, the total number of entries into the files, and the amount of communication and computer time that will be necessary. When all of the data is available, the estimated monthly charges can be predicted fairly accurately. The monthly charges for terminals, data storage, computer time, and the communication charge are estimated at $1,450 for the volume of work that is currently being done manually for sales, accounts receivable, and inventory maintenance. The new system will require only two clerks rather than six. Therefore, the total anticipated costs would be:

1 Supervisor @ $8,500.00		$ 8,500.00
2 Clerks @ 7,000.00		14,000.00
Cost of terminals, computer time, data storage, and communication charges.		17,400.00
Total Cost of Time-sharing System		$39,900.00

The estimated reduction in the cost of the new system would be the difference between the cost of the current method, $50,500, and the cost of the proposed method, $39,900. The figures indicated that there would be a cost reduction of $10,600.

The illustration cited is *simplified* as there are other factors which would also have to be considered. *The purpose of the illustration is to help you to understand what is meant by cost justification—the cost of the present system is determined and compared with the anticipated cost of the proposed system.*

Other Factors in Considering Time-sharing

Should the cost alone be the determining factor? No! In making the final decision both the merits and disadvantages of time-sharing would need to be carefully considered. The user would need to know how the software (programs) would actually process the data. What measures must be taken to make certain that the data is accurate as it is entered into the system? Will the quality of the statement and reports be as good as what had been produced manually? Is there another alternative that should be considered that would produce a greater amount of service for the same amount of money? Does the time-sharing company have programs available that will not only accurately maintain the number of items in stock but will also help in inventory management by analyzing the stock turnover and profit margin on the various items that the company carries?

Time-sharing may be selected as the best alternative even when there is not an apparent reduction in cost. One of the reasons most often cited is that the company making the decision is able to take advantage of the software provided by the time-sharing system and is able to improve their inventory control and forecasting. When time-sharing services are utilized, the user also has less trouble absorbing peak order volume. Once the information is entered into the system, many reports are available, at a nominal fee, which the user would be unable to produce economically if they utilized their own small computer system.

Any company considering the use of a time-sharing system should find out what programs are available that they might wish to utilize at some time in the future. Since they may wish to write some software for themselves, the types of languages that can be used on the system are also important. For example, BASIC, which was developed at Dartmouth College for use in time-sharing, is a very easy language to use. Since there are many versions of BASIC, not all of which have the characteristics of the Dartmouth version, the user should determine *which* one is being used.

The potential user should also be very concerned about his data. What security measures are taken to make certain that it is adequately protected? Some of the considerations expressed in regard to service bureaus are also valid when making a decision as to which time-sharing service to utilize. What kind of a reputation does it have? Has it been established very long? What do its other users say about its service? Does the system have enough capacity to add new users? If a system is utilized heavily and does not have sufficent capacity, the user may not be able to transmit data when it is most desirable to do so.

The distance that the user's terminal is from the computer is also important. Using satellites data can be transferred around the world with no problem. The charge that is made for the transmission of data is usually determined by the length of time that it takes to send the message and the distance it must travel.

The backup arrangement that the system has is also very important to the user. The Holiday Inn time-sharing system, for example, has one computer that has the ability to handle all of the messages, and a second one that is available as a backup system.

The only real disadvantage to time-sharing is that confidential data is stored off the premises and beyond the control of the business using the services.

Time-sharing Networks

Today there are many time-sharing systems. Some of the systems are dedicated to a particular type of service, such as banking, educational data processing, or hospital accounting. It was announced in 1972 that the North-west Hospital of Chicago became the one-hundredth hospital to automate its accounting procedures by using the McDonnel Douglas Automation Company's shared hospital computer system.

One of the oldest time-sharing systems is CYBERNET which was developed by the Control Data Corporation to interconnect their computers and make it possible for each of their centers to share programs and a common data base. If one of the computers in the system fails, its work assignment can be given to another computer in the network. Today there are twelve Control Data Corporation "super-computer systems" linked together which provide time-sharing services to all major cities in the United States. Since many of their specialized programs deal with engineering, mathematics, and research, about 50% of the utilization of the system is derived from the large corporation which has its own computers. For example, Ford Motor Company

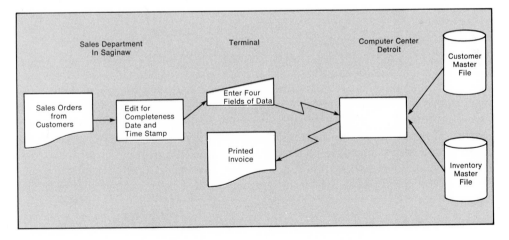

FIGURE 3–5. SALES INVOICING PROCEDURE USING TIME-SHARING

in Detroit, with all of its computer-power, still uses the CYBERNET system for their inventory parts control.

TYMNET is an international data communications network which was established in 1970. By April of 1973 it connected 37 large-scale computers in 54 cities throughout the world. To link the system, over 40,000 million miles of leased telephone lines are required. The largest single user of the system is the National Library of Medicine in Bethesda, Maryland.

Darthmouth College has had a time-sharing computer system in existence since May of 1964. In 1973 over 30 secondary schools and 21 colleges in 10 states were using its facilities through time-sharing.

A TIME-SHARING APPLICATION

Processing the Sales Order Manually

In a manual method it must be determined before the order can be processed if the customer has exceeded his credit limit. The next check generally made is to determine if the item number used on the order is valid. At that time the price and description are also compared with those on the master price listing. Next, it is determined if there is a sufficient quantity of the item on hand to fill the order. If not, the item will have to be placed on backorder. The mathematics on the sales order is also checked by using a small calculator and then, finally, if the items are on hand and the customer's credit is satisfactory, the sales invoice is typed.

Using a Time-sharing System

When a time-sharing system is utilized the customer is able to take advantage of sophisticated software, or programs, that have been developed, tested, and debugged. Therefore, what functions required in a manual method can be eliminated if a time-sharing system is used? The customer's master file, which contains all of the pertinent information about the customer, is maintained on disk by the time-sharing service. The inventory file, which is also stored on disk, contains the item number, price, product description, and quantity on hand as well as other information that is not pertinent to this application.

As indicated on the sales order form, illustrated in figure 3–6, there are only four different fields that must be keyed in on the terminal by the operator. They are the order number, customer number, item number, and the quantity.

L. C. SMITH CORPORATION

1314 LARCH STREET

SAGINAW, MICHIGAN 48603

⟨V⟩ ORDER NUMBER: *00987*			DATE: *July 14, 1975*	
SOLD TO: *James H. Henderlong* ⟨MF₁⟩ *1413 North Bay Road* *Green Bay, Wisconsin*				
⟨V⟩ *0127*			TERMS: *2/10, N/30*	
SOLD BY: *J. Green* 18				

ITEM NUMBER ⟨V⟩	QUANTITY ⟨V⟩	⟨MF₂⟩ DESCRIPTION	⟨MF₂⟩ UNIT COST		TOTAL COST	
00149	10	*Sink Unit – Walnut*	156	93	⟨C⟩ 1569	30
00177	20	*Well Unit – Walnut*	53	50	1070	00
00179	2	*Corner Unit – Walnut*	47	32	94	64
		⟨V⟩ Variable Items Entered from Terminal				
		⟨C⟩ Calculated by the Computer				
		⟨MF₁⟩ From Customer Master File				
		⟨MF₂⟩ From Item Master File				
TOTAL AMOUNT:				⟨C⟩	2733	94

FIGURE 3–6. SALES ORDER—PREPARED BY SALESMEN

The fields are marked on the sales order with a V to indicate that it is the variable data that must be entered into the system by using the terminal. (The actual sales order would not be marked as such.) The description and unit cost of the product will be printed on the sales invoice by using the data in the inventory master file. The customer's name and address will be added to the sales invoice from the accounts receivable master file. The terminal used in the application is illustrated in figure 3–4 (p. 141).

The operator will key in the four fields of variable information on the terminal. Before the data is transmitted it is displayed on the cathode ray tube. Any character can be changed by the operator without affecting the remainder of the data. The display increases the accuracy because the operator can see the *data in its entirety before it is sent*. After the operator has edited the information, it is transmitted to the computer at *maximum terminal speed rather than at keyboard speed*.

As an optional feature, the *entire sales order form* could be displayed on the screen. The displaying of the form helps the operator to visually verify that the data had been keyed in correctly. The operator inserts the variable information in the proper places, verifies the data visually, and then the variable data is transmitted to the computer. After the data is sent, the variable data is erased from the screen. The form, however, remains displayed on the screen.

After the data is transmitted, the sales invoices will be printed on the terminal's printer. The terminal pictured in figure 3–4 has a printer that is capable of printing 220 lines per minute *or*, if no shifting for upper case letters is required (monocase), the printer can achieve 314 lines per minute. No operator intervention is required because all of the spacing and tabulating necessary (to position the data in the correct location on the sales invoice) is done automatically.

Remote Job Entry

If time-sharing is to be utilized for applications that require large volumes of input and output, it may be to the advantage of the user to install what is called a RJE (remote job entry) station. Rather than using a terminal which only provides data entry by means of a keyboard and printed output in "page copy format" on a typewriter-like printer, there are many other options that are available. *If* the cost of transmitting the data is based on time and distance, it may be to the advantage of the user to secure additional equipment that will transmit and receive data faster. The terminal illustrated can be utilized with a magnetic tape data terminal which will increase the transmission rate to 2,400 words per minute.

Remote job entry stations frequently utilize card readers, punched paper tape readers, and magnetic tape data terminals as devices with which to transmit data to the remotely located computer. In addition, when a large volume of data is to be transmitted back to the sender for utilization in printed reports, faster printers can be added as part of the RJE station. The printers can usually print 250 *or more* lines per minute. A typical payroll application might be done in the manner illustrated in figure 3–7.

In the time-slice that is given to L. C. Smith, the payroll may be processed online, as the input is received, or all of the data can be transmitted, stored, and then processed in a *remote batch mode.* The results of processing are then transmitted back to Smiths as a continuous stream of output, and the checks may be printed on a printer capable of printing 250 lines per minute. The master file information, maintained on a disk file by Gateway, is updated to show the results of the current pay.

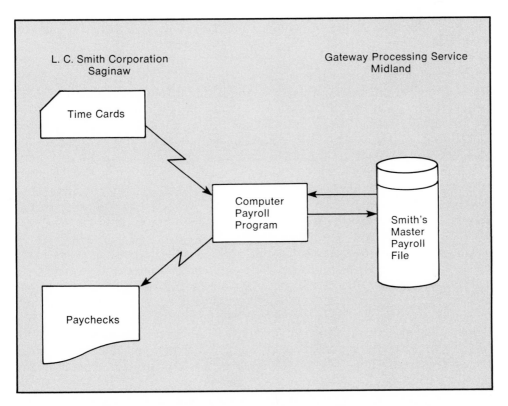

FIGURE 3–7. PAYROLL PROCESSING USING REMOTE JOB ENTRY CARD READER AND PRINTER

Advantages and Disadvantages of Time-sharing

When the time-sharing company is a large one, there are generally a number of applications that are already programmed, tested, and *debugged*. The small user has at his disposal a computer far more powerful than what could be economically justified for the volume of data which must be processed. Idle computer time is not a concern because the user is only charged for the amount of time that is utilized. If there is not an excessive amount of users on the system, the user feels that he has the exclusive use of the computer. Data can be transmitted today at a much faster rate and more economically, which makes it feasible for the small user to consider time-sharing. There are also many methods being employed today to make certain that the data is transmitted into the system accurately. When a sophisticated system such as TYMNET is used, if one computer is busy the user is automatically switched to a second or even a third computer. When time-sharing is used some of the steps between the occurrence of the event and the entry of the data into the system *may* be omitted. This, however, depends upon the location and type of terminal that is used in transmitting the data.

With any solution to a given problem there are generally disadvantages to the method selected as well as advantages. The company investigating a given time-sharing service must be careful not to become committed to a system that already has too many users. A backup system must also be available in the event that the computer is down. How the user's data is protected and backed up is also a point that must be examined carefully as there have been cases where user's files have been accessed by unauthorized individuals. Since the method used to charge for the services rendered varies between various time-sharing companies, the user must carefully examine each company's policy. In some cases the programs are designed for other users and do not meet the needs of a potential user. The cost of modifying the programs to meet his needs may be excessively high. Line-drop, which means data is lost, may occur as the data is transmitted. When this occurs, the data is retransmitted which takes additional time and delays processing.

When too many users are online to the same time-sharing system, an individual user may be put on "wait" until another user is finished transmitting. This occurs when the system is designed on a "first in" basis rather than having the user's terminal "polled" to see if there is data to be sent. There are also a maximum number of users which may be "connected" to a system at any one time. When some of the user's data is processed in a batch mode, the processing may be delayed if the system is overloaded. The question can then be raised: "What is the value of a computerized system if the results are less timely than when a manual system is utilized?" One example of "overloading" is the use of a time-sharing service by a large number of schools for the processing of student records. The grades, recorded by the teachers on prepunched, interpreted cards, were punched into cards. The length of time that it would take to transmit the grades using their RJE station would make it too expensive; therefore, the cards were taken directly to the computer center for processing. When the school system first utilized the time-sharing services, the grade reports were not available until three to four weeks later. Is the data timely for the purposes that the grades were intended at that point in time? There were many advantages gained by using the time-sharing service but timely grades was not one of the advantages.

Time-sharing has been presented only from the point of view of an alternative to be considered by a company that finds its present method of processing data inadequate. There are many other applications for time-sharing where the system is shared by many users *from one company* rather than many different companies utilizing the computational power, programs, and perhaps, the data base of the time-sharing service's computer. This is why that among the many possible uses that are available, time-sharing is the fastest growing segment of EDP. Other applications will be illustrated, along with the more specific hardware and software requirements of time-sharing, in module 11.

PERTAINING TO TIME-SHARING

3–17. When was the technology for time-sharing developed?

3–18. Is the user in a time-sharing system really aware that others are also using the system?

3–19. In a time-sharing system, what is the name of the device used to transmit and receive data from the computer?

3–20. What does the term *conversational* mode imply in a time-sharing system?

3–21. How many milliseconds is a typical time-slice?

3–22. What are the three general types of services requested by users in a time-sharing system?

3–23. How is a proposed system *cost justified*?

3–24. Discuss the following statement: Unless it can be shown mathematically that the time-sharing system will cost less to process the same volume of data as the system now being used, it should not be considered as an alternative.

3–25. In the invoicing application the user's master files were online to the computer which made it possible to provide a "computerized" check on what three items?

3–26. In time-sharing, is it possible for the remote user to utilize a variety of input and output devices?

3–27. Why might a large company elect to use the time-sharing services of another company?

3–28. In a time-sharing system the user usually pays a flat rate for being able to use the system plus an hourly rate for the actual computer time used. In addition, the user pays for the cost of transmitting the data over a common carrier, the connect time, and the rental of the terminals. What else might the user be required to pay for?

3–29. What is the difference between batch processing and online processing?

A SMALL COMPUTER SYSTEM

Today, another alternative that is available to a company that finds that it has outgrown its present manual or mechanical data processing methods is the acquisition of its own small computer. In acquiring a computer system there are certain basic factors that determine how expensive the selected system will be per month.

1. Memory—the computer's memory is used as storage for both the data and the program. The more memory that is available, the more costly the system becomes.

2. Access time—one of the basic considerations in any system concerns the length of time it takes to read and store data in the memory of the computer. The faster this can be done, the more expensive the system.

3. Computational time—how long does it actually take to execute a simple command such as to add, divide, or multiply? The faster the commands are executed, the more the user will likely pay for the system.

4. Other I/O devices—a very basic system may use a keyboard entry system for data, disk online auxiliary storage for master files, and a relatively slow printer. When additional or faster input and output devices are utilized, the cost of the system is increased.

Many of the very small computer systems are designed so that the amount of memory can be expanded in order to handle more sophisticated applications, which are required as the user gains experience in EDP. As more applications are added to the system, the first I/O devices may become too slow to handle the increased volume of data. The user then may exercise the option of changing to a faster printer and adding an additional input device to the system.

IBM SYSTEM/3 MODEL 6

The basic configuration of the IBM System/3 Model 6 uses a processing unit that contains a minimum of 8,000 characters of memory. Memory is usually rounded to the nearest thousand, or unit of four thousand, and is referred to as so many "K." In this case, if you wish to be very exact, the amount of memory is 8,192 characters or, as is more commonly stated, 8K.

The disk storage is in the upper drawer on the left on the configuration. The user is offered the option of having the capacity of storing around 2.5 million characters of data, or as much as 10 million characters online at any one time. One disk is removable, which means that one disk might be used for inventory records, another for payroll records, and still another for the accounts receivable file. One disk may contain more than one file of data. For example, the inventory disk may also contain the accounts receivable file. In terms of access time, two different models are available, one of which is almost twice as fast as the other. Why not select the fastest model with the largest disk pack? The reason is cost! How much data must be online and how

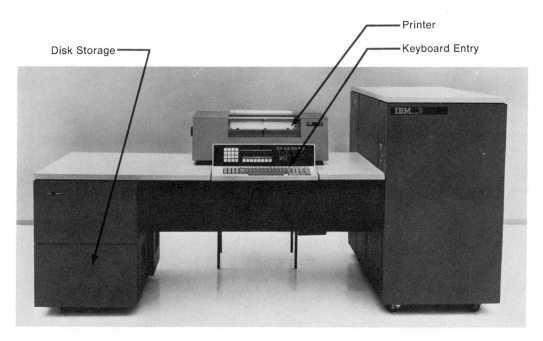

FIGURE 3–8. IBM SYSTEM/3 MODEL 6 (Courtesy of International Business Machines Corporation)

important is the access time? The trade-off, of course, is added cost for added storage and faster access. Each user must determine if the additional speed and capacity warranted the additional cost.

The printer, which usually is attached to the basic configuration, is also available in three different models. Model 1 is used primarily for scientific application which uses only single part paper. Model 2 prints essentially the same, from left to right, but is recommended for business applications that involve the use of multiple part forms. Model 3 prints in either direction—left to right or right to left—which increases the number of lines per minute that may be printed. On an average, a 100-character print line can be printed at either 26, 27, or 43 lines per minute depending upon which model is selected. Another printer is available which will permit the user to print on ledger cards as well as continuous form paper.

The keyboard used to enter data is much the same as a standard typewriter, except that it also has a special ten-key numeric keyboard.

As the needs of the user change, data entry may be by means of punched cards, a magnetic character reader, or a cathode ray tube.

APPLICATION PACKAGES

IBM has developed and tested in the field (which means using actual users) a number of different types of applications. Each application package is designed and tested to meet the needs of a certain type of user. For example, the Auto Dealer's Inventory package is designed *specifically* for the user who has a parts inventory of from 9 to 12 thousand unique parts and sells approximately 100 cars per month. The programs that are available as part of the package are based on the assumption that the user will have 12K of memory and 4.90 characters of online disk storage. It would be difficult to get much more specific in regard to the kind of user the programs are designed for or what volume of business can be handled by a very specific hardware configuration.

PROGRAMMING LANGUAGES AVAILABLE

The programs in the application packages are written in RPG (Report Program Generator), which is a very easy-to-use programming language. The programs may be modified by the user to make them more adaptable to his particular needs. Once the user becomes familiar with the basic package, additional programs may be written to perform some of the required data processing functions. The "application packages" are well suited to the needs of many small businesses who have not had any previous experience in either unit-record or electronic data processing.

A second language, BASIC, is also available on the System/3 Model 6 and is recommended for the use of engineers, financial analysts, and others who wish to use the computer for problem solving rather than the more routine processing of data.

Other Considerations

When the potential user is exploring the use of such a system, monthly rental of both the hardware (equipment) and software (application programs) can be accurately determined. The user is also able to see the reports that have been produced on a similar system. Usually included in the package is a general type seminar, or workshop, which gives an overview of the system. More specific workshops may be provided at a nominal charge involving, in this case, only the users of the automotive dealer's application package. Test time is generally available on similar System/3 Model 6 systems for both conversion of the user's files and modification of the available application programs.

There are, of course, many other manufacturers that offer similar types of service for the small computer user. This type of programming assistance and hardware configuration has not been available at a cost that is within the reach of the small user until rather recently.

Although the system is described as being small and usable by the small user (e.g., the automotive dealer), remember that as much memory is being considered in these systems as was available in many of the first- or second-generation computers. The small business that is expanding and in need of better data processing may not have been able to consider the second-generation 1400 system. Nevertheless, a small disk system, such as the System/3 Model 6 described, may be less expensive than a complete unit-record installation would have been in the early 1960s. It has far more uses than unit-record equipment and a greater capacity for problem solving.

Since the cost of the system is based upon the amount of memory, the time it takes to access online data, the amount of storage, and the number of I/O devices, the user should carefully determine his actual needs. A very definite advantage to a system, such as the one described is that it can be expanded as the needs of the user change; more memory, more disk storage with a faster access time, and additional input and output devices can be added.

3–30. Two users might have a System/3 Model 6. One user may pay a good deal more than the other user, yet both configurations look like the one illustrated in figure 3–8 (p. 155). Why is that possible?

3–31. Why is the keyboard data entry sufficient for a small user if the configuration also has auxiliary disk storage?

3–32. Were "application packages" such as the Automotive Dealer's Application Programs available for use with the second-generation computers? Discuss.

A LARGER SYSTEM/3 MODEL 10

When IBM announced the System/3 Model 10, it was featured as "a system to grow on" because it was available in three basic configurations.

1. A basic punched card system which utilizes a multi-function card unit, a central processing unit, and a printer.
2. A disk system which added online disk storage to the basic configuration.
3. A disk-tape system which is created by adding magnetic tape.

The System/3 is small enough for many first-time users yet can be expanded to keep pace with the data processing needs of the company. It has been well received, and it is predicted that it will be one of the computer systems that will be around for a long time. A group, NASU (National Association of System/3 Users) was organized in Los Angeles by Irwin Cohan, who reported that many of the members were first-time computer users. NASU meets regularly so that members may swap problems and programs. In addition to meetings, the group has both a newsletter and an applications library. Cohan felt that the organization has grown so rapidly because it meets the needs of so many members who are first-time computer users.

Application Customizer Service

The System/3 users, either Model 6 or 10, may also take advantage of what is called the "Application Customizer Service" which is offered by IBM. The System/3 user who is beginning to convert his present manual system, with perhaps some of the work being done by a service bureau, to a computerized system may wish to elect this option. The employees of the company who will be working with the new system are asked to fill out an application questionnaire and indicate their report specifications. In the case of L. C.

Smith, Keyser might elect to fill out questionnaires for their sales invoicing, accounts receivable, inventory accounting, and sales analysis since these were the areas of the company's greatest concern.

Filling in the questionnaires requires the user to take a *really good look at what is now being done.* Weaknesses of the present system can be determined that were not apparent to the user until this was done. One company reported that it had no idea that the customers were charged incorrect prices so often until they filled in the questionnaire on their sales invoicing system. To complete the questionnaires they must study their own system, which is where the design of any new system should begin. A small company that does not have personnel trained in systems work may overlook this part of the design procedure. The report specifications are nothing more than a *thoughtful analysis* of what is wanted from the new system. The information from the questionnaires and report specifications are entered into a computer which has been programmed to analyze the input and then produce programming aids which will assist the user in the conversion of his present system to the new System/3. The user will receive flowcharts and descriptions of both the system and the programs that will be needed to implement the new procedures. The user still writes, tests, and debugs the programs that will be needed. It can be done much faster, and probably more accurately, than if a relatively inexperienced individual were to design the entire system without assistance.

As an optional feature, the user may elect to have the source code (the program written in RPG II) provided for him. This would permit the user to convert faster, but it would permit less flexibility. Since a good deal of programming maintenance is usually required, it might be better in the long run for the user to write his own programs. Sooner or later the user's employees must learn to work with the equipment and the programming languages if the system is to be effectively utilized. Each firm must decide for itself the merits of writing its own programs against securing programs that are already available.

Other Assistance

Application briefs are also published by IBM for users in various industries which give very specific details pertaining to the volume of business, the hardware selected, and the design of the system. For example, one is available in the building supply industry which details the system and applications of the Building Supply Center, Inc., in Pensacola, Florida. This application brief would be of interest to the L. C. Smith Corporation if they were considering a System/3.

When alternatives are being considered, one of which is the utilization of a small computer system, the experiences that others in the same industry have had is good input (along with all the other factors) to consider when making the decision. The types of services (such as the Application Customizer Service) provided by the manufacturer must also be considered. The fact that a user's group existed, which has a newsletter and applications library, would also be reassuring. In January 1973 IBM began publishing a new magazine, DP/SOLUTIONS which contains primarily application-oriented information and articles on System/3.

THE COMPONENTS OF THE BASIC SYSTEM/3—MODEL 10

The 96 Card Column Card

The most "shocking" feature to so many people who are involved in the computer industry was the use of the "mini" card. The card contained approximately 20% more information than the "standard" 80 card column Hollerith code card, yet was about one-third the size. For over eighty years the 80 card column card had been *the* IBM card!

The code used to record information in the card is referred to as a BCD or *binary coded decimal* system. The card is divided into three tiers. The first is referenced by digits 1–32, the second tier by 33–64, and the third tier by 65–96. Figure 3–9 illustrates the tiers, printing, and punching positions.

The card layout form in figure 3–9 is one-fifth larger than the actual card which is shown in figure 3–10. The top portion of the card contains 128 print positions while the lower part of the card is divided into three tiers each of which can contain 32 characters of information. *B* and *A* represent zone punching while the 8, 4, 2, and 1 positions are referred to as *digit* punching positions. Numbers are represented by the correct combination of digit punches. For example, a 9 would be represented by an 8 and a 1 punch in the same card column while a 3 would require a 2 and 1 punch in the same card column. The 0 is represented by the *A* zone punch.

BCD Code

The binary coded decimal system, used to represent the alphabetic information and the special characters, is an easy one to work with. It is the same basic code that is used on some magnetic tape or data stored in a computer which utilizes a six bit code. *A bit is a binary digit and each location*

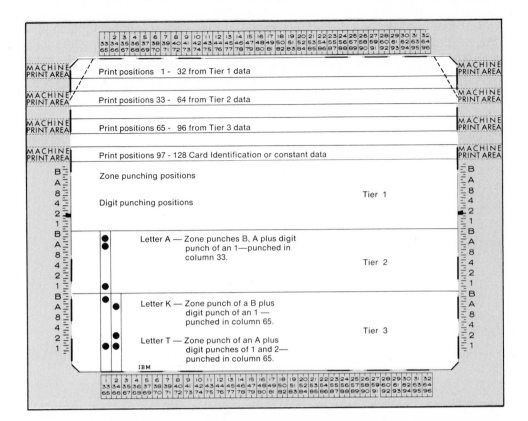

FIGURE 3–9. CARD LAYOUT
FORM FOR
SYSTEM/3
96 CARD
COLUMN CARD

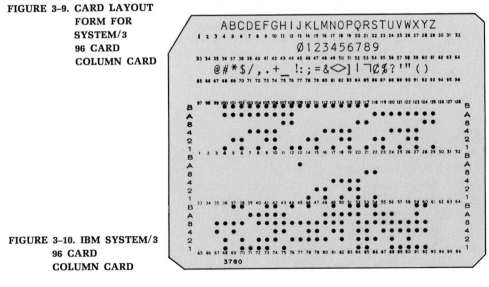

FIGURE 3–10. IBM SYSTEM/3
96 CARD
COLUMN CARD

in the card contains six bits that are used in the code. If a hole is punched in the card in a given location, the bit is "on." If there is no hole in a given location, the bit is "off." The BCD code representing the letters of the alphabet is as follows:

A–I ALL REQUIRE THE B AND A ZONE PUNCHES PLUS THE DIGIT PUNCHES NEEDED TO REPRESENT 1–9.

ZONE	DIGIT	LETTER
B, A	1	A
B, A	2	B
B, A	1,2	C
B, A	4	D
B, A	4,1	E
B, A	4,2	F
B, A	4,2,1	G
B, A	8	H
B, A	8,1	I

J–R ALL REQUIRE THE B ZONE PUNCH PLUS THE DIGIT PUNCHES NEEDED TO REPRESENT 1–9.

ZONE	DIGIT	LETTER
B	1	J
B	2	K
B	1,2	L
B	4	M
B	4,1	N
	• • •	
B	8,1	R

S–Z ALL REQUIRE THE A ZONE PUNCH PLUS THE DIGIT PUNCHES NEEDED TO REPRESENT 2–9.

ZONE	DIGIT	LETTER
A	2	S
A	2,1	T
	• • •	
Z	8,1	Z

What is needed to represent the letter *O*? The zone punch of a *B* and the 4 and 2 digit punches. Do you see the pattern that is used in the code? What punches are in a given card column to represent the letter *W*? The zone of an *A* plus the 4 and 2 digit punches are needed.

Why was a card designed that used a BCD code rather than the Hollerith code? Using the BCD code only six punching positions are required in any one column to represent the digits, letters of the alphabet, or special characters. Since this is true, more data can be punched in a smaller card than if the Hollerith code were used. The Hollerith code also requires a zone plus a digit, but nine rows are used for the digit and three for the zone punches. In contrast, the BCD card uses only two zone punching positions and four digit positions. With six punching positions available in any one location, 64 different combinations are possible. This permits the letters A–Z, the digits 0–9, and 28 special characters to be represented in the System/3 code.

As is illustrated in figure 3–10, the information that is punched in the card is printed in the corresponding print location in the card which makes handling the card much easier. Figure 3–10 is the actual size of the System/3 card and is punched with the digits 0–9 and the letters of the alphabet.

DATA RECORDER

The data recorder is used both to punch and verify the cards. Before starting the job, the program card, which contains the codes to control the necessary shifting, skipping, and duplication, is read and its contents stored in the data recorder's memory. As many as four different card formats, or programs, may be stored in the memory of the data recorder at one time. This permits

FIGURE 3–11. DATA RECORDER.
(Courtesy of International Business Machines Corporation)

the operator to switch from one program to another when a job requires multiple card formats.

The keyboard is arranged much like a standard typewriter, and the alphabetic keys are all in the same locations. For ease of operation, however, the numeric keys are arranged so that all of the digits may be reached by using the right hand. Because both digits and alphabetic characters are on the same key, the data recorder must shift from one mode to another depending upon whether the field contains numeric or alphabetic information. When a special character or digit is on the top of the key, such as the J key that is illustrated $\begin{pmatrix} 4 \\ J \end{pmatrix}$, the machine must be in numeric shift, or mode, in order to get the four punched in the card.

The data recorder is *buffered* which permits the operator to key in all of the data before any of the characters are actually punched in the card. If the operator senses that an error is made, the invalid character may be erased and the correct one rekeyed. The data recorder can function also as a verifier, which is an advantage to the small user because one piece of equipment can both punch and verify the cards.

The data recorder has a card hopper, a punch station, a read station, a print station, and a stacker. Overlapping of the punching and keying functions

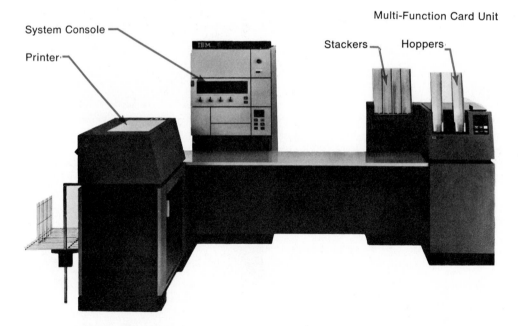

FIGURE 3–12. BASIC SYSTEM 13 CONFIGURATION. (Courtesy of International Business Machines Corporation)

can occur; that permits the operator to begin keying in the second card while the first card is being punched at the punch station. The read station is used in duplicating constant material from one card back into the following card. The print station prints on the card the data that was punched in the card in one of the three printing locations illustrated in figure 3–9 (p. 161).

Multi-function Card Unit

The multi-function card unit (MFCU) can do far more than read input cards into the system. The MFCU can read two files of cards, punch a file of cards, or read and then punch additional information into the same file of cards. In addition, data may be printed on the cards while they are at the print station. Selected cards can be stacked in any of the four pockets. The MFCU can also sort and merge card files.

The MFCU has two card hoppers which operate independently. Once a card is fed from one of the hoppers it passes through a read station where it is read column-by-column, three tiers at a time, until the entire card is read. The card is read by using solar cells which pass a light through the punched holes. The light is then converted to electrical signals which in turn cause the data punched in the cards to be stored in the memory of the computer. If the card is not to be read, as in the case of blank cards that are to be used for output, the sensors are not activated and the card passes the read station unread. Figure 3–13 illustrates the card path through the MFCU. After the card is read, it enters the wait station. The punch station contains 18 punching devices which make it possible to punch the card column-by-column, three tiers at a time. If the card is not to be punched, it passes through the station unpunched. The print station is composed of a series of printer wheels, each of which contains 63 characters plus one blank. Four lines of 32 characters each may be printed on the card. If the printing is not to be done, the card is immediately selected into one of the four output pockets. Which pocket the card will enter is determined by the user's program.

Cards from both the first and second hopper can be read, punched, printed, and sent to any one of the four stackers, regardless of the hopper origin (fig. 3–13). The traditional unit-record functions of reproducing, gang-punching, summary punching, interpreting, collating, decollating, and sorting can be performed on the MFCU, under complete control of the stored program.

Card Reading

Cards are read serially at the rate of 250 or 500 cards per minute.
As each card moves through the read station, light passes through the

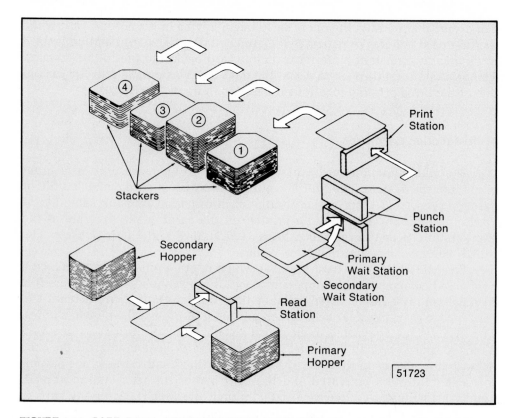

FIGURE 3–13. CARD PATH: MULTI-FUNCTION CARD UNIT (Courtesy International Business Machines Corporation)

punched holes in each column and is converted to electrical energy by an array of solar cells. There is one solar cell for each punch position.

The multi-function card unit is a combination of the abilities of the interpreter, reproducer, collator, and sorter; and it also performs its primary job of reading input into the computer. The user has two models from which to choose. The slower model reads 250 cards per minute while it punches and prints only 60 cards per minute. The faster model reads 500 cards per minute and will punch or interpret 120 cards per minute.

Selecting a Printer

When selecting a printer for use with the Model 10, the user can choose from five different printers which range in speed from 100 to 1,000 lines per minute. Type cartridges are available which permit the user to select the print character set which best meets his needs. The basic printer can print 96 characters on a line. The user, however, may elect to use either 120 or 132 horizontal print positions rather than 96.

The central processing unit which contains the memory of the computer starts at 8K and can be expanded to as much as 60K. Since the charge for the system is based upon the amount of memory that is available and the speed of the various input/output devices, the first-time computer user might well select the 8K system with a MFCU that reads 250 cards per minute. One of the basic printers, which prints at either 100 or 200 lines per minute, will balance the system and adequately meet the user's needs.

Accounts Receivable Application Using a Basic System/3 System

The accounts receivable problem that was illustrated in figure 3–3 (p. 135) will be flowcharted assuming that a basic System/3 system with a MFCU, central processing unit (memory), and a printer are used. With a conventional card reader the flowchart would be the same as in figure 3–3 except that the block labeled accounting machine would be "computer" and the reproducer's job of summary punching would be done by the card punch which is online (under the control of) to the computer.

When figure 3–3 is contrasted with figure 3–14, the advantage of using the MFCU is readily apparent since the operator has far less card handling. The job can be done much faster and with less chance of error. The approach used in the accounts receivable application is to read two separate files of cards. The master deck is placed in the primary hopper and the detail cards are placed in the secondary hopper. The customer's cards will be processed only if there is a master and one, or more, detail cards. If there is not a "match," the sensors are not activated and the cards merely pass through the read, punch, and print stations. No processing will occur! The matching ability of the collator is being simulated, the summary punching ability of the reproducer occurs as a new card is punched, and the interpreter's ability to print is executed as the data is printed on the new balance card.

System/3 Disk System

As the user finds that it is necessary to process more data, more memory and faster input/output devices may be added to the basic system. When online disk is added to the basic system, the disks and drives necessary to read the data on the disks are in a drawer beneath the MFCU. Figure 3–12 (p. 164)

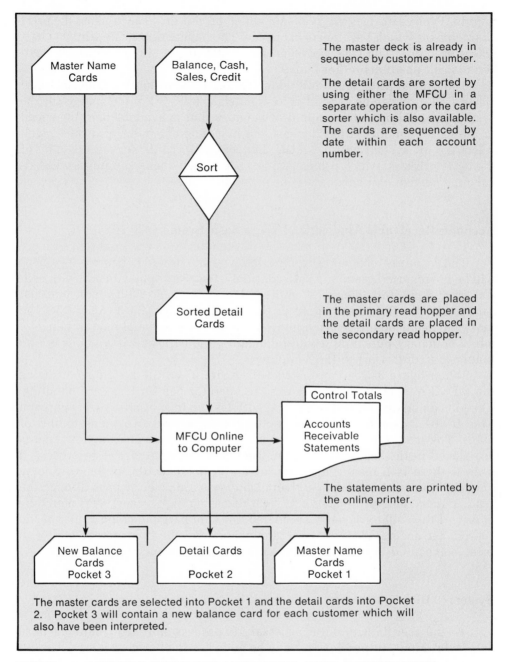

The master deck is already in sequence by customer number.

The detail cards are sorted by using either the MFCU in a separate operation or the card sorter which is also available. The cards are sequenced by date within each account number.

The master cards are placed in the primary read hopper and the detail cards are placed in the secondary read hopper.

The statements are printed by the online printer.

The master cards are selected into Pocket 1 and the detail cards into Pocket 2. Pocket 3 will contain a new balance card for each customer which will also have been interpreted.

FIGURE 3–14. ACCOUNTS RECEIVABLE APPLICATION—BASIC CONFIGURATION OF SYSTEM/3

shows the location of the disk unit. The disk configuration available can utilize either two, three, or four disks per pack and can provide online storage ranging from around 2.5 million to ten million characters of data. The same application, accounts receivable, is used to show the advantage of adding disk to the system. Figure 3–15 illustrates the processing changes that would be made when disk storage is added.

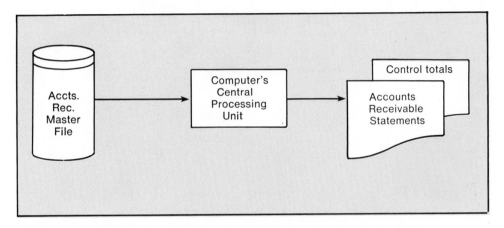

FIGURE 3–15. ACCOUNTS RECEIVABLE STATEMENTS USING A DISK SYSTEM

The accounts receivable master file is now maintained on a disk. Each customer has a record in the file which may contain a wide variety of information about the transactions he has had with L. C. Smith. The size of the record and the amount of information that it will contain is determined by the programmer and the analyst when they design the sales and accounts receivable systems. The customer's record will usually contain all of the unpaid invoices plus totals for the amount received on account, amount of returns, and sales.

As sales, cash, and credit memorandums are processed on a day-to-day basis, the accounts receivable master file will constantly be updated to reflect the events that are occurring. At any time management may request a listing of accounts receivable balances.

Disk-Tape System

The central processing unit's memory can be expanded, tape drives added, and additional disk storage added which will convert the installation from what might be termed a small installation to a medium-sized installation.

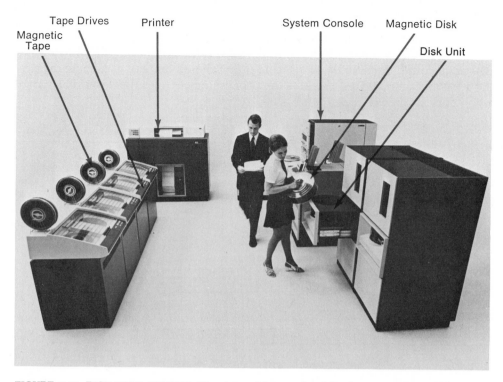

Tape Drives · Printer · System Console · Magnetic Disk · Magnetic Tape · Disk Unit

FIGURE 3–16. DISK-TAPE SYSTEM. (Courtesy of International Business Machines Corporation)

Figure 3–16 illustrates the operator mounting a disk pack which can contain up to 20.48 million characters of data.

The magnetic tapes will be used for input, output, and as a storage media. When the disk-tape system is used, a faster printer and MFCU are usually utilized. The disks and tapes illustrated in figure 3–16 are also compatible with the much larger IBM 360 and 370 systems.

When the basic system was used, the user wrote or obtained programs that were written in RPG II. With the larger systems, RPG II, which contains many attractive features, can also be used. Some of the languages, usually available on much larger systems, such as COBOL (Common Business Oriented Language), Basic Assembler, and FORTRAN IV are also available.

The System/3 has some interesting options such as the dual-feed carriage option which makes it possible for the printer to print two side-by-side forms at the same time. Each form is individually controlled by the user's program. In data processing the basic functions are to sort, merge, summarize, and calculate; all of these functions can be performed by using the MFCU and the central processing unit.

Optional Features

There are many optional devices that are available for use with the System/3. A card sorter, which is offline, is available, and it can sort either 100 or 1,500 cards per minute. A data entry keyboard can be added to the MFCU which will permit the operator to key in information to both punch and verify cards.

The System/3 is well suited to communications and can serve the company using the system in a number of different ways. The Model 10 also offers dual programming which, under certain conditions, enables the system to independently load and process two different programs simultaneously.

Many of the features, such as dual programming and communications, require complex software (programs) that are supplied by either the computer manufacturer or independent software companies. Features such as these are well beyond the reach of the first-time computer user.

Model 15

IBM announced a new System/3 Model 15 which has increased capabilities over the Model 10. The hardware components, central processing unit, disk, and tape systems are the same as those used with the Model 10. The big difference is *software!* The Model 15 will have a further expanded memory to permit the enlarged software package to be stored and still provide enough room for the users' programs and data. *A computer's ability comes from both hardware and software.*

REGARDING THE SYSTEM/3 MODEL 10

3–33. What are the three basic configurations available for the System/3 Model 10?

3–34. What is the smallest amount of memory, or core, that can be obtained with the System/3 Model 10?

3–35. What does the application customizer service do?

3–36. What is NASU?

3–37. What does MFCU stand for?

3–38. What basic data processing functions can be performed by the MFCU when under the direction of the CPU (the computer)?

3–39. How many characters of information can be punched in the System/3 card? How does it contrast in size to the *standard* card? What type of code is used for punching either special or alphabetic characters in the card?

3–40. What are the three vertical areas of the card called?

3–41. What combination of punches are required to punch a *B* in the card?

3–42. Why is a BCD code used rather than the Hollerith code?

3–43. Depending upon which *mode* the data recorder is in, what can it do?

3–44. How many different program formats can be stored at one time in the memory of the data recorder? Under program control what functions are automatically performed?

3–45. The MFCU has four pockets in which to put the processed cards. What determines where the card being processed will go?

3–46. Are all cards that enter the MFCU read?

3–47. When the disk system was used, what advantage should be apparent in regard to printing the accounts receivable statements for the customers?

3–48. When the MFCU was used in the basic configuration to read the cards in order to produce the accounts receivable statements, what functions were provided which had been previously assigned to unit-record equipment?

3–49. When magnetic tape is added to the system, along with the disk, the system then might be classified as a medium-sized installation (perhaps on the small side). The magnetic tapes are an excellent input, output, and storage media for what kind of files?

3–50. When the basic card system was used only a small amount of memory was probably available. What language was probably used for most of the programming?

3–51. When the larger Model 10 tape-disk system is used, more memory is available. On the larger model 10 computers, what languages (besides Report Program Generator) are usually available?

3–52. Can the languages listed for 3–51 (COBOL, FORTRAN IV, and assembler) be used on other computers?

3–53. What is the biggest difference between Model 10 and Model 15?

3–54. In your opinion, is the Model 10 of the System/3 a computer system that can "grow"?

A COMPUTERIZED ACCOUNTING SYSTEM

It was illustrated in module one that when manual methods are used good form design can make it possible to decrease the amount of time that is necessary to process data. The illustration was given of the imaginative and creative payroll clerk who redesigned the payroll forms so that the data could be typed *just one time* and be used to produce the payroll check, the employee's earning record, the current journal, and the year-to-date summary. It was pointed out that this decreased the time from two days to a half day.

This concept, which might be termed the "write it once" principle, has been utilized for a long time in many different types of mechanical data processing equipment. Today, the mechanical equipment is disappearing from the market and in its place is appearing electronic computerized systems. The electronic equipment is easier to maintain and is more capable than the mechanical equipment. Some of the new equipment, such as the NCR 399, still utilizes the same basic concept of entering the information *once* and having several documents prepared at one time.

NCR 399 SYSTEM

The NCR (National Cash Register) 399 System appeals to many small businesses because they feel comfortable with the system. It gives the small but growing company the type of records that it is familiar with but with far less effort. The system is also one that can easily be expanded as its data processing needs change. No special preparation is necessary to install the system. Figure 3–17 illustrates the NCR 399.

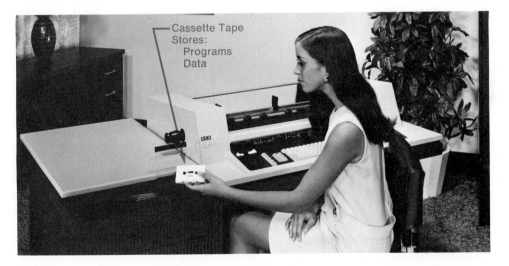

FIGURE 3–17. NCR 399 COMPUTERIZED ACCOUNTING SYSTEM. (Courtesy of National Cash Register Company)

How does the system work? First, let's learn a little more about the basic system and then find out some of the details that are involved in processing payroll. The 399 is a computer since it does have a memory that can store a series of commands which we now know is called the program. The memory of the 399 can start with as little as 8K and can be expanded to as much as 32K. The NCR 399 system can be expanded as the L. C. Smith's volume of data is increased.

Because workable, tested programs are available at a low cost, the system appeals to many small first-time computer users. Although the hardware is generally rented, the software is purchased. When the programs are purchased step-by-step, well-documented instructions are also available. The operator needs very little training because each detail of the procedure is clearly explained in the manual. When the 399 was first introduced, programs were available on *cassettes* for processing payroll, accounts payable, accounts receivable, and general ledger accounting. If the customer would like the programs adjusted to fit his particular needs, this can easily be done as there are systems analysts available to make the necessary program modifications. Today there is a library of special programs already written and field tested that customers may also select from.

Processing Payroll Using the NCR 399

Assume that it is time to process payroll and you are the employee who operated the NCR 399 at the Samaritan Hospital in Bay City, Michigan. The first step, if you are new at the job, would be to take out the documentation and follow it!

Next you would load the program into the computer. Figure 3–17 shows the cassette containing the program about to be inserted into the 399. After the program is loaded, the payroll journal (illustrated in fig. 3–18) is inserted into the NCR 399. In front of the journal is placed the employee's ledger card. The front of the card contains the pertinent data about the employee in *human-readable* form. More important to the system is the *machine-readable* data that is on a strip of magnetic tape on the back of the ledger card. This magnetic tape, which looks like stereo tape, contains all of the necessary data about the employee: name, address, number of exemptions, salary, hourly rate, quarterly earnings and taxes, voluntary deductions to be taken out, tax status, and many other fields of data. Depending upon the width of the ledger card, the employee's record can contain as many as 1,500 digits or 750 alphabetic characters.

In front of the ledger card will be inserted the payroll check. The program now takes over! The name, employee number, date, and check number are all automatically printed. You then enter the hours that the employee has worked. Now it is the computer's turn to calculate the employee's pay and to print the information on the forms. In addition the employee's record, which was read into memory from the magnetic tape, is updated. After the new values are added to the year-to-date totals (updating), the record is rewritten on the magnetic tape. The printing is done by a "ball" impact printer which moves along, stopping at the proper places, and prints at the rate of 24 characters per second.

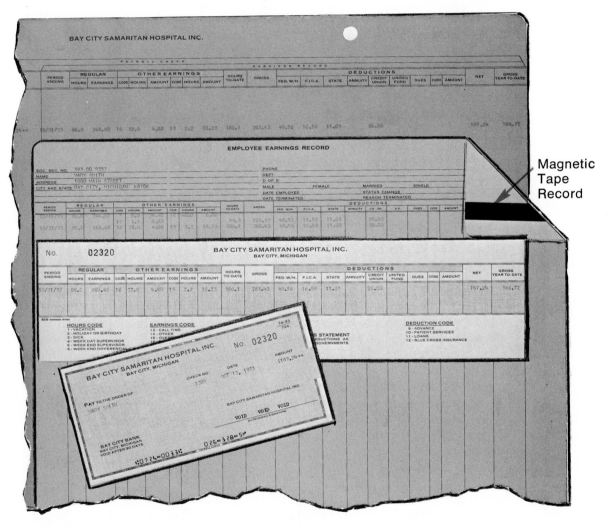

FIGURE 3–18. (Courtesy of the Samaritan Hospital)

The ledger card for the first employee will automatically eject and stack at the back of the machine. If continuous form checks are used rather than individual checks, the next check will be positioned automatically. The operator inserts the ledger card for the next employee and the same procedure will be followed for the second employee. The entire process is easy for the employee operating the machine as the forms are automatically aligned. In one operation readable copies of all three documents are prepared.

Annual Reports

What happens at the end of the quarter or at the end of the year? Each ledger card is read into the computer. This can be done rather quickly. As the cards are read, the information is stored on a cassette. After the data is accumulated on the cassette, the desired program is loaded and executed. Since the data is available for any use that is required, year-to-date payroll summaries, W-2 forms, and quarterly and annual reports can all be printed automatically.

The forms illustrate data which is printed for the hopsital's payroll system. However, each user can determine both the design of the forms and the data to be accumulated for each employee's record. In one operation the readable reports are prepared and the master file updated. For the company familiar with mechanical equipment, the electronic system is faster, quieter, and more convenient.

Expanding the System

Can the system be expanded? More memory can be added to the NCR 399 right in the customer's office. A printer, capable of printing up to 300 lines per minute, can also be added to the system. In addition, disk storage is available.

Each company can learn to write, test, and debug its own programs. Although an NCR analyst is available, and will make requested program changes, it may be desirable for the employee who operates the computer to learn to program it. Some companies may never choose to utilize the 399 in any way other than to do their accounting work. Other users will learn to program the NCR 399 computer and use its capabilities to perform many additional tasks.

The system can operate either as an independent computer or can serve as a terminal for transmitting data into a time-sharing system. The cassette tape can be used to record the data when it is to be sent to the larger "host" computer. When used in this manner the NCR 399 can be referred to as an "intelligent" terminal.

SUMMARY

Today a company that finds itself in the situation that the L. C. Smith Corporation did in the early 1960s has many alternatives from which to choose. As was indicated in the case study, they could not elect to use a computer system of their own. Today, however, there are *many small systems* that are within the budget of the small firm. In one text it would be impossible to cover all of the available systems.

Probably the wisest move that L. C. Smith made was to establish a data processing department and charge it with the responsibility of establishing long-range objectives. The in-service training seminars for management in the effective use of data processing methods would also have been extremely beneficial to the company. Most of the large corporations of today have already passed the point where general data processing seminars are necessary because management is well aware of the impact of electronic data processing on their firms. Special seminars are still needed, however, to keep management current with changes within the industry and *specifically* within their own organization. In the case of the charge made to Keyser and his task force there was one serious error made: top management should have been directly involved as a part of the task force. In addition, *studying in depth* the alternatives available is a *major* undertaking. Release time from other activities should have been given to Mr. Keyser so that he could more effectively serve as the project leader.

Although cost justification is important, it should not be the only factor that is considered. This is especially true when the company makes the initial change from a manual or mechanical method to an electronic system. To be realistic, some small companies may not actually determine the cost of both the present and proposed system. In addition, they may not consider all of the choices that are available. If they lack experience in electronic data processing, can they effectively judge which system provides the largest return on their investment?

When the small company elects to secure its own small system and use the manufacturer's software, they must determine how expensive it will be to maintain the programs. As the programs need to be altered, who will make the necessary changes? How difficult will it be to train their employees to maintain the programs?

How much computer power do they actually need now? Having the right amount to meet their needs is important. Management would not consider building ten warehouses which will not be needed for ten years as this would be a poor use of the company's resources. Selecting a system with more power than what is needed can also be a waste of resources. For this reason, the small system that can "grow" with their company may provide an answer to their expanding need for data processing.

A small company should also explore the possibility of using either a time-sharing system or a service bureau. Since the equipment and software is provided, this may still be the best alternative for some companies. Could you, at this point, make the decision as to which is the best alternative? Would you not need to know much more about what a computer *really is* and how you evaluate one system with another? What are some of the basic concepts and techniques that should be developed to effectively utilize this device which can do so many different things? To begin with, maybe the *components of the computer,* in terms of what they can and cannot do, *should be studied.* Much more should be learned about the central processing unit and the various types of software that are needed to make the computer function as man wants it to.

GLOSSARY OF NEW AND OLD TERMS TO CHECK YOUR KNOWLEDGE

Application Programs. Programs that are written to perform a particular function, such as to print the payroll checks, compute and print the accounts receivable statements, update a master file, etc.

Batch Processing. Processing, or executing, each program in its entirety before starting the next program. Processing the entire day's sales in a "batch" at one time. After the job is completed the next program is executed.

BASIC. A programming language developed at Dartmouth College for time-sharing applications.

Batch Total. A total taken on a specific field, such as regular hours, for a given number of transactions. This total is then checked with the computer's total after processing the transactions. If the two totals agree, it is another indication that the output is valid and that all of the transactions were processed.

Bit. A binary digit that is either in an "on" or "off" state. When the BCD code is used, the arrangement of the "on" bits determines what character is either stored in the memory of the computer or punched in the card.

Coding. After a program flowchart is constructed to show the logic of the program, the computer commands are "coded" by the programmer. The rules of the language being used must be followed. Each language, such as RPG, FORTRAN, and COBOL have unique rules that apply only to the particular language.

Central Processing Unit. Often referred to as the CPU, it is the portion of the computer which contains the stored program that is to be executed and the data. A more complete definition will be given later.

Data Base. Large online files that contain a substantial amount of data pertaining to one or more areas. For example, the personnel and payroll data could be combined to provide one large data base. Each employee would have a record in the data base.

Disk Files. A disk file contains a collection of records pertaining to a given topic such as payroll. When the disk file is online the records can be brought from the file into the memory of the computer for processing.

Debug. After a program is written it is tested. If there are logical errors in the program which produce invalid results, the errors must be eliminated. This is called debugging a program.

Flowchart. A graphic representation of the movement of data throughout the system. Flowchart can be used in either manual or automated data processing.

Multi-Function Card Unit. The device that reads, punches, and interprets the small 96-column System/3 cards. The MFCU also can function as a reproducer, collator, or sorter.

Online. A device, such as a card reader or printer, that is online is under the direct control of the program that the computer is executing.

Remote Batch Processing. Data from remote locations is received into the computer center through the use of time-sharing terminals. All of the data, for a particular application from a given customer, is accumulated for a given time period and then processed all at one time.

Terminal. A device used to communicate with the computer. Some terminals can be used only to receive, others only to transmit, and still others to provide two-way communication.

Time-sharing. The utilization of a computer system by a number of different users. The term usually implies that the user communicates with the computer through a terminal or remote job entry station.

Time Slice. The duration of time that each user is given. A typical time slice may be .15 seconds. During this time the user's program is brought into the CPU and executed. The input may be either online file data or what is transmitted to the system by means of a terminal.

ANSWERS

REVIEW QUESTIONS (p. 131)

3–1. A. A complete reassessment of their present system was needed before any major commitment should be made.
   B. They could not justify even a small computer system as it would be idle so much of the time.
   C. None of their employees had any experience working with computerized systems. They were hesitant about bringing in an outsider who was unfamiliar with their company to perform such a major assignment as designing an entirely new data processing system.

3–2. They received the expertise of the company that they were working with.

3–3. He felt it would be more understandable if the employee doing the procedure actually documented it. If the new method could be written down as a series of steps needed to accomplish the objectives, the employee understood it.

3–4. There are several things that are wrong. Mr. Keyser is given a *major* assignment, which is one of the objectives of the firm, and still expected to do numerous other jobs plus learning about the new technology. In addition, it is implied that since he is responsible to the controller, top management is not involved in the planning as they should be. What will happen to the committee's recommendations?

QUESTIONS ON THE ACCOUNTS RECEIVABLE APPLICATION (p. 136)

3–5. The output needs and format are determined first as they will dictate the input requirements.

3–6. The equipment is told either by a wired control panel (unit-record equipment) or the actual computer program where each field of information will be. There are a few applications, such as use of input for scientific programs, that permit free format, but in the vast majority of cases the input must be in the exact location that was defined.

3–7. The "X" punch was used.

3–8. Control totals were printed that could be checked back with existing totals. For example, the total of all of the amounts due must equal the total as shown by the accounts receivable department. The total payments received on account must agree with the deposits made during the periods for this purpose. Other totals were also checked.

3–9. Keypunch, verifier, sorter, collator, reproducer, accounting machine, and interpreter.

QUESTIONS FOR THOUGHT (p. 140)

3–10. Probably the major advantage is that the computer can be used for decision making rather than just as a "super-clerk" to process the routine business transactions. Too often the computer's real abilities are not challenged.

3–11. Cost is the major disadvantage. Another real disadvantage is that unless the firm's employees are experienced, poorly designed systems may be developed.

3–12. If the company moves from the area and it is necessary to select another bureau, it will be costly both in time and money.

3–13. No. Some of the clients were billed as much as $14,000 per month which would permit the client to rent a computer and the required equipment for themselves. The clients apparently feel that they could not duplicate the other services that were included in the price.

3–14. Batch

3–15. Approximately 5 to 6% of the business data processing is done by service bureaus.

3–16. Time-sharing

PERTAINING TO TIME-SHARING (p. 153)

3–17. The technology for time-sharing was developed in the late 1950s and early 1960s at the Massachusetts Institute of Technology.

3–18. No. Each user generally feels he has exclusive use of the system.

3–19. Terminal

3–20. The user can easily communicate with the computer. Often messages are printed or displayed which instruct the user as to what he is to do next.

3–21. 150 millisecond

3–22. A. Purchase of computer time only
B. Computer time plus utilization of the available software (programs)
C. Computer time, use of software, and use of an online common data base

3–23. The cost of the present system is compared to the anticipated cost of the proposed system.

3–24. Although a greater emphasis is currently being placed on the "cost" factor, there are still many other factors that must be considered, such as how many customers are lost when a firm takes five days to manually process an order while a competitor has an online order entry system that gets the major portion of the orders on their way in one day.

3–25. A. The customer's credit
B. The validity of the item number
C. The availability of the item ordered

3–26. Yes. *Remote job entry* stations often use magnetic tape or disk, fast printers, card readers and punches, as well as other devices.

3–27. Often a very large company finds that it is cheaper to use an existing tested program to solve a problem than to do all the programming and testing on its own system. In CYBERNET over half of the use of the system is by large users who have their own computer system.

3–28. The user might also be required to pay for file information which is stored online.

3–29. Batch processing implies that all of the data is received and then processed at one time. First, one job is fully executed; then another entire job is processed. Online implies that the data is processed as it is transmitted. If the user's time-slice ends, processing is interrupted until a new time-slice begins.

REGARDING A SMALL COMPUTER SYSTEM (p. 158)

3–30. The user who pays more may have elected to have a larger memory, more auxiliary disk storage with a faster access time, and the faster printer which can also print ledger cards. In addition, that same user may have elected to use the software application package provided by the manufacturer, while the second user has decided to write all of his own programs.

3–31. The master file information is stored on disk. This provides much of the information that is needed for each transaction. Only the variable data is actually entered through the keyboard. In payroll, for example, the employee's number and hours worked might be all of the variable data that is required. The constant data is available for each employee on the payroll disk pack.

3–32. No. Each user was pretty much on his own to write his own software. The vendors did provide a good deal of assistance, but not to the extent that is now available. Another point that perhaps should be made, however, is that now the software package is rented at a monthly charge, usually for a given number of months, whereas earlier assistance during the second-generation computer era was free.

REGARDING THE SYSTEM/3 MODEL 10 (p. 171)

3–33. CPU, MFCU, and printer
Addition of disk storage
Addition to the disk system of magnetic tape capabilities

3–34. 8k

3–35. Based upon the questionnaire and report requirements which were supplied by the user, a system design is created for the customer. The flowcharts, programs needed, and other detailed information regarding files, etc., are provided for the user by IBM. It makes the coding or writing of the actual computer programs much easier. One of the major benefits derived from the service is that the user must really look at what is now being done in using the present system.

3–36. A users' group organized nationally for all System/3 users. The initials stand for National Association of System/3 Users. At one time there was also a very strong users' group for the 1130 which was a very popular second-generation computer.

3–37. Multi-function Card Unit

3–38. The basic functions are sorting, merging, interpreting, summarizing data, punching the results in a new card, and calculating. The MFCU actually performs functions done by the sorter, interpreter, reproducer, and collator, plus reading cards.

3–39. Ninety-six characters of data can be punched in the System/3 card. It is approximately one-third the size of the standard card. A BCD (Binary Coded Decimal) code is used to record information in the card.

3–40. The card is divided into tiers.

3–41. The B and A zone punches plus the 2 digit punch are required to punch a *B* in a given column.

3–42. It takes less space to represent the same number of characters. The BCD code requires six bits for the code while the Hollerith code requires 12 rows to represent the digits, alphabetic characters, and special characters. The BCD code is limited, however, to 64 different digits and characters, whereas the Hollerith code could accommodate up to 4,096 different digits and characters.

3–43. The data recorder can be used to either punch or verify cards.

3–44. Four program formats can be stored. Skip, duplicate, and shift are automatically performed.

3–45. When the user writes the program which processes the card, it is determined where each type of card will ultimately be stacked. For example, the master cards are in pocket 1, detail in pocket 2, and new balance cards in pocket 3.

3–46. No. If the program controlling the MFCU does not activate the "sensors," the card will merely pass under the reading device.

3–47. Since the master disk file contains updated current information, a program is written that merely prints the statements from the data on the master file. No cards are required. The statements can be produced much faster and probably more accurately.

3–48. The functions provided are sorting or sequencing the decks, matching the decks (only matched cards were processed), and summary punching a new balance card on the MFCU rather than using the reproducer. The new balance card was also interpreted on the MFCU. The problem illustrated the sorter's, collator's, reproducer's, and interpreter's functions being done by the MFCU.

3–49. Sequential

3–50. Report Program Generator

3–51. COBOL
       FORTRAN IV
       An assembler language

3–52. Yes. Each assembler language is unique to the system but COBOL and FORTRAN IV are very widely used.

3–53. The hardware, or machines, are essentially alike. However, more powerful software was made available when the Model 15 was announced.

3–54. Yes. The size of the CPU can be expanded from 8k to currently 60k, faster printers can be added, plus additional auxiliary storage can be added using either (or both) disk and tape.

BASIC COMPUTER 4
AND PROGRAMMING
CONCEPTS

What Are the Functional Units of a Computer?

How Is Data Stored in the Computer?

What Is the Difference Between Binary and Hexadecimal Mathematics?

What Types of Computer Programming Languages Are There?

What Are Parity Checks?

What Do the Control Unit and the Arithmetic Unit Accomplish?

What Are the Components of a Medium Size Computer System?

What Are Some Common Programming Tasks and Techniques?

How Is a Program Compiled and Tested?

Dr. Carl Hammer's very serious viewpoint regarding computers (referred to in module 1) could almost be summarized in the statement, ". . . we are dealing here with a power that is inconceivable to the human mind. I think it is the greatest challenge that ever faced mankind."

The whirlwind evolution from the unreliable vacuum tube computers of the late 1940s to the present self-correcting models of today challenges many, and perhaps confuses even more, people. As computers proceed through their evolution, they are becoming still more reliable and faster and have an increasing capacity for storing programs and data. In addition, a wider range of input and output devices are becoming not only available but economically feasible for use in an increasing number of applications. More sophisticated programming languages are developing which make it easier to communicate effectively with the masked marvel, "Mr. Computer."

Art Buchwald was also quoted earlier as he portrayed computers as gobblers of data. It does seem that they digest input with no effort to produce usable output at a fantastic speed. In the punched card data processing material some of the details illustrated made it apparent that using mechanical or electronic equipment does not just cause beautifully finished accurate reports and other forms of output to appear at the wave of a wand. It is time that some of the mystery is removed from computers. No longer should they remain in your mind as only the "doer" of good things. A look should be taken inside of the computer to find out all that is going on!

More of the terminology of both the _hardware_ and _software_ must be learned if you are to understand why computers can control both a space flight and the quality of your morning coffee cake. What makes it possible for the airline clerk in Denver to find out if you can leave New York City at 4:10 on Tuesday? The term _hardware_ is used to specify the physical devices that make up the computer system, such as the computer, card reader, printer, etc.

The _software_ is composed of many programs and routines which serve to instruct the computer in the execution of a program.

What are the components, or parts, of any computer system? What is meant by the statement that programming languages are becoming easier to use in communicating with the computer? How are programs generally constructed? What is the CPU? How is a program compiled? These questions as well as many others will be answered in this module.

FUNCTIONAL UNITS OF COMPUTERS

Figure 4–1 shows the computer as many people perceive it—a mysterious device that reads input, processes it, and somehow produces an answer that may or may not be right.

There are three functional units of any computer system.
1. _Input_—a wide range of devices, from cards to cathode ray tubes, can now be used.
2. _Central Processing Unit_—the central processing unit is commonly referred

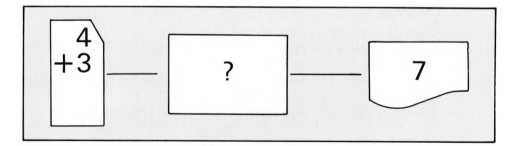

FIGURE 4-1. FUNCTIONAL UNITS OF THE COMPUTER

to as the CPU and contains the control unit, arithmetic and logic unit, input, output, and main memory. The term is also used to designate *just* the arithmetic and logic unit where the computations take place. When the term "idle CPU" is used it indicates that although the computer may be reading and writing records it is not doing any computations.

3. *Output*—the user can choose something conventional, such as a printer or a more exotic output device like a cathode ray tube.

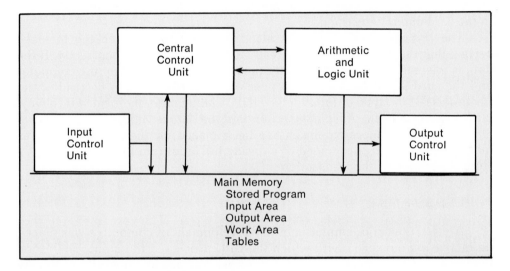

FIGURE 4–2. CENTRAL PROCESSING UNIT

Input

Input today can be in many forms because the user can now select from devices such as cards, magnetic tape, magnetic disk, paper tape, scanners that read typing or printing, mark readers, cathode ray tubes, wands that read price stickers, magnetic ink character readers, employee badge readers, terminal typewriters, touch-tone telephones, and many other devices.

Each user must decide what type of input will best serve the needs of the business. In selecting the input devices that can most effectively be utilized, consideration must be given to the volume of data that is to be processed and how the data is originally generated. Another consideration of prime importance is the amount of the company's resources that can be utilized for data processing equipment. In building a system, the input devices, central processing unit, and output devices should be as compatible as possible with one another. To illustrate the point, assume that most of the jobs assigned to the computer are to read cards, process the information, and punch out an answer. It would be pointless to get the fastest card reader on the market, a fast CPU, but save money by ordering the slowest card punch available. In the case cited, all processing is held back to the speed of the slowest unit—the card punch.

It is essential that the data which enters the system is accurate. For this reason the punched card has remained popular as an input device since there is a high degree of confidence that the data is accurate since it is first punched in the card *and then verified.*

The computer manufacturers also provide ways of checking to make certain that the data in the card is read and stored in the CPU correctly. If the data is misread or stored incorrectly the operator is notified by the computer and the card is put back in the hopper of the card reader to be read again. *Regardless of the type of input device that is being used, there must be a way, built into the system, of making certain that the data is valid.*

Recently far more emphasis has been placed on the input method, as more ways are being developed of entering the input into the system directly from the source of the transaction.

Processing the Input

At first, the major emphasis in the development of computers was placed on increasing the speed with which the CPU processed the input. Therefore, the computational speed of the computer became much faster with each new generation, while the speed of reading input into the computer was not increased as significantly. The term *millisecond,* first used to describe the speed with which computers could process data, was replaced by microsecond, then nanosecond, and finally picosecond. Now any of the four terms which are defined may be applied to the speed with which the computer can process data.

millisecond	1/1000 of a second
microsecond	1 millionth of a second
nanosecond	1 billionth of a second
picosecond	1 trillionth of a second

More emphasis is now being placed on developing faster input and output devices since the computer, due to its fantastic ability to process data, has been "I/O Bound." The term, "I/O Bound," is used as an explanation of the fact that the CPU can process the data so much faster than it can possibly read or write. Figure 4–3 illustrates the relationship between reading, processing, and writing data in a typical computer in the late 1960s or early 1970s.

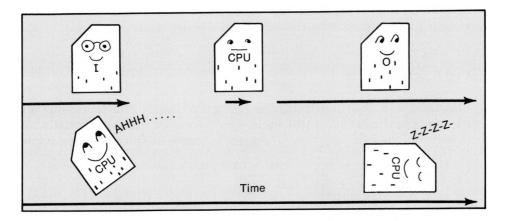

FIGURE 4–3. I/O BOUND

Increasing the speed with which information can enter and leave the computer is just one of the solutions which have been developed for solving the problem of the "idle CPU."

Output

Output methods are also becoming far faster, more dependable, and more varied. The slower card punch and printer are now supported by a wide range of other forms of output such as magnetic tape and disk, microfilm, voice, and video pictures.

When data is written as output from the memory of the computer it is generally checked to make certain that it is accurately written. For example, after a record is written on magnetic tape it is checked for accuracy, and if the computer finds that it has not been written correctly the tape is backed up and the record rewritten. Usually, unless there is a problem with either the tape or the equipment, on the second attempt the record is correctly written and verified.

The Console Typewriter

Many computer configurations have a console typewriter that is used primarily as a communication device between the operator and the computer. In a large installation it is not considered as an I/O device, while in a smaller installation a *very limited* amount of control information may be entered through the console. As the *operating system* is discussed, the console typewriter will be illustrated in its role as a device which provides a means of communication between the computer and the operator.

Central Processing Unit

Figure 4–2 (p. 193) illustrates the concept of the central processing unit which contains the I/O control units, central control unit, arithmetic and logic unit, and the main memory. The main memory, or storage area, contains

1. the stored program which is written by a programmer,
2. a logical record of input,
3. a logical record of output,
4. work areas and tables.

The *stored program* requests that information is read and specifies the device that is to be used to input the data. The data enters the computer from the input device by means of a *channel*, to which there may be connected one or more input or output devices. The data read is stored in the CPU in the area labeled *input control unit*, and then *one record* of information is stored in the main memory. After the command to read the input has been executed, an *interrupt* occurs which is really saying to the CPU, "the data is read, now what is to be done with it?"

As it is responsible for coordinating the input/output activities with the processing functions, the *control unit* receives the interrupt. The control unit also makes sure that no information is destroyed that should be retained, that all of the programmer's commands are executed in the correct sequence, and that the information leaving the computer and going to the various output devices is complete. The control unit is also responsible for the error messages which the operator receives when a problem occurs.

As you learn more about the computer and the various functions that it can do, you will appreciate more fully the complexity of the assignment given to the control unit. The control unit must keep track of the many activities of the CPU. Figure 4–4 illustrates the concept of the functions provided by the control unit.

In the *arithmetic* and *logic unit* the mathematical operations are executed. The entire logic of the computer is based upon its ability to compare two numbers and see if the second is *equal to, less than,* or *greater than* the first. In writing the commands, which will be evaluated in the logic unit, the programmer may also use Boolean logic which permits the use of *and, or* and *not.*

The sequence in which a program is executed is determined by the programmer. The programmer, however, may have wanted to do one of two

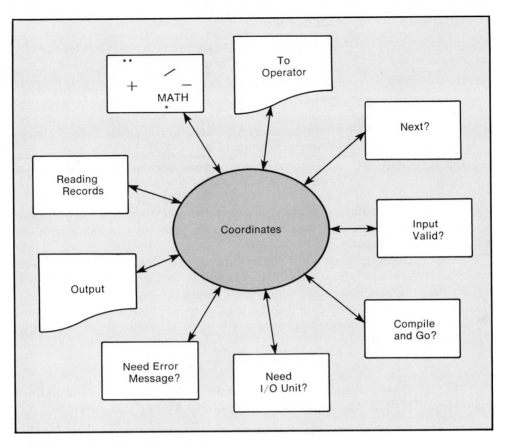

FIGURE 4-4. THE CONTROL UNIT

things depending upon if A and B are equal or not. The program which he wrote may have stated:

IF A = B THEN GO TO READ-NEW-CARD
ELSE GO TO DO-YOUR-MATH.

In the *logic unit* there must be an evaluation made to see if *A* is equal to *B* or not. The condition is either true or false. *All of the logic of a computer eventually breaks down to one small evaluation which is either true or false.*

If the condition *A = B* is true, the program control *branches* to the point where the command to read a new card is stored. If the condition is false and *A* is not equal to *B*, then the control of the program branches to where the commands to do the mathematics are stored. The following explanation of the components of the command may help you to understand it better.

NAME USED	EXPLANATION
A	Location of a field of data stored in the computer which is referred to as A by the programmer.
B	Location of a field of data stored in the computer which is referred to as B by the programmer.
READ-NEW-CARD	Location of where commands are stored which will read a new card of data. Meaningful names should always be used in programming.
DO-YOUR-MATH	Location of where commands are stored which will do some type of mathematical operations.

The *locations* referred to are actually called *addresses*. Just as you have an address where you live, data and commands have an address within the memory of the computer.

The programmer may write commands using *and, or,* and *not* to determine the sequence in which the statements will be executed. The illustrations are written in COBOL which is a high level language.

If both conditions are found to be true when evaluated in the *logic unit* of the CPU, the control of the program will go to the *address* referred to as READ-NEW-CARD.

IF A = B <u>and</u> C = D THEN GO TO READ-NEW-CARD

If *C* and *D* are not equal, the control of the program will go to the address called END-OF-JOB. The command is a *conditional* branching statement.

IF C <u>not</u> = D THEN GO TO END-OF-JOB

If *C* is equal to either *D* or *E* the control of the program will go to the commands stored at the address referred to as PUNCH-CARD.

IF C = D <u>or</u> C = E THEN GO TO PUNCH-CARD

The addresses illustrated are called *symbolic addresses*. When the programmer's statement is translated to actual computer commands the READ-NEW-CARD becomes an *actual address*, which the computer will branch to if the condition is true. Stored at that address will be the command which is to be executed.

SO FAR SO GOOD

4–1. What is the program that controls the computer?

4–2. What is the term that is used to refer to the computer and its various components such as the card reader, printer, tape drives, etc.?

4–3. What are the three functional units of the computer?

4–4. What does it mean when it is said that computers are "I/O bound?"

4–5. Can data be entered into a computer system at the time a transaction actually occurs?

4–6. What three major items are usually stored in the main memory of the computer?

4–7. What computer component is responsible for carrying out the programmer's program, coordinating all input/output activities, informing the operator of problems, etc.?

4–8. What type of logic permits the programmer to use *and, or,* or *not* in programming?

4–9. A programmer writes a statement such as "IF X = Y THEN GO TO READ-NEW-CARD" in his program. If the condition is true, *what kind of branching occurs?*

4–10. In the above question when the program is translated to computer commands, what does READ-NEW-CARD become?

STORAGE IN THE CENTRAL PROCESSING UNIT

Data entering the Central Processing Unit must be stored in the computer's memory. The storage of both the data and the commands involves two different factors

1. A device must be used to store the data. It was noted earlier that vacuum tubes were used by the first generation computers to store data and commands. Currently there are several methods used for storing data in the computer's memory.

2. A *binary coded decimal* (BCD) system is used to represent the data in order that more information may be stored in a given amount of space.

One of the more popular storage devices used today is magnetic core. Each core is capable of storing one binary digit (bit). Each individual core is either *on* or *off*. Since data is stored in each *location in memory,* the cores needed to represent the data, according to the code being used, are automatically turned on, while the cores not needed to represent the data are in an off state.

The doughnut-shaped magnetic cores, approximately the size of the head of a pin, are strung on very fine metal wires (see fig. 4–5). If several cores are all strung on one wire, how is just one selected to be on while the others are

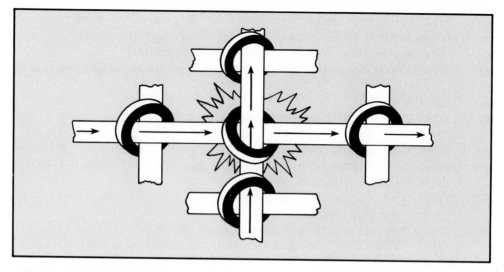

FIGURE 4–5. MAGNETIC CORE

off? To accomplish this, a second wire is run through each core at a right angle to the first wire. One-half current through *each wire* is required to turn the selected core on. Additional pairs of wires are needed for reading the data. Can you visualize the maze of wires needed in a computer with a large memory?

BINARY CODES

The two most frequently used codes are the ASCII (American Standard Code for Information Interchange) and the EBCDIC (Expanded Binary Coded Decimal Interchange Code) codes. The first code, ASCII, uses seven bits in each location which can represent up to 128 different letters, symbols, and digits. The ASCII code is supported by both ANSI and by BEMA (Business Equipment Manufacturers Association). The second code, EBCDIC, is an eight-bit code used to represent 256 unique letters, symbols, and numbers. The logic for using the EBCDIC code over the ASCII code becomes apparent when you see how data is stored using the EBCDIC code.

Pure Binary

Why binary? The system used for storing data in mechanical equipment such as adding machines, calculators, and cash registers is base 10. Since elementary school you have been working with base 10 but before you can understand another numbering system, ask yourself, "do I really understand base 10?" If a number is to be stored ranging from 000 to 999, 30 different devices are needed.

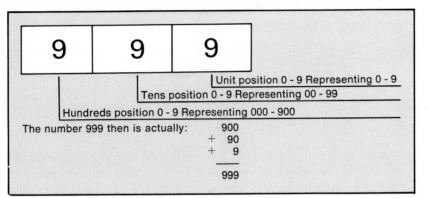

How many different storage devices are needed to represent 999 in pure binary? Pure binary uses one single bit, which is either *on* or *off*, to represent different numbers. As in base 10, the location in relationship to the decimal is what determines the values. Figure 4–6 illustrates the relative value of each location.

0	0	0	0	0	0	0	0	0	0	Off
1	1	1	1	1	1	1	1	1	1	On
512	256	128	64	32	16	8	4	2	1	Value
1	1	1	1	1	0	0	1	1	1	999

FIGURE 4–6. BINARY VALUES

How would 999 be represented in pure binary? As was illustrated in the discussion of base 10, 999 is 900 + 90 + 9. In pure binary it is necessary to use the following values (see *value* line of fig. 4–6):

$$
\begin{array}{r}
512 \\
256 \\
128 \\
64 \\
32 \\
4 \\
2 \\
\underline{1} \\
999
\end{array}
$$

As shown in the illustration, it took only 10 bits to store the number 999 when pure binary was used. When stored in base 10 it was necessary to have 30 different digits available in order to represent the same number. When less storage devices are used, it not only saves space in the memory of the computer but also makes the handling of the data much faster.

In binary, after the first location, which is either 0 or 1, each location has the value of two to one additional power. For example,

$$2^1 = 2$$
$$2^2 = 4$$
$$2^3 = 8$$
$$2^4 = 16$$

The major reasons for the computer using binary rather than base 10 are

1. to permit faster data handling,
2. to save space within the computer's memory.

Many computers use pure binary and do the required mathematics in *registers*. A *register* is part of the hardware, inside the CPU, that is not usually addressable by the programmer. Registers also have other very special uses which you need not be concerned with at this time. When registers are used, the data stored in the main memory is converted to pure binary, the mathematics is performed in one or more registers, and the answer is converted to the appropriate BCD code and stored in the location assigned for the answer.

STORING DATA USING THE EBCDIC CODE

The EBCDIC code utilizes eight bits to represent one special character or letter of the alphabet, either one or two digits, or one digit and a sign. The memory is composed of many magnetic cores which are strung on very fine wires. *Visualize* one *addressable* location as it appears in figure 4–7. The bits are stacked rather than being horizontal, as they were shown in pure binary. The value represented, however, is the same as the first four bits of the *pure binary code* (see figure 4–6 and observe the portion enclosed in the heavy lines).

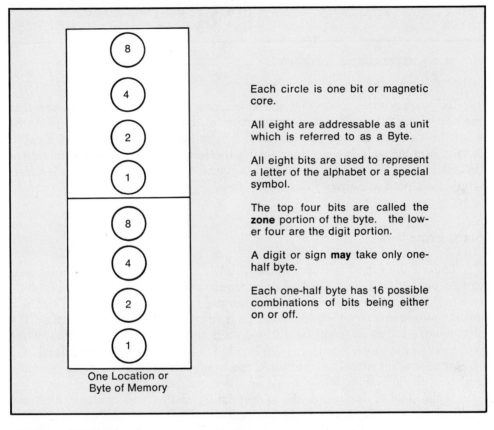

Each circle is one bit or magnetic core.

All eight are addressable as a unit which is referred to as a Byte.

All eight bits are used to represent a letter of the alphabet or a special symbol.

The top four bits are called the **zone** portion of the byte. the lower four are the digit portion.

A digit or sign **may** take only one-half byte.

Each one-half byte has 16 possible combinations of bits being either on or off.

One Location or
Byte of Memory

FIGURE 4–7. EBCDIC Code

Hexadecimal or Base 16

In each half-byte there are 16 different combinations available when the four bits, or core, are used to represent the hexadecimal numbers. Figure 4–7 illustrates how the bits are arranged within the byte. Figure 4–8 illustrates which bits are *on* to represent the numbers 0–F.

Bits On	Value	Represented by Hexadecimal	Bits On	Value	Represented by Hexadecimal
none	0	0	8	8	8
1	1	1	8, 1	9	9
2	2	2	8, 2	10	A
1, 2	3	3	8, 2, 1	11	B
4	4	4	8, 4	12	C
4, 1	5	5	8, 4, 1	13	D
4, 2	6	6	8, 4, 2	14	E
4, 2, 1	7	7	8, 4, 2, 1	15	F

FIGURE 4–8. HEXADECIMAL NUMBERS

To store a letter or special character, one hexadecimal digit is stored in the upper four bits, called the zone portion of the byte, and one digit is stored in the lower four, or digit portion, of the byte. Remember the Hollerith code? A very similar code is used for storing the letters of the alphabet using the EBCDIC code. The code is illustrated in figure 4–9. In the memory, the letters would be stored as shown in figure 4–10.

Storing Numbers

One of the nicest features about the EBCDIC code is that numeric data can be *packed* or *zoned*. Packed data requires less core because in one byte two numbers can be stored. Since the normal rules of algebra are followed in doing mathematics, each field, either packed or zoned, must have a sign. If a sign is not used in an input field, the data is treated as a positive field which will have in the lower portion of the last byte of the field an hexadecimal "C." If, due to mathematical calculations, the number stored in the field becomes negative, the sign will change to an hexadecimal "D."

If the field is unpacked, the zone portion of the field contains an hexadecimal "F" (see fig. 4–11). If the contents of the field becomes negative, the zone portion of the unit position of the field will also change to an hexadecimal "D."

Because a sign must be provided for, the formula for determining how many bytes are needed for a field is to add one for the sign to the number of digits in the field, and then divide by two. The field size needed for a four-digit number would be calculated as follows:

$$\text{Size} = (4 + 1) \text{ divided by } 2$$
$$\text{Size} = 2\frac{1}{2}$$

Letter of Alphabet	Hollerith		EBCDIC	
	Zone	Digit	Zone	Digit
A	12	1	C	1
B	12	2	C	2
C	12	3	C	3
J	11	1	D	1
K	11	2	D	2
L	11	3	D	3
S	0	2	E	2
T	0	3	E	3
U	0	4	E	4

FIGURE 4–9. ALPHABETIC REPRESENTATIONS

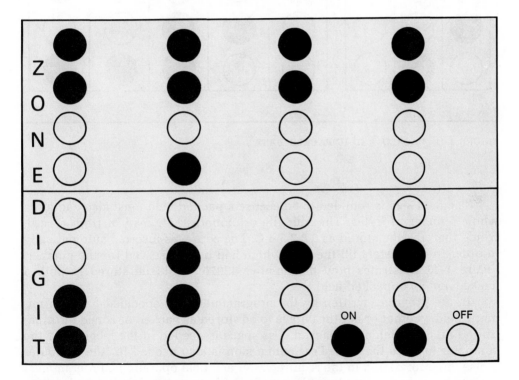

FIGURE 4–10. EBCDIC CODE USED FOR STORING LETTERS

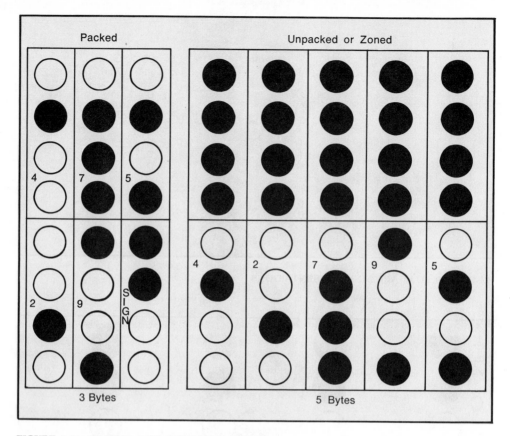

FIGURE 4–11 PACKED AND UNPACKED DATA

The field size is rounded to 3 because a packed field must also contain a whole number of bytes. The four digit number, 8234, read in from a card, would therefore be stored as *0 8 2 3 4 C*. The zero was inserted automatically in order to completely fill the field which had been reserved for the number. Figure 4–11 illustrates how the number 42975 would be stored in both a packed and an unpacked field.

In the program, written by the programmer, it is specified for each numeric field whether or not the data is to be stored as packed or zoned information. If numeric fields are packed, less space is needed in the memory of the computer to store the data. Less conversion is also needed for the computer to use the information in the required mathematical operations. Programmers need to know how to compute the number of bytes needed for packed data in order to determine the size of each field, as well as the record size needed, for both input and output files.

After the information is stored in the memory of the computer, each byte is checked to see if an *odd* or *even* number of bits are activated. If the computer being used has an *odd* parity check, there must be an *odd* number of bits turned on in each location that is used for storing data.

Each addressable location in the memory of the computer actually contains *nine bits* if the EBCDIC code is used. The ninth bit, which has been ignored up to now, is for providing a parity check. If the parity check is *odd,* an "A" is stored by turning on the 8-and 4-zone bits and the 1 digit bit. How many bits were turned on? Three. Is there an *odd* number? Yes! According to the table presented earlier, a "C" requires the 8 and 2 zone bits plus the 2 and 1 digit bits to be turned on. How many bits are on? Is four an odd number? No! Therefore when the "C" is stored, the ninth bit, the *parity bit,* is automatically turned on as it is part of the code used to store the data in the computer. After the data is stored, the computer automatically checks to see that each location has an *odd* number of bits activated.

If one of the bytes does not have an odd number of bits turned on, the computer will try to restore the information, since one bit somehow was not impulsed correctly. Parity checks are also used when writing information on magnetic tape, or disk, and transmitting data via telecommunications.

The programmer or operator is really not concerned with how the parity checks are actually made, but it is reassuring to know that they do exist. It is one more way that the basic computer design helps to insure the validity of information, either entering or leaving the computer.

Hexadecimal Mathematics

In hexadecimal mathematics, which uses base 16, how would 23 be represented? In base 10, 2 units of 10 are needed plus a 3 in the units position of the field. In base 16, to represent 23, *one unit of 16* is needed in the second position of the field plus a 7 in the unit position of the field. Twenty-three would therefore be written as 17—one unit of 16 plus 7. The values associated with each position of the digit are based on the power of 16, rather than the power of 2, which was used in pure binary. Figure 4–12 shows the relative value of the first four locations used for recording an hexadecimal number.

If numbers must be converted from hexadecimal to base 10, tables are available which are easy to use and understand. When a location within the CPU is given in a computer that uses an hexadecimal numbering system, it may be expressed in hexadecimal. Where is location 2123? Without using a table, the conversion would be:

16^3	16^2	16^1	-	To Power Of
4096 Times Digit	256 Times Digit	16 Times Digit	O - F	Value Represented
1	3	2	B	Example 132B
4096	768	32	11	Actual Value

FIGURE 4–12. HEXADECIMAL VALUES

$$
\begin{array}{rl}
2 = 4096 \times 2 = & 8192 \\
1 = 256 \times 1 = & 256 \\
2 = 16 \times 2 = & 32 \\
3 = 1 \times 3 = & \underline{3} \\
& 8483
\end{array}
$$

What would the number FEDA represent? The answer would be calculated by doing the following:

$$
\begin{array}{rl}
F = 4096 \times 15 = & 61{,}440 \\
E = 256 \times 14 = & 3{,}584 \\
D = 16 \times 13 = & 208 \\
A = 1 \times 10 = & \underline{10} \\
& 65{,}242
\end{array}
$$

The table given in figure 4–12 only includes the value of the first four locations. When the next four, which would continue to the left of those given, are specified they would be 16^4, 16^5, 16^6, and 16^7. You can see that very large numbers can be represented by a very few hexadecimal digits.

Addition and Subtraction in Hexadecimal

Addition and subtraction can easily be done using hexadecimal mathematics. Carryover and carryback involves 16 rather than 10 as is used in base 10. For example,

$$
\begin{array}{r}
123 \\
+ \text{ FF} \\
\hline
222
\end{array}
$$

To calculate the answer:

1. Add 3 + F (3 + F = 18). Since only 0 — F (15) can be recorded in one location, subtract 16 from 18 (18 — 16 = 2).
2. Carry 1 to the left and record the 2 in the unit position of your answer.
3. Add 2 + F plus the 1 which was carried. Again the answer is 18. Subtract 16 and record the 2. Carry 1 to the left.
4. The 1 carried plus 1 equals 2. Record the 2.

Why is 16 subtracted? Compare hexadecimal to base 10. In any one location from 0–9 can be recorded. If 8 and 4 are added, the answer is 12. What did you do? 12 — 10 = 2. A 2 was recorded in the unit position. One unit of 10 was carried to the next location.

In the subtraction of BA from hexadecimal 124, the following steps are taken:

$$
\begin{array}{r}
124 \\
- \text{ BA} \\
\hline
6A
\end{array}
$$

1. Since A (10) cannot be subtracted from 4, 1 must be borrowed. The *value of the 1 which is borrowed is 16.* Sixteen plus 4 is equal to 20.
2. Twenty—A (10) is equal to 10. *The answer is recorded as A.*
3. From the original 2 in column 2 as 1 has been borrowed. B (11) is to be subtracted from the remaining 1. Therefore it is necessary to again borrow 1 (which has the value of 16) from the left.
4. One plus the 16 borrowed is equal to 17. Seventeen minus B is equal to 6. The 6 is recorded.

Why learn addition and subtraction in base 16? When working with computers, it is sometimes necessary to understand the way that the data is actually stored within the computer. *The EBCDIC code using hexadecimal was selected for the following reasons:*

1. The EBCDIC code is used in a large number of computers and provides an opportunity to illustrate the use of packed fields.
2. Storage locations are often printed in the code which is used for the computer. It is sometimes necessary to add or subtract using the coded locations.
3. Once you learn to work in any base, other than base 10, it is simple to learn a new number base. If problems were given using the ASCII base 7 code,

you could apply the same principles as those presented and be able to add, subtract, or interpret the code.

Binary Mathematics

Addition and subtraction can be performed easily in pure binary. Remember each location in the register where the binary mathematics occurs either has a value of 1 or 0. In addition, the following "truth" table is used:

Binary Addition

FIELD A		FIELD B		SUM OF A + B	
0	+	0	=	0	
0	+	1	=	1	
1	+	0	=	1	
1	+	1	=	0	+ *Carry 1 to left*

The addition table, or truth table, is applied to a problem where A = 101 and B = 111. The mathematics is accomplished as illustrated:

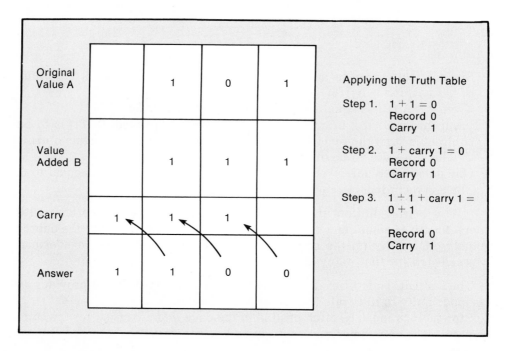

Is the answer 1100 correct? To illustrate that the answer is correct the same numbers are added in base 10:

	BINARY			BASE 10 EQUIVALENT
A =	1 0 1			4 + 0 + 1 = 5
B =	1 1 1			4 + 2 + 1 = 7
Answer =	1 1 0 0			8 + 4 + 0 + 0 = 12

Binary Subtraction

Since subtraction is the inverse operation of addition, the following table is used for subtraction.

	FIELD A		FIELD B		ANSWER
	0	—	0	=	0
	1	—	0	=	1
	1	—	1	=	0
Borrow 1	0	—	1	=	1

The subtraction table is applied in a problem in which A = 101 and B = 010.

The mathematics may be accomplished as illustrated:

					Applying the Truth Table for Subtraction
Borrowed			1		
Value of A Original Value		①→	0	1	Step 1. 1 − 0 = 1 Record 1
Value of B Which is Subtracted		0	1	0	Step 2. Borrow 1 Record 1
Answer		0	1	1	Step 3. 0 − 0 = 0 Record 0

Is the answer 011 correct? To illustrate that the answer is correct the same number is subtracted in base 10:

	BINARY	BASE 10 EQUIVALENT
A =	1 0 1	4 + 0 + 1 = 5
B =	0 1 0	0 + 2 + 0 = 2
Answer =	0 1 1	0 + 2 + 1 = 3

The answer to the subtraction problem could have been arrived at in a different manner, which is essentially the way the computer would have solved the problem.

Value of A	1	0	1
Original Value of B	0	1	0
Reversed Value	1	0	1
Add 1 to unit position			1
Resulting Answer	0	1	1

Subtraction by using the 2 compliment method:

Step 1. Reverse all bits in the number to be subtracted:

← B reversed = 1 0 1

Step 2. Add 1 bit to the unit position.

Step 3. Now add the original value of A, the reversed bits of B, and the additional 1.

Addition Using the "Truth" Table for Addition.

Step 1. (1 + 1) + 1 = 0 + 1
Record 1
Carry 1

Step 2. 1 carried + 0 = 1
Record 1

Step 3. 1 + 1 = 0 + carry
Carry 1

It may appear to you that the answer really was 1011. The subtraction, however, is done in a register containing 16 bits. Observe what happens:

```
   Original A = 0 0 0 0   0 0 0 0   0 0 0 0   0 1 0 1
   Original B = 0 0 0 0   0 0 0 0   0 0 0 0   0 0 1 0
  REVERSED B = 1 1 1 1   1 1 1 1   1 1 1 1   1 1 0 1
 1 Bit added =                                     1
     Carried = 1 1 1 1   1 1 1 1   1 1 1 1   1 1 1
      Answer = 0 0 0 0   0 0 0 0   0 0 0 0   0 0 1 1
```

When the final addition occurs in the high order position of the register (left-most location), an "end carry" takes place which results in the answer having a plus sign. If the answer *does not* result in a final end carry, the answer is negative. When this occurs, the bits in the *answer* are reversed and a 1 bit is added to the unit position. The resulting answer will then carry a minus sign.

TO REVIEW

4–11. What is another name for a binary digit?
4–12. What is often used in the memory of the computer to store one bit of data?
4–13. What code is recommended by the American National Standards Institute and the Business Equipment Manufacturers Association?
4–14. When the EBCDIC, or eight-bit code, is used how many different characters may be represented?
4–15. Give three reasons why a binary code (rather than base 10) is used for storing data within the computer?
4–16. Convert the following numbers that are expressed in binary to base ten. Refer to figure 6 for questions 4–16 and 4–17.
A. 0 1 0 1 0 1   C. 1 0 1 0 0 0
B. 1 0 0 0 0 0   D. 1 1 1 0 0 0
4–17. Convert the following base ten numbers to binary.
A. 48   C. 129
B. 57   D. 237
4–18. What is a byte?
4–19. Where is the zone portion of a byte?
4–20. In hexadecimal mathematics what is a *B*? a *D*?
4–21. In a packed field which contains a positive number, what hexadecimal number is stored in the digit portion of the last byte of the field?
4–22. How many bytes will be required for a seven digit *packed* field? How many bytes would have been required if the field was unpacked or in a "zoned" format?
4–23. Since all numeric fields must be signed, how will an unsigned field of data entering the computer be stored?
4–24. A computer has an odd parity check. An *A* is stored in the CPU, which uses the 16-bit hexadecimal code by turning on in the digit portion of the byte the 8 bit. In the digit portion of the byte, the 1 bit was turned on. What will occur and why?

4–25. In hexadecimal mathematics what value do the following numbers have?

A. 21B B. 12F C. 1111

4–26. Subtract the following:

$$\begin{array}{r} A123 \\ -1B42 \end{array} \qquad \begin{array}{r} FFFF \\ -DDDD \end{array}$$

4–27. Add the following:

$$\begin{array}{r} BBBB \\ +1238 \end{array} \qquad \begin{array}{r} C347 \\ +1B26 \end{array}$$

4–28. Add the following binary numbers:

$$\begin{array}{r} 101 \\ +111 \end{array} \qquad \begin{array}{r} 010 \\ +101 \end{array}$$

4–29. Subtract the following:

$$\begin{array}{r} 111 \\ -011 \end{array} \qquad \begin{array}{r} 101 \\ -011 \end{array}$$

PROGRAMMING CONCEPTS

The general concepts that are common to most computer languages are covered in this section. As a student you should be aware of the lack of uniformity that exists in the EDP world. Although programming standards have been developed by committees and endorsed by the different groups such as BEMA and ANSI, the standards are still optional on the part of both the manufacturer and the user.

When the concepts are presented, such as opening a file, a student can always say, "FORTRAN doesn't require files to be opened." The reply would be, "True, but COBOL, PL/1 and most assembler languages do!"

Types of Languages

Before covering the basic concepts and common programming techniques that are required in most of the more widely-used languages, the various types of languages and some of the more common terms must be explained so that we have a base of reference. The three types of languages are *machine, assembler,* and *compiler.*

Machine Language

Machine language is what the computer really understands. Before any program can be executed, the language used must be converted to machine language and stored in the memory of the computer. To use machine language you would need to understand exactly how each instruction works and assign locations for input, output, and the commands. The early first-generation computers could only be programmed in machine language. In using the commands the programmer needs to understand such things as how the computer adds, where the answer is after the add command, and how the computer knows where each field begins and ends.

Assembler Language

Assembler languages were an advancement over machine languages because they permitted the use of symbols rather than using only numbers for the programming commands. The programmer still needs to know how the computer will execute each command, but the detail of assigning locations for input, output, and instructions is unnecessary. When the program is *compiled* the programmer's symbolic commands are translated to machine language and the locations are assigned by a program called the compiler which is stored in the computer's memory. As the assembler program is read, the compiler assigns the locations and translates the symbolic commands to machine language commands. Although each assembler language is unique and can be used on only one computer, there are common characteristics that apply to many different assembler languages. Each assembler command generally creates only one machine language instruction. The assembler languages have unique names, such as BAL (Basic Assembler Language), Autocode, or SPS (Symbolic Programming System).

Are assembler languages used? Yes, there are several reasons why a programmer may code in an assembler language.

1. When a small-scale computer is used, the assembler language may be either the most practical language or the *only language* that may be used.
2. Coding in assembler sometimes produces a more efficient program that will compile and execute faster than when a compiler language is used.
3. Certain I/O devices, such as a mark reader, may not be supported by the compiler language that is used in the installation. In that case the assembler language will be used.
4. Certain comands that are needed are not in the compiler languages subset (rules). For example, the programmer wishes to put the card with an incorrectly spelled student name in pocket 2 while all cards with the names spelled correctly will be put in pocket 1. The language being considered for writing the complete program does not permit this to be done. A routine, called a subroutine, may be coded in assembler and then *called* into the compiler program.
5. Coding the required changes for the *operating system*, which controls the entire computer configuration, can usually be done only in assembler.

6. The programmer may like to code in assembler in preference to using a higher level compiler language.

After a program is *coded* in either an assembler or compiler language, the commands written on the coding sheets are usually punched into a deck of cards called a *source deck*. After the compiler is *loaded* into the computer's memory, the source deck is read, checked for errors, the locations are assigned, and the commands are translated to the appropriate machine language commands.

Compiler Language

Compiler languages are far more powerful, as one command may generate several machine language commands, and the programmer does not need to understand how individual commands are executed. With a few minor modifications, a compiler program written for one computer may be able to be executed on several different computers. The program usually can be written much faster since it will contain far fewer commands than if written in assembler. Some of the details, which are often referred to as "housekeeping," are added to the program from the *libraries* which are maintained to assist with the many "details" of programming. The more popular compiler languages are COBOL, PL/1 (Programming Language One), and FORTRAN.

Compiler programs generally contain far fewer commands and are easier to code than when other types of languages are used. The programmer does not need to know *how* the computer adds, just that it does add and does do the other required mathematics.

REVIEW QUESTIONS ON LANGUAGES

4–30. What are the three general types of languages?

4–31. Which type of computer language is the most powerful?

4–32. Which type of language was the *only* one available for programming the early first-generation computers?

A REVIEW OF MAJOR POINTS

Some of the major points should be related and brought together in a review before the responsibilities of the programmer and some of the common programming techniques are discussed. It may seem that the three items covered in the module are unrelated. Nevertheless, the *functional units, methods of storing data,* and the *types of programming languages* are all very much related. The functional units of the computer system were defined as: input, central processing unit, and output.

Input

From the various types of input available in the installation, the programmer selects the best form to use for the program that is being written. He may not have a choice, however, since the installation may have only one form of input available for his use. Regardless of the type of input being used, there are some common programming functions that must be performed before the data can be stored in the CPU:

1. Define the fields as either numeric or alphanumerical and indicate, by means of the program, if the numeric fields contain packed or zoned data.
2. If the field contains numeric information, the programmer should also specify the following information:
   a. Location in the field of the assumed decimal. Decimals are not punched in the input fields, but if the programmer specifies where they are assumed to be, the computer will keep track of the decimal and make it available for printed output.
   b. In case the field becomes negative, provision must be made to make certain that the computer will recognize that the field does contain a negative value.

Input Checking Methods

As an input record is read and stored in the CPU a parity checking method is used to make certain that the data is stored in the CPU correctly. If not, the control portion of the CPU makes certain that the record is restored and will then again check the parity of each individual byte in the record.

It seems that the computer manufacturers, through both the computer hardware and software, have done a great deal towards making certain that the input is read and stored correctly. The programmer and analyst also have a responsibility to make certain that the data is correct and the design of the procedure will usually provide for

1. checking of the source document,
2. recording and verifying the data on the input media,
3. batch totals.

Internal Checking Methods

Although most input is checked for validity, since it is read by the computer's input device, a programmer still has the responsibility of building internal checks into his program. A statement may be made: "but it just can't happen." One of the differences between really good programming and mediocre programming is the editing and internal checking features which are built into programs to catch the "but it just can happen" mistakes.

The Boolean logic of and, or, and not, along with the computer's ability to compare two values to see if one is greater than, less than, or equal to the other, are utilized in the program to provide the necessary editing and checking routines. The more sophisticated compiler languages have features or pre-written routines that may be called in which make the internal editing a much easier task.

The languages available should be looked at very closely by the user while the selection of a "first," or different, computer is being made. Since most compilers are very complex programs, they are usually supplied free, rented, or purchased from the computer manufacturer, rather than each installation writing its own.

Processing the Data

Before a program can be written with which to process the data, there are certain details that must be accomplished by the programmer and analyst. One, determine the input format that is to be used since the computer *must know* where the fields are in the input records. Two, determine the output that is desired. Generally the output format is determined first as this dictates what input must be used. Three, determine how the input must be processed. The amount of programming needed depends upon a number of different things such as the sophistication of the system and the languages being used.

PROGRAM FLOWCHART

Once it has been determined what input and output is needed, the logic of the program is defined by using a program flowchart which shows the sequence in which the computer will execute the program. A computer executes a program sequentially unless there is either a *conditional* or *unconditional* branch in the instructions.

The program flowchart provided uses the standard ASCII flowcharting symbols to illustrate a program which will read a card, calculate the employee's gross pay, and print a list of just those employees who have earned more than $500.

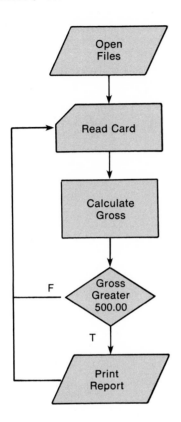

Card is read into the buffer area and then transferred into "main memory."

Calculations are made in the arithmetic unit. Often the mathematics is done in binary, however, the data may actually be stored as packed, zoned, or binary.

Condtional Branch. If the condition is true, an indicator is turned on which causes the print command to be executed rather than following the normal path which is to go back and read a new card. The control unit determines which command to execute, depending upon the status of an indicator which will be turned on in the logic unit if the condition is true.

Unconditional Branch. After the print report is executed, there is an unconditional branch to the location in memory where the command to read a card is stored.

After the program flowchart is constructed, the program is written in either an assembler or compiler language which is then translated to machine language and stored in the memory of the computer for execution.

The control unit takes care of coordinating the entire computer operation: reading input into an input buffer, transferring a record of data into the main memory, executing the logic of the programs, generating error messages to the operator when problems occur, transferring the information to the output buffer, and writing the output.

Why does the input go into an input buffer, *which is a temporary storage area,* rather than going directly into the area labeled main memory? Remember the discussion on *I/O Bound* and *idle CPU* time? Information usually can not be read into the memory of the computer nearly as fast as the CPU can

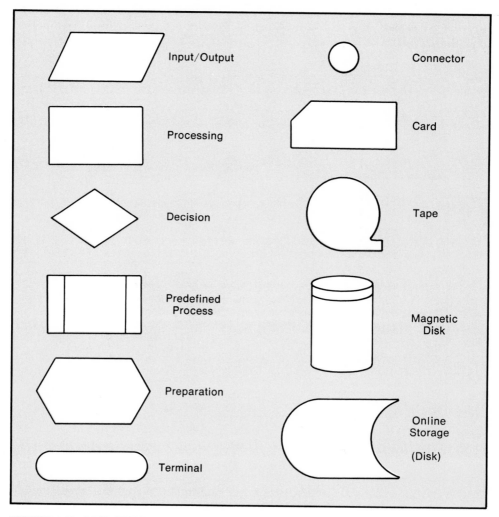

FIGURE 4–13. ASCI STANDARD FLOWCHART SYMBOLS

process the data. By providing input and output buffers the operations could be overlapped which means that record 3 is read and waiting to be processed, record 2 is processed and waiting to be written, and record 1 is being written as output. As soon as record 1 is written the control unit takes care of transferring record 2 to the output area, processing record 3, and reading record 4. For a brief period all three events are occurring simultaneously. The processing finishes first, then the reading, and finally the output is done!

The control unit has its work cut out for it because just the coordination of the various input/output devices being used and the overlapping of operations make it an awesome task.

The entire system is no more reliable than the validity of what is stored in one byte of the computer's memory. Since programs and data are either digits or characters stored according to a binary coded decimal system, it is possible to provide a parity check on information either entering or leaving the computer.

Output

The control unit takes care of transferring the processed data to the output buffer. The programmer is responsible for making certain that the information is in a form which can be easily utilized by the individuals who work with the output. The ease with which a report can be written and edited is directly related to the language that is used.

The amount of available memory determines the size of programs that can be written, as well as the number of different input/output devices which can be used in any one given application.

REGARDING THE REVIEW

4–33. What details should the programmer provide in the program regarding numeric data?
4–34. What type of things are provided for regarding the validity of the input that do not directly involve the computer?
4–35. What is a buffer?

COMMON PROGRAMMING TASKS

When coding is used to illustrate a given technique, COBOL will be used because the logic of the command can easily be seen in the coding. If a field name is used such as REGHRS, the *field must have been defined in the program.* The programmer must have told the computer what kind of information that the field contains and how the data is to be stored.

There is usually a common pattern that is followed by many programmers in doing the various functions that are required in the program. As was mentioned earlier, the exact functions that *must* be done, and the programming features that *may* be used, depend upon which language is used. If the programmer is not required to code for a given function, such as opening a file, when the program is compiled the commands are added to the program. A compiler is a program, usually supplied by the manufacturer, which translates the user's source code to machine language. The following "housekeeping" details are what the programmer must take care of before he can code the main logic of the program.

Declaring the Files

When writing a program, a file is defined as any input or output device other than the console typewriter. The program must tell the computer what physical devices, or files, are going to be used and how they will be utilized.

Opening the File

When the file is opened, the control system provides a check to make certain that the right disk or tape file is being used for the procedure. If the file did not have to be opened and a command was given to read a record from disk, what assurance would there be that the right disk file is being used? There would be nothing like trying to process payroll while reading the student history file. Often, it is unnecessary to open the files associated with the card reader, card punch, or printer.

Declaring Records

From the way the record is declared, the computer must know the name of the entire record and the location, size, and kind of data that is stored in each field. A unique *descriptive* name should be used for each field because the name should tell you something about the data that is stored in the field. Figure 4–14 illustrates a card layout format and how the structure (record) would be declared in COBOL. Without any knowledge of COBOL, it should be easy for you to see the relationship between the card design and how the record is described for the computer.

Declaring Work Areas

If a programmer needs to have answer areas that are not part of the input record or part of the output, work areas should be defined. Some languages

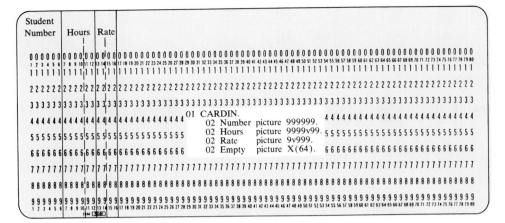

FIGURE 4–14. CARD FORMAT AND CODING

permit the computer to *default* and decide the attributes or characteristics of the work areas for itself, which can sometimes result in rather peculiar results. For example, one program had a command that stated:

COMPUTE NET-PAY = GROSS − WTAX − STTAX

In the solutions, the following values were used by the computer:

Compute Net-Pay = 50.00 − 5.00 − 2.38

Would you believe the answer of $42.63? The student who wrote the program didn't! The student wanted to say the computer couldn't subtract, but the fault was his as not all of the fields had been declared.

Declaring Tables

For the convenience of programming and saving commands, *tables* or *arrays* can be established in the memory of the computer. The computer will then generate an individual distinct address for each portion of the table. Tables can be used to help solve many types of problems. For example, when student tests are scored, the results are often stored in a table. After all the tests, or input, is read, the calculations are made and the results are printed. For each student the printed report may show his rank in the class and his percentage score. For each question it may print the right answer (if the student had answered the question incorrectly) plus tell the student how many other people in the class also missed the question. Such evaluations can be made only if tables are used to store the data in as the individual records are processed.

Printing Direction

If a printed report is to be one of the forms of output, the programmer must design the report and then write the source code to print the headings, subtotal, and total lines that are to be used for the report. It is also the responsibility of the programmer to tell the computer when each type of line is to be printed.

End-of-Job Routines

The program flowchart for the program which calculated the employee's gross pay and printed a report listing all employees who earned over $500 was a bit casual for a number of reasons. There should have been a way of determining when the last input card had been read and processed. In addition, some type of end-of-job routine is usually required such as printing totals or a message. It is considered a good technique to print some form of message that shows that a normal job ending has occurred. There are various methods used for detecting what is termed the "end file conditions." When the end-of-file is detected, a conditional branch command can be executed that will cause an instruction to print a message on the printer which might print "SJ010 completed satisfactorily."

Closing Files

What actually happens when files are closed depends upon the device that is being used. In using magnetic tape when the file is closed, a label is written on the tape and the tape may rewind automatically. A disk file may be opened as output and created during part one of a program, then closed, and reopened as input in the second part of the same program.

The functions described are only a small part of the detail that the programmer must be concerned with. Declaring files, structures, work areas, print lines, and tables are not part of the programmer's logic, but are necessary "housekeeping" detail. When all details are taken care of, the programmer is finally ready to code the logic of the program. In the module on operating systems, some of the techniques that can be used to save coding will be discussed.

Refer to the program in the COBOL module which computes the bowling averages and observe the first three divisions of the program. In those divisions the files are declared, structures defined, and work areas assigned. All of the logic of the program is expressed in the procedure division.

REVIEW QUESTIONS ON COMMON PROGRAMMING TASKS

4–36. In programming, what is a file?
4–37. When a record is declared, what information is being supplied by the programmer for the computer to use in working with the record?
4–38. What is an array?
4–39. Why might the programmer want to have a message print out on the printer when a job, which reads a tape file, processes the data, and then writes the answers out on a second tape file, is completed?

COMMON PROGRAMMING TECHNIQUES

In most cases only small sections of total programs are illustrated by using either the coding or the program flowchart. Again, COBOL is used to illustrate some of the more common programming techniques.

Loops

A loop is a series of one or more programming steps that are executed, according to a predetermined sequence, one or more times. An entire program is actually one large loop.

If a program is to punch 100 cards exactly like each card that is read as input, the hard way to write the program would be to write the statement to punch the card 100 times. There must be an easier way! A *count controlled loop* can be constructed and the coding done as illustrated by the partial program shown by figure 4–15.

The field name need not have been "count" because any name that is meaningful could have been declared as a numeric field, initialized as one, and then incremented by one each time a card was punched. When count is equal to 100, 100 cards will have been punched. Rather than using 100 commands to punch the cards, 4 commands were used to establish the count, check to see if it equaled 100, increment count (by 1), and then branch back to punch another card.

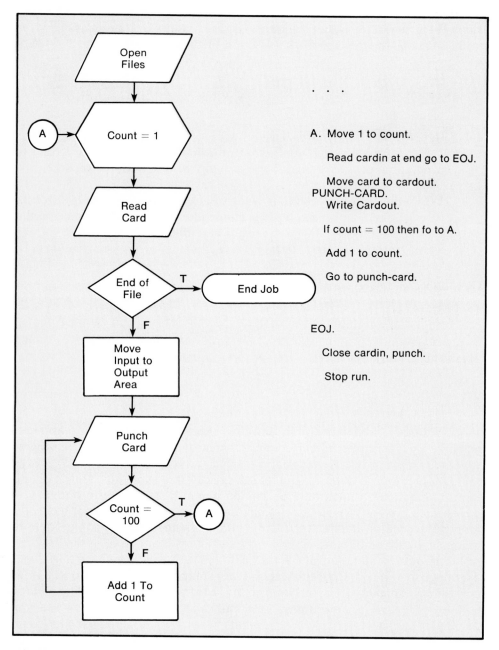

The flowchart contains the following elements:

Open Files

A → Count = 1

Read Card

End of File — T → End Job

F

Move Input to Output Area

Punch Card

Count = 100 — T → A

F

Add 1 To Count

. . .

A. Move 1 to count.

Read cardin at end go to EOJ.

Move card to cardout.
PUNCH-CARD.
  Write Cardout.

If count = 100 then fo to A.

Add 1 to count.

Go to punch-card.

EOJ.

Close cardin, punch.

Stop run.

FIGURE 4–15. COUNT CONTROLLED LOOP

The entire program is also a loop which will continue being executed until the end of the file is detected. When using some card readers, the end of file is recognized by reading a special card, such as a card punched with a /*, directly behind the last input card. In the "READ CARDIN *AT END* GO TO EOJ." statement used, actual machine language commands are generated when the program is compiled that will look for the special end-of-file card. When it is found, the conditional branch is executed and the program control branches to the location where the commands to close the files and end the job are stored.

Internal Programming Checks

Many different kinds of checks can be provided for in the program. A company has a policy that states that no one employee will have more than 20 hours of overtime. In the program a check should be provided:

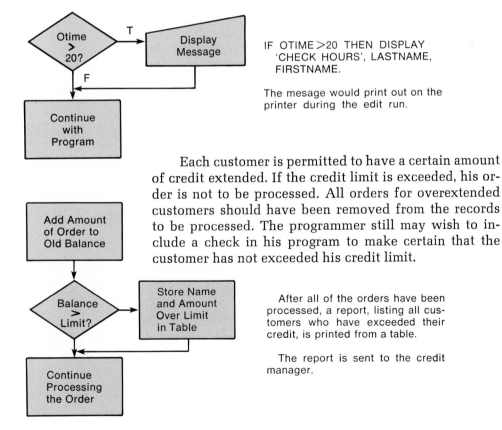

IF OTIME >20 THEN DISPLAY 'CHECK HOURS', LASTNAME, FIRSTNAME.

The mesage would print out on the printer during the edit run.

Each customer is permitted to have a certain amount of credit extended. If the credit limit is exceeded, his order is not to be processed. All orders for overextended customers should have been removed from the records to be processed. The programmer still may wish to include a check in his program to make certain that the customer has not exceeded his credit limit.

After all of the orders have been processed, a report, listing all customers who have exceeded their credit, is printed from a table.

The report is sent to the credit manager.

The student's number which is keypunched in the "drop and add" card is used to retrieve his record from the student master file which is maintained on disk. When the cards are processed, the job will be cancelled (unless the programmer provides an alternate course of action) if the student's number is incorrect.

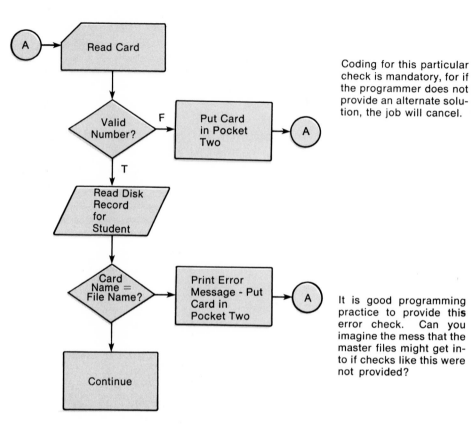

Coding for this particular check is mandatory, for if the programmer does not provide an alternate solution, the job will cancel.

It is good programming practice to provide this error check. Can you imagine the mess that the master files might get into if checks like this were not provided?

Editing of Input

A payroll system was designed which provides a master disk file that contains most of the needed information for the calculation of the payroll. Time cards are needed in the following cases:

1. All students and other part-time employees.
2. Hourly workers who work either less than, or more than, 80 hours. The payroll is calculated every two weeks.
3. A salaried worker who is not to be paid according to his established salary.

4. An employee who worked under an account number that is different from the one that is usually used. (Each employee's record on the master file contains the account number that he usually works under.)
5. Bonus pay cards.

The cards are edited by the computer program in the following manner:
1. The name on the card and the name on the master file must be exactly the same.
2. The student number on the time card must be the same as the student number in the master file.
3. If the student is a work study student (as identified by a special code on the card), then the program checks the following:
    a. Is a valid employer number code on the card?
    b. Is the account number 2155?
    c. Is the department number 569?
4. Each employee has a status code that determines how the pay is calculated. A check is made to determine if the status code on the card is the same as the code on the master file.
5. Completeness of the card.
    a. Are the fields used for regular hours, overtime hours, rate, card type code, and account number *completely* filled in with only *numeric* data.
    b. If the card code indicates that it is a "bonus" card, is the amount field filled in *completely* with only *numeric* data?
6. If the employee has only one card, does it have a 0 in the "card code" field?
7. If the card code field indicates that there will be numerous cards for the employee, a check is made to make sure that all of the cards have a 4 as the card code, except the last card for the employee which must have a 5 code.
8. Since the cards must be in absolutely correct alphabetical order, the sequence is checked.
9. A check is made to see that the first two digits of the account number are not 00.

If any of the conditions that are being checked by the edit program are found to be false, an appropriate error message, along with the name of the employee, is printed out on the printer. The processing of the payroll cannot continue until all of the error messages have been taken care of. In processing a payroll which will print approximately 1,000 checks, the edit program takes about a minute and a half to execute. Usually, there are one or two error messages printed out which can be resolved easily. The time spent in catching errors at this point in the payroll processing is well worth the time and effort.

It is not intended that you understand why the account number for work study students must be 2155 or why the cards must be in alphabetical sequence. The list is provided as a means of showing some of the ways input can be edited. If the input record is original data (used for the first time), regardless of the input media being used, there are probably edit checks that can be employed successfully to help prevent errors from getting in the system. For example, the First Savings and Loan Association in Saginaw indicated that 40% of its programming effort was directed towards checking and editing input.

Program Flowchart

Before any coding is done, a program flowchart should be constructed which shows the major logic of the program. In addition, after the program is written, tested, debugged, and becomes operational (used for real), the program flowchart is redone in final form and included in the *documentation* of the job. If another programmer, or the same programmer, has to "patch" the program at some time in the future, it is much easier to make the changes if the program flowchart is available. The statements included inside the symbol should be in "plain old English" that anyone can follow, and should not include technical terms that only a programmer or analyst can follow. Both management and the auditors should be able to look at the program flowchart and determine how the input is processed.

REVIEW QUESTIONS OF COMMON PROGRAMMING TECHNIQUES

4–40. What is a count controlled loop?
4–41. What is the difference between a conditional branch and an unconditional branch?
4–42. What is an internal program check?
4–43. A cash receipts card is being processed for a customer. The card contains the customer's number, name, the invoice number that is being paid, and the amount of the payment. The master file for the customer is read in. If the customer number is 10, then record number 10 will be read from the master file. What are two ways that the input card might be edited or checked? Think about what might be on the master file. State any assumptions that you make as you answer the question.
4–44. What are some of the uses for the program flowchart?

COMPILING AND TESTING A PROGRAM

When a request is made for a program, there must be a clear definition of exactly what is being requested and the objectives that are expected to be achieved as a result of the new or revised procedure. If the request is approved, formats will then be determined. A program flowchart is then made which will serve as a guide in coding the program.

The edit and error routines included should be designed to catch the unusual errors—the "it will never happen" variety, along with the routine errors that occur regardless of how many manual or machine checks are built into the system.

The source deck is keypunched from the coding forms. Some languages permit a free format to be used, which means that the source statements may be punched almost anywhere in the card; other languages require a very rigid format to follow for punching the source deck.

The compiler is then loaded into the computer. The term *loaded* means that the compiler is stored in the memory of the computer. As each source statement is read, the statement is both listed on the printer and checked for errors. The type of errors that will be detected are the routine clerical-type errors or a violation of the rules of the language. A few of the common type errors that will be detected are illustrated.

Common Programming Errors

1. In the declare statement for the input time card regular hours was spelled:

REGHRS

In the statement to compute the gross pay the following was coded:

COMPUTE GROSS = REGHR * RATE.

In the computer statement regular hours is misspelled, the computer had no way of knowing it is the same field as defined on the input card as REGHRS.

2. The following COBOL statement was coded:

COMPUTE GROSS = REGHRS * RATE.

In COBOL statements there must be a space before and after the field names that are used. A message will be printed regarding the "Gross=" part of the command.

3. Name had been defined as an alphanumerical field and then used in the following statement:

ADD 1 TO NAME

Since an alphabetic or alphanumerical field may not be used in an arithmetic command, an error message will be printed.

Each of the three errors illustrated fall into the category of careless errors that violate very basic rules of the COBOL language. The error messages printed are clearly stated and with a little practice can be easily interpreted by the programmer. All of the errors must be corrected before the program can be tested.

After all warnings are cleared up, the program is *linked* with other routines that are supplied by the manufacturer, loaded into the memory of the computer, and is then ready to be executed. The programmer must design test data that will cover any possible situation that can occur and then execute the program. The computer's results are matched against hand-calculated results to make certain that the program works.

Errors Not Detected during Compilation of a Program

The types of errors that will not be detected during the compilation of a program are:

1. *Omissions.* The programmer did not include a command to open the files, or the unconditional branch command to GO TO READ-NEW-CARD was omitted. The next command in sequence was executed which closed the files and ended the job. Rather than processing all of the data, the computer did exactly what it was told to do and processed one record and ended in a perfectly normal manner.
2. *Logical Errors.* The programmer did not express the logic of the program correctly. The statement may have said IF A = B THEN GO TO END-IT. What actually should have been coded to give the proper results was IF A *NOT* = B THEN GO TO END-IT.
3. *Careless Errors.* This type of error is commonly referred to as a "bone-headed error." A count controlled loop is constructed that is to be executed 100 times. The programmer declared a field called COUNT as a 2 position numeric field and gave it an initial value of 1. Each time the loop is executed one is added to count. Will the program ever get out of the loop! No! Since count can only get as large as 99, the test IF COUNT = 100 THEN GO TO CONTINUE-WITH-PROGRAM will never be *true.*

Since errors like the ones cited are made, knowing how to test a program is as important in programming, *or perhaps more so,* as being able to code.

Designing Test Data

In designing the test data, it is important that provisions are made for all the possible situations that can occur. If a complex program is being tested, it is not uncommon to test various sections of the program individually.

To cite a simple example pertaining to testing, suppose that the dean would like a list of all students whose grade point average is over 3.5. The input needed is the name of the student, the total credit hours attempted, and the number of honor points earned. All of the information is available in one card which is already in the file. In testing the program, what situations should be provided for when the test data is made up? Three cards would test everything that needs to be tested:

Card 1—Data that will calculate a grade point average of less than 3.5
Card 2—Data that will calculate a grade point average equal to 3.5
Card 3—Data that will calculate a grade point average that is greater than 3.5

The output, or report, should contain only the name and grade point average that was calculated from the third card. The calculations made by the programmer should be the same as the averages calculated by the computer. In a program as simple as this, the actual cards would probably have been used in the testing. Nevertheless, when complex programs are being tested, the actual files should not be used for a number of reasons. Often a programmer who works primarily on one system, such as the sales system, will maintain test files that can be used when new features are to be added to the system. The time spent in *complete* testing will result in fewer problems when the procedure, or system, becomes operational.

Documentation

After the testing, the programmer and the analyst are still not finished as *documentation* should be prepared which will serve a number of different purposes. The documentation includes the program listing, samples of the input and output, instructions to the operator, the revised program flowchart, an overview of the procedure, and many other different items. Each firm generally has its own standards of documentation which must be adhered to by the analyst and programmer. More information pertaining to documentation and its uses is provided in the module on *Designing Systems and Procedures* (p. 349).

Evaluation

One more task remains that should be done on a *continuing basis* as long as the program is being used. An evaluation of the effectiveness of the program must be made. Initially, an evaluation can be made to see if the program accomplished the major objectives which were part of the original problem definition. As the program is used over a period of time, the types of errors that occur should be noted, and for recurring problems, corrective action, often in the form of more internal program checks, should be taken.

SUMMARY

Many people still feel that all you must do is ask the computer to do something and it will be done. It does seem that way when management, through its terminal, can interrogate the master files and retrieve information. You should now be aware of the fact that the instructions given to the computer must be carefully planned. Although today's computers are much easier to program (since there are more powerful compiler languages that may be used to simplify the task), the computer will still do only what it is told to do and in the sequence in which the commands are given. The error messages that are received during the compilation of the program are relatively easy to understand. Nevertheless, there are some types of errors that can only be detected through careful testing. *The design of the procedure—to provide as many "error checks" as possible and the testing—is what makes good applications "happen."*

The entire configuration is managed by the control system. For a small-scale computer, the system may be relatively simple; while for a large system, it will be extremely complex. The manufacturers have provided (in both the hardware and software) ways of making certain that the data is read and stored correctly. The programmer and analyst must also assume their share of the responsibility and make certain that what is read into the system as input is correct. Internal checks and editing should be provided as often as possible.

Even in an extremely large, sophisticated program, the logic is always expressed in terms of a comparison being made between two values. In addition to the comparison, the *and, or,* and *not* operators may be used in the coding of the problem. The difficult part of programming is not the coding but the expressing of the intent of the program in a well-defined program flowchart. The programmer may not need to be aware of how data is actually stored internally. Nevertheless, the more he understands about the computer he is working with the easier his task becomes. When an unusual error occurs, sometimes the only way to understand why the results are invalid is to know how the data is stored and how the arithmetic and logical unit function.

AN ILLUSTRATION OF A MEDIUM-SIZE SYSTEM

In order to better explain the components of a computer system and how they must all "fit together" to meet the needs of the user, a medium-sized installation is illustrated. The explanation of the system will emphasize some of the items discussed in the module. Although it is good to work with the detail, it is also important to keep the perspective of what a data processing system involves—input, output, the central processing unit, *and the people.*

Today there are many good medium-size systems from which the user can choose. The UNIVAC 9480, although not the very newest or fastest on the market, is used as an illustration since it is typical of many other good computer systems. Each installation must be designed to meet the specific needs of the user.

Who selects the components that make up the system? Generally, it is the data processing manager and analysts, working with management, who make the decision. The components must be compatible and the cost of the system within the financial resources of the company. Its capabilities may be increased, as the needs of the company change, by expanding the memory, adding more peripherals, or both. Some of the features that are available as part of the system will not be presented until the more advanced computer concepts are covered. The specifications given for the central processing unit and the input and output devices will help to clarify some of the points that have been discussed in regard to the basic components of a computer system.

The hardware capabilities of any system are related to the amount of memory, the speed with which the calculations can be executed, and the time needed to access data. Equally as important as the hardware is the software that supports the system; and the features that are part of the operating system (which can be thought of as a master controller for the entire computer system) must be carefully analyzed. Some of the options available, such as multiprogramming which can be done on the basic 9480 System, will be covered in module 11.

The selection of the hardware and software is not as easy a task because it involves a comparison of various systems. Often "benchmarking" is done to evaluate one system against another. In benchmarking a "mix" of programs is used to evaluate the effectiveness of each individual computer. It is important that the mix is representative of the typical procedures to be run once the new system is installed.

The UNIVAC 9480 System can be tailored to the needs of the user. A smaller company, which has mostly sequential files, might select the 9480 System and include in the configuration the central processing unit, several magnetic tape drives, a card reader, card punch, and a printer. With the 9480,

FIGURE 4–16. UNIVAC 9480 SYSTEM. (Courtesy of SPERRY UNIVAC Computer Systems)

either magnetic tape or disk must be initially utilized as an auxiliary storage media for the required basic operating system.

As the company gains experience in EDP and begins to feel comfortable with a tape system, it would soon see how much more could be achieved with other means of mass storage for its master files; and therefore, might add disk drives as the next step upward. Additional units of memory may also be added to the system in order to accommodate larger, more sophisticated programs. With the expansion of both the hardware and software capabilities both batch and real-time processing may be simultaneously accomplished. Batch processing implies that one job is run at a time and is entered into the system from the centralized data processing center, while real-time processing indicates that the data is processed, from remote locations, as rapidly as it enters the system. The transition to the more sophisticated system, which permits the entering of data into the system from remote locations, can easily be achieved.

The CPU

The basic internal storage of the central processing unit starts at 65,536 bytes (normally termed 64K) and may be expanded to 262,144 bytes. Each byte contains eight bits plus the parity bit, and data is stored in the CPU using the EBCDIC code which means the numeric data may either be packed or zoned. Magnetic core is not used for the memory because a newer form of semiconductor storage is utilized.

The control section of the central processing unit governs the sequence in which the instructions are executed and taken care of, the interrupt handling, and the error checking. When an interrupt occurs, due to a number of reasons, the control unit makes sure the appropriate action takes place and then returns control to where the next instruction which is to be executed is stored.

The arithmetic section of the CPU permits arithmetic operations in both binary and decimal arithmetic, which can only be performed on packed data. The comparison needed to determine if a condition is true or false takes place in the arithmetic section. If the programmer has stored numeric data in a zoned format, the data must first be converted from zoned to packed before the mathematics can be performed. This conversion is done automatically when compiler languages are used. Whenever possible, knowing that the mathematics can only be done on packed decimal fields, the programmer should provide packed data.

The input/output section of the CPU takes care of bringing the data from the input device into main storage or transferring it from main storage to the output device. Data may be read in or written out at the same time as the CPU is executing other commands.

The instruction set of the 9480 includes 70 instructions, some of which have several different variations. When you think about it, 70 is not really very many. Nevertheless, extremely complex programs can be written utilizing the available commands. The user has the choice of using COBOL, FORTRAN, RPG, or an assembler language to code the programs. If assembler is not to be used, the programmer is not as concerned with how the instructions are executed. If the programmer does learn the assembler language and knows how the commands actually work, he will have a better understanding of the system.

Each component of the system is briefly discussed in its relationship to the material presented in the previous sections of the module.

Console

The operator console has a keyboard printer much like a standard typewriter. Use of any of the keys causes an EBCDIC character to be transmitted indirectly into the central processing unit. When a response is desired from the operator an attention indicator comes on the console to notify the operator. The console keyboard printer should not be thought of as an I/O device, *but as a communications device with which to communicate with the CPU.* Interrupt messages will print on the console typewriter as well as programmer supplied messages. For example, the console message to the operator might read: "If checks are to be printed, reply 1." Any other response, other than a 1, will cause the checks not to be printed. If the checks are or are not printed is determined by what command is executed after the evaluation is made in the logic unit of the CPU of the operator's response to the message.

Card Reader

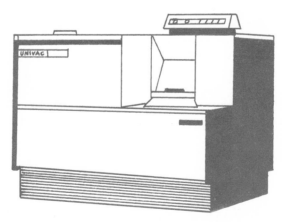

The UNIVAC 0716 Card Reader, which reads cards at 600 cards per minute, was selected to go with the system, *since the user had relatively few cards to read.* This particular reader can, as an optional feature, utilize cards which contain only 51 or 66 card columns. The 0716–02 Card Reader, which reads cards faster, could also have been used with the system. The UNIVAC Card Reader reads cards column-by-column whereas other card readers often read row-by-row. Since the CPU stored the cards in EBCDIC, the translate mode option was selected. This means that the standard Hollerith code punched in the card is converted to the EBCDIC code for storage in the CPU. The card reader can also be used with a system that stores the data in ASCII code, and then the required ASCII translate option would be specified. The I/O devices must all be carefully correlated with the capabilities of the central processing unit.

The 0716–02 Reader has two output stackers. *Error cards may be automatically selected into the second output pocket.* Since the stacker only holds 2,000 cards, the operator may wish to specify that he wants the second stacker to be used for processed cards when the first stacker gets full. When the first stacker gets full, the reader will automatically put the cards in the second stacker. When this is done, the stop-on-error feature is used, rather than pocket selecting the invalid cards so that invalid cards will not be mixed in with valid cards.

Magnetic Disk

When magnetic disk storage is added to the system, records can be accessed both randomly and sequentially. Frequently programs and routines can be stored in a library on disk, and when needed, brought into the CPU for execution.

With the 9480, the user has the availability of two different disk systems which permit him to determine what best suits his particular need.

Both the UNIVAC 8414 and 8424 Disk System (which are the options available to the user) have removable disk packs that allow the files which are not utilized in a particular application to be stored offline.

If the user selects the 8414 System, each pack can store 29,176,000 bytes of data and from 2–8 disk drives may be added for each subsystem that is utilized. Since the data is stored in an eight-bit byte, numeric information may be packed which increases the disk storage capacity. In contrast to the 8414, the 8424 has more data stored per pack and has a substantially faster access time.

Master files which require the addition and deletion of records, updating of balances, changing of certain fields of information, and the correction of data are better suited to disk rather than tape storage because far less CPU time will be required to do the required file maintenance.

Printer

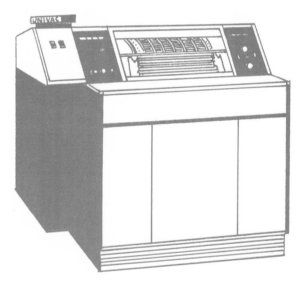

The UNIVAC 0768 Printer utilizes a print drum which contains the character set. Depending upon the model selected, the printer can produce from 840 to 2,000 lines per minute. The drum must rotate to move the desired character into the proper print position. The speed that can be attained from a printer depends upon whether the reports are to be single, double, or triple spaced, as well as the number of characters that are specified for inclusion on the drum. The model 00/01 Printer has a maximum of 63 different characters on the drum, whereas the 02/03 Printer has 94 different characters available. Both models, however, can print a maximum of 132 print positions per line. Depending upon the carriage control tape that is used, the printer can print either 6 or 8 lines per vertical inch.

Magnetic Tape

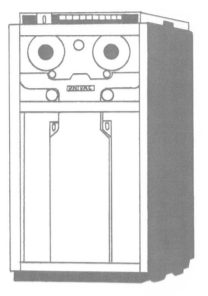

With the Uniservo Tape System selected, from 1 to 16 tape drives may be used with the system, and are available in either nine-track or seven-track models. The nine-track tape uses the same eight-bit EBCDIC code as the central processing unit, since the ninth channel is used for parity checking. The tape can be read either forward or backwards. The ability to read the tape backwards increases the speed that can be attained while sorting and merging tapes.

How the information is written on the tape is partially controlled by the program. Tape can be processed much faster if several records are read at one time and then processed. This factor, of how many records will be read at one time, is called blocking and is controlled by the programmer.

Card Punch

The 0604 Card Punch is capable of punching 250 cards per minute. The cards, which are punched row-by-row, may have the data punched in the card using the standard Hollerith code or according to the internal storage mode of the central processing unit. Since the cards may be referred to visually, they are generally punched in the standard punched card code.

When the cards are punched in the image mode (how the data is stored in the central processing unit) the information can also be "packed" in the card. In this mode the output card may contain as many as 160 digits of

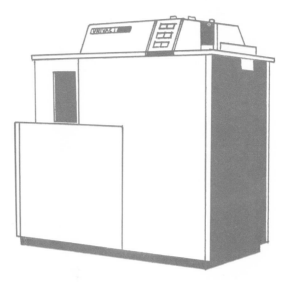

numeric information. When this is done rows 12–3 are used to represent one digit while rows 4–9 are utilized for the second digit.

The speed of the card punch may seem exceedingly slow, but with a system that utilizes both disk and tape, relatively few cards will be punched.

UNIVAC 9480 SYSTEM SUMMARY

Reference will again be made in the textbook to the UNIVAC system because only very general information regarding input/output devices and the central processing unit has been provided.

It is not important that you remember the speeds or the model numbers. What is important is that you understand that for any one given system, there are many options available. For example, the choices in the speed of the card reader or the printer selected for the system, the number of disk or tape drives to be added, the amount of memory, the way the data is stored, and the operating system that is to be used are but a very few of the options that are available. The key factors in the selection of a system are:
1. Does it meet the present needs of the company?
2. Can the system be expanded to meet future needs?
3. Are the components selected compatible?
4. What software is available with the basic system?
5. What languages are supported by the system?

6. Since contracts are usually carried with the vendor for the maintenance of the system, what is the reputation of the vendor in regard to maintaining the hardware?

Perhaps you can see now why the selection of the "right" system may require one *or more* years of intensive study. The study must involve many different individuals within the company in order to make certain that the basic needs of all groups are met.

DISCUSSION QUESTIONS

4–45. What is contained in the central processing unit?

4–46. Why are buffers used for reading input into and writing out of?

4–47. What is the difference between ASCII and EBCDIC code?

4–48. What advantages are there in "packing data"?

4–49. What is computer logic?

4–50. What is a register? What one use was given for a register?

4–51. What are some of the disadvantages of using an assembler language rather than using a compiler language?

4–52. Why is an assembler language sometimes used rather than a compiler language?

4–53. What all does the control unit actually do?

4–54. Do the programmer and analyst have a responsibility toward making certain that the input is correct?

4–55. Why are *loops* used in a program?

4–56. What are some internal programming checks that might be used?

4–57. In what ways could an input card be edited?

4–58. How and why should a program be tested?

4–59. Discuss. The UNIVAC 9480 system had just one basic configuration. All users have the same amount of memory and used the same I/O devices.

4–60. What is the difference between a conditional and an unconditional branch?

4–61. After a program is written and becomes operational, why should it continue to be evaluated?

GLOSSARY OF NEW AND OLD TERMS TO CHECK YOUR KNOWLEDGE

Address.   A location within the central processing unit. Each location, or byte, is addressable.

Array. Another name for a table. An array must be defined and then may be used to store data. Each location is addressable.

ASCII. American Standard Code for Information Interchange. A 7-bit code that is used to represent up to 128 unique numbers, symbols, and letters.

Assembler Language. A language that permits the use of symbols and mnemonics. The addresses for data and instructions are assigned when the computer compiles the program. Unless MACRO instructions are used, each command generates only one machine language command.

Binary. A number system that uses a single bit which is either on or off.

Bit. A binary digit. The smallest storage unit within the central processing unit.

Branch. The control of the program transfers to a location in memory where a command is stored and executes that command rather than executing the next command in sequence. A branch may be either conditional or unconditional.

Buffer. An area that is reserved either for information coming into main memory or leaving main memory. The data is stored in the buffer until it can be either processed or, in the case of the output buffer, until the output device is ready for the data.

Central Processing Unit. The central processing unit contains the control unit, arithmetic and logic unit, input unit, output unit, and main memory.

Channel. A physical device that transmits data from the input unit to the central processing unit or from the central processing unit to the output device.

Compiler. A program that checks the source statements for errors, translates pseudo-commands to machine language commands, and assigns locations for instructions and data.

Compiler Language. A powerful language that does not require the programmer to understand how each individual command actually is executed. One statement may generate several machine language commands. Many of the "housekeeping" details are supplied by the compiler.

Control Unit. Coordinates all computer activites. This includes the normal execution of a program as well as the abnormal conditions which may occur.

EBCDIC. Expanded Binary Coded Decimal Interchange Code. An 8-bit code which may reprsent up to 256 unique letters, symbols, or numbers.

Hardware. The computer and the peripheral equipment such as printers, card readers, tape drives, disk drives, and other I/O devices.

Hexadecimal. A 16-digit numbering system that contains the digits O-F.

Interrupt. A signal to the control unit that an event has taken place. The event could be one such as finishing reading an input record, or an unscheduled occurrence such as an invalid character entering the computer.

Loop. A series of programming steps executed one or more times.

Operating System. A combination of hardware and software (under the control of a supervisor or monitor program that reside in the central processing unit) that coordinates all the activities of the computer and its components.

Parity Check. A method using either an odd or even number to determine if data is stored correctly. For an odd parity check after a character is stored, the number of bits are counted that are on. The total number of "on" bits must be an odd number.

Software. The operating system, compilers, utility programs, and application programs that are necessary to make the computer function.

Stored Program. A program that was written, compiled, and then loaded into the central processing unit for execution. If the program is already tested, it may be loaded directly into memory from disk or tape.

Symbolic Address. A label or name used in the program that will be translated to an actual address when the program is compiled.

ANSWERS

SO FAR SO GOOD (p. 192)

4–1. Software
4–2. Hardware
4–3. Input unit
Central processing unit
Output unit
4–4. The CPU can process information far faster than the data can be read in or written out. This resulted in the CPU being idle a great deal of the time.
4–5. Yes, there are many different kinds of devices (called terminals) such as badge readers and cash registers which make it possible to enter data, as the transaction occurs, directly into the system.
4–6. Program
Input
Output
4–7. Central control unit
4–8. Boolean logic
4–9. Conditional
4–10. READ-NEW-CARD is translated to an actual *address* in the memory of the computer where a machine language command is stored.

TO REVIEW (p. 207)

4–11. Bit
4–12. Magnetic core
4–13. The ASCII which is a seven-bit code is recommended.
4–14. 256

4–15. A. Less storage area is needed with a BCD code.
   B. Mathematics is faster using BCD because less conversion is required.
   C. A system was needed that could provide for the storage of letters and symbols as well as digits.

4–16. A. 21
   B. 32
   C. 40
   D. 56

4–17. A. 110000
   B. 111001
   C. 10000001
   D. 11101101

4–18. A byte is one location within the computer's memory which contains 8 bits.

4–19. The upper four bits of a byte are referred to as the zone portion of a byte.

4–20. 11, 13

4–21. C

4–22. 4, 7

4–23. Unsigned numeric data is stored as a positive number.

4–24. After the *A* is stored incorrectly, the computer will make a check. In finding only two bits on a parity check will occur since 2 is not an *odd* number. Normally the data is restored and will be stored correctly on the next try.

4–25. A. 539
   B. 303
   C. 4369

4–26. 85E1   2222
4–27. CDF3   DE6D
4–28. 1100   111
4–29. 100   010

REVIEW QUESTIONS ON LANGUAGES (p. 210)

4–30. Machine languages
   Assembler languages
   Compiler languages

4–31. Compiler

4–32. Machine language

4-33. A. The size of the field
   B. How the data is to be stored—packed or zoned
   C. The number of places beyond the assumed decimal
4-34. A. Batch totals
   B. Verifying data on the verifier
   C. Editing, or checking, of the source documents before entering the data into the system
4-35. A buffer is a temporary storage area where information is stored before processing or leaving the computer.

REVIEW QUESTIONS ON COMMON PROGRAMMING TASKS (p. 219)

4-36. Any input or output device is referred to as a file.
4-37. The name of the record, the name of each individual field, the size of the fields, the number of places beyond the assumed decimal, and the relative location of each field. Note the use of EMPTY in figure 4-14 (p. 217). It is required in COBOL that an input card record describe all 80 card columns as that much space is reserved for the card in the CPU.
4-38. An array is another name for a table that may be declared to store data in as input files are being processed.
4-39. To show the operator that the job has come to a normal job ending and that all of the records were processed. The message could also provide some type of control, such as printing the number of records which were processed.

REVIEW QUESTIONS OF COMMON PROGRAMMING TECHNIQUES (p. 224)

4-40. A count controlled loop is a series of programming steps that will be executed a predetermined number of times.
4-41. A conditional branch is executed only if a given condition, or conditions, is true. For example, if a statement such as IF COUNT = 100 THEN GO TO A is used, the program control branches to the instruction stored at A only if the condition is true. Whenever an unconditional branch statement is encountered, such as GO TO PC, the con-

trol of the program transfers to the locations specified. PC was the location in the program where the command to punch a card was stored.

4-42. An internal program check is a check made within the program to determine if a condition is true, if a stated policy is adhered to, if the amount of pay is calculated for an employee within a permissible range, or if the customer's credit is within the range that is permitted. Many different types of internal checks can be made.

4-43. A. Does the name on the card agree with the name on the master file? If identified only by the account number, the number in the card could be wrong.
B. If there is not a corresponding invoice number on the master file that has not been paid.
C. Is the amount field completely punched in?
D. Does the amount field contain only the digits 0–9?

4-44. A. It may be used by management or auditors in determining how the input is being processed by a given program.
B. When a program must be patched, it helps to show the logic of the program to the person who is assigned the job of altering the program.
C. The programmer follows it when the program is coded.

DISCUSSION QUESTIONS (p. 237)

4-45. A. Main memory
B. Input control unit
C. Output control unit
D. Control unit
E. Arithmetic and logic unit

4-46. Information is read into and written out of buffers in order that the input, processing, and output functions of the computer may be overlapped.

4-47. The ASCII is a seven-bit code whereas the EBCDIC is an eight-bit code.

4-48. When data is packed, there is less conversion needed to do the mathematical operations. In addition, almost twice as much material can be stored in a given amount of bytes.

4-49. Computer logic is the computer's ability to compare two values to determine if one is higher than, lower than, or equal to the other. In addition, the programmer may use the logic *and, or,* and *not.*

4-50. A register is part of the hardware, usually at a low core address, which is used for a special purpose. Generally the programmer is unable to directly address the registers. The only function that has been given for registers at this point is their use in doing mathematical functions.

4–51. When an assembler language is used, the programmer must know exactly how each command will be executed. Unless MACROS are used, each command will generate only one command. Each assembler language is different. When using a compiler language (such as COBOL), the transition can be made from one computer to another much easier.

4–52. Assembler languages are used for the following reasons: Some programmers prefer to code in assembler. Computers with a very limited amount of memory may not have business-oriented compiler languages. In using a particular input or output device the compiler language for the system may not support the device. Changes to the operating system usually are made in assembler. A feature may be wanted in the compiler language which isn't available, so the routine may be coded in assembler.

4–53. The control unit coordinates all input/output activities as well as providing for the interrupts and error handling.

4–54. The analyst is responsible for the *total* design. Part of his responsibility includes making certain that the input into the system is accurate. The method of recording the data originally, the forms used, and method of verification are all part of the design of the system.

4–55. Loops are used to save coding. Less space in the memory of the computer is used to store the commands needed if loops are used.

4–56. The internal programming checks would vary with the application. For example, under 4.0 grading systems a check could be made to make certain that a calculated grade-point average is not greater than 4.0

4–57. An input card can be edited to make certain that only numeric information is recorded in each numeric field and that there are no blank card columns. A code may be given for making a salary change. If the code is used, the amount field must be filled in. The ways in which cards can be edited depends upon the information that is in the card.

4–58. Some types of errors, such as coding being omitted, will not be detected by the compiler. Logical errors are also undetected. A student should be taught early that one of the major responsibilities of programming is testing.

4–59. The UNIVAC 9480 system is modular and can have many different options. The system can be expanded by adding additional I/O devices, more memory, and by including additional features in the operating system.

4–60. A conditional branch is based upon a bit having a value of 1 if the condition is true. An unconditional branch always occurs whenever the statement is encountered.

4–61. Continued evaluation should occur even after the program is operational to determine if repeated errors are occurring, and, if so, corrective action should be taken. Also, if the system, or procedure, does not meet the objectives that were stated in the definition of the problem, some thought should be given to redesigning the procedure.

INPUT/OUTPUT DEVICES 5

When the computer was first invented, most people regarded it only as a speed calculator. It was not thought of as a common tool for business, industry, or the individual. There was no major concern expressed over the fact that the input and output was very slow. In fact, Thomas Watson, then chairman of the board of directors for the International Business Machines Corporation, first viewed the computer as a useful tool for research, but certainly did not envision the far-reaching impact it would have on all segments of the population. For this reason his company's attention was directed toward the further development of unit-record equipment rather than research on computers and their peripherals. His son, however, had much more faith in the computer and felt that it would become a major resource with a wide range of applications for both business and industry.

In the late 1940s and early 1950s the major thrusts in the development of the computer were speed, ability to store more data and commands, and increased reliability. Since it was most commonly used for a host of applications involving a large volume of input, concern was expressed by the users because the input and output devices were so much slower than the computational speed of the computer. In the more typical business applications (which require a large amount of input and output), it was not uncommon to find that the central processing unit was working only 10% of the time.

In computational or research laboratories the slow I/O devices were not as much a concern because a very limited amount of input was used, many calculations were made in the mathematical unit of the central processing unit, and relatively little information was produced as output. Today, in situations such as this, the basic configuration might still well be punched card input, the central processing unit, and a console (typewriter) for the very limited amount of output that is produced.

Magnetic tape was developed in response to the need for both faster I/O and a better offline storage media for data. One of the major problems with tape is that it can be accessed only sequentially. For this reason devices, such as disk, were developed which permitted random access of the records in the file.

The next step in the development of I/O devices was special devices for unique needs. For example, because the banks needed a way of processing the increasing number of checks, a special Magnetic Ink Character Recognition system was developed for the banking industry. The computer industry has also responded to some of the rather unusual needs of other industries. Often this is done by the manufacturer working with the user to develop unusual systems or methods that can be applied to other companies in the same industry. Just as computers were being improved to process data more effectively, input and output devices were being made faster, more reliable, and more adaptable to specific needs of the users.

Dissatisfaction was expressed by many users with the necessity of recording the information on a source document, transmitting the document to the centralized data processing department, and then, by some means, putting the data into machine processable form. Why couldn't the information be entered directly into the system as the transaction occurred? This technique would eliminate the necessity of transcribing the data into a machine processable form after it was received by the data processing department. In the case of sales, would this not give the customer faster service and make him a more satisfied customer? Could dollars be saved if the data could be entered from the point of sale?

In presenting the material on input/output devices, cards, tape, disk, and the printer will be covered in detail because they are still the most common form of input and output devices that are utilized. Other devices will be discussed more briefly.

As with any item that is purchased, it must first be determined what amount can be allocated to that particular expenditure. Although some of the more unusual devices would work very well for the small or medium-sized companies, they are probably unable to justify the use of some I/O methods due to the small volume of data to be processed and the amount of funds that are allocated to data processing.

In the selection of data processing hardware, there is always the conflict between "can we afford to do it" and "can we afford not to do it." Just as a computer is not a solution to all of management's problems, faster and better input and output devices have not solved all of the computer's problems. Other solutions to the "I/O bound problem" will be covered in the presentation on operating systems. Accuracy and security are also major topics that warrant consideration.

No one form of input or output meets the needs of all applications and all users. In each situation the benefits received must be weighed against the cost of the input or output devices to determine if the hardware can be justified economically. Unit cost, reliability of the data, security, ease of entering, processing, storing, and accessing of data must all be considered.

Since there is a direct relationship between how the procedures can be run, the amount of data handling, ease of handling controls and edit routines, and the type of input/output devices that are available, the sales invoicing procedure for the L. C. Smith Corporation will be reviewed. As each of the I/O devices is presented, the change in procedure, as well as the advantages offered by using the particular input, will be covered.

REVIEW OF SMITH'S SALES INVOICING PROCEDURE

Manual Method

The following steps were utilized in the manual method of processing the sales orders for the L. C. Smith Corporation. The source document (the sales order) was first manually edited and checked. Several processing steps were required in order to produce the typewritten sales invoice.

1. The order was submitted by the salesman. In the mail room the order was opened, date stamped, and routed to the credit department.
2. The credit department manually checked the credit rating from the listing of the accounts receivable provided by the accounting department. New customer's orders were delayed until a complete credit check was performed.
3. The sales department provided the following functions:
   a) The availability of the items ordered was checked by using an inventory card system. The cards were manually updated as items were sold.

b) A check was made for each item on the sales order to ascertain that the correct price and the description were used for each item.

c) A clerk multiplied each verified price times the quantity and then totaled the order.

d) From the edited sales order the sales invoices were typed.

As you recall, the major problems that were cited when the manual system was used were:

1. The average sales order took from four to five days to process.
2. The credit check was ineffective because current balances for the accounts receivable were not available; and customers too often were permitted to overextend their credit.
3. The manual inventory and price check were extremely slow, tedious, and subject to errors.
4. Customers often received the wrong merchandise.

Unit-Record System

When the punched card method was utilized (and you may assume by either L. C. Smith or by a service bureau such as Gateway) the system was fairly effective for the volume of transactions that were processed. Nevertheless, the *basic problems* of the credit and inventory check had not been solved by the use of the unit-record system.

You may wish to reread the entire section on a "Sales Invoice Procedure" (p. 105) to determine the way that the sales orders were processed when the unit-record equipment was utilized. The flowchart on page 111 illustrates the four steps which were used to process the sales order card and complete the procedure.

COMPUTERIZED METHODS

The computerized methods discussed will assume that the same sales order is used as the source document. The input card will still contain the customer's number, date, item number, order number, salesman's number, and quantity sold. The rationale for keypunching and verifying each variable on the input card is the same as it was for the unit-record method. The sales invoice which is printed using a computerized method is still essentially the same as the one illustrated on page 110.

First, the computerized method, using only punched cards and the printer, will be contrasted to the unit-record system. As L. C. Smith expand their installation to include magnetic tape and then disk, the tape and disk systems will be contrasted to the punched card methods. You *should be able* to see the relationship between the type of input/output devices used and the number of manual steps that are required as the various systems are presented.

Smith's Computer System

As the L. C. Smith Corporation continued to grow, they acquired a computer system which had a central processing unit, a card read/punch unit, and a printer. The magnetic tape units were added first, and then as the volume of sales continued to increase, magnetic disk drives were also installed. The system then had the general characteristics and capabilities of the UNIVAC 9480 which was detailed in module 4. Initially, all jobs were processed in a "batch" mode since their software did not support any other method.

Although L. C. Smith did have a separate data processing department and management had expressed interest in the development of improved data processing methods, they still did not spend the time *(before their computer arrived)* to do the required systems work which would enable them to more effectively utilize the capabilities of their new hardware.

Their procedures were "lifted" from the unit-record equipment without any real thought as to how the applications could be improved. The same type of conversion is still being done today by some companies when a newer, more sophisticated computer replaces the company's older and less powerful model. When conversions are made in this manner, the new hardware's capabilities are not challenged!

After the characteristics of card readers, card punches, and printers are covered, Smith's first computerized sales invoicing procedure will be contrasted to their unit-record procedure.

Card Read/Punch Units

In selecting the card read/punch unit to utilize with a system, the user will generally have a number of models to select from. Readers can read as many as 2,000 cards per minute and as few as 90 cards per minute. The one UNIVAC reader previously illustrated could read either 600 or 1,000 cards per minute depending upon which speed was specified by the user.

The card reader may utilize either brushes or photoelectric reading devices to read the cards. When either method is used, there is generally compare circuitry available to make certain that the information read at the read check station is the same as what is read by the second read check station. The chances of the information being incorrectly read for the same card at both stations and with the same identical error made each time are very unlikely. Figure 5–1 illustrates the read/punch stations (as well as the hopper and stackers) of a typical unit which can both read and punch cards.

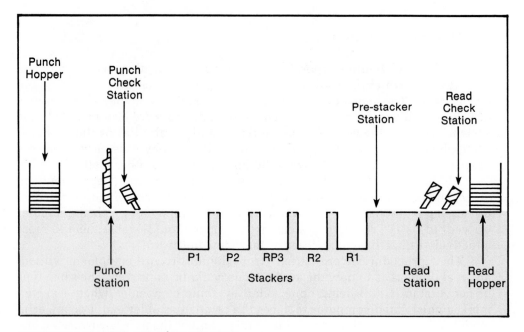

FIGURE 5–1. TYPICAL READ/PUNCH UNIT

The first three stackers on the right, labeled R1, R2, and RP3 can be used for the cards which are read as input, while those labeled P1, P2, and RP3 are utilized for the punched card output.

A few card readers, such as the System/3 MFCU, will permit the results of processing to be punched into the input card.

The common occurrences that require the attention of the operator while reading cards are:

Read Check

The read check occurs when an incorrect hole count, or parity check, is detected which indicates that the data was not read or stored properly. The read check is a standard feature on most card readers because if this feature were not available, the input might be stored incorrectly. When the read check occurs, the cards are removed from both the hopper and the stacker. With most readers the first card in the stacker is the card which was misread. The operator examines the card to make certain that it is valid and then places the card which caused the read check back in the hopper along with the rest of the unprocessed cards. Unless there is a physical problem with the reader, the card will generally be read and stored correctly the next time it is read.

Validity Check

A validity check will occur when a card contains an improper combination of punches in a given card column. This can result from a malfunction of the keypunch or from data being added to a card which already contains information. If the cards are verified, both of those problems should be detected by the verifier. If the cards are positioned incorrectly in the hopper, a validity check can also occur. In most cases, when a validity check occurs a new card must be punched to replace the invalid card. The computer run may have to be cancelled since the source document which contains the data punched in the card is not available in the computer center.

Feed Stops

A nicked or damaged card will cause the *feed stop* light to come on and the reader to stop reading cards. Sometimes the card that created the problem can be used, but more often duplication of the damaged card will be required before the job can continue.

Stacker Light

When any of the stackers being used are full, the computer will stop until such time as the cards are removed from the stacker and the card reader is restarted. An optional feature referred to in the discussion of the UNIVAC card reader was the automatic use of stacker two when stacker one became full. When the stacker light does come on and halts the operation, the entire system may go into a *wait* state until the operator empties the hopper. When the computer time on the system may be valued at 100 dollars *or more* per hour, how much time can be wasted waiting for the stacker to be emptied?

Transport Light

When the transport light comes on, there generally is a card jam within the transport area of the card reader. The transport area is the internal portion

FIGURE 5–2. STUDENT REMOVING CARD JAM ON 2540 READ/PUNCH

of the read unit which is between the card hopper and the stacker. If cards are stored correctly, handled by the operator properly, and the reader well maintained, the newer card readers tend to have few cases of actual card jams. When card jams do occur, an experienced operator should be secured to correctly solve the problem.

When the card reader is used to read large quantities of cards for processing as input, the reader requires almost the constant attention of the operator to fill the hopper and empty the stackers. When the hopper becomes empty, the card reader stops and causes the computer to go into a *wait* state until the operator either adds more cards or causes the job to terminate.

Reading Cards

The cards may be read either by the parallel or serial reading method. The parallel reading method reads the cards row-by-row while the serial method reads the data one card column at a time. When the parallel method is used, it takes the same period of time to read a card with one column of data as it does to read 80 columns of input.

When cards are read serially, a card with only a few columns of information can be read far faster than one which contains data in all 80 columns. As soon as the last defined column is read the card will be released and a new card will be advanced to the reading station. If certain fields are not required as part of the input for a given job, the programmer simply doesn't define those areas of the card. If the analyst had designed the card with a control punch in card column 80, it would require reading the entire card. Therefore, when working with a serial card reader there is a very real relationship between the card design and the speed of the card reader.

Stacker Select

In utilizing the stackers available for the input card it may involve a hardware feature, such as the automatic selection of invalid or incorrectly read cards, or may be the result of the programmer's commands.

The sales invoice job requires that the customer's master is merged with the sales detail cards before the invoices can be printed on the online printer. As the cards are read and the data processed, the programmer may be able to specify that the master cards go into stacker one while the detail cards will be placed in stacker two. This would save selecting the masters from the detail cards, as a separate operation, after the computer run is finished. Input cards are being used to make necessary changes to the student's record which is stored on disk and identified by the student's number. Cards with incorrect student numbers can be selected into stacker two while cards with correct numbers will be in stacker one. The documentation, or run sheet, for the job would tell the operator what corrective action is required for the cards in stacker two. Using options such as this will keep the job running and permit all corrections to be made at one time.

Other Features of Card Readers

A few card readers permit the use of two input files eliminating the need for a match-merge operation to combine the master and detail cards into one file for processing. When this type of card reader is used, both input card files must be sorted in the same sequence. The program language that is used will permit the programmer to easily specify that *only if* there is both a master and a detail card for the same student or account number is the card to be processed.

Some card readers will read data in the image mode which permits the data in the card to be *packed*. Since each character or digit is represented by a combination of six bits, two characters or digits may be recorded in each card column which expands the capacity of the card from 80 to 160 characters of data. When the image mode is used as input, the card was generally previously punched as computer output from another application.

In a computer installation which uses only cards for input, the more unusual features, such as having two input card read hoppers and being able to punch into the input card, are more beneficial to the user than when a number of different devices are used as input. When disk or tape is used the master file information is stored in that form rather than on punched cards.

Functions Performed by Card Readers

Card readers are generally used for the following functions:

1. *Reading Input.* In the case of a very small installation or a computational lab cards may be the only form of input that is used. In larger installations there are several approaches used to solve the problem of reading cards, since the relative speed of the card reader is very slow as compared to reading tape or disk.
2. *Reading Job Control Cards.* Job control cards are used as a means of communicating information regarding the procedure to the computer. The cards tell the computer when a new job is starting, when to end a job, what tape drives will be used for the input tapes, what drives will be used for output, as well as informing Mr. Computer about many other factors pertaining to the job. Some computer systems require extensive use of control cards while other systems make little or no use of JCL cards.
3. *Reading Control Information.* All of the information needed to print the students' grades is on the student master file. A control card may be required in order to print the semester and the date on the grade reports.
4. *Reading Source Decks during the Compilation of a Program.*

Advantages and Disadvantages

The punched card has been utilized for many years as a means of recording new information into the data processing system. Although card readers are relatively slow, the strong points in favor of the card seem to be: the data is easy to keypunch into the cards, can be machine verified, and is interpreted by the keypunch or interpreter so that the information is identifiable to the operators and others who must handle the card.

The disadvantages of the use of the card as an input media are the data must first be recorded on a source document, then transferred to the punched card which is a duplication of effort. As an input media it is very slow, and the rekeying of the data for the card verification is both time-consuming and costly.

Card Punch

When disk or tape is used in an installation, relatively few cards are punched. For this reason the card punch unit is generally much slower than the read unit. For example, the IBM 2540 read/punch unit will read 1,000 cards per minute and punch only 350 cards per minute.

If only the card reader is available for input, a large percentage of the applications will have punched card output for updated records and summarized data which may serve as input for the next procedure.

Most card punches have a *punch check* light which comes on when a parity error has occurred. In a five stacker read/punch unit, such as the one lllustrated in figure 5–1 (p. 250), it is not uncommon for the invalid cards to go into P1 while the valid cards will go into P2. The card punch also has a *feed check* light that will come on if nicked or torn cards are detected. If cards are not stored correctly and become warped due to excessive humidity or poor card handling, feed checks and punch checks will occur more frequently.

QUESTIONS ABOUT THE READ/PUNCH UNITS

5–1.   What devices are commonly used by the card reader to read the card?
5–2.   Why are two read stations found in a card reader?
5–3.   May the input card go into any of the five stackers of a typical read/punch unit?
5–4.   What usually happens when a parity check occurs while reading cards?
5–5.   What will cause the card reader's validity light to come on?
5–6.   When the *feed stop, validity check* or *read check* light comes on, will the reader continue to read cards until the operator notices that the light is on and stops the reader?
5–7.   What causes the transport light to be turned on?
5–8.   What is the difference between the parallel and serial method of reading cards?
5–9.   Can the programmer determine which stacker to use for the input cards?

5–10. What advantage would there be in having a card reader that could read two separate input files rather than requiring one combined file?

5–11. What advantage is there in being able to read cards in an image mode?

5–12. Discuss the following statement. In most installations the card reader is only used for reading input.

5–13. Why have many companies looked for other means of entering large amounts of input rather than using the punched card?

5–14. What has occurred when the *punch check* light comes on the card reader?

5–15. When a large volume of input cards are to be processed, does the card reader/punch unit require much of the operator's attention or time?

LINE PRINTERS

The printer is one of the most essential pieces of peripheral equipment in any computer system. The amount of actual printed material that is required varies depending upon what other output devices are available. Again, relatively speaking, the printer is a slow output device. Some of the solutions to the problem of using a slow printer with much faster magnetic tape or disk input will be covered in another section.

When a line printer was first used rather than the accounting machine as the printing device for data processing applications, it was viewed as a really "high speed printer" and is still referred to as that by many people. But as tape and disk output devices were utilized, they were found to be far faster than the printer. If a given company has a large computer installation and reads magnetic tape at the rate of 240,000 characters per second, the central processing unit will usually be able to process the data faster than it can be read into the CPU. A line printer capable of printing 2,500 lines per minute would produce a maximum of 5,500 characters per second. When this rate is contrasted with the input rate of 240,000 characters per second, a very definite problem exists. Unless some form of corrective action is utilized, the entire computer system will be slowed down to the rate of the printer. The 5,500 was calculated by using 132 characters per print line. The number of characters which can be printed on one line varies with the printer selected. Although the maximum number for any given printer could be either more or less, most of the more conventional printers print either 120 or 132 characters per line.

The illustration is extreme in some respects because certainly not all magnetic tape is read at the rate of 240,000 characters per second. On the other hand, if a printer is to perform at the rate of 2,500 lines per minute very definite restrictions are imposed in order to obtain that particular rate of speed. For example, the Control Data Corporation's 14031 impact printer can print at the following rates of speed:

PRINT SPEED	CHARACTER SET UP
1200 lpm	48
1500 lpm	36
2500 lpm	16

Why can faster speeds be obtained if a smaller character set is used? The printer selects the nearest character on the print chain or drum to print. When a 36 character set is used rather than a 48 character set, there are more of each character available on the chain or drum and therefore, on an average, less revolving of the chain or drum is required in order to find and print the desired characters. The 2,500 lines per minute is also possible only if the printer is operating in what is called a *burst mode*. The term burst mode implies that the printer constantly is seeking and printing information, with no interruptions permitted for other I/O, until the entire print job is finished. If lines are frequently skipped to correctly position the form vertically, the maximum rate which is specified will be decreased considerably.

FIGURE 5–3. IBM 3211 PRINTER. (Courtesy of International Business Machines Corporation)

Types of Printers

Printers can be divided into two broad categories—impact and nonimpact printers. Impact printers, although much slower, are by far the most common type of printer.

When an impact printer is used, printing occurs as the result of a metal character striking against an inked ribbon. The familiar typewriter is one example of an impact printer. Although print chains or drums are the most popular devices used, impact printers can use print wheels, wire matrixes, or ball printers.

Although the nonimpact printers are much faster, the quality of print is usually not as good as what is produced by using impact line printers. The

FIGURE 5–4. STUDENT CHANGING CARRIAGE CONTROL TAPE ON THE 1403 PRINTER

nonimpact printers usually require the use of special paper which is more costly than the more conventional paper used by the impact printers. Non-impact printers are, however, becoming more popular since they are much faster.

Carriage Tapes and Special Forms

Printers may require the use of a carriage tape which is used to help control the vertical movement of the paper. A program command starts the skipping of the form in the printer while the punch in the carriage tape tells the printer when and where to stop skipping, or advancing, the form. When internal reports are produced, stock paper and a standard list tape are usually used. If a large number of spaces is to be skipped, it is faster when a special carriage tape is used, rather than using a series of programming commands, since most systems permit the programmer to skip a maximum of three lines per command. When special forms (like the sales invoices) are used a special carriage tape is punched to control the vertical movement of the paper.

If each print job requires special forms and carriage tapes, the operator would spend a great deal of time changing forms and tapes. Some companies always use single part stock paper for all internal reports and then duplicate the number of copies that are wanted. The additional cost of duplicating is offset by getting more printed output in a given period of time, since delays were not required for changing paper to produce the correct number of copies.

Inserting New Forms in the Printer

When the operator mounts a new carriage tape and puts the new forms in the printer, the tape and the form must be correctly synchronized or else the printing will not be printed in the correct location. Most printers can be adjusted both horizontally and vertically so that the printing will more exactly match the form. Since the width of the forms can vary, the tractors which hold the paper are also adjustable. Many installations have a rule that the tractor on the left is not to be moved so that the programmer will always know where each print position will print on the form that is to be used. Also if only one tractor is adjusted, it takes less time than if both tractors must be moved.

After the operator has aligned the forms in the printer and is ready to start the printing operation, it is possible to single cycle the printer so that it stops after each line is printed. This permits the operator to check and make certain that the printing is correctly aligned before a large number of forms have been printed. If prenumbered forms are used, it is important that the

FIGURE 5–5. A STUDENT INSERTING GRADE REPORT FORMS IN THE 1403 PRINTER

first form is printed correctly because each form number must be accounted for as part of the "control" procedure.

The operator should make certain that the forms are stacking correctly as they are being printed. Some printers, such as the Control Data Corporation's 14031, have an optional power stacking feature that minimizes the need for the operator's attention. As with the use of many other devices, the operator learns to be aware of changes that occur. If the printer stops during the printing operation, an experienced operator should be instantly aware that this has occurred. When it stops the operator should check to see if the printer is out of forms or if a form check or some other type of error has occurred that will require his attention.

Controls are provided on almost all printers which allow manual adjustment of paper tension, form thickness, paper alignment, vertical print positioning, horizontal print positioning, and the advancement of forms.

LET'S REVIEW THE PRINTER

5–16. When contrasted to other I/O, is the printer considered to be slow or fast?

5–17. What are the two broad categories into which printers are divided?

5–18. What two devices are most often used for storing print characters by impact printers?

5–19. Do printers always print at their quoted maximum speed?

5–20. What is the advantage in using "stock paper" for internal reports?

5–21. How does the computer know how to vertically place the printing on the report?

5–22. Is a new carriage tape made every time the pay checks are printed?

5–23. Why might a company have a policy that all internal reports are to be printed on single part stock paper?

5–24. If the printer runs out of paper during a given procedure, what will generally happen?

A COMPUTERIZED SALES INVOICING PROCEDURE UTILIZING PUNCHED CARD INPUT

Because the L. C. Smith management wanted the procedures computerized as soon as possible, the functions performed by the calculator and accounting machine were replaced by the computer's ability to do mathematics and to control the online printer. The functions performed by the reproducer, collator, sorter, and interpreter were still needed in most of their applications.

Refer back to the flowchart on page 111 and observe the four steps which were required to print the invoice. The card-oriented computerized method still requires the use of a price master to complete the sales invoice card. Step one is repeated in the computerized method except that the computer will be used to multiply the price times the quantity rather than using the calculator.

Step two is the same in both systems since master name and address cards along with the sales cards must be used to print the sales invoices.

Step three is changed as the computer is now used rather than the accounting machine. The revised step three is flowcharted in order to illustrate the changes.

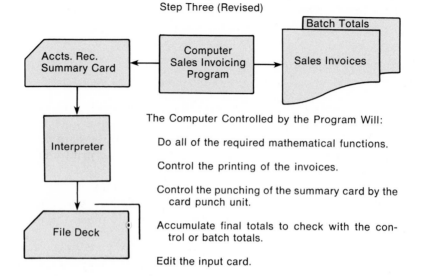

Step Three (Revised)

The Computer Controlled by the Program Will:

Do all of the required mathematical functions.

Control the printing of the invoices.

Control the punching of the summary card by the card punch unit.

Accumulate final totals to check with the control or batch totals.

Edit the input card.

Using the computer and the online printer rather than the accounting machine for step three would enable the job to be completed much faster. If the program used to produce the sales invoices was well written, there could be additional editing and checking features added as "bonuses" that could not have been done using unit-record equipment.

The final total for all invoices is printed out at the end of the job and will become a control total for other procedures which will use the accounts receivable summary cards. The total quantity of all items ordered is printed and *must* agree with the control total which was taken directly from the sales orders. The invoices will not be released from the data processing department until the computer total agrees with the adding machine control total.

Since the sales invoicing procedure requires a large volume of input and output in relationship to the small amount of processing required of the CPU, it is a perfect example of "I/O bound." The CPU is idle far more than it is working! Even if a second-generation computer, such as a 1401 or an 1130, were used rather than a third-generation computer, the processing would still be many times faster than it is possible to read the cards or print the sales invoices. Faster I/O devices and a more sophisticated operating system can help to decrease the amount of time that the CPU is idle.

The sales invoicing application has neither effectively utilized the computer nor efficiently dealt with the credit and inventory checking procedures.

A manual check was still done to determine if the customer's credit was satisfactory. The inventory was updated as a separate computer procedure, using the sales cards, after the invoices were printed. The daily inventory listing is used in the manual "items check." Although the item checking is still done manually, at least the data used is *timely*. The card-oriented system involved a number of manual operations, some of which should have been computerized, and a good deal of card handling.

As L. C. Smith gains experience in using computerized methods, it is anticipated that both the data processing department and management will realize that *just adding more peripherals is not the answer*. Time must be spent in analyzing their present system to determine what procedures, *either manual* or computerized, must be changed.

Magnetic Tape

Magnetic tape can be used as input, output, or as an offline storage media. There has been a remarkable improvement in magnetic tape since (1) there are now a variety of ways in which to prepare magnetic tape input; (2) the density of tape has increased; (3) the length of the IRG has decreased; (4) the access time for retrieving information is much faster; and (5) the performance of the tape has increased while the cost per unit of information stored on the tape has decreased.

In considering which tape drives to utilize with a given system, there are three major questions that must be answered.

1. What density of tape can be utilized?
2. What is the access time required to read a tape block or record?
3. What is the rate at which the data can be transferred from the tape into the memory of the computer?

FIGURE 5–6. MAGNETIC TAPE DRIVE.
       (Courtesy of Control Data Corporation)

Tape Density

The density of tape refers to the number of characters, or bytes per inch, which may be stored on one inch of tape. The first magnetic tape that was processed had a density of 200 BPI, the next advancement was to 556, and then it went to an unheard of density of 800 BPI. Now magnetic tape is also available at 1600, 3200, and 6250 BPI. One inch of 6250 density tape is capable of storing almost 80 cards of data. A tape drive can process, as an optional feature, more than one density of tape. It is not uncommon for the system to be able to read or write tapes at both 800 and 1600 bytes per inch. International Business Machine Corporation's tape drives which read and write at 6250 BPI can also process 1600 BPI tape. Tape must always be read at the same density that it was written. For this reason the external tape label that is positioned on the cover of the reel of tape indicates the density that was used in recording the information on the tape. For other than the really large-scale computer system, 800 or 1600 BPI is the most common density that is utilized.

In determining how much information may actually be recorded on one reel of tape, there are also several other factors that must be considered besides the BPI. The size of the record, the blocking factor that is used, and the required size of the gaps must also be considered. The tape illustrated in figure 5–8 would be able to store far more information and would be processed faster than the tape shown in figure 5–7. The use of the blocking factor is the major reason for the increased amount of data that can be stored since the BPI and the record size are the same in both illustrations.

If the tape is written as computer output, the size of the record is determined by the systems analyst and the user. For example, if a payroll master file is to be written on tape, the analyst will work with the payroll department in determining how much information should be recorded in each employee's master file record. A good deal of thought should go into determining what information should be stored in the master file because it is costly to store unused data on either tape or disk. The tendency sometimes exists for the user (the payroll department) to ask for more information than what is really needed.

Blocking Factor

The blocking factor is determined by considering the size of each individual record and the amount of memory that can be allocated for input and output. If a record contained 400 characters of information and a blocking factor of 20 is used, over 8,000 locations in memory will be required for each input buffer. If two buffers are used for input, over 16,000 locations of memory would be required. When very large computers are used, this is not a great deal of space. However, there are many installations that have smaller computers which would not be able to allocate this amount of memory to input. When working with magnetic tape, there is not an "ideal" blocking factor as the size of the block is determined by the amount of memory that is available for reading and writing the tape files.

Why are records blocked? Figure 5–7 illustrates a tape which has a record length of 400 characters, BPI of 800, and has a blocking factor of 1 (no blocking). The tape drive used to read or write the tape requires a gap of ¾ inch between records.

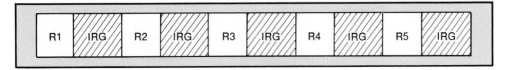

FIGURE 5–7. UNBLOCKED TAPE

There are two disadvantages in processing the tape as it is illustrated in Figure 5–7. One, since a blocking factor is not used, the tape will be processed much slower than if the records were blocked. Each time a record is read the tape drive must stop, store the data, and then start again. The gaps, referred to as IRGs (Interrecord Gaps) are provided so that when the read or write operation stops and starts, all of the data will be processed. It is physically impossible to read an individual record, stop, and start reading again without losing data if there is not a gap between the records.

If you were to stand and watch the tape being processed, you would not be able to actually observe the stops and starts. They do occur, however, and each "stop/start" takes time. Therefore, if a blocking factor of 5 is used, only one "start/stop" is required for each five records causing the tape to be processed faster.

The second advantage of blocking tape is that far more information can be stored on one reel of tape. Figure 5–8 shows a tape which is blocked using a blocking factor of 5. What can you observe at a glance? The same five records take far less space on the blocked tape than on the unblocked tape.

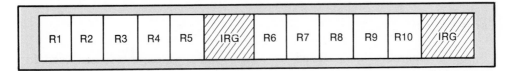

FIGURE 5–8. BLOCKED TAPE

Tape Codes

Magnetic tape may have either seven or nine channels. Data recorded on the nine-track, or channel, tape uses the EBCDIC (Extended Binary Coded Decimal Interchange Code). Eight bits, or channels, are used for the code and the ninth bit provides a parity check. In module 4 the EBCDIC code, as it related to storage of data within the Central Processing Unit, was explained. Figure 5–9 illustrates a portion of the EBCDIC code used to store data on magnetic tape.

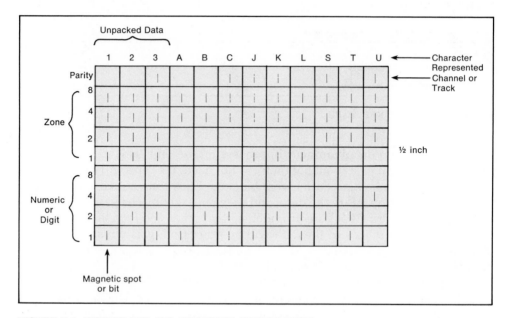

FIGURE 5–9. NINE-TRACK (OR CHANNEL) EBCDIC CODE

When the EBCDIC code is used, the programmer may specify that the data is to be packed which would permit one digit to be stored in the zone portion and a second digit to be stored in the digit portion of each individual location on the tape.

Parity Check

Seven-channel tape utilizes the ASCII code. Six channels are used for storing the data on the tape while the seventh provides a parity check. The parity check illustrated in figure 5–9 (*using the EBCDIC code*) assumes that the computer using the tape is an *odd* parity check computer. When magnetic tape is being used, the parity check provided is just another example of the many ways that those responsible for the advances in computer technology have tried to make certain that data either entering or leaving the computer is correct.

What happens when a parity check does occur? If information is being written on a magnetic tape and a parity check occurs, due to the fact that one or more bits were not recorded correctly, the tape is reversed, the data re-written, and the parity is retested. If the parity check again is not valid, the same process is repeated. Usually on the second attempt the material will be recorded correctly. The computer operator is not even aware of the fact that the parity check occurred because the *operating system* (control system usu-ally provided by the computer manufacturer) takes care of the recovery pro-cedure. If, however, after a given number of tries, the parity check is still not valid, the system will cancel the job and notify the operator that there is a problem. Either the magnetic tape, the drive, or the central processing unit has a problem that the recovery procedure provided cannot solve. When the job is cancelled, an appropriate message is printed on the console typewriter so that the operator knows why the job terminated.

Access and Transfer Time

When selecting tape, the user can usually specify the density and the number of tracks that are desired. Nine-track tape is usually provided for the tapes with the higher density that are used on the larger systems. The smaller systems may use seven-track tape since the data stored within the central processing unit may also use the ASCII code.

In the specifications provided regarding a particular tape drive, both the access time, which is measured by the number of inches per second that can be read, and the transfer time are available. The transfer time is the number of characters per millisecond that can be transferred from tape into the central processing unit. The Control Data Coporation 34201 tape drive that was illus-trated has the following ranges listed for the various models which are avail-able:

	HIGH	LOW
Access Time (inches per second)	200	75
Transfer Rate (bytes per millisecond)	320	41.7
Density (bytes per inch)	1600	556

The higher transfer rates and access times are available for the tapes with the higher densities. To determine the *actual* transfer rate, the actual amount of data stored per inch is calculated by using the density, record size, and blocking factor. The characters per inch can then be multiplied by the access time to determine the actual character transfer rate per second. You would find that a fantastic amount of data can be read from or written on tape in one second. The transfer rate given in the specifications is always the *maximum* rather than the actual since the maximum figure would be possible only if there were no interrecord gaps.

Why does each user not select the model with the highest access time and transfer rate? As the higher rates are obtained, the equipment becomes more complex. Due to this factor, the user pays a premium price for the additional speed and density. The user must determine, based upon his needs, what is required to most effectively process the available data. The access times and transfer rates given were by no means the highest that are now available. *The ranges were given to once again illustrate the fact that the compatibility of the system is important.* Because it is, a wide range of choices are available from most tape drive manufacturers.

TAPE REVIEW

5–25. Does it cost more or less to store data on tape today than it did five years ago?

5–26. How is tape density measured?

5–27. How many bytes per inch can be recorded on the highest density tape listed in the text?

5–28. To determine how much data can be stored on a reel of tape, is it only necessary to consider the density?

5–29. What are the two major advantages of blocking tape records rather than reading each record individually?

5–30. Is seven- or nine-channel tape used more frequently?

5–31. As the tape is being written, what happens if data is not correctly recorded on the tape?

5–32. In reading tape, how is the access time measured?

5–33. How is the transfer rate of tape usually measured?

5–34. What is a millisecond?

CONVERTING CARDS TO TAPE

Converting cards to tape is one method of initially recording information on the magnetic tape. Until 1965 it was the only method that could be used!

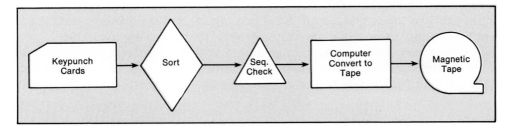

FIGURE 5–10. FIRST METHOD USED FOR CREATING AN INPUT TAPE

If tapes were created for computer input, the method illustrated in figure 5–10 was usually used.

In the method illustrated in figure 5–10, why are the cards sorted and sequence checked before they are converted to tape? Tape can only be processed *sequentially* which is the major disadvantage in the use of tape. Since the record sequence is a vital factor in the tape being processed correctly, it is essential that the tape records are either in correct ascending or descending order.

As computers became faster, tape could also be processed more rapidly, and utility programs were developed which made it easy to sort tapes into the desired sequence. The method shown in figure 5–11 was then utilized for the creation of tapes from cards. Step 1 reads the cards and transfers the data onto magnetic tape. In step 2 the output is sorted to the desired sequence. The

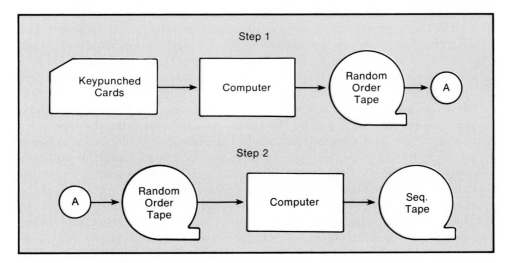

FIGURE 5–11. CONVERSION TO TAPE

tape sort in figure 5–11 is oversimplified as usually four tape drives (two for input and two for output) are utilized in a tape sort. Less drives can be used but the sorting process is more efficient when four tapes are available.

It was also common for an installation with a large computer to utilize a small computer for the conversion of cards to tape. The tapes were then used as input for the larger, faster computers.

KEY-TO-TAPE

In 1965 Mohawk Data Sciences Corporation introduced a data-recorder that made it possible to key information directly onto magnetic tape. The keyboard has the same basic arrangement of keys as the keypunch. Therefore, the right hand is used for recording all numeric data. The data-recorder can operate in three different modes:

1. *Entry Mode.* The data is entered into the memory of the data-recorder by the operator who keys in the information from the source document. The machine may be programmed to shift, duplicate, and skip automatically. When all of the information has been recorded from the document, the information is written on the tape. Since the data is stored in a buffer, sensed errors may be corrected. After the information is written on the tape, each bit is compared back with what is in the memory of the machine to make certain that the information was correctly recorded on the tape. An error light will come on if any difference is found. The time required to write, read, and compare the record of information is 150 milliseconds.
2. *Verify Mode.* The operator keys in the data from the source document and each character entered is compared with the information which was read into the memory of the machine from the tape. If the operator keys in a different character than the one that is in the memory, the error light will come on. When this occurs, the operator must check to make certain that what was keyed in was correct. If so, by following the correct procedure, the error may be corrected by the operator who is verifying the tape.
3. *Search Mode.* The tape is positioned at the beginning and an identifier is keyed in by the operator. The records are then read from the tape and compared with the identifier until a match is found. In search mode the data-recorder will read and compare 1,100 records per minute. When the match is found, the record may be corrected by the operator.

The 6400 Data-Recorder records the information on nine-channel tape at a density of 800 BPI and the record size is always 100 characters with a .6-inch interrecord gap. Model 1100 has essentially the same features but uses seven-channel tape and the data is recorded at a density of 200 BPI.

FIGURE 5–12. KEY TO TAPE DATA-RECORDER (Courtesy of Mohawk Data Sciences Corporation)

Although there are many advantages in recording the information directly on tape, the biggest advantage is that the conversion of cards to tape is eliminated. After the information is recorded on the tape it may be sorted by the computer into any desired sequence. In addition, although cards are relatively cheap, the expense of cards is eliminated. As with an audio tape recorder, magnetic tape used in data processing can be reused many times.

Mohawk Data Sciences had the field of key-to-tape data recording to themselves until 1968 when Honeywell also began to manufacture equipment that could record information directly on magnetic tape. Since that time, the key-to-tape market has expanded rapidly and there are now many different kinds of equipment available from a large number of manufacturers.

Other Approaches to Key-to-Tape

In some installations the first operator keys the information directly onto a mini-reel of tape while a second operator verifies the recorded data as it is

FIGURE 5–13. 2400 KEY-DISPLAY SYSTEM. (Courtesy of Mohawk Data Science Corporation)

being transmitted to a centralized tape. Several recording and verifying units can be utilized under the direction of a controller which will "pool" the data onto one large reel of tape.

Other systems place the entire responsibility for the accuracy of the data on one operator who keys the information from the source document into a buffer and then immediately verifies the data. If corrections are needed, they can be made as the data is verified. The verification can be done either by rekeying the data from the source document or by a visual method. In the visual method data is displayed on a video picture tube which is identical in appearance to a television picture tube. The display unit is generally referred to as a *CRT* or *cathode ray tube*. The operator checks the accuracy of the keyed data by comparing the displayed information with the source document. The advocates of this system, which places the responsibility for accurate data solely with one operator, feel that it is faster and more accurate because only one person is required to handle the documents. Studies have been made which indicate that the operator who keys the data originally is no more likely to repeat the same error or transposition than would a second operator. When one operator does both the recording and the verification, it is the specific responsibility of the *one* individual to correctly interpret doubtful characters.

Key–Display System

It is also possible to key in data, have it edited, processed by other offline peripheral equipment, and also recorded on magnetic tape. The Mohawk 2400 Key–Display System has this capability. The tape can be used as a storage media or as computer input to produce additional reports. A system such as this might record the variable information from the sales order into the system by using a keyboard similar to a typewriter. The operator verifies the data by referring to the CRT. The constant information, such as the customer's name and address, may be available from a magnetic disk file that can be accessed randomly. An offline printer can print the sales invoices as the recording operation is occurring. The variable data, along with the selected fixed information supplied by the magnetic disk, will be written on a tape for additional processing by the computer.

Editing functions and batch control totals can be done since the "controller" of the entire operation is actually a minicomputer that is dedicated to certain specified functions. The system may be designed to provide the editing and checking functions as well as to establish batch totals on certain fields of information. How systems such as these operate and what peripheral equipment is attached depends upon the jobs that are assigned to the equipment. The system may use only *one* keyboard station or *many* stations. A large multipurpose peripheral system, with many stations, may provide for keyboard entry, editing, sorting, printing, verifying, and then rewriting and consolidating the information on either tape or disk.

The data recorded by the 2400 system may also be communicated directly to a remote computer. The obvious advantage of such a system is that the data can be edited, checked, and condensed as the input is being prepared. Also, some of the more routine processing functions such as preparing and printing the sales invoices, can be done offline. This saves valuable CPU time for the more complex processing functions.

At one time magnetic tape was assumed to be a reel containing approximately 2,400 feet of tape. "Mini" reels are now also widely used. In addition, tape cassettes are also available for use in both recording and processing of information. The cassettes are convenient because they are easy to handle and store. It is anticipated that cassettes will be more widely used as more applications are assigned to the *dedicated* minicomputer. Dedicated is used to imply that the computer, which has a relatively small amount of memory, is assigned one specific task.

To summarize, the three basic methods of preparing magnetic tapes for input or storage of data are:

1. Conversion of data punched in cards to magnetic tape.
2. Stand-alone key-to-tape recorders. The data can be verified by either re-keying the information or by visually checking the displayed data on a CRT.
3. Key processing systems that can have one or more keyboard entry stations. The specialized functions that may be done such as editing and checking the validity of certain data fields are controlled by a minicomputer.

MORE QUESTIONS ABOUT TAPE

5–35. Does a reel of magnetic tape always contain approximately 2,400 feet?
5–36. How is tape processed?
5–37. What general type of program is used for most tape sorts?
5–38. Why are tapes sorted?
5–39. How many tape drives are utilized when sorting a tape?
5–40. When was a key-to-tape recorder first available?
5–41. What is a CRT?
5–42. How can a CRT be used in the verification of data?
5–43. Discuss the following statement. All people involved in data processing agree that one person should record the data and the second person should verify the data.
5–44. What additional functions can be done if a key processing system is used to record data rather than a stand-alone key-to-tape data recorder?
5–45. What is the "search mode" which is available on most key-to-tape data recorders?

TAPE HANDLING

The newer tape drives are designed to make the loading of tapes much easier since it is no longer necessary for the operator to thread the tape or follow complex instructions. In the newer models the operator mounts the tape reel, pushes a button, the reel latches, the window closes, and the tape threads automatically (see fig. 5–14). The automatic threading has not only made it much easier for the operator but has also decreased some of the prob-

FIGURE 5–14. STUDENT MOUNTING A TAPE ON AN IBM 3310 TAPE DRIVE

lems that were caused by improper tape handling. Accumulated data has indicated that less than 20% of all tapes actually wear out from normal machine use. Mishandling and improper storage account for most of the computer tape failures. When tape dropout (loss of data on the tape) occurs, the file must be rewritten. Tape can be tested to determine if it is reliable enough to use for recording and storing information.

Tape should be stored in dust-proof containers in an area where both the temperature and humidity are controlled. The tape is placed in the containers by holding the hub, or center, of the tape reel. The operator should not touch the tape or permit it to come in contact with any area which might cause the tape to pick up particles of dust or other foreign matter.

TAPE LABELS

An *external label* is attached to the container so that the operator can easily identify the tape. Sometimes the label is large enough to contain the history of the file—when it was used and by whom. When tapes were first used by computers as an I/O media, they were labeled only on the outside of the container. If the wrong container was used or the tape incorrectly labeled, the possibility existed that it could accidentally be destroyed. Tape had not been used for very long before it was decided that an *internal label* should be written on the tape.

Internal tape labels are created differently depending upon the computer that is used. It is the *software* provided by the computer manufacturer, however, that usually takes care of both the writing and checking of the labels. The label information is supplied by the programmer either as part of his actual program or by the *job control cards* that are required to run the program. The label usually contains the name of the file such as "Payroll Master File" or "Student Accounting Master File." The creation date and expiration date are also written on the tape as part of the label information. Tape may not be used for output until *after* the file's expiration date. If an operator attempts to do so, an error message is provided which serves as a warning. The exact label information that is required and the format in which it must be supplied depends upon the computer system being used. The three most common items used on tape labels are (1) name of the file, (2) creation date, and (3) expiration date.

WRITING AN OUTPUT TAPE

When a new tape is written as output, a tape is placed on the drive that has been assigned to the output file. The tape can either be a new tape, which has no information recorded on it, or a tape which has obsolete data which will be destroyed as the new file is written. As another protective feature, a file ring is used if a tape can be written on as an output file. The ring is generally a bright color such as yellow, green, or red and is attached to the outside of the reel of tape. It is easy to remember—*no ring, no write.* If a tape which is stored does not have a ring it must *not* be used as an output tape since the file contains data that is to be retained.

When the output tape file is mounted by the operator, it is automatically positioned in the location where data can be written. This location is found by the photoelectric cells in the tape unit which look for the *load point,* a reflective spot located 12 to 15 feet from the beginning of the tape. When the load point is found, the *header label* is written on the tape. As processing occurs each *block* of information is written on the tape followed by the required IRG. When the job ends, the *trailer label,* which is usually identical to the header label, is written on the tape. A tape has a label on both ends since it is possible, on most drives, to read tape either frontwards or backwards. If the tape is processed backwards, the trailer label can be checked to make certain that the right tape is mounted. Since the programmer can generally specify if the tape is to be rewound or not, time can be saved if it is not rewound and then processed backwards. The way in which the input tape is to be processed determines if it is wise to attempt to process it backwards.

At a point approximately 14 feet from the end of the tape is an end-of-tape mark which when sensed notifies the system that the physical end of the usable portion of the tape has been found. If this occurs before all of the records have been written on the output tape, there is still room for the trailer label to be written. The file would then be closed, and the reel of tape may or may not be automatically rewound. The rest of the records in the file would be written on a second reel of tape. As part of the label information, a volume number would be used so that the reels of tape would be processed in the correct sequence. As the output tapes are removed from the tape drive, the protective file ring is removed, an external label is placed on the container in which the tape is placed, and the tape is stored.

READING AN INPUT TAPE

When the tape is used as input, the label information written on the tape is checked by the computer system against the information supplied in the program that is utilizing the file. Is it the right input tape? If the program or job control cards indicate that the label should read "Student Master File" and the label on the tape is "Payroll Master File" the operator will receive an error message on the console. The message, which is identified by a number, might read "wrong tape mounted." If the operator is not sure of what he must do (first day on the job), he may look up the message in the operator's guide. It usually explains the message and tells how to respond to continue the job. Some systems may print a message and automatically cancel the job rather than waiting for the operator to respond to the message.

STORING TAPE

It is the responsibility of the data processing operations manager to make certain that the tape is handled and stored properly. Due to its high recording density, dust and dirt are probably a tape's worst enemies. The general condition in regard to cleanliness of the data processing center will have an effect on how successfully the tape is processed. Regardless of how tape is prepared, the cost of replacing the data would be expensive if the tape is accidently destroyed or damaged.

If the tape is a master file that is constantly updated it would be even more costly if the tape had to be replaced. For this reason the systems analyst and manager work out a method of maintaining "backup" files. As a few typical jobs are explained the security or backup method will also be covered.

REVIEW QUESTIONS

5–46. Is it as difficult today to mount a reel of tape as it was several years ago?
5–47. What is tape "dropout"?
5–48. Although the internal tape labels can vary from one system to another, what are three factors that are usually included in the label?
5–49. What does the file protection ring tell the operator?
5–50. Why are both header and trailer labels written on the tape?

TYPICAL TAPE APPLICATIONS

A system flowchart for a typical application using magnetic tape is illustrated in figure 5–15. Since tape can only be processed sequentially, both the student master file and the current grade file must be in the same sequence. The logical sequence for the records on the tape would be by student number.

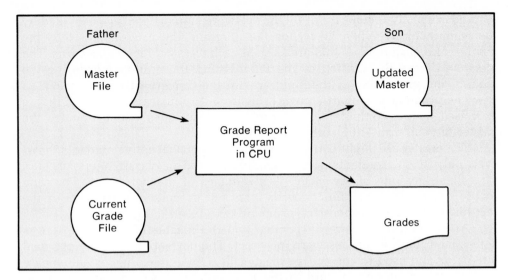

FIGURE 5-15. STUDENT GRADE REPORTS—TAPE SYSTEM

The master file contains the records for all of the students whose files are considered to be active and contains a great deal of information about each student. The data in the file is continually being updated by adding new information and correcting invalid or obsolete data.

The current grade file was created by a key-to-tape method, using the grade sheets as the source document. The records were then sequenced by student number.

Both a current file record and a master file record are read by the program into the computer. A comparison is then made in the logic unit of the CPU. If the two numbers are equal, a series of commands will be executed which will update the credits and honor points, record the new grade for the courses, and calculate a new grade point average. The information is updated in the memory of the computer, written out on a new master tape, and the student's grade report is printed before the program control branches to where the command to read a new current file is stored.

If the student number from the current grade file is not the same as the student number from the master tape, a command is executed which will write the master file on the new master tape exactly as it was read into memory. No grade report will be printed. A new master file will be read, and again in the logic unit of the CPU the numbers are compared to determine which series of commands are to be executed. If the records were blocked, the entire block, or physical record, is read into storage at one time. Each *logical record* (an individual record) is processed one at a time since the unblocking of the records is usually taken care of by the software support package provided by the manufacturer. When he writes the program, the programmer tells the number of *logical* records that are to be in each *physical* block of records. The blocking during the writing of the records and the unblocking during the reading and processing of the input are not the concern of the programmer.

The program flowchart shown in figure 5–16 illustrates the logic that is exercised by the computer in processing the tape files which updates the master file and prints the students' grades.

The master file might contain the records of 50,000 active students; however, only 10,000 students were actually enrolled in classes this semester. This illustrates one of the basic disadvantages of magnetic tape. For each record processed, four other records were not processed. Only 20% of the records read had any processing or updating of information.

After the grades were all printed and the master file updated, it was determined that five grades were incorrect. The corrections will be punched into cards and used to correct the master file. Obviously, the corrections are costly because only one record in 10,000 is updated. To help solve the problem, corrections and changes to the master file can be *batched* and processed all at one time.

Figure 5–15 (p. 279), the input master file, was labeled "father" and the output master file, "son." The "son" tape contains the updated current information and will be the tape that future reports are written from. The "father" is retained as a *backup tape*. If the new master, or "son," tape is destroyed, the "father" would then be used to recreate a new master tape. The grade report program would also need to be rerun since it is responsible for updating the new master file. The grades would not be printed because an option could be specified by the computer operator not to print during this particular computer run. Any other corrections or changes to the master file, which had been made since the grades were processed, would also have to be rerun.

For security reasons, the "father" and "son" tapes should not be stored in the same physical location. In some applications which involve frequent updating of the master file, the "son, father, and grandfather" are all retained. Another solution to the security problem is to copy the "son" tape after it is written and keep the copy of the updated master copy as a backup. In some of the more security-minded companies, the backup tapes may be stored in a bank vault rented for this purpose.

Are the Devices Compatible?

Study figure 5–16 and see if there is anything wrong with the basic configuration used for the job described. Magnetic tape input is used for both the

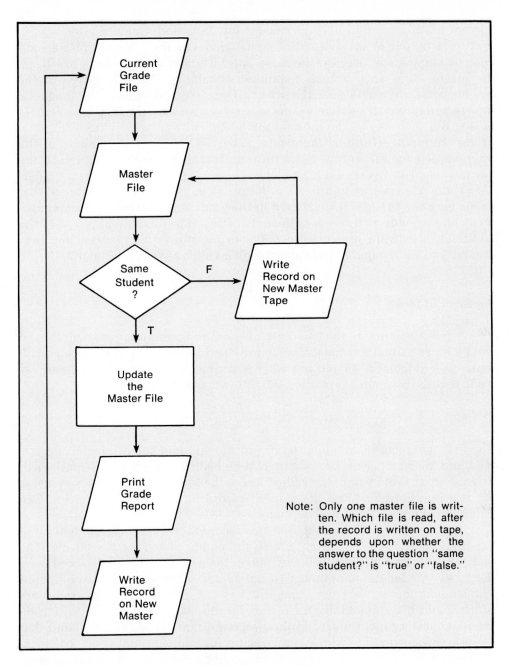

Note: Only one master file is written. Which file is read, after the record is written on tape, depends upon whether the answer to the question "same student?" is "true" or "false."

FIGURE 5–16. STUDENT GRADE REPORT—TAPE SYSTEM

current file information and the master file data, and a new master tape is written as output. What about printing the grades on the printer? Since a good deal of skipping is required because special grade report forms are used, the printer does not reach its maximum capability. Does the speed of the printer come anywhere near the speed of reading and writing the magnetic tape records? Even if relatively slow tape drives were used with a tape density of 800 BPI, it could be determined mathematically to what extent the tape drives were outperforming the printer. The CPU is idle a good share of the time waiting for the output to be printed. In some installations, due to the hardware and software that is available, there is no other way to print grades.

There are several solutions to the problem of the lack of balance that exists between the I/O devices used in the grade report application. Management must decide if there is sufficient justification for obtaining either the additional hardware or software that can be utilized to increase the productivity of the computer and solve problems such as the one illustrated.

An Error in Logic

A point was made that, as part of good programming practice, the "it can't happen" situations must also be provided for. In view of this statement, look again at figure 5–16 and see what is wrong. As you follow the logic, assume that the computer is reading the following records:

Current Grade File: 10, 20, 30, 35 . . .
Master File: 05, 10, 20, 21, 35 . . .

The first two records, number 10 current file and number 05 master file, are read into the memory of the computer. Which student record, or records, will be read next? From what file or files? Trace the logic of the program by using the program flowchart and the student record numbers that are given. Can you find the error? What will happen?

Need some help? When the first two records were read, the student number from the current file did not match the number from the master file. The record for student number 05 is written on the new tape, and the record from the master file for student number 10 is read into the memory of the computer. The student numbers are the same, the master file is updated, the grades are printed, and the updated master record for student number 10 is written on the new master tape. Control of the program branches to the command that reads a new current file which is the record for student number 20. The master file (20) is also read; and since the student numbers match, the same commands for updating the record and printing the grades are followed again. The current file read is for student number 30 while the master file is for student 21. The student numbers are not the same, so record 21 is written on the output tape and the record for student 35 is read and compared with the current file student number of 30. Will any more current file records be read? *No!* Nevertheless, the entire master file will be read and each record rewritten on the new master tape. The computer's time is being wasted because the entire job will have to be rerun after the master file is corrected to include the record for student number 30.

One more simple step in the program flowchart would have solved the problem and provided for the "but every student must have a master file" or "it can't happen" situation. Figure 5–17 shows where the additional step would be included.

This illustration also shows a common technique that can be used in "desk checking programs." After the program flowchart is constructed, test

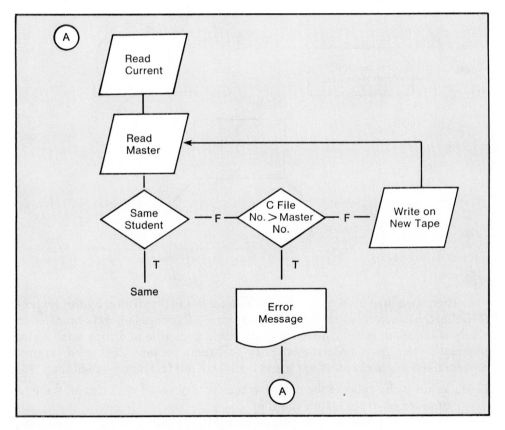

FIGURE 5–17. NECESSARY ADDITION TO THE PROGRAM LOGIC

data should be made up and the logic of the diagram followed as if the computer were processing the data. Doing this will help the programmer to find simple errors in logic that may have been overlooked. *Every programmer sooner or later plays the game of being the computer and processing data!*

STOP AND THINK

A master file which is maintained on tape contains records for 25,000 customers of a large department store. Each day the tape is updated to add the current charge sales to the customer's account. In the same procedure the amount that the customer paid on his account is subtracted from the balance due. Each day approximately 2,500 customers either charge items to their account or make payments.

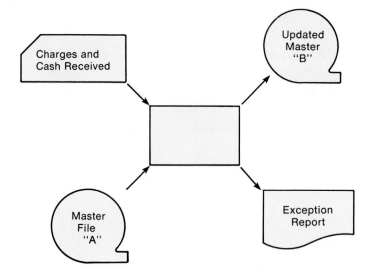

The procedure used to update the master file is illustrated by the *systems flowchart*. Management is trying to find ways of processing data more effectively since there is very little computer time available and they wish to implement several new procedures. They feel their present CPU is adequate if it were used more effectively. Can you answer the following questions:

5–51. What is the ratio of the active accounts processed each day to the total number of accounts on the file?

5–52. Could computer time be gained by updating the master file three times per week rather than six times per week?

5–53. What would be the best way to conserve computer time?

5–54. The exception report is used as follows: when a customer tries to use his charge account, the clerk calls and the exception report is referred to. What does it contain? When the update job is run only 1 to 2% of the customers' names will appear on the report.

5–55. Will running the update job only three days a week affect the validity of the exception report?

5–56. Discuss. Each day, as the new tape ("B") is written, the old tape ("A") is immediately made available as an output tape. Is this a good practice?

5–57. Why does a totally new master file need to be written?

5–58. If the job were revised and tape was used rather than the punched card input, would you recommend the elimination of the exception report?

5–59. Would there ever be a case when there was a card for a customer but no master file? What could be the problem?

5–60. Other than processing charges and cash receipts, what other changes would have to be made to the master file as part of the normal maintenance? (Assume that the file has only the customer's name, address, credit limit, balance, and number.)

THE SALES INVOICING PROCEDURE USING TAPE

When a computerized card method was used, there was still a great deal of card handling. The processing of the data was several times faster than when unit-record equipment was utilized, but the inventory was still updated as a separate procedure. Master cards were used for both the name and address of the customer and for determining the current prices and descriptions of the products. A manual check was still made to determine if the customer had a good credit rating or if he had overextended his credit.

If tapes are used, the entire procedure can be done faster with far more effective utilization of the computer. Assume that the system is still relatively small and key-to-tape equipment is not available. The cards are punched from the sales orders and are used in a procedure which now can be computerized. The credit of each customer is checked against his tape master file record to determine if the order can be processed or not.

Figure 5–18 illustrates the credit check procedure which is far faster than the previous manual method. It is also more accurate since it utilizes the master file account balances which are updated each day.

The sales invoice card contains the same data as was used for the card system. The sales order is keyed into the card in order that the card can be related back to the source document. In addition, this number can now be printed at the top of the sales invoices rather than using prenumbered forms. Now all three items—card, sales order, and sales invoice—have the same order number to use in auditing or checking the transaction.

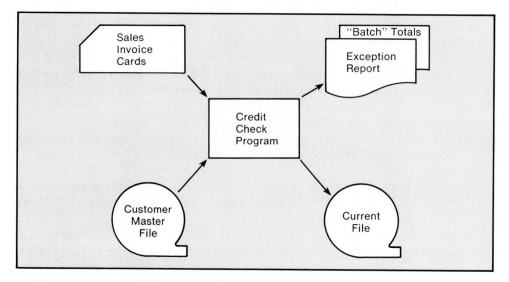

FIGURE 5–18. CREDIT CHECK AND EXCEPTION REPORT

The exception report shown in Figure 5–18 provides both a listing of new customers not yet added to the master file and old customers who have exceeded their credit limit. The amount of credit that each customer may have is established by the credit department and is one of the fields of data in the customer's master file. If the credit manager feels that additional credit should be extended, the order will be processed with the following day's "batch." The control total based on quantity is adjusted for the orders that are delayed due to referring some of the orders to the credit department.

Why was only an exception report printed? Since the credit manager is not concerned with the majority of the customers who do have sufficient credit to process their orders, the exception report saves the manager time and effort as he only needs to review the "exceptions."

Control Totals

A batch control total on quantity had been established by the sales department as they audited or checked the incoming orders to make certain that they were ready for keypunching. The control total is adjusted for the total quantity ordered by customers whose orders were sent to the credit department. The quantity total printed for the orders which can be processed is checked with the sales department's adjusted total. *The totals must agree!* Further processing of the current file is delayed until the two totals do agree.

The Current Tape File

Since the data on the sales invoice cards is now a part of the current file, the cards will probably not be used again. The tape contains all of the information from the cards *plus* some of the data from the customer's tape master file.

Other Considerations

In both the unit-record card system and the computer system which used only cards and the printer as the I/O media, a number of factors were ignored in order to keep the illustration as simple as possible.

1. How would the problem of one customer having two orders in the same day be handled? Keep in mind only one set of master cards was used during the match-merge operation.
2. How should the problem of having both a billing and shipping address be handled? One customer might have a billing address and several different shipping addresses.
3. How could the salesman's name be printed on the sales invoice? One salesman could have hundreds of different customers.

The three problems listed above must, of course, be handled in the unit-record and computer card system. The problems can, however, be solved much more easily when tape or disk is available. The salesman's name, as well as the shipping and billing addresses, can be maintained on the master tape since the record is not limited to 80 bytes of data. In addition, a credit history can also be included in each customer's tape record. Although the amount of data that can be recorded on tape is almost unlimited, the larger the record the longer it takes to process the file. The use of the tape must be carefully considered when determining what data is to be transferred from the master file to the current file. In this case, however, the tape is used only in the next operation and then replaced by a more complete current file tape which will contain all of the data needed for the invoicing operation as well as other related procedures.

INVENTORY UPDATE AND COMPLETION OF THE CURRENT FILE

The update procedure replaces step one which was used in the computer card system (see fig. 5–19). Several things are consolidated into the one update operation.

1. The current file is completed by adding the price and description from the inventory master file.
2. A check is made to determine if the item ordered is in stock or not. If not, a backorder file is created and the information pertaining to the inventory item is listed on the exception report.
3. If the item is available for shipment, the quantity on hand in the master file is decreased before the record is written on the new master file tape.

Since tape can only be processed sequentially, the current file input tape must be in the same sequence as the inventory master input tape. Therefore, the tape was sorted by item number before the update program was run.

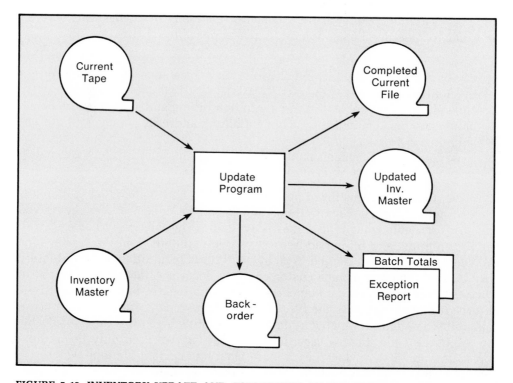

FIGURE 5–19. INVENTORY UPDATE AND COMPLETION OF THE CURRENT FILE

Program Logic

The logic of the program is the same as that expressed in the student grade report application.

1. The actual processing of data occurs when the item number is the same on both the current file and the master file.
2. If there is only a master file and no current file, the master file is written on the new tape exactly as it entered the memory of the computer.

This problem involves far more logic than the student grade report since there may be more than one current file for an inventory master file record. Programming checks would need to be added to the program to make certain that each current file actually has a corresponding master file.

Inventory Exception Report

The exception report lists the items which are either out of stock or below the *reorder point*. The reorder point is determined by the purchasing department which studies accumulated data. Data looked at are (1) how long it takes to get a shipment when the item is reordered; (2) the number of different suppliers that are available; (3) where they are located; (4) the quantity that should be reordered at one time; (5) the quantity that is normally sold in a given period of time; and (6) how stable the sales are for the particular item. Once all of the data is accumulated, the computer can be used to calculate the reorder point for the purchasing department. The reorder point for each product is then reviewed by the purchasing department, perhaps adjusted, and then made a part of the data in the master file.

Checking Control Totals

The totals printed at the end of the job would be checked back with the previous total taken. The total from the credit check program would need to be adjusted for the items that were backordered before it could be compared with the new total. The new total and the adjusted total must agree.

Far more is accomplished in the computerized tape system in a fraction of the time that was required for the unit-record method. Compare figure 5–19 (p. 288) with step one of the unit-record system. The sales invoicing procedure also is a good illustration of the fact that when large master files are available, some of the procedures can be merged together into one operation. Step one of the card system only completed the card. The tape procedure not only performed that function by completing the record and writing a new current tape, but also consolidated the inventory item check and update into the same procedure.

The discussion of batch totals relates back to a point covered earlier, which should be considered again. A system such as the sales system is made up of many procedures. Each procedure should be checked for accuracy before the next step is performed. If not, errors can compound to the point where it takes a great deal of time and effort to make the corrections. These changes may involve recreating and correcting the files and possible rerunning several of the applications. The more integrated the systems become, the more necessary it is to incorporate as many *controls* or checks as possible.

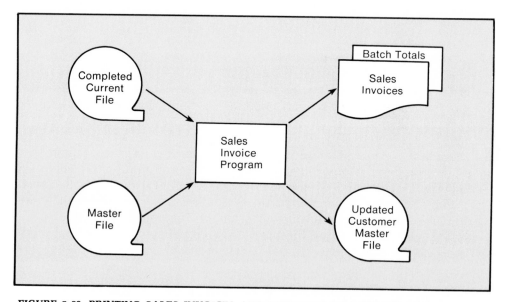

FIGURE 5–20. PRINTING SALES INVOICES AND UPDATING THE MASTER FILE

The output current file from figure 5–19 is first sorted in one operation by customer number and order number. Several tapes can be merged into one file as they can be sorted on one or more control fields.

The sales order number is printed on the invoice as a means of "linking" the invoice with both the order and the current file. If one customer has several orders, each order will print on a separate invoice. A control total is accumulated and printed at the end of the job to check with the total taken, both on quantity and dollars, in the procedure illustrated in figure 5–19. At the same time the customer's master file is updated to include the information from the current transaction. Probably what is added to the file is the date of the order, the total amount due, and the order number.

COMPARING THE CARD AND TAPE INVOICING METHODS

5–61. What manual step was eliminated?

5–62. What two procedures are combined in figure 5–20?

5–63. What are the advantages of printing exception reports rather than a complete report each day of all inventory balances?

5–64. Discuss the statement: batch totals or controls are not as important when the procedures become more sophisticated and use larger master files and integrate several procedures into one application.

5–65. What is the value in using the order number as the invoice number?

5–66. When unit-record equipment was used to prepare the sales invoices, the final step was to compare the sales order and the sales invoice as they are filed. Is there value in still doing this in the computerized tape system?

SUMMARY OF MAGNETIC TAPE

Magnetic tape can be used effectively as input, output, and as an effective storage media since one reel of tape has the capacity of storing thousands of cards. Since the cost of a reel of tape is relatively inexpensive, the cost per unit of information stored on the tape is very low. Recording data on tape is approximately one-tenth of the cost of recording the same amount of data in cards. With the increased density of tape and the price of tape going down, while the cost of cards is increasing, the one-tenth is a very conservative figure.

Tape in some medium- and large-scale computer systems is the fastest form of direct input and output equipment that is available to the system. The tape label and file protection ring make it impossible to destroy a tape by writing over it *without* the operator being aware that it is occurring. Since tape is relatively cheap and can be copied rapidly, it can and should be frequently duplicated and stored as backup. When disk is also used, the backup file is more economically stored on tape than on disk.

The standard reel tape, approximately 2,400 feet in length and one-half inch wide, can be written on by one tape system and utilized by another system. It can be mailed easily from one installation to another as special containers, made to protect the tape while in flight, are available. Some governmental reports can be submitted directly on tape rather than in printed form saving the computer's time as well as the expense of the paper. When this is done, the BPI and number of channels are specified by the governmental agency which will receive the report.

Tape can be prepared in a number of ways. Provision is usually made for correction of the tape if an error is sensed during the recording of the data.

The major disadvantage of tape is that it must still be accessed sequentially. If a record in the middle of a reel of tape is to be corrected, the entire file must be read and rewritten. Heat, humidity, and dust can all create problems that will cause the tape to be unreliable. It is important that the storage and processing areas are clean and that the operator is instructed on the handling, care, and external labeling of tapes. The use of tape cartridges can eliminate some of the tape handling hazards.

Since the advantages far outnumber the disadvantages, it is anticipated that tape will continue to be widely used for applications which utilize files sequentially and require little maintenance. Also, tape will continue to be used to backup both tape and disk files.

In designing their newest tape and disk drives, IBM made the two compatible so that the access time and the data transfer time would be the same for both devices. The user can use both tape and disk in the same application without being concerned that one device, which might be slower, is holding back the entire system. Tape might be used for the current file, which is sequential, while disk is used for the master file, which requires frequent maintenance.

Today, in a small system which can justify only tape or disk, disk would probably be selected rather than tape. Nevertheless, in making the decision the type of applications, the capacity of the central processing unit, and the capabilities of the other peripherals would have to be considered.

RANDOM ACCESS STORAGE

Introduction

When records can be accessed randomly, there is no longer the necessity for processing the entire file in order to retrieve and utilize one record of information. The sales manager, for example, may inquire directly into the online file to determine the status of an *inventory item* or of a *customer's account*. Many of the new applications have been made possible because large amounts of data can be stored online and accessed randomly by using a variety of communication devices.

Random access storage is not new and can be provided by the following devices:

Disk drives with removable disk packs   Drums
Disk drives with nonremovable disks   Data cells

Types of Disk Storage

The most widely used random access device today are disk drives which have removable disks. Magnetic disks have the same general appearance and are approximately the same size as a long-playing stereo record. The drive may utilize a single disk or a pack which contains more than one disk. Disk storage has become very widely used in both small- and medium-sized installations. Drives which had nonremovable disks were the first type of random access auxiliary storage that was utilized. The early models, by today's standards, were exceedingly slow because one access arm with a read/write head retrieved the records from *all* of the disks. The newer nonremovable disk drives access the information far more rapidly because there are multiple read/write heads. This type of disk storage is often utilized for teleprocessing and for large data bases that provide information for numerous applications. Very large computer installation may use both the removable and the nonremovable disk drives.

Magnetic Drum Storage

Magnetic drums have been utilized as an auxiliary storage media for several years. When they were first developed they were intended to serve as a high-capacity, intermediate-access storage device and were used primarily to store data that was often referenced, such as actuarial and income-tax tables. The drums are usually considered as a temporary storage area for data that is currently being used in an application rather than as permanent storage for files. The drums are not removable and usually provide far less storage than disks. Although the speed is not as fast as when the data is accessed in the CPU, it is still generally much faster than other random access devices.

Date Cells

Data cells contain removable strips of magnetic film which are capable of storing large amounts of data which can be accessed randomly. The film is

2¼-by-13 inches and can store 200,000 bytes of data on one magnetic strip. Before a record can be accessed, the strip of film must be selected from the subcell and wrapped around a small drum. Although the average time that it takes to access a record is far greater than either disk or drums, the cells do have the capability of storing a large volume of data *economically*.

The characteristics of the disk drives and packs will be covered since they are by far the most popular of the random access devices. When disks were first utilized for random access files, it was considered a very expensive way of storing data, and only the larger installations could justify its use. In a presentation, the theme of which was "Profitability thru Productivity," IBM made the following comparisons regarding the cost of storing data on their disks.

YEAR	COST PER MILLION BYTES PER MONTH	YEAR	COST PER MILLION BYTES PER MONTH
1956	$130.00	1971	6.50– 9.00
1964	88.00	1973	5.90
1966	13.00–25.00		

It is difficult to determine if the decrease in cost is due to the increasing number of users and applications or if the reverse is true. Due to the decrease in cost, far more users can justify applications that only one or two years ago would have been considered economically unattainable.

While the costs per unit of information have decreased, the performance of the equipment has increased. More data can be accessed and stored, ready for processing, in a shorter period of time. Improvements in the equipment have permitted the density of the data on the disk to be increased, which results in far more information being stored on one disk pack.

OPERATING SYSTEM

In discussing the ways in which the disk file can be organized and accessed, it is often necessary to refer to the operating system. The operating system is defined as a "combination of hardware and software which is directly under the control of a *supervisor*, which resides permanently in the memory of the computer." Part of the software are the many routines and subprograms, generally supplied by the manufacturer, which are called into the central processing unit and executed when they are needed. Some of the routines make the utilization of the random access files possible. The *supervisor* is also called by many other names such as the executive program or monitor. Essentially, the supervisor is responsible for coordinating all of the computer's activities. The operating system also includes the use of the Job Control Language, or JCL cards, which the operator uses to communicate certain information pertaining to disk to the computer. Some reference will be made to both the operating system and the necessary JCL cards as they relate to typical disk applications.

Selection of the Disk System to Be Used

When determining which disk system should be utilized, the drives may be compared on a number of different points:

1. The time that it takes to access and then store the data in the memory of the computer. The total amount of time that it takes to read and store the data is composed of the *arm positioning time,* the *rotational delay* (latency time), and the *data transfer time.*
2. The amount of data that can be stored on one disk pack as well as the total number of drives that can be attached to the system.
3. The method that can be used to organize and access the data on the disk. This depends on both the hardware (CPU) and the software (operating system).
4. The relative cost of storing data on the various drives when all of the factors are considered. The cost of the drives and the packs, the power requirements, increased cost of software (if any), and many other factors should be carefully compared.

Because the systems that can read and store the data at the higher rates of speed are more costly, each user must determine how important the increased productivity of one system over another is to his particular situation. For example, the Univac 9480 System offers two different disk systems which the user can select from, based upon his particular needs. A few of the characteristics of the two disk systems are compared:

	8414 SYSTEM	8424 SYSTEM
Capacity per Disk Pack	29,176,000	58,350,000
Average Arm Positioning Time (in milliseconds)	60	30
Latency Time—Average (in milliseconds)	12.5	12.5
Storage Transfer Rate (bytes per second)	312,000	312,000
Disk Drive Speed	2400	2400
Number of Disks per Pack	11	11

The specifications described are typical of the systems utilized by many of the users today, although there are both faster and slower systems on the market. For example, IBM's 3340 Disk System (see figure 5–21) has a data transfer rate of 1.25 million bytes per second in contrast to the 312,000 bytes per second listed for the 8414. The Univac 8414 lists an *average* access time of 72.5 milliseconds, while the IBM 5444 Model 2, designed for the System/3 Model 6, indicates an average access time of 269 milliseconds.

FIGURE 5–21. IBM 3340 DISK DRIVES. (Courtesy of International Business Machines Corporation.)

The IBM 3340 disks, which can contain either 35 or 70 million bytes of data depending upon which option is selected by the user, have their own access arms and read/write heads. The disk pack then becomes a *unit* and each file is always read by the same read/write head which originally created the data.

Perhaps one of the more interesting trends in regard to characteristics of the new disk systems is that although there have been faster and larger capacity systems announced, there also have been more new systems for the smaller user. *The small user was apparently overlooked for too long a time!*

Disk Organization

Figure 5–22 shows how the disk pack is divided into cylinders and tracks. The tracks are the recording surfaces of the cylinder and are numbered from 00 to 09. A cylinder of data is the amount that is accessible with one positioning of the access mechanism. This is an important concept since the movement of the access mechanism represents a significant portion of the time required to seek and transfer the data into the CPU. All ten read/write heads move in and out together, always accessing the same cylinder. Each is on a different track at any one point.

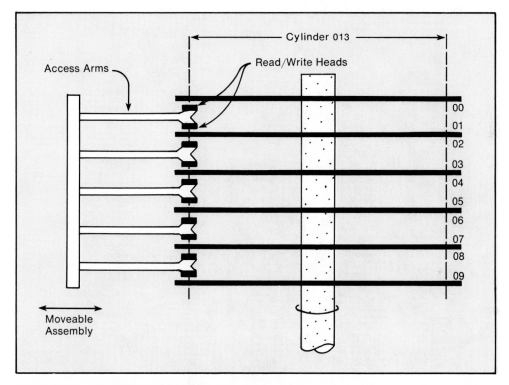

FIGURE 5–22. DISK ORGANIZATION

The arm positioning time referred to is the length of time that it takes to position the arm so that the read/write head can read the record. A minimum and maximum, as well as the average, time is usually listed, because the time that is required depends upon the distance the access arm has to travel. After the arm is positioned, it must wait until the disk revolves around so that the data can be read. This waiting to read the data as it passes by at 2,400 rpm is what is referred to as the latency or rotational delay time. It resembles catching the ring while riding the merry-go-round! The disk, however, is revolving somewhat faster and the reading of the records is accomplished much more accurately than "catching the ring."

Although the pack illustrated has six disks, only ten of the recording surfaces are utilized. One head on the access arm reads the lower surface of the disk while the other reads the upper surface of the disk.

The 2311 Disk Pack, illustrated in figure 5–23, is divided into 203 cylinders, each of which has ten tracks or recording surfaces and is capable of storing 7.25 million characters of information. That much data, however, is not actually stored on the pack for a number of reasons. One cylinder is re-

FIGURE 5–23. STUDENT CHANGING IBM 2311 DISK PACK

served for the VTOC (volume table of contents) for the pack, and three cylinders are usually reserved for "bad tracks."

When data is written on the disk, it is checked to determine if it was recorded correctly. If the verification is not correct the first time, the system will try writing the record, or block, again. After a number of attempts are made, it is determined that the most probable cause of the failure to write the record successfully is that a defective track is being used. If this is the case, the block of records will automatically be written on one of the cylinders provided for this purpose. The new location for the record will be kept track of by the system, regardless of how the file is organized, so that the records can be retrieved.

RANDOM ACCESS QUESTIONS

5–67. What are the four types of storage devices that are used for files which are to be accessed randomly?

5–68. Which one of the four types is the fastest method of randomly accessing data?

5–69. Which method is usually considered the slowest, yet is one of the most economical methods of storing data so that it can be accessed randomly?

5–70. What is the advantage of random access files over sequential files?

5–71. Discuss the statement: the cost of storing data on random access files has increased only slightly in the past ten years.

5–72. Do all of the disk drives with the removable disk packs transfer and access data at approximately the same speed?

5–73. The disk pack described had how many cylinders and tracks?

5–74. What is a cylinder?

5–75. Why is the amount of arm movement an important factor?

5–76. Give two reasons why the entire 203 cylinders on the pack cannot be used to store data.

DETERMINING HOW THE FILE SHOULD BE ORGANIZED

The way in which the file is to be utilized after the file is created should determine the best way to organize the file. There are three basic methods that may be used: indexed-sequential, sequential, and direct. The operating systems of some of the smaller disk systems, however, may not support the indexed-sequential method.

Indexed-Sequential Organization

The indexed-sequential method provides the most flexibility, but the user "pays" for it by not being able to store as much data in the file. In addition, the access or retrieval time is slower since a record which is to be processed must first be looked up in the index to determine on which cylinder and track it is located. For example, the record for student number 999 is to be updated because she dropped Drafting 101. The student number is the key. The system looks up 999 in the index and determines that the record's address is 0120407 —cylinder 12, track 4, record 7. In some systems, the record location is determined from a separate index which is on the track. When processing blocked records, the entire block of records is brought into the computer's memory, even if only one of the records is to be processed. This may seem like an uneconomical use of the computer's memory, but once the decision is made to block the records, all future applications for that file will have blocked records. Once a file is created, the organization and blocking factor remain the same unless the file is recreated.

Each time the file is used as either an input or update file, the programmer must indicate how the file is to be accessed. For example, the student's master file is created as an I-S file. Each situation requiring the use of the master file is evaluated to determine the best access method.

SITUATION	ACCESS METHOD
Corrections are to be made to a student's record for a wrong grade.	Random access.
Printing grades for all students.	Sequential access.
Print name and address stickers for all honor students. Ten percent of the students meet the requirements.	Sequential. Let the computer determine who they are!
Process the "drops" and "adds."	Random access.

When an indexed-sequential file is originally created, the data from which it is written must be in the sequence that the file is to be organized. The programmer indicates in the program that writes the new output disk file which field is to be the *key*. After the file is created, all of the records in the file are in sequence by student number and can be *accessed* either *sequentially* or *randomly.*

When the file is to be accessed *randomly,* the student number, since it is the key, must be a part of the input. Figure 5–24 indicates how the file is accessed randomly.

The drop and add cards used as input identify which student records are to be updated. After the first card is read, the index is checked to deter-

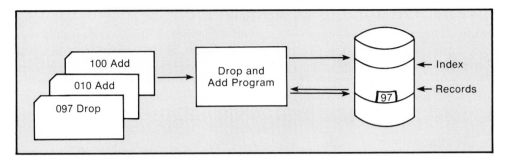

FIGURE 5-24. RANDOM UPDATE OF INDEXED-SEQUENTIAL FILE

mine where in the prime area of the file the record for student 97 is stored. The access arm is positioned, the record read, and the data is transferred into the CPU. The record is changed, or updated, in the CPU to delete the course which is indicated on the drop card. After the record is updated in memory, it is rewritten on the file in the exact location from which it had been retrieved.

Sequential Access

When the indexed-sequential file is to be accessed sequentially, processing is essentially no different than if the file were organized sequentially. In some systems the programmer may indicate which record is to be the first record processed which will permit entry into the file at that point. The rest of the file is then processed according to the sequence of the records on the file. Figure 5-25 illustrates a typical sequential application.

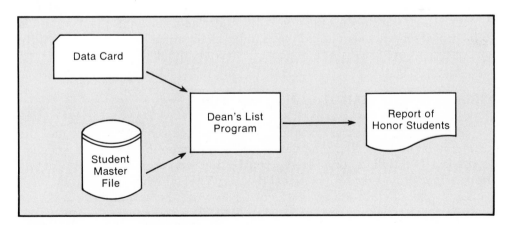

FIGURE 5-25. SEQUENTIAL ACCESS OF I-S FILE

Indexed-sequential files are well suited to applications that require the file to be accessed sometimes as a sequential file and at other times randomly. Although the I-S file is less efficient the advantage of being able to utilize the file either way offsets the disadvantages. As new records are added they are inserted automatically into the file in the correct location as the determination of where the data is to be stored is made entirely by the supportive software.

Direct Files

Direct files can only be accessed by using the *address* of the record to be processed. The address, which can be computed or entered as part of the input, must provide the cylinder, track, and record number of the record that is to be retrieved. A record can usually be retrieved faster than when I-S files are used since direct access files usually do not require the use of an index. In addition, more records can be stored on the disk since neither keys nor indexes have to be maintained on the file. Large data bases, especially those used in conjunction with terminals, are usually organized as direct files.

Sequential Files

Sequential files are essentially organized the same way as a tape file and are processed in the same sequence as they are recorded on the disk. Depending upon the operating system and the language being used, it is usually possible to start processing the file with any given record. Sequential files require less space for the same number of records because keys, or indexes, are not required. The file can also be processed faster than if it were organized as a direct or I-S file. If the disk file does not require additions and changes, and is to be processed only sequentially, it should be organized sequentially. Utility sort programs are usually available to sort sequential disk files.

CREATING AND MAINTAINING DISK FILES

When writing a direct, sequential, or indexed-sequential disk file, the system must be told where the data is to be stored on the disk pack assigned to the file. If the file is organized as an I-S file, one area is reserved for the index and another area for the actual records. The following information must usually be supplied to the system in order to write the output file:

1. The name, or serial number, of the pack that is used for the file. Whenever the pack is used as an input file the serial number is checked to make cer-

tain that the right pack is being used. If the wrong pack is mounted, the operator receives a very polite message on the console typewriter which generally reads, "wrong pack mounted."

2. The label that is to be used to identify a particular file. The label might read, "George's Test Pack" or "Student Accounting File," since each file must be provided with a unique label. The label is written internally on the pack and is used by the computer to make certain that the right file, for the application being processed, is available.

3. The area must be defined on the disk pack for the file which is being created. The cylinders and tracks that are being used for both the prime area (where the records are stored) and the index area must be specified. Before reading the file, the location specified in the VTOC is checked with the area specified by the JCL cards to make certain that the right cylinders and tracks will be used.

4. Both the file creation data and the expiration date must be defined for the system. Once the file is written, the areas specified for the file's use cannot be used for another output file until after the expiration date.

The *label* information is often provided by using the appropriate job control language cards. The information must be available for the computer to use in (1) protecting the file, (2) label checking, (3) recording the data pertaining to the file in the VTOC.

In the small- and medium-sized computer systems it is the responsibility of the data processing operations manager to provide a method for keeping track of where the files are stored on the various disk packs. For example, the inventory master file, the backorder file, and the vendor's master file are all physically on one disk pack. Each of the files is organized as an indexed-sequential file. The space on the pack may have been allocated as follows:

CONTENTS OF FILE	BEGINNING CYLINDER AND TRACK		ENDING CYLINDER AND TRACK	
VTOC	000	00	000	09
Inventory Master File				
Index	001	00	001	09
Record Storage Area	002	00	080	09
Backorder File				
Index	081	00	081	09
Record Storage Area	082	00	099	09
Vendor's Master File				
Index	100	00	100	09
Record Storage Area	101	00	120	09
Work Area	121	00	199	09
Reserved for Bad Tracks	200	00	202	09

The contents of the VTOC can be displayed at any time to determine the files that are on the pack, when they were created, how long they are to be protected, and the name (or label) of the file.

In installations which have very large scale computers and more complex operating systems, the operations manager is not concerned with where the file is actually stored. Through the JCL cards, the system is informed how much area is needed for the file, and then the actual assignment of the location on the disk is determined by the operating system.

Determining File Size

How do you determine how much space is needed for a given file? The answer to the question starts at the point where the analyst or programmer, working with the user who requested that the file be created, determines what fields of information are needed in the file. The file records are designed much like the way in which the card format was determined. Usually, some extra space is provided in order that additional data can be added to the file, because when the business expands, their data requirements change also. Although there should be room for additional fields, the record size should not be excessively large because it will decrease the number of records that can be read into memory at one time; not only will the file processing time be increased, but so will the cost of storing the data on the file.

Many of the disk systems provide for the utilization of the same eight-bit EBCDIC code as was used by both magnetic tape and the central processing unit for data storage. Numeric fields may be packed, two digits per byte, or zoned. Ideally, the records should be blocked so that an entire track can be read, or written, at one time. Packing the numeric field is another way of keeping the record smaller permitting more records to be written on one track.

Blocking Records

Once the record size is determined, a table supplied by the manufacturer can be used to find out how many records will fit on one track. If an indexed-sequential file is to be created with records that contain 400 bytes of data, the table for records with keys might indicate that the blocking factor is eight. Since each track contains 3,625 bytes of storage, you might wonder why nine records could not have been stored on the track. Certain data must be available to the operating system concerning the records stored on the disk. Since this data is usually stored in front of each disk record, not all of the bytes on the track are available for the programmer's use.

Processing Blocked Records

The programmer specified the blocking factor to be used for the file when it was created. When the file is used as input, one *physical* record, which may be a block containing eight *logical records,* is read and stored in a buffer. The logical records are then transferred, as needed for processing, into the main memory. After all eight logical records are *individually* processed, data from the second buffer is used to supply the records needed by the program. While data from the second buffer area is being processed, the first buffer receives another block of records. Both the buffering (which permits overlapping of the read, processing, and write functions) and the record blocking make the processing of the file much faster.

It has been determined, in the example cited, that the record size is 400 bytes and the blocking factor is eight. If the file is to contain records for 4,000 students, how many cylinders will be needed for the indexed-sequential file? Since there are eight records per track and ten tracks per cylinder, your first answer might be 50 cylinders.

Reserving Space for New Records

For an indexed-sequential file, 50 is *not* the correct answer because space must be reserved for adding new records. When the file is originally created, it is in sequence by the key indicated by the programmer. The key for a student file would usually be the student number. If only 50 cylinders had been provided, where would the record for a new student be recorded? When working with I-S files, the programmer determines how many tracks in each cylinder should be provided for *overflow.*

If new records are added on a regular basis, two tracks might be sufficient for overflow. If a file is very static and new records are seldom added, one overflow track might be enough. As records are added to the file, they are inserted in the right location of the appropriate track. Fortunately, the programmer and the operator need not be concerned about where the records are stored since the software which supports the I-S file organization takes complete charge of maintaining the record index. It is the operation manager's responsibility to make certain that adequate space, in terms of cylinders, is allocated for each file so that additional records may be added.

The number of cylinders required for a file is determined by the number of records that are to be added initially and the amount of activity, in terms of additions and deletions of records, that is anticipated.

File Maintenance

In the small- and medium-sized installations, it is the responsibility of the operations manager working with the analyst and programmer to provide a systematic method for the reorganization of the indexed-sequential files. The recreating of the file will bring all of the records in the overflow area back into the prime area. Figure 5–26 illustrates the two phases of the file reorganization.

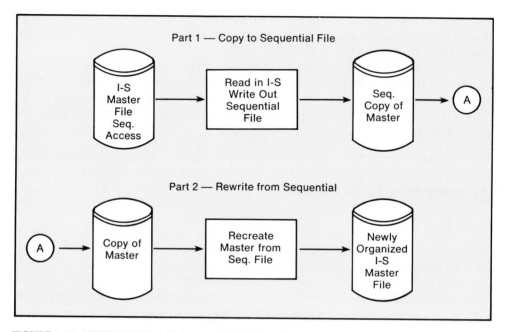

FIGURE 5–26. RECREATING AN INDEXED-SEQUENTIAL FILE

Part 1 *accesses* the indexed-sequential file sequentially and writes as output a file that is *organized* sequentially. Part 2 takes the sequential file and uses it as input to create the master file, which is again organized indexed-sequentially. If this is not done, the overflow areas will become full and a message will appear on either the console or the printer to inform the operator that no more records can be added to the file. The file must be recreated, as shown in figure 5–26, before the rest of the records can be added to the master file. The sequential copy of the master file is usually maintained as a backup file. Magnetic tape could be used rather than disk for the sequential file. A systematic plan for copying all disk files, not just the I-S files, must be provided so that if one file is accidently destroyed, the records are readily available on another pack or tape.

Maintenance programs need to be provided to make certain that the master files are both timely and accurate. Regardless of how carefully data is recorded and verified, errors will still occur. Therefore, the maintenance programs need to be able to correct, change, and delete records from the file.

How Can Disk Files Be Written?

1. *Card-to-Disk.* Just as with tape, there are many ways of getting the information recorded on the disk file. One method is to first punch cards, read the cards into the memory of the computer, and then transfer the information to disk.
2. *Key-to-Disk.* There are also many key-to-disk systems available that may be used to record the data directly on the disk. The Mohawk Key-Display system, illustrated in figure 5–13 (p. 272), can be used for keying data directly on either tape or disk. Visual verification of the data entered is provided by referring to the CRT display unit. Some key-to-disk systems can only place the data sequentially on the disk; while the larger multiple purpose systems, which have controllers or minicomputers, can provide for editing, sorting, and consolidation of the record data from several units into one large disk file that is organized in whatever manner is specified.

MORE QUESTIONS ABOUT DISK

5–77. What is the organization method called which permits the file to be accessed either randomly or sequentially?
5–78. What is the best file organization for a very large online file that is accessed from many terminals? Access speed is very important.
5–79. How are files organized which can only be processed in the order that the records are written on the disks?
5–80. How would an indexed-sequential file be accessed in order to process "drops and adds"?
5–81. What is the purpose of providing an expiration date for an output disk file?
5–82. How does the internal label get on the file?
5–83. How does the computer know where to write a new file on a disk pack?
5–84. What must be provided when creating an indexed-sequential file so that new records may be inserted into the file?

5–85. Can more than one file be stored on a removable disk pack?

5–86. An inventory file which is an I-S master file contains a great deal of information. Answer the following questions considering that each record has only the item number, price of the product or item, description, quantity on hand, and vendor's name and address:

    A. Which field would be considered as the key? The key is used in accessing the file randomly. It is looked up in the index to find out where the record is stored.

    B. Which field would be changed due to using the file as input for a normal job rather than changing it with some type of maintenance program?

    C. A change program would be needed to update what fields?

    D. What one field could not change if you still want to access the file randomly?

5–87. Why must an indexed-sequential file be copied to a sequential file and then rewritten at periodic intervals?

THE SALES INVOICE PROCEDURE—UTILIZING DISK

When the L. C. Smith Corporation added disk drives to its basic hardware configuration, the sales invoicing procedure could be accomplished in one operation or broken into a series of smaller procedures. If 15 different analysts were assigned the task of designing the application, utilizing as many controls and editing features as possible, probably 15 different systems would be devised. Figures 5–27 and 5–28 illustrate a two-step approach to printing the invoices and updating the files. The card was keypunched and verified from the sales order form. From the sales orders, an adding machine total was taken on quantity to establish a batch total. If the 129 Data Recorder were used, the total on quantity could have been taken as part of the keypunching operation.

The program illustrated in figure 5–27 edits, or checks, the following factors as it processes each sales order card.

1. An edit routine is used to determine that each field contains only numeric information.

2. Since the cards are to be arranged by order number, the numerical sequence of the cards is checked.

3. The validity of each customer's number is checked by using a numbering system which includes a "check digit." The computer will detect either a wrong digit or a transposition.

4. The validity of the item number is also determined by using a check digit.

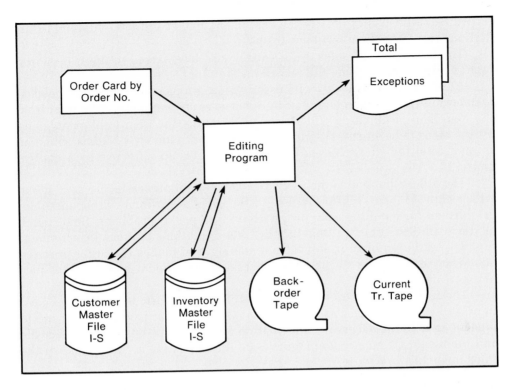

FIGURE 5–27. SALES INVOICE PROCEDURE—STEP 1

5. The customer's balance is checked against his credit limit to determine his credit standing.
6. It is determined for each item ordered whether there is a sufficient quantity of merchandise on hand to fill the order.

Any time the answer to the question (such as, "Is the account number valid?") is "false," the card will be selected into pocket two of the read/punch unit so that it will be recognized as an unprocessed card. In addition, an appropriate error message will be printed on the exception report.

When all the answers to the questions are "true," the inventory record on the master file is updated by decreasing the quantity on hand. In addition, the price and description of the product is transferred to the transaction tape record.

After each group of cards is processed for a given customer, the customer's master file is updated. The data from the current order is now a part of the master file because the order number, amount of the order, and date of the order were added to the customer's record. Added to the transaction tape record from the master file are the customer's name, address, shipping information, and other data pertinent to the sale.

The data from the sales order card is also transferred to the transaction tape record before writing the record on the tape.

After all of the cards are processed, totals are printed which will be used to determine if the correct number of items were accounted for. The total from the item field of *all* cards will be checked against the item total established by the sales department. In addition to the total number of items sold, the amount total for all *processed* orders is now available for use as a control figure.

The orders that match the cards which were not processed are sent, along with a copy of the exception report, to the sales department. Procedures are established for handling each of the different types of problems. Some, such as the invalid customer or item number, have solutions that can be arrived at rapidly. As the problem is solved in a manner that makes the order processable, it is again routed to the data processing department and becomes part of a new daily "batch."

The current transaction tape contains all of the information that is needed to print the sales invoices as the data that was in the cards was transferred to tape along with the necessary information from both the customer master file and the inventory master file. Figure 5–28 illustrates the second phase of the sales invoicing procedure.

The total taken at the end of the job must equal the amount total taken during the editing program.

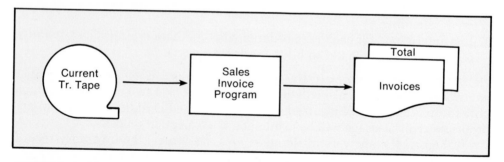

FIGURE 5–28. SALES INVOICE PROCEDURE—STEP 2

Some Comments

The illustration used is a simplified version of a sales application as some factors were omitted. The factors were omitted from consideration in order to present the concepts without getting sidetracked by the detail. If you have followed the illustration from the punched card application up to this point, you should begin to see that *verification* of the data and *editing* and *establishing controls* are essential to any method or to any application. The computer is an effective means of processing the data, but becomes more effective as more sophisticated peripherals, such as tape and disk, are utilized.

Regardless of how many controls are established and how often verification and editing of the data are done, some errors will still be made. Did the computer make them?

A visit was made to three installations which process their sales orders in approximately the same manner as illustrated by the disk method. Each of the three companies has tape, disk, a card reader, card punch, and a printer, and they all keypunch the data from the orders into sales invoice cards. The cards were checked by editing programs for the same items as were covered in the illustration, plus each firm had additional codes that were also checked.

The question was asked as to how many of the cards, or what percentage, were printed out on the exception report because of missing data, invalid codes, nonnumeric data in a numeric field, invalid account numbers, invalid item numbers, out-of-stock items, or customers who exceeded their credit limit.

The first company indicated that 2% of their sales order cards were rejected due to one or more of the reasons listed. The company also felt that they could decrease this number by adding a few more "check points" in the sales invoicing system. They had analyzed the different types of errors that were made in order to try to devise corrective procedures. The errors were traced back to the source to determine *who* and *why* they were made. This particular company had the least amount of computer power and had perhaps the most sophisticated sales invoicing system. They had a considerably smaller installation than the Univac 9480 (which was illustrated in module 4, p. 229).

The second company had a computer system very similar to the Univac 9480. Their error rejection rate, in any one computer run, was approximately 10% of the sales order cards. They were concerned, but had not analyzed the errors as extensively as the first company.

The third company had by far the most computer power since they had more core, or memory, than either of the other two companies and faster peripherals. Their answer to the same question was that they did not know since the percentage varied.

The illustration of the three companies is given only to point out again that it not only takes hardware to develop a good system but also "peopleware." Error analysis is essential to determine what kind of errors were made in order to provide corrective action.

It may seem at this point, when the disk sales invoicing system was contrasted to the unit-record or card computerized system, that the ultimate had been reached. There is still the time-consuming method of preparing the original input—keypunching and verifying the data from the source documents. Point-of-sale, POS, systems offer a variety of solutions to this problem.

OTHER INPUT-OUTPUT DEVICES

Introduction

The card punch, card reader, printer, magnetic tape, and disk drives might be considered as the basic peripheral equipment that is found in most installations today. A large percentage of the installations still have only those devices to use as computer input and output. Module 4, in presenting the Univac 9480 configuration, suggested that often a company starts with a very basic system and then builds by adding additional I/O devices. It has also been stressed that in designing jobs and selecting the right devices to use, the equipment should be compatible. When the speed of the card reader is contrasted to the newer disk or tape drives, it is easy to see why the computational ability of the computer is not being effectively utilized, when one device is extremely fast while another, in the same application, is extremely slow. The printer, when used with disk or tape drives, presents a problem because its speed in relation to the speed of disk or tape is extremely slow.

Some of the more technical points, such as access time, were presented in order to make you aware of the wide range of capabilities that exist among the different models of any one device. The discussion on both the density and speed of magnetic tape was intended to illustrate the many factors that must be taken into consideration before *actual performance* can be evaluated. The ease with which either tape or disk can be used depends partially upon which language is being used for programming. Some of the areas of responsibility of both the operator and the data processing operations manager were pointed out as they relate to file organization, backup, and security of the data.

The peripherals covered—cards, tape, disk, and the printer—have been illustrated in a traditional approach to data processing, where the data is recorded, edited, transcribed to a machine-processable form, verified, and then processed. The approach will continue to be widely used by many firms.

As management became more involved and wanted "total systems," it became apparent that much of the actual data collection should be done outside of the data processing department. While the industry was developing, the data processing manager often did not get involved with the actual data collection from either a budgetary or technical sense. Data gathering costs and techniques were thought to be someone else's problem—certainly not EDP personnel.

Today, EDP personnel are more concerned with the *recording, transmitting,* and *storing* of data than they had been previously. It is estimated that the actual processing of input by the computer is solving only 20 to 25% of the problem of dealing with the increasing volume of data.

As some other types of peripheral equipment are illustrated, think about other applications that the particular piece of equipment might be used for. How many of the devices tend to decrease the number of steps involved in the processing of data? Do the terms "source data automation" or "zero data conversion" apply?

Since there are new and exciting peripherals appearing on the market each day, it would be impossible to cover all of the choices that are now available to both the small and large EDP user.

The following general categories will be used in illustrating some of the other peripheral equipment.

GENERAL TYPE	EXAMPLES
Optical Readers	Optical Character Recognition (OCR) Optical Mark Recognition (OMR) Magnetic Ink Character Recognition (MICR) Point-of-Sale (POS)
Online Communication Devices	Input/Output Terminals Remote Batch Intelligent Terminals
Offline Peripheral Equipment	Printers Viewers
COM	Computer Output to Microfilm

Optical Character Recognition

OCR, the popular term for optical character recognition, is not new as Dr. Davis H. Shepard is credited with inventing the first practical optical reader in 1951. Four years later, in 1955, the *Reader's Digest* installed the first machine for commercial use.

OCR can read paper tapes, printed turn-around documents, and type-written forms. It provides a method of eliminating the need for transcribing the data from the source document into a machine readable form. The OCR documents are used as input and the human-readable numbers, letters, punctuation, and special symbols are converted into a computer-compatible binary code. Page documents can be prepared either by hand or by using a regular typewriter. Turn-around documents, such as insurance bills, utility bills, or credit-card billings, are printed as output by the billing company, sent to the customer, and then read as computer input by the OCR equipment.

In the selection of an OCR reader, the user should consider (1) the number of different types of characters (or fonts) that can be recognized, (2) the size and type of documents that can be handled, (3) the speed and reliability of the equipment, and (4) the relative cost of the equipment.

All OCR readers have limited capabilities as to the variety of characters that they can recognize. Therefore, the number of characters and typefonts a reader can recognize is directly related to the cost of the equipment. The font options that are available with the Control Data 959 OCR Page and Document Reader are illustrated in figure 5–29.

OCR readers may fail to recognize a character due to poor print quality, poor registration, or a number of other reasons. When this occurs, the machine either rejects the document or substitutes another character based on the preprogrammed logic. In some machines the level of reading accuracy can be altered and is a function of operating speed and cost. The rate of throughput is dependent upon the amount of characters on each document, print quality, the rate at which the machine recognizes a character, and the level of accuracy that is required.

Optical character recognition equipment can be connected online to a computer or can be used offline. When online, raw data is machine or hand-printed on the source documents. The documents, which may be of various sizes, include adding-machine tapes, cash-register tapes, cards, and printed forms which have been designed for applications using OCR equipment. The data on the documents may be typewritten, imprinted, preprinted, hand-written, or produced by an online printer. OCR devices can read typed or printed characters *directly* from the documents.

One of the earlier reasons cited for the lack of utilization of OCR equipment was the limitation as to the type of printing that could be used. Since Control Data Corporation, as well as other companies, have multifont OCR equipment, this reason is no longer valid. Another objection to OCR equipment is that unless a high volume of data is processed the equipment is too expensive for many computer users. Cases have been documented where substantial cost savings were achieved when OCR equipment was used as little as four hours per day. *Major commitments are necessary from the users to reorganize their data processing methods in order to take full advantage of the capabilities of the OCR equipment.*

Often the only way the data on the OCR document is verified is visually. When the document being read has been printed as the result of a previous procedure, this problem is also solved. For example, the Social Security Administration uses an optical page reader to read the names, social security

959 FONTS AVAILABLE

Font Option	Character Set Read
ANSI OCR–A SIZE–I	0123456789 | ⑀⑁⑂ ABCDEFGHIJKLMNOPQRSTUVWXYZ -{}%?.,:;=+/$*⑇█&'
Lower Case	abcdefghijklmnopqrstuvwxyz
RABINOW CHARACTERS	⅃⋈#▽△↑↓;=⑂
ANSI * OCR–A SIZE IV	ABCDEFGHIJKLMNOPQRSTUVWXYZ 0123456789⑀⑁⑂
ISO OCR-B	0123456789 –+⌗#
7B	0123456789 EP
7B MIRROR IMAGE	P8Γd2¥ES10
12F	0123456789 H–
407–1 (1403)	0123456789 ⌑–
1428	0123456789 H–,
1428 + ALPHA-MERIC	0123456789CNSTXZ⌿
E13B	0123456789⑆⑇⑈⑉
HANDPRINT	0 1 2 3 4 5 6 7 8 9 C S T X Z + – = | 1 7

* Requires Size IV Option

FIGURE 5–29. 959 FONT OPTIONS. (Courtesy of Control Data Corporation) numbers, and quarterly earnings of millions of wage-earners. The edited and verified output from thousands of businesses becomes the input (read by the OCR equipment) for the Social Security Administration. It might be noted as a point of interest that the report can be submitted on 800 BPI magnetic tape if certain other specifications are followed.

An OCR Illustration

The Control Data Corporation 959 OCR Page Document Reader, which is illustrated in figure 5–30, can scan data at the rate of 750 characters per second, which results in reading 720 full pages per hour or 18,000 single-line documents per hour. Full page documents can consist of up to 30 double-spaced lines of print. The font options available were illustrated in figure 5–29 (p. 315).

One of the more popular applications for OCR equipment is the processing of billings such as utility and insurance premium notices. The premium

FIGURE 5–30. 959 OCR PAGE AND DOCUMENT READER. (Courtesy of Control Data Corporation)

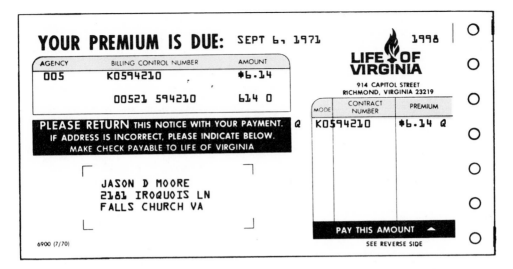

FIGURE 5–31. TYPICAL OPTICAL SCAN DOCUMENT. (Courtesy of Control Data Corporation)

notice was printed by the insurance company on its online printers and sent to the insured. When payment is received, the premium notice (illustrated in fig. 5–31) is read by the OCR. The operation may be online, which would update the master files and accumulate the necessary data for other applications as the documents were being scanned. The more common method is to process the documents offline and write a magnetic tape file which will then be processed online. The advantage of using the OCR equipment offline should be apparent. Although the reading rate seems high (750 characters per second), it is far slower than magnetic tape. Therefore, a considerable amount of CPU time can be saved if the documents are first converted to magnetic tape and then processed.

The advantages of using the OCR equipment offline are illustrated by figure 5–32, which shows both the traditional approach for recording a transaction and the OCR approach. The source documents in the traditional approach are edited, keypunched, verified, converted to tape, and then processed. When the optical character recognition equipment is used, the premium notice is already scannable, without editing, since it was produced as output by the billing company.

Since each batch of documents is scanned separately, batch totals can be utilized to check the cash received against the amount recorded from processing the documents. The elimination of the keypunching and verification steps not only decreases the amount of labor involved, but should also decrease the probability of errors.

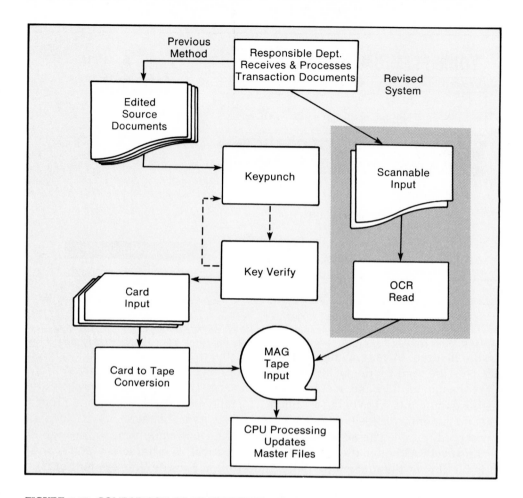

FIGURE 5-32. COMPARISON OF TRADITIONAL METHOD OF RECORDING A TRANSACTION WITH THE OCR METHOD. (Courtesy of Control Data Corporation)

Optical Mark Readers

Closely related to OCR equipment is the Optical Mark Reader (OMR), which is capable of recognizing a bar or mark placed on the document with an ordinary pen or pencil. The location of the mark on the document determines the value associated with the mark. Special forms of different sizes may be utilized which can be used in ordering merchandise, recording payments, securing personnel data, or recording grades. One of the more common applications with which you may be familiar is test scoring. The optical mark reader has the same basic function as OCR equipment: recording the data at the source where the transaction occurs in a machine-processable form.

Optical mark readers are available which are relatively low in price and capable of reading cards at a reasonable rate of speed. The optical mark reader illustrated in figure 5–33 permits the user to design his own forms by using a standard 80-card column card. Although the reader recognizes the 128-character Hollerith code, it can be made to recognize other codes at the user's request.

The reader can function as a terminal and is capable of reading up to 300 cards per minute. Errors are no problem because all corrections are made by erasing the mark that is in the wrong location and replacing it with a mark that is in the correct location. Since the cards are prepared at the location where the transaction or event occurs, the verification rests solely with the user. Data can be recorded conveniently at the source. For example, in the factory, the shop foreman can record both the raw materials and labor that are used on a given job. Students could, using the code, prepare computer source statements and data in their own homes. Doctors can record data pertaining to patients in machine-processable form at the patient's bedside.

FIGURE 5–33. OPTICAL MARK READER. (Courtesy of Hewlett Packard Corporation)

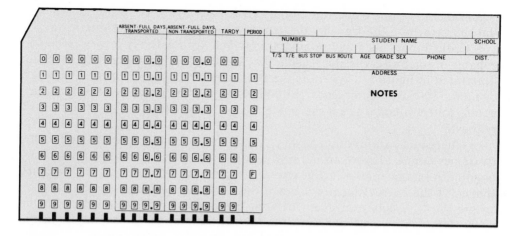

FIGURE 5-34. USER DESIGNED FORM FOR HEWLETT PACKARD MARK READER.
(Courtesy of Hewlett Packard Corporation)

As an optional feature, the Hewlett Packard Mark Reader can process either 40-column or 80-column cards without timing marks. When data is transmitted to the computer, either even or odd parity checks are available. A card designed for use by the mark reader is illustrated in figure 5–34. The card may be written on or printed in any place that is not specifically denoted as an input area.

The mark reader provides a relatively inexpensive way of transmitting data into the system and the potential uses for mark readers, such as the one illustrated in figure 5–33, are almost unlimited. The leased price for the model illustrated is less, on a three-year contract, then the monthly rental of a 129 Data Recorder.

For many potential users two basic problems still exist. One, since the only means of verifying the data is visually, errors may be difficult to detect. Two, if an employee is required to mark a large number of cards it becomes a routine, repetitive job which could result in an unusually high error rate. As with the design of any procedure, steps can be included to edit and verify the information when and where the transaction occurs.

Magnetic Ink Character Recognition

Magnetic ink character recognition (MICR) equipment, used primarily by the banking industry, deserves special consideration for several reasons. If it were not for the use of MICR equipment, it would be almost impossible for a bank to process the large volume of checks which are received each day. MICR equipment is somewhat unique as it serves as both a reader and sorter.

When a check is received by the bank, the amount of the check is encoded on the bottom of the check as illustrated in figure 5–35. A "batch" of checks is encoded by an operator who keys in the amount written on the check into a machine (encoder) which then writes the amount, in magnetic ink, at the bottom of the check. A batch ticket is encoded for each group of checks and placed behind the last check of the batch. The batches are usually small which is an advantage if the total printed by processing the checks is different than the batch control figure. Processing cannot continue until the difference is accounted for. It is far easier to check small groups of checks for an error than to check (at one time) a large group.

After the checks are encoded, all batches are processed as one procedure. The MICR reader reads the Federal Reserve routing number, the bank number, the customer's number, and the encoded amount. During the processing each batch is listed on the online printer along with a computed total, and any difference between the computed total and the batch ticket amount is printed on the report. As was previously stated, *all differences must be solved.*

The MICR reader can also be used to sort the checks by customer number, bank number, and the Federal Reserve routing number. Although the MICR reader can accommodate checks of different sizes, the encoded amount and the identification numbers must be printed in the same location on all checks.

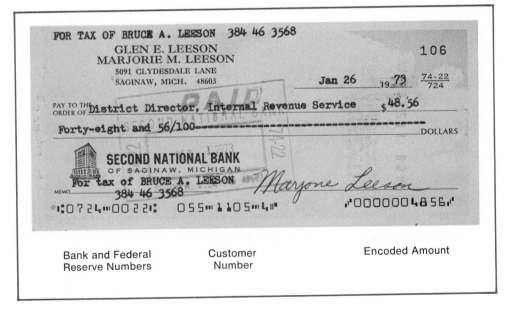

FIGURE 5–35. CANCELLED CHECK

Rejected checks are usually handled by keypunch operators who must punch a card containing all the MICR characters that appear at the bottom of the check. Baystate Computer Center in Massachusetts is now handling their rejected checks by using a CRT (cathode ray tube) keyboard rather than punched card. As checks are rejected by the MICR reader, an exception file is written on disk. The rejected documents are then given to a clerk who "calls up" each rejected check on the CRT screen. The display cursor (marker) moves directly to the first position of the record that was not read by the MICR reader, and the clerk determines why the check was rejected. The proper characters are then entered by the clerk to complete the record, and the disk file is automatically updated. The CRT system has eliminated key-punching and provides faster reconciliation of the batch totals.

The events that have occurred since the banking industry elected to use MICR equipment are an illustration of what might be expected more frequently in the future. Since it was necessary to process other bank's checks, the entire industry agreed where the identification numbers and the encoding would appear on the check. The type of font to be used was also agreed upon by all users. Legislation was then passed which made it mandatory to use checks that had the customer number and bank number printed in magnetic ink. *Standards were developed and implemented!*

When you compare how rigid the rules are for handling the punched card, it is interesting to note how few "jams" normally occur on the MICR equipment, which processes various size checks some of which are rather mutilated. Although people do fold, bend, and mutilate, it is seldom that a check cannot be processed on the MICR equipment. All MICR equipment recognizes only the *one type of font,* or printing, (illustrated by the check in fig. 5–35). Note the unusual apearance of the 4, 1, and 7. The marks around the amount, 0000004856, are amount symbols and are used to make certain that the computer processes the field as the amount of the check.

Point-of-sale

Point-of-sale devices can be terminals that record the data directly into a computerized system or a data collection device which accumulates the information on a reel of magnetic tape, a tape cassette, or perhaps a diskette. An IBM diskette, commonly called a "floppy" disk, is approximately eight inches square, weighs about one ounce, and can hold 1,898 128-character records. After the data is accumulated at the point-of-sale on the data collection device selected, the information can be transmitted to the EDP center.

One POS system utilizes a wand to scan color-bar-coded tags and labels which were prepared on the printer (see fig. 5–36). One pass of this "light pen" or wand over the price tag automatically records all pertinent information—

price, size, stock number, and style—for subsequent computer processing. The wand is part of a new electronic system developed by the National Cash Register Company for department stores, discount stores, and other retail operations. The system not only speeds up customer service, but virtually eliminates errors at the point of sale.

After all items have been recorded, the operator depresses a total key. This causes the terminal, or cash register, to automatically compute the tax and total the transaction. The cash register illustrated in figure 5–36 also multiplies to compute the price on multiple-item purchases. As the items are recorded, they are simultaneously entered on a data collector. At night the data collector transmits the day's transactions into the centralized data processing center.

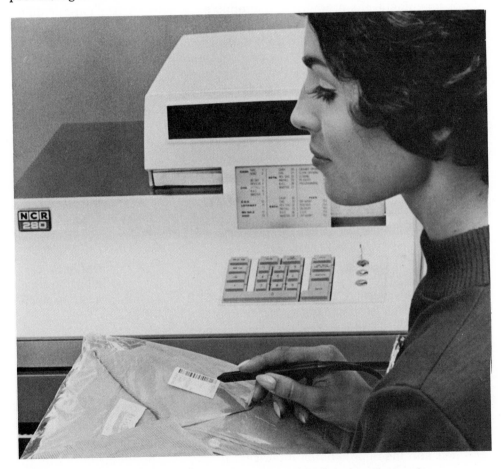

FIGURE 5–36. WAND READER. (Courtesy of the National Cash Register Company)

The system is so designed that the NCR 280 could function as a terminal and transmit the point-of-sale data directly into the computerized system. The electronic cash register is, in effect, a minicomputer. It performs instantaneously all computations and guides the salesperson, step-by-step, through the most intricate transactions by flashing instructions on a display screen.

Why Not More Use of Optical Readers?

There have been a great many articles written as to why OCR and OMR equipment has not been used more extensively. In current publications at various times entire issues have been devoted to describing the various types of optical readers, their advantages and disadvantages, and the comparison of one manufacturer's product with another's. The comparisons are made on price, performance, and major characteristics.

A considerable amount of new improved optical equipment has been introduced on the market. With the price of the optical equipment decreasing and the performance increasing, it may be more widely utilized. Perhaps when more of the optical equipment uses direct optical image processing through the use of laser and holographic techniques, it may be more accepted.

LET'S REVIEW OPTICAL READERS

5–88. An example was given for each type of optical reader. Set up a table to evaluate each of the following types of optical readers: OCR, OMR, MICR, and POS. For your table use the headings which are illustrated below.

Application Data Conversion Reliability of Data Variable Data Added at Source

5–89. For each method, *OCR, OMR, MICR,* and *POS,* think of at least one application for the device other than the examples used in the text.
5–90. What are the advantages of using a wand reader?
5–91. What does the term "zero data conversion" mean?

TERMINALS

Terminals may be divided into two major classifications—*input/output terminals* and the *remote batch intelligent terminals.* The input/output terminals are capable of receiving or transmitting data directly from or to the computer. Remote batch intelligent terminals will not only record the data but will do some initial editing, calculating, printing, and condensing before transmitting the data (in a batch mode) to the centralized computer.

According to the ANSI definition, a terminal is "a point in a system or communication network at which data can either enter or leave." Therefore, any device that can communicate data to or from the computer is a terminal.

Some computers have the potential to utilize terminals in terms of available memory, but do not have the appropriate software package to support the terminals.

The terminals may be telephones, badge readers, optical scan equipment, card readers and punches, remote printers, cathode ray tubes, keyboards which are operated in the same manner as a typewriter, wands, light pencils, magnetc tape, diskette, and plotters. Paper tape is still widely used in both sending and receiving messages.

The Telephone as a Terminal

One of the more interesting terminals is the telephone. Data can be entered into the system by dialing the computer and then using the touch-tone phone keyboard to input the information. The dehumanized aspects of computers can be overcome by using the telephone as an *audio response system* since the user hears a human voice rather than receiving the communication through a digital printout. Typical users of talking terminals are banks and retailers. In a retail application, the talking computer system provides a cheaper response than some other systems for checking credit ratings. In the event of a poor credit risk, a private answer is given over the phone to the clerk. An audio response system can also be used in factories for checking the status of inventories or jobs in production.

With all the apparent advantages, why has the popularity of talking computer systems grown so slowly? A few of the early applications date back to the 1960s, and by 1970 there were about 400 systems in use. It is anticipated that by 1975 there will be over 1,200 audio response systems. The major objections to audio response equipment seem to be the lack of hard copy and the limited speech capability of most of the systems. Another reason for the audio response's slow growth may be that the manufacturers who produce the necessary audio equipment are also producing other forms of terminals.

Playboy Clubs International use the touch-tone telephone to check the credit of their customers, and the answer is provided by the audio response system. A bonus in using the system for the Playboy Clubs was the ability to collect overdue accounts while the customer was in the club!

With a greater emphasis on data entry directly into the system from the location where the transaction occurs, a number of manufacturers have designed data entry systems. The systems can function as a terminal and transmit the data directly into the computer system, or can store the data in a condensed form on disk or tape for remote batch transmission.

Data Entry System—Remote Batch

The IBM 3735 (fig. 5–37) is a programmable terminal. The system is operator-oriented and designed for capturing data, document preparation, and intermediate to high-speed batched data transmission between remote locations and the central computer. The system consists of a modified Selectric keyboard-printer, a programmable control unit, and a disk buffer storage for programs and data.

In the order entry application the sales invoice is prepared by the operator at the remote location. Since the disk buffer provides for storing the user's data, as well as the program, only the variable information is supplied by the operator. For example, once the customer is identified, his name and address are printed automatically from the data stored on the disk. The stored program

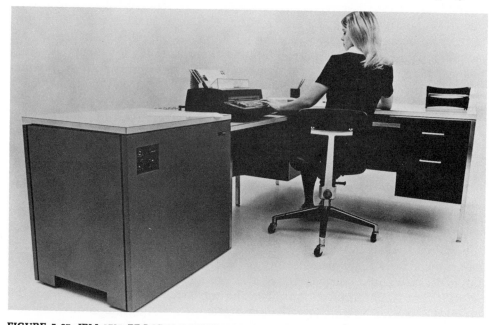

FIGURE 5–37. IBM 3735 PROGRAMMABLE TERMINAL. (Courtesy of International Business Machines)

provides all of the mathematical functions, and also controls the vertical and horizontal spacing of the form. Numeric fields are automatically justified, and punctuation such as the comma, period, and dollar sign can be provided for. The data is compressed so that only what is needed in future applications, made by the "host" computer, will be transmitted. This compression or editing of the information is often referred to as data "crunching." The host computer can be one of many different IBM computers. Although referenced as a programmable terminal, systems such as this are also called "intelligent" terminals since many different techniques of data checking and editing are utilized. Provision is made for automatic transmission between the terminal and the computer at night when the terminal is not being used and the host computer has more available time.

Input/Output Terminal

The terminal illustrated in figure 5–38 can display at one time 24 80-character lines on its cathode ray tube. When data is to be transmitted, the

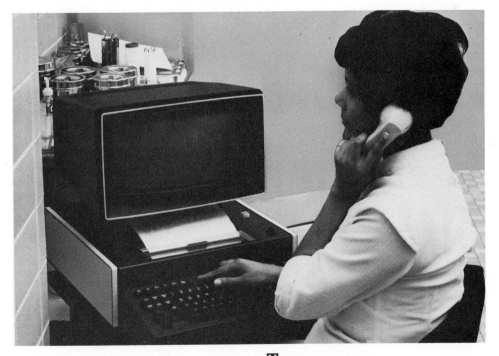

FIGURE 5–38. TELETYPE MODEL 40. (Courtesy of Teletype Corporation)

operator keys in the data and then visually verifies by reading the data displayed on the CRT. The available printer is capable of printing the 24 displayed lines in 4½ to 6½ seconds. When transmitting, the printed copy provides documentation of the data that was sent to the host computer.

When inquiries are made into the computer's online storage, such as to the status of a student's record, all or part of the record can be displayed on the CRT. If the counselor desired a printed copy for future reference, the student's record could also be printed.

The model 40 teminal illustrated in figure 5–38 is available in three basic configurations: keyboard/display, keyboard/display/printer, or receive-only printer.

Portable Terminals

With a portable terminal the computer is never any further away than the nearest phone. The Bendix Logiport/2 (fig. 5–39) has a 9-inch CRT which will display 16 80-character lines. The user plugs in the terminal, dials his friendly computer's number, places the phone on the terminal as indicated in figure 5–39, and is ready to converse with the computer. He will, of course, be asked to identify himself for two reasons. One, not just anyone should be

FIGURE 5–39. PORTABLE CATHODE RAY TUBE TERMINAL (Courtesy of Bendix Corporation)

able to access the data that is stored in the files. Therefore, each user has an identification number which will permit him to use the computer and access certain online files. Two, the identification number is also used to charge the user with the computer time that is utilized.

Why portable terminals? An insurance man calls on a new customer to sell an insurance policy. In the selection of the right policy for the customer, various charts and tables have to be consulted to determine the premium as well as other features of the policy. The insurance man checks the figures very carefully, making numerous calculations. He could have dialed the phone, entered a few digits of data, and instantaneously had the answer displayed on his terminal.

When a salesman is placing an order, he could either enter the entire order by using a portable terminal or use it as a means of checking the files to determine if the desired merchandise is available. Students or faculty may be able to check out terminals from the Learning Resource Center. The student will use the terminal to complete homework assignments, while the faculty member uses it to prepare new material for the students.

ABOUT TERMINALS

5-92. Define terminal.
5-93. List ten different devices that could be used as terminals.
5-94. What is an intelligent terminal?
5-95. Can all computers use terminals?
5-96. Give an example, other than those given, of a situation in which a portable terminal would be useful.

COMPUTER OUTPUT TO MICROFILM

COM (computer output to microfilm), like any other solution in data processing, is not the answer for all users to the problem of the printer and printed reports. When a system is being designed or redesigned, it should be considered as a possible solution to the avalanche of paper than most computer users find they are generating. The first step in determining if it can be an effective solution is to determine if the company considering COM has the type of documents that are applicable to being stored on microfilm. Good candidates for COM are account status reports, catalogs, price lists, and reports for management.

Many advantages can be cited for COM. As was mentioned earlier in the text, the cost of storing and retrieving data is no longer considered a minor one. In addition, the cost of paper, even stock paper, is continually rising. There is also an ecological problem of both using vast amounts of paper and then effectively destroying or recycling the paper after it has been used.

When the printer is used as an output media to produce reports there is no possible way for it to output the data as fast as the computer can perform the calculations. It was pointed out in a recent article pertaining to COM that a ten-thousand-page report in four copies would take a minimum of ten hours of CPU and printer time to produce. An equal amount of time would be needed to collate, burst, and bind the report into 52 two-inch books, which would weigh over 300 pounds. The same report could be produced via COM on 50 microfiche in less than three hours *without* tying up the computer. Additional copies can be made in 20 minutes, and all 4 copies can be neatly stored in a box the size of a cigar box and will weigh less than a pound.

How is the microfilm produced? One of the most common methods of producing the microfilm is to use computer-generated magnetic tape mounted on a tape drive connected to an Eastman Kodak KOM–90 microfilmer (see fig. 5–40). The microfilmer reads the data which is on the tape, displays it on the face of the cathode ray tube (which is part of the KOM–90), and photographically transfers the image onto 16, 35, 82.5, or 105 mm film.

FIGURE 5–40. MAGNETIC TAPE READER AND KOM-90 MICROFILMER. (Courtesy of Eastman Kodak Company)

While this transfer is taking place at a rate of approximately 90,000 characters per second, the computer is free to do other tasks. The rate of transfer is equivalent to 25,000 lines a minute, which is approximately seven times faster than output of the most sophisticated line printer.

The operator instructs the KOM–90 by inserting into the machine a job setup control card which determines image orientation, reduction rate, and the image length. Provision for retrieval of the data stored on microfilm may be by line coding, image count, or binary coding. Software is available for the KOM–90, which takes care of the indexing and retrieval system that is to be used.

The KOM–90 system uses nine-channel magnetic tape. A page, as represented on the magnetic tape, may have 64 lines containing up to 132 characters per line. The font style may be regular, with both upper and lowercase alphabetic characters—italic or boldface. The film is then used in a film processor to produce the microfilm. The form of microfilm produced depends upon the type of film that was created from the magnetic tape. The microfilm may be in the form of roll, magazine, jacket, microfiche, or aperture cards. Figure 5–41 illustrates the five types.

FIGURE 5–41. THE FIVE FACES OF MICROFILM—ROLL, JACKET, APERTURE CARD, MAGAZINE, AND MICROFICHE. (Photo Courtesy of Eastman Kodak Company)

Most microfilm is produced in the roll form. When used in a magazine, however, the film is not only protected but the information can be accessed faster because the film, when inserted in the reader, is self-threading. Small sequences of images may also be produced which can be stored (for ease of handling) in a "jacket." Medical records, student grades, and other information which may be updated and augmented frequently can be effectively stored in this manner. Microfiche is a single four-by-six-inch sheet of film that may contain as many as 270 pages of data. Buyers guides, service and parts information, as well as reports can be effectively stored and retrieved using microfiche.

Aperture cards use the standard punched card with a die-cut window that provides for the retention of the microfilm images. Information can be keypunched and interpreted into the aperture card, which make the filing and retrieval of the cards easy. An interesting application for aperture cards involves its use in a career information center. Each card contains up to nine pages of information pertaining to a given vocation. Students can visually select the card, which is indexed by occupation, and insert it into the viewer. The student may obtain a copy of any page by pressing a button on the viewer.

The viewer illustrated has a 14" x 14" screen which reads a pre-indexed self-threading film magazine. Within seconds the desired information can be retrieved and displayed. If a printed report is desired, the "print" button is pushed and a report, in any of 12 sizes, is available. There are, of course, many different models of viewers available that read the various types of microfilm, and not all are equipped with the print feature.

Surveys made of the opinions of employees who work with information retrieval, using COM, indicate that they have been favorably impressed with its speed and ease of operation. In a midwestern bank the employees, prior to COM, looked up the status of customers' balances from reports which were printed daily. When the microfilm viewers were used, rather than the large bulky reports, the employees felt the records could be accessed much faster. In addition, they felt their job was much more pleasant than it had been under the old system. The bank was *most* impressed by the *cost reduction!*

A special report in *Data Management* identified the characteristics of the potential COM user. The report indicated that a rather large computer configuration, which produces approximately 400,000 form plies a month, was necessary to support a COM system. The need filled by COM is the reduction of turnaround time needed for reports with initially high reference requirements. The reduction in printer, computer, and retrieval time, as well as the cost and physical volume of materials, were also cited as advantages. The article also indicated, however, that the smaller users, who have applications which are well suited to COM, should investigate the use of service bureaus. There are service bureaus in many areas which have both the facilities and

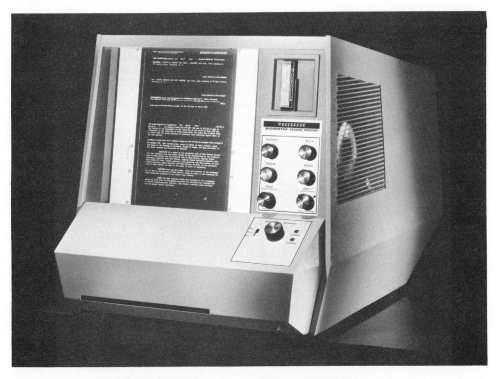

FIGURE 5–42. RECORDAX READER. (Courtesy of Eastman Kodak Company)

trained staff to produce microfilm, in a variety of forms, from computer produced magnetic tape.

OFFLINE PRINTERS

Various speeds and models are available in offline printers. The Mohawk Data Science printers, such as the one illustrated, may print either online or offline and range in speed from medium to high depending upon the model selected. The slower models may print as little as 250 lines per minute, while the faster models can print up to 1,250 lines per minute with a maximum of 160 characters or 16-inches on one line.

The magnetic tape used to print from an offline operation may be either 7 or 9 channel. The tape will contain all of the headings as well as the commands to control the vertical spacing of the forms and may have been prepared by using a data recorder or as the results of computer output.

FIGURE 5–43. OFFLINE PRINTER. (Courtesy of Mohawk Data Science Corporation)

The offline printer has the advantage of being able to print information which was the result of computer output without holding the CPU and faster input devices down to the speed of the online printer. While printing occurs offline, the CPU is free to do other computer functions or produce more magnetic tape or disk output.

COM AND OFFLINE PRINTERS

5–97. COM is an abbreviation for what output method?

5–98. Would it be wise to use COM for reports which are needed in a hurry?

5–99. If COM can be justified, what savings will result other than the savings in computer time?

5–100. How can a copy of a given page of a report be printed when microfilm is used?

5–101. Which of the statements listed below best describe the following terms: microfilm role, jacket, aperture card, magazine and microfiche
  A. Single sheet, four-by-six-inches, that can hold as many as 270 pages of data.
  B. Most common form of microfilm.
  C. The film is mounted on punched cards which may be written on, or punched, to permit the data to be quickly retrieved.
  D. Roll film in a container which permits self-threading in the reader.
  E. Small sequences of images stored for ease in handling. When the sequences are all stored together it resembles microfiche.

5–102. Discuss the following statement: it is impossible for a small company to effectively utilize the advantages of COM as so much equipment is necessary to convert magnetic tape to microfilm.

5–103. Other than COM, what is another way of saving computer time when very large printed reports are to be printed?

5–104. Discuss the following statement: offline printers can only print listed reports which do not require special headings or spacing.

SUMMARY

It should be apparent from the peripherals covered that many different types of equipment, with a wide range of abilities, exist today. There are many other devices that were not mentioned which also have a great deal of potential for different users. No one type of equipment is the answer to the needs of all users. Some of the devices, such as terminals, are easy to illustrate yet may require complex, costly operating systems in order that they may be effectively utilized. The ability of the central processing unit is dependent upon both peripherals and the operating system to achieve maximum throughput. Combining all factors, the throughput speed is generally in direct proportion to the total cost of the system.

A much greater emphasis has recently been placed in improvements of the peripherals. IBM's compatible 3330 Disk and 3340 Tape Drives are a good example of an improvement in speed, capacity, and concept. Companies that have gained experience in using computerized systems are constantly searching for a better method of getting the input into the system. Zero data conversion, with editing and batch totals, is possible through use of intelligent terminals.

As was illustrated, the ease with which a procedure can be executed depends not only on the ability of the CPU, but also on the type of I/O devices that are available. Contrast the many steps (some of which were manual) that were necessary when only card input and printed output were used in the sales invoicing procedure with the more sophisticated and integrated disk method. Not only is the disk method far faster, but a great deal of manual steps were eliminated by providing for more computerized editing and checking. These checks were made possible when online master files were used.

Optical character recognition might be used effectively to process typewritten sales orders. Optical mark recognition can read pen or pencil marks which would indicate the customer number, part number, and the quantity desired. Other data, required only for identification and checking purposes, could be handwritten on the document for visual reference, since the order is compared to the sales invoice which is prepared.

Although available for a long time, there seems to be a revival of interest in the optical readers, COM, and voice answerback. The computer technology is now such that terminals are within the reach of many users—and becoming more so each day.

Each user must be able to cost-justify the peripherals that are selected. How much does it cost, for example, to have peripherals that produce the sales invoice one day faster—can a company afford to or not to?

GLOSSARY OF OLD AND NEW TERMS
TO CHECK YOUR KNOWLEDGE

Access Time (tape).   The number of inches per second of magnetic tape which may be read.

BPI.   The density, or bytes per inch, that is used to record data on tape.

Block.   A group of logical records that are combined to form a physical record. The physical record is read all at one time but each logical record is processed individually.

Buffer.   A temporary storage area or device. The use of buffers help to maximize the rate of throughput in a computer system, since overlapping of operations can occur.

Burst Mode.   A method of reading or writing data which does not permit an interrupt to occur.

Carriage Tape.   A paper tape punched to correlate with each special form which helps to control the vertical movement of the form in the printer.

COM.   Computer output to microfilm. Refers to a method of producing microfilm, in a variety of forms, from computer-produced magnetic tape.

CRT.   Cathode ray tube which is used to display data. Under certain circumstances they may also be used for input.

Image Mode. The image mode permits the use of a binary coded decimal system for reading or punching data in cards. When this mode is used, numeric data can be packed in the card.

Impact Printers. Printing occurs as the result of a metal character striking against a ribbon. A common example is the typewriter.

Interrecord Gap. The space or gap between the physical records on the tape, which allow the tape drive to stop reading and start reading (or writing) without missing data.

Job Control Cards. Cards used to communicate the desired options for the job to be run on the computer. They also call in the program, tell where data is on tape or disk, terminate the job, etc.

Key (file.) The key is the field in the input record that is used as the address, to compute the address, or to find the address in an index of a disk file record that is to be retrieved.

Logical Record. One record on a file pertaining to a single subject, such as information pertaining to one student. The programmer is responsible for correctly defining the fields that make up the record.

Opitical Character Recognition (OCR). By optical methods, typewritten, printed, or handwritten characters may be recognized and read into the CPU.

Operating System. A combination of hardware and software that is directly under the control of the supervisor, which resides permanently in the memory of the computer. Among other things, it is responsible for coordinating all input/output activities.

Offline. Offline refers to either the storage of data in auxiliary devices rather than the CPU, or the processing of data by a method that is not directly controlled by the computer.

Parity Check. A check made to determine if the correct number of bits are turned on as data is read into, or written out of, the CPU. Auxiliary devices such as intelligent terminals may also make use of a parity check.

Peripherals. Input or output devices used in electronic data processing other than the CPU.

Physical Record. A block of logical records.

Point-of-Sale (POS). A term used to indicate that data, regarding a sale, is entered directly into the computerized system without being converted to another form.

Parallel Reading or Printing. An entire row is read or printed at one time.

Random Access. The ability to access any record in the file without first processing the records that proceed it.

Read Check. When a parity check is detected by the card reader. Valid data was read or stored incorrectly.

Sequential Access. All records in the file must be processed in the order that they appear in the file.

Serial Reading or Printing. A single character is either read or printed. If the term is used to refer to the card reader, the data is read column-by-column.

Standard Labels. A tape or disk label used to identify the file. It is checked before the file is processed to make certain that the right file is being used.

Tape Dropout. Loss of bits or bytes of data which make the tape data incomplete and unreliable. When this occurs a new tape must be created from the backup tape.

Terminals. A point in the system or communication network at which data can enter or leave.

Transfer Time. Bytes per millisecond that may be transferred from tape or disk into the CPU.

Transport Light. A transport light on the card reader generally indicates that there is an internal card jam.

Utility Program. A program, often provided by the manufacturer, which performs a task such as a sort, sort/merge, card-to-tape conversion, disk-to-printer listing, etc.

Validity Check. A validity check occurs when a card contains a combination of punches in a card column which are not recognizable as a valid character.

VTOC. Volume table of contents for a disk pack. It generally provides the file name, where it is located on the pack, the creation date, and the expiration date.

ANSWERS

QUESTIONS ABOUT THE READ/PUNCH UNITS (p. 255)

5–1. Cards are read by using either brushes or *photoelectric reading devices.*

5–2. The read check station and the read station both read the same card and the results are compared. It would be very unlikely that the same error would be made by both sets of reading brushes.

5–3. No. Generally, the input card may go into the three pockets referred to as R1, R2, and RP3.

5–4. When a parity check is detected, the read check light will come on and the card reader stops reading cards.

5–5. The validity check light will come on when a given card column contains an invalid punch configuration.

5–6. No. This is one of the "protective measures" that is built into most systems—the reader stops until the operator corrects the situation. Some large installations are set up in such a way that if the computer waits more than a given period of time the job is cancelled, the balance of the input is "flushed" through the reader, and the next job will start.

5–7. A "cardjam" has occurred.

5–8. The parallel method reads row-by-row while the serial method reads column-by-column.

5–9. Yes. The statement is generally true. Some languages do not support stacker selection on input. Usually a routine can be written in assembler language and then called into the program when needed by the programmer.

5–10. Less card handling would be involved because the cards would not have to be first merged on the collator and then separated after the job was completed.

5–11. The data may be packed on the card and more information can be stored.

5–12. No. Job control cards, control cards, and source decks are also read by the card reader. In a large installation, which utilizes a large-scale computer, the card reader may be used more for the three functions listed, but seldom for actually reading input.

5–13. The punched card is costly to keypunch and verify. The relative speed of the card reader, as compared to other devices that are available, is very slow.

5–14. A validity check has occurred when the output card was punched. In many cases the computer will try again. The correct output card will be put in one stacker, while the invalid card will go into a different stacker.

5–15. Yes. When a large volume of cards is read it takes the almost constant attention of the operator to take the cards from the trays, place them in the hopper, remove the processed cards from the stackers, and replace them in the tray. The operator also must watch the *read* or *validity checks, feed stops,* or selected cards.

LET'S REVIEW THE PRINTER (p. 261)

5–16. In most systems the printer is considered to be a very slow output device.

5–17. A. Impact printers
       B. Nonimpact printers

5–18. A. Print chains
       B. Print drums

5–19. No. Normally, various speeds are listed depending upon the size of the character set that is used on the print chain or drum and the method used for spacing the forms. Maximum speeds are generally specified for single-spaced numeric data which is printed in a burst mode.

5–20. To save "setup time," internal reports are generally printed on *stock* paper. A *standard* list tape is also used.

5–21. Vertical spacing is the result of the commands written by the programmer.

5–22. No. Carriage tapes are stored and then reused many times.

5–23. Less time is needed to change paper to produce the desired number of reports. Copies will be made of the one single report. Computer time can be saved.

5–24. The end-of-forms light will come on and the printer stops until the operator puts in more paper.

TAPE REVIEW (p. 268)

5–25. It costs much less to store data on tape today than it did five years ago.

5–26. The density of tapes is measured in bytes per inch.

5–27. The highest density tape listed has 6,250 bytes per inch.

5–28. No. It is also necessary to consider the size of the gaps required, the blocking factor, and the record size.

5–29. A. More data can be stored on tape.
  B. Since less stop/starts, or actual deaccelerations and accelerations are required, the tape may be processed faster.

5–30. Today, nine-channel tape is more widely used than seven-channel.

5–31. A parity check will occur.

5–32. Access time is measured by the number of inches that may be read per second.

5–33. Transfer rate is measured by the number of bytes per millisecond.

5–34. 1/1000 of a second.

MORE QUESTIONS ABOUT TAPE (p. 274)

5–35. No. A "standard" reel of tape contains 2,400 feet of tape. However, there are tapes available in varying lengths.

5–36. Tapes can only be processed *sequentially*.

5–37. A *utility* program is used in sorting tapes. This means that rather than writing a sort routine each time a different tape is to be sorted, the operator can use one basic program and supply the variables that are needed for the application being processed.

5–38. A tape file may contain records that contain a good deal of information. Several reports may be produced from one file. In order to process the tape and get the desired report, however, the sequence in which the records appear on the tape may have to be changed. This is especially true if master files are being used with a transaction tape.

5–39. If available, four tapes (two input and two output) should be used in order to achieve the best results.

5–40. 1965

5–41. Cathode ray tube, which is used to visually display data.

5–42. After the data is keyed in by the operator, the record is displayed on the tube. It is then visually checked against what is recorded on the source document to make certain that the keying operation was accurate.

5–43. Originally, this was done when the data was first keypunched and then verified in the card. The more experienced operator was usually the one to verify the data. Now, however, there is a trend to have one person both key in the data and verify the data. Some research has been done which indicates that it is as effective as having two people performing the two separate functions. The newer methods of recording data into the system, especially when the CRT is used, make it necessary to have one person do both operations.

5–44. The data may be edited and checked for accuracy, batch totals can be taken, and some processing of the data can be done which may involve the use of additional peripherals, such as a printer and disk being used by the "system."

5–45. An identifying key is used to compare on. When the same number is found in a tape record, the information in the record can be updated or corrected.

REVIEW QUESTIONS (p. 278)

5–46. No, because the newer tape drives usually feature automatic threading of the tape.

5–47. Tape dropout is loss of data on the tape. When dropout occurs, the tape generally will have to be recreated.

5–48. A. Name of the file
B. Creation date
C. Expiration date

5–49. It tells the operator that the reel of tape may be used for an output file.

5–50. In most systems the tape may be processed either frontwards or backwards. If the label is on both ends, it may be checked regardless of how the tape is processed.

5–51. 1:10
5–52. Yes. This was a common practice in order to more effectively utilize the equipment. In theory, the ratio would then be 1:5. Not as much time would be gained, since twice as many cards would need to be read, as if tape were used in place of the cards.
5–53. Use a key-to-tape recorder and eliminate the punched card from the procedure.
5–54. A listing of all customers who have exceeded their credit limit.
5–55. Yes. It is not as current as it would be if printed on a daily basis. This factor, however, would have to be weighed against the increased cost of running the job each day.
5–56. No. "A" should be retained as a backup tape. If "B" were to break or be destroyed in some way it would be very costly to recreate the master tape. "Dropout" can occur and make the tape unreliable, and even in some cases impossible to read.
5–57. Tape files can only be accessed sequentially. It is therefore impossible to merely find and correct the records that are to be updated. Also, in working with tape at any one point in time, it can either be input or output but not both.
5–58. No. It is needed to verify that the customer's account is valid. Any name on the list would represent an overextended account, perhaps a lost charge plate, closed account, etc. A very small percentage of the accounts will list out. When "real-time" is covered there is a far better solution but for now the printed report is necessary.
5–59. Wrong customer number punched in the card (poorly written on source document could have caused the problem). New customer whose master file was not yet created.
5–60. The name and address could change. A correction might need to be made because a charge was billed to the wrong customer. The amount of the credit limit is either increased or decreased depending upon the history of the transactions with the customer.

COMPARING THE CARD AND TAPE INVOICING METHODS (p. 291)

5–61. The credit check was computerized.
5–62. Inventory update and completion of the transaction tape.
5–63. A. Prints only the items that need attention, which saves time in utilizing the report.

B. Saves the computer time.

C. Saves paper.

5–64. When real-time procedures or systems are implemented, this is one of the major concerns—control. The more integrated the procedures become the more vital it is that the input is valid and that methods are used to prove the accuracy of each phase of the system.

5–65. It relates the source of the information, the order, to the output. The numbers can still be in sequence as the order number is stamped on the document as part of the conditioning for keypunch or key-to-tape processing.

5–66. Yes. Any deviation from quantity ordered and actually shipped should be noted. A price check can be made. If a salesman prepared the order it determines if he is quoting correct prices. Descriptions can be checked. Where they vary a great deal—one for tires, the other for tractors—some means should be used to confirm which item was wanted before the shipment goes out. The item number could be valid, but the salesman did not use the one that was needed to get the merchandise that is desired.

RANDOM ACCESS QUESTIONS (p. 299)

5–67. A. Disk drives with removable disk packs

B. Disk drives with nonremovable disks

C. Drums

D. Data cells

5–68. Drum

5–69. Data cells

5–70. In a sequential file the entire file must be processed to update only a few or perhaps only one record. When RAF are used, only the records desired for processing need to be read. Any one record can be assessed without reading the preceding records.

5–71. The statement is totally false. The unit cost of storing data is approximately 1/12 of what it was at that time.

5–72. No. As with many other types of hardware, there is a wide range of equipment available. The access time varies partially because different equipment is intended to appeal to different users. The System/3 Model 6 disk system for example is slower than many drives because it is intended to be utilized as a small low-cost system.

5–73. The disk pack described had 203 cylinders and 10 tracks.

5–74.   A cylinder is a specific location on the disk which can be accessed by the read/write heads. The cylinder is accessed by one positioning of the access mechanism.

5–75.   The arm movement takes more time than waiting for the record to become accessible or actually reading and transferring the data into the memory of the computer in order that it can be processed.

5–76.   A. The VTOC takes one cylinder.
B. Three cylinders are reserved in case some of the other cylinders become defective.

MORE QUESTIONS ABOUT DISK (p. 307)

5–77.   Indexed-sequential

5–78.   Direct

5–79.   A file that can only be processed in the order in which it is written on the disk is a *sequential* file.

5–80.   Randomly

5–81.   The area designated for the file is protected (until after the expiration date) against anyone accidently writing another file over the top of an unexpired file.

5–82.   The label is punched into a JCL card. When the file is written, the label from the card is transferred to the file.

5–83.   The cylinders to be used are indicated on one of the JCL cards. If enough areas were not reserved, an error message would be printed on the printer or console.

5–84.   An I-S file requires than an *overflow area* is established so that new records can be inserted into the file on the right cylinder and track.

5–85.   Yes. As many files as will fit may be stored on a disk pack. The one exception would be a very small one-disk removable pack, since a VTOC is not provided for.

5–86.   A. Item number
B. Quantity on hand
C. 1. Price of the product
    2. Vendor's name and address
    3. Description
D. Item number

5–87.   To get the records that are in overflow back into the main area of the file. If this is not done, the overflow areas will become full and no new records may be added. A special area can be designated as an additional overflow area, but this point was not covered in the text.

5–88.

	APPLICATION	DATA CONVERSION	RELIABILITY OF DATA	VARIABLE DATA ADDED AT SOURCE
A. OCR	Life insurance	None—all machine processable	As good as company's system.	None
B. OMR	Medical	None	Depends upon visual verification.	With pencil or pen all data is variable.
C. MICR	Check processing	Amount of the check	All preprinted except amount. Visual and batch total verification on amount.	Amount encoded
D. POS	Light pen or wand	None	As good as the accuracy of the operator who prepares the tags using the printer.	None

5–89. OCR Light bill, telephone bill, house payment, installment payments, credit card applications.

OMR Medical history, tests, surveys, class cards, grade reports, class request forms, government tax bills, monthly statements.

MICR Any application which would involve constant data that could be preprinted on the form. Only a limited amount of variable data would be added by hand and then encoded. Any applications that OCR is used for could be done using characters that are printed in magnetic ink.

POS Point-of-sale using a light pencil or wand. Any retail application. The secret to its success is having valid tags printed.

5–90. The procedure is faster than when the clerk must enter the data by keying it on the cash register. More data is therefore entered regarding the sale. The one weak spot in the entire system is that the tag could be wrong, since a clerk prepares it by keying information into a machine which then prints the tag. The system also can be used either online or to collect the data for batch transmission.

5–91. When the transaction occurs the data is recorded in a machine-readable form that requires no conversion for processing. The turn-around statement read by the OCR and the wand applications are both examples of zero data conversion. Another noncommercial application would be the utilization of sensor devices that transmit data directly into computers.

5–92. A point in a system or communication network at which data can either enter or leave.

5–93. Keyboard entry devices, telephone, badge reader, optical reader, voice response system, optical reader, card reader, paper tape reader or punch unit, cathode ray tubes, printers, wands, light pencils, magnetic tape transmission devices, diskettes, and plotters.

5–94. The data entered can be edited, verified in various ways, used in mathematical operations, added to provide control totals and condensed before it is transmitted. Transmission may be either online or remote batch.

5–95. Some computers do not have the hardware capability, while others do not have the software, or operating system, which will permit their use.

5–96. Sales personnel receiving and transmitting data, from various locations within their territory to the home office.

A doctor checks the online hospital file to determine the status of a patient who is in the hospital.

The corporation president is at a conference and wants information that is in the online data base.

The use that can be made of the terminal depends upon how the computer can be accessed, what programs can be called up, and how extensive the data base is that is available to the user.

COM AND OFFLINE PRINTERS (p. 334)

5–97. Computer output to microfilm

5–98. Yes. COM is often a very effective solution for the need of having a report, one that is to be referenced often, available sooner.

5–99. The cost of materials needed to produce the reports will be substantially less.

5–100. Many viewers, or readers, have the ability to produce a copy of what is shown on the cathode ray tube.

5–101. A. Microfiche
B. Microfilm roll
C. Aperture card
D. Magazine
E. Jacket

5–102. If a small company has applications that are well-suited to COM and are already using magnetic tape, they should investigate the possibility of using a service bureau.

5–103. The output can be written on magnetic tape and then taken to an offline printer.

5–104. No. The magnetic tape that was produced as computer output contains the necessary commands to print headings as well as to vertically position the paper.

DESIGNING SYSTEMS 6
AND PROCEDURES

THE L. C. SMITH CORPORATION TODAY

The corporation has continued to expand both their branch operations and product line as they were able to sell a substantial amount of stock due to their excellent reputation and growth record.

Although corporate reorganization has occurred at various stages of development, the data processing manager still reports directly to the controller since most of the computer applications are still financially oriented.

As you can see from the organization chart (fig. 6–1), the department has expanded a great deal in a relatively short period of time. Currently there are three major areas of responsibility within the data processing department: systems development, programming, and operations.

The department has "come of age" and no longer is everything done on a crash basis without the necessary planning and systems work. L. C. Smith has learned, sometimes the hard way, that "peopleware" must function before the hardware and software can be effectively utilized. It has also taken time

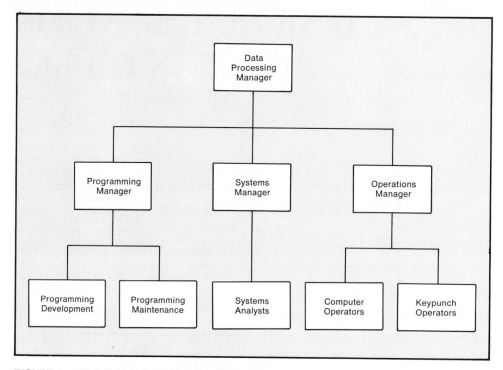

FIGURE 6-1. THE DATA PROCESSING DEPARTMENT

to educate management that if a data processing system is almost totally utilized when it is first installed, it probably is the wrong system for the company.

JOB DESCRIPTIONS

The job description of the data processing manager is beginning to look more "managerial" than the previous description given in module 2 when the position and department were first created. This trend is apparent in many companies today because much of the professional data processing literature now stresses that the manager *must manage*—it is not enough for the manager to be a good programmer or an analyst. Different talents are needed to effectively manage the men, machines, materials, and methods which are at his disposal. The following classifications and functions merely highlight what is found in the L. C. Smith Corporation Systems Manual.

Data Processing Manager

1. Develop a long range plan for the expansion of both services and facilities.
2. Submit an annual budget by April 1 of each fiscal year.
3. Schedule all requests for *feasibility studies*.
4. Approve and schedule all *systems studies*.
5. Determine the priorities for all operational procedures.
6. Keep all departments informed regarding the available data processing services.
7. Hire and train all data processing employees.
8. Supervise and evaluate all data processing personnel.
9. Provide in-service training opportunities for all data processing employees.
10. Provide in-service training seminars for personnel in other departments on the potential use of the computer within their areas.

Systems Manager

1. Develop standards for documentation for all systems and procedures.
2. Work with the users in the development of project proposals.
3. Assist with the development of feasibility studies.
4. Plan, schedule, and aid in the implementation of the systems studies.
5. Keep current on all new developments within the data processing industry.

Systems Analyst

1. Assist the task force in studying the present system. Generally, an analyst will serve as "project leader."
2. Work with the "task force" assigned to a project in developing alternate methods for revision of the system under study; each alternate method should include the cost of developing and implementing the new system, and also include the time that it would take to complete the project.
3. For each alternative listed:
   a. Develop all *systems flowcharts*.
   b. Develop the *macro program flowcharts* and the *decision tables*.
4. Supervise the *testing* of all systems and procedures.
5. Assist in the development of *training materials* that are needed for the implementation of the new systems.
6. Conduct *ongoing evaluations* of the new systems and procedures to determine if the objectives are achieved.

Programming Manager

1. Schedule all required programming.
2. Conduct training seminars for all personnel when changes are made in either the languages used or the operating system.
3. Work with the systems manager and operations manager to make certain that all procedures have adequate controls.
4. Supervise the training of all new programmers.

Programmers

1. Develop from the *macro* program flowcharts the detailed program flowcharts.
2. Code all programs in COBOL adhering to established standards for file and data names.
3. Test and debug all programs. *Documentation* of the test design is to be included as part of the *procedures manual.*
4. Work with the systems analyst in continuous evaluation of each major system.
5. The programmers in the program maintenance group will be responsible for making certain that all programs are properly *maintained* according to the established standards.

Operations Manager

1. Provide direct supervision of the operators.
2. Schedule all jobs based upon the predetermined priorities.
3. Maintain post-control books.
4. Determine the validity of all reports before they are released from the department.
5. Maintain a log of all problems that occur.
6. Order all supplies and materials.
7. Make certain that all hardware is adequately maintained.

Computer Operator

1. Follow the established schedule in running all jobs.
2. Follow the directions given in the operator's guide for processing all data.
3. Keep current on all programming and operating systems changes.

4. Maintain a daily log of all procedures. All problems are to be noted in the log.
5. Operate the peripheral equipment.
6. Maintain a neat and orderly work area.

Keypunch Operator

1. Punch and verify the data from the source documents.
2. Stamp all documents with the date and time that they are processed.
3. Keep all source documents in the sequence in which they were received.
4. Explicitly follow the directions for each job which are given in the keypunch operator's procedures manual.

As you review some of the job descriptions, you may have been unfamiliar with both the terms and the functions that are being performed. The job descriptions will be clarified for you as you find out more about not only the hardware but the functions of the data processing department and how it relates to other departments. The concept of the data processing department that is emerging in the L. C. Smith Corporation, as well as many other companies, is one of providing a communication service through information processing which will help to unify the entire corporate organization. *The data processing department has no function of its own since its basic purpose is to process the information for all other departments.*

TODAY AT L. C. SMITH

What kinds of problems are the systems analysts at L. C. Smith working on now? Seriously being considered is the use of COM (computer output to microfilm) for their price lists, which are now printed and sent out to all of their salesmen and branches. Their initial survey indicates that they do have a sufficient volume of reports printed to make it feasible to pursue the investigation. Their analysts are currently working with other members of the firm in developing a proposal which will contrast the cost of COM, using microfiche, to printed reports. They are also investigating the possibility of utilizing a service bureau which has COM equipment since they have a substantial number of other projects that must be programmed and implemented.

In addition, an investigation is being made to determine if they should perhaps phase out some of their keypunches and get some key-to-tape units. Should the key-to-tape equipment be "free standing" or function as a unit under the supervision of a minicomputer?

Still another group of analysts and programmers are investigating the possibility of getting a new "super large" computer system. Would this be better than getting a second computer and having it work in conjunction with their present computer?

The material that follows is presented to give you a better understanding of some of the basic functions of the data processing department and how it relates to the other departments within the corporation. As the computer's capabilities are utilized to a greater extent in providing management with more information, it is not uncommon to see the entire corporate organization change in order to provide better communication between departments by establishing a more functional form of management.

A FEW QUESTIONS

6–1. What is the major assignment that was given to the data processing manager?

6–2. Why was he asked to provide in-service training opportunity for all of the data processing employees in the department?

6–3. What was the first responsibility listed for the systems manager?

6–4. Has the job description for the computer operator changed much from the one that was given for the unit-record equipment operator?

6–5. How did the L. C. Smith Corporation regard the data processing department in relationship to all of the other departments?

FEASIBILITY STUDIES

When a division or department feels that their present data processing system should be changed, a request is made in writing to the data processing department manager. The first step that will be taken, in order to determine if a change in methods is warranted, is to schedule a feasibility study.

A Simple Feasibility Study

An individual could do a feasibility study to determine if the old car should be maintained or if it would be advantageous at this time to secure a new car. The costs of maintaining and operating the present car can be contrasted with the costs of several alternatives. One alternative might be to lease a car rather than to own one. Several makes and models of cars should be studied as possible replacement for "Old Bessie." The projected costs of keeping the old car should be weighed against the costs involved in each of the alternatives. Evaluation of the various choices of cars on the market and their anticipated performance is not nearly as complex as the evaluation of various methods of processing data. Should a complete, complex study be made? Answering that question is the purpose of a feasibility study—the first phase of a systems study.

Feasibility studies are generally conducted by a team of individuals who study an area or function with a view towards *improving its performance by using better methods.* The basic techniques and principles used in development of a feasibility study are almost universal. Although the term has been used widely in data processing, the concept applies to any function or problem.

The scope and depth of the study varies, as well as the time and personnel required, but certain basic concepts apply to all projects. The study may be made by a management committee, a systems task force, an analyst, or by using consultants.

The time involved in doing the actual feasibility study can vary from one day to several months. The written request may be for a simple change to be made in an existing procedure, in which case an analyst can investigate the request and submit recommendations in a very short period of time. If an entire system is to undergo a major change the feasibility study may require several months. Another factor pertaining to the time factor is the extent to which the individuals involved in the study are released from other responsibilities.

To make the discussion a little more pertinent, assume that a study of the current sales information processing system is requested in writing by the sales manager. The systems manager assigns one or more members of his staff to the preliminary investigation of the project. The systems staff members meet with the sales staff representatives to make certain the problem is clearly understood and to determine the scope of the suggested study. Any revisions to the original request that result from the meetings should be in writing. After these initial discussions the project will either be "dropped" or "scheduled." If scheduled, a small team with representatives from both the sales and systems departments will be primarily responsible for the feasibility study.

Under the modern concepts of systems development, it is imperative that *top management* be directly involved in the feasibility study, because their support will be needed for the continuation of the project. It is also vital that adequate time and personnel be committed to the project since some major decisions are made during the study.

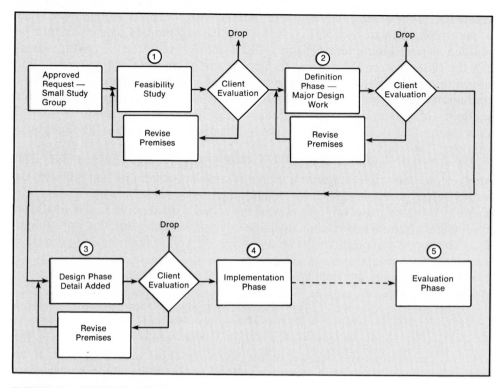

FIGURE 6–2. SYSTEMS DESIGN FLOWCHART

As indicated in figure 6–2, the project may be dropped after phase 1. There is not always a clear distinction as to exactly what will be done in phase 1 (the feasibility study) and phase 2 (the definition stage). Generally the basic design of the new system is outlined in phase 2.

When a data processing department was initially organized and the computer first installed, inadequate time was often spent on the first two phases of systems work, which often resulted in poorly designed systems. Therefore, after implementation, extensive changes were sometimes required. Management learned that shortcutting the feasibility study and the definition phase could well be a false economy.

Phase 2—Definition

If a complete study is recommended and approved, the definition phase continues with the investigation of the present system and tentative designs for a new system are developed. Phase 2 is conducted by a task force, or project team, which must determine what information is needed from the system. The informational needs are studied through direct communication with the individuals who are involved in sales and other related areas. A comprehensive investigation is made of the present sales system, the structure of the firm, and the environmental conditions in which it operates. During the investigation several alternate approaches to solving the problem should be explored.

Project Team

If phase 2 is begun, without looping back through parts of phase 1, the full project team is selected. Figures 6–3 and 6–4 show the traditional and systems approach in team selection. Since sales is interrelated with production, purchasing, accounts receivable, inventory, accounting, shipping and receiving, as well as other departments, the project team or task force should be composed of individuals from all of those areas. In a small company some of the "talents" may be combined and one person might represent more than one area.

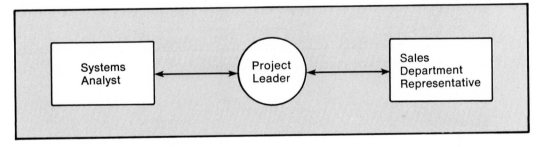

FIGURE 6–3. TRADITIONAL APPROACH

To conduct the sales investigation for L. C. Smith, the project task force could be made up of one or more systems analysts, a programmer who knows the language and the operating system, a representative from operations, a hardware expert who knows the capabilities of various I/O devices that are being considered, and representatives from the sales, accounting, manufacturing, and inventory departments. The systems approach will result in less duplication and a better design, which is more likely to be accepted because in the *early stage of development the departments that will be directly affected are represented.* In the traditional method, other groups are *consulted* but are not part of the task force.

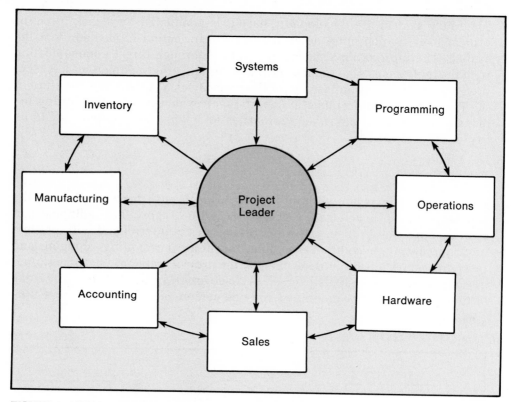

FIGURE 6–4. TASK FORCE UNDER SYSTEMS APPROACH

Constraints

Alternatives developed by the project team during phase 2 are compared to determine the best approach that is within the constraints imposed by the firm. The constraints may be:

1. *Time.* A deadline may have been established for the completion of the project which makes a complete study impossible.
2. *Budget.* A predetermined dollar amount has been made available for the implementation of a new system. The budget includes the initial cost of the study, implementation of the system, and the amount per month that may be allocated for personnel, equipment, and supplies.
3. *Personnel.* The firm may have decided that any change made in an existing system may not involve additional personnel. If only personnel from the existing departments can be utilized, more training will be required. There

also could be a problem of securing the talent that is actually needed for the new positions created.

Estimating Costs

The hardware, software, and personnel costs must all be allocated for each of the alternatives that are studied. The study must be able to show that the alternative selected will not only meet the stated objectives, but will also produce a return on the dollars invested in the project. This was not as true when the data processing departments were first organized and the computer technology was in its infancy. At that time, systems were sometimes justified on the bases that more timely and complete reports would be available for management.

When the transition to computers was in its early stages, due to the inexperience of the data processing personnel, the original projected costs were frequently understated. Like any other form of management, through experience they are better able to predict the costs of the alternatives of the proposed systems. Data processing management learned in a hurry to provide for the "little extras" that were previously overlooked.

Phase 2 Report

Phase 2 ends with a study plan that includes the *objectives, basic design, equipment configuration, timetable* and an outline for phase 3. Although the cost figures, equipment and personnel requirements, and the design are tentative, it can be determined with reasonable accuracy if the resources of the firm, or department, will support the proposal. Since it is not uncommon for the costs incurred by the data processing department to be charged to the department that utilize their services, the sales department will have to justify the additional costs.

Phase 3 Report

Phase 3 terminates with a report that includes the *precise objectives,* systems design, data requirements, equipment specifications, and personnel requirements. The recurring costs as well as the developmental and conversion cost of the proposal are justified in terms of dollars saved and dollars earned.

Acceptance by management of the report from phase 3 becomes a commitment for both the sales manager and the systems manager. A well-documented report must be prepared in order to avoid as many misunderstandings as possible. In some organizations, after the report is accepted, no changes can be made until the system is implemented. This forces the sales department to do their thinking *before* the final stages of the development of the new system.

Emphasis on Systems Development

The increased emphasis on the feasibility study, definition phase, and design portion of systems work is shown by the table of expenditures for the various data processing functions.

| | PERCENT OF TOTAL COSTS | | |
	1953	1969	1971
Equipment	80%	32%	25%
Operations	12%	38%	40%
Development	8%	30%	35%

STUDYING THE PRESENT SYSTEM

There are various viewpoints regarding how extensively the present system should be studied. There are analysts who feel that when a new method is to be created it is unnecessary to study the present system. The analysts who share this opinion feel that if the present method is studied, they may not be as open-minded to a really new innovative approach.

More analysts support the concept that the existing method should be studied to determine what is now being done, what the problems are, and then design an alternative that solves the basic problems and meets the stated objectives.

How should the analyst proceed to study the sales system? One way is to study the firm's *systems manual* or *procedural manual*. The manual will normally provide the following information:

1. The organization of the department being studied.
2. The job descriptions should be available for each function.
3. Flowcharts may be available. Flowcharting is used in many areas—not just data processing. Almost anything that is logical and orderly can be represented by a flowchart. The manual flowcharts will show the movement of the documents throughout the organization.

4. The function that each person performs on the sales order as it moves throughout the organization is usually illustrated by the flowchart and also explained in written form.

Systems manuals or procedural manuals were also used long before electronic data processing was established as a profession. The problem that exists in some organizations is that the "formal" structure appears in the manual while the informal "this is the way it is done" structure really exists: Another reason why the analyst cannot stay in his office and hope to find out how the present system actually operates is that the manual may not have been updated as changes have occurred. Most companies do have forms that are to be used when changes are made, but revisions are frequently made to the procedure but not *to the manual.* This may well be another *bonus* factor of electronic data processing—*a strong emphasis is placed on developing and maintaining good documentation.* Nevertheless, even simple manual methods need good documentation.

The second way to study the existing sales system is to actually trace the sales order through the company to find out what each person does to the order, why it is done, what problems occur, how long it takes each employee to perform a given function, how long the order stays on each desk, how the invoice is prepared, and what other reports are generated from the sales order or invoice information. Can the analyst stay within the sales department and find out the information that is needed? Obviously not.

In tracing the document through the various departments and determining the interrelationships that exist, the analyst should remember that he must ask the department managers if he may work with the various individuals within each department who perform the functions that are being analyzed.

When interviewing individuals, from whom the analyst must secure a good deal of information, it is helpful to formulate the questions that will be asked ahead of time. If a great deal of information is needed from one individual, it would be wise to send a written memo, or form, to the individual listing the points that will be covered. This will give the person being interviewed an opportunity to think about the answers to the questions, look up materials, and be organized when the interview is conducted.

After the interview, it is also considered a good practice to send a written confirmation to the individual interviewed as to the conclusions reached. This will achieve two purposes. First, it becomes part of the documentation (there is that word again). Secondly, it serves as confirmation of what was said; there will be no misunderstanding at some future date. If, however, only one or two questions are to be asked, such formal action is not required.

Forms can be used by the analyst which can also be very useful. The form would tell who was interviewed, why the interview was conducted, and the points that were pertinent to the study could be noted. The form would be considered part of the "working papers" of the analyst.

The analyst should also study all of the forms that are available for the sales order system. Do they contain the information that is needed? Are they easy to fill out? What reports are printed? Who uses the report? Sometimes it is discovered that the six-part report that has been printed for the past 12 years on a monthly basis is either an almost exact duplicate of another report or is one that no one uses.

The common methods of studying the present system are

1. studying the systems and procedure manuals,
2. interviewing the personnel involved with the current system,
3. observing the actual flow of the sales documents throughout the organization, and
4. studying the forms and reports.

Documentation

Why document? Documentation, or the recording of the pertinent data pertaining to a system, procedure, or task, is a good technique for anyone to develop. In a simple manual method there is need for good documentation. For example, Mary Smith works in a one-girl office where most of the procedures are manual. Why should Mary's manual procedures be documented? If she were to leave, she would be asked to train another individual to take her place, but what happens if she goes on vacation? Can anyone else do her job for her if there are not detailed directions to follow? Written directions pertaining to any topic such as how to change a tire could be considered documentation. For some people, maybe it is just one of the things you know how to do, but without documentation, would everyone know the step-by-step method that must be used to achieve the desired results? A favorite recipe is written down with all the ingredients and *very specific directions as to what to do and when to do it.* This is also documentation. Each phase of a systems study must be completely documented.

In data processing each installation has its own *standards for documentation.* If complete documentation is available, it is relatively easy to "patch" programs, operate equipment, train new operators, enter data, and for management to determine how the system actually functions. The documentation for a procedure should include (1) the objectives, (2) the systems flowchart, (3) the detailed program flowchart, (4) a program listing, (5) samples of both input and output, (6) directions for the operator, (7) directions for the keypunch operator, and (8) special instructions or controls that are to be utilized in the job. It is estimated that as much as 15% of the programmer's time may be spent on documentation.

REVIEW QUESTIONS

6–6. Can a feasibility study be conducted for any purpose other than changing a data processing system?

6–7. When is the major part of the creative work of a system study done?

6–8. The report for phase 2 will include what items?

6–9. When the report is given for phase 2, what three things can happen?

6–10. What are three constraints that might limit the type of design that could be developed?

6–11. Why is the "task force systems approach" better than the traditional approach?

6–12. What evidence is there that more emphasis is placed on systems development work today than when computers were first being utilized?

6–13. The acceptance of the phase 2 report actually accomplishes what objectives?

6–14. In general terms, what is a systems manual?

6–15. Is the organization illustrated in the manual exactly like the structure that is being used to manage the company?

6–16. What are the four ways that were given for studying the present system?

6–17. Why is it considered a good practice to send the points to be covered during the interview to the individual to be interviewed ahead of time?

6–18. Why should a memo be sent after the interview?

SYSTEM STUDY REVIEW

To review, a request has been made for a new sales system. The original request was made in written form. According to figure 6–2 (p. 356), the request could have been:

1. *Rejected.* Personnel may not have been available at the time the request was received to do even a feasibility study.

2. *Revised.* After the initial discussions the tentative request may be revised or dropped.

3. *Accepted.* If the original request is approved the feasibility study is then started.

It is also possible that the request could have come from top management, in which case phase 2 (the definition phase) may be started without going through the feasibility study since their request may be given top priority.

After the feasibility study is finished, the decision must be made to continue with phase 2, drop the suggested revision, or to do a more in-depth preliminary investigation. The original idea may have to be scaled downward to permit its eventual implementation.

When the report, which is documented, is submitted at the end of phase 2, it includes the data requirements, objectives and tentative design, and equipment and personnel costs. If the report is accepted by the sales department, it must be "sold" to management. Various media (e.g., overhead materials, slides, and charts) should be prepared to make the presentation as clear and concise as possible. In making the presentation to management, it is important that the analyst be able to communicate effectively.

If phase 2 is accepted by both the sales department and management, the major work of the task force is ended. The methods currently used were studied, the problems cited, and recommendations made in the form of the tentative design for the new system. The tentative design included the hardware, software, personnel, and data requirements. The analysts and programmers assigned to the study must take the tentative design and add the detail necessary to finalize the plans. Even though the task force may have been officially dissolved, the help of the various members on the team will be recruited as the detail of the design is developed.

The exact specifications for hardware and software must be determined, and how the changes may affect the existing corporate structure are detailed. The analyst is not only concerned with what happens within the data processing department, but how the decisions being made will affect all other departments. Therefore, the other departments which will be affected must be *involved in the decisions.*

The design may start with capturing the data at the source where the transaction occurs, which may be the district sales office in New York City, and recording the information directly into the system. Distance is no barrier! The district offices, then, should be where the analyst begins his detailed design. How will the data be entered? What hardware is needed? How will the accuracy of the information be determined? What retraining will the district sales personnel need if a system is used that will record the information from the district offices directly into the files of the home office?

Detailed Design

The analyst is creative and his imagination and initiative were utilized to their fullest in the definition phase when the tentative design was developed. *His work now is not as much creative as it is working with facts and details.* For example, in phase 2 it may have been decided to use magnetic disk storage. Now the details must be determined as to exactly what each file and each record will contain. In addition, decisions must be made as to how the information will be recorded and verified, what totals are to be established, how often the file should be updated, what security measures must be taken to protect the data, and who should have access to the information.

Determining how the variable information is to be entered into the system is probably one of the most difficult decisions to make. After the decision has been made, the proposed sales system is defined in terms of the procedures required to actually process the data. Each procedure is further studied in terms of the specific tasks that make up the procedure. For each task it must be determined; what personnel is needed; how the personnel will be trained; what equipment is needed; what materials will be required; how long it will take; when the results must be available; who should receive the results; what controls must be established to determine that the results are valid.

For example, the proposed sales system which is being designed is composed of many procedures, such as preparing the sales invoice, processing backorders, maintaining inventory records, analyzing the sales of each product sold, and so forth. Each sales procedure is divided into very specific tasks which must be defined in detail. The sales invoicing procedure is made up of the following tasks:

> Recording the sales order data into the system
> Credit check
> Inventory check
> Recording backorders
> Checking the validity of the invoice
> Distribution of the invoice
> Recording the invoice

Once the major commitment was made during the definition phase as to the type of system—time-sharing, batch computer processing, or point-of-sales entry into the system—the detail work can start. Top management must have been involved in making the decision as to the processing method to be used for the system. The detail design work is primarily accomplished by the programmer or the programmer/analyst. The analyst will usually supply the systems flowchart that gives a broad overview of the system and its individual procedures. The programmers are normally assigned the responsibility of doing the program flowcharts which illustrate, step-by-step, how the computer will process the data.

Designing the entire system may sound complex. It is true that making a commitment to a particular method is a very difficult decision to make. The detail work, however, is no more complex than defining one small individual task. Nevertheless, it is important that very minor details are not overlooked. How successful would the implementation of the new sales invoicing procedure be if it was discovered at the last moment that one small simple detail, ordering the new forms for the printer, had been overlooked?

Projected Timetable

How long did it take to get to this phase? How much longer, if the decision is "go," will it take before the new system is operational? No one simple answer can be given because there are many variables that must be considered. The study could have recommended a seven-year plan, a five-year plan, or perhaps a three-year plan, as a means of implementing the recommendations.

If at the beginning the decision had been made to request a study to determine if the sales system could be revised in such a manner as to incorporate some new hardware (perhaps terminals) but primarily use the existing central processing unit, *a three-year timetable may have been projected*. It could be similar to the one illustrated:

PHASE	MAJOR FUNCTION	ESTIMATED TIME
Phase 1	Feasibility Study	4 months
Phase 2	Tentative Design (definition)	6 months
Phase 3	Design Refinement (detailed)	6 months
Phase 4	Implementation	20 months
Phase 5	Evaluation	Continuing

After all the details have been developed for the design of the input, files, reports, and procedures, a presentation is once again made to the sales department. If the decision is "go," then the implementation phase will begin. By looking at figure 6–2, (p. 356), you can see that this is really the "point of no return." If the sales department and management accept the detailed design, implementation will start.

If the cost estimates and tentative design were well done in the definition phase, it is unlikely that the idea will be rejected at this point. If, on the other hand, not enough time had been spent on the definition phase and the estimates involving personnel, hardware, and software were underestimated by a substantial amount, the proposal could be rejected at the end of the detailed design phase. Although a good deal of time, effort, and cost have been invested in the project up to this point, it is better to drop the project if the initial design is poor than to proceed and implement the design.

IMPLEMENTATION AND EVALUATION

Phase 4, *implementation,* is far more involved than just writing, testing, and debugging programs. When the implementation phase is entered, it has already been established what hardware will be needed to support the system. In addition, the software and personnel requirements have also been determined.

A great deal of coordination must be achieved during this stage of development of the new system since on the "target date" (when the new system is to be up-and-running), everything must be ready. One difference between now and ten years ago is that reasonable estimates can be made as to how long it will take to study, design and implement a proposed change. Management has also accepted the fact that new systems do not appear overnight like mushrooms.

As part of the planning an actual timetable can be established that will tell when each detail must be started and *completed.* There are some things that must be done in a given sequence while other portions of the system can be implemented simultaneously. Certainly before the computer comes in the location in which it will be housed must be ready. It would be just a little backward to have the computer come in and then think, "oh, yes, it ought to go somewhere. Perhaps it will fit in the back of John's office." The site must be prepared and ready before the computer arrives. Parallel events could be training of the employees, preparation of the data base (files), and testing of programs. The coordination of the activities can be effectively shown on a chart that graphically shows the sequence and timing of each event. The chart or graph can also show the tasks which can be done simultaneously. The project leader will have the responsibility of coordinating all phases of the implementation.

Ordering Equipment

The computer is ordered along with all of the peripheral devices that are necessary. In determining the specifications many different factors were considered—the volume and type of data to be processed, the anticipated growth rate of the company, the estimated number of new applications for which the equipment will be used, the optimum method of accessing information, the long-range goals of the company in terms of type of data processing system that is ultimately desired, and the funds available for the hardware, software, and personnel.

Once the specifications are determined as to the amount of memory desired, peripherals needed, and the software required the determination of which manufacturer's equipment to use is also very difficult as there are many good computer systems available on the market.

This one factor alone—which computer to select—may take from one to two years of study. A large Texan firm recently paid $200,000 to a consulting firm for making such a study.

The equipment should be ordered soon enough so that it will arrive before the actual conversion date as the final testing should be done on the new system.

Site Preparation

Most computers require special consideration regarding the physical location in which they operate. The air conditioning system should provide both temperature and humidity control. If the room temperature goes beyond a certain point the computer may stop. This is a protective device in the design of the computer so that it will not be injured due to attempting to operate when it is overheated.

Usually special wiring is required in order to provide the system with a sufficient amount of power. Frequently, false flooring, which has removable sections, is used. All of the large connecting cables and channels required for the system can be installed underneath the flooring. When the equipment is rearranged, which normally does not happen until additional hardware is ordered, the flooring can be removed to provide easy access to the wiring. Since some of the equipment is extremely noisy, acoustical ceiling and walls should be considered a "must."

File Conversion

The new system may utilize both disk and tape while the former system had only punched card input and output. With the use of disk and tape a great deal of additional information will be available in the files which can be used to produce meaningful reports for management. Some of the constant information can be added to the files ahead of the conversion date such as the name and address of the firm, shipping information, billing information, credit history, and customer classification. The variable information such as the unpaid invoices and items on backorder should not be added to the file until the actual conversion to the new system. File conversion requires the scheduling of personnel ahead of time so that at the required time there is the necessary manpower available. One solution to the problem of the additional staff requirement is to contract with a service bureau in advance of the file conversion date for additional assistance in doing some of the required keypunching.

Training of Personnel

If the new system involves major changes such as use of terminals for inputting information into the system, the employees who will be utilizing the equipment need to be trained. Training manuals can be developed which will aid not only in the conversion process but in the training of new employees who are added when the system is operational.

It may sound like a simple thing, but how will the employees in the plant learn about the new badge reader that might be part of a new payroll system? Slide presentations might be prepared so that each employee can receive individualized instruction on the "do's and don'ts" of the new badge reader. Why "don'ts"? It may seem obvious to you that when the badge is stuck in the reader, you do not use nail clippers or gum in trying to remove the badge. *The key to success in data processing is to provide for "all things that will never happen."* In one installation a maintenance man was told to clean the room where the new badge readers were located. Fine—but no one told him *not* to squirt them with water from a hose. The system had been designed so that bells rang when problems occurred with the time and attendance system. Can you imagine what happened that day!

Ordering Supplies

The input and output forms required for the new procedure or system should be designed and ordered early enough so that they will be available when the system is tested.

In one installation during the final system testing there was an insufficient amount of paper for the printer. Since it was a "first" computer for the firm, the amount of paper required for the high speed printer had been inaccurately predicted. The only person happy about the whole arrangement was the controller as the programmers were saving computer listings and using the back of the paper for another compile.

Usually the manufacturer's sales representative will assist the user in determining the type and amount of supplies that should be ordered.

Programming

The macro flowcharts which illustrated the major concepts of the new system were submitted as part of the definition phase of the study. Each procedure now requires a *detailed program flowchart* or *decision table*. Decision tables, which are used as another method of expressing programming logic, are covered in the next section of this module. From the detailed program flowchart, the programmer will write the necessary source code. Developing a good complete program flowchart before starting to code is well worth the programmer's time.

Usually each installation will select one language for their application programs. If only one language is used, both programming maintenance and conversion, when necessary, to a new computer is much easier. Programs are also easier to maintain if *meaningful codes* are used by all programmers. In some installations "data dictionaries" are used which makes it necessary that all programmers use the same data name for any given file, record, field, or code.

There are three classifications of employees within a given firm: salaried, hourly, and part-time. The gross pay for each type of employee is calculated differently. Would you use X, Y or Z as the code to tell the computer what type of pay record is being processed, or would S, H, and P be more meaningful? If the firm does require the use of *uniform,* or standard, programming names, all programmers will be required to use the same code to distinguish the employee's classification.

Since the codes are often used by the individuals who are preparing input into the system, less errors will occur if they are meaningful and easy to remember.

Compiling and Testing

If the new computer is not compatible with the one currently being used, the contract may provide for test time on either the vendors or another customer's computer.

Testing should begin as soon as the first procedure is written as the complete sales system might involve 40 or 50 different programs. A single large program is often tested in segments which will make it easier to detect the cause of an error.

The user's computer should arrive early enough that all final testing can be done on their own system as two firms may have identical computers but their software may differ. This might permit one company, with the more elaborate software, to use more powerful programming commands and subroutines than the other.

The design of the test data is very important as all editing and error routines should be completely tested. The testing procedures should be well documented and the data retained for future testing of program changes which are made after the system becomes operational.

Documentation

Most of the documentation should be done prior to the actual conversion. Documentation can be done at several different levels to serve different needs or purposes.

A systems manual should be prepared for the new sales system that will contain macro flowcharts and a description which provides an overview of the system. For each procedure, within the system, a written explanation of the objectives of the procedure should be provided. The files are described, samples provided of both the input and output forms, testing procedures defined, and special codes, controls, and instructions are noted. In addition, in operations for the purpose of running and maintaining the program, there should be a folder or file for each procedure which contains:

1. *The Program Run Sheet.* The run sheets contain the directions for the operator. What forms and files are to be used, the format for the control card (if one is required), the job control language cards that will be required, and any special instructions are carefully explained. If error messages are written into the program by the programmer the run sheet should tell the operator how he should respond to the messages. Usually the run sheets will tell who programmed the procedure and who should be called in the event that a problem occurs while running the program. If Deb Schroeder is listed, since she coded and tested the program, she shouldn't be surprised to get a 3:00 A.M. phone call if the job aborts (terminates due to an error) at that time of the morning.

2. *Detailed Program Flowcharts.* When it is necessary to modify the program for any reason the program flowcharts are extremely helpful.

3. *Complete Current Listing of the Source Program.* The computer listing of the source statements will list each command that is coded by the programmer and assign it a sequential number by which it may be referenced. Often cross reference listings are also available which list for each field or file all of the statement numbers in which it is used.

4. *Samples of Input.* When cards are used, an actual sample may be included as part of the documentation. If a data error is detected, the operator can then determine if the card is correctly punched. The tape or disk file formats should also be available. Since master tape and disk files may be used in several different procedures, however, they are not fully described for each application.
5. *Samples of Output.* When a printed report is prepared as part of the procedure a sample is often included which shows the headings, part of the detail portion of the report, and the control totals.
6. *Control Procedures.* Usually a final total for a report must balance with a predetermined figure. If a data control clerk is not assigned the responsibility of determining the accuracy of the output, the computer operator may be responsible for checking the totals before the report is distributed. If the program uses only disk or tape, totals may be printed on the printer which must be checked to determine if the correct number of records were processed and that the procedure was executed in a normal manner. Some installations require that a statement always be printed which will indicate that the entire file was processed and the job terminated satisfactorily.
7. *Distribution of the Report.* Complete directions as to the distribution of printed reports must be provided.

When the details listed are provided in a folder, or notebook, for each procedure the operator has a ready source of reference. Operators are not programmed to run jobs; they are trained. Part of their training should be to *check* run sheets in order to avoid making careless errors which can prove to be very costly. Files are protected, but if the operator thinks the file is obsolete and that new data can be written over the top of the old file and he is wrong, how costly is the error? The carriage tape was to have been changed on the printer as the report is to be printed eight lines to the inch rather than the more usual six lines to the inch. If the tape is not changed, or the printer adjusted, the entire job must be rerun as the printing will not be positioned on the forms correctly. A job calls for one of three digits to be entered on the console typewriter, depending upon the type of report that is desired. The operator *thinks* he knows the codes but enters the wrong one. These things may seem simple but in a given installation hundreds of different applications may be run. Therefore, the run sheet should be checked prior to running the application in order to make certain that all of the detailed instructions are followed.

With good documentation new operators can be trained more easily. An operator who had just been trained to be the night operator of a small installation was in a car accident on the way to work. Do you just shut down the night shift? Since very good documentation was available, about 90% of the jobs were easily handled by a substitute who knew the hardware but not the procedures. Without good documentation the manager might have found himself in a new position—night operator.

In small installations where good documentation is even more important due to the size of the staff, it is more likely to find incomplete documentation. The larger installations by now have established fairly rigid standards for documentation as they have learned, perhaps the hard way, that complete documentation more than pays for itself.

Additional documentation is prepared for the individuals who will be working directly with the preparation of the input. If complete, the information can serve both as a reference and training manual.

Conversion

If at all possible, the procedure or system should be run parallel—both the old way and the new way.

This may be difficult, especially in a small installation, as it means additional work loads. In the material in module 11 pertaining to the First Savings and Loan's new system, it is indicated that they ran parallel for nine months to make absolutely certain that their new system was functioning correctly.

When the actual conversion is made, you generally do not find your analyst and manager leaving at 5:00 P.M. and saying "good night, operators; I hope it works." Even on a rather simple conversion from a unit-record sales system to a computerized system you might well find the manager, analyst, programmer, and operational manager all staying to check the parallel run. Nothing like hamburgers for dinner at midnight! You don't say, "Well, in 99% of the cases it seems correct." It is 100% or not at all. It is easier to run parallel when it is only the case of adding an additional procedure for a new report than it is when the entire system is to be converted to a new method.

Evaluation

As the programs are written, files converted, and reports are tested, the question can always be asked, "Are the stated objectives being achieved?" When the conversion actually is accomplished the questions must be asked again. As the new system is utilized it should continue to be evaluated. All errors should be noted and additional controls and editing added to correct any problems that might occur.

In the new sales system being utilized not all of the customers are charged sales tax on their orders. When tax is to be charged, the input card will contain both a tax code and the rate of tax. The error analysis indicates that frequently the tax code is used in the card without the tax rate field being keypunched. The programmer can add an editing feature to the program which processed the sales card to check the tax code field; and if it is not blank, to then determine if the rate field is blank. If the rate field is blank, an appropriate error message will be printed in order that the input card can be corrected.

If the errors are due to invalid information being entered from the source of the transaction, such as the salesmen entering wrong codes, a different form of corrective action is needed.

Each type of error should be analyzed as to *why* the error occurred. Is it a human error, improper programming, lack of control, operator error, or due to invalid data? The invalid data is the type of error that is the most difficult to correct.

SUMMARY

Refer again to figure 6–2 (p. 356) and review the different phases of systems work. Can you begin to see the scope of what is involved in designing a new method for accomplishing a given procedure? When you look at your paycheck or a statement from Standard Oil for the gas purchased during the month, think of the planning that went into that one simple output. Standard Oil might have spent three or four years designing a new billing system that would give the customer better and more accurate service, permit the station that sold the gas to be paid faster, and provide more controls so that only the person authorized to use the card may do so. What files must be maintained to provide the data that is on your check stub? How is the new input entered so that your gross pay can be calculated?

Are you thinking that this is an introductory course so why even mention designing systems and procedures? The beginning student should develop an awareness of the entire scope of data processing. Data processing does not begin and end in the computer room; it encompasses many different jobs, at many different levels, and, nowadays, in many different places. Maybe the most important person in the entire data processing network is the person on the terminal who is inputting the data as the transaction is actually occurring. The computer operators also play a vital part in the success of the operation. In the design of either a system or a single procedure a team effort must be made. Although creativity is required, hard work and attention to small details are what make a brilliant design work! The project leader and managers have a tremendous job in coordinating the development of the new system.

Many of the topics that have been briefly presented could have an entire book written about just the one topic, such as: the role of the computer operator, designing a system, selection of hardware, selection of software, the expanding role of the manager, or the documentation standards.

The case study is used to illustrate the steps for one small request made to the systems department for an additional sales report. No new hardware is needed. The techniques used in designing the new procedure are the same as those needed for designing a new system.

REVIEWING IMPLEMENTATION

6–19. Discuss the statement: when a system is to be implemented, one step is done at a time. For example, the files are all converted and then the programming starts.

6–20. Is the equipment selected during the implementation stage of the study?

6–21. Does a large- or medium-sized computer need any special considerations as far as the room in which it is to be located is concerned?

6–22. Is the training of operations personnel important?

6–23. What is coding? Give one illustration that is not used in the text.

6–24. Can a large program be tested before it is completely finished?

6–25. Of what value is "documentation?"

6–26. What is meant by "run parallel?"

6–27. Why should a continuing evaluation be made after the system is operational?

6–28. Discuss the statement: designing a payroll procedure involves only the operations within the data processing center.

DECISION TABLES AND COMPILES

Before giving the illustration of how a new procedure is actually designed and implemented, two terms which have been used should be clarified. What are *decision tables* and how are they used? What actually happens when a program is *compiled*?

Decision Tables

Although there are several different types of decision tables which may be used only a *vertical limited entry table* will be described. Some firms feel that the logic of a program is much easier to follow if decision tables are used rather than program flowcharts. The true advocates of decision tables claim that the logic is easier to follow, omissions in logic will not occur if correct procedures are used in developing the decision tables, and that you need not be an artist to construct the table. The techniques normally used in developing a decision table are to first expand the table to include every combination of true and false answers that can exist and then reduce the table to take out all redundancy. The three parts of a decision table are

> Decision Stub
>
> Action Stub
>
> Rule

The *decision stub* contains the questions. Is the light red? Is it raining? Has he earned $14,100? Is there school tomorrow? Do I have homework? The question is shown as being answered by true or false, or yes or no. Questions which are not relevant, due to a true or false answer from a previous question which alone decides the rule, are indicated by a dash (–). For example, if an employee already has earned $14,100, the current social security deduction is 0. Therefore, it is not relevant if the new year-to-date gross is equal to or greater than $14,100.

The *action stub* gives the action that is to be taken. The action might be *stop, branch to read-card, exit from loop, buy a new car.* In the illustration for the sake of simplicity only two considerations, or decisions, will be used:

> Is the light red?
> Is there a car in the way?

How many possible combinations are there?

Light Red?	T	T	F	F
Car in Way?	T	T	F	T

Any time there are only two decisions there can be only four possible combinations of true and false answers. If there are three decisions, there will be eight possible combinations; four decisions, sixteen combinations, etc.

The next step is to consider the action. This problem is relatively simple as you either *stop* or *go.* Put the two together, the decisions and the action, and you will have an exploded decision table.

	Rule	Rule	Rule	Rule
Decision Stub Light Red	T	T	F	F
Car in Way	F	T	F	T
Action Stub Stop	X	X		X
Go			X	

EXPLODED DECISION TABLE

The table can be reduced down to the following:

	Rule	Rule	Rule
Light Red	T	F	F
Car in Way	-	T	F
Stop	X	X	
Go			X

REDUCED DECISION TABLE

The decision table can be expressed by three rules:

1. If the light is red, you must stop.
2. If a car is in the way, you must stop.
3. If the light is not red and there is not a car in the way, you may go.

What considerations are part of the decision to go to a movie? To limit the illustration consider only the following:

No homework?
Have money?
Is it a good movie?

The action stub will either be:

Go to the movie.
Stay home.

Program Flowchart

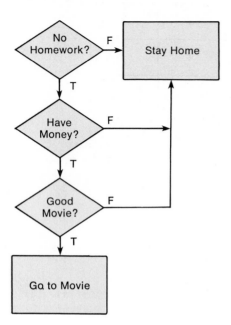

Decision Stub	Rule 1	Rule 2	Rule 3	Rule 4
No Homework	F	T	T	T
Have Money	-	F	T	T
Good Movie	-	-	F	T
Action Stub Go to Movie				X
Stay Home	X	X	X	

The decision table on "going to the movie" has been assigned to students by stating that they are to do a decision table which involves only three decisions on the topic of going to the movie. It is interesting to note the number of factors that are brought into the decision: have transportation, have money, does a friend want to go with me, is anything good on television, good movie, or can I get money. Seldom does the student start his decision table as I have started mine—*have homework?*

In using decision tables, each table should be relatively small. In payroll, the payroll register program would have one table to compute gross, one table for each of the taxes, and still other tables for determining the voluntary deductions.

Decision tables can be used effectively with a program flowchart to support the predefined processes. The next time you have any decision to make, try using a table. The technique is to first expand the table to include all possible combinations then condense it to avoid the redundancy. In professional magazines covering a number of different topics (not just data processing) you will now find decision tables being referenced as a means of formulating rules or a course of action to be followed.

TESTING A PROGRAM

Before a test can be made the program must be *compiled.* If the programmer wishes to test the program immediately after it is compiled, it is a three-phase process. In a disk-oriented system the computer will go from one phase to the next without the intervention of the operator. The correct Job Control Cards (JCL) must be used to tell the computer that this is a "Load and Go" compile. The three phases are

1. Checks for errors in the source statements. The routine clerical errors will be found but not the errors in logic.
2. Link-edits the program.
3. Tests the program.

The three phases appear as one since the computer will go from one into the other providing there are no *catastrophic errors.* An error is termed catastrophic when it is so bad that the compiler knows there is no point in continuing because the program will not be able to be executed. Other errors will be noted, but the computer will often try to execute as much of the program as it can even though there are some minor errors which are labeled "warnings." Compilers differ as to how many and what types of errors they will permit to be in the program and still make an attempt to run the program. RPG compilers *generally* will attempt to execute the program even though a great many errors have been detected. COBOL compilers will generally link-edit and run a program only if there are warnings. Also, unless the programmer specifies that he does not want it, during phase 1 a listing will print out on the printer which numbers each source statement. If errors are found, messages will appear on the printout, either at the end of the source statements or intermingled with the statements, similar to the ones illustrated.

802 E SIZE OF NUMERIC FIELD IS GREATER THAN 18. (18 is the maximum size for a numeric field in many languages.)
625 E INCORRECT FIELD NAME IN A MOVE STATEMENT: (The programmer called the field REGHRS when defining the field and then moved it as REGHR).

In the error statements the 802 and 625 identify the area of the program that the errors were found in. The *E* tells the programmer that it was an error message which was caused by a violation of the language's syntax (rules).

Hopefully, as the program compiles, none of the many different error messages will appear. The programmer is most delighted when the message reads:

SUCCESSFUL COMPILATION

When a compilation cancels due to catastrophic errors the analyst, in one installation, has the following message printed:

SORRY BUT I CAN'T COMPILE YOUR PROGRAM TODAY—
I AM JUST NOT IN THE MOOD.

One thing that can be said in favor of the message; at Christmas, MERRY CHRISTMAS is added to the message.

How compiles are executed differ with the system. If a disk system is used, the "load and go" compile will be as indicated by the flowchart in figure 6–5.

What happens during the link-edit phase? Programming has been made easier since many of the routines are available in the *library* which is stored on disk. The programmer writes a simple statement OPEN INPUT DISKIN. Let's look at the statement.

Open is telling the computer to open the file.
Input is stating that the file will be used as input.
Diskin is the name of the file. The programmer names the file.
He then consistently refers to the file as DISKIN in his program.

When the program is link-edited a whole series of commands are brought in due to the one simple "open" statement. First, commands are needed to check to make certain that the file of information is online. After this is determined, it must be established that the right area of the disk (cylinders and tracks) is being used.

When the read statement is used, commands will be added from the library to take care of the unblocking of the records. If the blocking factor is 20, the one read statement will read 20 logical records. A counter is maintained, and until those 20 are processed and the buffer is ready to be refilled no new physical record is read. Sound complicated? In COBOL all the programmer has to say is: READ DISKIN AT END GO TO END-OF-JOB-ROUTINE.

On the listing provided during the compilation of the program there is a long list of the various routines that have been incorporated into the user's program by the *linkage editor*. What is the linkage editor?—software. It is a routine that gets for you what you need out of the library which is stored on disk or tape. Your "library card" is the JOB CONTROL LANGUAGE card that tells the system to link-edit the program. In some systems the card will be // EXEC LNKEDT.

Phase 3 loads the linked program, which is now complete, back into the central processing unit for execution. The test data must be carefully constructed to cover all possible situations as complete testing of even the simplest program is an *absolute necessity*.

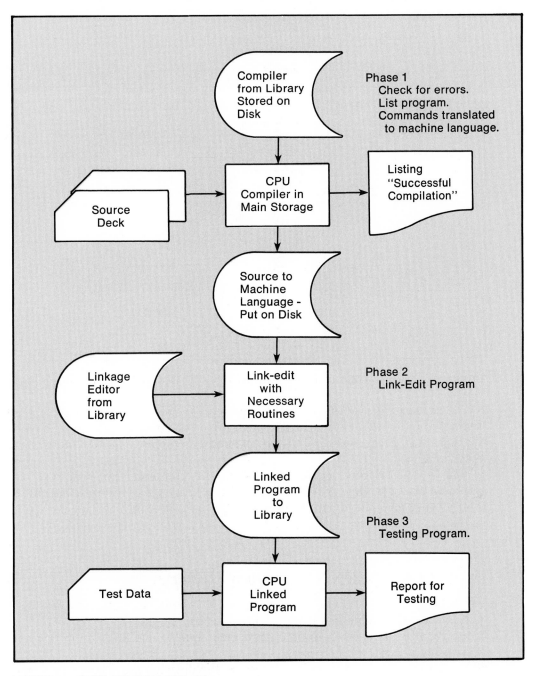

FIGURE 6–5. DISK COMPILE AND GO

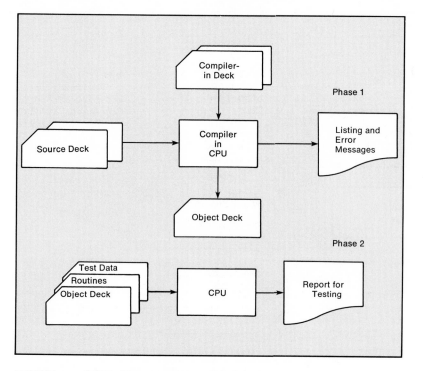

FIGURE 6–6. CARD SYSTEM COMPILE AND GO

In a card-oriented system, the load-and-go compile would be done as illustrated in figure 6–6. In a card system the error messages, during the compilation of a program, are often not as good as when a disk or tape system is used.

In a tape-oriented computer system the compilers and routines are stored on magnetic tape. The system works as illustrated with disk but rather than storing and getting information from disk, tape is used as the input device.

REVIEW OF DECISION TABLES AND COMPILES

6–29. A decision table has three parts which are called?

6–30. What is considered to be a good technique to use in developing decision tables?

6–31. If a decision table has four items on the decision stub, how many possible rules are there?

6–32. Are decision tables used in fields other than data processing?

6–33. If decision tables are used, does this always imply that program flow-charts will not be used?

6–34. Do all compilers work exactly the same?

6–35. As a general rule are error messages hard to read?

6–36. Refer back to figure 6–5 (p. 381) and determine what was stored in the main storage of the CPU during each of the three phases of the compile.

6–37. Where is the library that the linkage editor uses?

6–38. Discuss the following statement: currently computers are much more difficult to program as the programmer must take care of all of the small details that are necessary to make the program work.

DESIGN AND IMPLEMENTATION OF A PROCEDURE

The accounts receivable department manager felt that since all of the information needed for the aged accounts receivable trial balance was on the sales master disk file the procedure should be automated. If you are unfamiliar with an aged trial balance refer to page 394 and look over the report. In asking how this could be done, she was told that a memo should be sent to the data processing manager requesting that the procedure be computerized.

TO: Mr. Dale Keyser, Data Processing Manager   DATE: June 10

FROM: F. Gainey, Manager
           Accounts Receivable Department

RE: Aged Trial Balance Report

    In reading over the Sales System Documentation Manual it seems that all of the data required for the Aged Trial Balance is already available on the Accounts Receivable master file.

    The attached report illustrates the format that is currently used for the report. The report is printed each month and is used by both the accounts receivable department and the credit department.

    May I make an appointment with you as soon as possible to discuss the matter? It currently takes 10 - 15 hours per month to produce the report manually. It would seem a considerable amount of time could be saved if it could be printed by your department.

FIGURE 6–7. REQUEST FOR SYSTEMS WORK

Keyser agreed that this had been an omission in the sales system design. The addition of the requested procedure to the existing sales system was scheduled for immediate implementation as it would not involve a major programming effort.

Dennis R. McNeal, Systems Manager, was asked to see the accounts receivable manager and work out the details. He was asked not only to determine what the accounting department wanted in the report but to make certain that adequate controls were built into the design. Since there is additional information on the master file that might make the report more meaningful he was told to "brainstorm" the idea a little rather than just automating the former procedure.

Steps in Procedure Design

Step 1. *Problem Definition.* The present system was studied in order to see what currently was being done. The accounts receivable department was satisfied with the existing report. McNeal did suggest that additional information could easily be extracted from the file while the first report was being produced and stored in tables from which two additional reports could be printed.

The first summary, or additional report, would list customers that had only invoices which were over 90 days old. The report would give the name and address of the customer, the invoicing number, date of the invoice, number of days old, the salesman's number, and the amount that was due. Although there would be a relatively small number of accounts that would appear on the report, these were the ones that required *immediate attention*. Each salesman would be responsible for checking on his customers to determine the nature of the problem. It might be that some good "public relations" work is in order to get the amount paid and the customer's account active again.

The credit manager thought the idea would be great but asked why each salesman could not have his list on a separate sheet of paper. McNeal thought that sounded even better. McNeal said that a utility sort package, which was available as part of the computer's software, would make it very easy to have each salesman's list on a separate sheet, with a total for the salesman printed at the bottom. This might also prove interesting, for if one salesman consistently had an excessive number of individuals on his list the matter should be investigated by the district sales manager.

The second suggestion was to let the computer calculate the amount for an accounts receivable age group that would be considered as uncollectable. The results of the calculations would be summarized on a separate sheet.

The two additional items would take less than a minute of computer time to print yet would provide useful information to the individuals working with accounts receivable.

To avoid any possible misunderstanding, McNeal sent a memo confirming the decisions that had been reached at the meeting. He attached a copy of the design of the three reports to the memo and requested that both the credit manager and the accounts receivable manager send a memo back to him confirming that the new procedure and reports were acceptable.

After receiving confirmation that his interpretation of the meeting was correct, and that the reports were designed according to the wishes of the two departments that would work directly with the information, he sent a copy of the complete folder of information to a programmer, Betsy Smith. He asked her to start work on programming the procedure as soon as possible. McNeal had drawn up the macro flowchart shown in figure 6–8 which gave an overview of the new procedure.

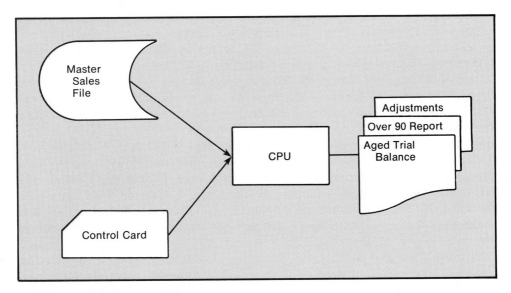

FIGURE 6–8. MACRO FLOWCHART

Step 2. *Determine Input/Output Needs and Formats.* All of the data that is needed for the reports is already in the accounts receivable master file. All fields were edited as the information was added to the file, so it is reasonably certain that the information is valid. Appropriate control totals had also been used as the file was updated. The programmer, Betsy Smith, realized that a control card would be needed to input the date for the report and to provide the Julian date for the determination of the age of each individual unpaid invoice. You will remember from the previous discussion of the master file that *for each invoice* the date, invoice number, and the amount of the invoice are all recorded. The date has already been recorded as the Julian date, so there is no conversion required. To get the age of each individual invoice, the invoice date is subtracted from the current date. On December 31 the Julian date entered would be 365. If an invoice had been recorded on the 320th day of the year, the age of the invoice would be calculated as 365–320 or as 45 days old. The amount would then be added to the 31–60 day old total field for the customer.

The control card had the following format:

> 1–13   Report date as it will be printed on the top of the report
> 14–16   Julian date

The print layout forms were put into final form and are included as part of the documentation. Before the programmer can write the program, the layout forms must be done so that he will know where to print the headings, report line, and totals. Since the report is for internal use only, stock paper is used and the headings are added to the report by the program. A standard control tape is used which allows a one-inch top and bottom margin.

Step 3. *Program Flowchart.* The program flowchart expresses the major logic of the program, while the decision table supports the predefined process. Both the program flowchart and the decision tables are included in the final documentation. Note: To keep the problem simple, the table and extra reports are not included in the flowchart of the problem.

Step 4. *Code the Problem.* After doing the program flowcharts, the next step is to code the problem in the language used by the installation. The illustration uses COBOL, which is the language that would have been used by the L. C. Smith Corporation at the point in time when the request was submitted. Read both the flowchart and the coding and see how much of the coding you understand. Can you pick out the file structures, control card, headings, and report line? Compare the report layout to the coding. All of the logic is expressed in the procedure division, since the first three divisions merely tell the computer the files and structures that are to be used. Compare the procedure division with the program flowchart and see if you can follow the logic. Since the printout from the compilation has the coding on it, the actual coding sheets are generally not part of the documentation.

Step 5. *Punch the Source Deck.* Each line of coding from the coding form will be punched into one card.

Step 6. *Compile the Program.* During the compilation of the program a listing is printed by the printer which shows the contents of each card in the source deck. The listing is retained as part of the documentation because it will be used if the program must be modified. Usually each programmer has a method of recording on each new printout the modification made and the purpose of the change. This is in addition to the data recorded on the documentation cover sheet.

Step 7. *Testing.* The programmer tested the aged trial balance report in the following way: The test pack, which is maintained for testing other accounts receivable programs, was used in testing the new program. Since there are only ten records on the test pack for the accounts receivable master file, it makes it easy to hand calculate the report, using the test data, doing exactly what the computer is doing as it evaluates the unpaid invoices for each customer. All of the invoices that are recorded in the test pack are unpaid. The totals are also added in the same way the computer will add the totals. The results of the hand calculations are compared with the computer printed report. In addition, the total of all accounts receivable ($20,351.34) must agree with a total which was established using the same data by another report that is known to be valid.

After the report is tested using the test pack of data it is run on the actual master file, and some of the accounts will be hand calculated as a final check that the report is valid. In addition, the final total must agree with the total from the accounts receivable summary report. Each individual account total can also be checked against the accounts receivable summary report. When the aged trial balance report is scheduled it will be run immediately after the accounts receivable summary report, and the two reports will be compared.

Step 8. *Documentation.* The procedure is documented according to the standards established by the L. C. Smith Corporation. The documentation that is maintained in the computer center for the use of the operator and programmer for running and maintaining the program is illustrated.

For each procedure a folder is filed by the number of the program. The aged accounts receivable program was assigned the number AR0246. In the library the program is also cataloged under AR0246. Once a program has been compiled and tested it may be cataloged in a library which resides on either disk or tape. When the program is used it is loaded into the memory of the computer and the steps of compiling and link editing the program can be omitted. The folder for AR0246 contains the following items which are illustrated:

1. *Cover Sheet.* As you examine the cover sheet you will see that there is a section provided for recording the revisions to the program. This, along with the name of the person to contact in case of problems, is probably the most important item on the cover sheet.
2. *Run Sheet.* The operator should *always* check the sheet to make certain that all directions are *explicitly* followed.

3. *Overview of the Program.* This could be eliminated from the documentation in the computer center, but it is essential that management has the information in their systems manual. The overview sheet should show how the procedure being documented fits into the total sales and accounts receivable system.

4. *Program Flowchart and Decision Tables.* When a program is changed for any reason it is very helpful to have the flowchart. The programmer can determine the logic of the program much easier by following the flowchart than by studying the program listing. Following the logic from either the listing or a written description of the program is far more time consuming. When changes are made in the program the *program flowchart should also be updated.*

5. *Program Listing.* The program listing is from an IBM 360/40 computer. The listing is needed if the program is to be modified or if for some reason the program is cancelled during execution.

6. *Input/Output Description.* The entire file need not be detailed as the fields can be determined by referring to the program listing. Some languages such as PL/I permit comments on each field's card as to what the data is used for. For example:

> 02 ECODE PIC '9', /* 1 for hourly, 2 for salaried */
> 02 STATUS PIC '9', /* 1 for single, 2 for married */

7. *Testing Methods.* When modifications are made to the program this material will be helpful because each time the program is altered it should be tested on the test data.

8. *Sample Output.* When special forms are used, the illustration will show the operator how the information is to appear on the form. The print layout form, or print chart, should also be retained because changes are easier to format from the layout form.

9. Some of the information required by the computer in order that it can run the jobs correctly is supplied by the operator using Job Control Language cards (JCL). The function of the cards required for the Aged Trial Balance report is given, as well as a listing of the actual cards (page 398).

   a. // JOB card. The major function of the job card is to provide the job name, kind of job, account to be charged, as well as the other information that is used in accounting for the computer's time.

   b. The // ASSGN cards are for assigning the files defined in the program to a physical device. SYS007 is a disk file and is assigned to disk drive 192. If drive 192 is not available the operator can change the assign card to 193 or 194.

   c. // DLAB cards provide the label information. This card must be exactly like the one that was used when the master file was created. The system checks to see if the name is right. If it is not correct an error message will be printed on either the printer or console typewriter.

d. The // XTENT cards tell where on the disk pack the index and the prime area are located. The XTENTs used to execute the program must be identical to the XTENTs used in creating the file.

e. The // EXEC AR0246 is used to load the program which is in the library into the central processing unit.

f. The date card is used as an illustration of how the card must be punched.

g. The /* informs the computer that the end of the file has been found. The /& will cause the termination of the job.

The documentation that is presented should be considered as a *minimum*. Study the illustrations that refer to the case study and the documentation.

DOCUMENTATION FOR AGED ACCOUNTS RECEIVABLE

Overview of the Aged Accounts Receivable

The program is designed to print a monthly report which totals the unpaid invoices for each customer by age. The age is determined by subtracting the date of the invoice from the current Julian date which is entered on the control card.

The age is calculated according to the following age groupings:

> thirty days or less
> thirty-one to sixty days
> sixty-one to ninety days
> over ninety days

The total of all unpaid invoices must agree with the total of the year-to-date Accounts Receivable report. The Aged Accounts Receivable report is to be run immediately after the year-to-date report.

Systems Flowchart

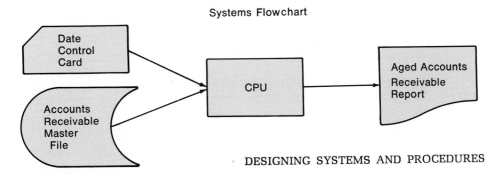

Systems Flowchart

Cover Sheet

Program Name	Aged Accounts Receivable
Program Number	AR0246
Language Used	COBOL
Author	B. Smith
Date Written	July 1975
Execution Problems Contact	B. Smith
Revisions	

By	Date	Reason

Note: Normally this is the first page of the documentation.

PRODUCTION RUN INSTRUCTIONS

JOB NUMBER	PROGRAMMER	DATE	FREQUENCY
AR 0246	B. Smith	July, 1975	Monthly

DATA CARD

1 - 13 Date for Heading
14 - 16 Julian Date

TYPE OF RUN

☐ MAINT.
☒ XX REPORT

PUNCH
No.

PRINTER

FORM TYPE	SPACING	CARRIAGE: ☒XXX STANDARD
3-part stock paper	☒XX 6 LPI ☐ 8 LPI	OTHER

DISK:	FILE NAME	ADDRESS	SPECIAL INSTRUCTIONS
ActRec	Diskin	CYL 2 - 69	

SPECIAL INSTRUCTIONS

1. Keypunch control card as indicated.
2. The report is to be run the first day of each month prior to the file update for current transactions.
3. Run immediately after AR 0245.
4. Check the final total with AR 0245 report total before distribution of the report.

OPERATION ACCEPTANCE: *M. Wackerly*

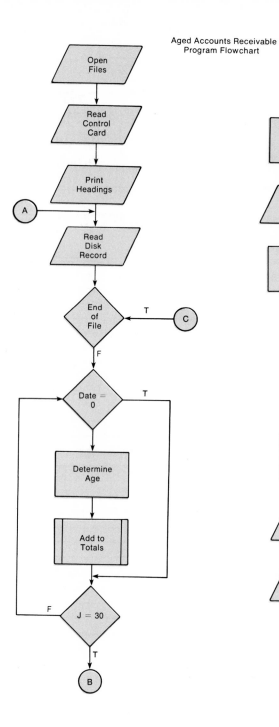

Aged Accounts Receivable
Program Flowchart

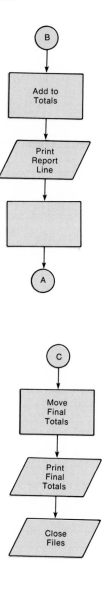

	RULE 1	RULE 2	RULE 3	RULE 4
Decision Stub:				
Computed Age < 31	T	F	F	F
Computed Age < 61	—	T	F	F
Computed Age < 91	—	—	T	F
Computed Age > 90	—	—	—	T
Action Stub:				
Add to Total A	X			
Add to Total B		X		
Add to Total C			X	
Add to Total D				X
Add to Total E	X	X	X	X
Exit	X	X	X	X

Input Requirements

The accounts receivable master file is to be used as input for the report. The report must be run the first of each month prior to the daily update of the file.

A date card is used which has the date punched as mmmm dd, yyyy in columns 1–13. The Julian date for the day the report is to be run is entered in card columns 14–16. It is essential that the date be correct because the ages of the unpaid invoices are determined by using the date.

Output

Three-part stock paper is used for the report. The print layout sheet illustrates where the data is to be printed. A sample report is printed from the test data. After determining that the report is correct, it should be decollated and sent to the accounts receivable department.

Testing Method

The program is tested using the test data for accounts receivables. Each customer's record was hand-calculated and compared to the printed report. The test data is retained for testing related sales and accounts receivable programs.

The total of all unpaid invoices must agree with the total of the year-to-date report.

SHARE PRINT CHART   PROG. ID. _AR0246_____   PAGE _____

(SPACING: 6 LINES PER INCH, DEPTH; 51 LINES)   DATE _____

PROGRAM TITLE __AGED ACCOUNTS RECEIVABLE_____

PROGRAMMER OR DOCUMENTALIST: __B. SMITH_____

CHART TITLE _____

Fold back at dot

```
                    L. C. SMITH CORPORATION

                AGED ACCOUNTS RECEIVABLE              XXXXXXXXXXXXX


       NAME                    0-30      31-60     61-90    OVER 90   TOTAL

XXXXXXXXXXXXXXXXXXXXXXXXXXXXXXXXXXXX   XXXXXX.XX  XXXXXX.XX  XXXXXX.XX  XXXXXX.XX  XXXXXX.XX












TOTAL ACCOUNTS RECEIVABLE     XXXXXX.XX  XXXXXX.XX  XXXXXX.XX  XXXXXX.XX  XXXXXX.XX
```

```
LINE NO. SEQ. NO.        SOURCE STATEMENT

    1    001010 IDENTIFICATION DIVISION.
    2    001020 PROGRAM-ID. 'ARO246'.
    3    001030 AUTHOR. B  SMITH.
    4    001040 ENVIRONMENT DIVISION.
    5    001050 CONFIGURATION SECTION.
    6    001060 SOURCE-COMPUTER. IBM-360.
    7    001070 OBJECT-COMPUTER. IBM-360.
    8    001080 INPUT-OUTPUT SECTION.
    9    001090 FILE-CONTROL.
   10    001100     SELECT DISKF ASSIGN TO 'SYS007' DIRECT-ACCESS 2311,
   11    001110     ORGANIZATION IS INDEXED,
   12    001112     ACCESS IS SEQUENTIAL,
   13    001130     RECORD KEY IS DACCTNO,
   14    001140     SYMBOLIC KEY IS ZNUM,
   15    001150     RESERVE NO ALTERNATE AREA.
   16    001160     SELECT PRINTF ASSIGN TO 'SYS006' UNIT-RECORD 1403.
   17    001170     SELECT CARDIN ASSIGN TO 'SYS008' UNIT-RECORD 2540R.
   18    002010 DATA DIVISION.
   19    002020 FILE SECTION.
   20    002030 FD DISKF
   21    002040     RECORDING MODE IS F
   22    002050     BLOCK CONTAINS 5 RECORDS
   23    002060     RECORD CONTAINS 536 CHARACTERS
   24    002070     LABEL RECORDS ARE STANDARD
   25    002080     DATA RECORDS ARE DF.
   26    002090 01  DF.
   27    002100     02  DACCTNO PICTURE XXXX.
   28    002110     02  DNAME    PICTURE X(26).
   29    002120     02  DADD     PICTURE X(25).
   30    002130     02  DADD2    PICTURE X(24).
   31    002140     02  DTSALES PICTURE 9(6)V99.
   32    002150     02  DTCASH   PICTURE 9(6)V99.
   33    002160     02  DTRETURN PICTURE 9(6)V99.
   34    002170     02  DTABLE.
   35    002180        04  DDATE    OCCURS 30 TIMES, PICTURE 999.
   36    002190        04  DINVNO   OCCURS 30 TIMES, PICTURE 9999.
   37    002200        04  DAMT     OCCURS 30 TIMES, PICTURE S9(5)V99.
   38    003010     02  DCRLIMIT PICTURE 9(5)V99.
   39    003015     02  SALESMAN PICTURE 99.
   40    003020     02  JUNK     PICTURE X(4).
   41    003030 FD PRINTF
   42    003040     RECORDING MODE IS F
   43    003041     RECORD CONTAINS 80 CHARACTERS
   44    003042     LABEL RECORDS ARE OMITTED
   45    003043     DATA RECORDS ARE PRINTO.
   46    003044 01 PRINTO.
   47    003045     02  FORM     PICTURE X(80).
   48    003046 FD CARDIN
   49    003047     RECORDING MODE IS F
   50    003048     RECORD CONTAINS 80 CHARACTERS
   51    003049     LABEL RECORDS ARE OMITTED
   52    003050     DATA RECORD IS CARDS.
   53    003051 01  CARDS.
   54    003052     02  DATE PICTURE X(13).
```

```
 55    003053     02   JDATE PICTURE 999.
 56    003054     02   FILLER PICTURE X(64).
 57    003055 WORKING-STORAGE SECTION.
 58    003056 77  TA  PICTURE S9(7)V99 VALUE 0.
 59    003057 77  TB  PICTURE S9(7)V99 VALUE 0.
 60    003060 77  TC  PICTURE S9(7)V99 VALUE 0.
 61    003070 77  TD  PICTURE S9(7)V99 VALUE 0.
 62    003073 77  TE  PICTURE S9(7)V99 VALUE 0.
 63    003075 77  GTA PICTURE 9(7)V99 VALUE 0.
 64    003076 77  GTB PICTURE 9(7)V99 VALUE 0.
 65    003077 77  GTC PICTURE 9(7)V99 VALUE 0.
 66    003078 77  GTD PICTURE 9(7)V99 VALUE 0.
 67    003079 77  GTE PICTURE 9(7)V99 VALUE 0.
 68    003090 77  ZNUM  PICTURE XXXX VALUE '0001'.
 69    003100 77  AGE   PICTURE 999 VALUE 0.
 70    003105 77  J   PICTURE 99 VALUE 0.
 71    003106 77  LINEC  PICTURE 99 VALUE 40.
 72    003108 77 FILLER PICTURE X(3) VALUE SPACES.
 73    003110 01  FIRM.
 74    003111     02   FILLERX PICTURE X(29) VALUE SPACES.
 75    003112     02   FNAME PICTURE X(23) VALUE
 76    003113          'L. C. SMITH CORPORATION'.
 77    003114     02   FILLERX PICTURE X(28) VALUE SPACES.
 78    003115 01  HONE.
 79    003120     02   H1  PICTURE X(28) VALUE SPACES.
 80    003130     02   H2  PICTURE X(24) VALUE
 81    003135          'AGED ACCOUNTS RECEIVABLE'.
 82    003140     02   H3  PICTURE X(8) VALUE SPACES.
 83    003150     02   H4  PICTURE X(13).
 84    003160     02   H5  PICTURE X(7) VALUE SPACES.
 85    003180 01  HTWO.
 86    003190     02   M1  PICTURE X(11) VALUE SPACES.
 87    003200     02   M2  PICTURE X(4)  VALUE 'NAME'.
 88    004010     02   M3  PICTURE X(20) VALUE SPACES.
 89    004020     02   M4  PICTURE X(4)    VALUE '0-30'.
 90    004030     02   M5  PICTURE X(4)  VALUE SPACES.
 91    004040     02   M6  PICTURE X(5) VALUE '31-60'.
 92    004050     02   M7  PICTURE X(5) VALUE SPACES.
 93    004060     02   M8  PICTURE X(5) VALUE '61-90'.
 94    004070     02   M9  PICTURE X(4) VALUE SPACES.
 95    004080     02   M10 PICTURE X(7) VALUE 'OVER 90'.
 96    004090     02   M11 PICTURE X(3) VALUE SPACES.
 97    004100     02   M12 PICTURE X(5) VALUE 'TOTAL'.
 98    004105     02   M12 PICTURE X(4) VALUE SPACES.
 99    004110 01  HTHREE.
100    004120     02   N1      PICTURE X(3)   VALUE SPACES.
101    004130     02   NNAME   PICTURE X(27).
102    004150     02   NTA     PICTURE -------.99.
103    004170     02   NTB     PICTURE -------.99.
104    004190     02   NTC     PICTURE -------.99.
105    005010     02   NTD     PICTURE -------.99.
106    005030     02   NTE     PICTURE -------.99.
107    006010 PROCEDURE DIVISION.
108    006020     OPEN INPUT DISKF, CARDIN, OUTPUT PRINTF.
109    006030     READ CARDIN AT END GO TO EDJ.
110    006040     MOVE DATE TO H4.
```

```
LINE NO. SEQ. NO.
    111   006090 01-READ.
    112   006100     READ DISKF AT END GO TO EDJ.
    113   006110 02-READ.
    114   006130     PERFORM CHECK THRU CK2 VARYING J FROM 1 BY 1
    115   006131     UNTIL J = 31.
    116   006132     COMPUTE TE = TA + TB + TC + TD.
    117   006133     IF TE = 0 THEN GO TO 01-READ.
    118   006136     MOVE DNAME TO NNAME.
    119   006140     MOVE TA TO NTA.
    120   006150     MOVE TB TO NTB.
    121   006160     MOVE TC TO NTC.
    122   006170     MOVE TD TO NTD.
    123   006175     MOVE TE TO NTE.
    124   006180     IF LINEC = 40 THEN PERFORM HEADR.
    125   008010     WRITE PRINTO FROM HTHREE AFTER ADVANCING 1.
    126   008020     COMPUTE LINEC = LINEC + 1.
    127   008030 ZEROR.
    128   008040     MOVE 0 TO TA.
    129   008050     MOVE 0 TO TB.
    130   008060     MOVE 0 TO TC.
    131   008070     MOVE 0 TO TD.
    132   008080     MOVE 0 TO TE.
    133   008100     GO TO 01-READ.
    134   009010 CHECK.
    135   009020     IF DDATE (J) = 0 THEN GO TO CK2.
    136   009030     COMPUTE AGE = JDATE - DDATE (J).
    137   009040     IF AGE < 31 THEN ADD DAMT (J) TO TA,
    138   009050     ADD DAMT (J) TO GTA,
    139   009060     GO TO CK2.
    140   009070     IF AGE < 61 THEN ADD DAMT (J) TO TB,
    141   009080     ADD DAMT (J) TO GTB,
    142   009090     GO TO CK2.
    143   009100     IF AGE < 91 THEN ADD DAMT (J) TO TC,
    144   009110     ADD DAMT (J) TO GTC,
    145   009120     GO TO CK2.
    146   009130     IF AGE > 90 THEN ADD DAMT (J) TO TD,
    147   009140     ADD DAMT (J) TO GTD,
    148   009150     GO TO CK2.
    149   009170 CK2.
    150   009180     EXIT.
    151   010050 HEADR.
    152   010055     WRITE PRINTO FROM FIRM AFTER ADVANCING 0 LINES.
    153   010060     WRITE PRINTO FROM HONE AFTER ADVANCING 3 LINES.
    154   010070     WRITE PRINTO FROM HTWO AFTER ADVANCING 3 LINES.
    155   010080     COMPUTE LINEC = 0.
    156   010110 EOJ.
    157   010112     MOVE 'TOTAL ACCOUNTS RECEIVABLE' TO NNAME.
    158   010115     COMPUTE GTE = GTA + GTB + GTC + GTD.
    159   010120     MOVE GTA TO NTA.
    160   010130     MOVE GTB TO NTB.
    161   010140     MOVE GTC TO NTC.
    162   010150     MOVE GTD TO NTD.
    163   010160     MOVE GTE TO NTE.
    164   010170     WRITE PRINTO FROM HTHREE AFTER ADVANCING 3 LINES.
    165   010180     CLOSE DISKF, PRINTF, CARDIN.
    166   010190     STOP RUN.
```

```
                          L. C. SMITH CORPORATION

                    AGED ACCOUNTS RECEIVABLE           JULY 31
            NAME        0-30        31-60       61-90      OVER 90      TOTAL
    JOHN REED           9000.00      500.00     1000.00      500.00    11000.00
    RITA SMITH           199.23         .00      500.00       98.00      797.23
    PAUL BLAKE              .00      922.11         .00        5.44      927.55
    BRAD GREEN          -200.00         .00         .00      100.00     -100.00
    JERRI BROWN          888.88         .00      463.19      888.88     2240.95
    FRANK BLAINE            .00         .00         .00     2209.11     2209.11
    SALLY REED           419.00         .00      500.00      100.00     1019.00
    JANE BROWN             .00         .00     1499.99      200.00     1699.99
    BETTY ROBERTS         98.98      200.00         .00       50.00      348.98
    JAMES LOVE            93.42         .00       16.13       98.98      208.53


    TOTAL ACCOUNTS RECEIVABLE
                       10499.51     1622.11     3979.31     4250.41    20351.34
```

```
JOB CONTROL CARDS FOR AGED ACCOUNTS RECEIVABLE PROGRAM

// JOB ARO246    F6 PR    002  AGED ACCOUNTS RECEIVABLE

// ASSGN SYS007,X'192'

// ASSGN SYS006,X'00E'

// ASSGN SYS008,X'00C'

// VOL SYS007,SYS007

// DLAB 'ACCOUNTS RECEIVABLE MASTER FILE              ACTREC'           X
          0001,74001,99365,'                 ',ISE

// XTENT 4,1,000001000,000001009,'ACTREC',SYS007

// XTENT 1,2,000002000,000060009,'ACTREC',SYS007

// EXEC ARO246

JULY 31,19   212                /*DATE CONTROL CARD--CHANGE EACH MONTH*/
```

GLOSSARY OF NEW AND OLD TERMS
TO CHECK YOUR KNOWLEDGE

Action Stub. The portion of a decision table that contains the action such as GO TO READ-CARD, EXIT FROM LOOP, or COMPUTE TAX.

Analyst. An individual who studies a given system or procedure and determines the best method or methods to use in the solution of the problem.

Decision Stub. The portion of the decision table that contains the decisions which are made. Each decision is answered by using a T or F.

Decision Table. A table of possible courses of action that can be taken depending upon the decisions that are made.

Documentation. The materials needed to illustrate an application. Included should be the statement of the problem, flowcharts, samples of input and output, and operating instructions.

Feasibility Study. A study which is made to determine if an existing system should be changed in order to incorporate better methods and improve performance.

Hardware. The computer and the related I/O devices.

Linkage Editor. Part of the software that is stored on disk or tape. When a compile is performed it is loaded into the CPU and is assigned the task of link-editing the program.

Load and Go. A common term used when a program is to be compiled, link-edited, and tested without first producing an object deck.

Macro Program Flowcharts. Macro flowcharts provide the major concepts of a program or procedure.

Management. The persons who manage a business.

Object Deck. A deck of cards that contains the machine language translations of the source code.

Procedure. A precise step-by-step method of effecting a solution to a problem. Complex systems are divided into procedures which may in turn be divided into tasks.

Rule. The decisions made and actions taken determine the rules.

Software. The compilers, operating system, application, and utility programs that are necessary for the computer to function.

Syntax. A set of rules governing a computer language that must be followed in coding a program.

Systems Flowchart. A systems flowchart illustrates the files needed for input and output generated from the processing of the data.

Systems Manual. Contains information on the operation of a system. Sufficient detail is provided so that management can determine the data flow, forms used, reports generated, and controls exercised. Job descriptions are also generally provided.

Systems Study. A comprehensive study made of an existing system with recommendations for alternate methods of more effectively achieving the stated objective.

ANSWERS

REORGANIZATION OF THE DATA PROCESSING DEPARTMENT (p. 354)

6–1.   He was asked to develop a long-range plan for the expansion of both the services and facilities of the data processing department.

6–2.   You should be aware that the field of data processing is constantly changing. Each time a firm secures new hardware, or software (the operating system) changes, employees must be aware of what changes were made and how it affects their jobs.

6–3.   Develop standards for documentation. This implies that perhaps within the company the standards were not developed or were felt to be inadequate.

6–4.   The description has not changed but the operator's job has—keeping up to one large-scale computer may take two or three operators per shift. It is an extremely demanding job.

6–5.   The data processing department was considered almost as a service bureau whose function was to provide services to the other departments within the company.

REVIEW QUESTIONS (p. 363)

6–6.   Yes. A feasibility study could be conducted to determine if a new machine should be purchased for the plant or if the present machine should be retained. Is it feasible to reorganize the company or should the present structure be retained? Since the definition is essentially "to study an area or function with a view towards improving its performance by using better methods," a feasibility study can be conducted for any purpose.

6–7.   During phase 1 and phase 2.

6–8.   A. Data requirements
       B. Objectives
       C. Tentative design, equipment, and cost

6–9.   A. It can be accepted as is and phase 3 would then be scheduled.
       B. It can be rejected. The team assigned to the study would be asked to revise or to perhaps present a totally new approach.
       C. The entire project can be terminated.

6–10. A. Time
       B. Budget
       C. Personnel

6–11. It involves the people who will be directly affected by any change in the sales system.

6–12. A greater percentage of the total cost involved in the various data processing functions is allocated to development.

6–13. It becomes the commitment for both the sales and systems departments.

6–14. The systems manual shows how the department is organized and what each individual within the department actually does.

6–15. No. The structure, job descriptions, and methods of performing certain functions could have changed, but the manuals have not been updated accordingly.

6–16. A. study the manual   C. observation
      B. interview employees   D. study reports and forms

6–17. If the individual is aware of the points to be covered he can get the materials together that will be needed and organize his thinking. It would save time and also make the interview much more productive.

6–18. It confirms what actually occurred at the interview. It may prevent any misunderstanding at some time in the future.

REVIEWING IMPLEMENTATION (p. 375)

6–19. The statement is untrue, because it would take entirely too long to convert if this were the case. A chart or schedule is made up that indicates the sequence that different parts of the implementation will occur in. Many different things can be done parallel to one another.

6–20. No. The selection is already determined. It is ordered and scheduled to arrive in time for some of the testing to be done on it.

6–21. Yes. With the exception of the minicomputer, most computers need an air conditioned room, special wiring, and raised flooring. Other considerations make life more pleasant, such as the use of acoustical tile and wall coverings, attractive use of color, etc.

6–22. Yes. A good deal of attention should be given to the training of the employees, especially those who play a major role in preparation of input and the use of equipment. They should know how each step is to be done and made to feel comfortable with the new equipment and procedures.

6–23. Coding is condensing of information. The student may select some very simple codes to use as an answer, such as 1 for freshmen, 2 for sophomore, etc. Another code might be a V for veteran and a blank for a non-veteran. The code should be simple and easy to remember.

6-24. Yes. Often a large program can be tested in segments. Each program is tested individually before the entire system is tested.

6-25. One form of documentation, the systems manual, provides the overview for the entire system for management. Other documentation is prepared for the computer operators and the individuals who will work with magnetic tape units, keypunches, or the terminals.

6-26. Both the old and new method are used. The results are compared. In the case of payroll, the net pay, taxes, and deductions should be the same regardless of which method is used.

6-27. To determine if it really does meet the objectives. Also an error analysis can be done to determine if more controls should be built into the system.

6-28. No. Part of the systems work will be done in the factory. How effective are the badge readers or timecards that are being used? The system design starts at where the transactions occur.

REVIEW OF DECISION TABLES AND COMPILES (p. 382)

6-29. decision stub
action stub
rule

6-30. A good technique is to first explode the table, study it, and then reduce it to eliminate duplication.

6-31. 16

6-32. Yes. Decision tables are used in solving many different kinds of problems and in many areas other than data processing.

6-33. No. The case study will illustrate the use of a program flowchart which can almost be thought of as a macro program flowchart. The predetermined process is supported by a decision table.

6-34. No.

6-35. No. The messages are, for most compilers, very understandable.

6-36. Phase I—The compiler
Phase II—The linkage editor
Phase III—The compiled and linked program written by the programmer

6-37. The library is on disk and the editor is actually a program that is stored when needed in the CPU.

6-38. The statement is completely false because with each generation more is done by using routines stored on tape, disk, or in card decks. The one exception is the true minicomputer.

RPG 7

Report Program Generator (RPG) is extremely well suited to procedures that read files, involve little mathematics, and create reports. The files can be defined with a minimum of effort, and the instructions necessary to write the headings, detail, and total lines are also easily coded. RPG, however, does not currently support the use of compound mathematical formulas. For this reason, programs that are mathematically oriented, rather than report oriented, are easier to write in FORTRAN, PL/I, or COBOL.

Since RPG is not a machine-oriented language, the programmer is required to know very little about how the computer will actually execute the commands. Programmers who have had experience writing in other languages feel that there are many unique features about RPG, since many details are automatically taken care of by the compiler.

RPG was first introduced for use on the IBM 1400 series computers, and then later used for other small-scale computers which had a rather limited amount of memory. Although RPG was available in the early 1960s and used on a variety of computers, not much was written about it until its utilization by the System/3 computers. The System/3 line, introduced by IBM in 1969, still supports RPG as its principle language. However, the larger System/3 can also use COBOL and FORTRAN. Since its origination, RPG as a language has become far more complete and functional.

Coding in RPG is considered by some programmers as being more tedious because very rigid formats must be followed in coding the four major types of statements which describe the files, input and output formats, and provide the calculations. Four different *specification forms* are used to provide the following functions:

1. *File Specifications.* The function of this form is to describe to the computer the characteristics of each file, give it a user-supplied name, and tell the specific piece of hardware that will be used.
2. *Input Specifications.* For the input files described, each record is broken into fields. For each field, the computer is told where in the record the field is located and if it contains alphanumeric or numeric data.
3. *Calculation Specifications.* The major logic of the program is expressed by using the commands available. In this section, arithmetic operations are performed, data is moved from one field to another, and comparisons are made. The programmer specifies the conditions under which each command will be executed.
4. *Output Specifications.* Headings, detail lines, and total lines can easily be established for the printer. The conditions are given under *which each type of output* is to be printed, when a card is to be punched, or when a disk or tape file will be written.

Once the specification sheets are coded, the source deck is punched from the sheet and the program is compiled. As the execution logic of an RPG program is explained, you will see how many things are done automatically and seemingly not under the more "direct" control of the programmer. Therefore, programmers who have experience in the more traditional languages, COBOL, FORTRAN, and PL/I, sometimes have trouble accepting the fact that so much is done automatically and not at the specific request of the programmer.

RPG LOGIC—AN OVERVIEW

As a general rule, without going into exceptions and detail, once the problem is compiled, the logic of RPG takes over in the execution of your program. The logic will be detailed in this section, but for now accept that a program, using card input and printed output under RPG I, would be executed in three phases:

1. As input record is read and usually one or more indicators are turned on.
2. Next, control goes to the commands generated from the calculation specifications. Which of the commands will be executed? The computer will pick the commands to execute depending upon what indicators are on.
3. After selecting the proper calculations, moves, or comparisons to make and executing those, the program control passes to output. Here, again, decisions are made by the computer based upon which indicators are on. Will headings be printed or will only a detail line be printed?

For a point of reference, phase 1 will be referred to as input time, phase 2, calculation time, and phase 3, output time.

RPG I and II

The first version of RPG, RPG I, was rather limited in scope because certain features now permitted in RPG II were not available. Tables could be utilized in RPG I by using a key and a command called LOKUP, but the use of indexes was not permitted. Information could be written as output only during "output time," which made the establishment of loops requiring the use of repeated calculations and output for one input record impossible to construct. Therefore, RPG II permitted the writing of output during calculation time, which made the construction of loops requiring an output operation easy to code. Subroutines, written in RPG II, can now be called into the main program by an RPG command. In RPG I, however, the subroutines had to have been coded in the computer's assembler language to be utilized in the main RPG program. Many other additional features, not available in RPG I, were added to RPG II.

Is RPG Widely Used?

The true advocates of RPG II feel it is now a complete language which permits the programmer to do, with relative ease, almost everything he wishes. Some programmers feel it will become the language of the future. Currently, its use is not limited to only IBM computers since other manufacturers' computers also have RPG compilers. It is presently more widely used among the small-scale user than by the large-scale users. In an installation where FORTRAN and COBOL are also available, RPG still might be the easiest way to generate simple reports from existing data files. For scientific or statistical analysis, FORTRAN probably can be used more effectively.

REVIEW QUESTIONS

7–1. What are the four major specification sheets used for coding RPG?

7–2. For what kind of computer user was RPG first designed?

7–3. In general, what did RPG II attempt to do for the RPG users?

7–4. What types of programs, or problems, are best suited to RPG?

7–5. Does the programmer have as much control over the way the program will be executed as he might have in a more conventional language?

7–6. What is an indicator? If you can't answer the question, refer to the end of the module and use the glossary.

7–7. What is meant by the statement, "RPG is not a machine-oriented language?"

RPG LOGIC

It is important that you understand the logic that the computer follows in execution of an RPG program. On figures 7–1 and 7–2, used to show the logic or program cycle, an explanation is given as to what causes these events to take place. Is it the programmer's responsibility to code the command, or is the instruction added to the object code as the program is compiled? Before considering the diagram, *level breaks* (L1–L9) and the *last record* (LR) indicator will be explained.

The last record indicator (LR) is turned on when the end of the file is found. If a card file is used, the end of the file may be detected when the /* card is read. On tape or disk, an end-of-file marker follows the last record, and when it is read the LR indicator will automatically come on providing that on the file specification sheet an "E" was coded in column 17 to indicate that it is the programmer's wish to terminate the job with that particular file.

Level Breaks

There may be as many as nine level breaks, numbered L1–L9, provided automatically in an RPG program. If an input card had the following fields, four level breaks could be used:

REGION NUMBER	L4
DIVISION NUMBER	L3
DEPARTMENT NUMBER	L2
MAN NUMBER	L1

Since man is the smallest unit, L1 is used for the man control break number. Men work in departments (next in the hierarchy) so L2 is coded for the department level break. The departments are within divisions, which means that L3 will be used for the division level break and L4 for the region numbers. The level breaks are indicated on the input form and will be covered in detail at the end of the module. Why would you want to know when these level breaks occur?

Perhaps management would like a sales report showing the total by man, by department, by divisions, and finally by each region. When an L4 occurs, which resulted in the computer detecting a change in region number, any L1 event will be executed, then all L2s and L3s. Finally the L4 events will take place. As you will see, level breaks can be used to tell the computer to either do certain calculations or write various types of output at the point in time indicated by the control level. If used effectively, indicators turned on by level breaks can save the programmer a great deal of coding.

Examples of L1 and LR

A report is to be produced from the cards, all five, which will total the sales for each man and print his total sales. At the end of the report, the total sales for all men is also to be printed. The five cards would produce the following report:

Sales Report

001	599.00
002	108.18
Total Sales	707.18

When the computer was reading the cards shown in the illustration, the following events took place:

CARD READ	AMOUNT ON CARD	MAN	EVENT WHICH TOOK PLACE
1	500.00	001	500 added to Man Sales and to Final Sales.
2	99.00	001	99.00 added to Man Sales which now has 599.00. The 99.00 is also added to Final Sales.
3	80.00	002	* * * * L1 OCCURRED * * * * This means: 1. PRINT TOTAL of 599.00 2. CLEAR MAN SALES to 0. 3. Then proceed as usual by adding 80.00 to Man Sales and Final Sales.
4	10.00	002	10.00 added to each total.
5	18.18	002	18.18 added to each total. * * * * LR TIME * * * * 1. L1 taken care of first which means the total 108.18 is printed. 2. LR activities occur so the literal Total Sales and the amount, 707.18, will print. 3. Job ends. Files closed automatically.

L1–L9 and LR indicators are only two of the types of indicators that may be used in RPG. The secret to successful programming in RPG is to use indicators correctly and effectively.

ARE WE COMMUNICATING?

7–8. The sales manager would like a ten-year sales report which will be prepared from magnetic tape. The tape was sorted by day, month, and year. If RPG were used, what level indicators would be used for *day, month,* and *year?* The level breaks will be used to cause a total to print for each day, for each month, and for each year. Why is L1 used for day, L2 for month, and L3 for year?

7–9. What indicator will be used to print the ten-year total for sales?

RPG Logic Cycle

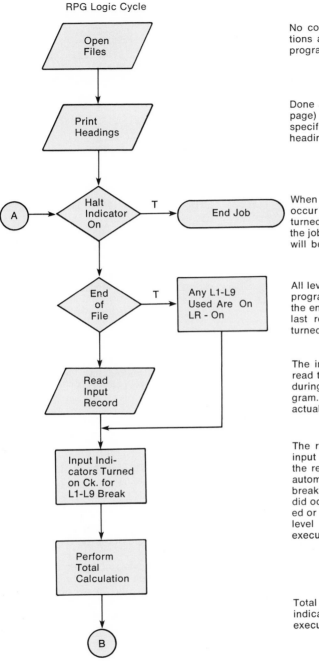

No coding required. Instructions are generated when the program is compiled.

Done automatically if 1P (first page) is used on the output specification sheet for the heading desired.

When various error conditions occur a halt indictor (HO) is turned on automatically and the job terminated. The causes will be discussed.

All level indicators used in the program are turned on when the end of file is detected. LR, last record indicator, is also turned on.

The instructions necessary to read the record are generated during compilation of the program. No read command is actually coded.

The record read turns on the input indicator specified for the record. A check is made automatically to see if any break has occurred. If one did occur, the data is not stored or processed until after the level break instructions are executed.

Total calculations for the level indicators that are on are executed.

FIGURE 7–1

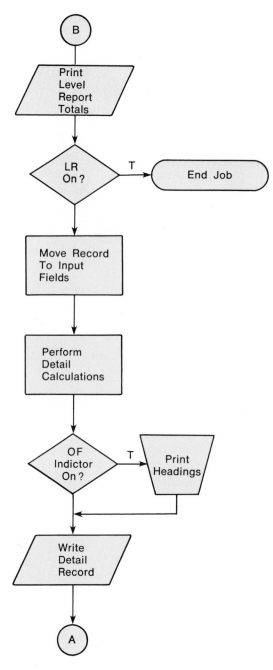

Totals are printed for all level indicators that are on.

The LR indicator was turned on
earlier when the end-of-file was detected. Files are closed. No coding is rquired to close the files.

After the level break activities take
place, the input record is stored in
the individual fields established by
the input specification sheet.

Detail calculations are performed.
Detail calculations are those other
than the L1-L9 or LR calculations.

If the OF indictor is on, the headings are printed before the detail
line. The OF indicator is turned on
whenever the print command would
cause the detail line to print past
the point where the last detail line
is to be printed on the page.

The moving of the data to the output line is done automatically. The
programmer need not code the
moves. The detail records are those
not coded with a level break or LR
indicator.

FIGURE 7–2

7–10. How is the indicator referred to in 7–9 turned on?

7–11. Before the final ten-year total is printed, at LR time, what three events must take place prior to the printing of the total?

RPG LOGIC CYCLE

Use of the Logic Cycle Diagram

Until you work with RPG, some of the statements on the diagram may not be meaningful. Nevertheless, study figures 7–1 and 7–2 and determine in view of what you do know about computers and programming what you can discover about how RPG works. Refer back to the diagrams as you code your RPG problems.

Coding In RPG

Four major coding forms must be used as indicated earlier in the text. It is absolutely essential that each item entered on the coding form be in the exact card column that is indicated for the information. If this is not done, an error message, which is called a *note*, will be printed during the compilation of the program. The *entire statement* is ignored if an error is detected on *any element* of the statement. This rigid coding format is perhaps a disadvantage, but it is necessary to effect the savings in commands which result from using RPG. Before explaining the specification forms and rules in detail, a problem will be illustrated to give you an overview of RPG.

AN ILLUSTRATION USING RPG

Problem Definition

The secretary of the Delta Products Company bowling league has requested that the data processing department automate the procedure for computing and listing the new bowling averages each week. The secretary is not familiar with data processing but did ask that the system be easy to implement, require little keypunching, and produce a report that would list the bowler's name, total pins, total games, and average. The bowler who has the highest number of pins for the week is listed on the report as "bowler of the week."

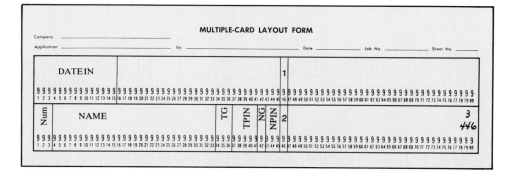

FIGURE 7-3

The programmer/analyst assigned to the job submitted the card design, illustrated in figure 7–3, and the report design, illustrated in figure 7–4, to the secretary. The secretary approved the use of input and output formats.

The cards are punched with the first four fields of data as output from the first week's computer run. After the cards are interpreted, the secretary records the games and pins for the second week on the cards. The keypunch operator reads the data on the card and keypunches it into the same card. After the card is verified it will become the second week's input. The "3" and "446" illustrate how the data for each bowler would be written on the *actual* card. The four digits of new data are then keypunched into the card.

Since the date card is used to supply the variable information for the report heading, the program may be run from an object deck or by calling it in from the library. This will make it unnecessary to recompile the program each week.

Since two input formats are used, the computer must know how to identify *each card type*. For that reason, a "1" is punched in card column 46 of the date card and a "2" is used in 46 of the bowler's card.

FIELD NAME	CONTAINS
NUM	Bowler's number
NAME	Bowler's name
TG	Total games to date
TPIN	Total pins to date
NG	Games bowled this week
NPIN	Total pins for the week
2	In all cards to tell the computer it is the bowler's card and not the date card

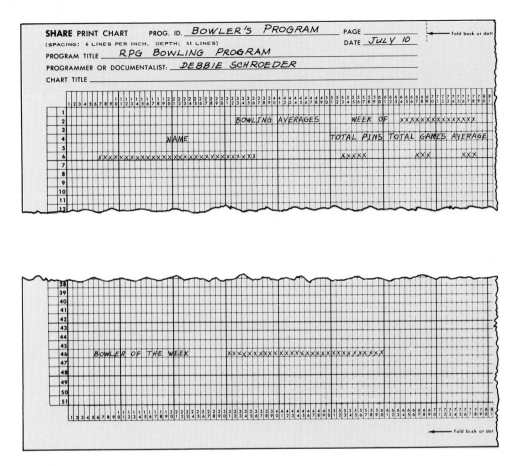

FIGURE 7–4

The report illustrated in figure 7–4 will be printed on 8½-by-11 inch stock paper. It is essential that the report layout be done before the problem is coded in order to show the programmer exactly where the output is to be printed.

Program Flowchart

The program flowchart in figure 7–5 provides the major logic of the program and is used as a guide in coding the procedure. If it is necessary to "patch" the program at some time in the future, the program flowchart is also very useful to the programmer making the required changes. For this reason,

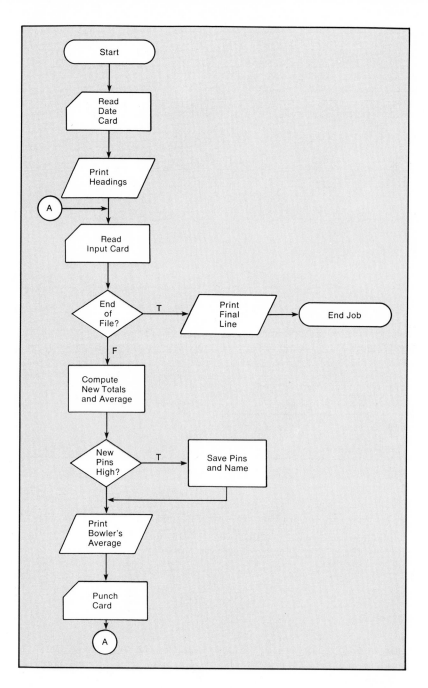

FIGURE 7–5

the program flowchart becomes part of the *documentation*. The amount of detail given on the program flowchart depends partly on the standards of the installation and the experience of the programmer. It should be detailed, and in *nontechnical terms,* so that it can be easily understood by both the client, the bowling secretary, and the programmer.

Coding for the Bowling Program

The four basic coding sheets needed for the illustration are coded. Given for each line of the coding is a simple explanation of what is being accomplished. The *File Description,* figure 7–6, names the three needed files: *Cardin* to read the input cards, *Cardo* for punching output, and *Printo* for the printed report.

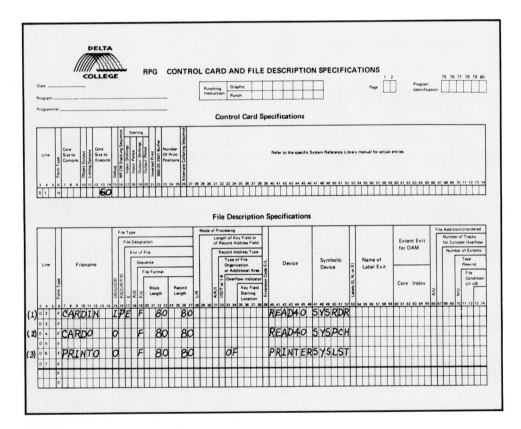

FIGURE 7–6

(1) The name used is CARDIN. The programmer may use any name, up to eight characters long, for the file name. The following codes were used to describe the file:

Card Columns	Code	Tells the Computer
15	I	Input file
16	P	Primary file
17	E	End job when file ends and finds /*
19	F	Fixed record length, cards always are fixed
22-23, 26-27	80	Length of record and block
40 - 46	READ40	Signifies card reader
47 - 52	SYSRDR	Symbolic name for card reader, SYStem Reader.

(2) The file is named CARDO

15	O	Output file
19	F	Fixed length for file
22-23, 26-27	80	Length of record and block
40 - 46	READ40	Signifies card punch
47 - 52	SYSPCH	Symbolic name for card punch, System Punch.

(3) The file name is PRINTO.

15	O	Output file
19	F	Fixed length
22-23, 26-27	80	Length of print line which could be greater or less than 80.
33 - 34	OF	When a punch is used in channel 12 of the carriage tape the OF indicator turns on when an attempt is made to print the detail beyond that point.
40 - 46	PRINTER	Used to signify use of Printer
47- 52	SYSLST	Symbolic name, System Printer (list).

The *Input Specification,* figure 7–7, details the two input cards, telling the computer what indicators to turn on for each type of card and naming the individual fields.

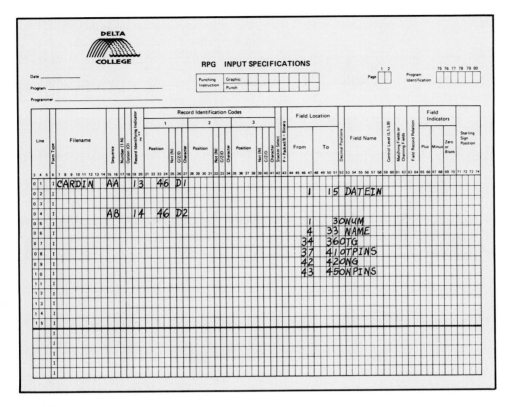

FIGURE 7-7

The name of the file must agree with the name used on the file specification form. Each file name is used **only once** regardless of the number of card types.

Card Columns	Code	Tells the Computer
15 - 16	AA	Sequence—alphabetic letters used when no particular card sequence is necessary.
19 - 20	13	Indicator to be turned on when a digit of a "1" is punched in card column 46. Any number from 1-99 could be used but **keep track of which indicators you use!**
44-47, 48-51	1 - 15	Location in card where the field is found. This must agree with your card format form.

RPG   **417**

52	Blank, zero or digit	Blank—for alphanumeric field. Zero—for numeric whole number. Digit—numeric, tells places beyond the assumed decimal.
53 - 58	DATEIN	Field name—any name supplied by the programmer **up to six** characters in length.

All of the logic is done using the *calculation specification* form, illustrated by figure 7–8. The computer is told *when to do something* by using one or more indicators.

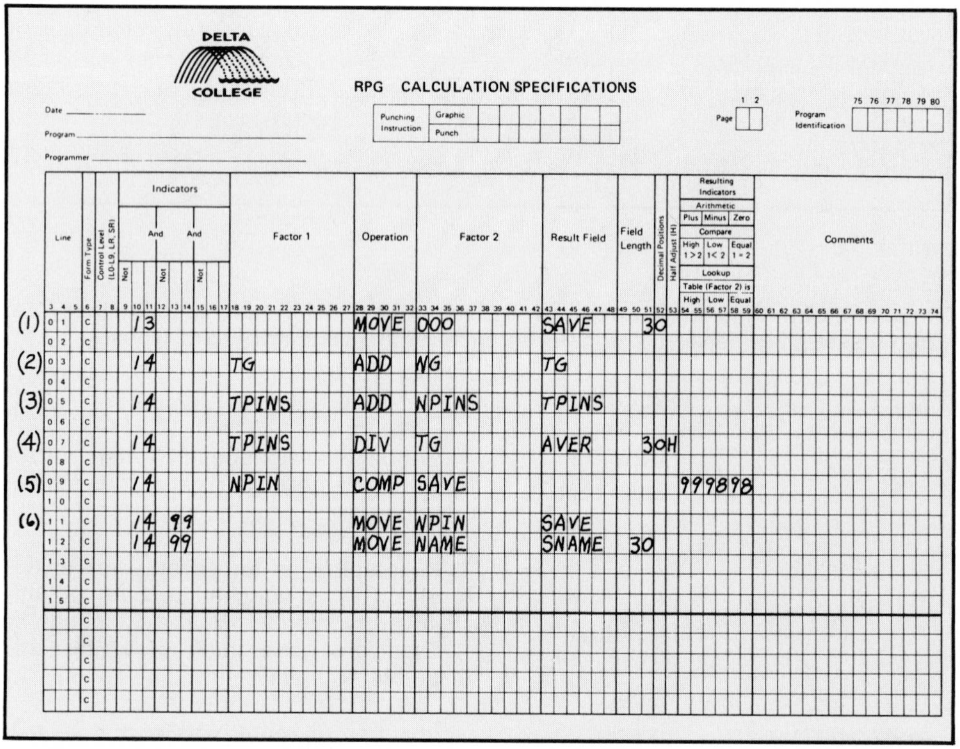

DELTA COLLEGE

RPG CALCULATION SPECIFICATIONS

Date
Program
Programmer

	Line	Form Type	Indicators	Factor 1	Operation	Factor 2	Result Field	Field Length	Decimal Positions	Half Adjust (H)	Resulting Indicators (High / Low / Equal)
(1)	01	C	13		MOVE	000	SAVE	3	0		
	02	C									
(2)	03	C	14	TG	ADD	NG	TG				
	04	C									
(3)	05	C	14	TPINS	ADD	NPINS	TPINS				
	06	C									
(4)	07	C	14	TPINS	DIV	TG	AVER	3	0	H	
	08	C									
(5)	09	C	14	NPIN	COMP	SAVE					99 98 98
	10	C									
(6)	11	C	14 99		MOVE	NPIN	SAVE				
	12	C	14 99		MOVE	NAME	SNAME	30			
	13	C									
	14	C									
	15	C									

FIGURE 7–8

Card Columns	Indicator	Tells the Computer
(1) 10 - 11	13	On indicator 13, which is turned on by the date card, MOVE 000 to SAVE. SAVE is a new field. The 3 in 51 tells the computer to reserve 3 locations in the CPU. The "0" in 52 specifies it is a numeric field with no places beyond the assumed decimal.
(2) 10 - 11	14	On indicator 14, which is turned on by reading the input cards, a number of steps are accomplished. In 2, the new games are added to the old games. The result field now has the total. The former value of TG was destroyed!
(3) 10 - 11	14	The new pins for the week are added to the former total. Since TPINS is also used in the "Result Field," the former total pins is replaced by the new total.
(4) 10 - 11	14	The average is determined by dividing total games into total pins.
(5) 10 - 11	14	The current bowler's pins for the week, NPIN, are compared with SAVE. SAVE will become the high number of pins. If NPIN is high, **99** is turned on.
(6) 10-11, 13-14	14, 99	If 99 and 14 are **both** on, NPIN replaces the former total in SAVE; the current bowler's name is stored in SNAME.

Both headings and detail lines are described on the output specification form illustrated by figures 7–9 and 7–10. One or more indicators are used to tell the computer when to print or punch.

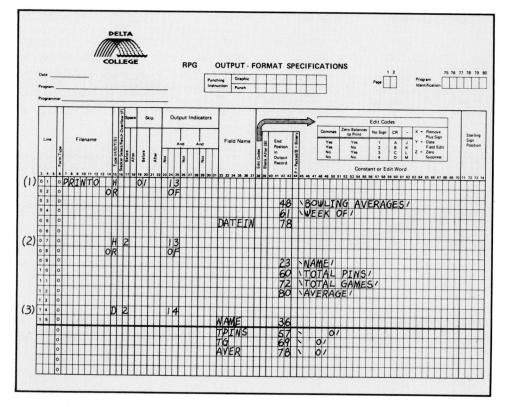

FIGURE 7-9

(1) Card Columns	Code	Tells the Computer
7 - 14	PRINTO	File name.
15	H	Heading.
19 - 20	01	Skip to channel 1 of carriage tape.
24 - 25	13	Indicator 13 is turned on when the date card is read. Heading will print when 13 is on.
14 - 15	OR	Gives an alternate condition under which the headings will be printed.
40 - 43	48	The ending print position of where the field specified will be printed.
45 - 70	Constant or Edit word	Tells computer to print the constant or literal "Bowling Averages" in the location specified.

(2)	15	H	Again specifies a heading to be printed on either 13, the date card indicator, or OF the overflow indicator.
	17	2	Double space before printing.
(3)	15	D	Specifies a detail line to be printed, when the 14 indicator is on. The 14 is on when an input card is read.
	32 - 37	NAME	The field of data to be used is printed in the output position indicated. The contents of the symbolic address name is moved to the output location and then printed.
	40 - 43	36	Ending print location for the contents of the field specified.
	32 - 37	TPINS	Total pins are moved to output location prior to printing. ' 0' is an edit word which will cause the lead zeroes to be suppressed.

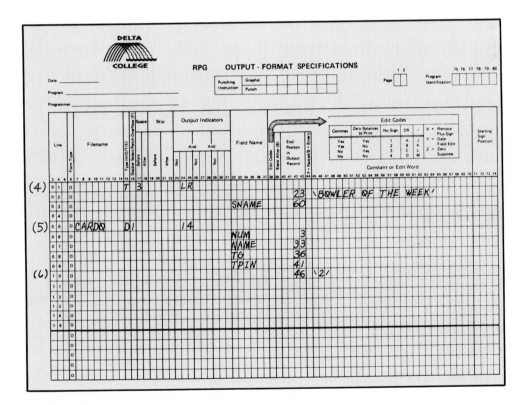

FIGURE 7-10

Card Column	Code	Tells the Computer
(4) 15	T	The **total line** will be printed at LR (last record time). In this problem, LR is turned on as the card reader reads the /* card.
(5) 7 - 14	CARDO	File name which specifies the card punch.
15	D	Detail time which is specified by indicator 14, which is turned on by reading the input card.
32 - 37	NUM	The field name that contains the data to be punched in card columns 1 - 3 of the output card.
(6) 45 - 47		'2' specifies that a 2 which is treated as a nonnumeric literal is to be punched into card column 46.

THOUGHT STARTERS

Before you read more of the detailed rules pertaining to RPG, see if you can answer the following questions by studying the bowling program. Read the material pertaining to the coding of the four required forms several times. See how the output specification form tells the computer about the report which was designed by the systems analyst. The input specification form detailed for the computer the two card formats that will be used as input. The logic of the program flowchart is provided by the calculation specification. The questions are not presented to discourage you, but to show you how much you can learn from observation and thinking.

7–12. What are the four specification forms used?

7–13. In the example what name was assigned to the card reader? How many characters may be used in the filename? The filename used on the file specification form must also be used on what other form?

7–14. In the example what symbolic device name was used for the card reader? The specific model number for the card reader used in the illustration is called READ40 and refers to the 2540 IBM card reader.

7–15. How will the overflow indicator, OF, get turned on?

7–16. If a System/3 were used, what number would be used for the block and record length?

7-17. Must the print line always be specified by a record length of 80?

7-18. What is the correlation between the input specification form and the file specification sheet?

7-19. What does alphabetic sequence on the input form, such as AA and AB, specify?

7-20. How, or when, will the 13 indicator get turned on?

7-21. How long does the 13 indicator which was turned on by reading the date card stay on?

7-22. How will the 14 indicator get turned on?

7-23. In answering this question, refer back to the Input Specification form. What differences in the data stored in each field can you detect from the way the following fields are coded:

	FROM 44–47	TO 48–51	52	FIELD NAME 53–58
A.	10	13	0	NUMBER
B.	14	17	2	HRS
C.	18	38		NAMEX

7-24. What actually is the symbolic name "TG" when it is used by the programmer in the calculation commands?

7-25. A. When indicator 13 is on, what one thing happens in the calculation section?
    B. What happens during the output phase of the cycle when the 13 indicator is on?

7-26. How large is the *new field* called SAVE?

7-27. What does the 0 in 52 of the calculation sheet specify?

7-28. A. What command is used to add new games to the previous total games?
    B. Where is the resulting answer stored?
    C. What happened to the previous total games?

7-29. What command is used when you wish to divide?

7-30. Looking at the calculation specification sheet, how are the fields under Factor 1, Operation, Factor 2 and Resulting Field coded and then punched in the source deck? Are they right or left justified?

7-31. Why are two indicators used for (6) on the calculation sheet?

7-32. Look first at the program flowchart and then at the calculation specification sheet (5) command. What does (5) compare to on the flowchart?

7-33. What indicators must be on if the "true" commands indicated on the flowchart are to be executed?

7-34. What indicators could have been used on the compare command?

7–35. Print lines are printed at three different points in time based upon the indicators used. Tell which indicator was used to print the headings? Detail lines? Total lines?

7–36. A. What is the ending print position for the constant, or non-numeric literal, "Bowling Average?"

B. How did the programmer know to use Ending Print Position 48 for the constant "Bowling Averages?"

7–37. What does the "2" in 17 of the Output Specification sheet indicate?

7–38. In the output specification form columns 45–70 can be used for what two purposes?

7–39. What indicator must be on to punch a card?

SPECIAL FEATURES OF RPG

In the introduction it was indicated that RPG is unique in many respects. Certain commands, necessary in many languages can be omitted. For example, commands are not needed to open or close files. This could present a problem if the programmer wanted to write a disk file, close it, and then reopen it as input, since two programs would have to be written. In other languages, such as COBOL or PL/I, one program could be written to write then read the file.

The programmer is not required to use either read or write commands. Somehow it just happens! Of course, what does occur is that the commands are generated during the compiling of the program and will become part of the object program.

Conditional branching is not as easy to identify in RPG as in other languages. Many languages will contain a statement containing an "IF" and "GO TO" which can easily be related to the program flowchart; *RPG uses indicators*. Consider the more traditional coding as compared to the RPG coding for the partial program flowchart provided in figure 7–11.

In figure 7–11, A and B are compared by using the COMP command. Since A, or Factor 1, is higher than B, or Factor 2, the 13 indicator will come on. However if A = B or A < B indicator 14 will be turned on. A GOTO statement is also available to use with branching commands.

DO YOU KNOW?

Do the mathematics that the computer would do, in the illustration, to solve for "X" in each of the three problems. Note that "X," which is the

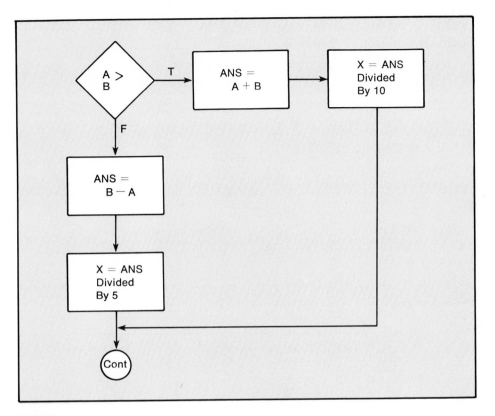

FIGURE 7–11

More Traditional Coding

IF A > B THEN COMPUTE ANS = A + B
COMPUTE X = ANS / 10
GO TO NEXT-STEP.
COMPUTE ANS = B - A.
COMPUTE X = ANS / 5.
NEXT STEP.

RPG Coding

Line	Form Type	Control Level (L0-L9, LR, SR)	Indicators					Factor 1	Operation	Factor 2	Result Field	Field Length	Decimal Positions	Half Adjust (H)	Resulting Indicators			Comments
			And		And										Arithmetic			
				Not		Not									Plus / High 1>2	Minus / Low 1<2	Zero / Equal 1=2	
															Compare Lookup Table (Factor 2) is High / Low / Equal			
0 1	C							A	COMP	B					13	14	14	
0 2	C	13						A	ADD	B	ANS	62						
0 3	C	13						ANS	DIV	10.	X	62						
0 4	C																	
0 5	C	14						B	SUB	A	ANS							
0 6	C	14						ANS	DIV	5.	X							
0 7	C																	
0 8	C																	

RPG   **425**

answer, is in the *result field*. Keep in mind also that X is solved for in two different ways, depending upon the values of A and B.

7–40. If A = 12 and B = 10, what will X equal?
7–41. If A = 5 and B = 5, what will X equal?
7–42. If A = 3 and B = 6, what will X equal?

UNIQUE CHECKING FEATURES

In RPG a check is made, if the programmer codes the input specifications correctly, for

1. missing cards which are part of an identified sequence;
2. invalid, or unidentified, cards; and
3. sequence errors.

The file name CARDIN, which will be used in the illustration showing some checking features, is shown in figure 7–12.

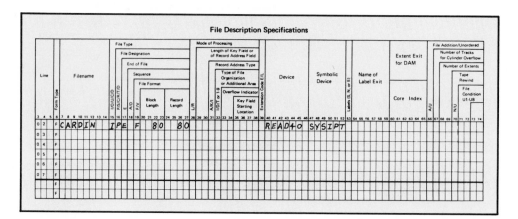

FIGURE 7–12

The input cards for the file referred to as CARDIN, are detailed on figure 7–13, the card layout form. Complete details are not given regarding each card. It is important to note that since multiple records are used in the file, each card has an *identification code*. The number punched in card column 1 will tell the computer what record it is reading and the information will be stored according to the specifications given for that particular record. The identification card code could be a digit, a letter or a zone punch.

1	Num	Name & Address
9 9 9 9 9 9	9 9 9 9 9 9 9 9 9 9 9 9 9 9 9 9 9 9 9 9 9 9 9 9 9 9 9 9 9 9 9 9 9 9 9 9 9 9 9 9 9 9 9 9 9 9 9 9 9 9 9 9 9 9 9 9 9 9 9 9 9 9 9 9 9 9 9 9 9 9 9 9 9 9 9
1 2 3 4 5 6	7 8 9 10 11 12 13 14 15 16 17 18 19 20 21 22 23 24 25 26 27 28 29 30 31 32 33 34 35 36 37 38 39 40 41 42 43 44 45 46 47 48 49 50 51 52 53 54 55 56 57 58 59 60 61 62 63 64 65 66 67 68 69 70 71 72 73 74 75 76 77 78 79 80

2	Num	Cum. Grade Point & Other Data
9 9 9 9 9 9	9 9 9 9 9 9 9 9 9 9 9 9 9 9 9 9 9 9 9 9 9 9 9 9 9 9 9 9 9 9 9 9 9 9 9 9 9 9 9 9 9 9 9 9 9 9 9 9 9 9 9 9 9 9 9 9 9 9 9 9 9 9 9 9 9 9 9 9 9 9 9 9 9 9 9
1 2 3 4 5 6	7 8 9 10 11 12 13 14 15 16 17 18 19 20 21 22 23 24 25 26 27 28 29 30 31 32 33 34 35 36 37 38 39 40 41 42 43 44 45 46 47 48 49 50 51 52 53 54 55 56 57 58 59 60 61 62 63 64 65 66 67 68 69 70 71 72 73 74 75 76 77 78 79 80

3	Num	Current Grades—1 Class per Card
9 9 9 9 9 9	9 9 9 9 9 9 9 9 9 9 9 9 9 9 9 9 9 9 9 9 9 9 9 9 9 9 9 9 9 9 9 9 9 9 9 9 9 9 9 9 9 9 9 9 9 9 9 9 9 9 9 9 9 9 9 9 9 9 9 9 9 9 9 9 9 9 9 9 9 9 9 9 9 9 9
1 2 3 4 5 6	7 8 9 10 11 12 13 14 15 16 17 18 19 20 21 22 23 24 25 26 27 28 29 30 31 32 33 34 35 36 37 38 39 40 41 42 43 44 45 46 47 48 49 50 51 52 53 54 55 56 57 58 59 60 61 62 63 64 65 66 67 68 69 70 71 72 73 74 75 76 77 78 79 80

FIGURE 7–13

Each student must have one name card, one cumulative grade-point average card, and one or more current grade cards. The Input Specification form, figure 7–14, is needed to provide the computer with the identification codes and the *record formats*.

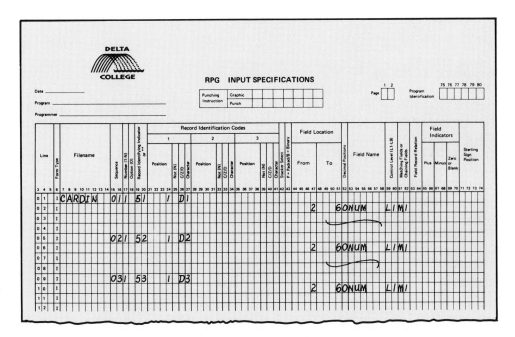

FIGURE 7–14

The cards are sorted by student number before the job is run. For each student, the name card is first, followed by the grade-point average card, and then the individual grade card or cards. Each individual field that the programmer wishes to use in his program must be identified by giving its location and name.

OBSERVATIONS

7–43. How does the programmer indicate the sequence of the cards, within each student's number, to the computer?

7–44. In card column 17 what does the use of the "1" and the "N" signify?

7–45. In the illustration, either indicator 51, 52, or 53 is turned on, depending upon which card record was read for the individual student. What indicator numbers could have been used?

The sequence is given in columns 15–16 of the input specification form. This will tell the computer *for each student* what card must be first, second, and third. In card column 17 it indicates if the card is mandatory or not. The "1" indicates that there *must* be one (but only one) card of this type. An "N" is used to indicate that there *must* be one but there *may* be more than one record of this type for each student.

Sequence Checking

If the cards enter the computer for student 00001 as illustrated in example 1 what will happen if the Input Specification had been coded as shown in figure 7–14. If you refer back to the logic cycle you will see the question "Halt Indicator On?" If the answer is "Yes", the job terminates. When the "3" card is read out of sequence the HO (Halt Indicator) is turned on. The computer was told on the Input Specification form that the cards would be in sequence, based upon the code used in card column 1, of 1, 2, or 3. The cards obviously are out of sequence.

Example 1   Example 2

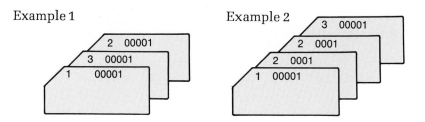

In example 2, the cards are all for student 00001. The HO indicator will again come on since the programmer specified that there was to be only one type "2" card for each student.

When the cards in example 3 are read, an unexplained code is detected. Was this a keypunching error or a card from another job? It doesn't really matter since the computer views it as invalid. The computer is looking for only "1", "2", or "3" codes. Our old friend, the HO indicator, again comes on and the job will terminate.

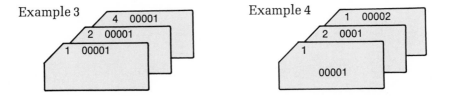

In example 4 there are no grade cards. Since the "N" in card column 17 indicated that there must be one or more, the job will terminate.

The four examples show the result of having the cards within a student group out of sequence, two cards of a given format read when only one was specified as being required, an undefined input card and a missing input card. In other languages, the programmer would have to code input checks such as these into his program. These might be termed "bonus" features available by using sequence numbers in card columns 15 and 16. The programmer may set up routines to turn the "HO" indicator off in order that an error message might print describing the problem rather than having the job terminate. In the cases illustrated, however, would you want the job to continue and get invalid results, or is it better to have the job cancelled?

Other Sequence Errors

The problems identified thus far have been involved with sequential problems within a set of cards for a given student. If the File Description form had specified that the cards were to be in either ascending or descending order by student number, the error depicted in 5 would be detected.

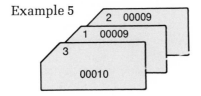

The card set for student 00009 is out of sequence. If the report is to be sequential or if a master file is to be accessed sequential in the same application, input cards out of sequence would present a major problem. This situation will also cause the HO indicator to come on if an M1, M2, or M3 indicator is specified for the fields to be checked. In this illustration an M1 was used adjacent to the student number field on the Input Specification form. Other uses for the M1, Matching Record, Indicator will be discussed at the end of the module. When sequential errors of this type are detected, the job is normally cancelled.

Level Break

Since the L1 indicator is also used next to the student number field, an L1 break will occur whenever a new student number is read.

Example 6

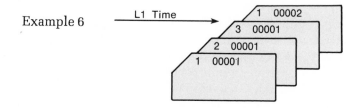

In example 6, when will an L1 break occur? What can the L1 indicator be used for? The L1 occurs when the "1" card for student 00002 is read. The computer has been comparing and testing to see when a new student number is encountered. At "L1" time, the programmer might wish to punch a new cumulative credit card or to print a line on the printer. *All detail processing is suspended until after all activities specified by an L1 indicator have taken place.*

MORE QUESTIONS

7–46. In order to be able to use a level break in the calculations or output specifications, how must the input specification form be coded?

7–47. A report is to be totaled by day, by month, and by year. What would you use as the level indicator for each field?

7–48. What instructions must be generated as the program is compiled to permit the changes in levels to be detected and to then cause control level activities to occur?

7–49. What types of input checks will be provided if the programmer uses a numeric sequence code and specifies if one or more cards will be required for each card format?

CONTROL CARD SPECIFICATION

Each system differs on what information must be included on the card. For some systems, it is necessary to code only the memory size needed to execute the program. Before compiling a program, the control card requirements for the system being used should be determined.

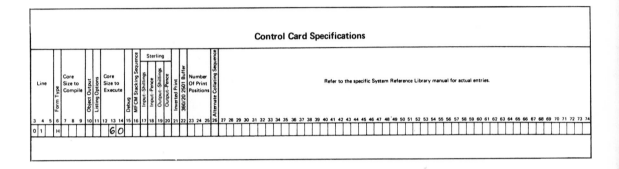

It is *essential* when the cards are punched to punch the card type in card column 6. In this case, an "H" for heading is used. The card is placed in the source deck in front of the File Specification cards. Punching line and page numbers are optional. Some installations require that they be used as part of their "programming standards."

Although some of the rules were given on the "Bowling Average" program, each of the four major forms will be covered. Information necessary to code problems using the card reader or punch, the printer and sequential disk will be discussed. Other forms of file organization will not be covered as this is not intended to provide the complete RPG Syntax.

The rules covered are based on RPG I and will be valid for most installations that use RPG. The sections that follow are intended as a reference to be used in coding problems.

RULES FOR CODING RPG

File Description Specification

FIGURE 7–15

Card Column	Specification—Rules—Uses (figure 7-15)
6	F must be used for form type.
7	* would indicate a comment card.
7 - 14	FILE NAME, left justify the field.
	1. Eight characters or less.
	2. The first letter must be alphabetic. Numbers may be used but not special symbols.
	3. No blanks between characters.
15	FILE TYPE.
	1. Input.
	2. Output
	3. Update which applies only to direct access files.
	4. Combined only applies to multifunction machines which permit output to be punched in the input card.
	5. Display which applies only to RPG II.
16	FILE DESIGNATION. For sequential file, it is required for input specification.
	1. Primary. There must be only one primary file for each job.
	2. Secondary. When sequential files only are used, all input files which are not designated as the primary file are secondary files.
17	END OF FILE. An "E" is used on the file that you wish

to have turn on the LR indicator when the end-of-file marker is detected. Generally, the "E" is on the primary file.

18	SEQUENCE. A for ascending sequence, D for descending sequence. A sequence letter is used only for input files. It is applicable for use in working with matching record. MR is discussed in a special example at the end of the module.
19	FILE FORMAT. F (fixed) is used unless variable length disk or tape records are utilized. In all problems illustrated, fixed length records are used.
20 - 23	BLOCK LENGTH. Only disk or tape records are blocked. If 10 tape records of 80 characters each are in one block, the block length would be 800.
24 - 27	RECORD LENGTH. The standard IBM card is always 80. Tape, disk, and printed records vary in size.
33 - 34	OF. Use the overflow indicator for the printer if you wish to print headings each time you reach the predetermined end of the page.
40 - 46	DEVICE. Relates to a specific I/O unit.

READ01	2501 Card Reader.
READ20	2520 Card Reader.
READ40	2540 Card Reader.
MFCU1	Multi-function Card Unit.
MFCU2	Secondary hopper of MFCU1.
PRINTER	Online printer.
DISK11	Disk drive.

The correct device code for each installation must be used. The RPG manual for the hardware being used will provide the information.

47 - 52	SYMBOLIC DEVICE. Some systems do not require that the symbolic name be used. These names are determined as the system is operated. The ones commonly used are:

SYSLST	Printer
SYSRDR	Card Reader
SYSIPT	Card Reader
SYS001- SYS254	Any I/O unit. A number is used to designate tape and disk files. Some systems limit the largest number used to SYS015.

INPUT SPECIFICATION

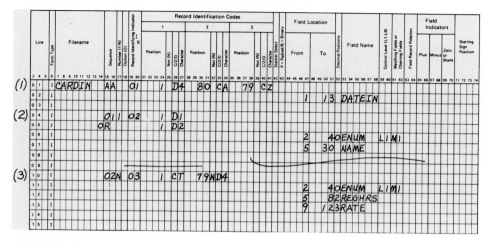

FIGURE 7-16

Card Column	Specification—Rules—Uses (figure 7-16)
6	An I, the letter, must be punched to indicate that it is an input specification card.
7	* is used to designate a comment card.
7 - 14	FILE NAME. The same name as the one used in the file specification sheet must be used. For multiple record files, the name is used only one time.
15 - 16	SEQUENCE. 1. **Alphabetic** letters can be used when no given card order is required. The cards specified may or may not be used in the application. A missing card type will not cancel the job. 2. **Numeric,** starting with 01 to nn, provides the sequence that the cards, within a set, must be in. Sequencing checking is then provided. 3. Alphabetic sequence entries must be coded before the numeric entries.
17	NUMBER 1. A "1" indicates that only one record of a given format should be present in each card group. 2. An "N" indicates that one or more records of a given format may be present.

3. Use a "1" or "N" **if numeric entries** were used in 15 - 16, **NOT** with alphabetic sequencing.

19 - 20   RESULTING INDICATOR. Any indicator from 01 - 99 may be used. A code is established that can be used on:
1. Calculation commands.
2. Output commands.

21 - 24   RECORDING IDENTIFICATION CODES. Either the AND or OR relationship may be used.
1. In example (1) of figure 7-16 an **extreme case** is used. The 01 indicator will come on only if there is a digit of a "4" in card column 1, a character of an "A" in 80, and also a "Z" in card column 79. All three conditions must be present to turn on indicator 1.

    Generally, one or two codes are sufficient to identify a given record.

2. Example (2) of figure 7-16 illustrates the **OR** relationship. The "02" indicator will turn on if the card has either a 1 or 2 punched in card column 1. The OR must be punched in card column 14 and 15.

3. NOT may also be used. In example (3) the not is utilized. The 03 indicator will come on if there is a "T" in card column 1 **and NOT a "4" in column 79.** Both conditions must be present before the indicator will be turned on.

4. More than three AND relationships may be used by utilizing additional cards. Several OR relationships may also exist for one input record. Each OR is on a separate card.

44 - 51   FIELD LOCATION.
1. **FROM.** Justify the field to the **right.** Enter the first card column of the field.

2. **TO.** Justify the field to the **right.** Enter the last card column of the field.

52   DECIMAL POSITION.
1. Blank for alphanumeric data. Mathematics **can not** be done with fields so designated. Two alphanu-

meric fields, or an alphanumeric and non-numeric literal, may be compared, however.

2. "O" specifies a numeric field.

3. A number, such as 1, 2, or 3, specifies the number of places beyond the assumed decimal.

53 - 58   FIELD NAME.
1. The name of the field may be up to six characters in length.

2. **Left justify** the name.

3. Only alphabetic characters or numbers may be used for field names.

59 - 60   CONTROL LEVEL.
1. L1 - L9. L1 for lowest and L9 for the highest when 9 levels are used.

2. If only 3 levels are used, L1, L2, and L3 are used with L3 indicating the highest level.

61 - 62   MATCHING FIELDS.
1. Use M1, M2, or M3 to specify record-matching for two input files.

2. It is also used to specify sequence-checking for the fields of a single input file.

CALCULATION SPECIFICATIONS

The commands used on the Calculation Specification form fall into three general categories: *moves, arithmetic commands* and *comparisons*. It must be specified by the use of indicators the conditions under which each command will be executed. The logic is carried out in the manner in which the Calculation Specifications are coded. On the program flowchart, the indicators may be added to the "working copy" to assist in planning the procedure.

General rules for use of the Calculation Specification form are:
1. Indicators are used to implement the program logic.
2. Indicators may be turned on by:

a. A level break being detected.

b. End-of-file condition.

c. Result of any arithmetic command.

d. Result of a compare command.

e. An input record.

3. Level breaks commands are coded after detail calculation and in the order of L1, L2 . . . L9, LR.

4. In coding information in Factor 1, Factor 2, Operation and Result Field, left justify the data name, code or literal.

5. Non-numeric literals are enclosed in single quote marks (' ').

CALCULATION SPECIFICATION ILLUSTRATIONS

Very often the first calculation specification command is SETOF. Figure 7–17 illustrates how indicators are turned off. Three indicators may be turned off in one command by using columns 54–55, 56–57 and 58–59.

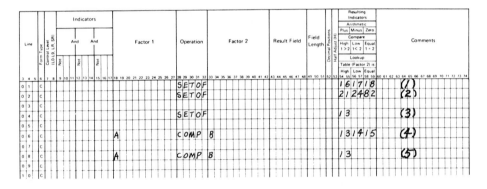

FIGURE 7–17

In (4) of figure 7–17 all three indicators are used so if A is not greater than B, 13 will be turned off and either 14 or 15 will be turned on. In (5) when only 13 is used, if A is not greater than B, 13 may *remain* on from a prior comparison of B to A. In order not to have invalid results, SETOF must be used.

Many programmers as a matter of routine always SETOF *all indicators* turned on by arithmetic operations or compare commands.

In figure 7–18, assume that A is a four digit number, with two places beyond the decimal and is equal to 45ʌ50. Field B is also a four digit field with three places beyond the assumed decimal and contains 3ʌ755. The "04" indicator is on from reading the input record. The ʌ indicated where the decimal is assumed to be.

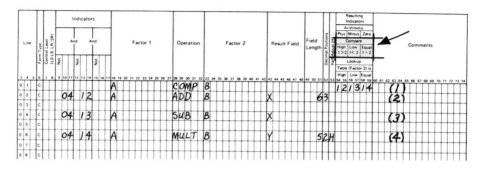

FIGURE 7–18

1. Field "B" is compared to "A." Depending on the value of the contents of A and B, the following will occur:

	Turned On:
A > B	12
A < B	13
A = B	14

The 12 indicator is turned on since A is greater than B. ONLY the command with the "04" and "12" indicators specified will be executed.

2. ADD. ADD is the command used to add. Factor 2, "B," is added to Factor 1. The answer is in the result field. "X" is a new field, **not defined on the input specification form,** so must be described. It is six positions in length with three places beyond the assumed decimal.

What will the field "X" contain after the command is executed? The answer is A + B, which would equal 49.255. "X" is a symbolic address which can be referenced if we wish to use the data stored at the location assigned to "X" in another instruction.

3. SUB. SUB is the command used for subtraction. **IF** this command were executed due to "A" being less than "B," what would "X" equal? The answer is X = A – B, which would be 41.745. Since X was described in

2, no field length should be specified. It is only the **first time** a data name is used that the size and type of data is described for the compiler.

4. MULT. MULT is the command used when you wish to multiply. IF this command were executed due to "A" being equal to "B," "Y" would have the value of:

$$Y = A \times B$$

In multiplication, the field size is determined by adding the number of digits in the multiplier and multiplicand—in this case, field "A" plus "B." Why was "5|2" used in 51 and 52? The answer, if you did it with paper and pencil, could contain no more than three whole numbers and five numbers beyond the decimal. The computer works the same way! In this case, "5|2" was used because the programmer wants the answer ROUNDED to two decimal places. The "H" in 53 tells the computer to half-adjust, which means round to the precision indicated. What did the computer do?

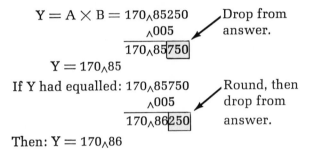

$$Y = A \times B = 170_\wedge 85250 \quad \text{Drop from}$$
$$_\wedge 005 \quad \text{answer.}$$
$$\overline{170_\wedge 85\boxed{750}}$$

$$Y = 170_\wedge 85$$

If Y had equalled: $170_\wedge 85750 \quad$ Round, then
$$_\wedge 005 \quad \text{drop from}$$
$$\overline{170_\wedge 86\boxed{250}} \quad \text{answer.}$$

Then: $Y = 170_\wedge 86$

LEARNED TO DATE

7–50. REGHRS and RATE were specified on the input card. In a calculation, the following statement was used:

    REGHRS   MULT   RATE   GROSS   6|2H

A. Why was "6|2" specified in card columns 52–53?
B. What does the "H" in 53 tell the computer to do?

7–51. What is the exact spelling you must use to multiply, subtract, and add?

7–52. In figure 7–18, if A = 10 and B = 20, which command would have been executed?

7–53. In figure 7–18, if A = 4 and B = 4, which command would be executed?

7–54. In one logic cycle, would (2), (3), and (4) all be executed?

MORE CALCULATIONS

In figure 7–19, A = $4_\wedge 12$ and B = $3_\wedge 06$. Each field was defined on the input specification form as a $3_\wedge 2$ field. The input card turned on the 99 indicator.

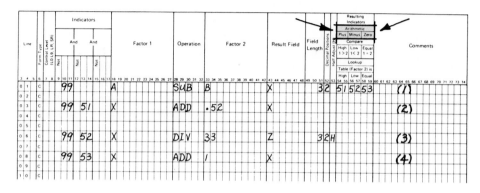

FIGURE 7–19

1. Field B is subtracted from A with the following results:

    X = A – B
    X = 4.12 – 3.06 = 1.06 | It is still just the assumed decimal! |

The answer is a positive 1.06. All fields not specified as negative are treated as positive. However, if the field becomes negative, the answer field will indicate that it is a negative field. In this case, a positive 1.06 will cause indicator 51 to come on.

2. If this command were to be executed, it is the same as:

    X = X + .52

As the command is executed, the former value 1.06 is replaced by the new answer 1.58. Does the computer really do mathematics any differently than you do with pencil and paper? Why in figure 7–19, isn't (3) executed? The reason of course is that after (1) was executed field X is positive which turns on indicator 51. Only the commands which are to be executed if 51 is on will be carried out during this card cycle.

3. DIV. DIV is used as the divide command. In division, Factor 2 is divided **into Factor** 1. The answer is stored in the result field. The command is the same as:

$$Z = X \div 33$$

In division, you should provide an answer area with whole numbers before the assumed decimal as large as the number of digits in the field you are dividing into. The places beyond the decimal point depend upon the precision desired.

4. Doing the problem with paper and pencil, the formula would be:

$$X = X + 1$$

After the command is executed, the former value of X is replaced with the answer.

DO YOU KNOW?

7–55. In figure 7–19, if A = 3 and B = 3, which command would be executed after (1)?

7–56. In figure 7–19, if A = 2 and B = 3, which command would be executed after (1)?

7–57. In division, which factor is divided into the other factor?

7–58. In figure 7–19, would (2), and (3) and (4) all be executed during the same logic cycle?

MOVES

When MOVE is used, FACTOR 2 is moved *from right to left* into the result field. If C, the result field contains 982.46 and 1.52 is moved from factor 2 into C, C would then contain 981.52, since only the three digits 1.52 would have replaced any of the original digits in C. The programmer must watch moves such as this since they are somewhat unique to RPG. In PL/I or COBOL, if the same move had been made, field C would have contained 001.52.

In figure 7–20, A = 4.20, B = 3.62, and C = 9.99. In RPG there are several types of moves, but only the MOVE command and an alternate method for zeroing fields will be covered. A, B, and C used in the illustration were part of an input record which turned on the "04" indicator.

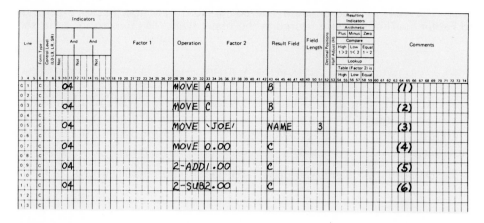

FIGURE 7–20

What is different about these commands and the arithmetic operations covered up to now? *Right!* Factor 1 is not used! Remember A = 4.20, B = 3.62, and C = 9.99.

1. The contents of A is moved to B. B now is equal to $4_\wedge20$. After the move, A also contains $4_\wedge20$.

2. The contents of C, $9_\wedge99$, is moved to B. B now contains $9_\wedge99$ as does C.

3. The nonnumeric literal is moved to a new field NAME. Stored in the address specified by NAME is Joe.

4. Zeroes are moved to C. C equals $0_\wedge00$ after the move. Note that **in literals,** a **real** decimal is used. In input and CPU storage, the decimal is still only assumed.

5. Z-ADD. Zero and add is the command. C is first zeroed out, then the literal $1_\wedge00$ is moved in. After execution, C = $1_\wedge00$.

6. Z-SUB. Zero and subtract. C is zeroed out, then $2_\wedge00$ is subtracted. C, after execution, is a negative $2_\wedge00$.

QUESTIONS REGARDING MOVES

7–59. What section of the coding form, normally used in calculations, is not used for the MOVE, Z-ADD, and Z-SUB commands?

7–60. As the result of a MOVE, the contents of what field is stored in the result field?

7–61. What happens to the result field specified when a Z-ADD command is executed?

In moving data, be careful. Unless both the sending field, *factor 2,* and the receiving field, *result field,* are the same size, invalid results can occur. This also applies to the use of the printer and edited fields. Keep field sizes the same when moves are involved.

OUTPUT SPECIFICATIONS

The Output Specification Form is used for the printer to establish headings, detail lines, and total lines. Each *type* of print line usually uses different indicators. Output for card output, disk, and tape are also specified. Looking at the form you can tell that the file name must be used and it must agree with the name given on the File Specification Form. The type is specified, vertical print commands given, and indicators are used to tell *when* the output is to be printed. Either a field name may be used to tell the computer to use the data stored at that symbolic address or a literal may be indicated in columns 45–70. This same area, 45–70, is used for establishing edit words.

In an RPG program, output must also be specified along with input and file specifications. A program may not require calculations.

Printed Output

Before coding for output, the form layout must be completed. In the design given on figure 7–21, there are two headings, the detail lines which are to be printed at L1 time, and an LR total line.

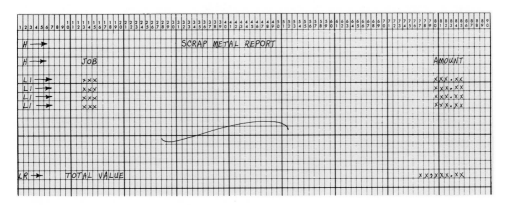

FIGURE 7–21

The coding needed to produce the report is indicated on the output specification form in figure 7–22.

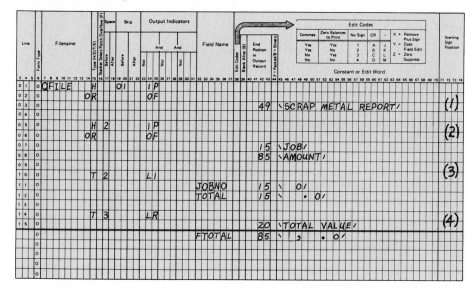

FIGURE 7-22

In describing the form, the coding will be described from left to right, for each of the four types of lines printed.

	Card Column	Contents	Does What
1.	7 - 14	OFILE	Name of the file specified on the file specification form.
	15	H	Indicates it is a **heading line.**
	19 - 20	01	Skip to channel 1 of carrier tape (new page).
	24 - 25	1P	Printed on the first page before any other events take place.
	14 - 15	OR	Also print on **OF.** The indicator is specified by using OF in columns 24 and 25 of the FD.
	49	'SCRAP METAL REPORT'	Is the actual data which will be printed.

All of the specifications refer to one print line. Directions are given for spacing, when, and what to print.

2. The same indicators are used, first page and overflow. The only difference is that under Space before a 2 is used. It does exactly what is stated— double space and then print the line. What line?

Card Column	Contents	Does What
42 - 43	15	Ending location of where 'JOB' will print.
42 - 43	85	Ending location of where 'Amount' will print.

3. This is a total line, "T" in 15. The printer will double space and print the line at level one time. What will be printed? The **contents** of the field called JOBNO and TOTAL.

Card Column	Contents	Does What
45 - 49	' 0'	Establishes an edit word. Lead zeroes will be suppressed. If the value of JOBNO were zero, nothing would print since the 0 is in the last location of the edit field. ' ' always encloses an **edit word** or a **literal.**
45 - 52	' . 0'	The data will move in around the . point. Lead zeroes will also be suppressed. A value of 00999 would print as 9.99.

Other special characteristics may be established in the edit field such as dollar signs, minus signs, commas, periods, asterisk, DR or CR symbol, and edited blanks.

4. Another total line is described that will print at LR time. The literal TOTAL VALUE will be printed ending in column 20. The value of the FTOTAL field will be edited to include both a comma and a decimal. If FTOTAL contains 0001342, it will print at 13.42. However, if stored in FTOTAL is 0134269, 1,342.69 will print.

Basic Rules—

Match Field Size—A field in the calculation section described as "7|2", seven digits in all with 2 places beyond the assumed decimal, *must* have 7 locations plus the editing characteristics (i.e.: FTOTAL is a 7|2 field). To include a dollar sign, the comma and period would require:

'$bb,bbb.b0'

The small *b* is a space when you keypunch! Ten print locations are required for the edited data.

Don't make the fields larger than needed. Some *unusual* things may happen if you do.

ABOUT PRINTED OUTPUT

7–62. What must both an edit word or constant be enclosed in on the output specification form? What columns are used?

7–63. Where else will the filename used on the output specification form be used?

7–64. Different types of print lines can be specified. Under type, in 15, what does the H, D, and T represent?

7–65. Before or after refers to spacing the print form. What would happen if a 3 is in *before* and a 2 is in *after* on the same command?

7–66. JOBNO was first defined on the Input Specification Form. Why is an L1 used next to JOBNO?

7–67. FTOTAL was first defined in the calculation specifications. What was added into the field?

CARD OR DISK

Each device would have been described on the File Specification Form. This type of output is much easier to specify as there is less detail.

The file name on figure 7–23 is CARDO. The card is punched at detail time when the 04 indicator is on. The data to be punched is contained in the CPU at the *symbolic addresses* of EN, HRS, RATE, and GROSS. Where did the data EN, HRS, and RATE probably come from? It was either read as input or occurred as a result field in a calculation. Gross was calculated. EN, HRS, and RATE were part of the input record that turned on indicator 4.

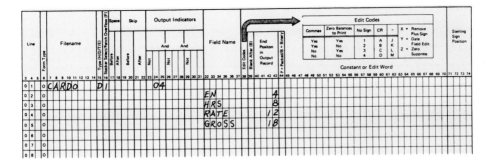

FIGURE 7–23

Disk Output

The file DISKO in figure 7–24 is written at detail time *if* indicator 04 is on. Note the B in 39. When B is used in this manner, the field is set to zero *after* the record is written.

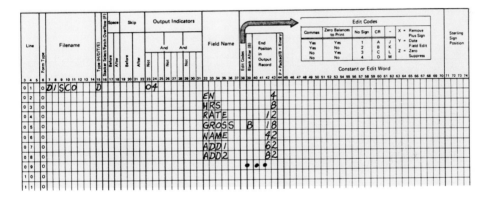

FIGURE 7–24

Once Again, Level Breaks an Illustration

An input record contains a part number, a job number, and material used. Management wants to know at the end of the day how much material of a given type (part number) was used for each job. A job is a given order being worked on. The cards are sorted by part number, then by job number. One card will be punched containing part number, job number, and total material used for that part number for each job. A second output card will contain the job number and the daily total of all material used on that job. The card formats are shown in figure 7–25.

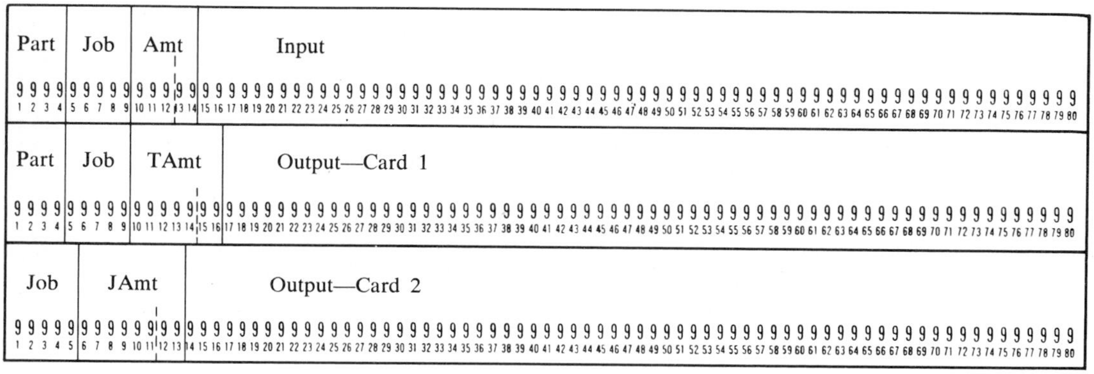

Part	Job	Amt	Input
9999	99999	99999	99 9999999999999999999999999999999999999999999999999999999999999999
1 2 3 4	5 6 7 8 9	10 11 12 13 14	15 16 ... 80

Part	Job	TAmt	Output—Card 1
9999	99999	99999	99 9999999999999999999999999999999999999999999999999999999999999999
1 2 3 4	5 6 7 8 9	10 11 12 13 14	15 16 ... 80

Job	JAmt	Output—Card 2
99999	99999	99 9999999999999999999999999999999999999999999999999999999999999999
1 2 3 4 5	6 7 8 9 10 11	12 13 14 ... 80

FIGURE 7–25. CARD LAYOUT

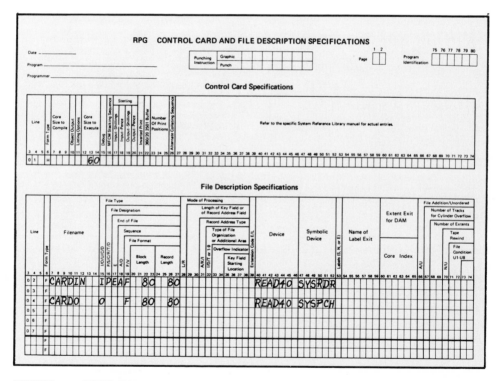

FIGURE 7–26. FILES USED

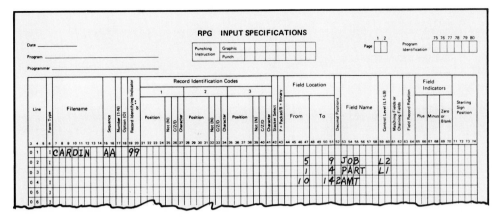

FIGURE 7–27. INPUT INTO FIELDS

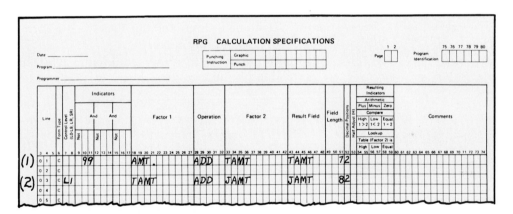

FIGURE 7–28. MATH IS REQUIRED

1. At detail time when 99 is on the amount from the card is added to the total amount. TAMT will contain the total material for a given **part number** used on one job.

2. When the part number changes, a L1 occurs. The amount in TAMT is then added to a total called JAMT.

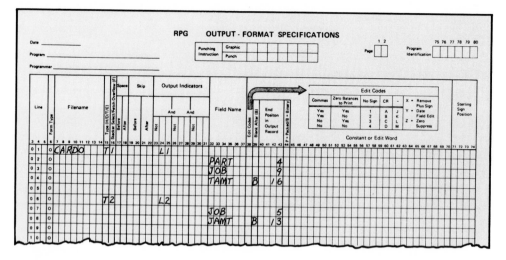

FIGURE 7-29

QUESTIONS REGARDING THE JOB

7-68. Why is it essential that a "B" be used in 39 for the TAMT and JAMT fields? The "B" was not used for the other fields.

7-69. When cards are read as illustrated in figure 7-30, what happens at the point of time which is indicated by the arrow?

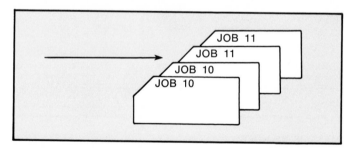

FIGURE 7-30

Level breaks must be thought of in regard to "timing." At level 3 time, L1, then L2, and finally L3 events will occur. If you were programmed as follows:

L1 WASH HANDS
L2 COMB HAIR
L3 EAT LUNCH

When lunch time, L3, occurs you will first wash your hands, then comb your hair, and then eat lunch. Unless, of course, L3 is also contingent upon other indicators such as 04, money available for lunch! It could be: L3 04 EAT LUNCH.

Matching Record

When a multifunction card unit is used, or master tapes or disk records used along with cards, matching record can be used effectively. The employee has both a master card and a detail card that we wish to process. Stacker 1 is used for the master file and Stacker 2 for the detail file. The input and output records are shown by figure 7–31. As you read the coding sheets you will see that only if there is both a card record and a master disk record for an employee will processing occur. MR is used on both the calculation and output specifications.

FIGURE 7–31. FILE LAYOUT

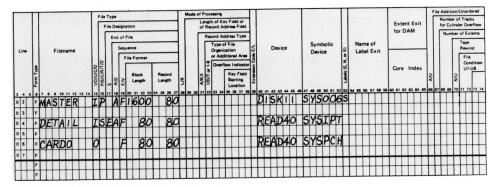

FIGURE 7–32. DESCRIBES THE FILES

QUESTIONS ABOUT THE FILE DESCRIPTION

7–70. Why is the "E" in card column 17 of figure 7–32 used for the detail file?

7–71. How many records are contained in each block of the master file?

7–72. Why is an "S" used in column 53 (fig. 7–32)?

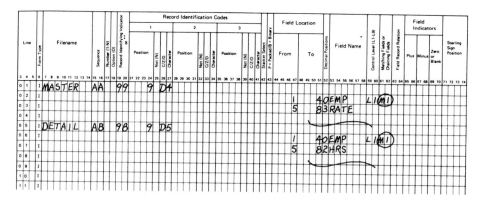

FIGURE 7–33. TELLS ABOUT THE FIELDS

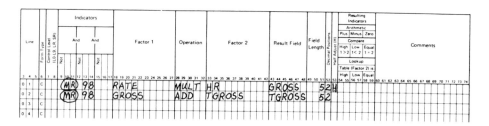

FIGURE 7–34. DOES THE MATH

1. When MR is used on figure 7–34 the calculation will be done only if there is both a master and a detail card.
2. However, each employee may have more than one detail card.
3. MR is used for matching record. The M1 (on the input specifications) causes a comparison to be made to determine if there is both a master disk record and a detail card for the employee. If not, no calculations will occur.

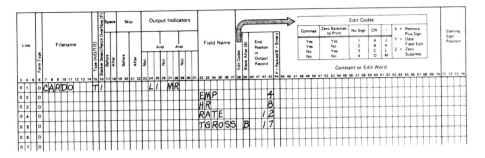

FIGURE 7–35

The output card will be punched on the MR indicator only if the L1 indicator is also on. If the input records read in this job were as shown by figure 7–36, the only output punched would be for employee 0001, 0004 and 0005.

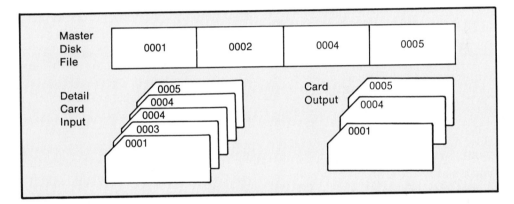

FIGURE 7–36

REGARDING MATCHING RECORD

7–73. If either M1, M2 or M3 is coded on the input specification form, what indicator can then be used on the calculation and output specification forms?

7–74. In a card-oriented system, what is the advantage of using matching record when you are using a multi-function card unit?

7–75. What conditions must be present before a card is punched?

7–76. A. What would happen if the time cards were arranged as follows:

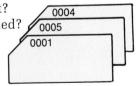

B. Why in this case is that a desirable feature?

Many features of RPG, some of which were illustrated, save the programmer a good deal of coding. You may find it interesting to look at both the COBOL and FORTRAN "Bowling Averages" program and contrast the program flowchart and coding to see the amount of detail that RPG required in contrast to the other two languages.

If the program involves relatively few mathematical commands and uses existing files for the creation of reports, the coding can probably be done faster in RPG than in either FORTRAN or COBOL. For a midterm exam at Delta College the same problem was given to RPG, COBOL and PL/I students. The RPG students finished in one hour, the PL/I in approximately 1½ hours and the COBOL in 2½ hours. This illustrates the point that less coding is generally required if RPG is used for report-oriented problems.

Diagnostics during the compilation of the program are good and easily understood by the programmer. In some computer systems, execution-time errors are not as easily identified as in other languages. The programmer need not understand how the computer actually executes the commands to effectively use RPG.

If you continue studying RPG and work with RPG II, many additional features and advantages will be discovered. Whether it becomes *the* language of the future is yet to be determined; however, its usage, and the respect programmers have for it, continues to grow.

As with any language, rigid adherence to the rules or syntax is essential. How well RPG serves you depends upon how creative you can become in applying it to problems you wish to solve. Each language has limitations that you must work around! The success of any RPG application depends upon a complete analysis of the problem being done before the program flowchart and coding is attempted.

GLOSSARY OF NEW AND OLD TERMS
TO CHECK YOUR KNOWLEDGE

Address.   Location in the memory of the computer.

Assumed Decimal.   The point in input or in the memory of the computer that a decimal point would occur. Although not actually present, the computer will keep track of the decimal as if it were present.

Detail Calculations.   Calculations to be performed at other than L1–L9 or LR time. Usually when a given input record is read.

Detail Print Line.   An output line printed using indicators other than L1–L9 or LR.

File. In RPG, a file refers to any I/O device. It is also a collection of records.

Indicator. Any number from 1 to 99 may be used as an indicator. Indicators are used in RPG to tell the computer that a given situation exists. They may be turned on by: reading a given type card, an arithmetic operation, a compare command, or a level break.

Last Record Indicator (LR). The LR indicator is turned on when the end-of-file marker is found if on the file specification sheet an "E" is coded in column 17.

Level Indicator. The level indicators allowed are L1–L9. The indicator is specified next to a field on the input specification sheet. For example, the man number field has an L1 next to it. Each time the data stored in the man number field changes, L1 is turned on and remains on for the duration of the cycle.

Note. An error message generated during an RPG compile which aids the programmer in determining the error made. Only clerical type errors and violation of the basic rules are noted during compilation of the program.

Output Stream. A continuous stream of information is established by the computer which will be written out all at one time. It is established by moves, filling in unused areas with blanks, moving literals, etc. The computer collects all the information, edits when told to, and then writes the entire stream of data at one time.

Overflow Indicator (OF). The use of "OF" is indicated on the file specification sheet and then utilized on the output specification form to inform the computer to print headings again. The OF indicator is usually turned on when the computer attempts to print a detail line past the punch in channel 12 of the carriage tape.

RPG. The abbreviation used for the report program generator language.

Specification Sheet. A form used to code RPG statements. Each column has a very specific function. Punching and coding using the sheets becomes very rigid because the exact column indicated must be used.

Standard Labels. A label created for a disk or tape from a job control card. The label is written on an output file and checked on an input file.

Symbolic Address. A name used, such as REGHRS, that will generate an address when the program is compiled.

Symbolic Device. Name used to indicate an I/O file; i.e.: SYSRDR used to specify the card reader. The names to be used are determined when the system is generated.

System/3. A series of computers, relatively small in scale, introduced by IBM in 1969. An interesting departure was made as a 96-character card, which used a BCD code, was introduced with the system.

PROGRAMMING PROBLEMS

Problem 1.

The sales department of a company using a card-oriented system has requested that the completed sales order cards for the month be used to total the sales of each major product class for each salesman. The company has three major product classifications which are identified by the *first digit* of the item number:

$$CODE\ 1 = PRODUCT\ A$$
$$CODE\ 2 = PRODUCT\ B$$
$$CODE\ 3 = PRODUCT\ C$$

The request indicated that the output was to be in punched card form.

SYSTEMS FLOWCHART

The input must be sequenced by salesman's number. Both the input and output cards are illustrated below:

From the input card, the programmer will only have to identify and work with the following fields of information:

FIELD	CARD COLUMNS	CONTAINS
MAN	14–15	Salesman's number
CODE	16	The first card column of item number contains the product code.
SOLD	50–56	The total amount of the product that was sold by the salesman.
	57	"D" punched in all cards. Turn on 99.

The program flowchart is provided. Before you start to code the problem, answer the questions on page 458.

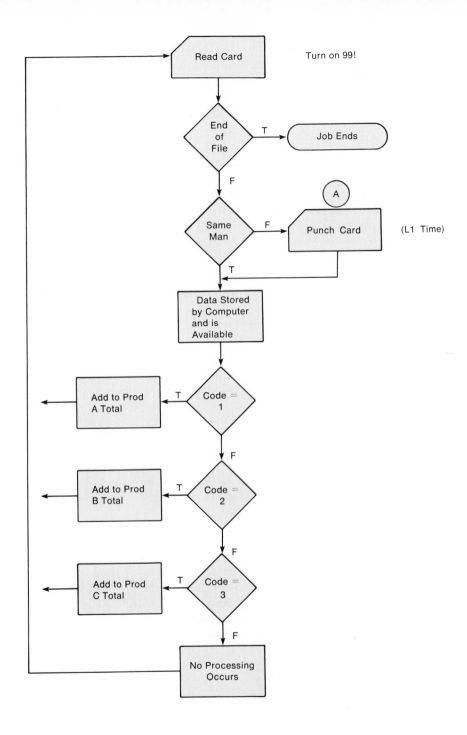

Turn on 99!

Read Card

End of File — T → Job Ends

F

A

Same Man — F → Punch Card   (L1 Time)

T

Data Stored by Computer and is Available

Add to Prod A Total ← T — Code = 1

F

Add to Prod B Total ← T — Code = 2

F

Add to Prod C Total ← T — Code = 3

F

No Processing Occurs

A. When you code the problem, do you have to compare on CODE three times? In RPG, when you compare two values you can determine if one is higher than, equal to, or lower than the other. How about comparing on "2"?

B. How would you test the program? Indicate how many cards, and in general, what situations you would need to test.

C. When the job becomes operational, what documentation for the job would you recommend?

D. If the cards had been used in previous jobs which totaled the sales for the month and printed a report showing the total for each item as well as the total sales for the month, what control could be built into this job to make certain that all cards were processed? It is not asked for, because your first programming problem should be simple!

E. What would happen if a card without a "D" in card column 57 is read by the computer? This question assumes that you used the "D" in 57 as the card identification and turned on indicator 99 whenever a valid card is read by the computer.

F. What happens in this application, as you were asked to code it, if an invalid product code is punched in the card? Should this occur at this point in time if the cards were already used in another application which updated the inventory?

G. What will cause the program control to go to the end-of-job routine? In this problem the job is merely terminated. On your system how do you know that the job has come to a normal job ending and not aborted due to an invalid card or some other reason?

H. After the card is punched for the first salesman, how are the areas used in the CPU to total the sales for each product set back to zero?

Problem 2.

The sales department, after receiving the output from problem 1, indicated that the output was incomplete. They feel they want a printed report like the report layout form that is illustrated. In addition, they would like the commission for each salesman to be calculated and printed. The commission report had been a separate report. To combine the two reports, however, will eliminate card handling and computer time will also be saved. Commissions are calculated as follows:

PRODUCT A, at 7.5%
PRODUCT B, at 8.42%
PRODUCT C, at 6.33%

PRINT LAYOUT FORM

		COMMISSION REPORT			
	SALESMAN	PRODUCT A	PRODUCT B	PRODUCT C	COMMISSION
	XX	XXX,XXX.XX	XXX,XXX.XX	XXX,XXX.XX	XX,XXX.XX
	XX				

Directions:

1. Remove from your program the file specification and output commands for punching the output card that you coded for problem 1.
2. Setup the required headings for your report. Cause the headings to print on 1P and OF.
3. The following logic replaced the punched card output section of the program flowchart for problem 1. The diagram below is inserted at "A" of the program flowchart.

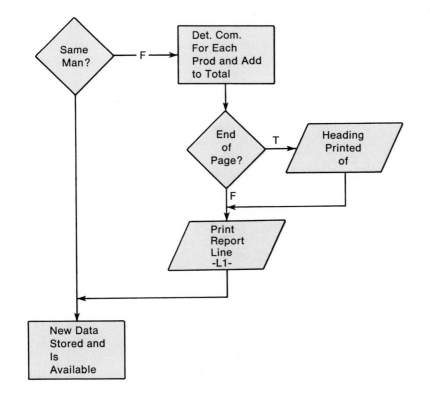

Questions:

A. What additional steps would you now have to take to test your program?
B. What would you add to your documentation?
C. Could you use a predefined process symbol effectively on your revised program flowchart?
D. Does this type of situation actually occur when the systems analyst or programmer works with clients?

Does it occur more frequently today in a well-organized installation than it did five or ten years ago?

Many programs are patched for a variety of reasons, but in this situation the client had not clearly defined his needs before submitting the request to the data processing department.

Problem 3.

The sales department was pleased with the new report. They did feel, however, that totals should be added to the bottom of the report. They would also like a page number printed at the top of each page. RPG has an automatic feature that will start with page equal to 1 and then increment it each time the headings are reprinted. The word PAGE is used as the data name.

The data control clerk will add the final totals for the product sales and make certain that it agrees with a predetermined total for the monthly sales.

Directions:

1. Do a detailed program flowchart that will not reflect both the changes asked for in problem 2 and problem 3. When will you add the amounts to the three final totals that are now requested? There are two approaches that may be used.
2. Print the final totals at LR time. What control could be established by printing the total of all commissions?
3. Code the changes that are requested.
4. In this case, when the sales department requested that totals be printed at the end-of-job, should they really have had to make that request?

Problem 4.

The academic dean would like a report listing all of the students who have a 3.5, or above, grade-point average. Letters are to be sent to each student on the list. The dean's secretary will secure the address of each student on the report and type the addresses on envelopes. The dean will send a letter to each student congratulating him on his achievement. At the end of the report a total representing the number of students on the report will print.

INPUT

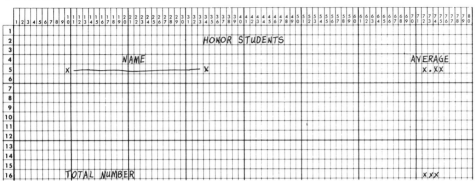

	HONOR STUDENTS
NAME	AVERAGE
X —————————— X	X.XX
TOTAL NUMBER	X,XX

Directions:

1. Do the program flowchart and code the problem. Although the final flow-chart would not have the indicators on it, put the indicators that you will use on the flowchart. This will assist you in your planning and coding.

Questions:

A. How would you test the program?
B. Is this an effective program? How could the program be improved upon, in terms of reducing work, if the input were tape or disk and contained the complete record (name, number, address, honor points, classes taken, etc.) for each student?
C. If only a card system were available, could the program still be improved in terms of reducing the work done by the secretary?

Problem 5.

Each employee must have a master card and one or more time cards. The cards were sequenced by employee number within each department.

A report is to be printed which gives the gross pay for each employee and the total for each department. As indicated, a final total for all departments is also printed.

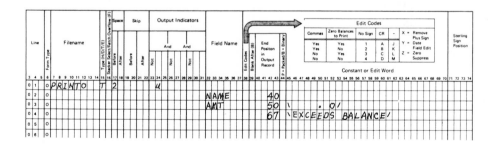

Directions:

1. Compute the gross for each man. The OTIME hours are actually adjusted for the overtime premium, so are paid for at the regular rate.
2. If the employee earns $500.00 or more, print a literal next to his amount which states "CK AMT." To do this efficiently you should be aware of the fact that the entire print line is printed at L1 time and the printing is controlled by that indicator. Each individual item, however, can be contingent upon another indicator.

   The example illustrated *is a similar situation.* At "L1" time, the data stored in name and the amount will print. If indicator "96" is on the literal "Exceeds Balance" will also print. If "96" is not on, the literal will not print, but the name and amount will still print at "L1" time.

3. At L2 time the department total, and the literal indicated, will print.
4. At the end of the job a final total for all departments is to be printed.
5. Before the problem is coded, do a program flowchart. On the chart show what indicators you will use in solving the problem.

ANSWERS

REVIEW QUESTIONS (p. 406)

7–1. A. File specifications   C. Calculation specifications
       B. Input specifications   D. Output specifications

7–2. The small-scale computer user. For individuals who purchased a 1401, after using an accounting machine, either the 402 or 407, RPG was a natural language to use for the conversion.

7–3. Many new features were added to the language which made it a more complete and versatile language.

7–4. Programs which read files and create reports but require a limited amount of calculations.

7–5. No. Certain tasks, such as opening files, closing files, reading records, writing records, etc., need not be coded. Programmers who have programmed a great deal in other languages sometimes have a problem accepting the logic of RPG.

7–6. Indicators are used on commands to tell the computer that you wish the command to be executed or not executed. Indicators may be on as the result of (A) A level break, (B) Reading the end-of-file marker which turns on LR, (C) Using a compare command in the calculation specifications, (D) Any arithmetic operation, and (E) Reading an input record.

7–7. The programmer needs to understand the logic of RPG and the commands that are available in RPG, but he need not understand exactly how the computer will execute any given command. In contrast, when using an assembler language, the programmer must know exactly how each command he codes will be executed.

ARE WE COMMUNICATING? (p. 408)

7–8. *L1* is used for day, since it is the smallest unit; for month, the next unit, *L2* is used; and year, the major unit, is indicated by the *L3*. Days are within months, months within years. If the 402 or 407 has been covered, the totals may be referred to as minor, intermediate, and major totals.

7–9. The LR indicator will be used.

7–10. The computer, when attempting to read the input record, encountered the end-of-file marker.

7–11. A. The L1 total line is printed.
     B. The L2 total line is printed.
     C. The L3 total line is printed.

THOUGHT STARTERS (p. 422)

7–12. A. file
     B. input
     C. calculation
     D. output

7–13. Cardin, eight, input specification form.

7–14. SYSRDR

7–15. The OF indicator is turned on whenever a detail line would be printed beyond the point where a punch is positioned in channel 12 of the carriage tape.

7–16. 96 if the BCD card is used by the System/3.

7–17. No. The number relates back to the size of the line on the print layout form. In the illustration, the report is centered using only 80 print positions. The print line, however, could be as large as 120 or 132 (or greater), depending upon the printer being used.

7–18. The same file name must be used for the card reader on both forms.

7–19. The cards could be in any sequence. It is also not mandatory that both types are used in a given problem. In the problem, however, the date card would be placed in front of the input card since the 13 indicator is used to print the heading prior to printing the detail printing.

7–20. Each time a data card, with a punch of a 1 in card column 45, is read.

7–21. One logic cycle which will encompass both calculation and output time. Actually, it is turned off when a new input card is read. In this illustration, the 14 would then come on as soon as the second card is read. The remainder of the input cards have a "2" in column 45, so on each cycle the 14 indicator is turned on.

7–22. Each time a bowler's card with a punch of a "2" in card column 45 is read.

7–23. The key to each answer is the contents of column 52.

A. NUMBER is a four position field without an assumed decimal.

B. HRS is also a four position field but it contains two digits before the assumed decimal point and two digits after.

C. NAMEX is a field which may contain alphanumerical information.

7–24. "TG" is the symbolic *address* where the data is stored within the memory of the computer. Before the program is executed it will be translated *to an actual machine address.*

7–25. A. Zeroes are moved to a new field called SAVE.

B. For the first time, headings are printed.

7–26. Three numeric digits may be stored in the field.

7–27. A numeric field with no places beyond the assumed decimal.

7–28. A. The command, ADD.

B. The field referred to as TG, total games.

C. The ADD command is destructive, as used in 2, since the old amount is replaced with the answer.

7–29. DIV

7–30. Left justified.

7–31. The commands are to be executed only if a detail card was read and if the new bowler's pins are higher than the pins stored. The compare command in (5) tested this factor.

7–32. The question in the diamond, "New Pins High," of the flowchart.

7–33. 14, 99

7–34. Any indicator from 1–99 which was not used for other functions. In the illustration, this would mean any but 13 or 14.

7–35. Headings   13 or OF

Detail lines   14

Total lines   LR

7–36. A. 48

B. He referred to the print layout form that was designed prior to the coding. This tells him what print locations to use.

7–37. To double space before printing the line.

7–38. Columns 45–70 can be used to establish either *edit words* for numeric fields or *constants.*

7–39. The 14 indicator must be turned on.

DO YOU KNOW? (p. 424)

7–40. 2.20

7–41. 0

7–42. 0.60

OBSERVATIONS (p. 428)

7–43. In card columns 15 and 16, the sequence number is given: 01 for the first card of the group, 02 for the second, and 03 for the third.

7–44. The "1" indicates that there must be one, but only one, of this type of card. The "N" indicates that there is to be one or more.

7–45. Any numbers from 01–99 may be used providing they have not been used to indicate some other factor.

MORE QUESTIONS (p. 430)

7–46. The desired indicator, L1–L9, must be coded, next to the appropriate field, in columns 59–60.

7–47. Year   L3

Month   L2

Day   L1

7–48. Using the year as an example, the year from card 1 is stored and compared against the year from card 2, etc. The command needed to store the old number and compare it to the new number read is generated as the program is compiled. A branch is also generated to the commands to be executed at L3 time. Control then branches back to the next command in sequence which would normally be a detail calculation. When numerous levels are used, a great many commands are added to the program. A level 4 control break would first force L1, L2, and L3 events to take place prior to execution of the L4 prior commands.

7–49. A. Missing cards.

B. Invalid codes.

C. Cards within a group that are out of sequence.

D. Duplicate cards of a given format if the coding specifies only one card is to be read for each group.

E. If comparing on a control field by using M1, M2, or M3 control groups, sequence errors can be detected.

LEARNED TO DATE (p. 439)

7–50. A. Gross is a new field which has not been defined prior to the execution of the command used to multiply rate times reghrs. The programmer wants four numbers before the assumed decimal and two places beyond the assumed decimal.

B. Round the answer to the precision indicated. In the question, two places beyond the decimal.

7–51. Multiply   MULT
Subtract   SUB
Add   ADD

7–52. The command indicated by (3) because indicator 13 would have been turned on since B is larger than A.

7–53. The command indicated as (4) because indicator 14 is on. Fourteen is turned on since A and B are equal.

7–54. No, since only one of the three indicators (12, 13 or 14) will be on during any one cycle.

DO YOU KNOW? (p. 441)

7–55. The (4) command, since 53 is turned on as a result of the answer obtained in (1), being 0.

7–56. The (3) command, since the result of the arithmetic operation in (1) is minus.

7–57. Factor 1 is divided by factor 2.

7–58. No, since only one of the three indicators (51, 52 or 53) will be on during any one cycle.

QUESTIONS REGARDING MOVES (p. 442)

7–59. Factor 1

7–60. The contents of the field specified in Factor 2 is moved to the field specified in the Result Field.

7–61. The Result Field is first changed to zeroes and then the data from the field specified in Factor 2 is moved into the Result Field.

ABOUT PRINTED OUTPUT (p. 446)

7–62. Both edit words and constants must be enclosed in single quote marks. The coding is done in columns 45–70.

7–63. On the File Specification Form.

7–64. heading, detail, total

7–65. The computer would triple space, print, then double space.

7–66. The total for each job is to accumulate and print out at L1 time.

7–67. The total field at L1 time or the amount from the input card at detail time.

REGARDING THE JOB (p. 450)

7–68. Since the field is used as the result field and new amounts added, it must be reset to zero before the computer begins to total the amounts for a new job or part number.

7–69. An L2 occurs which means that the L1 commands are executed first:

A. TAMT added to JAMT.

B. Punch card type 1, TAMT set to zero.

then: Card type 2 is punched at L2 time, JAMT set to zero.

ABOUT THE FILE DESCRIPTION (p. 452)

7–70. The job should terminate when there are no more detail (time) cards.

7–71. 20

7–72. To indicate the use of standard labels.

REGARDING MATCHING RECORD (p. 453)

7–73. MR or matching record, can be used *only* if M1, M2, or M3 is used on the *input specifications.*

7–74. Save collating cards prior to the computer run.

7–75. Both MR and L1 must be on.

7–76. A. The HO indicator would come on and the job would be terminated.

B. If the cards are out of sequence the computer would assume that 0004 disk record was unmatched and read 0005. The entire job would be invalid since there is a sequence error in one of the input files.

COBOL 8

AN INTRODUCTION TO COBOL

COBOL, the acronym for Common Business Oriented Language, permits coding in English-oriented statements making the logic of the program relatively easy to follow. As the name implies, it is a language well suited to most business problems, and is often selected as the in-house language for *application programming*. Mathematical power is generally given in most versions by permitting the use of compound formulas.

Why was COBOL developed? Could you communicate effectively with 100 or more employees if each spoke a different language? This was the dilemma the federal government was in! Their computers were programmed in a vast variety of languages which made the development of workable *standards* impossible. Therefore, transfer of computer personnel from one location to another was exceedingly difficult. In an effort to solve the problems created by lack of a standard language, the executive committee of the Conference on Data Systems Languages (*CODASYL*) was convened by the federal government on May 28, 1959. The committee was composed of computer

469

users, manufacturers, and federal government representatives. COBOL-60 resulted from the work of this committee.

A revised version, COBOL-61, conflicted with the previously developed COBOL-60. Nevertheless, all subsequent versions have been refinements and clarification of COBOL-61. Maintenance and improvements are accomplished by means of the COBOL Maintenance Committee, which was established in 1964.

ANS COBOL

COBOL-65 was turned over to the American National Standards Institute (ANSI) for the development of standards. This version that was developed is referred to as ANS (American National Standard) COBOL. In order to provide flexibility with respect to implementation, three levels were established. The levels range from the minimum level, which requires only three features—the basic nucleus, table handling, and sequential access of files—to full COBOL which must also provide for random access of files, an internal sort feature, report writer, segmentation, and the availability of the COBOL library. The features listed are defined as follows:

Nucleus defines the character set and the elements contained in each of the four COBOL divisions, which are the *Identification, Environment, Data,* and *Procedure* divisions.

Table handling permits the establishment and use of tables through *subscripts* and *indexes.*

Sequential access is used to read or write a file in a serial manner. Reference is made to a record by its physical location in the file.

Random access can be used to retrieve records stored on a direct-access device, such as magnetic disks or drums, by use of a programmer-supplied key.

Sort gives the ability, within a program, to sequence file records in either ascending or descending order.

Report writer permits the programmer to specify the conditions under which headings, total lines, and detail lines will be printed. *Source data* is specified in the report structure, which eliminates the need for actual coded move commands.

Segmentation permits a program, which may require more core than what is available, to be executed in parts. Each part, as defined in the Procedure Division, is brought into memory at object time, as called for by the program logic.

Library gives the user the ability of accessing prewritten sections of source programs, such as statements defining a card structure during the compilation of a program; the statements copied, by using the copy function from the *library,* will appear on the listing as if coded by the programmer. *Subroutines* can also be called in from the *library.*

USA and JOD

Other standards for COBOL, referred to as USA, were published by a committee working under the United States of America Standards Institute (USASI). Although the name has been changed, reference is still made to USA or USASI Standard COBOL. Still another authentic publication was published by the Programmer's Language Committee of CODASYL in the CODASYL COBOL/Journal of Development (JOD). This *subset* was less limited than the USA *subset*.

Is there a standard COBOL? Since most compilers for COBOL were developed prior to the printing of the USA, ANS, or JOD standards, none of the compilers conform completely to any of the published standards. The manufacturers who develop the compilers still view the standards as the minimum, and each individual compiler written may include additional features unique to a given computer. In addition, due to the time that it takes to develop new standards to deal with new situations, both the user and the manufacturer are developing new features to add to the existing subsets.

What would be the advantage? If only one standard were developed and really adhered to by both the manufacturers and the users, the advantages would be:

1. COBOL would have complete independence. *Emulators, simulators,* and translators would be unnecessary when converting to a new computer.
2. The training of programmers would be simplified and the programmers would also be more productive.
3. *Source programs* would be compatible with all of a firm's computers. This would require less programming maintenance.
4. Technological advances could be capitalized on more fully and part of the mystique surrounding the computer would be removed.

Would it be wise? A completely standardized programming language could result in the following disadvantages:

1. Time lag. As new features are needed, such as the utilization of communication facilities, the time required to convert the need to part of the standard subset is too slow. Consequently, each firm patches their compiler to provide for needed features.
2. Unless only one level were established, there would not be computer independence. If only one level were established, one of two results would occur: either only the computers with a large amount of core would have the compilers, or COBOL would lack the power and features needed by the large-scale computer users.

There may never be, and perhaps should not be, only one common *subset,* when you consider the disadvantages. Nevertheless, COBOL is probably the closest of any of the languages to being uniform or standard.

Government Support

In an effort to support the concept of a standard language, the federal government requires that COBOL be available for any computer it purchases. The Navy Department has done a great deal of work to make COBOL available for all computers, even those with a very limited amount of core. This is why COBOL is used around the world—on land and on the sea! Features developed by governmental groups are often available at no cost to other interested users. In a recent survey, however, it was reported that a large percentage of programming in the government's installations is still being done using assembler languages!

Degree of Differences

Once a programmer learns a given COBOL subset, it is relatively easy to change to use a different COBOL compiler. Generally, an experienced programmer can read through the manufacturer's manual, which contains the COBOL subset, and determine rather quickly the differences. The major difference will be in the level of COBOL that is supported and how many of the eight features are available in the compiler being used. The power and features available are generally directly related to the size of the CPU and the support given to COBOL by the individual computer manufacturer.

DISCUSSION TOPICS

8-1. Is there just one authentic standard COBOL?
8-2. Why was the CODASYL committee formulated?
8-3. Do all COBOL compilers have the same features?

GENERAL CHARACTERISTICS OF COBOL

Since COBOL is a high-level compiler language and relatively machine independent, the programmer is free from many of the machine-oriented restrictions of an *assembler language* and is able to concentrate on the logical aspects of the problem.

COBOL has four divisions that must be in the sequence of Identification, Environment, Data, and Procedure in the *source* program.

Identification Division

It serves only to identify the name of the program. Documentation can be provided by using the author's name, date written, and remarks.

Environment Division

This division serves primarily to provide information about the hardware to be used. All files, which are the I/O devices to be used in a program, are identified and given a unique name. This name, supplied by the programmer, is then used in a number of different commands that relate to the files. The source and object computer to be used are also identified in this division.

Data Division

In the *File Section* the characteristics of the input and output records are described. Each record is detailed as to the size of the fields and the type of data contained in each of the fields. Working-Storage is used to define constants and to set up intermediate answer areas. In addition, *arrays*, headings, and report printing lines can easily be established.

Procedure Division

The logic of the program is coded in this division as it contains the *imperative commands*.

Coding

After a little experience, the coding of the first three divisions becomes almost a mechanical process and can be done rapidly. If the library function is available, the *copy statement* can be used effectively as a means of both reducing coding and forcing adherence to established standards. Since the

Procedure Division contains the program logic, the coding should be checked against the program flowchart, or decision table, to make certain the commands will be executed in the correct sequence.

AN ILLUSTRATION OF A COBOL PROGRAM

Is the logic easy to follow? Before presenting the rules, formats, and details of the language, an illustration is presented to relate COBOL to the procedure design steps you are familiar with.

Problem Definition

The secretary of the Delta Products Company bowling league has requested that the data processing department automate the procedure of computing and listing the new bowling averages each week. The secretary is not familiar with data processing, but did ask that the system be easy to implement, require little keypunching, and produce a report that would list the bowler's name, total pins, total games, and average. In addition, the bowler of the week who has the highest number of actual pins is listed at the bottom of the report.

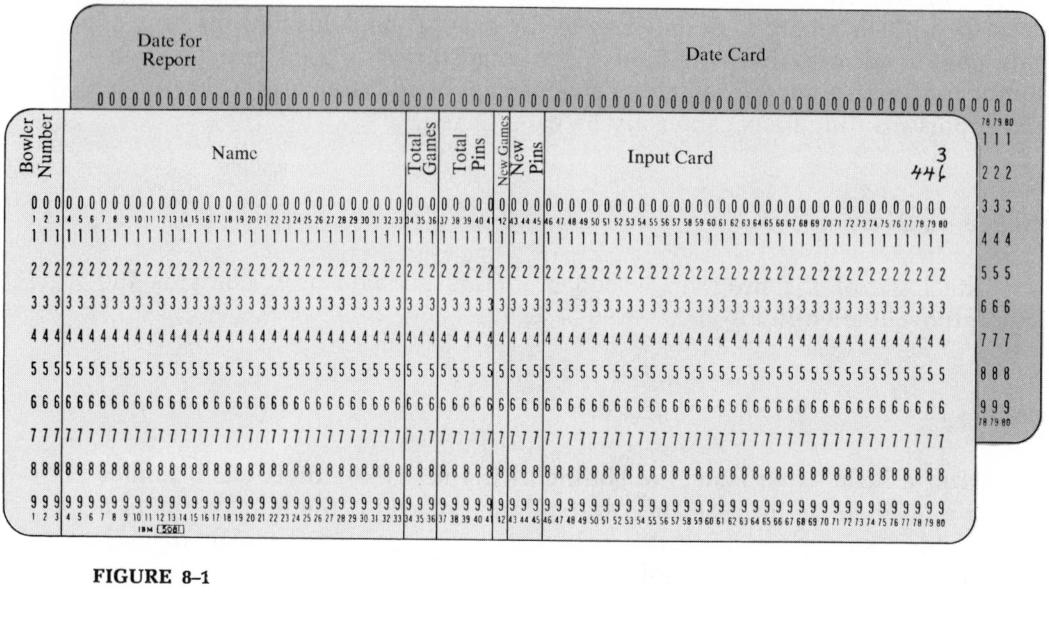

FIGURE 8–1

The programmer/analyst assigned to the job submitted the card design shown in figure 8–1 and report design illustrated in figure 8–2 to the secretary. The secretary approved both the input card and report design. The card formats in figure 8–1 illustrate the two input cards. The first four fields are punched by the computer as output of the first week's computer run, interpreted, and then given to the secretary who writes the number of games and pins for the week on the right of the card. The "3" and "446" illustrate how the data would be written on the card. The four digits of new data are keypunched into the card and then verified on the verifier. (The cards then become the input for the second week.)

Since a date card is used to supply the variable information for the report heading, the program may be run from an object deck or by calling it in from the library. This would make it unnecessary to recompile the program each week.

The report will be printed on 8½-by-11-inch stock paper. It is essential that the print layout be done before the problem is coded in order to show the programmer exactly where the output is to be printed.

Program Flowchart

The program flowchart (diagram 1) illustrates the major logic of the program which the programmer will use as a guide in coding the procedure. If it is necessary to "patch" the program at some time in the future, it is also very useful to the programmer making the required changes. For this reason, the program flowchart becomes part of the documentation. The amount of detail given on the program flowchart depends partly on the standards of the installation and the experience of the programmer. It should be detailed, and *in nontechnical terms,* so that it can be easily understood by both the client, the bowling secretary, and the programmer.

Coding

After the program flowchart is completed, the problem is coded. In coding, the rules or COBOL *syntax,* for the computer being used must be followed *exactly.* A low-level COBOL compiler for a computer with limited core might not permit the use of compound statements, whereas the typical higher-level COBOL compiler usually does. For example, you wish to add A, B, and C to get X. One COBOL might require:

Add A To B Giving X.   Add C to X.

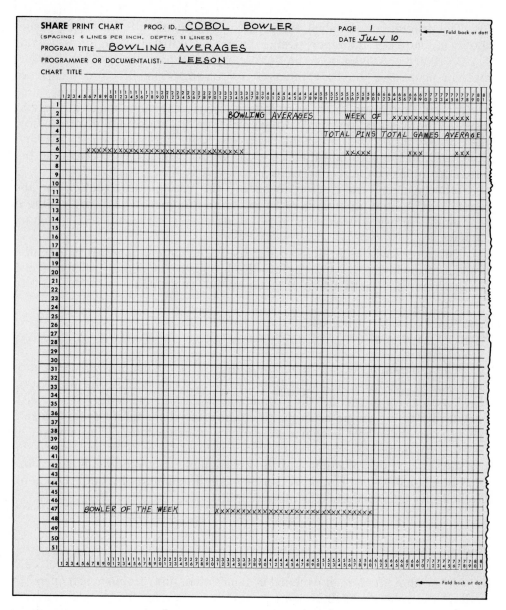

FIGURE 8–2

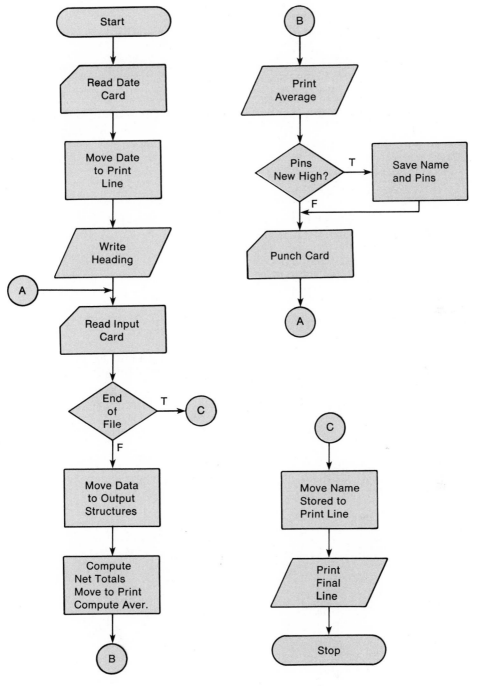

Diagram 1

The second COBOL might permit:

$$\text{Compute } X = A + B + C.$$

The source coding illustrated will compile, with minor modifications, on many computers. Changes, if required, are most likely to be needed in the Environment Division.

Study the coding for the bowling program. Does it tell the computer to do what is indicated by the program flowchart? Is the logic easy to follow? *All of the logic is expressed in the procedure division.*

```
IDENTIFICATION DIVISION.
PROGRAM-ID. 'BOWLING'.
AUTHOR. LEESON.
REMARKS. STUDY THE PROGRAM, THEN ANSWER THE QUESTIONS
THAT FOLLOW THE CODING.

ENVIRONMENT DIVISION.
CONFIGURATION SECTION.
SOURCE-COMPUTER. IBM-360.
OBJECT-COMPUTER. IBM-360.
INPUT-OUTPUT SECTION.
FILE-CONTROL.
    SELECT CARDIN ASSIGN TO 'SYS004' UNIT-RECORD 2540R.
    SELECT CARDOUT ASSIGN TO 'SYS005' UNIT-RECORD 2540P.
    SELECT PRINTO ASSIGN TO 'SYS006' UNIT-RECORD 1403.

DATA DIVISION.
FILE SECTION.
FD CARDIN,
    RECORDING MODE IS F,
    LABEL RECORDS ARE OMITTED,
    DATA RECORDS ARE DATE-CARD, INPUT-CARD.

01  DATE-CARD.
    02  IDATE           PICTURE  X(15).
    02  IFILLER         PICTURE  X(65).

01  INPUT-CARD.
    02  ISAME.
        04  INUMBER         PICTURE  999.
        04  INAME           PICTURE  X(30).
        04  ITOTAL-GAMES    PICTURE  999.
        04  ITOTAL-PINS     PICTURE  9(5).
    02  INEW-GAMES          PICTURE  9.
```

```
    02   INEW-PINS          PICTURE   999.
    02   IFILLER            PICTURE   X(35).

FD CARDOUT,
    RECORDING MODE IS F,
    LABEL RECORDS ARE OMITTED,
    DATA RECORD IS OUTPUT-CARD.

01  OUTPUT-CARD.
    02   OSAME.
         04   ONUMBER       PICTURE   999.
         04   ONAME         PICTURE   X(30).
         04   OTOTAL-GAMES  PICTURE   999.
         04   OTOTAL-PINS   PICTURE   9(5).
    02   OFILLER            PICTURE   X(39).

FD PRINTO,
    RECORDING MODE IS F,
    LABEL RECORDS ARE OMITTED,
    RECORD CONTAINS 80 CHARACTERS,
    DATA RECORD IS PRINT-LINE.

01  PRINT-LINE.            PICTURE   X(80).

WORKING-STORAGE SECTION.
77  WSNAME        PICTURE   X(30)   VALUE SPACES.
77  WSPINS        PICTURE   999     VALUE 0.
77  FILLER        PICTURE   X(7).

01  HEADING-1.
    02   F1        PICTURE   X(32)   VALUE SPACES.
    02   P1        PICTURE   X(16)   VALUE
                   'BOWLING AVERAGES'.
    02   F2        PICTURE   X(6)    VALUE SPACES.
    02   P2        PICTURE   X(9)    VALUE 'WEEK OF
    02   PDATE     PICTURE   X(15).
    02   F3        PICTURE   X(2)    VALUE SPACES.

01  HEADING-2.
    NOT CODED.

01  DETAIL-LINE.
    02   F1        PICTURE   X(5)    VALUE SPACES.
    02   PNAME     PICTURE   X(30).
    02   F2        PICTURE   X(19)   VALUE SPACES.
    02   PTOTAL-PINS  PICTURE   ZZZZ9.
```

```
        02  F3                PICTURE  X(7)       VALUE SPACES.
        02  PTOTAL-GAMES      PICTURE  ZZ9.
        02  F4                PICTURE  X(6)       VALUE SPACES.
        02  PAVERAGES         PICTURE  ZZ9.
        02  F5                PICTURE  X(2)       VALUE SPACES.
    01  FINAL-LINE.
        02  F1        PICTURE  X(5)              VALUE SPACES.
        02  P1        PICTURE  X(18)             VALUE
                  'BOWLER OF THE WEEK'.
        02  F2        PICTURE  X(7)              VALUE SPACES.
        02  FNAME     PICTURE  X(30).
        02  F3        PICTURE  X(20)             VALUE SPACES.
PROCEDURE DIVISION.
    OPEN INPUT CARDIN, OUTPUT CARDOUT, PRINTO.
    READ CARDIN INTO DATE-CARD AT END GO TO PRINT-HIGH-
        BOWLER.
    MOVE IDATE TO PDATE.
    WRITE PRINT-LINE FROM HEADING-1 AFTER ADVANCING 0
        LINES.

READ-INPUT.
    READ CARDIN INTO INPUT-CARD AT END GO TO
        PRINT-HIGH-BOWLER.

MOVE-DATA.
    MOVE ISAME TO OSAME.
    MOVE INAME TO PNAME.

COMPUTE-NEW-TOTALS.
    COMPUTE OTOTAL-GAMES  = OTOTAL-GAMES  + INEW-GAMES.
    COMPUTE OTOTAL-PINS   = OTOTAL-PINS   + INEW-PINS.
    COMPUTE PAVERAGES     = OTOTAL-PINS   / OTOTAL-GAMES.
    MOVE OTOTAL-GAMES TO PTOTAL-GAMES.
    MOVE OTOTAL-PINS TO PTOTAL-PINS.

WRITE-REPORT-LINE.
    WRITE PRINT-LINE FROM DETAIL-LINE AFTER ADVANCING
        2 LINES.

NEW-HIGH.
    IF INEW-PINS > WSPINS THEN MOVE INAME TO WSNAME,
                              MOVE INEW-PINS TO WSPINS.

PUNCH-CARD.
```

```
MOVE SPACES TO OFILLER.
WRITE OUTPUT-CARD.
GO TO READ-INPUT.

PRINT-HIGH-BOWLER.
MOVE WSNAME TO FNAME.
WRITE PRINT-LINE FROM FINAL-LINE AFTER ADVANCING
    3 LINES.
CLOSE CARDIN, CARDOUT, PRINTO.
STOP RUN.
```

THOUGHT STARTERS

Before reading some of the more detailed rules pertaining to COBOL, see if you can answer the following questions by studying the illustration of the bowling program. The questions are presented not to discourage you but to cause you to think. Programming in COBOL is logical and follows basically *simple rules.*

8–4. Looking first at the input card format and then the coding under 01 INPUT-CARD, determine why PICTURE 999 is used for INUMBER while PICTURE X(30) is used for INAME. There are two significant points that you should be able to figure out because PICTURE tells you field size and type of data stored in the field.

8–5. Study the coding under 01 INPUT-CARD and 01 OUTPUT-CARD and see if any standard, or convention, was used that might be considered a company policy. Look also at the 77's in the Working-Storage Section.

8–6. When the statement MOVE ISAME TO OSAME was executed, how many *bytes* of data were moved?

8–7. How is a constant, or, as it is called in COBOL, *nonnumeric literal,* coded so that it will print where it is desired? To answer, read the HEADING-1 section under Working-Storage and compare it with the 01 on the print layout form.

8–8. In what order are the four major divisions?

8–9. What is the 2540R? the 1403? Refer to the SELECT statements in the Environment Division.

8–10. For the SELECT statement for CARDIN, what other two statements must be used in the DATA DIVISION for CARDIN? *Read the SELECT statements and File Section of the Data Division to determine the answer.*

8–11. At what point in the program will imperative commands actually be generated that will execute the program logic?

8–12. After studying the coding under NEW-HIGH, under what condition will you store a new bowler's name in WSNAME?

8–13. If the INEW-PINS for the new bowler is equal to 438, and 500 is already stored in WSPINS, what command is executed after the computer evaluates the following condition test:

IF INEW-PINS > WSPINS THEN . . .

8–14. What command in the coding is an unconditional branch?

8–15. Did the design of the bowling procedure meet the requirements requested by the secretary? To answer the question, refer back to the problem definition and consider the total design.

8–16. Can you determine what problem would exist in the printing of the averages if you had 100 bowlers which required a printed report of approximately three pages? Read the Procedure Division coding to see if you can determine the answer.

Formats Presented

Since the COBOL presentation in this text is not intended to provide the reader with the entire subset, only the commonly used commands will be presented. The COBOL statements discussed will be based on IBM/360 COBOL and are generally compatible with IBM/360 and other COBOL compilers. Where there is a deviation from the IBM DOS American National Standard (ANS) COBOL, it will be indicated. Adjustments necessary for other compilers, other than the two illustrations given, are generally minor. The areas the student should check on before coding a problem are indicated. The information presented should serve as good reference material to use in coding problems, since many of the basic rules of COBOL are given.

CODING RULES

Before going into specific formats for the COBOL statements, there are some general rules pertaining to coding with which you should become familiar.

As you study figure 8–3, which is the COBOL coding form, you will observe that the squares are indicated horizontally by the number 1–72. These numbers also identify either the card column that *must be used* or the column that the *programmer wishes* to be used.

COLUMNS	FUNCTION
1–3	The use of the page number is optional.
4–6	The line number, when used along with page number, aids the programmer in keeping the source deck in sequence. Although optional, it is a good practice to use both the page and line numbers.
7	A dash (–) is used *only* if a *literal* is continued from one line to the following line.
8	Card column 8 is referred to as the A MARGIN and must be used for certain items such as division and section names, paragraph names, 01 record names, 77's, etc.
12	Card column 12 indicates the B MARGIN. Most statements must begin at the B MARGIN *or beyond.* For example, the GO TO statement must start in at least card column 12 but could start in any column beyond 12.
72	Is the last column that may be used as part of any COBOL statement. Anything beyond 72 will print on the program listing but is not considered by the compiler in compilation of the program.
73–80	May be used to identify the deck. PAR005 might identify the source deck for the fifth payroll report program in a payroll system.

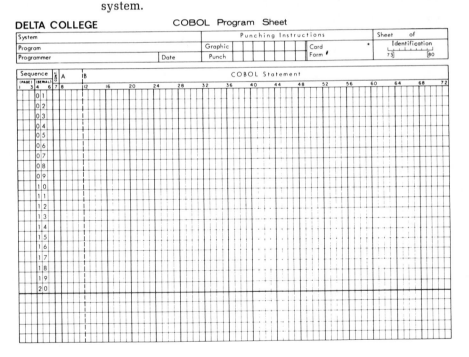

DELTA COLLEGE   COBOL Program Sheet

FIGURE 8–3

As you follow the coding examples provided, you will see that additional indentations are used. The practices illustrated make it easier to follow the logic, read the program, and to check for clerical-type errors.

Other General Coding Rules

The space is a separator and is used to tell the compiler that the end of a word or special symbol is found. *Arithmetic* and *logic operators* are also separated from the *variables* or constants in the expression by spaces.

The period is used to mark the end of a COBOL statement and must be used unless the statement is a compound statement. Compound statements have a period at the end of the last COBOL sentence.

A comma is considered optional and used only to increase the readability of the program.

Special spacing rules will be noted as they apply to the statements being used.

The allowable COBOL characters are given in figure 8–4 along with their function. The blank is often represented in COBOL notation by a small "b." The dash is treated as an alphabetic character in the formation of data, file and paragraph names.

Cobol Character Set			
Blank		Greater than	>
Letters	A-Z	Less than	<
Digits	0-9	Dollar sign	$
Plus sign	+	Comma	,
Minus or dash	—	Period or decimal	.
Multiplication or asterisk	*	Quote	'
Exponentiation	**	Left Paren	(
Division or slash	/	Right Paren	)
Equal	=	Semi-colon	;

FIGURE 8–4. COBOL CHARACTER SET

COBOL SYNTAX

How Are Statements Coded?

A reference guide is always available to help the beginner. However in order to use the guide, you must be familiar with the format notations. The following techniques are used in many COBOL reference guides, manuals, and texts.

CAPITAL LETTERS | *Reserved words* appear in all capital letters and must appear exactly as shown. A list of reserved words is given in figure 8–5. These words can only be used as specified in the format notations.

lower-case letters | The programmer supplied names are in lower-case letters. Any name which complies with the COBOL syntax and the standards established by the programmer's company would be used *providing it is not a reserved word.*

[   ] | Items enclosed in brackets are optional.

{   } | The programmer, depending upon the situation, must select one of the items from the list of items within the braces.

• • • | The use of ellipses indicates that the item preceding it may appear once or as many times as needed.

To illustrate:

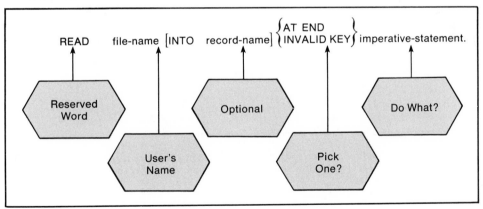

ACCEPT	DE	INDICATE	PAGE	SELECT
ACCESS	DECIMAL-POINT	INITIATE	PAGE-COUNTER	SENTENCE
ACTUAL	DECLARATIVES	INPUT	PERFORM	SEQUENTIAL
ADD	DEPENDING	INPUT-OUTPUT	PF	SIZE
ADVANCING	DESCENDING	INSTALLATION	PH	SORT
AFTER	DETAIL	INTO	PICTURE	SOURCE
ALL	DIRECT	INVALID	PLUS	SOURCE-COMPUTER
ALPHABETIC	DIRECT-ACCESS	I-O	POSITIVE	SPACE
ALTER	DISPLAY	I-O-CONTROL	PRINT-SWITCH	SPACES
ALTERNATIVE	DISPLAY-ST	IS	PROCEDURE	SPECIAL-NAMES
AND	DIVIDE		PROCEED	STANDARD
APPLY	DIVISION	JUSTIFIED	PROCESS	STOP
ARE			PROCESSING	SUBTRACT
AREA	ELSE	KEY	PROGRAM-ID	SUM
AREAS	END		PROTECTION	SYMBOLIC
ASCENDING	ENDING	LABEL		SYSIN
ASSIGN	ENTER	LABELS	QUOTE	SYSOUT
AT	ENTRY	LAST	QUOTES	SYSPUNCH
AUTHOR	ENVIRONMENT	LEADING		
	EQUAL	LESS		TALLY
BEFORE	ERROR	LINE	RANDOM	TALLYING
BEGINNING	EVERY	LINE-COUNTER	RD	TERMINATE
BLANK	EXAMINE	LINES	READ	THAN
BLOCK	EXHIBIT	LINKAGE	READY	THEN
BY	EXIT	LOCK	RECORD	THRU
		LOW-VALUE	RECORDING	TIMES
CALL	FD	LOW-VALUES	RECORDS	TO
CF	FILE		REDEFINES	TRACE
CH	FILES		REEL	TRACK-AREA
CHANGED	FILE-CONTROL	MODE	RELATIVE	TRACKS
CHARACTERS	FILE-LIMIT	MORE-LABELS	RELEASE	TRANSFORM
CHECKING	FILLER	MOVE	REMARKS	TRY
CLOCK-UNITS	FINAL	MULTIPLY	REPLACING	TYPE
CLOSE	FIRST		REPORT	
COBOL	FOOTING		REPORTING	UNIT
CODE	FOR	NAMED	REPORTS	UNIT-RECORD
COLUMN	FORM-OVERFLOW	NEGATIVE	RERUN	UNITS
COMMA	FROM	NEXT	RESERVE	UNTIL
COMPUTATIONAL		NO	RESET	UPON
COMPUTATIONAL-1	GENERATE	NOT	RESTRICTED	USAGE
COMPUTATIONAL-2	GIVING	NOTE	RETURN	USE
COMPUTATIONAL-3	GO	NUMERIC	REVERSED	USING
COMPUTE	GREATER		REWIND	UTILITY
CONFIGURATION	GROUP	OBJECT-COMPUTER	REWRITE	
CONSOLE		OCCURS	RF	VALUE
CONTAINS	HEADING	OF	RH	VARYING
CONTROL	HIGH-VALUE	OH	RIGHT	
CONTROLS	HIGH-VALUES	OMITTED	ROUNDED	
COPY	HOLD	ON	RUN	WHEN
CORRESPONDING		OPEN		WITH
CREATING	IBM-360	OR		WORKING-STORAGE
CYCLES	IDENTIFICATION	ORGANIZATION	SA	WRITE
	IF	OTHERWISE	SAME	WRITE-ONLY
DATA	IN	OUTPUT	SD	
DATE-COMPILED	INCLUDE	OV	SEARCH	ZERO
DATE-WRITTEN	INDEXED	OVERFLOW	SECTION	ZEROES
			SECURITY	ZEROS

ANS COBOL has additional reserved words. In addition each manufacturer's compiler may include some additional words. It is always wise to check the manufacturer's COBOL Subject for the system being used.

FIGURE 8–5

READ statements, complying with the required format, may be coded as follows:

```
READ Cardin INTO Card-one AT END GO TO end-of-job.
READ Diskfile AT END GO TO Print-Report.
READ Diskfile INVALID KEY GO TO Error-Routine.
```

Illustration of Statements

For each statement the format notation is first given. Until the programmer gains both experience and confidence, *the format for the statement should always be checked.*

Following the format notation will be an example of how the command would be coded in a typical program. Where deemed necessary, an explanation of the command and the related rules will be given.

The statements which start with a four-space indentation must begin at, or beyond, the B margin. Those statements which begin at the margin require coding which starts at the A margin. *The following material is intended both for reference and as a guide in better understanding some of the basic rules of COBOL.* In some cases not all options are given since the material presented is only an introduction to COBOL. Enough commands and rules, however, are given to enable you to code some fairly complex programs.

Identification Division

```
IDENTIFICATION DIVISION.
PROGRAM-ID.  'example.'
```

1. The user supplied program name must contain no more than eight letters or digits. Special characters may not be used.
2. The above two statements must be used. The statements, such as DATE-WRITTEN and REMARKS may be used to provide internal documentation.
3. ANS version of PROGRAM-ID would not require the quote marks around the word example.

```
AUTHOR.  Marjorie Leeson.
INSTALLATION.  Delta College.
DATE-WRITTEN.  July 10.
REMARKS.  You may give the basic concept of the program or any other
          remarks that you care to make.
```

```
ENVIRONMENT DIVISION.
CONFIGURATION SECTION.
SOURCE-COMPUTER.   IBM-360.
OBJECT-COMPUTER.   IBM-360.
```

1. ANS requires IBM-360-F30, F30 representing the computer model.
2. With some compilers, the entire CONFIGURATION SECTION can be omitted.
3. No space before or after the dash (–) in words such as OBJECT–COMPUTER.

```
INPUT-OUTPUT SECTION.                (DIRECT-ACCESS)
FILE-CONTROL.                        {UNIT-RECORD  }    device number.
    SELECT file-name ASSIGN TO 'SYSnnn' (UTILITY     )
```

SELECT cardin ASSIGN to 'SYS004' UNIT-RECORD 2540R.

1. Cardin is the name of the file and complies with the rules for data names which are:
    a. Use only A–Z, 0–9 or the dash (–). No blanks or special characters may be used. The dash may not be at the beginning or the end of the data-name.
    b. No more than 30 characters may be used. One of the characters must be alphabetic.
2. 'SYS004' will also be used on the *job control cards* to assign the card reader, specified by the 2540R, to the file. Use of 2540P would specify the card punch, 1403 the printer and 2311 disk drives. *The device numbers will vary with each system.*
3. UNIT-RECORD indicates the use of the card reader, card punch, or printer. Direct–access is used for disk. Utility may be used for tape or disk.
4. If you wish to compile a program, you must find out what numbers are used to specify the input/output devices in your installation. Some systems require less information in the SELECT statement as more of the detail is given in the job control cards.

The files, names and devices as they would appear in ANS COBOL are as follows:

SELECT cardin ASSIGN SYS004–UR–2540R–S.

SELECT cardo ASSIGN SYS005–UR–2540P–S.
SELECT report ASSIGN SYS006–UR–1403–S.
SELECT mdisk ASSIGN SYS007–UT–2311–S.

1. UT used for reading or writing a sequential disk file.
2. UR specified the card reader, punch, or the printer.

REVIEW QUESTIONS

8–17. What two statements must be in the Identification Division?
8–18. What does the SELECT statement tell the computer?
8–19. List all of the reasons that the following *file name is not valid.*

—DISKIN'IS'THE'NAME'OF'THE'MASTER FILE**

8–20. Do all compilers require the use of the CONFIGURATION SECTION?
8–21. You wish to use the card reader and code the following statement:

SELECT cardin ASSIGN TO 'SYS006' DIRECT-ACCESS 1403.

What is wrong with the statement?

Data Division

```
DATA DIVISION.                          Special notes:
FILE SECTION.                           The entire FD is one statement.
FD file name,                           BLOCK CONTAINS is used only for
                                           tape and disk.
                             ( F )      RECORD CONTAINS is optional
    RECORDING MODE IS        { V }         but provides a good check
                             ( U )         whether the record is as long
                                           as what you think it is!


   [BLOCK CONTAINS integer RECORDS    ]
   [RECORD CONTAINS integer CHARACTERS]
                              (STANDARD)
    LABEL RECORDS ARE         (OMITTED )
    DATA RECORDS ARE record names . . .
```

FD cardin,

      RECORDING MODE IS F,
      LABEL RECORDS ARE OMITTED,
      DATA RECORD IS card.

Note: ANS, or COBOL for a very large system, may include some of the information from both the FD and the SELECT statement on the *JCL* cards.

1. Cardin, the file name, must also be used in the FD. Every SELECT must have an *FD* and *01*.
2. The recording mode is F as card records always have a *fixed* size. For disk and tape, V (varying) *may* be used.
3. LABEL RECORDS ARE OMITTED is used for the card reader, the card punch and the printer. When STANDARD is used for disk and tape it indicates that a label will be created in order that the information put on disk or tape can be utilized in future programs.
4. DATA RECORD IS card. You may use RECORDS ARE or RECORD IS. In the example the *record* name is called card. There must be an 01 for card. The 01 is the group name that applies to the record that is going to be described in terms of fields of data.

```
01   Card.
     02   Name.
          04   First          PICTURE  X(10).
          04   Last           PICTURE  X(16).
          04   Middle         PICTURE  X.
     02   Reghrs              PICTURE  99V99.
     02   Rate                PICTURE  9V999.
     02   Filler              PICTURE  X(45).
```

How do you visualize the record called *card* that is described? The card layout in figure 8–6 should show the relationship between the 01 card description and the actual card.

01   Card.   Is a *group* item that identifies the entire *record*. No picture clause is used as *elementary* items tell about each item in the group.

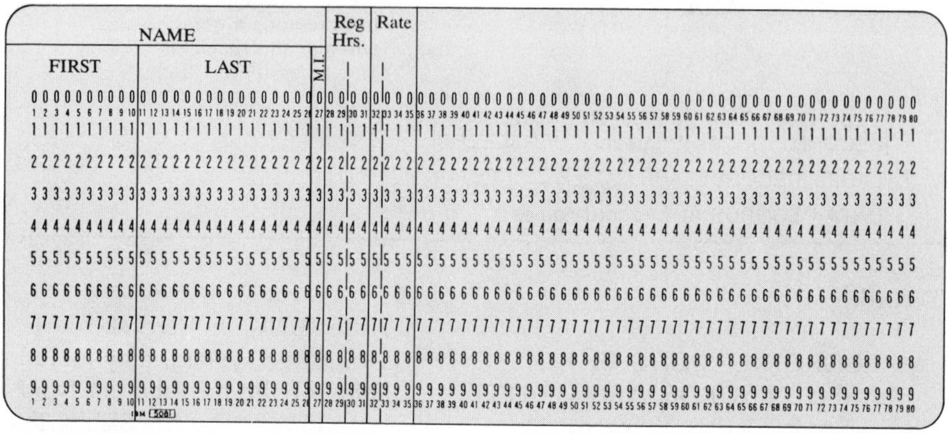

FIGURE 8–6

02 Name. Is also a group item that identifies all 27 card columns, or bytes, of the entire name field.

04 First. Is an elementary item within the group called name. The number associated with an elementary item must be at least 1 larger than the group item to which it belongs.

PICTURE *The picture clause tells 3 things:*
A. The size of the field.

B. The type of data it contains:

> 9 for numeric
> A for alphabetic
> X for alphanumeric

C. If numeric, where the *assumed decimal point* is, a "V" is used for this function. DO NOT count the V as part of the field size. S99V99 is a 4 position field with 2 places before and after the assumed decimal point. The S in front of the field tells the computer please don't lose the sign for the field and if the field becomes negative be sure and keep track of that fact!

Since the *usage* clause was not used for the card on any of its fields, the *default* is to *display* which means that numeric fields will be stored as zoned or unpacked data. Records in the File Section of the Data Division for either the card reader, card punch, or the printer *must have display usage*. The usage clause can be used for disk or tape to tell the computer that you want a field to be binary, packed decimal or floating-point.

NOW TELL ME

8–22. Why is regular hours defined 99V99 while rate is defined with a PICTURE 9V999?

8–23. How many card columns does a field described S999V99 take? How many bytes in core will the field take if it is stored *unpacked*?

8–24. In general terms what does the FD do?

8–25. What does the PICTURE clause for a given field tell the computer?

Working-Storage Section

```
WORKING-STORAGE SECTION.
```

1. This section, if needed, must be coded after the FILE SECTION.
2. The section contains single fields, tables, work areas, constants and the formats for printing reports.
3. The 77's in working-storage must be coded before the 01's.

77 GROSS	PICTURE	9(5)V99	VALUE 0.
77 LINE-COUNT	PICTURE	99	VALUE 25.
77 BOND-AMT	PICTURE	99V99	VALUE 18.75
77 NAME-IS	PICTURE	X(13)	VALUE 'CHARLIE BROWN'
77 NAME	PICTURE	X(13)	VALUE SPACES.

1. In numeric fields when the value clause is used the programmer may use 0, to establish the field to that initial value, or give it a numeric value. Line-count is given an initial value of 25.
2. If the field is alphanumeric it is initialized by using the word SPACES or by using a *nonnumeric literal*. Note that alphabetic constants must be enclosed in quote marks.
3. Except for unusual cases called 88's, the use of VALUE is restricted to the WORKING-STORAGE SECTION. *Don't* use the VALUE clause in the FILE SECTION.

Following the 77's in the WORKING-STORAGE SECTION you will generally find level 01's. They may be used to provide storage for an entire structure, to establish headings that may be printed upon the request of the programmer (in his program of course), to establish tables, or to meet a variety of other data storage needs. The illustration establishes a heading to print the *nonnumeric literal* PAYROLL REGISTER in the center of an 80-space page. The size of the printline was determined in the File Section in the 01, following the FD that is used to describe the printer.

```
01 Used-for-heading.
     02 Filler          PICTURE X(32) VALUE SPACES
     02 Heading-1       PICTURE X(16) VALUE 'PAYROLL REGISTER'
     02 Filler          PICTURE X(32) VALUE SPACES
```

The size of the printline was established at 80. If the programmer moves this information into the printline and it is less or greater than 80, a warning will be given when he compiles the program. Therefore, always count what is coded under an 01 to make certain you have accounted for all of the spaces that you indicated were in the record. Count also to make certain that each nonnumeric literal is the size that is specified in the PICTURE clause. What do you think would happen in the following?

```
77 CAN-YOU-ANSWER     PICTURE X(10) VALUE
     'I HOPE THAT YOU CAN ANSWER'.
```

Did you answer correctly? *The size of the nonnumeric literal is not 10 as indicated in the PICTURE clause. A diagnostic message will be printed when the program is compiled.*

Editing in Working-Storage

Numeric items may be edited by using what is called an *edit mask*. The mask is set up in the print structure in WORKING-STORAGE. A partial list of the report-form edit characters is given in figure 8–7.

9 V	Same as numeric form.
.	Inserts decimal and aligns source item.
Z	Used to suppress lead zeros.
,	Comma.
*	Asterisk protect.
$ + −	If more than one is used, they may float to the left of the first significant digit.
+ −	May appear on either end of edit word but not on both ends in the same mask.

FIGURE 8–7

SENDING FIELD		RECEIVING AREA	
PICTURE	DATA VALUE	EDIT MASK	WILL PRINT
S99V99	−1246	−ZZ,ZZ9.99	−12.46
S99999	00123	ZZ,ZZ9.99	123.00
S999999V99	128642	$$$,$$$.99	$1,286.42
S999999	128642	$$,$$$,$$$.99	$128,642.00

In counting the spaces needed for the editing mask, all characters are counted. The first mask requires the use of 10 print positions; the second, 9; the third, 10; and the fourth, 13. A standard rule for use of the floating symbols is to include at least one more character than the size of the sending field. For example, if the sending field were PICTURE 9999V99 and the receiving field were coded $,$$$.99, a warning message would result as the receiving field is not large enough to accept all of the numeric data and still print a $ sign. Correctly, it should have been coded at least $$,$$$.99.

In coding for a nonnumeric literal that is very long, a dash is used in column 7. A single quote mark must also be used in column 12. Figure 8–8 illustrates a literal continued on the second line.

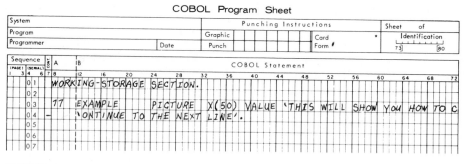

COBOL Program Sheet

FIGURE 8–8

WORKING-STORAGE REVIEW

8–26. Where in the working-storage section are the 01's coded?

8–27. You wish to print a heading for a report that reads:

Fall Semester Honor Students

The printline size that you are using for the report is 100 horizontal spaces. Code the heading line.

8–28. In the detail line of the report, a field is to be printed with dollar sign, comma, and a decimal point. The sending field is defined PICTURE 9999V99. Code the receiving field.

8–29. The WORKING-STORAGE section is coded after what section of the Data Division?

Tables in Working-Storage

01 TABLE.
    02 SALES-AMT OCCURS 10 TIMES   PICTURE   9(5)V99.

1. The OCCURS clause is used to tell the compiler that the programmer wants 10 areas of 7 bytes each.

2. In referencing each area, a *subscript* must be used. The subscript must be enclosed in ( ) and is punched SALES-AMT space (1). No space is before or after the 1. Each square of the table illustrated represents 7

bytes of core storage. When SALES-AMT (1) is used, the compiler generates an address that references the first location in the table. When the *subscript* is 10, the *address* will be that of the 10th location in the table.

3. The subscript must be a whole, positive number. If a variable is used, the numeric value of the variable then determines which location in the table is being addressed. Visualize the table as it is illustrated in figure 8–9.

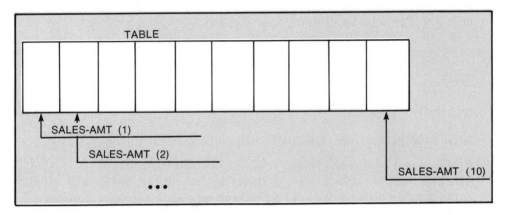

FIGURE 8–9

Why are tables used? Tables save a great deal of coding and are an extremely useful feature to assist the programmer in solving problems. A "mini" illustration is given at the end of the module to show how a table is initially established, set to 0, filled and then used. When tables are used to store data, records can be processed in random order without first sequencing the files. After the table is filled, statistical analysis of the stored data can be made. The subscripts must be whole, positive numbers which may be part of the input record or generated by the program.

How do you perceive a table? Think of a table as an apartment house. Can you find your friend if you know only the address of the apartment house? When the apartment number is also used, the *unique address* of your friend is then available. The apartment number is the *subscript* for the apartment building which is compared to the table. Since within the computer no postman or other tenants are available from whom you can find out where your friend lives, a valid subscript is necessary to store or recover data from the table.

```
PROCEDURE  DIVISION.
NOW-THE-LOGIC-STARTS.
```

1. The above NOW-THE-LOGIC-STARTS is a *paragraph,* or *procedure name,* and is used to generate an address which may be used in branching. Paragraph names also serve as a means to better document the program.
2. Paragraph names can contain 30 characters and no blank spaces or special characters may be used other than the dash (–).

```
OPEN        ( INPUT   )
            { OUTPUT }        file-name . . .
            ( I/O     )
```

OPEN INPUT cardin, OUTPUT cardout, printo.

1. All files must be opened before they can be used.
2. The file name must be used exactly as written in the SELECT statement.
3. A file may be opened, closed and then reopened in the same program.

```
CLOSE       file-name.
```

CLOSE cardin, cardout, printo.

Close all files at the end of the job. Generally this is the next to last statement in the program.

```
READ    file-name    [into data-name]    )AT END      (    imperative statement . . .
                                          )INVALID KEY(
```

READ cardin INTO datecard AT END GO TO end-of-job-routine.

1. Cardin is the file name.
2. Datecard is an 01 record name. If more than one structure is specified for an input file, it is wise to use the into option.

3. AT END must be used with cards and other sequential input files. On card files the condition is often recognized by many computers when the /* control card is read. On sequential tape or disk, the end-of-file marker is found which will cause a branch to the routine specified.

WRITE Ocard.
WRITE Disko.

1. The simple WRITE statement will write a sequential card or disk file from the *record* specified. The record name must be the 01 associated with the file.
2. Always *write a record, read a file!*

WRITE Print-Line FROM Heading–01 AFTER ADVANCING 0 LINES. The carriage control command used, 0 LINES, will cause the heading to be printed at the top of a new page. Spacing of the form in the printer takes place prior to the actual printing. The heading is then moved into the 01 Print-Line structure and printed.

The following integers may be used for spacing control:

0 LINES   Skip to Channel 1 of the carriage tape.
1 LINES   Single space.
2 LINES   Double space.
3 LINES   Triple space.

$$\text{MOVE} \quad \begin{Bmatrix} \text{Data-name-1} \\ \text{non-numeric literal} \\ \text{numeric-literal} \end{Bmatrix} \quad \text{to data-name -2 . . .}$$

MOVE Reghrs TO Print-field.
MOVE 'Joe' TO Pname.
MOVE 0 TO Reghrs.
MOVE 0 TO Ta, Tb, Tc.

1. A MOVE takes the contents of the field specified, or the literal, and moves the data to the second field specified.
2. The MOVE 0 TO Ta, Tb, Tc moves zeroes into all three fields.

3. Moves are accomplished differently for alphanumeric data than moves for numeric data.

  a. Alphanumeric and alphabetic information is moved from left to right. If the receiving field is larger than the sending field blanks are automatically placed in the unused bytes at the right. In figure 8–10, Name is the sending field and was defined as PICTURE X(6).

  b. In numeric moves the data is moved from right to left. Zeroes will fill the unused bytes to the left of the numeric information. In figure 8–10, Reghrs is a PICTURE 99V99 field and contains 79.56 hours. The receiving field is Print-field and was defined as PICTURE 9(4)V99. Numeric material aligns on the assumed decimal. Remember the decimal is not actually punched in the card.

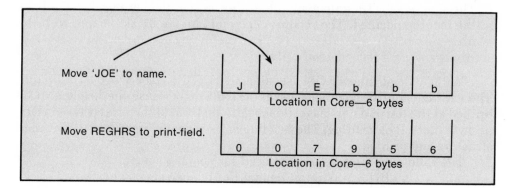

FIGURE 8–10

DISPLAY 'not valid card ', AcctNo UPON CONSOLE.

1. The message printed on the typewriter would read:

   NOT VALID CARD 0001

if the value stored in the data-name AcctNo is equal to 0001.

2. If "UPON CONSOLE" is omitted, the command will usually default and print the message on the printer.

```
GO TO        procedure-name.
```

GO TO Compute-Fica. The use of GO TO as presented is an unconditional branch to the procedure, or paragraph name, Compute-Fica.

```
COMPUTE      data-name-1      =    ⎧ data-name-2          ⎫   . . .
                                   ⎨ numeric-literal       ⎬
                                   ⎩ arithmetic-expression ⎭
```

COMPUTE Gross = Rate * (Reghrs + Otime * 2).

1. *All data names must be defined as part of input, output, or in the WORKING-STORAGE section.*
2. The unknown is always to the left of the equal sign. *Only one data-name can appear to the left.*
3. Arithmetic is accomplished according to the *hierarchy* illustrated in figure 8–11.

Top Priority:	( ) are cleared. Parenthetical expressions are executed, innermost to outermost, before any other mathematics take place.
Next:	** Exponentiation is taken care of.
Then:	* and / Multiplication and division are at the same level.
Finally:	+ and – Addition and subtraction are at the lowest, but same, hierarchy.

FIGURE 8–11

4. In the arithmetic statement given to compute the gross pay, the mathematics would be accomplished in the following manner:
   a. Clear ( )   Step one: OTIME * 2.
                   Step two: Add results of step one to Reghrs.
   b. Multiplication   Step three: Multiply the results of step two times RATE.
   c. The answer is then stored in the field called GROSS.

Other Arithmetic Statements

Some compilers do not permit use of the compute statements so mathematics is done using the add, subtract, multiply and divide statements. In any of the arithmetic statements, either data-names or numeric literals may be used. The statements are illustrated in figure 8–12.

	ADD	Reghrs	TO	Otime	GIVING	Total.
or	ADD	10	TO	Reghrs.		
or	SUBTRACT	X	FROM	Y	GIVING	Z.
	SUBTRACT	2	FROM	Y.		
	MULTIPLY	Rate	BY	Reghrs	GIVING	Gross.
	DIVIDE	Gross	BY	2	GIVING	Half-pay.
	DIVIDE	X	BY	Y	GIVING	Z.

FIGURE 8–12

When the GIVING option is not used in the ADD or SUBTRACT command, the second operand is destroyed and replaced with the new value. When GIVING is used, the other operands, other than the one specified in the GIVING option, contain the same numeric values after execution as before execution of the command.

CAN YOU DO MATHEMATICS?

8–30. You wish to first add A and B, the results are then multiplied by 58.96. This is coded as:

COMPUTE Ans = (A + B) * 58.96.

Why are the ( ) needed?

8–31. Grosspay is computed with the following variables:

Reghrs = 40 hrs.
Otimehrs = 10 hrs. (double time paid for overtime)
Rate = 3.00

A. Compute Grosspay = (Reghrs + (Otimehrs * 2)) * Rate.
B. Compute Grosspay = (Rate * Reghrs) + (Rate * (Otimehrs * 2)).
C. Compute Grosspay = Reghrs + Otimehrs * 2 * Rate.

Compute the answer for each of the three cases. Which answer is incorrect? Why? In example B are the inner ( ) needed? Why might they be used?

"IF" AND "PERFORM" STATEMENTS

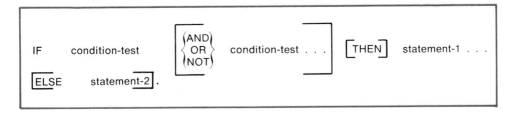

IF A > B THEN GO TO Start-over.
IF A = B THEN COMPUTE X = Y + 10,
ELSE COMPUTE X = Y + 49.52.
IF A NOT = B AND C NOT = D THEN
    COMPUTE X = A + B,
    GO TO Read-New-Card.

1. The majority of the program's logic results from using IF statements which may cause conditional branches to occur.
2. Generally each decision point on the program flowchart is coded by using an IF statement.

```
PERFORM     procedure-name.
```

PERFORM Print-Heading-Routine. Use of this statement causes a branch to the Print-Heading-Routine paragraph. If within the heading routine, *there is not* a branch, control automatically comes back to the statement which *immediately follows* the PERFORM Print-Heading-Routine.

```
PERFORM procedure-name-1   VARYING data-name-1   FROM  {numeric-literal}  BY
                                                       {data-name    }

{numeric-literal}   UNTIL  condition-test.
{data-name    }
```

PERFORM Punch-Card VARYING J FROM 1 BY 1 UNTIL J = 11
GO TO Read-New-Card.

1. The command will cause a branch to the paragraph called Punch-Card.
2. The Punch-Card paragraph has the following coding:
    Punch-Card.
        WRITE Cardo FROM Wscard-structure.
3. Figure 8–13 should help you to visualize how the PERFORM statement used would actually be executed.

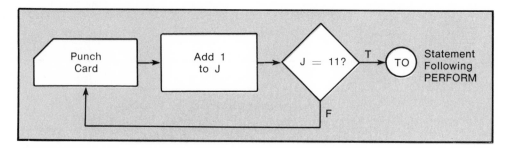

FIGURE 8–13

4. A perform using the VARYING option is a good way of setting up *count controlled loops*. They can be used effectively when clearing a table, filling a table, printing from a table or searching a table. There are, of course, many other uses for PERFORM statements.
5. There are several other versions of the PERFORM including nesting of the VARYING option.

NOTE	comment.

NOTE-Tax-Computations. Note the following coding is used to compute Federal Income Tax. This statement will only list out but does not generate any commands. It serves as documentation which will assist the programmer in following the logic. Until the new paragraph name, "Fed-Tax-Comp" is encountered all statements in the paragraph are considered as comments.
    Fed-Tax-Comp.

            IF Tax-Status = 'S' THEN GO TO Single.
            Compute Exemp = Eno * Amt-Each.
            Compute Taxable = Gross — Exemp.

            . . .

STOP	$\begin{cases} \text{Run} \\ \text{'Non-numeric-literal'} \\ \text{Numeric-literal} \end{cases}$

STOP RUN. This statement will cause immediate termination of the job.

STOP 'Got to Calc'. When STOP is used in this manner it will cause "Got to Calc" to display upon the console. The computer is *generally* in a wait state until the operator responds to the message. This is an effective way of getting a "pause" into the program. A more likely message might be to "put forms in printer."

USING TABLES

Part of the coding for the problem, such as the *required* statements before the SELECT statements, has been omitted. The problem will illustrate basically three different things: (1) how to establish the table to zero; (2) how to fill the table by reading cards; and (3) how to use the table to determine the percent of the total sales that each individual man sold.

The program flowchart is given in figure 8–14. It is used to provide an overview of the program logic. Detailed flowcharts are also given for each phase of the problem.

The card reader and the printer required for the problem need to be declared by using SELECT statements. Each SELECT statement must also have its own FD and 01 record. In addition, the table must be defined, the printline established, and work areas established for the sales total and a percent field. J, which is used as the *counter* for the PERFORM statements, also requires a 77.

In the example used, it illustrates the use of only five cards of input.

. . .

```
    SELECT Cardin ASSIGN to 'SYS004' UNIT-RECORD 2540R.
    SELECT Printo ASSIGN to 'SYS005' UNIT-RECORD 1403.
```

. . .

```
DATA DIVISION.
FILE SECTION.

FD Cardin,
    RECORDING MODE IS F,
    LABEL RECORDS ARE OMITTED,
    DATA RECORD IS Sales-card.
```

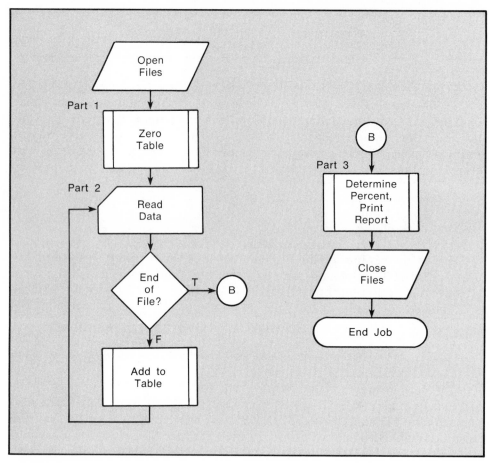

FIGURE 8-14

```
01  Sales-card.
    02  Man              PICTURE 99.
    02  Sold             PICTURE 9(3)V99.
    02  Not-used         PICTURE X(73).

FD Printo,
    RECORDING MODE IS F,
    LABEL RECORDS ARE OMITTED,
    RECORD CONTAINS 80 CHARACTERS,
DATA RECORD IS Pline.

01  Pline                PICTURE X(80).
```

WORKING-STORAGE SECTION.
```
77   Percent        PICTURE 999V99        VALUE 0.
77   Tsales         PICTURE 9(5)V99       VALUE 0.
77   J              PICTURE 99            VALUE 0.

01   Table-In-Core.
     02   Sales-Amt      OCCURS 6 TIMES        PICTURE 9(5)V99.

01   Print-Line.
     02   Filler         PICTURE X(10)         VALUE SPACES.
     02   Print-Number   PICTURE Z9.
     02   Filler         PICTURE X(20)         VALUE SPACES.
     02   Ppercent       PICTURE ZZZ.99.
     02   Filler         PICTURE X(52)         VALUE SPACES.
```
PROCEDURE DIVISION.
     OPEN INPUT Cardin, OUTPUT Printo.
     PERFORM Zero-Out VARYING J FROM 1 BY 1 UNTIL J = 7. (See
     figure 8–16)

Fill-Table. (See figure 8–15)
     READ Cardin AT END GO TO Eoj.
     COMPUTE Sales-Amt (Man) = Sales-Amt (Man) + Sold.
     COMPUTE Tsales = Tsales + Sold.
     GO TO Fill-Table.

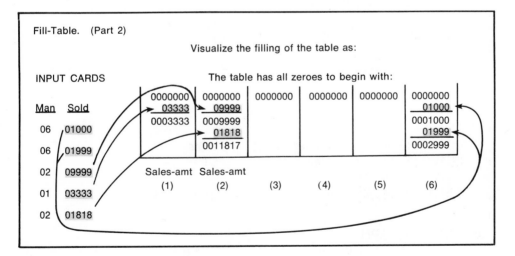

FIGURE 8–15

Zero-Out. (See figure 8–16)
    MOVE 0 to Sales-Amt (J).

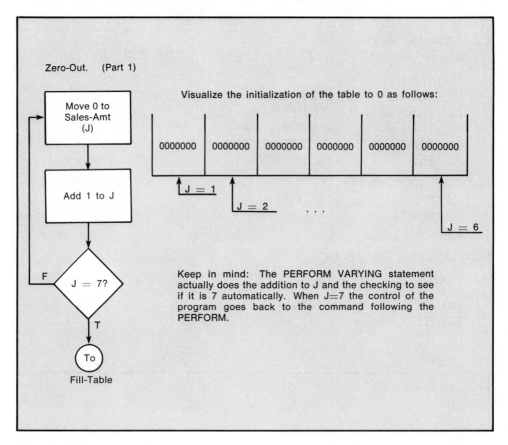

FIGURE 8–16

Calc-Per. (See figure 8–17)
    COMPUTE Percent = Sales-Amt (J) / Tsales * 100.
    MOVE J to Print-Number.
    MOVE Percent to Ppercent.
    WRITE Pline FROM Print-Line AFTER ADVANCING 2 LINES.

EOJ.
NOTE-PARAGRAPH.
    NOTE THE FOLLOWING COMMANDS WILL FIRST COMPUTE THE
    PERCENTAGE AND THEN PRINT THE REPORT.

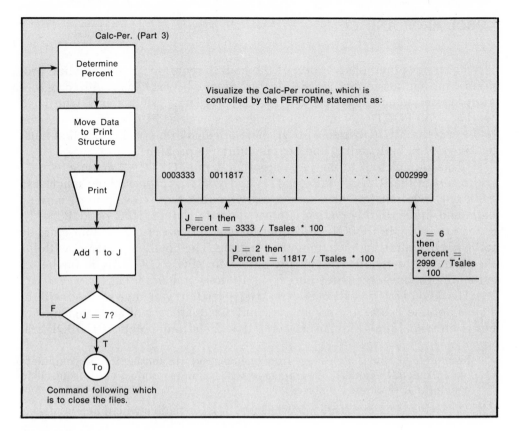

FIGURE 8-17

Compute-First-Then-Print.
    PERFORM Calc-Per VARYING J FROM 1 BY 1 UNTIL J = 7.
    CLOSE Cardin, Printo.
    STOP RUN.

MINI PROBLEM REVIEW QUESTIONS

8–32. Since the computer will execute any paragraph that it passes through, why is the Zero-Out routine not coded after the PERFORM Zero-Out ... statement?

8–33. What is the data name "man"?

8–34. In the example, how does the value of the subscript "J" change?

COBOL PROS AND CONS

From your own observation of the coding required for the bowling program, you will agree that a great deal of detailed work was required before the program actually got into solving the problem. Programmers who have worked with FORTRAN and other languages such as PL/I sometimes object to the fact that COBOL is so wordy. There are also rather rigid rules that must be followed in both coding and keypunching the problem.

Take a quick look at the same program in the FORTRAN module (p. 525) and again in the RPG module (p. 415) and you will observe how much less coding is required for these languages. Opening files, closing files, moving data, and other routine coding is not required in either RPG or FORTRAN, but is necessary in COBOL. RPG does have a very strict format that must be followed in coding and punching the program. The bowling program, with little mathematics required, is ideally suited to RPG. FORTRAN is far better suited to problems involving more computations and less I/O.

Until you have a basis of several languages that you have worked with to a considerable extent, the advantages and disadvantages of any language are not readily apparent. Most users agree that the strong points of COBOL are:

Programmers can easily change from one computer to another if both computers have COBOL compilers. Programmers will be more productive if required to code primarily in one language.

The source programs, with a few changes, are compatible with different models of computers.

Management, the client, and auditors can usually follow the logic of the program from the computer printout *if* documentation is added through notes and paragraph names. It also helps if standards are developed for file and data names.

Compile time diagnostics are usually good.

The disadvantages of COBOL depend to a degree upon *each user's level of COBOL and the extent to which it was supported by the computer manufacturer.* Execution time debug routines are not as good in COBOL as in some other languages. Many users feel that more abbreviations, as well as a free format for coding, should be permitted. There are fewer mathematical functions and editing routines available than in some of the other compiler languages. The conflict still exists as to whether there really is a common or standard COBOL. *Since committee action is required, time lags do exist in getting new features "standardized."*

Most experienced programmers agree that there is not yet an ideal language for all situations. Nevertheless, COBOL is used in thousands of installations as the *primary language*. With continued efforts and increased support of the manufacturer, some of the basic weaknesses of COBOL may be solved.

GLOSSARY OF NEW AND OLD TERMS
TO CHECK YOUR KNOWLEDGE

A Margin.   Indicates the use of card column 8 on the COBOL coding form. Certain statements must start at this margin.

Address.   A location within the CPU. Each byte may be addressed individually or as part of a field or record.

ANS COBOL.   COBOL standards published by the American National Standards Institute.

Application Programming.   Programming done generally by the installation's programmers for typical applications, such as payroll, accounts receivable, inventory, etc.

Arithmetic Operators.   The +, –, *, / and ** used in programming to indicate addition, subtraction, multiplication, division, or exponentiation. The ones illustrated are used in COBOL, FORTRAN, PL/I, and other languages.

Array.   A table established in the memory of the computer, which can be used to store data. Each element of the array can be addressed individually.

Assembler Language.   A low-level language that differs in characteristics for each computer. It is necessary to know how each command actually works in order to program in any assembler language.

B Margin.   Indicates the use of card column 12. Certain statements must start at this margin or beyond.

Byte.   A location in core where one character or two digits may be stored.

Character Set.   The digits, alphabetic characters, and special characters that are recognized within a given language subset.

Clause.   A part of a COBOL statement used to describe structures or give initial values to items.

COBOL Subset.   COBOL rules, within perhaps a much larger set of rules, which apply to a particular compiler.

CODASYL.   Conference on Data Systems Languages. The committee was convened by the federal government and asked to develop a standard language.

Compiler Language.   A high-level language which permits the programmer to write programs with little or no knowledge of the way the commands will actually be executed. The languages are usually powerful, since one statement may generate many machine language commands.

Copy Statement.   A COBOL clause used to bring the desired commands or structures into the programmer's problem from the appropriate library.

CPU.   Central Processing Unit. The memory of the computer where the commands, data, and the supervisor are stored.

Edit Mask.   A print format established for numeric data which includes the use of the allowable special characters. The numeric value of the sending field moves into the field around the editing characters. Some of the special characters "float" and are printed next to the first significant digit.

Emulator. An optional computer feature, generally rented from the manufacturer or a software company, which is a combination of both software and hardware. Its function is to permit the user to take source programs (written for another computer) and compile them on the new computer. The new computer will act like the old computer in the execution of the compiled program.

Environment Division. The division that indicates the file names and hardware which will be utilized in the program. Other features are also included in this division.

File Section. Describes the input and output records in terms of field sizes and types of data contained in each field. The characteristics of the file are also given in the FD for the file.

Hierarchy. Order in which the arithmetic operations, within a formula, will be executed.

Identification Division. The portion of the COBOL program that includes the program name. The other information included is for program documentation.

Imperative Command. A command that generates one or more actual computer commands.

Indexes. Pointers used to identify the location of data within a computer.

JCL. Job control language cards needed to tell the computer the options you wish to exercise, i.e., LINK, DECK, etc.

JOD. Journal of Development published by the Programmer's Language Committee of CODASYL. The journal gives the recommended standards for new features added to COBOL.

Library. The library or libraries reside either on tape or disk and contain complete programs which have been compiled, tested, and debugged. The library also contains subroutines that may be called into larger programs and source statements.

Literal. Another name for a constant.

Nonnumeric Literal. A constant that is either alphabetic or alphanumeric, and which is always enclosed in single quote marks: 'This is a nonnumeric literal'.

Object Deck. A deck may be punched, at the option of the operator, during the compilation of a program that contains the machine language translation of the source program.

Occurs Clause. This clause tells the number of times a described field is to be repeated in a table that is being established within the CPU. Each field within the table has an unique address. The clause may also be used to specify tables in cards, tapes, or disk.

Paragraph Name. In COBOL, statements, or sentences, make up paragraphs. Each paragraph has a user-supplied name which may be used in a branching instruction. They are also referred to as "procedure names."

Record. A unit of information, within a file, made up of fields. For example, the data pertaining to one employee in a payroll file is a record.

Reserved Word. COBOL words that have a particular meaning in the COBOL statement. They may be used only in the manner prescribed and may *not* be used for data names, paragraph names, or file names.

Simulator. Allows a program written for one computer to be run on another computer. The simulator is the program, or software, used to accomplish the conversion.

Source Data. When using the report writer feature the term "source" is used to represent the sending field. The programmer need not write a move command. The data in the field will be moved prior to printing the report line, since the commands generated during the compiling of the program will add the instructions necessary to achieve the desired results.

Source Program. A program written in a pseudo computer language which must be translated to machine language prior to execution of the program.

Standard. A uniform method of accomplishing a given task.

Subroutines. Prewritten routines, either provided by the manufacturer or written by the user, which may be called into larger programs. They are generally stored in a library residing on disk or tape.

Subscripts. A value used to formulate a unique address for each field within a table.

Syntax. The rules governing statement structure in a language.

USA COBOL. COBOL standards developed by the United States of America Standards Institute (USASI).

Usage Clause. Used in COBOL to tell the computer how data is to be stored: binary, fixed decimal, zoned numeric, etc.

Variable. A value that changes, such as hours worked, during the execution of a program.

PROGRAMMING PROBLEMS

Problem 1

The sales department of a company using a card-oriented system has requested that the completed sales order cards for the month be used to total the sales of each major product class *for each salesman*. The company has three major product classifications which are identified by the first digit of the item number:

Code 1 = Product A
Code 2 = Product B
Code 3 = Product C

The request indicated that the output was to be punched in cards.

SYSTEMS FLOWCHART

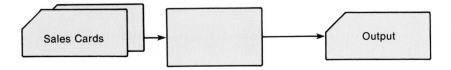

The input must be sequenced by salesman's number. Both the input and output cards are illustrated below:

From the input card, the programmer will only use the following fields of information:

FIELD	CARD COLUMNS	
Sold by	14–15	
Item No.	16	(First cc of field)
Total Sold	50–56	

The program flowchart is given in figure 8–18.

QUESTIONS

A. How would you test the program? Indicate how many cards and, in general, what situations would be tested by the test input.

B. When the job becomes operational, what documentation for the job would you recommend?

C. If the card had been used in a previous job which totaled the sales for the month and printed a report showing the total for each item as well as total sales for the month, what control *could be* built into this job to make certain that all cards were processed?

D. Under what circumstances would a message print out on the console? Why is the message coded if the item numbers all start with either a 1, 2, or 3?

E. What will cause the program control to go to the end-of-job routine?

F. Why should the total areas for A, B, and C be set to 0 initially and between card groups?

G. Why after reading one card do you compare to see if the stored salesman number is equal to the card man number? Won't it, at that point, always be the same?

Note: There are always different approaches that can be used to solve a problem. In this problem, a switch (as talked about under programming concepts) could be used to avoid use of two read statements.

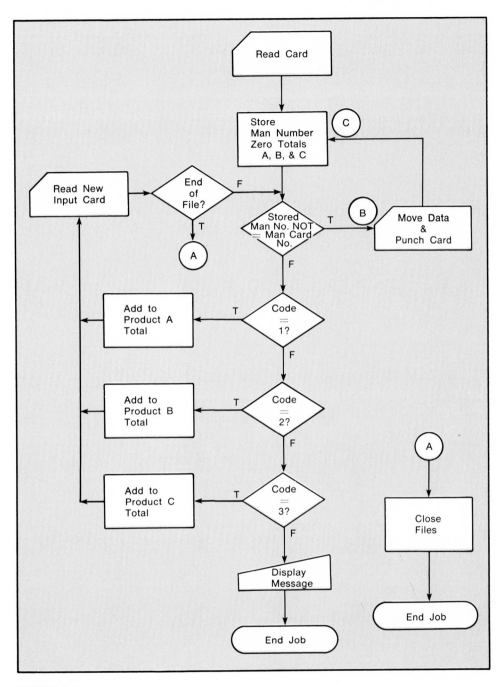

FIGURE 8–18

Problem 2

The sales department, after receiving the output from problem 1, indicated that the output was incomplete. They feel they want a printed report like the report layout form that is illustrated. *In addition, they would like the commission for each salesman to be calculated and printed.* The commission report had been a separate report. To combine the two, however, will eliminate card handling and computer time. Commissions are calculated as follows: product A, at 7.5%; product B, at 8.42%; and product C, at 6.33%.

Directions:

1. Code the additions that will be needed to problem 1. *Remove your SELECT, FD, and 01 for your punched card output and replace it with the printer specifications.*
2. Set up the headings in WORKING-STORAGE. Be sure to add the 77's which will be required. Print the headings and 25 detail lines per page.

SALESMAN	PRODUCT A	PRODUCT B	PRODUCT C	COMMISSION
	COMMISSION REPORT			
XX	XXX,XXX.XX	XXX,XXX.XX	XXX,XXX.XX	XX,XXX.XX
XX				

The following logic replaces the punched card output section of the program flowchart for problem 1. The added commands would be inserted at the point indicated as B:

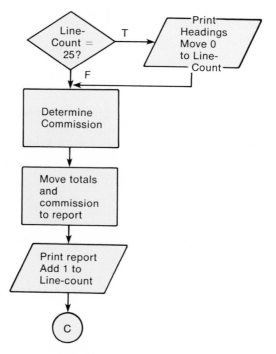

QUESTIONS

A. What additional steps would you take to test problem 2?
B. What would you add to the documentation?
C. Could you use a predefined process symbol effectively in your final revised program flowchart? Its use would keep the major logic of the problem easier to follow.

Problem 3

The sales department was pleased with the new report. *Nevertheless, they did feel that totals should be added to the bottom of the report. They would also like a page number printed at the top of each page.*

The data control clerk will add the three totals for product sales and make certain it agrees with a predetermined total for the monthly sales.

Directions:

Do a detailed program flowchart, to replace the one given in problem 2, that indicates the additional steps needed at B.

Do a detailed program flowchart for the end-of-job routine that is now needed.

Code the changes that are requested.

Problem 4

The academic dean would like a report listing all of the students who have a 3.5, or above, grade point average. Letters are to be sent to each student on the list. The dean's secretary will secure the address of each student on the report and type the addresses on envelopes. The dean will send a letter to each student congratulating him on his achievement.

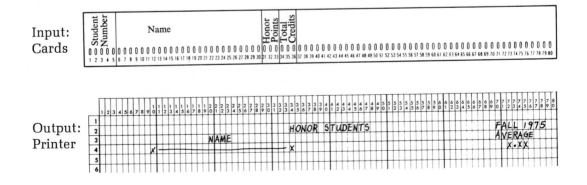

Input: Cards

Output: Printer

QUESTIONS

A. How would you test the program?
B. How could the program be improved upon, in terms of reducing work, if the input were tape or disk and contained the complete record (name, number, address, honor points, classes taken) for the student?
C. Could the work be reduced if only a card system were used?

Directions:

Do the program flowchart and code the problem.

Problem 5

Using the same input card as defined in problem 1, write a program that will do the following:

1. Read the cards which are in *random sequence* and accumulate the sales for each salesman in a table. Disregard the type of product sold.
2. *a.* You have only ten salesmen and they are numbered from one to ten.
   b. Before you start reading cards, be sure to zero out your table.
3. After all cards are read and the total for each man is accumulated in his area of the array, determine the percentage of the total sales each man sold.
4. At the end of the report, print out the total sales and the total of all individual percentages.
5. Design your report using the following headings:

Sales Analysis

Man Number	Amt. Sold	Percentage
XX	XXXXX.XX	XX.XX

6. Do a program flowchart. There are actually three parts to the program:
   a. Filling the table by adding each man's sales to his portion of the table.
   b. Determine each man's percentage of the total sold and print a detail line giving his number, amount sold, and percentage.
   c. Printing the final totals for the report. The fields to be totaled are the amount sold and each man's percentage.

ANSWERS

DISCUSSION TOPICS (p. 472)

8–1. Not really. Each manufacturer may add features to the basic COBOL standard. There are also two published standards: ANS and USA. The

Journal of Development also publishes changes recommended by the Programmer's Language Committee of CODASYL.

8–2. The committee was formulated at the request of the federal government. The intent was to develop a language that could be utilized effectively by all computers.

8–3. No. There are eight basic features that have been standardized. The lowest level compiler may contain only three of the eight. It is not uncommon to find that even some of the larger computers do not have the internal sort or report writer feature. Some large users who do have the report writer feature do not use it as they feel it does not provide the most efficient way, in terms of computer commands generated, of handling the writing of headings, detail, and total lines.

THOUGHT STARTERS (p. 481)

8–4. A. Numeric data is indicated by the use of a 9, whereas alphanumeric data is indicated by an X.

    B. The number within the ( ) indicates the size of the field.

8–5. A simple standard was used for coding all data in the input area, with the first letter of the name as I; an O was used for output data, a W for working-storage, and a P for an item in the print structure. This enables the coder to know where the field of information is from.

8–6. 41 bytes.

8–7. The intent was to center "Bowling Averages" in an 80-space line. Therefore, fields were defined and filled with spaces to set up the desired heading.

8–8. A. Identification.

    B. Environment.

    C. Data.

    D. Procedure.

8–9. A. 2540R refers to a given model for a card reader. The 2540R reads 1,000 CPM. It should be stressed that an installation's I/O model numbers may differ from the ones used in the illustrations.

    B. 1403 refers to a printer that prints 600 LPM.

8–10. Each SELECT statement must have its own FD (File Description) and 01 statement. The 01 defines the records into fields.

8–11. In the Procedure Division with the "Read Cardin Into Date-Card At End Go To Print-High-Bowler" statement. The student may answer with the "Open File" statement. It would be pointed out that opening the files is generally termed "housekeeping" and not part of the logic.

8–12. If the number of pins from the card is greater than the previous high stored.

8–13. Move Spaces to OFILLER.

8–14. "Go To read-input."

8–15. Yes, as three conditions were given:

A. Ease of input—only four card columns of data are keypunched.

B. Report requested is produced.

C. High bowler featured at the end of report.

It should be noted that even a simple procedure should have a post-implementation evaluation!

8–16. No provision was made for a line-count or for reprinting the headings. Depending on the system, this could produce a report that had a bowler's name and average printed on the perforation.

REVIEW QUESTIONS (p. 489)

8–17. A. The name of the division, IDENTIFICATION DIVISON.

B. The Program-ID statement.

8–18. The file name, Cardin, associated with both the physical device, 2540R, and the logical unit, 'SYS004'.

8–19. A. The name exceeds 30 characters.

B. A dash (–) can't be at the beginning or end of the data name.

C. No blanks are permitted within the name.

D. No special characters, other than the –, can be used.

8–20. No. Some compilers permit it to be excluded.

8–21. A. The card reader should be the 2540R.

B. It is also referred to as UNIT-RECORD.

NOW TELL ME (p. 491)

8–22. The regular hour field has only two places beyond an assumed decimal, whereas the rate field has three places beyond the assumed decimal.

8–23. Five bytes, since the S or V are not counted if the field is unpacked. Of course the V never is!

8–24. FD gives the computer more facts about the data in the file. Is it blocked or unblocked? Is the record size fixed or are there records that vary? How many characters in a record? What is the name that will be used in the program for that particular file? Are the labels for disk or tape created in the usual manner?

8–25. The picture clause tells the computer if the field is numeric, alphabetic, or alphanumeric. In addition, the field size is determined. If the field is numeric, how many places are there beyond the assumed decimal?

WORKING-STORAGE REVIEW (p. 494)

8–26. After the 77's.

8–27. 01 Heading.

02	F1	Picture	X(36)	Value Spaces.
02	P1	Picture	X(28)	Value

'Fall Semester Honor Students'.

02	F2	Picture	X(36)	Value Spaces.

8–28. 02 Receive-Data Picture $$,$$$.99.

8–29. The file section.

CAN YOU DO MATHEMATICS? (p. 500)

8–30. The ( ) indicate that A and B are to be added before the results are multiplied by the constant.

8–31. A. $180.00.
      B. $180.00.
      C. $100.00.

C is the incorrect answer as the computer takes Otimehrs * 2, then times the rate. To this the regular hours are added.

No, but they do aid in showing more clearly how the answer will be calculated.

MINI PROBLEM REVIEW QUESTIONS (p. 507)

8–32. It would perform the loop six times as requested and then execute the command one more time, since the program control passes through the paragraph. In this case, J would equal seven. The address of Sales-Amt (J) would then be invalid since the table was established with an "OCCURS 6 TIMES" statement. The program would therefore terminate at execution time.

8–33. A variable.

8–34. The value of J changes as the PERFORM statement is executed.

FORTRAN 9

FORTRAN I, which is the acronym for *FOR*mula *TRAN*slation, was first released in 1957, and its use was limited almost exclusively to scientific, engineering, and statistical applications. Restrictions in the early FORTRAN made financial applications virtually impossible. FORTRAN today is almost universal in its application, and is acceptable, with minor modifications, by most large-scale as well as small-scale computers.

FORTRAN was one of the first computer languages to use a "modular concept" because subroutines required for mathematical functions could easily be "called" into the user's program. This enabled the programmer to use a routine in his program, common to many applications, without actually coding it for himself. The modular concept has been broadened to include the many library functions that are available today. In addition, the use of subroutines by FORTRAN lead to the development of the second-generation computer's operating system. These same concepts paved the way for the sophisticated software of the third-generation computers.

Many of the weaknesses of FORTRAN I were corrected as FORTRAN II, III and FORTRAN IV were developed. A "standard" FORTRAN IV, published by a working group of the USASI (United States of American Standards Institute) and accepted by the major computer manufacturers, is now available. In reality, however, different manufacturers' FORTRAN may be quite different. There are tests that have been published to help users determine if their version is truly standard FORTRAN IV. FORTRAN IV is compatible with most earlier versions of FORTRAN. Therefore programs which follow the rules of FORTRAN I or II will usually compile successfully on a computer which has a FORTRAN IV compiler.

Many versions of FORTRAN were developed during the era of the second-generation computer. It made it possible to "batch" compiles to avoid loading the compiler, which often was stored on cards, into the computer for each individual compile. The diagnostics during compilation of the program left much to be desired and execution-time diagnostics were almost non-existent.

FORTRAN IV, developed for the third-generation computers, provides much better diagnostics during the compilation of the program although the error messages are still usually not as easy to understand as in COBOL or PL/I. Execution-time messages usually are not as explicit as to the cause of the problem as some of the other compiler languages.

WATFOR, which was originally developed for the IBM 360 at the University of Waterloo in Waterloo, Ontario, addressed itself to the problem of providing better diagnostics and faster compiles. Therefore, the WATFOR compiler makes use of many time-saving debug procedures. An update of WATFOR, called WATFIV, is now available on a time-sharing service basis and includes even better diagnostics than WATFOR. It has been reported that compiles are up to eight times faster using WATFIV than when using some of the "standard" FORTRAN IV compilers.

FORTRAN is a powerful compiler language. When you contrast the bowling program, written in FORTRAN, with the same program written in COBOL and RPG, you will find that far fewer source statements are required in the FORTRAN program. Less coding is required in FORTRAN because the mathematical statements are powerful and far fewer "housekeeping" commands are needed. For example, in FORTRAN it is unnecessary to open or close file, declare files and work area, or to move data from input to output.

WHAT IS FORTRAN?

9–1. What is FORTRAN the acronym for?
9–2. Do many computers have FORTRAN compilers?
9–3. Are all FORTRAN compilers the same?
9–4. What is WATFOR?

AN ILLUSTRATION OF A FORTRAN PROGRAM

Can you follow the logic of the program that is illustrated? Before presenting the rules, formats, and details of the FORTRAN language, an illustration is presented which will relate it to the procedure design steps with which you are familiar.

Problem Definition

The secretary of the Delta Products Company bowling league has requested that the data processing department automate the procedure of computing and listing the new bowling averages each week. The secretary is not familiar with data processing, but did ask that the system be easy to implement, require little keypunching, and produce a report that would list the bowler's name, total pins, total games, and average. In addition, the bowler of the week who has the highest number of actual pins is to be listed at the bottom of the report.

The programmer/analyst assigned to the job submitted the following card and report designs to the secretary for his approval. Figure 9–1 illustrates the two formats that will be used for the input cards. In card one, the first four fields are punched by the computer as output from the first week's computer run. After the cards are interpreted, the secretary writes the number of games

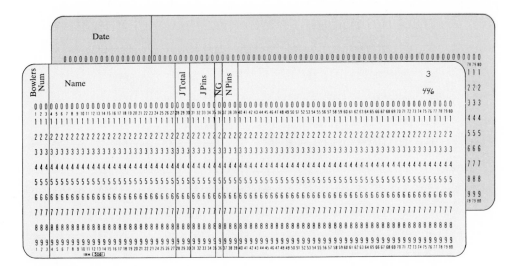

FIGURE 9–1

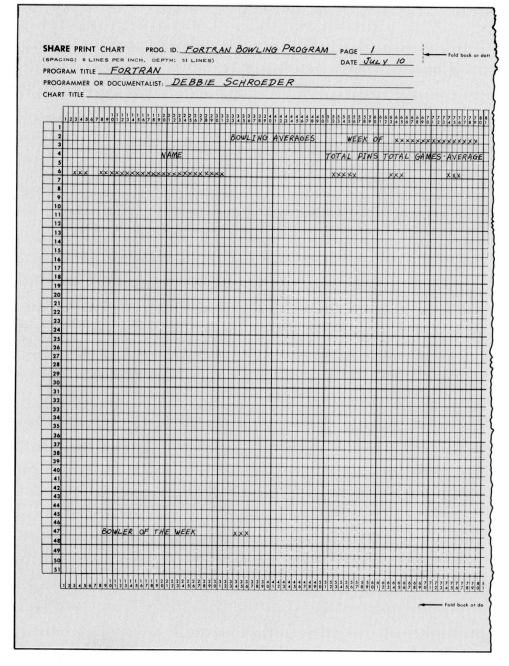

FIGURE 9–2

and pins for the second week on the right side of the card. The "3" and "446" written on the card in figure 9–1 illustrate how the data is recorded on the card. The four digits of new data is then keypunched into the card.

Using the date card to supply the variable information needed for the report heading will permit the program to be cataloged and then executed from the library. Either cataloging the program or making an object deck will save recompiling the program each week.

The secretary also approved the print layout, illustrated in figure 9–2, for the report which will be printed on 8½-by-11 stock paper. It is essential that the layout be done before the problem is coded in order to show the programmer exactly where the output is to be printed.

Program Flowchart

The program flowchart provided in figure 9–3 illustrates the major logic of the program which the programmer will use as a guide in coding the procedure. If it is necessary to "patch" the program at some time in the future, it is also very useful to the programmer making the required changes. For this reason, it becomes part of the documentation. The amount of detail given on the diagram depends partly on the standards of the installation and the experience of the programmer. It should be detailed, and in nontechnical terms, so that it can be easily understood by both the client, the bowling secretary, and the programmer.

Coding for Bowling Program

Statement Number	FORTRAN Statement
C	BOWLING PROGRAM CODED IN FORTRAN
05	FORMAT (I3,6A4,I3,I5,I1,I3)
10	FORMAT (4A4)
20	FORMAT (1H1,31X,16HBOWLING AVERAGES,6X,9HWEEK OF 4A4)
30	FORMAT (1H0,18X,4HNAME,27X,11HTOTAL PINS ,12HTOTAL GAMES ,7HAVERAGE)
40	FORMAT (1H0,2X,I3,2X,6A4,20X,I5,6X,I3,8X,I3)
50	FORMAT (1H0,4X,18HBOWLER OF THE WEEK,7X,I3)
60	FORMAT (I3,6A4,I3,I5)
	JSAVE = 0

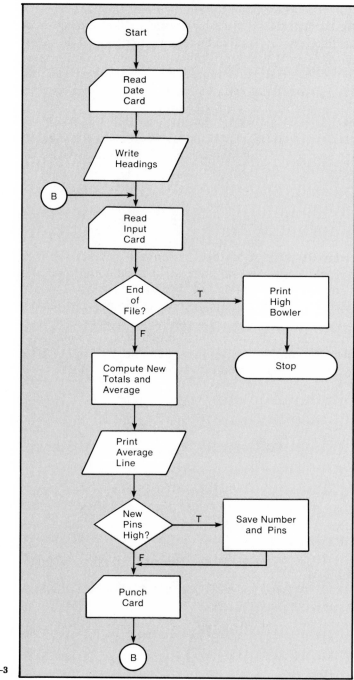

FIGURE 9–3

```
        READ 10,D1,D2,D3,D4
        PRINT 20,D1,D2,D3,D4
        PRINT 30
99      READ (1,5,END=199) NUM,N1,N2,N3,N4,N5,N6,JTOTAL,JPINS,
        NG,NPINS
        JTOTAL = JTOTAL + NG
        JPINS = JPINS + NPINS
        JAVER = JPINS / JTOTAL
        PRINT 40,NUM,N1,N2,N3,N4,N5,N6,JPINS,JTOTAL,JAVER
        IF (JSAVE — NPINS) 100,101,101
100     JSAVE = NPINS
        JNUM = NUM
101     PUNCH 60,NUM,N1,N2,N3,N4,N5,N6,JTOTAL,JPINS
        GO TO 99
199     PRINT 50,JNUM
        STOP
        END
```

FORTRAN STATEMENTS

The format statements specify how fields are positioned within a record. The information provided by the statement tells the length of the field, where it is located and the type of data contained in the field. The coding for statement 5 of the Bowling Program describes the input data card. Check and see if the format statement does not accurately tell the computer about each bowler's input card.

---

5   FORMAT (I3,6A4,I3,I5,I1,I3)

SPECIFIED AS	DATA CONTAINED IN FIELD	CARD COLUMNS
I3	A 3-position number which contains the bowler's number.	1–3
6A4	Six alphabetic fields each four positions in length. Six adjacent fields provide space for the bowler's name.[1]	4–27

[1] One of the unusual aspects of FORTRAN IV is that an alphanumeric field must be broken into units. The unit size varies depending upon which computer is utilized. Generally, the maximum size is from four to six characters.

SPECIFIED AS	DATA CONTAINED IN FIELD	CARD COLUMNS
I3	A 3-position number which contains total games bowled to date.	28–30
I5	A 5-position number which contains total pins to date.	31–35
I1	A 1-position number which contains the games bowled for the week.	36
I3	A 3-position field which contains the numbers of pins for the week.	37–39
	Undefined. Either the data isn't used in the program or the area contains blanks.	40–80

20 FORMAT (1H1,31X,16HBOWLING AVERAGES   ,6X,9HWEEK OF   ,4A4)

SPECIFIED AS	DATA CONTAINED IN FIELD	PRINT POSITION
1H1	The first location of a print line is for carriage control. 1H1 advances a new form.	1
31X	Skip 31 positions. Blanks will be contained in the locations indicated.	2–32
16H	Specifies 16 alphanumeric characters, "Bowling Averages", are to be inserted in the print line. H, for Hollerith, is used to specify the literals or constants used in printing headings or other data.	33–48
6X	Skip 6 positions. Blanks will be inserted into the print line being described.	49–54
9H	Specifies the 9 alphanumeric characters, "Week Of" to be inserted into the print line.	55–63
4A4	Print 4 alphanumeric fields, each 4 positions long, of variable information. The date from the card is the variable data that will be printed.	64–79
	Spaces or blanks will be automatically moved into the print positions from location 80 on.	80

Does this describe the first heading as shown on the report layout form?

JSAVE = 0 is used to establish a field to compare the number of pins each bowler gets for the week. The first bowler's pins are higher than 0 so will be stored there when command 100 is executed. Each subsequent bowler's pins are compared with the number stored in JSAVE. When a new high is detected, the new bowler's number and pins are saved.

```
READ  10,D1,D2,D3,D4
```

Read according to FORMAT 10 (4A4) a card containing four alphanumeric fields. Each field is identified by use of the names D1, D2, D3, and D4. The four fields contain the date. D1 is a *symbolic address* used to retrieve the data stored in the location specified. When the program is executed, all symbolic addresses have become the absolute addresses which are necessary if the computer is to retrieve data or execute instructions.

```
PRINT  20,D1,D2,D3,D4
```

Print according to FORMAT 20 will, during execution of the program, move the date into the locations specified in the format statement, advance a new page, and then print the heading.

```
99  READ  (1,5,END=199)  NUM,N1,N2,N3,N4,N5,N6,
          JTOTAL,JPINS,NG,NPINS
```

The data, as specified in FORMAT 5, is read from the input card and stored in the computer. Each field is identified by a unique name so that the stored information can be utilized by the programmer by referencing the name he assigned to the field. When the end-of-file is detected control goes to the command labeled statement 199. What did the program flowchart show was to happen at the end of the file? Does the command located at 199 do this?

Did you see the field names used before? Yes! The fields had been labeled on the design of the input card. NAME, however, had to be subdivided into 6 fields of 4 positions each and is now referred to as N1–N6.

```
JTOTAL  =  JTOTAL  +  NG
```

This command needs no explanation. JTOTAL is the total games to date and NG the number of games bowled this week. After execution JTOTAL contains the new total. The previous value was destroyed. The unknown is always to the left of the equal sign.

```
PRINT 30,N1,N2,N3,N4,N5,N6,JPINS,JTOTAL,JAVER
```

The bowler's name, pins to date, games to date and average, which was calculated by JAVER = JPINS / JTOTAL, are printed according to FORMAT 30. FORMAT 30 described the detail line which was planned for on the print layout form.

```
                          Neg  Zero  Pos
        IF (JSAVE – NPINS)  100,  101,  101
```

IF statements are generally used wherever a diamond appears on the program flowchart. An IF statement may provide 3 locations to which the control may branch. An evaluation is made of the expression (JSAVE — NPINS).

IF: JSAVE = 325
       NPINS = 416
WHAT HAPPENS: Unknown = 325 — 416
                Unknown = —91
Unknown: Negative—Control branches to 100
           Zero   —Control branches to 101
           Positive —Control branches to 101

"Unknown" as it is called in the example is never available for your use. Its value is checked to determine if it is a negative, zero or positive value. If negative, control passes to the point in the program where the commands to save the number and new high number of pins are stored. If zero or positive those commands are bypassed and a card is punched which contains the bowler's number, name, total games and total pins.

```
                GO TO 99
```

GO TO 99 is an unconditional branch to statement 99. At that address is stored the command to read a new input card.

Terminates the program.

```
STOP
```

Final required statement in a FORTRAN program.

```
END
```

THOUGHT STARTERS

Before reading some of the more detailed rules pertaining to FORTRAN, see if you can answer the following questions by studying the illustration of the Bowling Program. The questions are presented not to discourage you but to cause you to think. Programming in FORTRAN is logical and follows basically *simple rules*.

9–5. What card does 60 FORMAT (I3,6A4,I3,I5) describe?
9–6. Can you determine, without looking at the card layout form, where the data is located for each field?
9–7. What type of data is contained in each field of the 5 FORMAT statement?
9–8. Study the FORMAT statements and the explanation and then answer the following:
    A. What kind of data is field "A" used for?
    B. What is the "X" used for?
    C. An "I" is used to specify what kind of data?
    D. In 16HBOWLING AVERAGES, what does the 16 tell the computer?
9–9. What two statements are necessary to establish the printline in the CPU and then print the line on the printer?
9–10. Why are three FORMAT statements necessary for the card input and output?
9–11. What variable data was keypunched on the card each week?
9–12. Did the design of the procedure to print the bowler's averages meet the basic criteria for the job?
9–13. What command adds the new pins to the former total number of pins?
9–14. Which command provides a conditional branch that is contingent upon the number of pins for the week?
9–15. In the program, when will control go to statement 100?

9–16. IF (JSAVE — NPINS) 10, 20, 30
    A. What statement will the program control go to if NPINS is greater than JSAVE?
    B. What statement will the program control go to if NPINS and JSAVE are equal?
    C. What statement will the program control go to if JSAVE is greater than NPINS?

9–17. What must be used as the final statement in a FORTRAN program?

9–18. What type of branching command is illustrated by "GO TO 99"?

9–19. What actually will be stored at the symbolic address 99?

9–20. Why isn't a statement number used on the command which reads the date card?

9–21. Does the program flowchart for the program show in any way where statement numbers will be needed?

9–22. When will the command specified by the 199 be executed?

FORTRAN CODING FORMS

The coding form illustrated in figure 9–4 is easy to use as there are few restrictions placed on the programmer. If a comment, for program documentation, is desired a "C" is used in card column 1.

One through 5 is reserved for the statement number. Generally a number is used only on FORMAT statements and instructions to which the program branches. The statement numbers, which are actually *symbolic addresses*, need not be in sequence.

Column 6 is used only if a FORTRAN statement cannot be contained on one card. A dash is used in Card Column 6 on the continuation cards.

The programmer may code his statements in columns 7 through 72. Most FORTRANS allow considerable freedom in coding. One programmer may code a statement as: X=A+B; the second programmer may prefer: X = A + B.

Columns 73 through 80 are reserved for program identification. Whatever is coded in 73–80 is not considered by the compiler in translation of the program to machine language.

Source Program Characters

The FORTRAN character set will recognize the digits 0–9, the alphabetic characters A–Z and the following special characters:

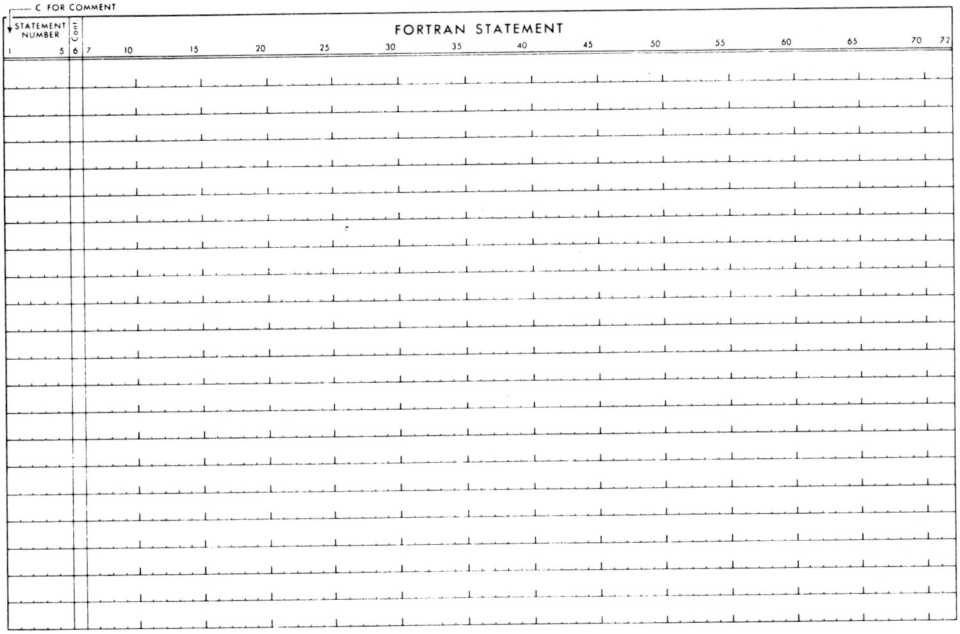

FIGURE 9–4. FORTRAN CODING FORM

(blank)	$ dollar sign
— minus	= equal
* asterisk	(left parenthesis
. period	) right parenthesis
, comma	' quote mark
+ plus	/ slash

For some computers, such as the IBM 360, the program may be punched using either the EBCDIC or BCDIC card code. If BCDIC is used, a special card is used with the source deck which instructs the compiler to translate the BCDIC to the EBCDIC code for internal storage. This feature was incorporated into the language in order that source decks punched with the BCDIC code could be compiled without repunching on a computer which utilized a FORTRAN IV compiler.

It is always wise before punching special characters to make certain that the special symbols on the keypunch that are used to punch the source deck produce the punch configuration required by the computer which will be used to compile the program.

FORTRAN Mathematics

As the name FORTRAN implies, formulas may be used when writing mathematical expressions. In so doing, the following characters are used:

+ addition
− subtraction
* multiplication
/ division
** exponentiation

The *hierarchy*, or priority, in FORTRAN, as in most other computer languages, is

1. exponentiation has top priority;
2. next in priority is multiplication and division; and
3. after all else is accomplished, steps involving addition and subtraction will be performed.

In the formula X = A + B * 10 / 2, A is equal to 3 and B is equal to 4.

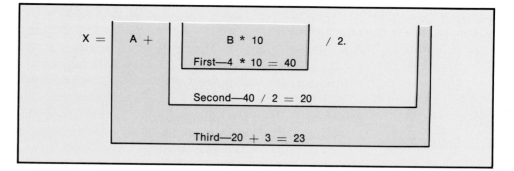

FIGURE 9–5

Figure 9–5 illustrates the mathematical hierarchy. After execution of the entire formula, X is equal to 23. The statement, besides showing the arithmetic hierarchy, shows some of the power of FORTRAN as many machine language commands will be generated in producing the final answer. An assembler language would require a minimum of 4 source statements. More may be required depending upon the computer being used and how the data in fields A and B is stored.

When the steps to be accomplished have equal value, as illustrated in figure 9–6, *the mathematics is done from left to right.*

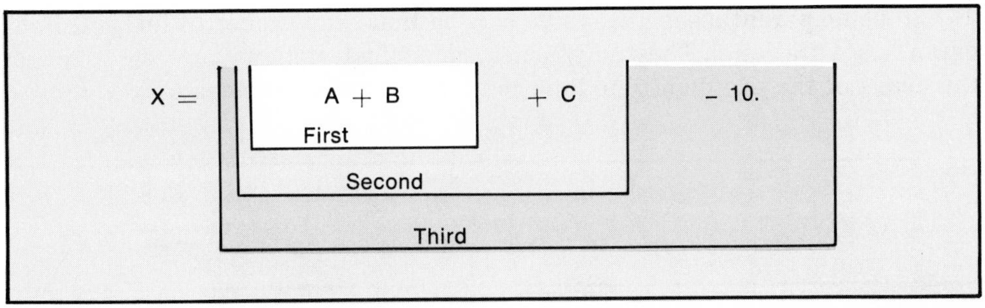

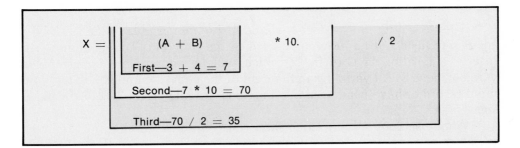

FIGURE 9–6

Parentheses

The priority given is valid *unless parentheses are used.* Figure 9–7 uses the same variables and constants as figure 9–5 but a different value for X is obtained when parentheses are added to the formula as parentheses are always cleared first.

FIGURE 9–7

In solving for X the answer differs depending upon whether the ( ) are used or not used. In some cases it may make no difference if parentheses are used or not. One programmer may code:

$$GPAY = (REGHRS * RATE) + (OTIME * RATE)$$

The second programmer writes:

$$GPAY = REGHRS * RATE + OTIME * RATE$$

The results produced are identical. The programmer who used the ( ) in his formula may feel their use adds clarity.

In using parentheses always be certain that the number of left and right parentheses are equal. They may be nested as illustrated in figure 9–8 to reflect the needs of the problem. The innermost ( ) are always cleared first.

L3	L2	L1	R1	L1	R1	R2	R3
Z = (	(	(A + B)	/	(C – D)	)	+ .15	) 39.624

FIGURE 9–8

Since there are two sets of "innermost" parentheses, A + B is executed then the operation C — D is performed. The sequence that the computer uses in accomplishing its work is:

1. A + B
2. C — D
3. (Results of A + B) / (Results of C — D)
4. Results of step 3 are added to .15.
5. The results of step 4 are divided by 39.624.

After execution the answer is stored in Z. *Any variable to the left of the equal sign need not be previously used in the program.* The computer will reserve a location in core for Z which will be addressable by using the variable name Z. All variables to the right of the equal sign must be part of an input record or have been used in a previous formula on the left of the equal sign.

What else does solving for Z show you? In an expression there may be *variables* or *constants*. The variables in the formula were A, B, C, D and Z; the constants, .15 and 39.624. The *one* unknown is always to the left of the equal sign.

LEARNED TO DATE

9–23. Are the > and < signs valid FORTRAN characters?
9–24. Can the programmer, using an IBM third-generation computer, use only the EBCDIC code in punching the source deck?
9–25. What symbols are used to do the following mathematical operations:
    A. addition   B. multiplication   C. division   D. subtraction
9–26. In terms of priority, how will each factor listed be executed in an

arithmetic expression? Rank each item. Use 1 for the highest priority and 4 for the lowest priority in answering:

A. addition or subtraction   C. clearing of parentheses

B. multiplication or division   D. exponentiation

9–27. In an expression, where must the unknown be coded?

9–28. Is A + B = C − D a valid FORTRAN expression?

9–29. What rules or facts regarding arithmetic have you learned to date? There are five facts, or sets of facts, that have been illustrated.

Were you able to identify the five basic arithmetic rules which were asked for in 9–29? If not, it might be wise to refer back to the discussion on FORTRAN mathematics in order that you know the rules which pertain to the following items:

1. Arithmetic hierarchy.
2. Use of parentheses.
3. Unknown must be to the left of the equal sign.
4. Only *one* unknown can be used.
5. Any variable used on the right of the equal sign must have been defined as part of input or appeared on the left of the equal sign in a previous statement.

DATA REPRESENTATION

Numbers stored within the CPU may be indicated as either fixed-point or floating-point. Different compilers differ on the number of significant digits that either type of numbers may contain. The significant digits are those that appear to the left of the decimal point. It is always wise to check in the programmer's manual for the current FORTRAN release being used to determine the precisions that may be utilized. The significant digit sizes that are used as an illustration appeared in one of the 360-40 FORTRAN releases.

Fixed-Point Numbers or Integer Mode

1. May contain no decimal points.
2. Are indicated in the FORMAT statement by use of the letter "I". FORMAT (I3,I4) would indicate a 3 position field in card columns 1–3; I4 would be adjacent to the first field and would contain 4 digits.
3. The character set for a fixed-point constant permits only the numerals 0–9 and the plus and minus sign. The sign, if used, must be to the left of the significant digits.

4. The data name for a fixed-point variable must *begin* with one of the letters I through N.
5. An integer, fixed-point number, may have no more than ten digits. The maximum value that it may contain is 2,147,483,647. It is contained in four locations in the CPU and is of the magnitude $2^{31}-1$.

Floating-Point or Real Number

1. A constant is written with a decimal point unless "E" notation is used.
2. The actual *input* for *variables* may be written with or without a decimal.
3. An F is used in the FORMAT statement to denote a floating-point number. FORMAT (F8.2,F6.2) for a punched card input format would tell the computer that:

Field 1:
F8.2
   a. Card columns 1–8 were used.
   b. Two places beyond the decimal point are indicated.
   c. The input could be punched as 12345.67 or 01234567. In the second case, the computer assumes the decimal point is between the 5 and the 6.

Field 2:
F6.2
   a. Is immediately adjacent to field 1.
   b. Therefore the data is in card columns 9–14.
   c. The data could actually be punched with or without the decimal point.

4. If a decimal is actually written in the variable field, the number of digits the field can then contain is decreased by 1. A F4.3 field with the decimal would be recorded .123. The numeral following the "F" is the total field size.
5. Variable names used for floating-point must start with a letter other than I through N. This means A through H and O through Z may be used.
6. The character set permitted for floating-point constants includes the numbers 0–9, arithmetic signs, and the decimal. The letters "D" and "E" may be used as indicated in 7 and 8.
7. *Single precision* numbers may contain no more than seven significant digits. The maximum single precision number would be 9999999. *Double precision* may be denoted for a constant in the following manner:

$$.123456789123D+14$$

The "D" indicates the use of double precision and the 14 is the total number of digits. The number is read then as:

$$+12345678912300.$$

Single precision, however, will be used in the problems and illustrations.

8. "E" may be used to denote an exponent. For example, 1,000,000,000 which is 10^9 may be written as 1.0E9.

Unless a minus sign is used as part of input data or as part of the constant, the field is assumed to be positive. If the result of a mathematical computation produces a negative value, the field sign in the CPU will change to the minus sign representation. In the example A = 4 and B = 5.

$$X = A - B$$

"X" will have a value of minus 1 after the command is executed.

In FORTRAN, as with any computer mathematics, the normal rules of algebra, in regard to the sign, are followed.

REVIEW QUESTIONS

9–30. FORMAT (I4,F6.2)
   A. What kind of number does I4 represent?
   B. What kind of number does F6.2 represent?
9–31. Are the following names valid for fixed-point, integer mode?
   A. GROSS   B. JNUM   C. NUM   D. BAL
9–32. Are the following names valid for floating-point, real numbers?
   A. NETPAY   B. X   C. JBAL   D. GRPAY
9–33. Are the following constants valid for fixed-point?
   A. 12.48   B. −123   C. 123.456   D. 123456789012   E. 126   F. 123−
   G. $120.00
9–34. Are the following values valid for floating-point numbers?
   A. 1248   B. −123.   C. 123456789.012   D. .12674D+14   E. 1.0E6
   F. $99.98
9–35. A. How is .12674D+14 read?
   B. What is the precision called?
9–36. A. How is 1.0E6 read?
   B. Who would be most likely to use this type of notation for constants?

MIXED MODES

Another very basic rule that should be followed in FORTRAN coding is: *do not mix modes.* During the compilation of a program, an error may not be detected when modes are mixed, but the precision of the answer may be invalid.

$$X = A + B * 10$$

Are the modes mixed? Yes, 10 is a fixed-point value. To avoid mixing modes, 10. should be used in the equation solving for X.

$$X = A + B * J$$

How are the modes mixed? A, B, and X are all floating-point variables while J is fixed-point. Any data name starting with a letter from I–N is a fixed-point variable, whereas all other letters denote floating-point variables.

In referring back to the bowling program, do you now see why JAVER was used for average rather than AVER? All numeric values in the bowling program are whole numbers. Therefore, all numeric field data names begin with I through N.

If a value is read in as an integer, such as J, it may be used in an assignment statement to a floating-point number, such as X = J. The value stored in field J is moved to X. X may now be used, along with other floating-point variables and constants in an expression.

VARIABLE NAMES

Variable names are used by the programmer as symbolic addresses. The computer will then generate an actual address for each variable. The rules for naming variables are:
1. The first character must be alphabetic. Some special characters are considered as alphabetic, such as the $ and).
2. Six characters is the maximum length.
3. The first letter denotes the mode:

> I through N—Fixed-point
> A through H and O through Z—Floating-point

4. Use meaningful names as they will aid in following the program logic such as: GROSS = (HRS * RATE) + (OTIME * RATE * 2.)

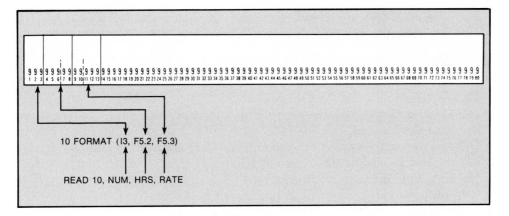

FIGURE 9–9

FORMAT STATEMENTS

Each different record design must have its own FORMAT statement. If in a program a card was read, calculations made, and the results were punched in a card of the same exact design as the one used for the input card, one FORMAT statement would be sufficient.

There is a direct correlation between the FORMAT statements and the READ and WRITE statements. The FORMAT statement is a *declarative* statement that reserves space for the data. In addition, the computer is told what kind of information is being stored in the reserved space. The data name associated with each individual field allows retrieval of the information for either calculations or output. Reading a card requires two statements: A FORMAT statement to inform the computer how the record is to be stored, and the READ statement that will actually cause a command to be generated to read the card. In figure 9–9 note the correlation between the card design, the FORMAT statement, and the READ statement.

The FORMAT specification codes are:

I   Fixed-point fields. No decimal points in the data.

F   Floating-point fields. Decimal points punched or assumed.

A   Alphanumeric data. A large field must be broken into the field size permitted by the compiler. In this text a maximum of four is used.

X   Indicates a skipped field. The size is given before the "X." Output fields specified with an "X" are filled with blanks.

H   The "H" is used to establish an alphanumeric constant called a literal.

The FORMAT specifies the number of characters in the field, an "H" for Hollerith, and then the actual characters in the literal are given.

Figure 9–10 illustrates the use of all of the codes described:

1. NUM will be punched in 1–3 of the output card. The NUM indicates that it is an integer.
2. GROSS, as implied by the name, is a 6-position field with 2 places to the right of the decimal.
3. The employee's name will be punched in 16 card columns. Units of 4, however, must be used in the output specification. 4A4 gives the factor number as 4, A for alphanumeric data and a 4 for the size *of each* of the four fields.
4. No output field is designated for the 48 blank card columns, since 48X specifies that 48 blanks are to be automatically inserted into the output area.

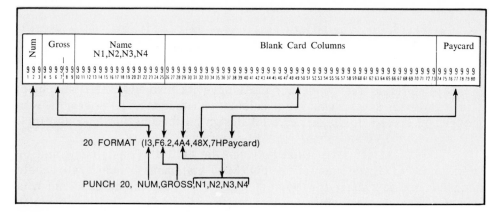

FIGURE 9–10

5. No output field name is used for the literal. The 7HPAYCARD tells the computer that the literal is 7 positions long, the "H" for Hollerith indicates that any (up to 7) of the valid FORTRAN characters may follow the "H" code.

PRINTED REPORTS

When reports are to be printed the first character of the FORMAT statement is reserved for advancing the paper in the printer. The following codes apply.

FIRST CHARACTER	ADVANCE BEFORE PRINTING
Blank	One line
0	Two lines
1	To first line of a new paper
+	No advance

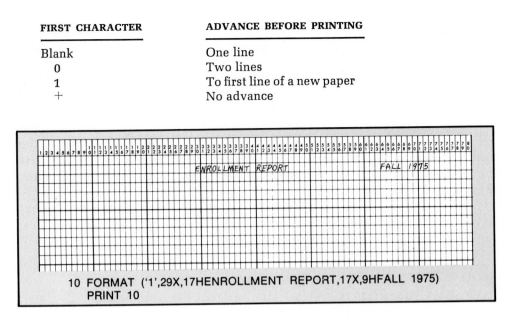

```
10 FORMAT ('1',29X,17HENROLLMENT REPORT,17X,9HFALL 1975)
   PRINT 10
```

FIGURE 9–11

Figure 9–11 shows a desired heading that is to be printed and the coding that is required to first set up the printline and then to print the desired heading. The FORMAT statement uses a '1' to denote the advancement of a new form in the printer, 29X will cause 29 spaces to be moved into the printline and 17H is used to specify a 17 position Hollerith field. The data moved into the location prior to printing is "Enrollment Report." Spaces are moved into the next 17 locations. Following the 17 spaces is the literal "Fall 1975" which was specified by the coding 9HFALL 1975.

The PRINT 10 statement is sufficient as no variables were used in the heading. However, in the bowling problem when a variable date, 16 characters long, was used the PRINT statement needed was

```
PRINT 20,D1,D2,D3,D4
```

The 20 referred to the FORMAT number of the statement which described the heading to be printed. Why were four fields specified for one date? As stated before alphabetic information is handled in units, each of which contains four characters.

In the bowling program the second READ statement used was

READ (1,5,END=199) NUM, N1,N2,N3,N4,N5,N6,JTOTAL,JPINS,NG,NPINS)

The 1, the first digit inside the parentheses, is the number of the logical unit. READ may be used to denote the card reader, tape or disk. A separate logical unit number is then used to denote each individual input device.

The programmer is responsible for finding out what logical unit numbers are assigned to each device. If READ is used without a logical unit number, the system assumes that the card reader is to be used. The second number, 5, is the FORMAT number. END=199 will cause a branch to statement 199 when the end of the file is detected.

WRITE also can be used, with a logical unit number, for any output device. Although several options are available for reading and writing files, the statements illustrated will be used:

READ 10,A,B,C	For card reader
READ (1,10,END=199) A,B,C	For card reader
PUNCH 20,A,B,C	For card punch
PRINT 30,A,B,C	For printer

Routines are often available that may be called into FORTRAN programs which allow cards to be read in a free format. As implied by the name "free format," the data may be punched anywhere in the card. Whenever a blank follows a digit, the computer knows that a field just ended. When another digit is found, it recognizes the start of a new field. Some versions of FORTRAN permit the use of "free format" without using a routine or function. Students find the use of the "free format" feature helpful when punching test data as field justification is no longer a problem. Most experienced data processing programmers and analysts tend to feel the utilization of an input card format makes editing easier and also helps to provide better control over accuracy.

CAN YOU READ AND WRITE ACCORDING TO FORMAT?

9–37. 10 FORMAT (I4,F8.2,F8.2)
  A. Do all FORMAT statements need a line number?
  B. How many fields are described by the FORMAT statement 10?
  C. The field specified by I4 will contain what kind of number?
  D. The field specified by F8.2 will contain what kind of number?
  E. Are the ( ) around I4, F8.2, F8.2 required?
  F. Are the commas required?

G. Could the statement have been coded 10 FORMAT (I4,2F8.2)?

9–38. What is wrong with the statement: "Read10,A,B,C"? The question relates back to the FORMAT statement given in 9–37.

9–39. 20 FORMAT (I4,10X,15HFORTRAN IS EASY)

				Output Card Punched by the Command: PUNCH 20, A
9 9 9 9	9 9 9 9 9 9 9 9 9	9 9 9 9 9 9 9 9 9 9 9 9 9 9	9 9 9 9 9 9 9 9 9 9 9 9 9 9 9 9 9 9 9 9 9 9 9 9 9 9 9 9 9 9 9 9 9 9 9 9 9 9 9 9 9 9 9 9 9 9 9 9 9 9 9	
1 2 3 4	5 6 7 8 9 10 11 12 13 14	15 16 17 18 19 20 21 22 23 24 25 26 27 28 29	30 31 32 33 34 35 36 37 38 39 40 41 42 43 44 45 46 47 48 49 50 51 52 53 54 55 56 57 58 59 60 61 62 63 64 65 66 67 68 69 70 71 72 73 74 75 76 77 78 79 80	

A. What will be punched in card columns 1–4?

B. What will be punched in 5–14?

C. What will be punched in 15–29?

D. What does the "H" stand for?

E. What will be in 30–80?

9–40. 15 FORMAT ('1',16X,44HFORTRAN SHOULD BE FUN BUT IT DOES
   –TAKE WORK)
   PRINT 15

A. What will the '1' cause to happen?

B. Why is nothing required but PRINT 15?

C. What will actually be printed on the paper?

D. Could "1H1" be used for the print control rather than '1'?

9–41. READ can be used for card, tape or disk. How would the computer know which you actually want to use?

9–42. Is there an alternate way that cards can be keypunched rather than adhering to a rigid card format?

9–43. After reading and processing all of the input cards, the totals are to be printed and the job ended. How will the computer be told to branch to Statement 200 which will achieve the desired results?

   200 PRINT 15, TOTALA, TOTALB, TOTALC
   STOP
   END

9–44. 15 FORMAT (I4,F8.2,F6.2)

   READ 15, X, GROSSPAYAMT,JRATE

Each variable is wrong *if* FORMAT 15 is correct. Why is each of the following variables incorrect? X? GROSSPAYAMT? JRATE?

9–45. Alphabetic information is punched in 1–20 of the input card. How would the FORMAT statement be coded? Write an appropriate READ statement to read the card.

"IF" AND "DO" CONTROL STATEMENTS

There are various statements which are classified as "control statements." However, the two most powerful are IF and DO.

IF has two formats; the first:

	Negative	Zero	Positive
IF (A – B)	10,	20,	30

provides up to a three-way branch. As previously stated control goes to one of the statement numbers depending upon the evaluation of the results of (A — B). If (A — B) produces a negative answer, the program control will branch to 10; if zero, to 20; if positive, to statement 30. The expression inside of the ( ) may contain any valid arithmetic expression. *It may not, however, include an equal sign.* All of the following are valid:

$$\text{IF (A — B * .10) 98, 97, 97}$$
$$\text{IF (Z * .8 / .3249) 10, 20, 30}$$
$$\text{IF (J) 5, 10, 15}$$

In each case, the statement numbers must be the number of the commands you actually wish to execute depending on the evaluation made. The value obtained from the expression inside the ( ) is never usable.

The second form of the IF statement, called the "logical IF," provides a two-way branch. *Relational operators* are used in the logical IF statements to determine where the control will go. The relational operators are

SYMBOL	MEANING
.LT.	Less than
.LE.	Less than or equal to
.EQ.	Equal to
.NE.	Not equal to
.GT.	Greater than
.GE.	Greater than or equal to

When a relational symbol is used an evaluation is made to see if the condition is true. If so the branching command is executed. Consider the following example given in figure 9–12.

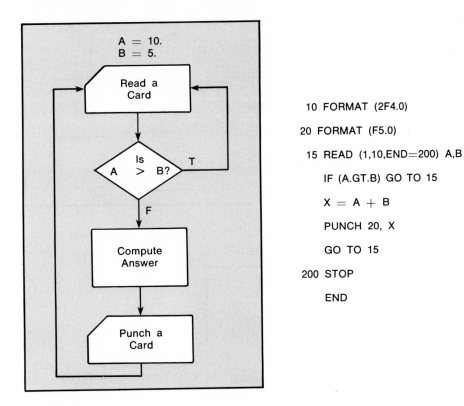

A = 10.
B = 5.

Read a
Card

Is
A > B?   T

F

Compute
Answer

Punch a
Card

10 FORMAT (2F4.0)

20 FORMAT (F5.0)

15 READ (1,10,END=200) A,B

　　IF (A.GT.B) GO TO 15

　　X = A + B

　　PUNCH 20, X

　　GO TO 15

200 STOP

　　END

FIGURE 9–12

Both the coding and the diagram in figure 9–12 clearly show that if A is greater than B a new card is read. How will the control of the program reach Statement 200? How, when reading cards, is the "End" of the file detected?

All of the following IF statements, using relational symbols, are valid:

IF (A.LT.B) GO TO 200
IF (A.EQ.10.) GO TO 15
IF (A.NE..44) GO TO 200
IF (B.LE.13.)　GO TO 15
IF (A*B.GT.100.) GO TO 15

"DO" statements are used to execute a count controlled "DO Loop." The form of the statement is illustrated in figure 9–13.

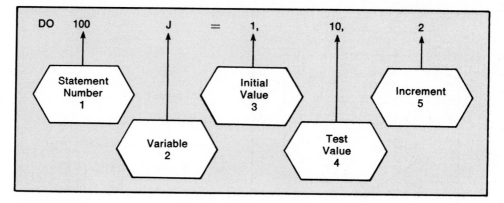

FIGURE 9–13

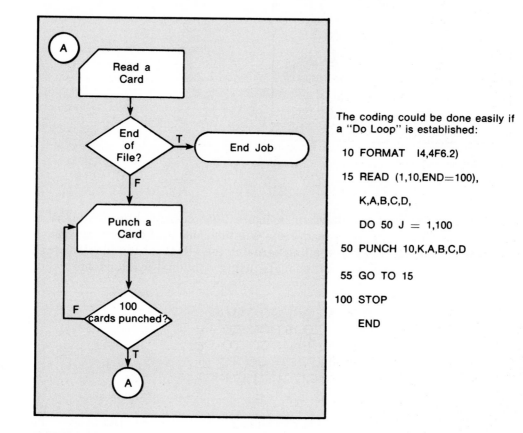

The coding could be done easily if a "Do Loop" is established:

```
10 FORMAT  I4,4F6.2)

15 READ  (1,10,END=100),

   K,A,B,C,D,

   DO 50 J = 1,100

50 PUNCH 10,K,A,B,C,D

55 GO TO 15

100 STOP

   END
```

FIGURE 9–14

In Figure 9–13:

1. The statement number closes the loop.
2. Any name may be used as long as it conforms to the rules of naming an integer variable.
3. An initial value is given. A constant, such as 1, can be used or an integer variable.
4. When the test value is exceeded, the command following *100* will be executed.
5. If an increment is not used, 1 is assumed.

A programmer wishes to read a card and punch 100 exactly like the one read, read a second card, punch 100, etc. The program flowchart, figure 9–14, illustrates the problem. The "loop" is established by: DO 50 J = 1, 100.

1. All statements from the point where the "Do" appears in the program to and including statement 50 are to be executed as part of the loop.
2. The *counter* J is established at 1.
3. The loop is to continue until J is greater than 100.

Is there anything that would prevent the loop from being executed 100 times? Yes, if an unconditional branch is within the Do Loop, an exit is made from the loop when the branch is executed. There are times, however, when it may be advantageous to have a conditional branch within the "Do Loop."

DO Loops may be nested as long as each loop is completely contained by the loop that it is nested in. The amount, or depth, of nesting permitted depends upon the compiler being used. If a programmer wanted to read exactly 100 cards and for each input card punch 5 new cards, a nested "DO" could be used. The problem can be perceived as illustrated in figure 9–15.

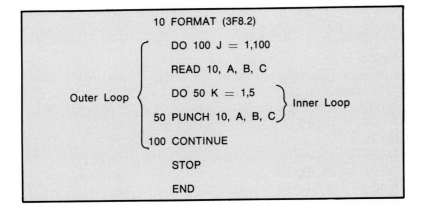

FIGURE 9–15

How many cards are actually punched? Five hundred cards will be punched as each time one card is read as part of the outer loop, the inner loop is executed five times. In executing DO 100 J = 1,100, one is added to J each time the loop is executed. A comparison is made to determine when 100 is reached. When J = 100 the control passes from the loop and the next statement is executed.

CONTINUE is often used as the last statement of the "Do" loop or range. It does not create any actual machine language instructions and is therefore referred to as a "dummy statement." Its use can prevent illegal statements from becoming part of the loop. Note that the FORMAT statement is not inside the loop. A problem illustrating more DO statements and an *array* is given at the end of the module.

DO YOU KNOW "DO" AND "IF"?

9–46. In each case A = 10 and B = 4. Which statement will control branch to in each of the following?

Neg. Zero Pos.
A. IF (A) 10, 20, 30
B. IF (B — A) 10, 20, 30
C. IF (B * 2. — A) 10, 20, 30
D. IF (A + B) 10, 20, 30
E. IF (B — 4.) 10, 20, 30

9–47. Again A = 10 and B = 4. Which statement will be executed next, after the "IF" in each case?
A. IF (A.GT.B) GO TO 99
GO TO 101
B. IF (A.EQ.B.) GO TO 99
GO TO 101

9–48. Does the logical IF provide a two-way branch?

9–49. How does the branching capability of the IF(J) . . . compare with the Logical IF statement?

9–50. The DO statements illustrated will each punch how many cards?
A. DO 50 J = 1,10,3
50 PUNCH 10, A, B, C
B. DO 50 J = 1,10
50 PUNCH 10, A, B, C
C. DO 50 J = 1,10
GO TO 99
50 PUNCH 10, A, B, C

9–51. Can DO loops be nested?

9–52. Most of the program logic is derived by effectively using what FOR-TRAN statement?

9–53. How many times will the loop be executed if J is equal to 6?

DO 100 I = J,100

OTHER CONTROL STATEMENTS

STOP   Is used at the logical end of the program. The program terminates when the STOP command is executed.

END   Is at the physical end of the program. At compile time it signals to the computer that all of the source deck has been read.

GO TO   The GO TO statement is used in branching instructions to transfer the program control to a given instruction. The instruction to branch to is designated by using a statement number.

PAUSE   The execution of the PAUSE statement halts the computer and awaits operator intervention. The following could take place:

     10 FORMAT ('1',19HMOUNT NEW DISK PACK)
     5 LOGIC—MANY STATEMENTS WOULD BE CODED
                        AT THIS POINT

     PRINT 10
     PAUSE
     GO TO 5

Unless the system has a time limit, it will wait for operator intervention. The PAUSE statement will cause the computer to wait until the operator responds to the message. In this case the operator should mount the new pack and then depress "Start" or "EOB" on the console. This will cause the computer to branch to statement 5.

END = nn   In a READ statement, such as READ (1,5,END=500) A,B,C, when the end-of-file is detected control transfers to the command designated as statement 500.

DIMENSION STATEMENT

Another *specification* statement besides FORMAT is DIMENSION. A DIMENSION statement reserves space in the computer for a table, or *array*.

Array is another name for a table. Consider the following case: on a card is punched the student's number and a test score. The cards are in random sequence. The programmer is told to write a program to add each student's test scores together and divide by 5. A report of average test scores is to be printed. Five is the number of tests each student took. The student numbers range from 1 through 99. All 99 numbers are assigned to students who took all 5 tests. The program flowchart is provided in figure 9–16.

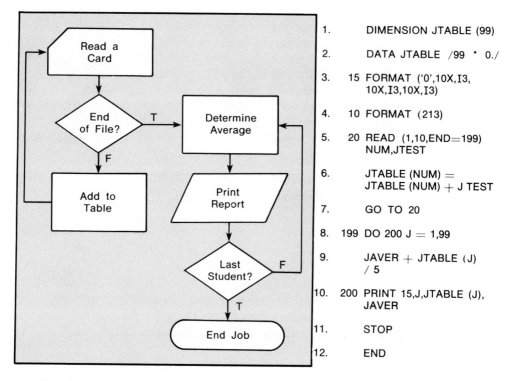

FIGURE 9–16

A DIMENSION statement must be used to establish a table that has 99 individual locations in which each student's total points may be accumulated. The student number is the *subscript* used to identify which location within the table that the test is to be added to. The input card has NUM, (student number), in 1–3 and his test score in 4–6. The report is to provide the student's number, and both his total points and average.

Since the scores are to be added to each student's area of the array, it must be initialized to zero. A DO Loop can be used to establish the table to zero if the DATA statement which is illustrated is not available.

Explanation of the Coding Related to Figure 9–16

LINE NUMBER	STATEMENT	ACCOMPLISHMENT
1	DIMENSION	Reserved enough space in the CPU to store the test scores for 99 students.
2	DATA	Establishes each area of the table to zero.
3	15 FORMAT	Describes the report which is double spaced and will print the student number, test total and average.
4	10 FORMAT	The input card is described.
5	20 READ	Reads the input file.
6	JTABLE (NUM) = ...	Adds the student's test score to his accumulated average. Each student has "reserved" for his test scores an area within the table.
7	GO TO 20	Unconditional branch to read a new card.
8	DO 200 ...	Establishes a DO Loop which will be executed 99 times.
9	JAVER = ...	Is one of the commands within the loop.
10	PRINT 15 ...	Prints the Report.
11	STOP	Executed after the loop is done 99 times.
12	END	Required final statement in the program.

Figure 9–17 will assist you in visualizing how the table is filled.

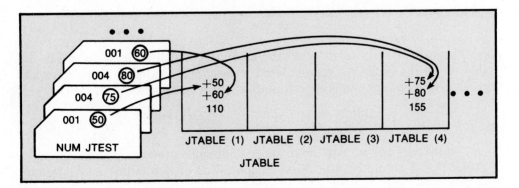

FIGURE 9-17

The student number when used as a subscript for JTABLE generates a unique address for each location in the table. When a DIMENSION statement is used to establish a table, the parts of the table are accessible only if a subscript is used. In TABLE (NUM), NUM is the subscript. A subscript must be:

1. Enclosed in ( ).
2. An integer.
3. A positive number.
4. It may be an integer constant or variable.

Figure 9–18 shows how the report is printed.

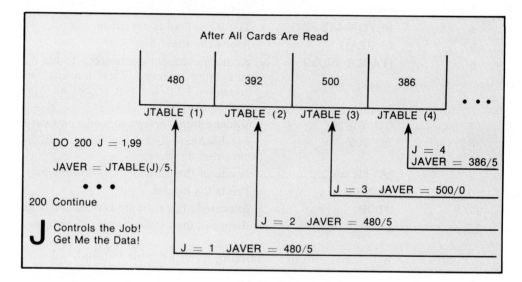

FIGURE 9–18

The value of J is used to tell the computer which address to use in the table to get the data, the accumulated test scores, needed. J also represents on the printed report the student number. For when J = 1:

Student	Points	Average
1	480	96

Tables, or arrays, can have more than one dimension. For example, TABLE (2,3,4) would be visualized as consisting of two tables, each containing three rows and four columns. Figure 9–19 illustrates the three-dimensional table.

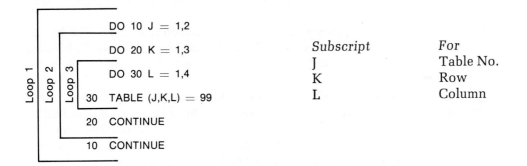

FIGURE 9–19

Let's assume that the value 99 is to be stored in each area of the array. Nested DO Loops could achieve this easily:

	Subscript	For
DO 10 J = 1,2	J	Table No.
DO 20 K = 1,3	K	Row
DO 30 L = 1,4	L	Column
30 TABLE (J,K,L) = 99		
20 CONTINUE		
10 CONTINUE		

Loop 1   Loop 2   Loop 3

Regarding The Loop

How many times is Loop 3 executed? If you answered 24, you are correct as loop times = 2 (tables) * Row * Column. How many different locations are reserved within the table in the CPU? Again 24!

The numbers in the table, (1,1,1) for example, indicate, in this problem, the values of J, K, and L, which make it possible to access that position in the table.

The concept of tables is sometimes difficult to visualize. Once you grasp the concepts involved, you can utilize tables in programming for many different purposes. It makes it possible to effectively process data which is in random sequence. Once the data is in the table, many different kinds of statistical analysis may be performed, using the information. By using an internal sort, data stored in tables can be arranged in any desired sequence. In the test average illustration the table might have been sorted so that the student with the highest score would print first, second high score next, and so on, until all student's scores were printed.

FUNCTIONS AND SUBROUTINES

A function may be either *external* or *internal*. An internal function uses a name to represent one arithmetic computation that is actually coded in the main FORTRAN program. An external function can contain a series of commands that were written and compiled as a separate program, which may be called into the larger program. If a very large program is to be written, several programmers can be assigned to the task, and each will work on one or more functions. All functions are then utilized by the main program.

Both types of functions use a CALL statement. The programmer using an external function must be told what *parameters or values* are required in the CALL statement. External functions can pass to the main program only one solution or value.

Subroutines are also prewritten programs which may be called by the programmers into the main programs. A subroutine is more versatile because it can solve for *more than one* unknown and "pass" the results back to the calling programs.

Subroutines and external functions can be utilized by having the routines stored on disk, tape, or cards. The FORTRAN subroutine concept created an entire new modular approach to programming. Subroutines and functions can be called into the program from the library, making it unnecessary for each programmer to include the source statements in his program. Compiles will be faster because the subroutine commands were previously checked for errors and are assumed, by the computer, to be ready for incorporation into the caller's main program.

REVIEW QUESTIONS

9–54. What happens when the STOP statement is executed?
9–55. What type of branching command is the "GO TO" statement?

9–56. What does the PAUSE statement do?

9–57. Is "END = 99" part of a WRITE statement?

9–58. What are DIMENSION statements used for?

9–59. Tell how many locations are within each table.
   A. DIMENSION (5,5)
   B. DIMENSION (4,2,6),
      1. How many different tables are there?
      2. How many rows does each table contain?
      3. How many columns does each table contain?

9–60. To access any data stored in a table what besides the name of the table must always be used?

9–61. Any integer or integer variable used as a subscript must be what kind of number?

9–62. What statement is very effective in working with tables?

9–63. The table established by DIMENSION (10,20,5) has how many dimensions?

9–64. What "condition" must be true if "Do Loops" are to be nested?

9–65. Subroutines are prewritten programs. Are they compiled and debugged prior to being called into the main program?

REVIEW OF STATEMENT TYPES

1. *Arithmetic*—be sure you know:
   a. The unknown is always to the left. Only one unknown is permitted.
   b. The arithmetic operators are: +, −, *, /, and **. Parentheses are used to make certain, based on the arithmetic hierarchy, that the steps are executed in the desired sequence.
   c. Two arithmetic operators can't appear adjacent to each other:

      WRONG—X = A * − 2.   RIGHT—X = A * (−2.)

   d. The modes are real, integer, and double precision. Real is often referred to as floating-point and integer as fixed-point. *It is better not to mix real and integer modes in an expression.* This is especially true if you are uncertain of how the compiler will treat them.
   e. All variables used in the expression must have been "defined" as part of an input record or have appeared to the left of the equal sign in a previous equation. Some FORTRAN compilers also permit definition of variables by the use of explicit specifications. For example:

      INTEGER * 2 NUM /13/

NUM is now defined as a 2 position field which has an initial value of 13. Real numbers (of both single and double precisions) and arrays can be similarly defined.

    f. Complex equations may be used. If continued to the second card, a dash is used in card column 6.

    g. In regard to the use of the sign, the normal rules of algebra apply.

    h. All fields read that are unsigned are stored as positive numbers.

2. *Input/Output Statements.* Included in this group are the READ/WRITE statements. PRINT, TYPE, and PUNCH may also be used. An I/O statement really has two parts, the FORMAT used to read into or write out of and the actual READ or WRITE statement.

3. *Specification Statements.* Two types have been covered: FORMAT and DIMENSION statements. Often these are referred to as declarative statements, since they are used to reserve space in the computer for I/O records, work areas, arrays, and subprograms. They do not actually generate commands.

    a. *I/O Formats* are used to describe where within the records the fields are and the type of data contained in each field. The FORMAT statement also gives the mode of any numeric data. There are also other FORMAT codes, other than the ones presented, that may be provided by the compiler you will be using. For example, a T FORMAT code may be used in establishing both horizontal print locations and literals:

> 5 FORMAT (T28, 'IF PERMITTED IT IS EASIER')
>   WRITE (6,5) or PRINT 5

IF PERMITTED IT IS EASIER will be printed beginning at position 28. Some of the newer FORMAT codes permit more flexibility and ease in the handling of both numeric and alphabetic data. The reference manuals for the computer being utilized will enable you to determine which FORMATS are available for your use. Output specifications can establish headings, report lines, and total lines which include both variables and nonnumeric literals.

    b. *Dimension Statements* are used to reserve space for and establish the size of arrays.

4. *Subprogram Statements* enable the user to name and define *functions* and *subroutines.*

5. *Control Statements.* IF and DO are the two most powerful. The IF statement has other versions besides the two covered. The "Logical IF" was developed for two way branches. The program logic is easier when the "Logical IF" is used rather than the IF (J) 10,20,30 format.

    Other control statements include PAUSE, STOP, CONTINUE, GO TO, and END.

CONCLUSIONS

Although not all of the statements were covered, you should still realize that FORTRAN has relatively few commands. The mathematical commands are powerful and easy to work with, and if data names are used wisely the program logic is easy to follow.

Both the IF and DO are considered powerful statements. Although numeric information is easy to work with, unless double precision is used the number of allowable significant digits could cause a problem in working with certain kinds of programs. Depending upon the compiler being used, alphabetic input and output is sometimes more difficult to work with in FORTRAN than in many other languages.

In contrasting FORTRAN with COBOL, RPG, or PL/I, less coding for most applications is required in FORTRAN than in the other three languages. In general, working with disk is not as convenient when using FORTRAN as it is when the other languages are used.

There are many versions of FORTRAN, and the faster ones with additional features, added to the basic or standard FORTRAN, require more memory to be available for the compiler, but tend to have better direct access file handling and diagnostics. Some FORTRANS can also be used at a terminal in what is termed a "conversational mode." FORTRAN is still utilized more for scientific and statistical problems than for information retrieval or financial applications.

The computer manufacturers usually have available as part of their software support a FORTRAN compiler for almost any size computer, and therefore it is an almost universal language.

GLOSSARY OF NEW AND OLD TERMS
TO CHECK YOUR KNOWLEDGE

Address. A location within the central processing unit. Each location in the CPU is addressable.

BCDIC. A binary coded decimal code that was used in many second-generation IBM computers.

CONSTANT. A value that does not change during the execution of the program.

COUNTER. An area in core which is established as a numeric field. It is usually incremented each time a given event or task takes place.

DECLARATIVE STATEMENT. One that reserves space and establishes the size for each field. Pointers, or word markers, are established to distinguish the individual fields within the record. Declarative statements do not generate commands associated with the logic of the problem.

DIMENSION STATEMENT. A statement used to establish a table in the CPU. The format is DIMENSION TNAME (100). The table is called TNAME and has 100 addressable locations.

DOCUMENTATION. Detailed information maintained for each procedure to enable program modifications to be made more easily. It also provides management with background information pertaining to each procedure and/or system.

DOUBLE PRECISION. When double precision is indicated for real numbers the significant digits allowed are usually increased from 7 to 16.

EBCDIC Code. An eight-bit code utilized in third-generation IBM computers, which permits the "packing" of numeric data in the CPU.

FIXED-point. A FORTRAN term which indicates that only whole numbers are being used. The term integer may also be used.

FLOATING-point. Real numbers that may contain whole digits and decimal fractions.

FORMAT Statement. Provides information regarding the individual fields within a record. During the compilation of the program, provision is made for space within the CPU for each file specified by a FORMAT statement.

FORTRAN. A powerful compiler language well suited to scientific and mathematical applications. It is the acronym for FORmula TRANslation.

Function. An external function is a precoded routine that may be coded and debugged in a separate compile. The function may be stored on cards, tape, or disk and called into main programs by the use of the CALL statement.

IF. A FORTRAN statement which provides up to a three-way branch. The "logical IF" is limited to a two-way branch.

Logical Unit Number. A number assigned to a physical device. The logical unit for the card reader could be 5, the card punch 6, tape 7, disk 8, etc. If a logical unit number is used, the programmer must determine what numbers were assigned to each I/O device.

Mode. Refers to the use of integer (fixed-point) or real (floating-point) numbers.

Operating System. A combination of hardware and software under the direct control of the supervisor, or control program, that coordinates all input/output activities.

Relational Operators. Symbols used to determine if one number is less than, equal to, or greater than the second number. Relational operators are used in the "logical IF" statement to determine which of two commands will be executed.

Release. Compilers for a given computer are frequently updated by the computer manufacturers. Each new version that has new features added has a release number.

Significant Digits. The digits to the left of the decimal place.

Single Precision. In FORTRAN, when single precision is used, the significant digits allowed in a real number are generally limited to seven.

Subroutine. Prewritten and tested programs that may be called into larger programs. Several answers may be calculated by the subroutine and "passed back" or returned to the main program.

Symbolic Address. A number or name used which will generate an actual computer address when the program is compiled. A data-name, statement number, and format number are all symbolic addresses.

Variable. Values that change as a program is being executed. They normally are either values read as part of the input record or values computed in an arithmetic statement.

WATFOR. A version of FORTRAN developed at the University of Waterloo in Waterloo, Ontario. WATFIV is a revision of WATFOR.

FORTRAN Problem 1. (Directions on page 563)

PROBLEM DEFINITION:

You are to determine if there is enough in the bond account for each employee to purchase a bond for himself. Some employees may have enough in their accounts to purchase more than one bond. The input card contains the employee's number and the amount that is in his bond account. As you can see from the program flowchart, if there is less than $18.75 in the employee's account, the card is not processed.

When there is $18.75 or more in the bond account it must be determined how many bonds can be purchased. The program flowchart illustrates how this can be done. The employee is listed on the report along with the number of bonds that are to be purchased for him. A new card is punched which contains the amount remaining in his account after the bonds are purchased. Since the output card becomes the input for other procedures in which the unprocessed cards are also used, the output format must be identical to the input format.

FORMAT OF BOTH THE INPUT AND OUTPUT CARDS

PRINTED REPORT

PROGRAM FLOWCHART

FORTRAN Problem 1

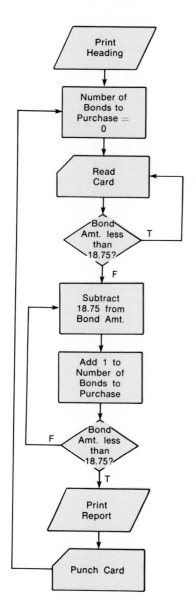

PROGRAM FLOWCHART

FORTRAN Problem 2

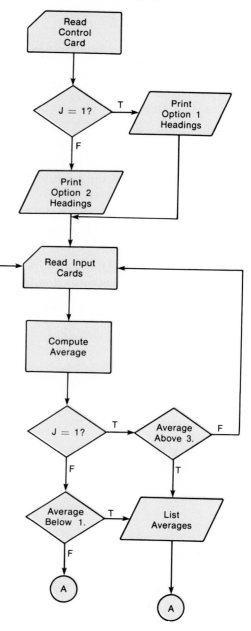

FORTRAN Problem 1. Directions:

1. Code the problem.
2. Use NO to represent the number of bonds that are to be purchased for each employee.

Think about:

1. Why must the output card be in the same format as the input card?
2. In a card-oriented payroll system would there be more data on the input card than what is identified for use in this problem?
3. If 2 is true, would the output punched really be valid?
4. How, during the program being run, would additions be made to the bond account?
5. Should the heading be printed more than one time? Why?

FORTRAN Problem 2

To provide flexibility the program has two options, depending upon the value of J which is entered from a control card. The program flowchart (page 562) illustrates the logic that is to be followed in coding the problem.

Directions:

1. If J is equal to 1, then the first heading illustrated on the report is printed. The report will list only those people with an average above 3.00.
2. If J is equal to 2, the second heading will be printed, and a listing is made of those students who have a grade-point average of less than 1.00.
3. The second heading is printed for either option.
4. Code the problem following the logic presented on the flowchart.
5. Both options would need to be tested to test the problem completely. This would require that J is entered for the first computer run as 1 and for the second run as 2.

INPUT CARDS

J
9 9 9 9 9 9 9 9 9 9 9 9 9 9 9 9 9 9 9 9 9 9 9 9 9 9 9 9 9 9 9 9 9 9 9 9 9 9 9 9 9 9 9 9 9 9 9 9 9 9 9 9 9 9 9 9 9 9 9 9 9 9 9 9 9 9 9 9 9 9 9 9 9 9 9 9 9 9 9 9

Num	Crs	Pts	
9 9 9 9 9	9 9 9 9	9 9 9 9	9 9 9 9 9 9 9 9 9 9 9 9 9 9 9 9 9 9 9 9 9 9 9 9 9 9 9 9 9 9 9 9 9 9 9 9 9 9 9 9 9 9 9 9 9 9 9 9 9 9 9 9 9 9 9 9 9 9 9 9 9 9 9 9 9 9 9 9

Why are floating-point, or real numbers, used for CRS and PTS, when each field contains only whole numbers? Each field is to be coded as an F4.0 field. The student's average, which is calculated, is to be carried three places beyond the decimal point. On the output format the average field will be defined as F5.3.

```
OPTION 1:
        STUDENTS WITH AN AVERAGE ABOVE 3.00

OPTION 2:

        STUDENTS WITH AN AVERAGE OF LESS THAN 1.00

    STUDENT NUMBER                              AVERAGE
        XXXXX                                   X.XXX

        XXXXX                                   X.XXX

        XXXXX                                   X.XXX
```

FORTRAN Problem 3

You are to read the tax rate cards into a table. To do this use a DO loop. The cards are in sequence so that the rate from the first card is stored in TABLE (1), the second TABLE (2), etc. Use K to index your DO statement. As card one is read K will equal 1; for card two, K equals 2, etc. What will you use for the subscript for TABLE in your "DO loop?"

The program flowchart (page 566) illustrates the logic *created by* the DO statement. You need not test for the value of K because the DO statement automatically increments K and tests to see when to exit from the loop.

INPUT CARDS

Rate
9 9 9 9 9 9 9 9 9 9 9 9 9 9 9 9 9 9 9 9 9 9 9 9 9 9 9 9 9 9 9 9 9 9 9 9 9 9 9 9 9 9 9 9 9 9 9 9 9 9 9 9 9 9 9 9 9 9 9 9 9 9 9 9 9 9 9 9 9 9 9 9 9 9 9 9 9 9 9 9
1 2 3 4 5 6 7 8 9 10 11 12 13 14 15 16 17 18 19 20 21 22 23 24 25 26 27 28 29 30 31 32 33 34 35 36 37 38 39 40 41 42 43 44 45 46 47 48 49 50 51 52 53 54 55 56 57 58 59 60 61 62 63 64 65 66 67 68 69 70 71 72 73 74 75 76 77 78 79 80

Num	Salary	J	
9 9 9 9	9 9 9 9 9 9 9 9	9 9 9	9 9 9 9 9 9 9 9 9 9 9 9 9 9 9 9 9 9 9 9 9 9 9 9 9 9 9 9 9 9 9 9 9 9 9 9 9 9 9 9 9 9 9 9 9 9 9 9 9 9 9 9 9 9 9 9 9 9 9 9 9 9 9 9 9 9 9 9
1 2 3 4	5 6 7 8 9 10 11 12	13 14	15 16 17 18 19 20 21 22 23 24 25 26 27 28 29 30 31 32 33 34 35 36 37 38 39 40 41 42 43 44 45 46 47 48 49 50 51 52 53 54 55 56 57 58 59 60 61 62 63 64 65 66 67 68 69 70 71 72 73 74 75 76 77 78 79 80

Field J on the input card identifies which of the tax rates stored in the table are to be used for the employee whose card is being processed. If J on the card is equal to 4, then TABLE (4) is referenced and the appropriate rate is used in the calculation. The salary is the employee's annual salary. The report is a weekly report. Input cards are used only for the salaried workers who worked during the week of the report.

PRINTED REPORT

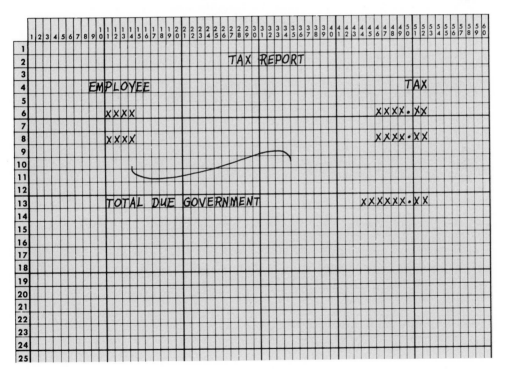

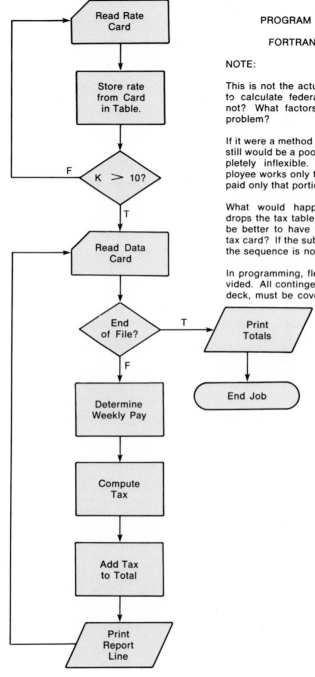

NOTE:

This is not the actual method employed to calculate federal income tax! Why not? What factors are lacking in the problem?

If it were a method that could be used, it still would be a poor one since it is completely inflexible. Suppose your employee works only two days and is to be paid only that portion of his salary?

What would happen if the operator drops the tax table cards? Would it not be better to have the subscript on the tax card? If the subscript is on the card, the sequence is no longer important.

In programming, flexibility must be provided. All contingencies, like a dropped deck, must be covered!

FORTRAN Problem 4

You have taken out a loan on a new house and would like to know the total amount of interest that will be paid over the life of the loan. A report like the one given below is to be printed out.

PAYMENT	OLD BALANCE	PAID	INTEREST	TO PRINCIPAL	NEW BALANCE
1	20000.00	200.00	116.67	83.33	19916.67
2	19916.67	200.00	116.18	83.82	19832.85
.	.	.	.	.	.
.	.	.	.	.	.
.	.	.	.	.	.

TOTAL INTEREST PAID   XXXXX.XX

Use the following facts in coding the problem:
1. The loan is for $20,000.00.
2. Each monthly payment is $200.00.
3. The interest rate is .07 per year. The banker's method is used for computing interest. Each month is based on 30 days or 1/12 of a year.
4. The field called "TOPRIN" is the amount of the payment minus the calculated interest: $200.00 — 116.67 = 83.33.
5. At the end of the loan, print out the literal 'TOTAL INTEREST PAID' and the total amount of interest that was paid.
6. Will your final payment be for $200.00? Probably not. This must be considered when you write the program.

DIRECTIONS:

1. Do a print layout form.
2. Design an input card that contains the amount of the loan, the interest rate and the monthly payment amount.
3. Do the program flowchart.
4. Code the problem.
5. Answer the questions pertaining to the problem.

   A. Why is it better to use an input card rather than establishing the value directly in the program? You could code the problem something like:
   PRINT 10 (Headings)
   BAL = 20000.00
   PINT = .07
   PAY = 200.00

   B. How would you test the program? Would you use the actual value of the loan, $20,000.00, in your test?

FORTRAN Problem 5

Sales cards which have been used in prior jobs contain the following fields that will be used in this application.

Card Columns	Field	
8–10	MAN	Salesman's number
21–28	SOLD	Total Amount of Sale

The cards are in random order, and each salesman has numerous sales cards that are to be processed:

PART 1

Read the cards and add the SOLD field to the area of the table that is reserved for the salesman whose card is being processed. Since there are 80 salesmen, whose numbers range from 1 to 80, reserve 100 locations in the CPU. We may hire more men! Make certain the table is initialized to zero before the sales are added.

After all cards are processed, PART II of the program will be executed. What subscript will you use to add the SOLD field to the correct area of the table? If MAN = 4, then SOLD is to be added to TABLE (4)!

PART 2

A. A DO loop is to be used, Again, for flexibility of adding more employees, use 100 as the value used to terminate part II of the program. Use J as the index, or counter, for the loop.
B. For each man:
   (1) Determine his commission according to the following method:

IF	RATE
TABLE (J) < 10000.01	.07
TABLE (J) > 10000.00 but < 20000.01	.08
TABLE (J) > 20000.00	.09

   (2) Print a line on a report. You may omit headings:

Man Number	Sales for Month	Commission
1	XXXXX.XX	XXXXX.XX
2	XXXXX.XX	XXXXX.XX
Value is printed from J	from Table (J)	is COMPUTED

   (3) Add his sales and commission to FTOTAL and FCOM.
C. Include, as the first statement in the DO loop, a check to see if the salesman, represented by the current value of J, actually sold anything. If in the table there are only zeroes, create a branch to the CONTINUE state-

ment. This bypasses the commission calculation and PRINT command. You are still within the loop, J will still increment, and processing will continue.

PART 3

Print a line that states monthly totals and then prints FTOTAL and FCOM.

DIRECTIONS:

1. Do a program flowchart and a print layout form.
2. Code the problem.
3. Indicate how you would test the program.

ANSWERS

WHAT IS FORTRAN (p. 522)

9–1. FORmula TRANslation.
9–2. Yes. FORTRAN can run on computers with a very minimal amount of memory. It could be described as an almost universal language.
9–3. No. There are tests that can be made to determine if the user has a true "standard" FORTRAN IV compiler. The standard gives the minimum attributes that the compiler should have.
9–4. A version of FORTRAN which was developed at the University of Iowa. It has gained wide acceptance because it compiles faster and has better diagnostics than standard FORTRAN IV.

THOUGHT STARTERS (p. 531)

9–5. The output card.
9–6. Yes, I3 would be the first 3 card columns; 6A4, the next 24 card columns; I3, the next 3 card columns; I5, the next 5 card columns. Unless an "X" is used to specify skipped columns, all fields must be adjacent.
9–7. I3—numeric; 6A4—alphanumeric: I3—numeric; I5—numeric
9–8. A. Alphanumeric
B. You wish to skip areas in either input or output records.
C. Numeric
D. The literal following the H (for Hollerith) contains 16 characters.

9–9. FORMAT
PRINT

9–10. Three different card designs were used: the date card, weekly input card, and output card.

9–11. The games bowled and pins for the week were keypunched.

9–12. Yes, because the request was for a design which had little keypunching and a printed output that listed, along with each bowler's average, the high bowler for the week.

9–13. JPINS = JPINS + NPINS

9–14. IF (JSAVE — WPINS) 100, 101, 101

9–15. Whenever NPINS is greater than JSAVE.

9–16. A. 10
B. 20
C. 30

9–17. END

9–18. Unconditional

9–19. A command to read a new card.

9–20. The program never branches back to that point in the program.

9–21. Yes. Each location that is branched to requires the use of statement numbers.

9–22. When the end-of-file for the card input file is detected.

LEARNED TO DATE (p. 536)

9–23. No, they are not part of the allowable special symbols.

9–24. No. Generally, by using a special card either the EBCDIC or BCDIC code may be used.

9–25. A. +
B. *
C. /
D. −

9–26. A. 4
B. 3
C. 1
D. 2

9–27. To the left of the = sign

9–28. No. Only one unknown to the left of the = sign is allowed.

9–29. A. The priority in which the steps required in the program will be performed.
B. The rules pertaining to the use of parentheses.
C. The unknown is always to the left of the equal sign.

D. Only one unknown on the left of the equal sign.

E. Any variable on the right of the equal sign must either have been an input field or have been used on the left of an equal sign in a previous equation.

REVIEW QUESTIONS (p. 539)

9–30. A. Fixed-point
      B. Floating-point
9–31. A. No
      B. Yes
      C. Yes
      D. No
9–32. A. No
      B. Yes
      C. No
      D. Yes
9–33. A. No
      B. Yes
      C. No
      D. No
      E. Yes
      F. No
      G. No
9–34. A. No
      B. Yes
      C. No
      D. Yes
      E. Yes
      F. No
9–35. A. 12674000000000
      B. Double precision
9–36. A. 1,000,000
      B. Scientists and mathematicians

CAN YOU READ AND WRITE ACCORDING TO FORMAT (p. 544)

9–37. A. Yes
      B. 3

C. Fixed-point or integer

D. Floating-point

E. Yes

F. Yes

G. Yes

9–38. "A" denotes a floating-point field while I4 describes a fixed-point field.

9–39. A. bbb4

(It should be noted that in FORTRAN lead zeroes are usually suppressed.)

B. Nothing

C. FORTRAN IS EASY

D. Hollerith

E. Nothing

9–40. A. A new sheet of paper will be advanced to print line 1 in the printer.

B. No variables are to be printed.

C. FORTRAN SHOULD BE FUN BUT IT DOES TAKE WORK.

D. Yes

9–41. A logical unit number is used in the READ statement. The logical units are usually assigned a number during the system generation.

9–42. Yes, if the "free format" feature is available, either as a function or subroutine, during the compilation of the program.

9–43. END = 200 should have been coded as part of the READ statement.

9–44. X Mode is wrong for I4—should be I through N.

GROSSPAYAMT Only six characters are permitted in a variable name.

JRATE Mode wrong

9–45. 99 FORMAT (5A4)

READ 99, N1, N2, N3, N4, N5

DO YOU KNOW "DO" AND "IF"? (p. 550)

9–46. A. 30

B. 10

C. 10

D. 30

E. 20

9–47. A. 99

B. 101

9–48. Yes

9–49. The IF (J) ... statement will provide for a three-way branch while the logical IF is limited to a two-way branch.

9–50. A. 4 cards punched (1,4,7,10)
B. 10 cards punched
C. 0 cards punched

9–51. Yes

9–52. The IF statement.

9–53. 95 times

REVIEW QUESTIONS (p. 556)

9–54. Execution of the program stops.

9–55. An unconditional branch command

9–56. Halts the system. This will give the operator time to perform a task such as putting a different form in the printer.

9–57. No

9–58. DIMENSION statements are used to establish tables (or ARRAYS) in the memory of the computer.

9–59. A. 25
B. 48
1. 4
2. 2
3. 6

9–60. Subscripts

9–61. Only *whole, positive* numbers may be used as subscripts.

9–62. The DO statement which can be used to set up a loop.

9–63. Three

9–64. The inner loop must be completely contained in the outer loop. There can be no "overlapping" of the loops.

9–65. Yes. One of the advantages in their use is that they are usually already compiled and debugged.

OPERATING 10
SYSTEMS

Operating systems are defined in many ways. One definition often used is "Software which controls the execution of computer programs and which provides scheduling, debugging, input/output control, accounting, compilation, storage assignment, data management, and related services."

Some of the characteristics of operating systems were available in the second-generation computers, but it was really the third-generation computers which "put it all together." The history of computers and their evolution through various generations becomes more relevant when discussed in terms of operating systems.

To use first-generation computers, which did not have operating systems, the programmer had to really understand exactly how each command was executed. He would write a program, which included *all* of the necessary routines and commands, and then sit in front of the computer console as the data was processed. Since the programmer was the only one who knew how the computer would react while his program was running, his presence was necessary—especially during the testing of a program. If the computer stopped, the programmer would analyze the error, make the necessary corrections to the program or to the data, and then continue the run. This often took a long period of time because there was no "hint" as to what the problem was. In a complex program it often became a case of trial and error to find the cause of the problem.

The computer operator would be of little help, because there was little standardization between programs and good documentation and console directions were rare. As programmers and managers gained experience in data processing, documentation was improved and program libraries were developed. These changes made it possible for an operator to run the programs without the programmer actually being present.

The first-generation computers, by today's standards, were exceedingly slow. It might have taken the computer two hours to execute a job which required ten minutes of the operator's time to set up. As second-generation computers became faster, the same job was run in approximately 15 to 20 minutes. Nevertheless, it still required ten minutes to set up the job. You can easily see from the illustration what had happened. While run time had decreased, the percentage of set-up time to the execution time of the program had increased from 8% to 50%. This was one of the major reasons why operating systems *had to be developed*.

By the end of the second generation most larger computers were under the control of monitors or "control programs" which mainly controlled the input/output activities. It was, however, an introduction into two different computer states, the supervisor or control state and the problem state, which distinguishes the second-generation from the third-generation computer.

During the "control state" certain input/output functions were performed by the *supervisor*, which was one of the names used to refer to the early operating system. The frequently used routines which were executed by the supervisor relieved the programmer of having to write a command for every single machine language command that was needed to successfully process the data. Many of these functions, performed during the control state, were part of what was known as the Input/Output Control System or IOCS. By using the control programs, more standardization was attained and less operator set-up time was required.

During the problem state the programmer's commands are executed. Today, however, if an *interrupt occurs,* the computer is no longer controlled by the programmer's commands but by the operating system. For example, the computer is told, by means of the programmer's program, to read a card. If the operator had failed to turn on the card reader, an *interrupt will occur* which returns the computer to the "control state." The supervisor takes over and determines that the appropriate action would be to notify the operator to turn on the card reader.

The second-generation computer supervisors were uncomplicated when contrasted to today's operating systems. Keep in mind, however, that for a second-generation computer, 64K was a terrific amount of memory. *Since the nucleus of the operating system must reside in the memory of the computer,* could much memory be allocated to the operating system?

Today's third-generation operating system is exceedingly complex. The operating system of today is a set of programs and related hardware devices, under the control of a supervisor or control program, *which helps to insure maximum throughput.* Throughput is the amount of data which is processed, starting as input and ending as some form of output. The programs, which are part of the operating system, are usually stored in a disk or tape library, and the supervisor is responsible for calling into memory the needed routines.

When a new computer is acquired, or changes are made to the existing configuration, a new operating system may be *generated.* This is referred to as a *SYSGEN.* The user selects from the many features available the ones that are to be included in his unique operating system. Why doesn't he take all of the features which are available? The more complex the operating system becomes, the more memory must be allocated to the supervisor.

What are some of the more common features? How can the third-generation operating systems make the computer more productive? How do they help the operator communicate more easily with the computer and consequently decrease the amount of "down time"? These and other questions will be answered in the provided material that pertains to operating systems.

TYPICAL OPERATING SYSTEMS

A small-scale computer may have a very minimal operating system which deals primarily with input/output activities. A true "mini" computer may not have an operating system since it may be dedicated to a particular task. In most medium- and large-scale computers, however, the operating system controls *the total computer environment.* What are the components of an operating system for a medium-size system, such as the UNIVAC 9480, IBM 360, or some of the IBM 370s? In a disk operating system (DOS) the *control* and *processing programs* which constitute the system are stored on disk.

Control Programs

The control programs consist of the *supervisor, job control language* (JCL), *and an initial program load routine* (IPL). In most disk operating systems, *everything is under the direct control of the supervisor.* The supervisor which *must* be in the memory of the computer provides the following functions:

1. Allocates CPU time. The allocation of the arithmetic and logical unit's time becomes important when *multiprogramming* concepts are introduced.
2. *Handles all system interrupts and, when needed, returns the appropriate message to the operator.* In most cases corrective action is automatically taken without the operator being aware that an interrupt occurred. An interrupt is a break in the normal execution of a program or routine which is accomplished in such a way that the usual sequence can be resumed from that point at a later time.
3. Loads or invokes the input/output error routines.
4. Loads the transient area, as needed, to provide such functions as opening and closing of files. The transient area is reserved for routines from the library.

Other functions provided by the supervisor, which are somewhat more technical, will not be covered.

Interrupts

The supervisor takes care of I/O, program, supervisor call, and machine interrupts.

1. *I/O Interrupts.* A signal is sent to the control unit of the computer notifying it that the data requested has been read or that the output has been written. The CPU then takes appropriate action.
2. *Program Interrupt.* An unusual condition occurs when the computer is in the problem state (under the control of the user's program). A program interrupt, for example, will take place when the computer is told to divide by zero. Program interrupts are also invoked if the command being executed has an invalid address or instruction. The program interrupts in some systems fall into 15 different classifications. If there is not a corrective action which can be taken for a particular type of program interrupt, the job is automatically cancelled. From the message printed on the console, the operator can determine which type of program interrupt occurred.
3. *Supervisor Call Interrupt.* An instruction that the program used, while in the problem state, caused the supervisor call interrupt to take place. One example would be notification that the program is finished and that the supervisor can bring in a new program for execution. This causes a switch from problem state to supervisory or control state. When the new program is stored in the memory of the computer and begins to execute, the computer is once again back in the problem state.
4. *External Interrupt.* It is seldom that the operator is required to do so, but if he uses the "interrupt key," which is on the console, an external interrupt takes place.

5. *Machine Interrupt.* When the actual computer hardware malfunctions, a machine interrupt is invoked. In some situations, corrective action is taken by using a routine, retrieved by the supervisor from the library which covers the particular problem. If the problem is such that it can not be recovered from, the job will be cancelled by the supervisor and an appropriate message will appear on the console. In certain cases, when the system doesn't know what to do, the computer still just stops—giving no indication as to the cause of the problem.

What is the *real* significance of the interrupts and the supervisor? Before operating systems were developed, the events that would today cause a problem or machine interrupt took place, *but no corrective action or error message* was available as standard system action. The program simply stopped functioning and it was entirely up to the programmer to diagnose the problem. Today the supervisor will use a routine, available in one of the libraries, to attempt to solve the problem. If it is necessary for the job to be cancelled, the error message which is printed helps the programmer, or operator, to determine what the problem is.

MESSAGES TO THE OPERATOR

The messages printed on the console are important for a number of reasons. Since many of the messages are generated by the supervisor, as the direct result of an interrupt, less time is required to solve the problem because the cause is fairly well stated. Some messages may be printed out when the computer is operating in the problem state, since they were coded in the program by the programmer. The operator can also tell, by referring to the printed message, what job is currently being executed. The console printout serves as a "log" of when each job was run and what interrupts, if any, occurred during its execution. Figure 10–1 illustrates an analyst determining the meaning of a message which was printed on the console during the testing of a new program.

Interrupt Messages

The messages illustrated are ones that would be generated by an IBM 360 computer. The origin of the message is important to the operator because it indicates *when the interrupt occurred.* The message printed on the console might read:

4n84D   NEED FILE PROTECT RING

FIGURE 10–1. AN ANALYST STUDIES A MESSAGE PRINTED ON THE CONSOLE DUE TO A PROGRAM INTERRUPT.

The first digit, or letter, of the message indicates the origin of the message. Some of the first position indicators are:

0   Supervisor or IPL
1   Job Control
2   Linkage Editor
3   Librarian
4   Logical IOCS

The "4," therefore, indicates to the operator that the condition which caused the message to be printed occurred during the period of time that the logical input/output control system was executing some of its routines. It could have been checking to make certain that the right disk pack was mounted, that the right area of the disk for a given file was being utilized, or that the key used to retrieve a record from an indexed-sequential file was valid. There are over 50 different things that are checked by the operating system that fall into the logical IOCS category.

The fifth, or last, position of the message number tells the operator what type of message it is. The following codes are used.

CODE	MEANING
D	A decision must be made, regarding the action to be taken, by the operator.
A	Action must be taken by the operator.
I	No action is required. The message is to provide the operator with necessary information.

In the back of the manual, IBM System/360 Disk Operating System Operating Guide, the message numbers are listed in numerical order. The operator finds the message number and then determines the page number that it is explained on. The message used as an illustration seems clear enough, but what decision must the operator make and how must he respond in order to continue the job? When the operator refers to the correct page, he finds the following information regarding 4n84D.

4n48D   NEED FILE PROTECT RING

Cause: An output file requires a file protect ring.
Action: Type CANCEL, or CANCELV, to cancel the job, *or*
place a file protect ring in the reel and type IGNORE to continue processing.
Default: Job canceled.

Any action other than placing the file protect ring in the reel and typing IGNORE on the console will automatically cancel the job. In regard to the file protect ring, you will remember from the material on magnetic tape that the rule is "No Ring, No Write." The cause of the problem which created the message was that fact that the operator had mounted, for an output file, a tape which did not have a file protect ring.

Another message to the operator might read "1C33A Program Not Found." Applying the information already learned, what can you determine about the message? The "1" indicates the message was generated due to a problem with a job control language statement. The final "A" tells the operator that action must be taken. The operator finds the following information in the manual.

1C33A   PROGRAM NOT FOUND

Cause: The phase name specified on the EXEC statement is not in the core image library.

Action: Convert phase name in EXEC statement, or reply CANCEL to terminate the job.

Default: Job canceled.

What does the message really mean? The EXEC card, when properly used, will bring a cataloged program from the library into the memory of the computer. Assume that the card had been punched: EXEC PAYRG2. When the card is read, the supervisor searches the directory of the core image library to find a program called PAYRG2. Unfortunately there is not a program by that name cataloged. Therefore, the message illustrated is returned to the operator. The operator, in checking his run book, may find that the card was incorrectly keypunched and should have read EXEC PAYRG3. He then, according to the manual, can either correct the card and continue, or cancel the job.

REVIEW QUESTIONS

10-1. With what generation of computers were operating systems first used?

10-2. What resides in the memory of the computer that "controls" the operating system?

10-3. There are two different computer states. When a program interrupt occurs, the computer is returned to what state?

10-4. In the problem state is the computer functioning under the control of a program, stored in its memory, such as one written by a programmer to compute the payroll?

10-5. Since the printed messages are relatively clear, less time is required to recover from an interrupt than when operating systems were not available. What is the end result of the savings in time?

10-6. The number of a message which ends in "D" requires a decision. How does the operator know what choices he has?

10-7. Are all interrupts the result of an abnormal occurrence?

10-8. What does the first digit of the interrupt message tell the operator?

10-9. If two companies have the same exact model of computer, does it mean that their operating systems are identical?

THE LIBRARIES

If all of the routines and programs, which make up the operating system, had to be stored in the main memory of the computer at one time, millions of bytes of memory would have to be available. Only the supervisor, which handles interrupts, schedules the I/O, communicates with the operator, loads the programs, provides error recovery routines, and provides a variety of other services during the execution of the programmer's program, resides in the memory of the computer.

Under the DOS supervisor's direction are three libraries which store both the *control programs and routines as well as the processing programs.* When the system is generated, the user can determine how much space is to be allocated to each library. How much space is allocated is determined by the amount of available online disk storage. If an installation has a limited amount of online disk storage, the libraries will be smaller and more of the user's programs will be maintained as object decks rather than being stored online in the library.

Another solution to the lack of online disk storage space for the libraries is to maintain some of the programs in what is called a "private library." The private library need not be online unless a particular program that is stored on the disk pack is required. If the user wishes to provide more security for certain programs, such as those dealing with personnel files, they may be stored in a private library, which is stored offline, except when the program is to be executed.

The core image, relocatable, and source libraries must all be on one pack, which is generally called the System Resident Pack, or SYSRES, and online whenever the computer is running.

The three libraries are managed by a *librarian function* which takes care of cataloging new programs, deleting obsolete programs, reallocating the size of the libraries, and performing other maintenance functions.

Core Image Library

As the name implies, the programs stored in the core image library appear exactly as they will in the memory of the computer—all routines have been incorporated into the programs and they are ready to be executed. The core image library contains the following types of programs:

1. *Initial Program Load* (IPL). In a sense, when the computer is first turned on its memory is one big blank and is capable of doing nothing. When the operator depresses the LOAD key on the console a series of events are

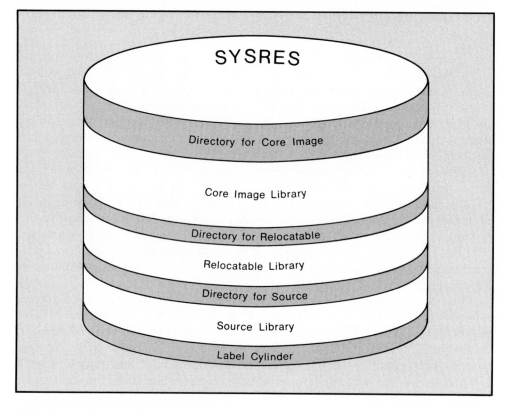

FIGURE 10–2. SYSTEM RESIDENT PACK

initiated. The IPL routine is first loaded from the library into the memory of the computer and the operator is then asked to enter the date and time. After the date and time are entered, a series of commands are executed by the computer which result in the supervisor being loaded into the memory of the computer. At this point the computer can begin to function and perform the many jobs that it will be asked to do!

2. *The supervisor is also located in the core image library.* As stated earlier, the supervisor is responsible for allocating the CPU time, handling all system interrupts, loading or invoking the input/output error routines, and loading the transient area to provide for such functions as opening and closing of files.

3. *Job Control Language Programs.* The commands or programs initiated by the job control language (JCL) statements are called into the memory of the computer between job steps. For example, compiling and executing a program actually involves three different job steps—each of which is initiated by using

the required JCL commands. The first job step is to compile the program, and the JCL cards, or commands, are used to tell the computer what options are desired and to load the compiler from the core image library into the memory of the computer. After the source statements are read, which includes checking them for errors and translating the commands into machine language, a second job step occurs during which time the programmer's commands are link edited with the necessary routines from the relocatable library. This step is initiated by the // EXEC LINKEDT card, which causes the linkage editor to be loaded from the library into the memory of the computer.

The third job step, which is the execution of the program, is initiated by the // EXEC card which is responsible for loading the link-edited program, from the core image library where it is stored, into the computer for execution.

The job control statements give job-to-job transition and may be entered either by using the console, card reader, magnetic tape, or disk. For a number of reasons, job control statements are usually initiated by using punched cards. A few of the options that may be executed by using JCL cards will be covered in a separate section.

4. *Linkage Editor.* When the job control statement // EXEC LINKEDT is read, the supervisor calls in the linkage editor program that is stored in the core image library. The linkage editor must edit all programs that are to run in the system. One of the most helpful things that it does is to bring, from the relocatable library, subroutines that can be linked with the user's program. This means that each programmer need not code each and every statement that is required in his program, since frequently used routines can be incorporated into the program by the linkage editor. As operating systems have become more complex, programming in compiler languages has become much easier because more routines are provided in the libraries.

5. *Utility Programs.* In most libraries there are a large number of utility programs, generally supplied by the computer manufacturer, which perform needed services, like displaying records from tape or disk on the printer, sorting the records, merging files, displaying the table of contents of any disk pack, initializing a disk pack which includes giving it a distinctive identification that may be checked to determine if the right pack is mounted, duplicating a source deck, giving each card a sequence number, and so forth. It usually requires only one or two job control language cards to call in a utility program for execution. For example, to display the contents of a disk pack on the printer, the user must use the name that the utility is cataloged under, tell where the information is on the disk pack, how many cylinders or tracks are to be displayed, and how many bytes long the record is. Once this is done, following the correct JCL format, the information stored on disk is printed, record by record, on the printer. This utility can be very helpful when a programmer is debugging a program.

6. *Language Translators.* The compilers, or translators, for languages such as COBOL, FORTRAN, PL/I, RPG, and Assembler are stored in the core image library. During the compilation of a program the COBOL compiler, for example, would be brought into the memory of the computer when the // EXEC COBOL job control language card was read by the card reader. New features are often added to languages when a SYSGEN (the operating system is generated) is done. For example, PL/I (Programming Language One) started with release 1. After a few years there had been several different releases, each with new features added that were unavailable in the previous versions. Unless SYSGEN's are done to incorporate the new features into the operating system, the languages, like any other part of computer technology, can become obsolete.

7. *User's Application Programs.* The programs are written, compiled, tested, and then stored in the core image library. They may be executed by using a // EXEC program-name card. Depending upon the system being used, it generally takes only a few seconds for the supervisor to look up the name of the program and call it into the memory of the computer. When a program is changed, it is recataloged using the same program name. The first version is flagged for deletion and the new version is stored in the library.

There can be many other features of an operating system which may be stored in the core image library. The ones which were listed are the basic, or core, programs needed for the supervisor to do its many functions.

Periodically, it is necessary to regenerate the system to incorporate new language features and additional options, previously not required or desired by the user, into the operating system. For example, the user may now wish to have the languages updated and an optional feature called an EMULATOR added to the system's software.

EMULATORS

An emulator causes the new computer to act as if it were the computer previously used. For example, if a 1401 emulator is available for the UNIVAC 9480, the programs coded in 1401 assembler could be used without being recoded in the 9480 languages. This feature enables programs coded for the 1401 to run, without reprogramming, on the new system. The emulated programs will run faster on the third-generation computer than they did on the 1401, which was a second-generation computer, but not as fast and as efficient as if it had been recoded.

In order to emulate, the supervisor must be enlarged, the emulator programs added to the core image library, and some additional hardware features installed. A SYSGEN is required to add the new features to the operating system. Each time the system is regenerated in a disk operating system it provides a good opportunity to do some "house cleaning" and delete unused programs and routines from the libraries. The software programmer, who does the SYSGEN, along with the operations manager and several other people will determine which features should be incorporated into the system.

REVIEW ON THE CORE IMAGE LIBRARY

10–10. Are all three types of control programs *(the supervisor, job control language, and initial program load routine)*, which are part of the operating systems, included in the core *image library?*

10–11. Must the initial program load routine be used, after the computer has been turned off for any reason, in order that the date and time may be entered and the supervisor reloaded into the memory of the computer?

10–12. Is it true that job control language commands are used during the execution of an application program written by a programmer?

10–13. The linkage editor is responsible for editing the program and linking it with subroutines. Where are the subroutines usually stored?

10–14. What is the function of the librarian programs?

10–15. Does the private library always have to be online?

10–16. Must the SYSRES, or systems resident pack, be online if the computer is to function?

10–17. What does the SYSRES pack contain that the supervisor must have access to in order to do the functions for which it is responsible?

10–18. What general type of program can read any tape record and print it, without formatting it or adding headings, on the printer?

10–19. The user's frequently used application programs are stored in the library so that they may be quickly brought into the memory of the computer and executed. What card is used to bring the program from the library into the memory of the computer?

10–20. Is an emulator a combination of software and hardware which makes one computer look, or act, like another?

10–21. Is the operating system regenerated to update the languages, add new software features to the operating system and delete from the system unused programs and routines?

THE RELOCATABLE LIBRARY

The relocatable library does not have self-contained, ready-to-use programs, such as are found in the core image library. The modules or routines stored in the relocatable library are stored in *object code,* which means that the source statements, written by a programmer, were checked for errors, translated into machine language, and then cataloged into the relocatable library. There are both *object modules,* which can be called into the user's program, and *input/output logic modules,* used for the read and write routines, stored in the library. The I/O logic modules do not become a part of the user's program, but are stored, when needed, in the transient area of the computer and function under the direct control of the supervisor.

Object Modules

Why use subroutines? There are many reasons why subroutines, and functions, are useful. First, the often-used routines are coded and compiled one time, and then may be used by all programmers. Often there are things that a programmer wants to do which can not be done in the language that he is using because the appropriate commands are not available. When this occurs, a routine can be written in the computer's assembler language, stored as a subroutine, and then called by the programmer into his program. For example, in PL/I there is no way to select an input card into pocket two of the card reader. In many applications, where a card is used to retrieve a record from a disk file, it would be nice to be able to put the cards with invalid keys (wrong student numbers) into pocket two while the processed cards go into pocket one. A subroutine was written and cataloged under the name "Pocket," which can cause the unprocessed cards to go into pocket two. Although the routine was written in basic assembler language, it can be called into a PL/I program by using the following statement:

Call POCKET (Control, Cardin);

The programmer who wrote the subroutine supplied all of the programmers in the installation with documentation which gave the name of the subroutine and detailed instructions on how it could be used. Although the parameters (control and cardin) may be names supplied by the user, the documentation gave explicit instructions on their use.

When subroutines are used, rather than using source code to perform the routines, the program will compile faster because fewer statements are checked for errors and then translated into machine language. When the program is link edited, the linkage editor edits the program and retrieves the needed subroutines from the library and incorporates the commands into the user's program.

Input/Output Logic Modules

The read and write routines which are part of the IOCS (Input/Output

Control System) are stored in the relocatable library. Having the read and write routines as part of the operating system has made programming much easier for the application programmer, since he need not be concerned with programming for a variety of I/O channel and device characteristics. Standardized input/output commands can be used, regardless of the characteristics of the device being used, which increases the programmer's efficiency.

For example, the programmer wants to process the student grade file (labeled "Student Grades") which is on a disk pack called STUACT. Ten logical records make up one physical record, which means that a blocking factor of ten was used when the file was created. The programmer in his program writes a very standard open file statement which reads: OPEN INPUT STUFILE.

When the open statement is executed a program is loaded from the relocatable library into the *transient area* of the computer. The transient area is located in the main memory of the computer and is reserved for I/O and error checking routines which are stored on the SYSRES pack. As the routines are needed, such as the open file routine, the supervisor takes care of making certain that they are loaded into the computer and executed.

After the program needed for opening the file is loaded into the transient area, commands are executed which check the file information supplied by the job control cards against the data stored in the volume table of contents (VTOC) for the "Student Grades" file, which is stored on the STUACT disk pack. If the VTOC has one address and the JCL cards have another, an appropriate message will be printed on the console. All of the information pertaining to the file, such as the pack number (STUACT), the label ("Student Grades"), the cylinders and tracks used for the file, the creation date, the expiration date, and the organization method, is found on the JCL cards. The data pertaining to the file from the cards must agree in *every detail* to the corresponding information stored for the file on the pack's VTOC. The information must also be the same as what is stored on the SYSRES pack's label cylinder. If there is any discrepancy in any of the information a message will be printed on the console.

All of the checking is generated due to the open file statement that created a *supervisor call interrupt* which caused the computer to switch from the *problem state to the supervisor state.* The supervisor reacted accordingly and loaded the required program from the *relocatable library* into the transient area of the computer where it was executed. *After the file information was checked, control returned to the application program where the command following the open statement was executed.*

Other input/output logic modules are available to take care of blocking and deblocking tape or disk records, reading and writing of physical records, error checking, label writing, and many other I/O activities. The programmer needs to consider only the logic of reading, processing, and writing the *logical records*. The detailed commands necessary to perform the actual functions which are required are already programmed and available as part of the operating system in the relocatable library.

CONCERNING THE RELOCATABLE LIBRARY

10–22. Does the relocatable library contain complete application programs written by the installation's programmers?

10–23. What should be considered as a potential subroutine?

10–24. The input/output logic modules are not incorporated into the user's program. How are they executed?

10–25. Is the label information for files usually found on the SYSRES pack as well as in the VTOC of the pack which contains the file?

10–26. The two different kinds of routines stored in the relocatable library are:

SOURCE LIBRARY

In the source library are stored sections of programs, entire small programs, structures, file declaration statements, and file descriptions. In COBOL, for example, the statements may be brought into the application program, which is being compiled by using a copy statement. For example, a programmer uses a copy statement, in the manner illustrated, to bring in a card structure, which is stored in the source library.

01 CARDIN COPY 'MASTCARD'.

When the compiler reads the statement, the coding stored in the source library is retrieved and displayed in the user's program as illustrated:

```
          01 CARDIN COPY 'MASTCARD'.
*1210     01 MASTCARD.
*1220         02 NAME                Picture X(30).
*1230         02 ADD1                Picture X(25).
*1240         02 ADD2                Picture X(25).
```

Copying structures and small programs from the source library not only saves coding, but it forces the programmer using the structure to use the same *uniform* names that are used in the library. Many large installations use the copy statements in programs for exactly that reason. The user, unless he renames the fields, must refer to the fields as NAME, ADD1, and ADD2. As more programming standards are established in an installation, the easier it becomes to maintain programs.

Entire source decks can be stored in the source library. The programmer can call out any statement that is desired, update the statement, and then rewrite the statement back into the library. Some installations are doing this for their COBOL source programs. The statements are displayed on a cathode ray tube, updated by the programmer, and then rewritten back in the source library. When all source statements are corrected, the program must be recompiled and cataloged for execution in the core image library. The source library is merely storing the source code.

The source code for MACRO statements is also stored in the source library. For example, when the programmer uses a GET statement in an assembler program, a whole series of commands are brought into his program from the source library. These statements are the ones necessary to actually read the file. The programmer uses only a very simple "Get" statement.

ABOUT THE SOURCE LIBRARY

10–27. What statement is used, in a COBOL program, to bring source statements from the library into the user's program?
10–28. Less coding is required when copy statements are used. What is another advantage of using copy statements?
10–29. Once the supervisor is loaded into the memory of the computer, do the libraries need to be online?

SUMMARY OF LIBRARIES

Libraries can be stored on disk, drum, data cells, or magnetic tape. They are far more efficient when stored on a random access device because the required program or routine can be found and brought into the memory in less time.

Since the supervisor is the only part of the operating system that resides in the memory of the computer, the libraries are essential to the computer's operation and must be online whenever the computer is in use. As more features are added to an operating system, the larger and more important the libraries become. Larger operating systems may have only one library but it includes all items discussed under the three separate titles *plus many more features.*

The system's library must be maintained just as does any other library. Each routine or program in the library must have a unique name in order that it can be cataloged in the appropriate directory.

JOB CONTROL LANGUAGE

The job control language (JCL) is also considered part of the operating system. Remember, one of the prime reasons that operating systems were developed was to improve communication between man and the computer. The job control language statements permit the operator to communicate his wishes to the computer in a language that both parties can understand.

Job control language statements always relate to the system and not to any given language. Therefore, the sequence of the JCL cards is the same regardless of the language being used. The statements under DOS are far less complex than those required under the larger OS system. OS is used to denote a more complex operating system, for a larger than average sized installation, which has a good deal of computer memory. The operating system might actually be referred to by many different names, depending upon the computer being used, such as MVT, SCOPE, VOS, and so on.

People in data processing have mixed emotions about JCL cards, for they are viewed as being good from the standpoint that the larger systems can delay making assignments to devices until the program is run, which gives a program true *device independence.* For example, the source program statements merely identify certain characteristics of a file. If the file is a sequential file the operator can assign it to either tape or disk, depending upon which serve his needs the best at the time the program is executed. This flexibility is not permitted, however, in some of the smaller systems because the devices must be assigned in the *program, not in the job control language.* JCL statements, however, do provide the system with greater flexibility in running jobs.

The JCL statements are also viewed with disfavor because they are fairly complex when used for the larger computer systems. Rigid rules govern how the statements are to be written and even a very minor infraction will cause the computer to reject the card.

Typical Job Control Language Options

Although some typical job control language options are given for DOS, it is not intented that you learn how the card is punched or the sequence in which the cards must be used. It is intended, however, that you begin to understand a few of the different options for which the JCL cards are used. Remember also that each different computer manufacturer has its own particular operating system and JCL statements. The following typical JCL cards and their usage are given as examples of their many uses.

1. To execute a cataloged program which requires the use of punched card input and printed output the following job setup is used.

// JOB PARO14 PR F1	A job card identifies the fact that a new procedure is to be started. It can also provide the computer with data for job accounting—who used the computer and for what purpose.
// EXEC PARO14 (Data goes here)	The program, stored in the core image library under the name PARO14, is located in the library and stored in the computer.
/*	End of file.
/&	End of job. The time that the program took to execute is listed on the console. If another job was not stacked behind the job, a message, "Waiting for Work," might also print on the console.

If disk had been used, additional job control cards, such as those illustrated in the documentation of the Aged Accounts Receivable problem would also be used. Their function is to tell the computer what disk pack is to be used, where the data is stored, when the file was created, when the data will no longer be protected, and what label was used when the file was created.

2. To catalog a program, the following job setup is required.

// JOB PARO14 PR F1	The job cards tell the computer that a new job is starting.
// OPTION CATAL	The supervisor is informed that the program is to be cataloged in the core image library.
PHASE PARO14,*	PARO14 is the name that the program will be cataloged under.
// EXEC COBOL Source Deck.	The COBOL compiler is brought into the memory of the computer to check the source code for error and to translate it into machine language, or object, code.
/*	End of source deck.

`// EXEC LNKEDT`
`/*`
`/&`
	The linkage editor is brought into the memory of the computer to edit the object code and to incorporate needed routines from the library into the application program.

3. To catalog the structure, previously used as an illustration of how to use the "copy" statement and retrieve structures from the source library, the following JCL cards would be used:

`// JOB MML245 BE SJ`	The job card identifies the new job and charges it to student MML who is enrolled in Data Processing 245. The BE tells the accounting system that it is an evening college class, and the SJ stands for "Student Job."
`// EXEC MAINT`	Cataloging into the source library is considered a maintenance function of the "librarian."
`CATALS C. MASTCARD`	Catalog into the source library under the name "Mastcard."
`BKEND C. MASTCARD`	The source statements must go between book end—BKEND.

Source statements punched in regular 80 card column cards.

`BKEND C. MASTCARD`
`/*`
`/&`

4. Other options specified by using JCL cards.

`// PAUSE   HAVE A COKE`	The message, "Have a coke," will print on the console. The computer will go into a "wait" state until the operator responds to the message.
`// PAUSE   PUT 2 PART STOCK PAPER IN THE PRINTER`	This is a more appropriate use of the pause statement.
`// ASSGN SYSLST, IGN`	The statement makes the printer, which is referred to as SYSLST, not function or print until the end of the job, or until it is reassigned.

// OPTION NOLIST	The use of this option card will cause the normal listing of the source program not to occur for this particular job.
// EXEC DITTO	Brings in a utility program called "ditto" into the computer. The operator must specify, either by using a card or the console, which ditto function is wanted.
// OPTION DECK	Rather than testing the program in what is called load-and-go, an object deck will be created. The object deck can then be tested to make certain that the program is working correctly.

There are many more job control language options which are available to the operator. How some of the options are used depends upon which ones were declared as "standard" when the system was generated. Remember at the time that the SYSGEN is done, the user can select which options are to be included in the operating system. One small part of the selection process is to determine which options will be "standard." The following JCL options might have been selected as standard.

ERRS	During the compilation of a program the source statements are checked for errors.
LIST	The source statements are to list out on the printer.
LOG	The JCL cards will list out on the printer.
XREF	Each field and file will be listed alphabetically. After the name each statement number that the name is used in will be listed.
SYM	A symbol table showing pertinent data about each field and record is printed as the program is compiled.

If the operator does *not want* a symbol table, the option card would read // OPTION NOSYM. Had the option not been made a standard option, the operator would specify // OPTION SYM when he wanted the symbol table to be printed. Only an absolute extreme optimist would specify NOERRS when his or her program was to be compiled!

Job control language cards do provide a way of communicating the wishes of the operator to the computer. Additional JCL cards are used for assigning the files to disk or tape drives, doing utility sort programs, cataloging subroutines, and doing compiles.

Usually the cards for the frequently run jobs, which use either tape or disk, are set up and filed. Each time the job is run the same decks can be used.

Usually the cards have a sequence number in the last eight card columns, which assists the operator in keeping the cards in sequence. From the illustrations used to catalog programs you might feel that this is unnecessary since so few cards were used; however, when sort/merges are done, 30 to 40 JCL cards may be needed to properly identify all of the files which are being used.

JCL REVIEW

10–30. Be able to discuss the statement: "all computer job control languages are alike."
10–31. Do you use the same JCL setup to catalog into all of the libraries?
10–32. What do the source statements go between when a program is cataloged into the source library?
10–33. What useful purpose does the pause statement serve?
10–34. What was the intent, or purpose, in developing job control languages?
10–35. Discuss the statement "Printing the sales invoices is a daily procedure. Each day new job control language cards are punched to run the procedure."

MORE COMPLEX OPERATING SYSTEM CONCEPTS

Multiprogramming

In introducing the computer and basic programming concepts, a point was made that most computers are I/O bound, since the computational ability of the computer is far faster than its ability to read or write. Although I/O devices have become much faster, the computer can still do the required mathematical and logical operations faster than data can enter, or leave, the computer.

By using selector and multiplexor channels, and the control units, which are under the jurisdiction of the supervisor, it is possible to use buffers and actually read more data into the memory of the computer, in a shorter period of time, since there is no waiting for records to be processed. When more than one output device is used, the channel concept also helps to increase the computer's ability to output data more efficiently.

Second-generation computers had very limited memories, while the third-generation computer's memories got larger and larger. It is not uncommon for a large installation to order another megabyte of core—remember, for a second-generation computer 64K was really a large amount.

Man's ability to utilize the computer more effectively also increased. This is demonstrated by the development of the sophisticated software, namely operating systems, which make it possible to do multiprogramming and time-sharing. Figure 10–3 illustrates the multiprogramming concept.

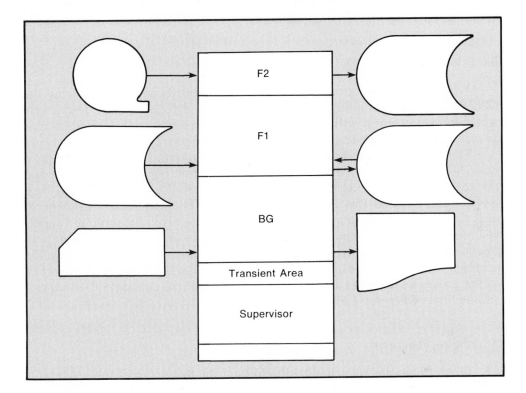

FIGURE 10–3

Partitions in Multiprogramming

Figure 10–3 illustrates a typical DOS multiprogramming application. The memory of the computer is divided into *fixed partitions.* Each partition is executing a separate program which shares the use of the CPU. The computer gives the appearance of executing all programs simultaneously, but *only one program at a time is using the CPU's computational or logical ability.* Since the read/write activities are so much slower, multiprogramming utilizes the CPU to a much greater extent than when only a single program is being executed.

Although the partition size is fixed, the amount of memory in each partition can be reallocated between jobs by the operator to accommodate larger programs, by using a special job control language card or by entering the commands through the console.

The supervisor is at the low-core address immediately following the unlabeled area that is reserved for rather "special" uses, which we need not be concerned with. The next area is the transient area which stores the error handling, opening, and closing routines.

Job Priority

While BG, or background, has the lowest priority in terms of using the CPU's computational ability, it is usually assigned the slowest I/O devices, which indicates that it will not want to do mathematical or logical operations as often as those programs that are assigned the faster I/O devices.

The program stored in the next area, foreground 1, has the *highest priority*. Foreground 1 is doing a disk update by reading in a current file and the corresponding master file, performing a series of calculations, and then rewriting the master file. Foreground 2, F_2, has the next highest priority. F_1 uses the CPU to do the required calculations. When it is finished, the supervisor finds out if F_2 has any computing that needs to be done. If so, foreground 2 gets a turn. After F_2 finishes, if F_1 doesn't want the use of the CPU again, the program in BG will have an opportunity to do some calculations. Unless one of the programs involves a great deal of mathematical calculation, there will still be times when the CPU is idle.

Scheduling Programs

When programs are scheduled to be run, the balancing of the program is important if maximum use of the CPU is to be achieved. It would be poor scheduling to have all three programs primarily involved in reading and writing files, without requiring many calculations, then loading in three new programs that all require a great number of computations. An individual, called a "scheduler," is responsible for determining what jobs will be run together. Priorities are determined by management, but the balancing of the jobs is done by the scheduler.

Limitations of the System

The illustration of a typical DOS multiprogramming application assumes that all jobs are still run in a "batch" mode and initiated through the card reader by using the correct JCL cards. There are limitations to a multiprogramming system of this type because, before a job can be link edited and cataloged, the partitions in which it will run must be determined. This could be a problem when you wish to run two jobs RIGHT NOW and they both need F_2! In the illustration, background has the printer and card reader assigned to it, so all jobs requiring those I/O devices must be run in background, which has the lowest priority unless a reassignment is made through the console, which of course takes time.

The data management capabilities are also somewhat limited, since there is no real device independency. If an I/O device is to be changed, the program must be recataloged, since the file was assigned to a physical unit in the program. Since both the logical record length and the blocking factor are given in the program, they must be recataloged if the record size is changed. If the size of the master payroll file is changed, 30 to 40 programs which use the file will have to be recataloged. Since 90 to 95 percent of all jobs that are run in a typical installation use cataloged programs, there are a great many programs in the library that need *normal maintenance.* When a large number of other programs need recataloging, scheduling the necessary computer time may present a problem.

If the system is regenerated and the size of the supervisor is changed, all cataloged programs must again be recompiled, since under DOS the location of the programmer's instructions are established when the program is cataloged.

The programmer is forced to be concerned with the amount of core needed because the partition assignment must be made before the program is cataloged. The partitions generally vary in size as well as in priority.

Increased Throughput

In multiprogramming, each program may take a little longer to run, but the total amount of system throughput will be increased tremendously over a system that has only one partition. The size of the supervisor, and the number of routines in the libraries, must be increased when the ability to do multiprogramming is added to the computer's software, since more "managing" of the system is required. Additional protection is needed for the data stored in the memory of the computer to make certain that it is not destroyed, or utilized, by a program other than the one that read, or created, the information.

Multiprogramming under Larger Systems

The larger operating systems have the ability to execute at one time more than three programs. The limit is now in excess of 60, and still increasing as new systems are announced. A master scheduler is often a part of the larger operating systems and is used to determine which jobs should be run. All jobs are loaded into a *job queue,* which is a storage area on disk, and given both a job class and priority.

The master scheduler does communicate with the operator, through either the console typewriter or a cathode ray tube, to tell him the sequence of the jobs which will be run so that he can ready the necessary I/O devices— mount tapes, disk packs, put special forms in the printer, and so forth. It may take two or three operators, per computer, to respond to the console messages and take care of the I/O requirements.

In some systems, when a program wants a particular file, the operator is notified. If his response is not quick enough, the master scheduler brings in the next job in queue, according to priority, rather than waiting for the file. The first job will be rescheduled and executed if, at that time, the I/O devices are ready. A large system cannot afford to wait!

The memory of the computer is dynamic, which means that there are not fixed partitions. As the master scheduler loads a program into memory, the storage locations are assigned. Therefore, as jobs are cataloged, no locations are specified, which make it unnecessary to recatalog programs if new features, which increase the size of the supervisor, are added to the software.

Changes in the record size and blocking factor of files can more easily be made, since the required information is part of the job control language rather than the programming language.

As soon as a computer can operate under multiprogramming, an entirely new world opens up! Again, with additional software, the computer can do teleprocessing and other real-time applications as well as supplying management with more timely, reliable data from data bases, which are also managed by the operating system.

REVIEW QUESTIONS ON MULTIPROGRAMMING

10–36. In DOS there are three partitions. Based upon their priority, name and rank the partitions from the highest to the lowest.
10–37. In multiprogramming can all three programs do their computations at the same time?
10–38. Does a DOS system offer "device" independence?
10–39. In a larger operating system how does the master scheduler execute the jobs (or programs)?
10–40. Each individual job may take a little longer to execute under multiprogramming. If this is true, what is the advantage in having the ability to do multiprogramming?
10–41. In multiprogramming are there ever more than three partitions?

SPOOLING

SPOOLing, which is the acronym for Simultaneous Peripheral Operations On Line, uses the principle for which buffers and channels were introduced. Buffers and channels were originally introduced in order that the CPU could become more productive, since it would have a continuous stream of input for processing and output for writing. In addition, buffers made it possible to overlap operations, since reading, processing, and writing could occur simultaneously.

Buffer one is filled with a block of records, called the physical record, and while this data is being processed, buffer two is being filled. The IOCS keeps track of the *individual logical records* which are processed. When the entire block is processed, which is done without interruption, the data in buffer two is utilized by the CPU while the first buffer is being refilled.

The theory of SPOOLing is to provide for a *continuous stream of input and output,* which will make the I/O devices far more productive. It has been determined that when the printer is utilized under SPOOLing it can produce up to 40% more printing. There are many different software packages, such as POWER and HASP, which support SPOOLing and utilize the basic principle illustrated by figure 10–4.

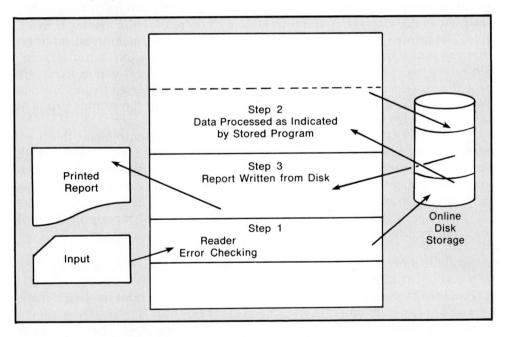

FIGURE 10–4. BASIC CONCEPTS OF SPOOLING

Figure 10–4 illustrates the basic concepts of SPOOLing, since there are three distinct phases, or steps, to a job which requires a slow input media, such as the card reader, as well as a slow output media. *Step one* reads the input into the CPU where the normal IOCS routines for error checking will occur. The data is written out on disk where it will remain until the job which requires its use is called from the queue into the memory of the computer for execution. The data may be read along with the JCL cards for the job and then remain stored on disk for a considerable period of time, or it may be processed immediately. When it is processed depends upon how many other jobs, with higher priorities, are already in the queue. When SPOOLing is done, an individual job usually takes longer but the total amount of system through-put is increased.

When the job which requires the input is loaded into the memory of the computer for execution, the data is read from the disk file. This in effect has made the input a continuous stream of information, from a *fast input device* rather than being processed directly from the card reader, which is a much slower device. After the data is processed the output is stored on disk. *Step two* then involves reading the input from disk, processing the data by using the application program, and storing the output on disk.

Step three will be accomplished as soon as the printer is available. Since all printed output is stored on disk and then printed according to the priority assigned to the job, one continuous stream of output for the printer is available. The printer operates at maximum speed in a burst mode with *no interruptions* for the duration of the print job. If you listen as a job is printed using SPOOLing and compare it with a job that is not SPOOLed, you can actually hear the difference in speed even though the same printer and computer are being used. There are no hesitations—under SPOOLing the printer prints at top speed for the entire duration of the job.

When SPOOLing is used in a multiprogramming environment that executes jobs on the basis of priorities, the operator can assign a job a high priority. If a request is made for a job to be executed immediately, the operator can, by using the JCL commands which are available, assign the job a high priority and, in addition, put all of the other jobs in queue on hold. If the job, however, requires a slow input media and a printed report, all three of the steps required in SPOOLing will still need to be executed.

1. Read the input into the memory of the computer and write the data out on a disk—part of SPOOLing software.
2. Process the input from disk and write the resulting output on a disk file—user's application program working in usual manner.
3. Read the output disk file from step 2 and print a report—part of SPOOLing software.

10–42. What does SPOOLing stand for?
10–43. Under SPOOLing is a continuous stream of output made available by storing data first on disk and then printing the report from the data stored in the disk file?
10–44. Does an individual job take more time to execute when it is SPOOLed or when it is executed in a one partition nonSPOOLing computer?
10–45. Under SPOOLing is the printer more productive?

REAL-TIME SYSTEMS

In a real-time system transactions are immediately entered into the system and processed in time for the results to have an immediate effect upon the situation. The key word in the definition is *immediate*. When batch processing is used, even under multiprogramming, the results of the processing may be from the previous day's transactions and do not have "an immediate effect upon the situation."

In contrast, consider what might happen in a real-time sales application. A salesman has a portable terminal that he takes with him when he calls on a customer. When a sale is made, the salesman enters the transaction into the sales recording system by using the terminal. The entry of the data may have one of many different *immediate* effects:

1. If the customer has previously overextended his credit, the salesman may be *immediately* notified that the order cannot be processed until the customer pays his overdue invoices.
2. The customer's credit may be fine, but one of the items that he has ordered is not available. The salesman can *immediately* find out if the customer would prefer the item to be placed on backorder or to order a substitute item.
3. If the customer's credit is satisfactory and all of the items are on hand, the inventory is *immediately* updated. Another salesman who places an order for the same item five minutes later may find that the items are unavailable.
4. If the salesman enters an invalid item number he *immediately* is informed of his mistake, and he can make the necessary correction.

The entire transaction may take only 10 to 15 seconds to complete, yet both the salesman and the customer know *immediately* the outcome of the transaction rather than waiting for perhaps as many as four or five days for the transaction to be processed. As with any system there are both advantages and disadvantages. Real-time systems take a very large complex operating system plus large online data bases if they are to be effective. If computers are dedicated to only the real-time application, rather than also being assigned batch jobs, their operating systems can be less complex.

In the system illustrated in figure 10–5 the system is not only a real-time system, but also a time-sharing system. The terminal's controller allocates a small time-slice to the terminal that makes a request to utilize the computer. As was indicated earlier in the text, the typical time-slice might be 150 milliseconds, which is more than adequate for processing the salesman's order.

The users batch jobs can process in both background and foreground one. In the application cited the data base, which is accessed by the terminals, must have information pertaining to both the customer's accounts receivable and to inventory.

Data Base

The term data base has been used frequently in the textbook to refer to large quantities of online information which may be accessed randomly. Is

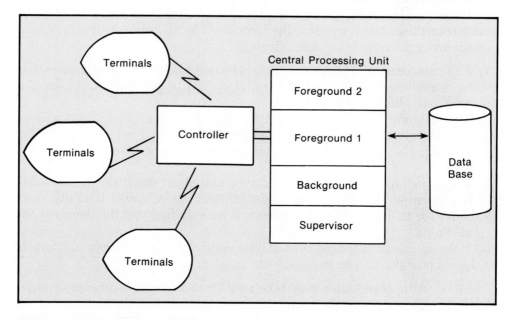

FIGURE 10–5. REAL-TIME SYSTEM

there a difference between a *true data base* and a *master file* which may be accessed randomly?

Usually when the term master file is used, it refers to records pertaining to one type of information. For example, in an installation there may be *individual* master files for payroll, accounts receivable, accounts payable, personnel information, inventory, and numerous other applications. When individual master files are used there is a redundancy of information, since certain fields which are used in one file are duplicated in another file. In both the payroll and personnel files there would be the employee's name, address, social security number, salary, number of exemptions, length of service with the company, plus the numerous other fields of information that are duplicated in both files.

When individual files are maintained, it not only takes more processing time to update the same information in several files but it is also more difficult to maintain the integrity of the information. Information in files is useless unless it is *current, complete,* and *reliable.* When numerous master files are maintained, it is not only more costly, but there also exists a lack of uniformity in how data is stored from file to file and the data names that might be associated with the fields.

With the technological advancements, which made it *feasible* to store an almost unlimited amount of data online, software was developed which could be added to the operating system that could "manage" and utilize the massive file of information that serves the needs of many different areas of the company. From the user's or programmer's point of view, he still deals with the information as if it were an individual random or sequential file.

The benefits, however, provided by having a data base rather than individual files, are numerous, since the consolidation of the information reduces the redundancy, permits easier updating of the information, better control over the data, greater flexibility, and more standardization. If a data base can be justified in terms of the volume of data that is processed, there will be a reduction in the cost (per unit of information), that is stored.

The trend among the larger companies today is *towards the development* of a true data base since few companies have actually made a total commitment to the concept. The commitment can be full or partial—where there begins a gradual integration of the files by combining certain naturals, such as payroll and personnel. A full commitment would involve a considerable revision of existing practices, more personnel, and additional hardware and software. In making a decision of this magnitude, a study would be undertaken to determine the long-range goals and how it should be phased in. Once the data base was established, the management of the information becomes a task of the operating system.

10–46. In a real-time system are transactions entered into the system in time for the results to have an immediate effect upon the situation?
10–47. In a real-time system is it necessary to have online disk storage?
10–48. In a time-sharing system what allocates a time-slice to each user?
10–49. Is a true data base and a master file the same thing?
10–50. Are there software packages available which provide for data base management that are considered to be a part of the computer's operating system?

VIRTUAL MEMORY

What is virtual memory? Virtual memory or storage is disk or drum storage that is utilized as an "extension" of the computer's real memory. The concept of virtual memory is used to enlarge the *real memory* of the computer by utilizing a much larger amount of lower-speed memory, which is stored on either disk or drum by memory swapping. Segments, or "pages," of memory are swapped back and forth in such a manner that the real memory of the computer is expanded to many times its actual capacity. The unit of either *program* or *data*, usually 2K or 4K in size, swapped back and forth, is known as a page. The process of swapping data or program commands back and forth is referred to as "page-in," since the page goes from disk to real memory, and "page-out" as a page leaves the memory of the computer and is stored on disk.

Until IBM announced virtual memory, or storage, in late 1972, little had been written about its merit. Virtual memory, however, had been utilized in the United States as early as 1961, as a feature of the Burrough's 5000 series. Since that time it has been a part of the Burrough's product line, but other manufacturers, other than IBM and RCA who made very limited usage of the concept, seemed to pay little heed to its potential and had a tendency to view it as just another "interesting computer feature" until IBM's big entry into the virtual memory field.

The use of virtual storage makes it possible to utilize the CPU a greater percentage of the time, since more and larger programs can be executing at one time in the memory of the computer. It is only necessary to have one page (which is either 2K or 4K) of the program or the data being executed in real memory of the computer at one time. The distinction between real and virtual memory is largely unnoticeable to the programmer or operator. It has made it possible to program for larger, more sophisticated programs more easily, since the programmer need not be concerned about the amount of memory that is available in a partition.

The difficult part of any such memory organization is keeping track of what part of the program is in real storage and what part has been "paged out" and is on disk or drum. A hardware device known as Dynamic Address Translation is utilized for this purpose, and additional operating systems were also designed to facilitate the new concept. Under the virtual storage concept, throughput is usually increased from 10 to 20%, whereas each individual job requires a slightly longer time to execute.

QUESTIONS ON VIRTUAL STORAGE

10–51. Why does the virtual memory, or storage, concept permit the user to run larger programs than could be run without VS?

10–52. What is "paging out?"

OPERATING SYSTEMS SUMMARY

The full potential of the central processing unit is beginning to be utilized because man had demonstrated his ability to develop improved software, which has enabled the computer to do multiprogramming, real-time applications, data base management, and to expand its memory by utilizing drum or disk storage. Regardless of how complex the new applications become, it should be apparent that the computer is still controlled by man. For what is the operating system but a set of programs and related hardware devices, under the control of the supervisor, which help to provide maximum throughput. The supervisor, which allocates the CPU time and handles all of the system interrupts which either print a message or provide a recovery routine, is also a mere program written by man.

GLOSSARY OF NEW AND OLD TERMS TO CHECK YOUR KNOWLEDGE

Core Image Library. The core image library contains many types of programs that are self-contained, ready-to-run programs. The supervisor, compilers, user's application programs, etc. are stored in the core image library.

Data Base. A collection of data available to the user as if it were a single integrated data base regardless of its actual physical description.

Emulator. A combination of hardware and software which permits one computer to look, or act, like another.

IOCS. Input/Output Control System. The IOCS provides the routines for such basic functions as blocking, unblocking, error checking, reading and writing physical records, and label checking.

IPL. When the computer is IPLed the initial program loader is stored in the CPU. It requests that the date and time be entered and then proceeds to store the supervisor in the memory of the computer.

JCL. Job control language. JCL cards and commands are used as a means of communication with the computer. Through the JCL statements the operator or programmer can tell the computer what options are desired for a particular task.

Logical Record. One disk or tape record pertaining to a given topic. For example, one student's record. Each logical record is *processed* individually.

Multiprogramming. Multiprogramming provides the ability to store more than one program in the memory of the computer at one time. The programs take turns doing the actual computations that are required. When slower I/O devices are used, multiprogramming *gives the appearance* that it is executing the programs simultaneously.

Operating System. A set of programs and related hardware devices, under the control of a supervisor, which helps to insure maximum throughput.

Page. A record which may contain either data or commands that is stored on a random access storage device. The page size is usually 2 or 4K.

Page Frame. A location in the real memory of the computer that can store one page, which usually consists of either 2 or 4K, of commands.

Physical Record. A block of logical records that are read, stored, or written as a unit of information. The IOCS takes care of both the blocking and unblocking of the records.

Real-time. A method of entering and processing the system's transactions so that the results may have an immediate effect upon the situation.

Relocatable Library. Subroutines that can be incorporated into other programs and the IOCS routines are stored in the relocatable library.

Source Library. Structures, file descriptions, MACRO statements, etc., are stored in the source library. It is used almost exclusively by COBOL and assembler language programmers.

SPOOLing. Simultaneous Peripheral Operations On Line.

SYSGEN. A systems generation is done in order to add to, or delete from, the existing operating system. The user has many options to select from in determining what features are to be included in the operating system.

System Interrupt. A break in the normal execution of a program or routine which is accomplished in such a way that the usual sequence can be resumed from that point later on.

Virtual Memory. Virtual memory is a technique for managing a limited amount of high-speed memory and generally a much larger amount of lower-speed memory in such a way that the distinction is largely unnoticeable to the programmer or operator.

ANSWERS

REVIEW QUESTIONS (p. 582)

10–1. Second

10–2. The supervisor

10–3. The computer is returned to the control or supervisor state.

10–4. Yes

10–5. More throughput or you might have answered the computer becomes more productive.

10–6. A manual or operating guide is available that can be used to determine the cause of the interrupt, what action can be taken, and what will happen if the message is not responded to correctly.

10–7. No. An I/O interrupt is a very normal occurrence as the control unit is merely notified that conditions are such that data may be read into or out of main memory. In many cases a supervisor call interrupt, such as signaling the end of a program, is also very normal.

10–8. The first digit of the message tells the operator, in a general way, the type of problem that has occurred.

10–9. No. When the operating system is generated (SYSGEN) the user selects the features that he wishes to have included. Certain basic features may be the same but one operating system may be far more powerful than the other.

REVIEW ON THE CORE IMAGE LIBRARY (p. 587)

10–10. Yes

10–11. Yes, for most systems. Some computer systems now have added software that may make it, under certain circumstances, unnecessary.

10–12. No. JCL commands are executed between job steps and to initiate new programs not as a part of the user's program.

10–13. The subroutines are stored in a relocatable library.

10–14. Librarian programs provide such services as cataloging new programs, condensing the library and do other forms of maintenance.

10–15. No. Private libraries can be stored offline. This provides additional security for the programs in the private library.

10–16. Yes

10–17. Programs such as the compilers, error routines, the linkage editor, etc.

10–18. A utility program

10–19. The // EXEC *program-name* JCL card. The format of the card will vary with the system.
10–20. Yes
10–21. Yes

CONCERNING THE RELOCATABLE LIBRARY (p. 590)

10–22. No. The application programs are stored in the core image library.
10–23. Almost any task, that is frequently used in a number of different programs, should be considered as a good subroutine.
10–24. The I/O logic modules are loaded into the transient area of the computer by the supervisor when they are needed by the user's program.
10–25. Yes
10–26. Subroutines and input/output logic modules are the two different kinds of routines stored in the relocatable library.

ABOUT THE SOURCE LIBRARY (p. 591)

10–27. Copy statement
10–28. Uniform or standard data names must be used by all of the programmers that use the copy statement to access a file.
10–29. Yes. The supervisor is like the tip of the iceberg. Relatively speaking it takes little memory to store the supervisor yet it may have, under its direction, in the libraries, millions of bytes of storage which contain routines, subroutines, and complete programs.

JCL REVIEW (p. 596)

10–30. *The statement is false* as each manufacturer's JCL cards differ. The Control Data card used to call in the COBOL compiler is COBOL. rather than // EXEC COBOL. The termination card is a 7, 8 and 9 punched in card column 1 rather than a /* card.
10–31. No. To catalog into each type of library requires a different job control language "setup."
10–32. BKEND's (Bookends)

10–33. It puts the computer into a wait state which permits the operator to change paper, mount a new disk pack, etc.

10–34. Job control languages were developed as a means of improving communications between the operator and the computer.

10–35. *The statement is false.* A number of cards will be needed since two master files are used plus a current file. The cards are punched and setup and then kept on file. On the face of the job card any special instructions, such as to change the date card, may be written.

REVIEW QUESTIONS ON MULTIPROGRAMMING (p. 600)

10–36. F1, Foreground 1, highest priority; F2, Foreground 2, the second highest priority; BG, background, the lowest priority.

10–37. *No.* Only one program can actually do mathematical computations at one time. They share, by priority, the CPU's computational ability.

10–38. No. The I/O device is assigned by the program not by the job control language statements.

10–39. The master scheduler executes the jobs according to job and class priorities.

10–40. Under multiprogramming there is far more throughput since the CPU is idle a much smaller percent of the time.

10–41. Yes. Under 370 OS partitions are not used as the memory is dynamic. A great many programs may be in the memory of the computer at one time.

REGARDING SPOOLING (p. 603)

10–42. SPOOLing stands for Simultaneous Peripheral Operations On Line.

10–43. Yes

10–44. Each job takes longer when it is SPOOLed but there is a decided increase in the amount of throughput.

10–45. Yes

QUESTIONS REGARDING REAL-TIME AND DATA BASE (p. 606)

10–46. Yes. This is perhaps the biggest value of a Real-Time system over a batch operation.

10–47. Yes. Random access files must be online in order to have a real-time system.
10–48. The multiplexor
10–49. No. A master file has only one type of data, such as payroll information, while a data base contains information pertaining to several systems.
10–50. Yes

QUESTIONS ON VIRTUAL STORAGE (p. 607)

10–51. The entire program need not be in the memory of the computer at one time under VS. A page, consisting of either 2K or 4K, is all that must be in the memory of the computer at one time.
10–52. A page of either data or commands is written out on disk in order that room is available for "paging in" commands or data which are needed.

TIME-SHARING 11

The Components of Time-Sharing

Time-Sharing at:
   First Savings and Loan Association
   Dow Chemical Company
   Blue Cross of Florida, Inc.

BASIC

A Time-sharing Language

Rules of BASIC

Simple Statements.

Time-sharing was defined in module 3 (p. 140) as a method used to place the computer's capabilities at the immediate disposal of a number of independent remotely-located users, each of which feels that he has the exclusive use of the system. Time-sharing may also be real-time, where the results of processing the data are available in time to have an effect on the transaction.

Dow's STR (Sales Transaction Recording) system, which will be used as an example of time-sharing, is also an online real-time system. When the information pertaining to the sale is entered through the terminal, the information is immediately processed. If there is an error in transmitting an invalid product identifier, or customer number, an alternate method of processing the data, which is built into the system, takes immediately corrective action. If the customer's credit is overextended, or the product unavailable, the salesman is notified immediately so that "the results of processing the data are available in time to have an effect on the transaction."

Time-sharing requires the following components: terminals, controller, central processing unit, and a method of transmission.

TERMINALS

The terminal may be an intelligent stand-alone "mini" computer which has built-in sequence control and instruction functions to guide the operator through each transaction, step-by-step. The intelligent terminal may also perform the necessary arithmetic operations, such as item extension, tax, and discount calculations, editing of the data, and so forth. In the case of credit transactions, the operations differ depending on the system, since some have an independent credit authorization terminal, while others permit online credit verification through the terminal. When the intelligent terminal is used for POS, it has been estimated that more than 80% of the information required in data processing can be captured at the point of sale. The three intelligent terminals which were discussed in some detail in module 5 are:

1. *NCR 280 Cash Register.* The cash register, illustrated in conjunction with the wand reader, can be used as an intelligent online real-time terminal. In the application presented, the data was accumulated and transmitted in a batch mode to the time-sharing computer.
2. *NCR 399 Minicomputer.* Deriving its intelligence from the tape cassettes which are read into its memory, it can be used in either an online real-time application or as a stand-alone computer.

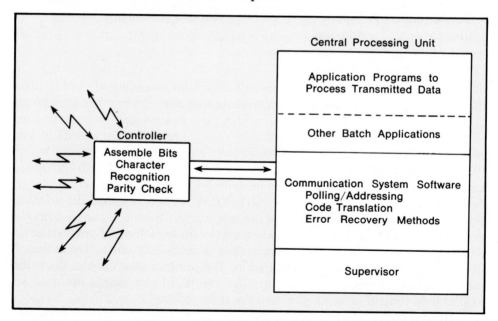

FIGURE 11–1. RELATIONSHIP OF CONTROLLER TO CENTRAL PROCESSING UNIT

3. *IBM 3735 Programmable Terminal.* The functions of the terminal were illustrated regarding its use in preparing a sales invoice. While the invoice was being printed, it could also have been online to the host computer.

The second type of terminal is the input-output terminal, which can either transmit data, receive data, or do both functions—send and receive.

Whether the terminals will be used online in real-time applications, or used to transmit data which is processed in a batch mode, is determined by the objectives which are defined in the system study. For example, the study done by the First Savings and Loan Association, which is presented in this module, started on the premise that an online real-time system was needed. Other studies by other companies might start with the question, "Can an online real-time system be cost justified?" The material presented regarding the Dow Chemical Company presents a different situation, since their system study indicated it was what should be used, but at the time the software and hardware available made it totally unrealistic to implement.

CONTROLLER

Figure 11–1 illustrates the concept of the controller, which is also called the "Frontend Processor." At one time the controller did little more than assemble the bits, which were transmitted from the terminal, into recognizable characters. In addition, the data transmitted was checked for parity errors. The most common method of correction utilized for a parity error was to ask the sending terminal to retransmit the message. The controller also acted as a "buffer," between the very slow transmitting device, the terminal, which usually sent or received only ten characters per second, and the super-fast data handler, the computer.

Two of the very basic terms used in time-sharing, or communications, should be defined:

1. *Polling.* A method of inquiring if a terminal has data to be transmitted. The polling can be done by line, by terminal, or by a predetermined priority.
2. *Addressing.* The computer asking the terminal if it is ready to receive a message.

The communication software package, which is in the CPU, has included in it a message scheduler that determines how often to poll the terminal and to transmit data back to the terminal. The message scheduler can have priorities built-in, which makes it more complex than if polling were done purely on a sequential basis.

Today the controller is being given more of the basic communication functions, such as the polling and addressing functions, error detection and recovery, storing the data received or transmitted in queue, plus their original functions of bit assembly and character recognition.

The area of communication controllers is being researched considerably, because it is anticipated that by 1978 65% of all computers will have data communication capabilities. In contrast, today, only 25% of the computers in use have terminals which are used to communicate with the computer. The use of low speed I/O terminals is anticipated to double, since it is the stable, already-tested, standby of the industry. The number of intelligent terminals in use will expand tremendously because, for many users, time-sharing is becoming feasible as online storage costs are decreasing, transmission times are faster, software is available, and so on.

The use of intelligent terminals and communication controllers, with expanded capabilities, will make it possible for the host computer to be even more productive. There is not a clear, sharp distinction today between exactly what is assigned to the terminal, what the controller should or should not do, and what remains for the host CPU to do as its share in the sophisticated data processing cycle of today. As more hardware and software is being developed for data communication, the user and the manufacturer, sometimes working together, are redefining the roles of the terminal, controller, and host computer.

TRANSMISSION METHODS

Often referred to as the medium, the transmission method for time-sharing can be one of the following: wire, radio, coaxial cable, microwave, satellite, and light beams. Over 80% of all data transmitted, to and from terminals, is by means of wire and in a majority of the cases it is over the Bell system. A terminal may be connected to the system in such a way that it need only be turned on to communicate with the host computer. Other terminals, such as the portable illustrated in module 5, require the use of a data set that is used to dial the computer. The data set, or phone, is then placed on the coupler, which is on top of the terminal, and communication can begin.

The communication lines are available from different common carriers, such as the Bell system, in two basic forms:

1. Public: direct dial switched networks.
2. Private: leased or dedicated lines.

If the first method is used (the direct dial switched network) it is exactly the same (talking to the computer) as when you make a long distance phone call. Within the two methods, there are substantial differences among the types of lines in terms of quality, transmission rate, and cost that deserve careful consideration. The choice is made depending upon the volume of data to be transmitted, the location of the terminals in relationship to the computer, *and the other communication needs within the company.*

CENTRAL PROCESSING UNIT

A considerable amount of memory is usually required if the computer is to be used for both time-sharing and batch processing. A special software package, in addition to the basic operating system, must be available to enable the computer, in the user's time-slice, to bring the necessary program into the computer, execute its instructions, and then output the data to the correct user. All of this takes place in the user's time-slice which may be 150 milliseconds. The development of one software package, called PROFITS, is illustrated in the material pertaining to the First Savings and Loan Association. The PROFITS software package took more than two years to develop, using the combined efforts of an advisory committee, the manufacturer's systems analysts, and the programmer/analysts from the First Savings and Loan Association.

CASE STUDIES

Introduction

Three firms, each of which is heavily committed to the concept of time-sharing, were selected for in-depth study. Each firm was sent a questionnaire which dealt with many of the topics covered in the textbook. Except for Blue Cross of Florida, Inc., visits were made to the installations to discuss the system with the individual who had been instrumental in its design. In addition, the system's documentation was studied to gain an overview of the time-sharing system.

The three case studies are presented to you, the student, as a means of relating a great many topics that have been covered in the text, to "real world" applications. Often there is a difference between what is presented in a textbook as theory and what exists in an actual application. As you read the three case studies you will see that many of the items presented in the text are actually major factors in the design and implementation of the system. The materials have been edited by Mr. Lloyd Smith, Manager, Business Information

Services, Dow Chemical Company of Midland, Michigan; Mr. A. James Devers, Vice-President, Systems and Programming, First Savings and Loan of Saginaw, Michigan; and Mr. Charles Scott, Manager, EDP Planning for Blue Cross of Florida, Inc. Without the assistance of these three men, and their staff, it would have been impossible to present the case studies.

Each of the three cases represents a little different use of the terminal in a time-sharing application. In addition, *only a very small portion of the total time-sharing system is presented.* Blue Cross of Florida, Inc., had been involved for a number of years in the use of terminals. Therefore, their systems study was related to how "to do the job better." Their particular application at this point is time-sharing but not real-time. It could, however, become a real-time system. Their terminals function in a "conversational mode" while the other two applications do not use that technique for guiding the operator through entering the information into the system.

The Dow Chemical Company application illustrates the use of long-range planning and the gradual implementation toward their "ultimate goal," a real-time online sales system, which was conceived long before it was possible to be implemented. The Dow application today is a true online, real-time, time-sharing system in the fullest meaning of the terms.

The First Savings and Loan Association study provides an illustration of an interesting development of software plus a good, solid approach to long-range objectives. It also illustrates the meaning of constraints, for their analysts see so much potential that, as yet, can not be achieved due to the problem of "cost justification."

All three companies have excellent documentation that includes: a complete overview of the system for management, instructions for the machine operators, detailed documentation for the program maintenance group, and very precise, detailed documentation for the terminal operators. Blue Cross and Dow use intelligent terminals whereas the First Savings and Loan Company's terminals only receive and transmit data.

The hardware configuration for Blue Cross and Dow represent very large installations with extremely complex operating systems. First Savings and Loan's configuration is a medium-size installation, perhaps a little on the small size, where excellent utilization has been made of the existing hardware.

FIRST SAVINGS AND LOAN ASSOCIATION OF SAGINAW, MICHIGAN

Introduction

Due to the efforts of a group of Saginaw men, the First Savings and Loan Association was started in March 1887. The building and loan concept was not new, for in 1815 a group of men in England organized a small home-owning society. Each member of the society contributed a fixed amount each month, and in a short time enough money was available to buy a home for one of the members. After securing his home, the member continued to pay the same fixed sum each month, and eventually all members of the society secured homes.

The Saginaw men, working through their representative William S. Linton, were able, in 1887, to get the Michigan Savings and Loan Act passed, which made it possible for the People's Building and Loan Association to become a reality.

If you could read through their early records, which are beautifully hand-printed, you would find that their assets in 1887 totaled $7,793.34, and that they had paid an unheard of sum of $50.00 *a year* for rent.

Through the years the Association, which changed its name in 1947, has matched its phenomenal financial growth with its physical growth. Its downtown offices were completely modernized in 1955 and an ultra-modern branch office was constructed in 1957. When they first utilized electronic data processing equipment, their assets exceeded 130 million and they had added two branch offices.

Today there are twelve modern offices, all of which have online real-time terminals to serve their many customers. Their assets have grown from the first year's total of $7,793.34 to over 250 million.

Their timely financial statements, prepared by modern EDP equipment, provide a sharp contrast to one of their early hand-printed statements which is framed and on display in their downtown office.

The Systems Study

The data processing department, whose manager reports directly to the controller, is divided into two areas: systems development and operations. A decision had been made before the systems study was started that the only solution to the problem, created by their rapid expansion, was the acquisition of a real-time system.

The systems study, which took approximately one year, was concerned primarily with the basic question of how to develop, in the most efficient way possible, an online real-time system to meet their expanding data processing requirements.

A study was made of the equipment available from all of the major computer manufacturers. Since the hardware costs for comparable real-time systems were found to be approximately the same, their study focused upon the following factors:

1. The software support available from the manufacturer for the specific applications required for a savings and loan institution.
2. The amount of reprogramming which would be necessary in order to convert from the UNIVAC 1004 and 1005 systems being used to a new online real-time system.
3. The amount of technical support available, in the immediate geographical area, for the system which would be selected.

After considering the proposals submitted by the various manufacturers, a decision was made to use UNIVAC equipment. The three strongest arguments in favor of selecting UNIVAC equipment were:

1. Less conversion costs because the new system would be compatible with their present equipment.
2. UNIVAC was in the process of developing a real-time software package for financial institutions.
3. Their relationship with UNIVAC had been very satisfactory, for they had received excellent *protective maintenance* on their hardware and assistance in developing new software.

Service Bureau or In-House?

After the decision had been reached to use UNIVAC equipment *if* an in-house installation could be *cost-justified*, an analysis was made that compared the cost of developing their own system against the utilization of a service bureau's existing services.

Two constraints which had been initially imposed upon the development of a new system were *time* and *budget*. The system had to be up-and-running within a given time period, and they also had to be able to prove it was to their *financial* advantage to develop an in-house system rather than using a service bureau. Their cost analysis indicated that per unit of work processed it would be cheaper to utilize a service bureau. Nevertheless, there were two major disadvantages in using a service bureau over developing their own system:

1. The service bureau's existing "package" did not include the financial reports and analysis which were part of First Savings and Loan's long-range planning.
2. The systems which were available were inflexible.

The decision was made to develop their own in-house system on the strength of the intangible benefits which would be derived from the new system, such as faster and more complete financial data available for management.

A certified public accounting firm was also asked to study the question of in-house versus service bureau and came up with the same conclusion as the one reached by the systems analysts assigned to the study. Although it was more costly initially to develop their own system, the long-range benefits available to management would more than offset the additional costs.

PROFITS

An advisory committee was established, consisting of representatives from 14 different savings and loan institutions, to assist in the development of software for the basic data processing requirements for similar financial institutions.

Since First Savings and Loan of Saginaw had been selected as a "pilot" for the development of a real-time software package, a systems analyst from UNIVAC was assigned to work with the programmer/analysts who were now involved in the design stage of the study.

The PROFITS (Personalized Real-time Oriented Financial Institution Time-sharing System) advisory committee met twice a year. At their meetings a presentation was given by the systems study team, detailing a feature of the system being developed. If the majority of the committee felt the feature should be included as part of the software, the cost of developing the program module was absorbed by UNIVAC. If less than half of the group wanted the module, First Savings and Loan would develop it at their own expense. The project team approach, working with the advisory committee, resulted in all 14 savings and loan institutions implementing the system.

Implementation

From April through November of that year the real-time system was implemented while both the new system and the old system were run "parallel" to make certain that the results obtained from the online system were valid. During the nine months there were relatively few problems and management was well satisfied with the new system. It is unusual for a company to run parallel for that length of time, since it is costly to maintain both systems simultaneously.

Passbook Savings

The tellers who used the Bunker-Ramo terminals were instructed on their use before the system went online, and they had little difficulty adjusting to the new equipment. A well-documented terminal operations manual, which details each type of transaction, is available to each teller. If a customer wishes to make a deposit to his savings account, the teller can determine from the first two digits of the account number the type of account that is being processed. The documentation pertaining to the types of savings accounts provides the following information regarding the 01 prefix code:

"01 Accounts
Regular passbook savings, *blue* book, 5¼ daily interest, credited quarterly. Investments and withdrawals may be made any time."

In the SAVINGS INVESTMENT section of the teller's documentation manual the following detailed instructions are provided for the teller:

"Investments with the Passbook

1. Obtain the customer's passbook.
2. Prepare the investment ticket neatly and properly.
3. Post the investment in the passbook.
4. Return the passbook to the customer.
5. Retain the investment ticket—teller stamp and file in numerical order with other investment tickets."

Included on the bottom of the instruction sheet is an illustration of a completely filled in and teller stamped investment ticket.

In the terminal operations manual for savings/mortgages the instructions, necessary to do step 3 ("Post the investment in the passbook") are detailed, step-by-step, telling the operator exactly what must be done. When the customer, pictured in figure 11–2, came in to make her deposit the teller would have been following these instructions:

"Step	Transaction Keys	##
1. Account number	Account #	01
2. Balance pick up	Balance	10
3. Book in machine		
4. Amount of deposit	Amount	20"

The teller, who has been through a training session and has also worked under the supervision of an experienced teller, needs no further instructions to understand the documentation. Since, however, we have not been through the sessions, a little more explanation is needed so that we understand what the teller does and how the computer responds to each step.

Since the customer has a "blue" passbook, as illustrated in figure 11–3, the teller knows immediately that it is a regular passbook account. The ac-

FIGURE 11–2. FIRST SAVINGS AND LOAN ASSOCIATION TELLER MAKING AN
ADDITION TO A PASSBOOK SAVINGS ACCOUNT.

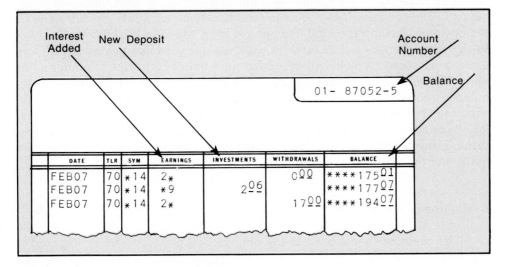

FIGURE 11–3. CUSTOMER'S PASSBOOK

count number, 01870525, is entered on the transaction keys, along with the code "01," on the transaction type key.

The account number is the key used by the computer to retrieve the customer's record from the indexed sequential master disk files which are located in the computer center at the main office.

If the key is valid, the customer's record will be brought into the computer's memory for processing. Step 2, which tells the operator to enter the customer's balance, which, according to the illustration, is 17501 is then followed. Entering the balance is a *validity check*. The computer will check to make certain that account number 01870525 has a balance of 17501. If not, the teller is notified that the "validity check" has detected an error. One of two conditions could be present:

1. The account number was entered wrong. Therefore, the wrong customer's record is now in the memory of the computer!
2. If the account number was entered correctly, then the only other possibility that exists is that the customer's balance was entered incorrectly by the operator.

It may be an unfair question, but would you, the student, have thought to enter the balance merely to provide a validity check? Without such checking features, the wrong customer's balance could have been updated.

If the validity check proves to be accurate, which means that the balance entered agrees with the amount on the disk record, the next step is followed by the teller which is to insert the passbook into the terminal. The teller follows step 4 by entering 20 for the transaction code and 17.00 as the amount of the deposit. The program that processes the passbook accounts checks to see if the customer has interest that has not yet been added to the customer's book. In this case there is a 2.06 interest that has not yet been posted to the customer's passbook, which will be added automatically to the customer's balance. The new investment of 17.00 is then printed on the passbook and the balance increased to 194.07. The customer's record in the memory of the computer has also been updated, and when the record is rewritten on disk it will contain the results of the new transaction. The only actual input entered through the terminal is: customer's number, balance as shown on the passbook, and the amount of the deposit.

Evaluation of the System

The customer benefits from the change because less time is required to complete his passbook transactions. Prior to the implementation of the new system, the teller was required to remove the customer's ledger card from the file, look up the amount of the unrecorded interest, post the interest, compute the balance, post the new deposit, and again compute the balance.

The tellers have reacted favorably to the new system, which is probably due in part to the excellent documentation that is available. Each procedure lists the steps necessary to perform the operation and, when needed, diagrams are used to show the status of the different switches and code condition keys.

The teller enjoys the fact that much of the old "balancing out" procedure, which is necessary at the end of each day, is now done automatically. The computer provides a summary, by teller, for each terminal, which totals each type of transaction, such as investments, withdrawals, payments, and so on. Under the new system, the teller can count and record the amount of cash on the "tellers daily cash count" form and be finished balancing out in approximately 15 minutes, which is 30 minutes less than it took under the old method.

Management has been well pleased with the new system because they do receive more complete and timely reports. The daily transaction report was also provided under the former method, but it was not available until six or seven days after the day's transactions had occurred. Now the same report, *produced automatically by the system*, is available by 8:00 A.M. of the following day.

Most of the errors that have occurred have been caught before the account is actually updated. Over 40% of the coding for programs that process the various types of transactions is involved in some way with the verification of input. In addition to the *one check* described for *one type of transaction*, it might also be noted that the customer's number contains a check digit.

File Security and Maintenance

After all of the transactions have been processed for any given day, the indexed sequential disk master file is copied to two sequential tape files which are stored in an *offsite vault*. In addition, as each entry into the system is processed online, each transaction is recorded on a sequential tape file. If for any reason the master file must be recreated, this can easily be done by using the sequential master file and transaction tapes.

All requests for programming changes must be made in writing and properly authorized before they can be made. The testing procedure for the changes use "live data" rather than test data. The prior day's transaction tape and the master file (copied from the backup master tape) are used to reprocess all of the entries for the day being tested. Any reports, or totals taken, from the testing run must agree with those previously received from the normal processing of the same transactions.

The hardware necessary to support the 25 terminals, located in 12 different branches, includes the following equipment:

CPU	The UNIVAC 9400 has 98K of wire plated memory which stores data using the EBCDIC code.
3 8414 Disk Drives	Capacity per removable pack—29,176,000 Storage transfer rate—312,000 bytes per second.
3 UNISERVO VI—C Magnetic Tapes	BPI 800, IRG .6″, Tape speed, 42.7 inches per second, data transfer rate 34,160 bytes per second.

1004 & 1005 Subsystems

The 1005 Subsystem, which is shown in figure 11–4, has some interesting features which once again illustrates that there are many different unique pieces of hardware which are available to meet the needs of the data processing user.

The UNIVAC 1005 Subsystem has a processing unit, with 961 characters of core storage, which has arithmetic, logical, and editing capabilities. Its peripherals consist of a 615 card-per-minute reader and a line printer which prints 600 lines per minute. The subsystem can function independently off-line as a separate computer system, or it may operate under the control of the

FIGURE 11–4. UNIVAC 1005 SUBSYSTEM. (Courtesy of First Savings and Loan Association.)

9400. When online, a special wired control panel (plugboard) is required. At any time, however, it may be switched to an offline mode and will operate as a free standing system. An additional unit of 961 characters of core, as well as other peripherals, may be added to the subsystem.

With the configuration that First Savings and Loan now has, more terminals may still be added to the system.

The DOS has the capability of running up to five jobs simultaneously. This particular disk operating system differs, however, from the one detailed in module 10, since there are no fixed partitions. The jobs with the highest priorities are loaded first, after the supervisor, and occupy the necessary space in memory. The memory of the computer used by the First Savings and Loan Association is divided as follows:

Memory Required	Function
20K	Supervisor which controls the entire operating system.
45K	Controlling program required to process data from the real-time terminals.
33K	Batch jobs which are loaded in, as needed by the operator.

Although up to five jobs may be run simultaneously, if a particular batch job requires 32K it would be impossible, while that job was running along with the real-time application program, to load another job into the CPU. Once the terminals are no longer in operation, however, 78K could be utilized for batch jobs. Depending upon the memory requirements of the jobs that are loaded into the CPU for execution, it might be possible to run five simultaneously.

The controlling program, which coordinates the terminals, polls each terminal to see if there is a request to transmit. A time-slice, which provides more than enough time to bring the program module needed by a terminal into the CPU and process the data that is transmitted, is given, upon request, to each terminal polled. Each terminal operator feels as if he had exclusive use of the computer.

Long-range Plans

The real-time system has been successful because it met the original design objectives which were to be able to more effectively process the customer's data and to provide management with more timely and complete information.

The terminals currently being used transmit only numeric data into the system at a relatively slow rate of 15 characters per second. If CRTs could be cost justified, the systems analyst would like to replace their current terminals with alphanumerical display terminals. Ultimately, they would like to have available a central information file, or data base, that management could inquire into by using a terminal. Since there is available time on the system, they would like to provide real-time data processing services to other savings and loan associations.

SUMMARY

The illustration given shows how a software package, in this case PROFITS, is developed through the joint cooperation of the user and the manufacturer. The First Savings and Loan Association of Saginaw, which initially developed the software, now has a sophisticated, and accurate, online real-time system which meets their original objectives.

ABOUT FIRST SAVINGS AND LOAN

11-1. What basic decision had been made before the actual systems study was started?

11-2. Since hardware costs were comparable, their study concerned itself with what three major factors in determining which system would be utilized?

11-3. In designing their system, the two constraints were?

11-4. Initially which was less expensive, developing their own system or using the services of a service bureau?

11-5. What group helped to determine the modules, or features, that should be included in the real-time software?

11-6. How long did they run parallel?

11-7. What is done as a verification measure that the right customer's account was retrieved from the file?

11-8. How is the customer's master file organized?

11-9. If a customer who is making a deposit has not been in to make a deposit for a year or more, what will happen if he now deposits $40.00 in his account?

11-10. What percentage of their programming effort involves coding to check the validity of the input into the system?

11–11. How is the master file backed up?

11–12. How is a programming change tested?

11–13. What is the 1005 Subsystem?

11–14. A job which requires 48K to run is wanted "right now" by the president. What will he be told if it is 12:00 A.M.?

11–15. Are all the commands needed to process the data entered from the terminal available in the CPU at one time?

11–16. Why would they like to replace their present terminals?

THE DOW CHEMICAL COMPANY

Introduction

The Dow Chemical Company, which is more commonly referred to as Dow, was organized in 1897, primarily to extract chemicals from the native brine deposits of central Michigan. Today its product line, which is highly diversified, includes over 1,800 different products and services which are sold throughout the world. The company's products are marketed directly through Dow's sales force and distributed to government, industrial, agricultural, and household consumers. Most of its sales activity, which is well in excess of two billion dollars per year, is centered around a *sales transaction recording* system which is online to its corporate headquarters in Midland, Michigan. Play the "what if game" and think about how their sales would be processed *if* computers were not available. Could the job be done today without computers? What hardware and software discussed in the text do they utilize in their effort to provide fast, reliable service to their customers? Is their service fast and reliable? What would you think if you were told that the *average* time that it takes to start an order on its way to a customer, from the time it is placed with the salesman, is 20 minutes?

Business Information Services

At Dow some of the data processing functions are under Business Information Services, which is accountable to an executive vice president who is also the director of U.S. Area Operations (fig. 11–5). This may seem strange to many individuals, since many firms today, including the L. C. Smith Corporation, have their departments under the vice president of finance. Dow supports the rationale that the "whole job" should be automated using the very best data processing methods and equipment that can be *cost*

FIGURE 11–5. BUSINESS INFORMATION SERVICES. (Courtesy of Dow Chemical Company.)

justified. When dealing with sales, the "whole job" does start in the production division. The long-range goals of the sales transaction recording system include a gradual integration of the production department's data, including inventory maintenance, into the data base used for sales transaction recording.

Where some firms, in their data processing department, have a very distinct division between the systems development group and the programmers, Dow has merged the two operations into a combined effort. Therefore, the two major divisions within Business Information Services are *operations* and *systems development.*

Evolution of Data Processing at Dow

Business Information Services (BIS) has been involved in the use of manual, punched card, and computerized methods. As they progressed through the various stages of their development, they have probably, at one time or another, utilized almost every type of equipment, or technique, that has been discussed in the textbook. The sales transaction record system, referred to as STR, will be used to illustrate some of the points, concerning both hardware and software, that have been presented. What does Dow do that is similar to what has been illustrated, and how do some of their philosophies and practices governing data processing differ?

The Systems Study for STR

When the BIS manager, Lloyd Smith, was asking how long it took to design and implement the system, he stated that it was hard to actually determine the length of time that it had taken, since STR was an evolutionary process which resulted from well-defined long-range planning.

A project task force had been appointed to do a feasibility study on the development of an online real-time sales order entry system that would essentially meet the following criteria:

1. Provide faster and more accurate sales processing by capturing the information into the system from the point where the transaction occurred.
2. Decrease the *unit cost* of preparing a sales invoice.
3. Provide an integrated system that would update all of the related information pertaining to the sale.
4. Provide better management information.

The feasibility study indicated that a complete systems study should be conducted in order to design an integrated sales system. Therefore, a system study was conducted by a project task force which consisted of representatives from the departments that would be directly involved in the STR system, plus the programmer/analysts and data processing operations personnel. Long-range goals were established during the definition phase of the study, which provided for a complete online real-time operation that would integrate sales, marketing, production, accounting, shipping, and inventory information into one large data base.

The constraints that seemed to make it impossible to achieve the long-range goals more immediately were:

1. The high cost of storing such a massive amount of data online.
2. The cost of transmitting the data, via the transmission media available, from remote locations into the system.
3. Cost of the terminals which would be needed to enter data from the source where the transactions were occurring into the system.
4. The incompatibility of data coding structures used for the various files, such as inventory, sales, and production.

At the time the concept was initially conceived, neither the hardware nor software was available that would support the system. It was at least seven years ago that Dow first made a presentation of how effectively all of the files and records would be updated as a sales order was entered into the system. At that time, the software packages simply were not developed sufficiently to support such a complex design.

Since the design stage of their system study, there has been a continuous implementation and phasing in of the long-range applications.

The original STR system, which used teletypes and message switching, was run on a pilot basis and phased in over a period of 18 months. After the original testing was accomplished, using testing procedures that were *completely documented,* the pilot system was run parallel with the former method of recording sales into the system. At Dow, as with many other companies, the project team which originated the design will maintain and make additional improvements to the system. Since the personnel on the project team may change, a *strong* emphasis is placed on good documentation that follows standardized procedures.

Training for the New System

Training sessions which cover the basic concepts involved in the STR system are conducted for new salesmen. Generally, during the training sessions for new salesmen, an excellent video tape presentation is shown which details the entire system from the time the order is placed until the delivery truck rolls up to the customer's door.

For terminal operators, three day training sessions are provided in Midland. At this point, the cathode ray tube terminals have been in use for about a year and there have been no real problems. The employees seem to enjoy being able to enter the information directly into the system by using the terminal.

The System Today

Over a period of five or six years there have been many improvements in the original system. Nevertheless, the initial step in the process is still manual, since the inside salesman must manually record the order, which is usually placed over the phone, on a uniform sales entry form. On the sales form is recorded the typical sales information, which includes a ship to and bill to address, terms, rating, routing information for shipping, shipping date, customer's purchase order number, the quantity, product code, unit of shipment, and special shipping instructions. The success of the entire system depends upon the correct use of the codes. Some of the codes used for the special

FIGURE 11-6. ENTERING SALES ORDERS. (Courtesy of Dow Chemical Company.)

shipping instructions would be unique to the chemical industry because the special handling of certain chemical products is a "must." The codes are visually checked before the data is entered into the system by means of the terminal.

Since each item must be keyed in with a *field identifier*, the operator may enter the data from the sales order in any sequence. Before the data is transmitted, the entire invoice of information is displayed on the CRT, in the format in which it will appear on the sales invoice, in order that it can be visually checked by the operator.

Other Accuracy Checks

Additional checks are built into the system, such as the use of self-checking numbers, for both the product number and the customer number.

When a self-checking number is used, a mathematical formula is applied to the number which will detect an error. For example, a customer is assigned the number of 2367. It is determined that the check digit for the number is 2. The number is then recorded as 23672. If any other combination of the digits 2367 is used, which might involve a transposition or a wrong number, the mathematical formula will indicate that the number is invalid. Any time sequential numbers are used, check digits and a computerized mathematical formula may be utilized to check the accuracy of the transmitted data. As a point of clarification it might be noted that check digits are not restricted to terminals since a keypunch may have a check digit feature added as an optional feature.

The program which processed the sales data also checks on the reasonableness of certain fields of data, such as quantity. The price of the product is available in the data base and is added to the information which is transmitted in order that it may be used in calculating the total cost for each item purchased plus the invoice total. The "ship to" and "bill to" codes enable the correct names and addresses to be extracted from the data base and utilized, when needed, to process the customer's order.

How about the freight charge? The order is displayed on the terminal in the shipping area, where the shipping clerk enters the appropriate information, via her terminal, which then permits the freight charges to be calculated based upon information that is available in the online file.

As a final check on the accuracy of the data—along with self-checking numbers, a visual check, and checks for the reasonableness of the data—the entire record is transmitted back to its origin in order that the completed invoice may be compared to the original source document.

At present the integrated data base is utilized for recording information pertaining to sales, accounts receivable, accounting, marketing, and shipping. Field names in programs which reference existing files must be those that are identified in the "data dictionary." The use of a data dictionary not only enforces standardization but also provides a cross reference listing of all programs utilizing each field of data.

Making Programming Changes

Source decks are used originally in compiling the program. When a program is to be modified, however, the program is "called" into the testing library. All changes are made from a remote job entry station which reads the card required to make the change. The source statement is called into the computer's memory from the library, the change is made, and the statement in its corrected form is rewritten. Since the programmers no longer handle the

FIGURE 11–7. ENTERING FREIGHT CHARGES. (Courtesy of Dow Chemical Company.)

source decks, there is far less chance of an error being made. Program listings are available on microfiche, which enables the programmer or operator to check the complete source statements for any program.

While the program is in the test library, all required testing is done. A major emphasis at Dow is the development and maintenance of both complete program test files and documentation.

System Backup and File Security

If the system were "down" for any period of time, a second identical system is available in the Computational Research Lab. Both the "Comp" Lab

FIGURE 11–8. ENTERING PROGRAM CHANGES USING THE RJE. (Courtesy of Dow
Chemical Company.)

and BIS have identical IBM 370/155's. An additional 155 configuration is
scheduled for BIS, for Dow's logging system indicated that during a peak
period their CPU had been utilized at 99% efficiency.

As a security measure, a "checkpoint" is taken after each sales order
transmission, which means that if the system has a failure, no more than one
order would need to be retransmitted. In addition, the complete STR files are
backed up from disk to tape once a day.

Each terminal user has an identification code which is used as a security
check to make certain that only qualified individuals, *and terminals,* access

certain areas of the data base. A given protocol must be used in the identification process because first the terminal, then the application, and finally the user is identified to the system by using the correct codes in the right sequence.

Since a complete loss of power can be harmful to a computer system, Dow has two separate substations that provide electrical current. On some systems, if power were to be cut off completely, without an alternate source, the disks could be damaged and the data stored in the memory of the computer might also be destroyed.

Operating System

The IBM 370/155 currently being used has in excess of two million bytes of memory. An interesting wall panel in one of the conference rooms shows the core map of the computer and the specific locations and amount of memory needed for each feature of the operating system. The master scheduler, for example, consumes 82K, while HASP, which gives the computer the ability to SPOOL, needs 93K. Multiprogramming is provided for, and up to 15 different programs may be loaded simultaneously into the memory of the computer.

DOW SUMMARY

If each of you could visit Dow, you would be impressed with the tremendous amount of computer power and peripherals that you would see. The BIS system, which is only one of Dow's computer systems, has a large scale IBM 370/155 computer, 24 3330 disk drives, 2 online printers, numerous tape drives, terminals, RJE stations, and numerous offline devices which support the system.

Upon viewing the film presentation of the STR system and talking to the men who designed the system, you would become more impressed with the ingenuity of the system's programmers and designers who perceived the entire concept before either the hardware or software had been developed.

Is Dow's service fast and reliable? Only a small portion of the many checking features that are built into the system have been presented. It has been indicated, however, that relatively few errors have been made in order handling since the STR system became operational. Although an order could be on its way in as little as 5 minutes, the average time that it takes to receive, process, and start the order on its way to the customer is 20 minutes. The customers have indicated that they feel they are receiving fast, reliable service.

11–17. Under the STR system what is the average time that it takes to process an order?

11–18. What is the STR system?

11–19. How does Dow seem to regard documentation?

11–20. How are terminal operators trained?

11–21. How does the original data get into the STR system?

11–22. How does the terminal operator check the validity of the information which is entered on the terminal?

11–23. What is the final verification step provided for any sales order entered into the system?

11–24. List at least three checking features which are built into the system.

11–25. How are the freight charges entered into the system?

11–26. What is microfiche (on which Dow stores their source program listings?)

11–27. Be able to discuss the security measures which were taken by Dow and referenced in the textbook.

11–28. Did Dow seem to have a very large, or complicated, operating system?

11–29. How are changes made in operational programs?

11–30. Why is uninterrupted power so important to a computer?

11–31. How often is a checkpoint established?

11–32. From the material presented, would you assume that Dow had been involved with computers for any length of time?

11–33. Is there anything that is different, at least from what many companies do, in where the BIS is located with the corporate structure?

11–34. What is HASP?

BLUE CROSS OF FLORIDA, INC.

Over 75% of Florida's hospitals are now online to Blue Cross of Florida's data processing center. The totally automated system sends and receives information from hospitals to the Blue Cross headquarters in Jacksonville. The Blue Cross subscriber benefits because admission notices and *their approvals* are processed much more rapidly. The terminals used are compact, quiet, neat, and use a minimum of paper, and when used in the hospital admissions offices, the patient receives fast, complete service.

The hardware needed to support the system includes an IBM 370 computer which utilizes an OS operating system. The software package includes

IMS (Information Management System) and multiprogramming capabilities. Presently, the terminals are polled at night with an IBM 2702, and the data received takes an average of 4 to 5 hours of 370 processing time. With other communication controllers planned, it is anticipated that the daily processing time of admissions information received from the terminal will be decreased to approximately 30 minutes per day.

The Systems Study

The data processing department is well established at Blue Cross of Florida, and is under the jurisdiction of a vice-president of data processing who reports directly to the corporation's senior vice-president. Under the data processing vice-president are five managers: EDP planning, systems and programming, systems development, data control, and operations. It is interesting to note that although there are over 500 employees in the data processing department, over half of the employees are listed under the data control manager.

When Blue Cross of Florida began a systems study in 1971, which was centered primarily around their terminals, neither electronic data processing nor online communications, between the Florida hospitals and the centralized data processing department in Jacksonville, was new to them. For a number of years their communication system, which had been installed in 1960, was considered to be adequate for their particular needs. Nevertheless, since the communication system had been installed in 1960, a number of different events had occurred. There had been a tremendous growth rate in both the number of hospital admissions and the number of claims which had to be handled by the EDP system. As the computer technology had advanced, their hardware and software, other than their communication system, had become far more sophisticated. Southern Bell was also involved in a situation where they could no longer supply new (or upgrade the existing) low speed communication systems of the kind Blue Cross of Florida were using. These were the major reasons that a system study, which took approximately two years to complete, was authorized. The major thrust of the investigation was centered around finding terminals which would transmit and receive data at a faster rate, provide an adequate backup system, and still be compatible with their present hardware and software. The major guidelines, or constraints, which affected the study were:

1. *System Compatibility.* A suitable configuration must have the characteristics which make it "look" like the present terminals to the current system. It must be capable of operating at the same speed as the present terminals,

so that major modifications to the system's software are unnecessary. Potentially, it must be able to transmit and receive data at faster rates when the operating system is modified.

2. *Cost.* The new equipment must be reasonably priced and competitive with the rates of the equipment currently being utilized.

3. *Appearance.* Since the terminals will be in the hospital business offices, they must be appropriate for that environment. Compactness and low noise level are appealing qualities for such applications.

4. *Simplicity of Operation.* The devices must be simple to operate in order that the training of personnel can be achieved in a relatively short period of time.

5. *Additional Sophistication.* Although the system must perform as if it were the present hardware, it must be capable of expansion in terms of advanced applications and technical improvements.

6. *Reliability and Maintenance.* Reliability and service capabilities must be such that a minimum amount of interference is experienced as a result of equipment failures.

Conclusions Reached by the Study Teams

The in-depth study led to a number of conclusions regarding the replacement of the terminals which were used by Blue Cross of Florida. It was determined almost from the very beginning that some type of "buffer arrangement" would be needed in order to handle the current volume of admissions as well as for the additional applications which were planned. After an investigation into the various storage medias that were available, it was felt that magnetic tape cassettes would be the most reasonable in terms of cost. Cassettes would also provide the capabilities which were required in order to meet the new system's *defined objectives.*

What happened in relationship to their search for hardware to meet their specifications supports the statement which was made earlier in the text: "Improvements in both hardware and software have often been initiated due to requests submitted to the manufacturers by users." Blue Cross of Florida wanted the following:

1. Tape cassettes to receive data regarding processed claims transmitted from the computer system in Jacksonville to the local hospital. The data received could then be printed by the terminal printer from the cassette to produce the desired "hard copy." The data would be transmitted at night and then printed offline. Printing offline would decrease the required connect and transmission time.

2. A second tape cassette would be used during the day to record admissions. During the evening the terminal would be polled by the computer and the data transmitted from the second cassette into the centralized system.
3. The printer would print the data in the format designed for the system, as it is recorded on the tape. The terminal must also have the capability of printing from the tape a second copy of the data transmitted.

When the study began magnetic tape cassette units were not available as part of printer terminals. One vendor responded immediately to Blue Cross's need and developed an integrated magnetic tape cassette/printer terminal. Blue Cross of Florida was chosen as the pilot test site for the new terminal, and two models were installed, at no cost, for field testing. While the pilot was valuable to both Blue Cross of Florida and the manufacturer, the internal corporate problems of the vendor caused the project team doing the study to look further for their terminals.

In the fall of 1972, contact was made with Texas Instruments, Inc., which had developed a twin-cassette/printer terminal. An evaluation model was installed in October 1972, where it operated successfully *without disturbance to the communications system* (constraint number one—system compatibility). Figure 11–9 illustrates the twin-cassette terminal selected by Blue Cross of Florida.

Training Operators

The EDP department of Blue Cross of Florida opened the first of nine day-long training sessions with a dramatic presentation of the new terminal. At the session, attended by 41 hospital admissions employees, the room was suddenly thrown into darkness. As the "Hallelujah Chorus" broke the silence of the room, drapes were drawn back, and a spotlight bathed a Texas Instruments Terminal in a glow of light. Hospital personnel who attended each workshop received a framed certificate of accomplishment for their participation.

Perhaps not as dramatic, but equally well done, are the manuals (documentation) which give a clear, concise explanation of each operation that the terminal is used for. Figure 11–11 illustrates the documentation, showing how data is entered on the cassette by using the keyboard terminal. The instructions, numbered 1–13, are easy to understand and the keys referred to are shown in the keyboard layout, which is given in figure 11–10. The control panel pictured at the bottom of each instruction sheet shows *exactly* how each switch is to be positioned for the operation being performed.

Similar instructions are available in the manual for printing replies, cleaning the tape transport area, erasing tapes, entering data, printing extra copies

FIGURE 11-9. COURTESY OF TEXAS INSTRUMENTS, INC.

of the admission data, set-up to transmit data, admissions format, end-transmission format, no-transmission format, and error correction.

All admission format codes are clearly defined in the documentation. For example, under RL, Relationship to the subscriber, the following codes are used:

> SUB —Subscriber (Do not use "same")
> SPO —Spouse
> SON—Son
> DAU—Daughter
> STE —Stepchild
> OTH—Other (explain in Miscellaneous)

In the miscellaneous format up to eight lines of data may be transmitted.

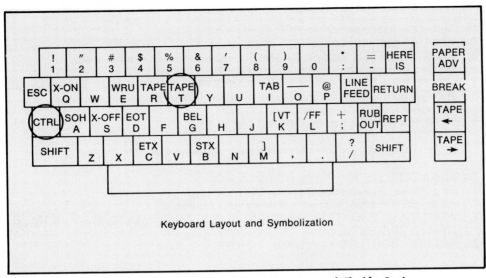

FIGURE 11–10. KEYBOARD LAYOUT. (Courtesy of Blue Cross of Florida, Inc.)

Entering Data

As indicated in the documentation, given under "Entering Data," the FORMAT tape is mounted on cassette 1, while a scratch tape is used on cassette 2. The data entered will be recorded on the tape, which is mounted on cassette 2. The tabs on the tape container, used on drive 2, must be closed, which essentially tells the system that the tape may be used as an output tape. As with regular magnetic tape or disk, it is impossible to accidentally destroy data if the output tapes have been labeled and cared for properly.

The format tape is responsible for displaying, field by field, the name of the data which is to be entered. For example, the first field to be entered is the "plan code." Printed on the terminal will be "PC." The operator then keys in the appropriate three characters as indicated by the "plan code" being used. Next will appear "LN," which tells the operator to enter the last name of the patient. Line-by-line, the format is displayed so that the operator can see what data is to be entered. Until the operator becomes familiar with all of the codes, the admission format in the documentation should be referred to.

Corrections are easy to make. If the operator senses an error *before it is recorded* on the tape, the correction is made as follows:

Code	*Operator Entered*	*Correction by Typing*
LN	JONHSON	*JOHNSON

Entering Data

1. Turn ON—LINE switch to OFF (lower right corner).
2. FORMAT tape on CASSETTE—1 transport.
3. Erased SCRATCH tape on CASSETTE—2 transport. Tabs closed.
4. Bottom four switches (no.'s 12, 13, 14, 15) to LOCAL.
5. CASSETTE—1 to PLAYBACK and CASSETTE—2 to RECORD (switch no. 3).
6. Rewind both cassettes and press switches 2 and 5 to LOAD/FF.
7. RECORD CONTROL switch (no. 11) ON.
8. TAPE FORMAT switch (no. 9) to CONT.

Terminal is now ready for entry through the keyboard

9. Strike CTRL key and T key simultaneously.
10. Enter data. At end repeat CTRL/T.
11. After last transaction create dummy end record.
12. After typing END TRANSMISSION in MS field strike CTRL/T, CTRL/B, CTRL/S, RUBOUTS.
13. RECORD CONTROL switch (no. 11) OFF.

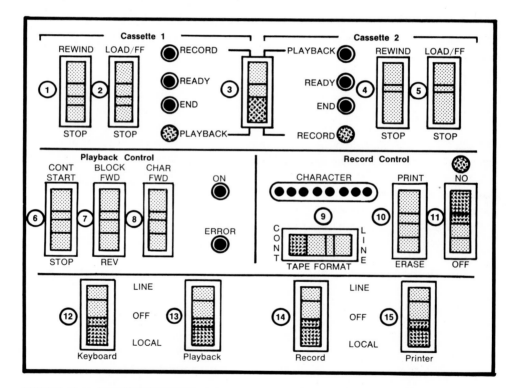

FIGURE 11–11. DOCUMENTATION—HOW TO ENTER DATA. (Courtesy of Blue Cross of Florida, Inc.)

If the error is detected in a preceding field, the operator enters a plus sign to void the record and then retypes the entered message, beginning with the "PC."

Evaluation of the System

Did the system meet the objectives? It was compatible with the present system. The data, however, can be transmitted at 120 characters per second as compared to the 10 characters per second for the previous terminals. As far as appearance, you may judge for yourself. Do they look professional and well suited to a hospital environment?

With the documentation and the training sessions that were provided, the operators had very little trouble adjusting to the new system. Both the patients and the hospital personnel reported that they were favorably impressed by the new system. The time required to process claims was decreased by one day.

Using a cassette to store the format for data to be entered presents a challenge to provide additional applications.

When the system was first installed, 5% of the input contained errors. The error rate is decreasing due to the constant analysis of the type of errors being made. Once it has been determined what kind of errors recur most frequently, special assistance is given to the operators in order to solve the problem.

The long-range plans include expanding the terminals into physicians' offices and additional applications using the terminals. When the communication controllers are added, remote control and continuous polling, rather than polling only during the evening, will be possible. This would also provide for the reduction of the 370's time needed to process the data which is received from the terminals.

DO YOU KNOW THE ANSWERS?

11–35. When the data recorded on cassette 2 is to be transmitted during the evening hours, why is a scratch tape put on cassette 1?

11–36. How long did the study take?

11–37. When were terminals first used by Blue Cross of Florida?

11–38. Why was the system so well received by the hospital employees who worked as operators?

11–39. What is the printer used for?

11–40. Discuss the statement: At the time Blue Cross of Florida defined their needs as a cassette/printer terminal, there were many different models to choose from.

11–41. Why was it necessary to do a systems study in this area?

BASIC

BASIC, which is the acronym for *Beginner's All-purpose Symbolic Instruction Code*, was developed by John C. Kemeny of Dartmouth College for use on its GE 235 computer system. Because of its easy-to-learn features, BASIC has been made available for many other types of computers. The language, therefore, is a machine-independent, high-level language that can be easily learned. Although it is a simple language, well-suited to time-sharing, it does have the ability to do complex mathematical problems. Remember, it was one of the two languages for use on the very small System/3, and was recommended for the user's problem-solving applications.

Although BASIC was developed for use on terminals, if possible, long problems should be punched into tape or cards and then transmitted to the computer by means of a common carrier. Programs that are to be executed frequently, should be stored in the library, available for the time-sharing user, and called into the computer's memory for execution from the terminal.

The original BASIC language contains very few *words* which are used to compose the BASIC *statements*. BASIC does, however, contain powerful arithmetical facilities, many language diagnostics, several editing features, a library of common mathematical and matrix functions, and simple input and output procedures.

BASIC *was designed for the individual who knew nothing about the computer and yet wanted to use it as a "tool" in solving mathematical problems.*

Basic Syntax

Although not all of the syntax will be presented, you will obtain enough background in BASIC to write a few simple, short programs by studying the rules and examples that are provided. As with most programming languages, there are differences in the compilers used for BASIC, and what might be allowable on one computer is not part of the language syntax used for the second computer.

A few of the general rules will be covered before the BASIC words and statements are explained.

1. All statements should be numbered. The statement number provides a point of reference and may be used in branching statements.
2. The following operators are used for the arithmetic commands:

+	Addition	LET A = X + Y
−	Subtraction	LET A = X − Y
*	Multiplication	LET T = A * B
/	Division	LET X = A / B
↑	Exponentiation	LET X = A ↑ 2

3. The priority of the arithmetic operators, ranked from the highest to the lowest is:

   a. ↑   b. / and *   c. + and −

   Note: As with other languages, if two operators of the same value are used in the expression, the mathematics is accomplished from left to right.

4. Data names can contain one letter which may be followed by a number.
5. Constants may be either numeric or alphabetic.
   a. Numeric constants may be an *integer,* such as 10, or a *real* constant which contains a decimal point. For example, .3333 and 48.76 are real constants.
   b. Alphabetic constants may be used for headings, explanation of the meaning of an answer, or as indication that the program ended satisfactorily:

   "SOLVING FOR INCOME TAX"
   "FEDERAL TAX ="
   "END OF PROBLEM 8"

6. In testing conditions, the BASIC language recognizes the following rational operators. In some versions of BASIC the symbol may be used, whereas other versions require the use of the letters.

Symbol	Letters	
>	GT	Greater than
>=	GE	Greater than or equal to
<	LT	Less than
<=	LE	Less than or equal to
<>	NE	Not equal to
=	=	Equal to

The BASIC words and statements illustrated will enable you to construct a simple program.

Word | Usage and Illustration

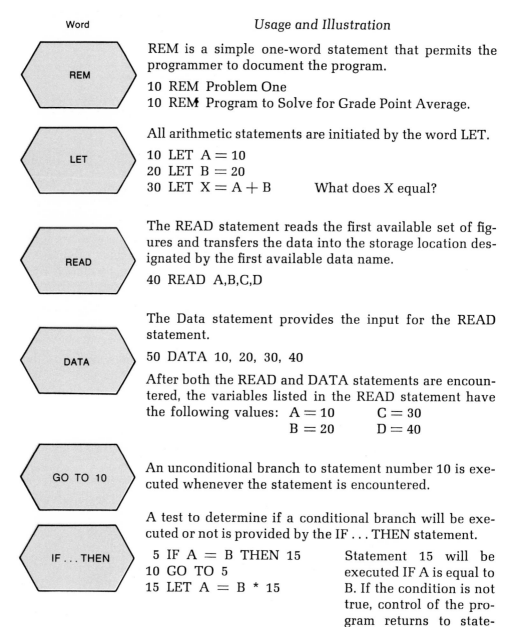

REM is a simple one-word statement that permits the programmer to document the program.

10 REM Problem One
10 REM Program to Solve for Grade Point Average.

All arithmetic statements are initiated by the word LET.

10 LET A = 10
20 LET B = 20
30 LET X = A + B   What does X equal?

The READ statement reads the first available set of figures and transfers the data into the storage location designated by the first available data name.

40 READ A,B,C,D

The Data statement provides the input for the READ statement.

50 DATA 10, 20, 30, 40

After both the READ and DATA statements are encountered, the variables listed in the READ statement have the following values: A = 10   C = 30
                                                                            B = 20   D = 40

An unconditional branch to statement number 10 is executed whenever the statement is encountered.

A test to determine if a conditional branch will be executed or not is provided by the IF . . . THEN statement.

 5 IF A = B THEN 15   Statement 15 will be
10 GO TO 5   executed IF A is equal to
15 LET A = B * 15   B. If the condition is not
                             true, control of the program returns to statement 5.

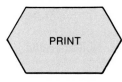

The PRINT statement may be used to print both variables and constants.

10 READ A, B	Read two variables, A and B.
20 DATA 10, 20	A will equal 10 and B 20 after the statement is executed.
30 LET X = A + B	X will equal 30 after the statement is executed.
40 PRINT "THE ANS IS," X	Printed will be: THE ANS IS 30
50 END	Program is terminated.
RUN	Control transfers to the computer. The commands are translated to machine language, the program executes and THE ANS IS 30 types on the terminal.

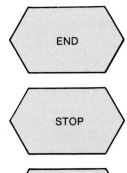

Every BASIC program must be terminated with an END statement.

The STOP statement terminates the execution of a program.

The FOR and NEXT are used to initiate and close a loop. The loop starts with the FOR statement and ends with the NEXT statement.

```
10  LET  X = 0
20  FOR  J = 1  TO  100
30  LET  X = X + 10
40  NEXT  J
```

Some simple rules for the FOR statement are:

1. Every FOR statement must have an associated NEXT statement that names the same variable.
2. Any number of statements may appear between FOR and NEXT.

3. FOR loops may be nested, but the inner loops must be completely contained in the outer loop.
4. The variable, J in the example, may not be changed in value by the statements within the loop.

From the commands illustrated, it is apparent that BASIC is a simple language to learn and no knowledge of the computer is required to be able to master the statements. The same techniques apply to the designing and implementation of a problem using BASIC as for any other language. The problem must be defined and a program flowchart constructed.

There are commands that were not covered which allow the programmer to use arrays, functions, subroutines, and other I/O devices for inputting data and writing output. As a student, you should be able to see, after even this brief on introduction to BASIC, that it is an easy language to learn because the rules are so uncomplicated.

REVIEW OF BASIC

11–42. Why was BASIC developed?
11–43. Can BASIC only be used by students who have a complete understanding of how computers function?
11–44. Is BASIC a "powerful" language?
11–45. When is the REM statement used?
11–46. In the BASIC statements used in the text, all arithmetic statements begin with what word?
11–47. Whenever READ statements are used there must also be one or more DATA statements. What is the purpose of the DATA statements?
11–48. What will occur in the program when the "GO TO 15" statement is executed?
11–49. What is wrong with the following statement? IF A = B THEN GO TO 120?
11–50. What closes the loop when the FOR statement is used?
11–51. Is BASIC used on computers that process data in a batch mode rather than in a time-sharing mode?

GLOSSARY OF NEW AND OLD TERMS
TO CHECK YOUR KNOWLEDGE

Addressing. The host computer determines if the terminal is ready to receive a a message.

Check Digit. The final digit of a number which is used in a mathematical formula to determine if the number has been recorded accurately. If wrong digits are used, or if a transposition of digits occur, the error is detected by the computer.

Controller. The controller acts as a buffer between the very slow transmitting device and the computer. Its functions are not clearly defined at the present time. There currently is a trend to have the controller to do more editing and summarizing of the data than what was done earlier by the controllers.

Polling. A method of inquiring whether a terminal has data to be transmitted. The polling can be done by line, by terminal, or by a predetermined priority.

Real-time System. In a real-time system, the results of processing are available in time to have an immediate effect on the transaction.

ANSWERS

ABOUT FIRST SAVINGS AND LOAN (p. 628)

11–1. A real-time system should be utilized to meet their data processing needs.

11–2. A. Software support available
B. Amount of reprogramming which would be necessary
C. Technical support available

11–3. Time and budget

11–4. Service bureau

11–5. An advisory committee which represented 14 different savings and loan associations.

11–6. Nine months

11–7. The balance is entered on the terminal and checked against the balance, which is in the record that is brought into memory from the master file.

11–8. Indexed-sequential

11–9. The interest which he has earned will be automatically added and posted to his passbook as the teller follows the steps outlined for "Investment with Passbook."

11–10. Approximately 40% of the coding deals with checking the validity of input.

11–11. The master file is copied onto a tape file which is then stored in an offsite vault.

11–12. On "live" data by using the master file and the transaction tape. The master file is recreated off the backup file.

11–13. A small computer which can either stand alone or be utilized as part of the 9400 system. It functions as the card reader, punch, and printer.

11–14. When the terminals are online, there is not enough memory left for a batch job of that size. The terminals can be used offline, but then everything has to be entered again because the master files are not updated. The president would be told to wait. It would be a good time to bring in the idea that what is needed is a data base and CRTs—then he could get what he wanted when he wanted it.

11–15. No. During the terminals time-slice the module needed is brought in from the library into the CPU.

11–16. The present terminals are very slow in transmitting data, and they can transmit or receive only numeric data.

REGARDING DOW (p. 638)

11–17. 20 minutes

11–18. Sales Transaction Recording

11–19. There is a great deal of emphasis placed on good documentation at Dow. Since there is not always continuity of personnel in the project team assigned to a system, the documentation must be such that a new person can understand the entire system by studying the documentation.

11–20. A three-day training session is provided. In addition, each operator has an operator's handbook that provides detailed instructions for the operation of the terminals.

11–21. The terminal operator enters the information, using the sales order as the source document, on the terminal.

11–22. The entire sales order is displayed before the data is transmitted into the system.

11–23. The sales invoice is transmitted back to the point of origin in order that the data on the sales order can be compared to the information on the invoice.

11–24. A. Self-checking numbers.
B. Reasonableness test.
C. Sight checking data as it is entered into the system.
D. Code checking before it is entered by means of the terminal.
E. Comparing the sales order with the completed sales invoice.

11–25. The shipping clerk entered the information from the shipping department's terminal.

11–26. Microfiche is a form of microfilm which may contain up to 270 pages of data. By using the viewer the required data can be rapidly retrieved.

11–27. A. Alternate power supply.
       B. Identification code for console operators.
       C. Backup of master file to tape each day.
       D. Checkpoint restart after each transaction.
       E. Second computer system which can also handle the online trans-actions.
11–28. Yes. A few of the memory requirements for features such as HASP were cited, which, by implication, should indicate the complexity of the operating system.
11–29. RJE's are used to read the corrected statement into the source program, which is stored in the test library.
11–30. A sudden loss of power can damage the hardware plus result in a loss of data.
11–31. After each transaction.
11–32. Yes! It should be apparent that there is a great deal of expertise involved in the development of the STR system. Dow has used unit-record equipment and first-, second-, and third-generation computers.
11–33. Yes. The manager reports to the executive vice president, who is also director of the United States area operations.
11–34. HASP is one part for the total operating system that is responsible for SPOOLing.

DO YOU KNOW THE ANSWERS? (p. 645)

11–35. During the evening, replies will be transmitted from the computer system to the terminal. These replies are written on cassette 1 which has been labeled with "replies" and the current date.
11–36. Two years
11–37. 1960
11–38. Possible answers were included: training sessions, ease of following documentation, terminals were quiet and easy to operate.
11–39. Printed report serves as a record of what was actually transmitted to Blue Cross of Florida. Replies that are sent back are confirmation, or status, of claims.
11–40. This statement is false. Selection was limited and required participation of various vendors.
11–41. A. Growth of number of claims
       B. Improved technology possible
       C. Southern Bell couldn't upgrade their present system

11–42. BASIC was developed as a time-sharing language by John Kemeny of Dartmouth College.

11–43. No. BASIC was designed as a simple language that could be learned easily *by beginners*.

11–44. BASIC is a very powerful language. The newer versions, referred to as BASIC "plus" or "extended" BASIC, have even more powerful features than the original Dartmouth BASIC.

11–45. The REM statement is used to introduce remarks into the program. The remarks can be called "internal documentation" and are there to help the programmer remember what the variables mean and what the various sections of the program are designed to accomplish.

11–46. LET. However some versions of BASIC now permit the programmer to omit the "Let" from the arithmetic statements.

11–47. The DATA statement contains the value to be associated with the variable named in the READ statement.

11–48. When the GO TO 15 statement is executed the control of the program branches unconditionally to the command stored at the address assigned to statement number 15.

11–49. The statement "IF A = B THEN GO TO 120" is invalid as the "GO TO" is not part of the IF statement. The statement should read IF A = B THEN 120.

11–50. The "loop" established by using the FOR statement is closed with the NEXT statement.

11–51. Yes. An increasing number of computers now have BASIC compilers.

REFLECTIONS AND TRENDS   12

The original Neiman-Marcus store in Dallas, Texas, has long had the reputation of having unique speciality items for the man or woman on your Christmas list who has everything. There is generally a fine gift item available at one of the Neiman-Marcus stores that they do not have! One such item, Honeywell's Kitchen Computer, for the hard-to-buy-for lady on your list, appeared in their 1969 Christmas book under the caption: "If she can only cook as well as Honeywell can compute." One of the news releases read:

> MENU MAGIC—Truly a gift for the housewife who has almost everything is this Honeywell mini-computer featured in the 1969 Neiman-Marcus Christmas catalog. For just $10,600—which includes a two-week course in programming know-how—the lady who finds this kitchen computer under the tree can not only keep track of her household accounts, but by pushing a couple of buttons can obtain a scientifically planned menu with options for dieters and fussy eaters. If substitutions are desired, just push another button, as Sunny Griffin is doing in the picture, and out come other suggestions. Milady also can program her favorite recipes into the small computer and save hunting for "that recipe in one of those books over there."

FIGURE 12–1. HONEYWELL'S KITCHEN COMPUTER. (Courtesy of Neiman-Marcus.)

Unfortunately for the ladies, none of the kitchen computers were sold when they were listed in the Christmas book for 1969. What if they are again advertised at a price that is a little more within the reach of the average shopper?

Will there eventually be a computer center in every home? In 1967, the March 15 issue of *Forbes* quotes an executive of Texas Instruments, who estimates that the home in the future may contain as much as $10,000 worth of electronic devices. The prediction is also made that by 1980 the market for such equipment will challenge the auto industry for the largest single share of the consumer's income.

How can the equipment be used? The Honeywell Kitchen Computer ad already illustrates that it is a reality now that the computer could be used in menu planning and household budgeting. Other household members, upon learning the programming language, could use the computer to solve any type of mathematical problem.

It is also a reality *today* that students can have a terminal in their home connected to a university's computer which would permit them to take advantage of both the center's data base and software. The terminal need be no more than an inexpensive touch-tone unit that can be attached to any telephone. Unless a printer were available on the student's terminal, the computer center would need an audio-response system to respond to the student's inquiry.

When portable terminals were discussed, it was indicated that salesmen and consultants might well bring a terminal with them when they call on clients. The degree to which they can actually access and utilize information depends upon their company's software and data base. The full potential of the computer is just a phone call away.

The computer industry is now at the crossroads! To better understand the route that might be taken, it is important that you understand the events that have occurred, as well as exactly where the industry now stands.

WHERE HAVE WE BEEN?

It is strange that both the punched card and Lou's business started to function in the year 1888! Certainly Dr. Hollerith, when he designed the card to automate the simple job of summarizing data for the U.S. Census Bureau, had no way of comprehending the wide range of uses that his punched card would ultimately be assigned.

Lou could not have envisioned the extent to which his simple logging business would have expanded until eventually it became a vast corporation with an extremely diversified product line and more than 200 branch operations. Since not all of the changes that occurred in Lou's company have been covered in the text, a summary of the major events is included to bring you up to the present. Many companies have developed in their utilization of data processing in much the same way as did the L. C. Smith Corporation which:

1. Started as a small sole proprietorship with a very limited need for data processing.
2. Expanded to the point where manual methods used for data processing were no longer capable of providing the information which management needed to effectively manage the company.
3. Utilized mechanical devices, such as typewriters, posting machines, billing machines, and calculators, along with accounting systems which used the "write it once principle," to fill their data processing needs.
4. Skipped the first-generation computers because they felt only the "industrial giants" in the late 1940s and 1950s could economically justify their usage.

5. Used both punched card data processing and the service of a service bureau to effectively process their increased volume of data.
6. Invested in a second-generation computer, which had a limited amount of memory, was programmed in an assembler language, and utilized as peripheral equipment only punched card I/O and the printer.
7. Updated their data processing system by acquiring a third-generation computer which utilized a DOS (Disk Operating System), which was controlled by a supervisor which resided in the computer's memory. Due to better communications between the computer and the operator, more throughput was obtained. There was also far less idle CPU time. In addition, random access disk files and sequential tape drives were added to the system. Smith's programmers now had their choice of three powerful compiler languages to use: FORTRAN, COBOL, and PL/I.
8. Added more memory, faster I/O devices, and a full operating system which made multiprogramming possible.
9. Acquired an IBM 370 computer which was capable of utilizing virtual storage. Program segments were swapped back and forth between real and virtual drum memory. Larger programs could be written since there seemed to be, under VS, an unlimited amount of memory. Although each program took a little longer to execute, the throughput was again increased. Since their feasibility study indicated that COM (Computer Output to Microfilm) would be an effective method to use in distribution of their price and parts lists, they entered into a contract with a service bureau to use their magnetic tape output to produce microfiche. A key-to-disk system, controlled by a minicomputer, was installed for recording source data onto magnetic tape.
10. Is now involved in a systems study to determine if
    a. a time-sharing system, which would centralize their entire data processing operation, can be economically justified;
    b. a second computer should be acquired which would process the information from the terminals and act as the "slave" to the "master" computer, or if one large computer should be used to meet all of the needs of the company.

REVIEW QUESTIONS

12–1. What unusual item did Neiman-Marcus offer in their 1969 Christmas book?
12–2. Why do you feel that none were sold, other than the price might have been beyond the reach of the "average" shopper?

12–3. List the various phases that the L. C. Smith Corporation went through in the development of their data processing system.

12–4. How will the microfiche be used?

12–5. What is the scope of the systems study in which the L. C. Smith Corporation is currently involved?

WHERE ARE WE NOW?

Since it is predicted that by 1978, 65% of all computers will have terminals, many companies must *now* be involved in system studies similar to the one L. C. Smith is presently conducting. The companies doing such studies are focusing their attention on two major areas.

1. *Hardware and Software Selection.* Selection of the CPU and the related software which will most effectively meet their data processing needs may require an intensive study over an extended period of time. After studying module 10 it should be very apparent that the computer system derives as much, or more, of its ability from its software as it does from its hardware.

2. *Source Data Entry into the System.* An intensive study will be made by many companies to determine if it is economically feasible to utilize some I/O device which will permit the entry of the data into the system, without transcription, from the point where the transaction is occurring.

Hardware

Today, in many different areas such as retailing, banking, education, research, transportation, and manufacturing there are both "systems" and I/O devices available that can provide for the entry of the data into the system *when* and *where* it occurs.

Terminals can be defined as any device that is used to communicate *with* the computer. At the present time there are numerous *"point of sale"* *systems* which utilize either a wand, another type of scanner, or the cash register to enter the sales transaction directly into the system. Simultaneously, sales, accounts receivable, and inventory can all be updated. The banking industry has been another major area where several manufacturers have recently announced both new hardware and software for online real-time systems. In laboratories, manufacturing, education, hospitals, and in many other areas new terminals are being developed to meet specific needs. The terminals may be either a *sensor* or a digital device. (A sensor is a device that receives and responds to a signal or stimulus.)

A great deal of emphasis has been placed upon improving the "old faithful" I/O media: cards, tape, disk, and printed output. For example, contrast the early keypunch to the modern 129 Data Recorder which can accumulate up to six different control fields of data; be used as either a keypunch, verifier, or interpreter; store the program formats for six different jobs; and buffer data which permits the operator to make corrections.

Magnetic tape and disk have not only increased in the density with which data can be stored but have dramatically decreased the access time which is required to retrieve the data. New forms, such as magnetic tape cassettes and the "floppy" disk, were developed to meet specific needs.

Renewed interest developed in the use of the scanner and mark readers, especially when they are used in conjunction with terminals and time-sharing. Many of the major manufacturers have developed improved scanners and readers which process both original and turnaround documents.

Improved methods have been developed for working with COM, which may make it possible for more companies to justify its use as an output media.

The performance of today's CPUs is almost unbelievable. Perhaps you now are beginning to believe that the UNIVAC 1108 outperforms human beings at the rate of ten million to one. Maybe you also share Dr. Hammer's feelings that "we are dealing here with a power that is inconceivable to the human mind." You may also agree with Dr. Hammer that it "is the greatest challenge that has ever faced mankind."

Today, however, there are two worlds: the world of the minicomputer and the world of the "supercomputer."

WHAT IS A MINI?

The first minicomputers were introduced in 1962 in the aerospace industry, and included such machines as the Arma Micro Computer, the Burroughs D210, and the Univac Add-100. Commercial minicomputers manufactured by Honeywell, Scientific Control Corporation, Xerox Data Systems, and Systems Engineering Laboratories appeared on the market in 1966. It was not until 1970 that IBM made its entry into the mini market with the System/7. Today there are more than 50 firms that manufacture computers which may be classified as minis, with the leading manufacturers being Digital Equipment Corporation, Varian, Hewlett-Packard, and the Computer Control Division of Honeywell.

There is no one simple definition for a "mini." There are, however, some common characteristics that apply to computers which can be classified as minis. The minicomputer is usually defined in terms of price, physical size, memory capacity, and word length. Today, although a computer may meet the general qualifications related to the term mini, the performance of the machine may be much greater than what the name would imply.

Characteristics of Minicomputers

In the late 1960s a mini was defined as a computer which was priced under $50,000. Although the performance of the minis has dramatically increased, the cost has substantially decreased so that a more reasonable figure to use in the definition would be $20,000—or less.

The minicomputer's data and instructions may be stored by using magnetic core, thin film, or semiconductor memories. The memory size is generally quoted as ranging from 1,000 to 65,000 *words*. The two most popular word sizes are 8 and 16 bits. In a 16-bit machine each 16 bits is an *addressable* unit or word.

The minicomputer performs exceedingly well for it generally has fast processing rates, relatively short word lengths, and versatile input-output structures. The cost of a mini is in direct relationship to the word length, number of instructions, and degree of versatility of the input-output structure.

Read Only Memory

Minicomputer manufacturers frequently make use of *read only memory* (ROM). The ROM is a method of storing data in a permanent (nonerasable) form which may be part of the basic hardware or an optional feature of the minicomputer selected for a given application. ROM is faster and cheaper than either magnetic core or semiconductor memory and can be utilized in two different ways:

1. To store, protect, and decrease the execution time of programs and execute routines that allocate the processor's time to either application programs or frequently used subroutines.
2. To store microprograms that define the processor's instruction set. In this case, every instruction is a permanent subroutine in a ROM.

If every instruction is a wired-in subroutine in a ROM, a different set of computer instructions may be obtained by changing the ROM. At one time, ROMs were wired at the factory to execute the programs specified by the users. After shipment to the user, the ROMs were practically impossible to modify. Today, however, many of the minis allow reprogramming of the

ROMs in the field by either the user or the manufacturer's customer engineer. The read only memory provides a very powerful tool for the computer designer as it:

1. Costs much less than the standard read-write core memory.
2. Is five to ten times faster than read-write core.
3. Is more reliable because the program is protected from overwriting.

Read only memory is employed by different minicomputers in varying degrees. The memory of a dedicated computer may consist primarily of ROM. It is anticipated that an increasing number of minicomputers will be programmed for one specific task, such as medical filing and accounting, law office paperwork, small engineering programs, inventory control, sales accounting, and so forth, in which case extensive use would be made of ROM.

Frequently, a minicomputer is described as being a 19-inch cube. The Honeywell 700 minicomputer which is being given a pre-customer checkout (see fig. 12–2) by a technician, is 11-inches high, 19-inches wide, and 22-inches deep. The dimensions given are enough space to contain logic, a sizable portion of memory core, and the power supply unit.

THE RUGGED MINI

The "mighty minis" are rugged! Minis are designed to withstand environmental and operational conditions that would bring an ordinary computer to a quick halt. The mini continues to perform through high and low temperatures, shock, vibration, high altitude, and contaminated atmospheres. For example, it is not unusual for a mini to have a 10° to 50° C operating range. Many ordinary applications, which the minicomputer will be assigned, subject the computer to a wide temperature variation. In a geargrinding shop, where one mini "works," the morning temperature is 30° F, and after the heat-treating furnaces are fired up the temperature increases to about 100° F.

All modern minicomputers are vibration and shock-tested to ensure that parts don't fall off under normal operating conditions. The shock tests are simple—the machine is hit with a hammer or dropped from a height. Throughout the tests the computer is expected to continue to perform its function.

Many minis are expected to function in environments that contain airborne contamination such as dust or iron filings. While most conventional computers function in humidity controlled atmospheres, the mini is provided no such luxury and must continue to execute its programs in areas where the

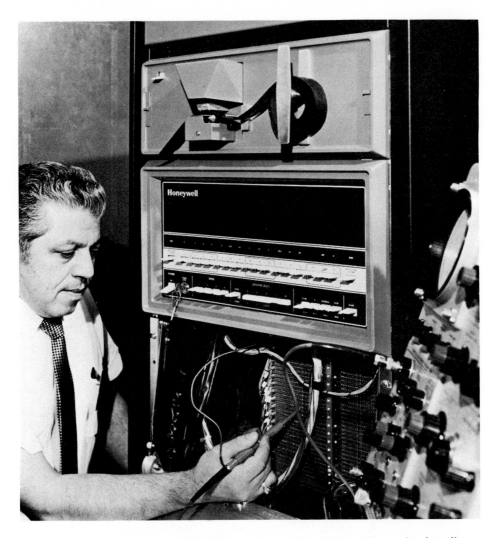

FIGURE 12–2. PRE-CUSTOMER CHECKOUT—A Honeywell technician takes a signal reading on a System 700 minicomputer prior to shipment from the firm's plant in Framingham, Mass., where the systems are being built. The System 700 family includes eight functional systems for sensor, communications, and multipurpose use. (Courtesy of Honeywell.)

humidity may be close to 100%. The mini must also be insensitive to both electromagnetic and radio-frequency interference. The mini, however, must not emit excessive radio-frequency noise which might affect other instrumentation.

Some manufacturers may provide both a "rugged" mini, which is built to the specifications necessary for its use in the shop or in the field by the military, and a "dressed-up" mini (for commercial applications) which does not meet the rigid standards of its "rugged" counterpart.

Usually the minicomputer with a small amount of memory must be programmed in an assembler language, although for the larger minis FORTRAN, BASIC, and RPG are often available. Until IBM's entry into the mini market, many of the manufacturers did not provide software support, therefore much of existing software was developed by users' groups. Now, however, an increasing amount of software is available as part of the mini's "package."

MINI QUESTIONS

12–6.   What would be a sensor terminal?
12–7.   What are the characteristics of a computer classified as a "mini?"
12–8.   Was IBM a "leader" in the minicomputer world?
12–9.   Are most minicomputers manufactured by the "big" computer manufacturers?
12–10. What is a word?
12–11. What is ROM?
12–12. Do the minicomputer manufacturers usually supply the software for their computers?

WHERE ARE THE MINIS?

By the end of 1972 minicomputers accounted for 54% of the total number of computers in use, as compared with 40% in 1971. It has been predicted that within the decade there will be a 400% market growth in the use of the minicomputer. While the industrial usage of the minicomputer at one time accounted for more than half of its applications, the *estimated* breakdown in 1972, according to an article in *Business Automation,* was:

	Percentage
Industrial	40
Laboratory	20
Commercial	15
All Others	25

The commercial and other usage of the minicomputer is increasing perhaps more rapidly than the other areas. In the "all others" group you are apt to find the mini *anywhere.* In *Computerworld,* an article reported on a mini-computer which was "bowling over" the league secretaries at Dolphin Lanes in Broward County, Florida. According to the Dolphin Lanes proprietor, Herm Tilman, two days work for a secretary using the computer is reduced to 40 minutes. Eight cents is charged for each bowler's record, and if the volume of bowlers reaches 5,000 a week, the project will break even.

What are some of the other unusual tasks that are assigned to the "minis"? The following list will give you an idea of the range of activity that the "mighty mini" is engaged in.

Dr. Ronald L. Webster, associate professor of psychology at Hollins College in Roanoke, Virginia, is using a mini in the treatment of stuttering. Presently, the computer is working as a judge of speech sound accuracy. The stutterer does the exercises in a programmed text while the computer listens, tells him whether he is correct or not, and signals when to go to the next step. It is anticipated that performance goals will be developed which must be met by the student at each step of the program.

In Australia a computer-controlled slot machine monitoring system is being used to detect illegal manipulation of the machines, and can also assist the club's manager in his accounting duties.

Datamation reports that the minicomputers are getting smarter. A Data General Supernova minicomputer check-mated an IBM 360/91 in just 25 moves. The Supernovas had a memory capacity of 32K, while the IBM system had a capacity of more than 2 million bytes. The match held at Columbia University was between the Supernova, owned by the Department of Electrical Engineering and Computer Science, and the IBM computer, which belongs to Columbia's computer center.

In England, a Honeywell mini has been operating an experimental driver-less taxi. The passenger inserts a magnetically encoded ticket into a slot in the taxi and he is swished to his destination. The article in the July 1973 *Datamation* did not report on the driving record of the mini!

The Prughs of Silver Spring, Maryland, have a minicomputer in their home. Thomas Prugh, who is an electronics engineer, has had the mini doing just about everything in his home—computing taxes, preparing menus, and assisting his children with their homework. He believes that it should be the basis of a home control center and should be able to open and close the windows and garage door, answer the telephone, and do a variety of other routine household activities.

A PDP-8 by Digital Equipment Corporation was set up in Scotland to control an automated potato picker.

In the Institute of Human Physiology at the University of Bologna, in Italy, an eight-thousand word memory computer is being used to conduct experiments relating to the neurons in the optic nerve system to light stimuli.

In the Pacific Northwest a minicomputer-based system is helping to prevent needless destruction of trees along power line routes. The U.S. Department of the Interior is using a minicomputer to help calculate precisely which trees along the patches of high-voltage power lines must be cut because they endanger the power lines.

The rugged Honeywell DDP-516s are aboard U.S. Coast Guard cutters that act as weather gathering stations. Since the balloon-tracking weather activities are normally conducted only four times daily, other duties have been assigned the DDP-516, such as oceanographic research, navigational activities, assisting in helicopter landings, and as satellite data reduction stations.

In the Food Fair Store in Baldwin Hills, California, the mini is linked to the cash register to produce a totally new control system. The ticket on each item is color coded by departments. Rather than entering the price of the product, the clerk enters the item number. Since 60% of all sales are groceries, the system is programmed to assume a grocery sale unless the clerk indicates that it is other than groceries. A display panel on the register flashes the correct price so that it is readable to both the customer and the clerk. Items that are charged for by the pound are weighed and the total price is displayed for the customer.

For taxable items, as determined by the code, the correct amount of tax is automatically charged. The customer at the completion of the transaction is given an accurate detailed record of the transaction which includes the item code number and the price for each purchase. The inventories are instantaneously updated which allow accurate electronic ordering. The manager, by using a MID (Managers Interrogation Device), can determine the inventory on hand of any product. The minicomputer in charge of the entire operation is a Honeywell DDP-516 with a 4K memory that can be expanded up to 16K.

The unusual applications listed are only a beginning, as the minicomputer is also found sorting trash, at baseball games and horse races, in the air, controlling shipping on the St. Lawrence River, and in mines checking the safety factor of the mines' roofs. Digital Equipment Corporation and Data General have the longest list of unusual applications. Some of the other manufacturers have increased their sales but only in the more traditional areas.

MORE MINI QUESTIONS

12–13. According to the article in *Business Automation*, what area or application utilized the mini the most in 1972?
12–14. In 1973 what percent of the computers were minis?

FIGURE 12–3. Located in the factory are two CIP/2200 minis (pictured on the right), two 10-mega
byte disk storage devices and the card reader. Throughout the plant are other input/
output terminals which are also part of the Process Control Division's inventory
and production control system. (Courtesy of Cincinnati Milacron)

12–15. Be able to discuss this statement: minicomputers are used for only a
very few scientific applications.

12–16. What does the term "dedicated" mini mean?

INDUSTRIAL APPLICATIONS

The minicomputer is probably used most extensively in industrial applications in the following three areas:

1. *Numerical Control.* The computer is used to control the operations of automatic machines, such as drilling or boring machines.
2. *Process Control.* The computer is used for the automatic regulation of operations or processes. The operation control is applied continuously in order to keep the value of a variable constant. Adjustments to regulate the operations are under the direct control of the computer.
3. *Recording.* Recording information pertaining to production at the source where the transaction occurs.

Numerical Control

In using numerical control for directing the operations of a milling machine, a computer program is written by an individual who understands: the milling machine; the design of the part to be produced; the tool speeds; and the characteristics of the metal being used. The programmer must also know the computer language that will be used for writing the programs. Before the program is written the data is entered on a chart of coordinates, which will make the coding of the computer program relatively easy.

The computer translates the program into a series of commands which are punched into a control tape that will be used to direct the milling machine in producing the desired parts. Such techniques apply not only to very small, close-tolerance parts, but also to large components which could be ruined by a single mistake in a long operation.

When the first tape is produced it must be "debugged" and tested the same as any other computer program. The milling machine operator and the programmer go through the operations together and make any required changes in the program. The computer would again be used to produce a corrected tape. There are several advantages in using numerical control, one of which is that all parts produced using a given tape will match perfectly.

Process Control

Plastic injection molding machines are utilized today for manufacturing everything from buttons to car bumpers, from hard hats to camera lenses. Several of the mini manufacturers have both the hardware and the software to control plastic injection molding manufacturing processes. In order to manufacture parts that will pass inspection at each stage of the manufacturing processing, the temperature and cavity pressure within the machine must be accurately controlled. Within each cycle (the time that it takes to mold one part within the cavity of the machine) the temperature and pressure must gradually increase to a given point and then decrease for the cooling part of the cycle.

Figure 12–4 illustrates the basic concept of the process, and indicates the greater degree of accuracy that can be obtained when the process is controlled by the minicomputer. On the diagram, "time" indicates the length of time that it takes to produce one part. The "PSI," or pounds of pressure per square inch, starts at zero and returns to zero after the part is produced. It is essential that the correct pressure is maintained at each processing stage. Sensors are used which constantly feed information pertaining to the cavity pressure and temperature into the computer. If the deviation is greater than the tolerance indicated on the diagram, the computer immediately calculates the needed

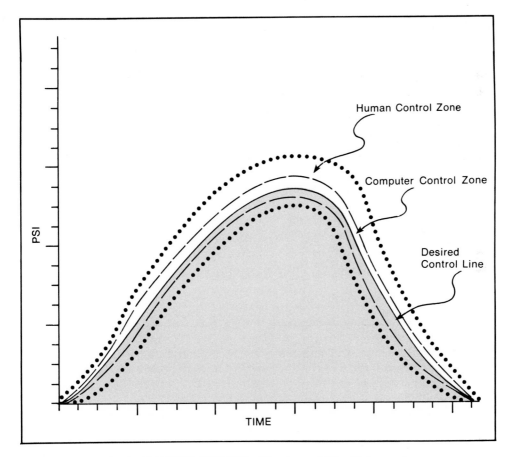

FIGURE 12–4. CAVITY PRESSURE CONTROL. (Courtesy of Glen E. Leeson.)

adjustment. The computer's response, as indicated by the much smaller computer control zone, is far faster than an operator's response would be if he were assigned the task of watching gauges or dials and had to make the proper adjustments based upon the readings he observed. The variation due to human response is shown by the much wider "Human Control Zone." The optimum, or desired pressure, is the "Desired Control Line."

Before the plastic injection molding machines were controlled by the minicomputer there was too much setup time required, material wasted, operator intervention required, and "down time."

Plastic injection molding is used as an illustration of process control for a number of different reasons. It is a relatively simple example of an application where sensors are used to detect a change in a physical condition under which a product is manufactured. When the change causes a deviation from the allowable tolerance, corrective action is set in motion by the computer, which reacts far faster to the stimuli than could an individual. A second reason for using the example is that it illustrates the point made that minicomputer manufacturers are now developing the software necessary to support the mini in *very precise applications*. For example, IBM's software for their plastic injection molding "package" for the System/7 is really two applications in one. It not only monitors and controls the temperature and pressure of the cavity, but also provides production statistics on cavity pressure, cycle count, and cycle time statistics.

The manner in which IBM made their presentation at "Profitability thru Productivity," in Detroit, Michigan, also is an indication of a change in the world of computers. At one time, management might have accepted that "it will produce a better product" or it "will very soon pay for itself" as rationale for investing in a computer. Today management wants more precise facts on what can be expected from the computerized system. IBM presented the following benefits which were the actual averages compiled from field testing the System/7 by a number of different users:

CONTROL BENEFITS PROVIDED BY THE SYSTEM/7	AVERAGE FOR PARTICIPATING COMPANIES
Reduced Cycle Time	15%
Increased Utilization of Equipment	4%
Reduced Setup Time	1.5%
Reduced Scrap	1.5%

The justification for the equipment was based upon the fact that *on an average* the machines became anywhere from 5 to 15% more productive. The costs, based upon one System/7 controlling ten machines, for both the hardware and software was broken down to the cost per hour per machine which, at the time of the presentation, resulted in 54 cents for the first year and 26 cents for the second year. The second year costs are much less because the entire cost of the software and machine setup expense is prorated over the first year. Mathematically, it was determined that the cost of the system will be paid for if there is a 1.3% increase in normal productivity. Any increase above 1.3% will result in a profit to the company on their investment in the computerized system. This is the type of justification that management looks for today when an investment is being considered in any computer.

Sensor-based minicomputers are ideal for a wide range of applications in processing and manufacturing control. The range of specific applications is tremendous and includes additional fields such as hospital patient monitoring, camera film manufacturing, papermaking, laboratory data acquisition, steel making, glass manufacturing, and weather observations.

Recording Data from the Shop Floor

The information based upon the study made of the Dow Chemical Company indicated that it was their philosophy to record data when and where the event or transaction was occurring. One of the illustrations was of a terminal in the freight room, which permitted the clerk to add the freight to the customer's record directly from the shipping room.

Many other companies have the same philosophy, and it is not uncommon to find the minicomputer out in the factory, where the raw materials and labor factors can be applied to the cost of the product at the same time as they are physically added to the product (timely, relevent information).

IBM has developed the necessary software, referred to as a transaction processor, to enable the System/7 to be used to process information from data collection devices. The devices are used to record both the material and labor that is applied to production.

The 2791 Area Station can be used to either record data into the system or retrieve production information from the system. The area station is kept simple to operate so that no special training is needed to utilize the 2791. It is both durable and rugged. The keys are also large enough, and spaced in such a manner, that an employee in the shop has no difficulty entering data.

The area station operates in a "conversational mode," for when any of the large function keys, such as "stock in," are depressed the employee's instructions are displayed in the center of the panel.

In the illustration an employee has just depressed the "attend" key which caused the instruction "Insert Badge" to appear in the center of the panel. The time that the employee is starting on the job is 0830, which automatically displays on the bottom of the panel.

If raw materials are to be added to job number 123, the employee would depress the "Stock Out" key which would cause the instructions, which the employee must follow, to appear on the panel. A prepunched and interpreted card for the material being added to the production is inserted into the card read slot at the top right of the area station. The variable information (quantity and job department number) keyed in by the employee is displayed automatically on the panel for verification. A "clear" key is available, which makes it possible to eradicate any invalid information, since the data does not enter the system until the "Enter" key is used.

The 2791 is durable, simple to operate, and used mostly on the shop floor for adding the appropriate labor cost of production. The system is flexible and can be programmed to display the information pertinent to any given application. Information is recorded into the system at the source where the transaction occurs. Since 60 to 80% of the cost of production is added in the factory, why not record the information at that point? The necessity of transmitting the data to the centralized location and transcribing it into machine processable form is avoided.

The 2791 can also be used to retrieve information from the system by using the "inquire" key. If the printer shown in figure 12–5 is also avail-

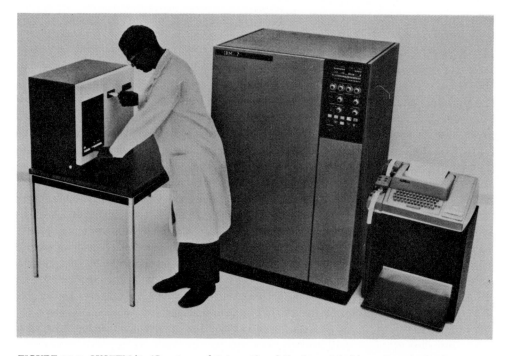

FIGURE 12–5. SYSTEM/7. (Courtesy of International Business Machines Corporation.)

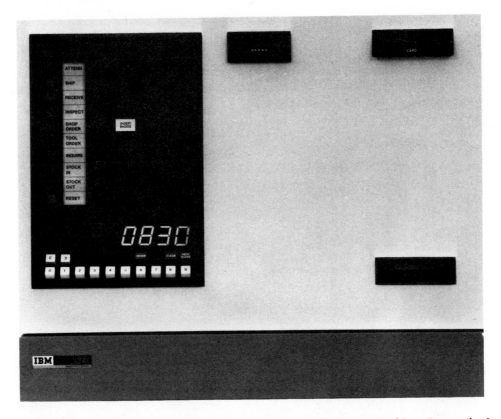

FIGURE 12–6. 2791 AREA STATION. (Courtesy of International Business Machines Corporation.)

able, the response will be printed. For example, the foreman might wish to know how much cost had been added to date to job 419. By inquiring into the system, following the directions which are displayed, the information desired would be almost instantaneously available. What information can be retrieved and how it will be displayed depends upon what provisions were made in the computer program.

The System/7 meets the qualifications for a minicomputer and can function as a standalone system, or it can operate as a satellite processor linked to other IBM computers. The System/7 is organized into 16 bit words which each have 2 additional parity check bits. The smallest memory size available is 2K and the largest currently is 16K. Inside the cabinet that houses the CPU is also the disk storage unit. Depending upon which model is selected, a maximum of approximately 2.5 million characters of information can be stored online by using two disks.

In the two examples given, process control and recording data from the shop floor, the minicomputer is dedicated to those tasks and unavailable for other applications. There are many more industrial applications, such as research and development, design work, drafting, product testing, quality control, inventory management, and monitoring of production lines, that are also assigned to the industrial minicomputer. With the trend developing for the computer manufacturers to develop the necessary software, there will be many other industrial uses.

INDUSTRIAL APPLICATIONS

12–17. How is the computer used in most numerical control applications?

12–18. What is one of the major advantages in using numerical control?

12–19. How does numerical control differ from process control?

12–20. What feeds the data pertaining to the temperature and pressure within a machine to the computer?

12–21. Why are there fewer spoiled parts when the machine is computer controlled rather than operator controlled?

12–22. How precise was IBM when it listed the benefits derived by the users who field tested the System/7 and its plastic injection molding software?

12–23. Why should a minicomputer be on the "shop floor"?

12–24. When data is entered into the system by using the area station that is on the "shop room floor," how does the person entering the data know if it was recorded correctly?

12–25. What devices are used to enter data into the system from the area station?

OTHER MINICOMPUTER APPLICATIONS

Education

Today in education the minicomputer is turning up just about everywhere —in classrooms, laboratories, counseling, and learning resource centers. Figure 12–7 illustrates the use of a minicomputer which is dedicated to computer assisted instruction. Computer Curricula Corporation of Palo Alto, California, has developed the software that makes it possible to use the minicomputer in a number of different subject matter areas. The software tailors each lesson to the student's achievement level and either progress or diffi-

FIGURE 12–7. COMPUTER ASSISTED INSTRUCTION. (Courtesy of Cincinnati Milacron.)

culty is reported to the classroom teacher. The same minicomputer may be used to challenge the very bright student who needs supplemental work or may provide drill and practice work for the student who needs special help in areas of difficulty.

The hardware is all contained in the one cabinet and includes the central processing unit, drum or disk memory, and equipment which makes it possible to use eight or more terminals. A typical system may provide daily instruction for up to 500 students a day.

Computer assisted instruction (CAI) allows the student to communicate with the computer in a conversational mode. After the student is identified, the lesson begins. Since much of the software uses a "systems" approach, each student starts at the point where he previously left off. Therefore each member of the class may be working on a different lesson. How successful computer assisted instruction is depends upon the *software and not upon the hardware*. There have been some outstanding programs developed which enable students to proceed at a much faster rate than they would be able to in a traditional classroom.

Computer assisted instruction, although a fairly recent application for the minicomputer, is not new. As early as 1963, the Education Data Services Department of the Palo Alto Unified School District was given the responsibility for developing the computer's role in education. Inservice training was provided for both faculty and staff in the use of the computer in education. In several different areas it was recognized that the computer had tremendous potential as an instructional device.

In 1966 a computer-based teaching system was developed at Stanford University and used in the Brentwood School in East Palo Alto. In the research project about 150 first-grade students were given a half hour a day online instruction in reading and arithmetic. The students used terminals which allowed them to respond, by using either a light pen or the keyboard, to the questions that were projected on the terminal's screen. If the student responded correctly, the next question was displayed. Wrong answers, or an excessive delay on the part of the student, brought an explanation. The computer kept track of scores, analyzed the results, and provided a progress report for each student. During the same period of time many other research projects were being conducted to determine if the computer could be used effectively as a teaching device.

Since CAI has been in existence for a considerable period of time, why has it not been utilized more frequently? Until it became possible to utilize a minicomputer, it was necessary to: use a large-scale computer exclusively for CAI; or, have a large computer with multiprogramming capabilities available. For the hardware alone the unit-cost *per terminal* was estimated at anywhere from $2.00 to $5.00 an hour. The Stanford research in CAI, cited in the example, had received a large federal grant which made it feasible for the school sytems involved in the project to pursue this form of instruction.

There has also been a lack of really good software for CAI. Today there are several projects, such as PLATO, which is sponsored by the University of Illinois, and Dartmouth's Time-Sharing system which are encouraging the development and *sharing* of the necessary software. More software is also available today from commercial companies such as the Computer Curricula Corporation.

In the counseling center the student interacts with the computer in finding out about various occupations in which he might be interested. The student is asked by the computer to respond to a series of questions. After the answers are analyzed by the computer, a list of vocations that the student might be interested in pursuing is either displayed or printed. Some systems will also have available audio tapes and printed materials to provide the student with additional information. The success of the system again is dependent upon the software. The program must be written in such a way as to allow the student to enter enough variables so that the analysis is meaningful. Timely, relevant data must be available in the online storage in order to provide the student with worthwhile information.

Think about the program flowchart which would be needed to code the problem. The student enters many different variables that must be matched against the qualifications cited for anywhere from 300 to 400 different vocations. The vocations that the student seems most qualified for will then be printed or displayed.

At the present time, however, there are relatively few counseling centers that have minicomputers for vocational counseling. The cost of *developing and maintaining the software and the files,* rather than the cost of the hardware, is the reason it has not been utilized to a greater extent. In this area also, research projects are being conducted which encourage schools to share existing software.

In the laboratory the computer is used as a tool to assist the student with the mathematical calculations that are necessary. When used for short problems, the student may elect to write the programs. For longer calculations prewritten programs may be utilized. The use of computers has stimulated more interest in laboratory work because much of the drudgery is gone. With the cost decreasing, and the software relatively easy to write, there should be in the future a much greater utilization of the minicomputer in the laboratory.

Where students and faculty have been able to use the minicomputer, time-sharing, or a larger computer in a batch mode to assist in problem-solving, new applications have been developed. The computer is viewed by students who do have access to it in much the same way as an audio tape cassette, slide projector, or overhead projector—just another learning media.

Computers will be used in education in ways that are not yet even thought of. In some learning resource centers dedicated minis will be as common as tape recorders and slide projectors are today.

12–26. What is CAI?

12–27. Since CAI is individualized instruction which permits the student to proceed at his own pace, why isn't it used more widely?

12–28. Was CAI used prior to 1971?

12–29. In using the minicomputer for vocational counseling, what problem is involved in file maintenance?

MINICOMPUTERS IN BUSINESS

The minicomputer is used by both the small and large company. For the large company it is generally dedicated to one specific task, while the small company use their's as a general purpose computer. The three areas in business in which they are most widely used are

1. as a standalone accounting system,
2. a multi-purpose terminal, and
3. a frontend processor for a communication system.

FIGURE 12–8. HONEYWELL SYSTEM 700. (Courtesy of Honeywell.)

Standalone Systems

As with the selection of a larger computer, the potential minicomputer user should be concerned with: the execution speed in terms of how many sales invoices or paychecks can be produced on the system in a given period of time; the compatibility it has within a "family" of computers; which options are standard and which ones are the "extras"; what software is available for the system; how much the system can be expanded; how reliable is the hardware; what types of field service contracts are available for maintenance of the equipment on the site; what training is available for employees; and how reliable is the manufacturer? These are not easy questions to answer. It is suggested that the small user compare one system with another, but can this be done if the individual has no prior experience with computers?

Refer back to the materials presented regarding the NCR 399 and the IBM System/3 Model 6, which were detailed in module 3, and see how many of the questions can be answered by referring to the textbook material or from your knowledge of the two companies. Do the companies (NCR and IBM) have both sales and maintenance offices in your area? What is their established reputation? There are good systems available for the small user from many of the more established computer companies, such as Burroughs, National Cash Register, Honeywell, and IBM. In addition, there are many companies who manufacture only minicomputers who also have software for their systems.

Some of the systems developed by the newer companies in the minicomputer fields are unique and offer some highly-specialized applications for the small user. For example, Comp-Acct, Inc., has been involved in the development, design, and marketing of cash, inventory, and time control systems which are operated in conjunction with the dedicated minicomputers. As early as 1968 the founders of the company felt that the fast-food industry was losing millions of dollars annually because there was not a practical, automatic system for gathering operational data at the point-of-sale. Therefore, an accounting system was developed which consists of electronic cash registers, a dedicated minicomputer, and the required software. Currently one minicomputer can handle from one to six terminals.

Since the cash register serves as the minicomputer's terminal, the point-of-sale use of a menu-pad and pencil is eliminated The system computes the price of each item, adds the prices, determines the sales tax, subtracts the total sales from the amount received by the customer, and indicates his change. The panel mounted on top of the register makes it possible for the customer to see the price of each menu item, the total charge, and amount of change which he will receive. By checking the panel, the customer is satisfied that he is correctly charged for the products ordered and the clerk is assured that he has accurately recorded the sale. A register tape is also given to the customer, which identifies the customer's number, date and time of the transaction, menu items purchased, total sales, sales tax, amount he paid, and the change received.

The system does far more than record the POS transactions. The software provides for automatic inventory control, and a detailed breakdown of all store activities is also available at the touch of a button. Since the employee uses the system to ring in and out, the need for employee time clocks, time cards, and handwritten daily labor records is eliminated.

The terminal, or cash register, has four basic types of color-coded keys.

1. Numeric keys for entering variable information, such as the quantity sold or amount of cash removed from the register and deposited.
2. Menu item keys, such as "Big Mac," "Lg Fries," "Choc Shake," etc.
3. Function keys used in entering or retrieving data from the system. Typical keys read, "Total," "Enter Date," "Waste Report," "Payroll Report," "Employee Meal Report," etc.
4. The miscellaneous keys are used for functions, such as "in," "out," "cancel," and "price changes."

In using the system, the clerk need not memorize menu item prices, remember price changes or specials, add or calculate the tax, or figure the amount of change. The customer is generally happy with the system because it provides faster service.

Information, such as the inventory of any item on hand, can be available upon the request of the manager because the recall is instantaneous. All the manager must do is push the appropriate button on his terminal and the computer goes to work! Immediately a printed report of recorded information is produced. A duplicate printout is retained in the register to be used as a permanent record. The manager no longer has to prepare cash sheets, statistical reports, time card audits, or employee schedules.

Some of the reports available from the system are: the register read report which provides data pertaining to the number of customers, cash sales, tax collected, cash in the drawer, cash value of promotional giveaways, and the cash value of the employee's meals. A product analysis is available which indicates the quantity and dollar value of the menu items sold. On the basis of the report the manager can determine if certain items should be dropped from the product line or promoted in order to increase sales. The grand total report provides the accumulated totals for the number of customers, net cash sales, tax collected, gross cash volume, value of promotional giveaways, employee's meals, waste, and overrings. The report can be used as a permanent record and provides the information needed for federal and state tax forms. Additional information is obtainable from the system through use of the payroll, last-hour sales and labor, automatic hourly sales, waste product, and employee meal reports.

After reading the material regarding the use of the minicomputer in the "fast food" industry, you might assume that by now every business must have a mini! Less than 10% of the businesses with 250 or fewer employees, however, now have a computer. There are over 400,000 prospects in that category! Think of the potential whole new industry that is there!

Many of the computer manufacturers are looking toward the small business minicomputer market as an area in which to expand. For example, General Automation, which has been involved in industrial and more specialized minicomputer applications, has indicated that they will soon announce their mini-based business system, which will utilize the SPC-16 family of computers. The SPC-16 minicomputer will have both a fixed and removable disk, up to four keyboard CRT terminals, and an optional printer. The system may operate as a standalone system or may be modified to communicate with either an IBM 360 or 370.

Recently, General Automation surveyed several hundred service bureaus which use IBM 360/30 (and up) hardware. They were interested in determining if the service bureaus would sell, service, design the system's software, implement the applications, and perform the education and guidance functions necessary to convert users to the SPC-16. The response to the proposal from the service bureaus has been very favorable.

Often when the small business owner reaches the thousand dollar a month mark for the bureau's services, he begins to consider the acquisition of a computer system. If the service bureau is a distributor for the General Automation minicomputer, it will be able to provide the client with a "packaged system" for his future needs. In a sense the bureau will not have lost a customer, but will have retained the client on a more limited basis. The client will have the economy and flexibility provided by having his own data processing center. The transition will be easy because he will continue working with the service bureau who is already familiar with his applications. It is logical to assume that the service bureau, with whom the client has been working, will be able to provide the services needed more effectively and economically than a consulting service, which has no knowledge of the user's business.

General Automation is also planning to establish a software pool. All software developed for the SPC-16 will be available to other users through service bureaus.

Often consulting firms do "specialize" in the type of minicomputer they install for new users. Other minicomputer manufacturers have enlisted the aid of companies, who specialize in writing software, to develop the systems which are needed to support their hardware.

Due to the increased software and consulting services available, more small companies will begin to look seriously at a small standalone minicomputer data processing system. It should become one of the most rapidly expanding segments of the computer industry. The trend in the business-oriented minicomputer development seems to be that the "typical" mini will consist of the central processing unit, a limited amount of online disk storage, and a serial printer. The printer also has a standard typewriter keyboard which is utilized to input data into the system. The mini configurations can be expanded by: adding more memory, increasing the amount of online storage, using a faster online printer, and adding CRTs.

MULTI-PURPOSE TERMINALS

General Automation in designing their SPC-16 business-oriented system anticipates that the minicomputer will function both as a standalone computer and as a terminal to a larger, more powerful host computer.

In module 5, figure 5–37 (p. 326) illustrated a "programmable terminal" which is essentially a minicomputer. It enables the branch office to process their data when it is needed. They can produce their own documents, such as sales invoices, payroll checks, and accounts receivable statements. The condensed, edited information to be transmitted to the "host" computer for further processing is stored on disk. Generally the minicomputer terminal will be polled at night by the host computer to determine if there is information which should be transmitted.

Figure 12–8 (p. 678) illustrates the extent to which a minicomputer-based system could develop. The system illustrated can be used for data collection, extensive data processing, and data transmission to a large host computer, all under the control of the 716 which is the CPU for the System 700 family of minicomputers. The configuration includes: four magnetic tape drives; four disk drives; type 716 central processor with a paper tape reader, paper tape punch, and teletypewriter; 300 lines per minute printer; and a card read/punch unit.

FRONTEND PROCESSORS

The voice-oriented telephone network has become the largest single method used for data communications. Although it is anticipated that it will be one of the largest growth areas, the majority of business computers presently in use are not designed to handle data communications effectively. The original frontend processors (or controllers) did little more than assemble the transmitted bits into characters. It has also been debated by some of the computer manufacturers whether the data communication function should be handled by software or hardware. Today many of the computer manufacturers have developed minicomputers which can function as a frontend processor. In a large system the minicomputer may be dedicated to performing only its data communication functions.

It is recognized that the large central processor should be relieved of as many of the routine, nonproductive functions as possible, in order that its capabilities may be used more effectively. Figure 12–9 illustrates the approach that most companies are now taking when they use a minicomputer as a frontend controller or processor. The minicomputer will generally take care of: the polling and addressing functions; error detection and recovery routines; the storing of data received from the terminals in the queue awaiting transmission to the host computer; and the retrieving of data from the queue which is to be sent to the terminals. When intelligent terminals, such as the IBM 3735 or the NCR 399, are used the data is edited and condensed before it is transmitted between the host and minicomputer by using the I/O channel.

Using the "Delta" concept, the verified, assembled messages are queued for transfer to disk (see fig. 12–10). The main I/O channel is used only to notify the host computer what type of message was received and where it is

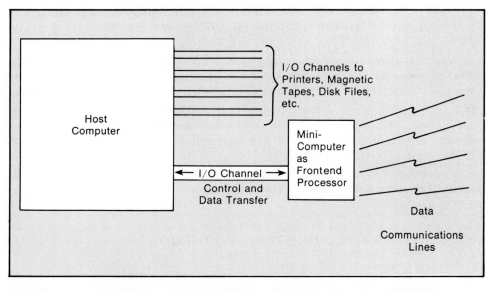

FIGURE 12–9. TRADITIONAL APPROACH USING MINICOMPUTER AS A FRONTEND PROCESSOR

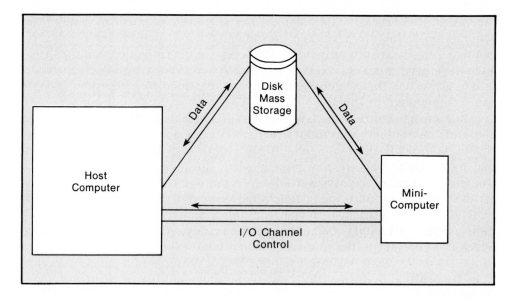

FIGURE 12–10. "DELTA" CONCEPT USING MINICOMPUTER AS A FRONTEND PROCESSOR

stored on the disk. Messages to be transmitted to the terminals are handled in the same manner. From the host computer the message is stored on disk and then read from the disk and transmitted to the terminal by the minicomputer. The I/O channel is used to notify the minicomputer where the data is stored on disk and what type of message is contained.

Under the more traditional approach, when the main system (host computer) receives an *interrupt*, messages usually stop being processed. The terminal user may receive an abrupt break in service which may be very irritating to the user. Under the Delta concept, the messages can continue being received from the terminal and are stored on disk. When the host computer resumes processing, the stored messages will be taken care of. Messages which are on disk to be transmitted can continue to be sent. When the interrupt occurs the terminal user may be notified that only partial service is available until the host computer is again functioning.

QUESTIONS ON MINICOMPUTERS IN BUSINESS

12–30. Are the questions that should be answered pertaining to the selection of a minicomputer any different than those raised when a larger computer system is being considered?

12–31. For what industry did Comp-Acct, Inc. develop a highly specialized system?

12–32. Besides processing their sales, the system provides what additional information to the manager?

12–33. In order to actually maintain an up-to-the-minute inventory of all items on hand, what must occur each time a *hamburger* is sold?

12–34. What else can the manager's cash register be used for besides entering data into the system?

12–35. Do the majority of small businesses now use a computer to process their data?

12–36. General Automation may use an unique approach for marketing their business minicomputer systems. What is it?

12–37. What does a "typical" business minicomputer system consist of?

12–38. Can a multi-purpose terminal function both as a "standalone" processor and as a terminal which transmits data to a "host" computer?

12–39. In what way will an increasing number of minicomputers be used in business systems?

12–40. Under the more "traditional" system how are minicomputers used in data communications?

12–41. What advantage is there in using the "Delta" concept rather than the traditional system?

MINICOMPUTER SUMMARY

The minicomputer is appearing everywhere in the industrial areas as a key to better products and productivity. It was illustrated that their usage must be justified in the same manner as a computer used for a business application. Also management must be able to clearly define the problem if they are to consider the utilization of a minicomputer to aid in its solution.

Although the minicomputer is currently very widely used in both numerical and process control, there are many other areas in which it is also utilized in industry. Continued expansion is expected in its use in the areas of tool scheduling, monitoring, and control; automated quality assurance and assembler; instrumentation calibration, inspection and testing; total manufacturing control and process control. The minicomputer will also begin to make inroads into some of the more traditional manufacturing areas.

In business the dedicated minicomputer will be utilized to a much greater extent than it is now. Two areas of anticipated growth are its utilization as a frontend processor and as an intelligent terminal. The small businessman will be more tempted to develop his own computer center with a minicomputer now that software and systems support is provided by many of the manufacturers.

Since the cost of the minicomputer, when contrasted to a regular computer, is extremely low, minis will be available for utilization by non-data processing personnel who wish to use their computational ability. Since they are inexpensive, management will not be concerned with idle CPU time. In colleges and universities the minicomputer will be utilized in many new and different ways.

An association of minicomputer users will undoubtedly be formed. The membership will be encouraged to "brainstorm" new and different applications to which their minis can be assigned.

There is a great deal of speculation that it will be the minicomputer that leads (or pushes) the way to the second industrial revolution. The change that it brings may have a tremendous impact on our very way of life!

Or will it be the "super" computer that will be responsible for creating the vast changes that are to come? What does a really "super" computer look like today?

A LARGE-SCALE SYSTEM: THE B 7700

Although the statement might be untrue tomorrow, today the "super" computer is a Burroughs B 7700 computer, which is installed at Michigan Bell Telephone Company's accounting center in Saginaw, Michigan (see fig. 12–11). According to the *Detroit Free Press,* a Burroughs spokesman stated: "To our knowledge, it's the largest commercial computer available (as a standard purchase) in the world." Other larger business computers have been built, but as a special, single order.

The article continues: "Although Burroughs has had B 7700s operating for its own use, the Saginaw installation is the first for a customer. The spokesman said three or four more of the approximately 5 million dollar computers have been ordered." (I don't think the hard-to-buy-for lady on your list will get one of these.)

The B 7700 will maintain a data file of more than 1.25 million customers, reading approximately 350,000 records each day and updating about 250,000 records. Every month it will add, delete, or change 100,000 customers' records; process 25 million toll calls, and generate a bill for each telephone.

What does the installation look like? If you are not an employee when you enter the building, it is necessary to have someone "sign for you." One of the Burrough's systems analysts assigned to the installation signed for me! Assigned to the B 7700 in Saginaw are two Burroughs systems analysts and six customer engineers.

There are two sets of locked doors that you must pass through to enter the data processing center—each requires a different key or pass. Currently, the center is "off limits" to all visitors. As you enter the center it seems large enough to hold an inaugural ball! Somehow the installation looks "uncomputerish," since the operator consoles are freestanding and in the center of the room. Again no flashing lights are visible because the central processing

FIGURE 12–11. BURROUGHS 7700. (Courtesy of Burroughs Corporation.)

unit is behind closed doors and is part of a long row of similar looking units. You are surrounded by an array of random access disk files, magnetic tape files, printers, card readers, and card punches.

The Michigan Bell installation does not utilize the full capabilities of the B 7700, since far more components could be added to the system. What you do see are central processors, input/output processors, a maintenance diagnostic unit, disk optimizer, head-per-track disk files, adapter cluster for data communications, a long row of stacked removable disk pack files, an equally long row of magnetic tape drives, seven online printers, six card punches, and several card readers. The four operator consoles stand in the center of the room, surrounded by the vast array of hardware.

It is anticipated that when the system gets fully implemented, *on an average* of 25 different programs will be the CPU in various stages of execution at one time—each sharing the computational ability of the CPU.

What are some of the unusual or different features of this "super" computer? Other systems might have similar features, but some of the concepts introduced now are different from others that you have studied throughout the text. Many of the concepts are available on only *very* large computer systems.

Understanding the B 7700

In designing the system, the hardware and the software were designed together by a single design team. Burroughs feels that the system is neither "hardware-oriented" nor "software-oriented" but is *user-oriented*. The system is distinguished by an exceptionally efficient and useable balance of the system's resources.

The architecture, or design, of the B 7700 is different than many of the computers on the market. The CPU's memory consists of 60 bit words. Twelve of the bits, however, have special functions, such as providing a parity check, so only 48 bits are actually used for storing data. If a parity check detects a one-bit error, the error is self-correcting. An error involving more than one bit, however, is irrecoverable and an interrupt will occur.

The high-speed memory consists of 1,048,576 words or *6,291,456 eight-bit bytes. A requestor of memory* may address and gain access to the entire contents of the high-speed memory. At rates of up to 6.75 million bytes per second a single input/output processor is capable of transferring data simultaneously between main memory and the peripheral controls.

Observe the illustration of the system provided in figure 12–12. When the CPU was defined earlier in the text, it was stated that it consisted of the control unit, arithmetic and logic unit, input unit, output unit, and the main memory. What is different about the diagram? The CPU no longer is responsi-

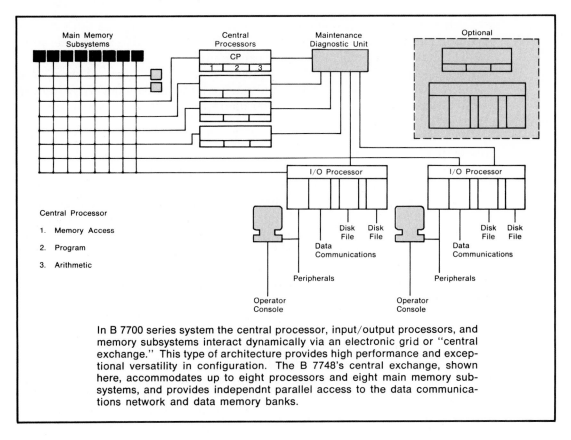

Main Memory Subsystems

Central Processors

CP
1   2   3

Maintenance Diagnostic Unit

Optional

Central Processor

1. Memory Access

2. Program

3. Arithmetic

I/O Processor

I/O Processor

Data Communications

Disk File   Disk File

Data Communications

Disk File   Disk File

Peripherals

Peripherals

Operator Console

Operator Console

In B 7700 series system the central processor, input/output processors, and memory subsystems interact dynamically via an electronic grid or "central exchange." This type of architecture provides high performance and exceptional versatility in configuration. The B 7748's central exchange, shown here, accommodates up to eight processors and eight main memory subsystems, and provides independnt parallel access to the data communications network and data memory banks.

FIGURE 12–12. ARCHITECTURE OF THE BURROUGHS B 7700

ble for the input/output activities, since there is a *separate I/O processor.* By freeing the central processor from concern about the input/output operations, it can become far more productive. I/O interrupts, which occur in other computer systems, do not occur. Also, by employing *fail-soft* measures, along with the separation of the I/O processor from the CPU, it is hoped that the system can keep running 100% of the time.

What is *fail-soft* and how can it be achieved? The term can be defined as, "capable of recovering automatically from a failure." Error detection circuits (hardware) are used throughout the system. The errors detected are recorded for software analysis. The master control program has the ability to recognize the faulty "module" in the system and exclude it. Because of the modular concept in the design of the system, if a faulty circuit chip is determined in a particular unit of main memory, that portion is bypassed until the problem can be found and corrected. To have full fail-soft capabilities there must be a minimum of two central processor modules and two I/O processors.

The maintenance diagnostic unit can be utilized *while the system is running* to test the components of the system. When the problem of the faulty module has been found, corrected, and retested, the module is then ready for a new assignment—made by the master control program.

Maximum Configuration

As many as eight memory modules may be arranged on the exchange with a combined total of up to eight requestors of memory. There can also be a *combined total* of eight central processors and input/output processors. At present the maximum number of high-speed, medium-speed, and low-speed peripheral devices that may be attached through controls and exchanges to a *single input/output processor is 255.* Each card reader, card punch, line printer, paper tape reader, paper tape punch, operator's display terminal, and free-standing magnetic tape unit is considered as a device. Each station on a magnetic tape cluster or disk subsystem is also considered as *one device.*

Besides the 255 peripheral devices, there may be included a vast network of remote terminals, controllers, and computers that can be accommodated by up to 1,024 remote lines, serviced by the four programmable data communications processors that can be *controlled by a single input/output processor.* The larger systems can service networks exceeding 6,000 lines.

Virtual Storage

When a program is compiled, the Burroughs compiler segments all programs and catalogs them in a segment dictionary. The program segments are stored on disk files. The execution software (another name for supervisor) refers to this dictionary at the time a program is being executed and calls segments into main memory from the disk file storage as they are needed. Therefore, programs can be written without regard to the size of main memory or to the segment locations.

Very fast access is obtained when the program segments are needed, because *head-per-track* disks are used. A track is defined as the groove (or cylinder) in which the data is stored. Rather than using only one access arm (as was illustrated in module 5), a series of arms are used each having multiple heads. If head-per-track had been illustrated in module 5 it would have shown 203 individual read/write heads for each of the 10 recording surfaces. The access time for the head-per-track disks ranges from 2 to 10 milliseconds. Contrast this access time with the ranges given in the discussion of disk, which is found in module 5. *Each input/output processor* could have as much as *eight billion eight-bit bytes* of information available on head-per-track disks.

Additional disk memory modules, which have removable packs, are combined into random-access memory banks which can contain from 15 million to 16 *billion* 8-bit bytes of data per input/output processor.

Master Control Program

The master control program, or operating system, is capable of dynamically controlling its own resources and the scheduling of its jobs. It is capable of processing a number of jobs concurrently in less time than it would take to process the same jobs individually. The master control program is capable of coordinating the execution of many programs, or jobs, in the processor or *processors*. It is also able to take *executive action* (error recovery routines) to meet virtually all processing conditions. It is responsible for the reallocation of modules to an assigned task when one module becomes defective (fail-soft).

Operator's Console

The operator's console is the communication link between the operator and the B 7700 system. It consists of switches (used in halting, clearing, or starting the system) and an inquiry keyboard. The keyboard is arranged much the same as a standard typewriter. Messages to the operator from the system are displayed on the video screen. Each input/output processor must have its own operator's console.

Other Features

The system is capable of doing code translations in both the I/O processor and the data communications processor. For example, EBCDIC can be translated to BCL (a special Burroughs six-bit code) or BCL can be translated to EBCDIC.

Slow card input is transferred to either disk or tape for processing. The card image files are then assigned to different pseudo card readers, which are treated by the master control program as if they were real card readers. Printer and punched card output is also written on tape or disk and then printed or punched when it is convenient. (Essentially, this is SPOOLing.)

The sequence of jobs to be run is determined by the master control program (operating system). The scheduler feature of the master control program takes into consideration the optimal program mix, the priority ratings, and the system requirements.

High-level languages, such as COBOL, ALGOL, FORTRAN, BASIC, and PL/I, may be used. The user may specify the locations of his critical disk files in order to make the maintenance and reconstruction of the files easier. Protected disk files allow a user to gain access to the last portion of valid data written in a file before an unexpected system halt. The reason for using duplicate disk files is to avoid the problem of fatal disk file errors. The master control program maintains more than one copy of each disk file. If a record cannot be retrieved, an attempt is made to recover the copy of the record.

B 7700 SUMMARY

There are many additional features of the system that could be presented. The most impressive features of the system, however, are:

1. Dividing the CPU into:
   a. Central processor—program, execution, memory
   b. I/O processor
2. The fail-soft features
3. Greater file protection

It is not anticipated that you will remember many of the detailed facts presented. Nevertheless, you should be well aware of the tremendous amount of data which can be stored and processed when the system is being utilized. Up to now, its full capabilities have not been utilized in any of the installations.

B 7700 REVIEW

12–42. On an average how many programs will be running concurrently once the B 7700 system is fully implemented?
12–43. What advantage is there in dividing the CPU and having a central processor and an I/O processor?
12–44. Why is the system "fail-soft"?
12–45. Why is head-per-track disk storage faster to access than the more conventional disk storage that utilizes only one access arm per recording surface?

12–46. Per I/O Processor what is the maximum number of I/O devices that can be attached?

12–47. How many communication lines can each I/O processor accommodate?

12–48. Virtual storage is used in a somewhat different manner as when the program is compiled it is broken into segments. Where are the segments cataloged?

12–49. The scheduler determines which jobs can run concurrently based upon predetermined priorities. What else does it consider in determining which jobs should be run concurrently?

12–50. Is card input read directly into the I/O processor?

12–51. Does Burroughs feel that the system is "hardware-oriented" or "software-oriented"?

MICROCOMPUTERS

Have you thought about a computer that you could easily hold in your hand? Figure 12–13 illustrates a single SOS chip which is an entire *processor*. It really doesn't look like a computer because there are no blinking lights or switches! Does it act like a computer? The LSI-12/16 is an 8-bit digital microcomputer which can have from 1K to 32K words of memory. A *microcomputer,* or microprocessor, is defined as a computer which has its entire processor on a single chip! The single chip contains the equivalent of 3,000 to 5,000 transistors.

When the LSI-12/16 was announced, it was the first computer to make use of the new silicon-on-sapphire technology, which originated in the aerospace industry. In using SOS, more circuitry can be placed on one chip, which means that less *area* and less *power* is needed for the processor. The single chip in figure 12–13 replaces the entire SPC-12 processor board shown in the background.

The board which is illustrated in figure 12–14 can be purchased alone, and it is a computer! The single 7¾-by-10-inch printed circuit board contains the *processor* (the single chip), memory, operator console, and systems operation features. On the one board there can be from 1K to 4K of random access memory and up to 8K of read only memory (ROM).

The board can also be purchased in the simple enclosure which is pictured. In addition to the board, it contains a battery for power backup and card slots for additional I/O. Why is a battery included? General Automation has chosen to use semiconductor memory, which makes it far easier to program the ROM. Semiconductory memory has a high volatility, however, which means that all data in memory is lost in the event of a power failure. The

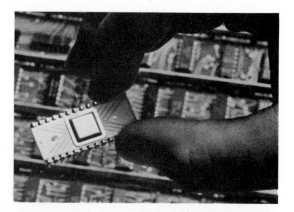

FIGURE 12–13. SINGLE SOS CHIP

FIGURE 12–14. LSI-12/16 MICROCOMPUTER. (Courtesy of General Automation, Inc.)

auxiliary battery backup system is activated immediately upon loss of power and will retain the contents of the memory for up to 15 hours.

Since the lady of the house did not get the Honeywell Kitchen Minicomputer, maybe the less-than-$1,000 microcomputer might be on her Christmas list. What could it do in the home? According to General Automation, Inc., some of the applications that it might find are:

1. Totally automated meter reading for gas, electricity, and water service.
2. Total control of environmental quality, including heating, cooling, humidity control, and air filtering.
3. Control of lighting and security systems for fire and theft protection.

4. Replacement of telephone books with a tie-in to a central telephone company computer for a file search for telephone numbers of "Yellow Pages" information.
5. Automatic control of appliances, including their use while home owners are away from home.

In business and industry, it can be used like a minicomputer as a front-end data communication processor; intelligent terminal; controller for building security systems; building environmental controller; controller in a hospital to monitor patients in intensive care; cash register replacement; or as a fire and burglary alarm system.

Since microcomputers are much smaller and cheaper than minicomputers, entirely new application areas are developing for their use. Although the microcomputers are usually slower than the mini, they are lower in cost, more flexible, and require less design time. The major application areas where the micros are taking over from the minis are as peripheral device controllers for card readers, floppy disks, cassette tape units, and line printers; general controllers; and standalone electronic cash registers.

MICROCOMPUTERS REVIEW

12–52. What is the silicon-on-sapphire "chip," which is shown in figure 12–13?
12–53. What is the major advantage in using the silicon-on-sapphire chip?
12–54. What is a microcomputer?
12–55. Do you feel that someday microcomputers will be used in the home?

THE FUTURE?

Information and applications have been provided for the various size computers, from the smallest to the largest: the microcomputer, the minicomputer, the small-size computer system, the medium-size computer system, and the "super"-size system. Which type of computer, or system, will have the greatest impact on our future?

When branch operations were first started, such as when Lou opened his second lumberyard, the data processing functions were centralized—the home office did it all. Phase 2, due to the inability of the home office to process large quantities of information manually, resulted in a decentralization of many of the data processing functions. Phase 3 again centralized the data processing functions in order to economically justify the utilization of medium- and large-size computer systems. Hundreds of pages of printed material have appeared in professional data processing literature pertaining to the advantages and disadvantages of centralization versus decentralization.

Many companies are now in the final stages of implementing the recommendations of system studies which indicated that centralization would be the best possible solution for their data processing needs. The systems study, however, may have taken two or three years to complete. An additional four or five years may have been required to fully implement the recommendations. Computer technology, in the period of time needed for the implementation, has changed radically.

Will phase 4 be the decentralization of the data processing functions, due to the greater realization of what the minicomputer can really do?

A NETWORK OF MINICOMPUTERS

When many large computers have a problem in their circuitry, or with an I/O device, the entire system may become inoperative until the problem is isolated and corrected. Often a computer system must stop processing information while customer engineers do protective maintenance. In data communications, when a standby computer is not available, the entire communications network may be down awaiting the host computer's recovery.

Many people, such as Captain Grace Hopper, who have been involved with computers over a long period of time and fully understand their architecture, feel that a network of minicomputers can often do the job more economically than one large "super" computer.

Minicomputer networks can be achieved in different ways. Under one method, each minicomputer is treated as a "module" of the total computer system. Adding another minicomputer to the network would be similar to securing more memory or I/O devices for an existing medium- or large-sized system. A second approach would permit the minicomputers to transmit data to one another through their input-output channels so that each acts as if the other were just another I/O device. A third approach dedicates each minicomputer in the network to a particular function. Each minicomputer would have access to only a given segment of the data base.

In a network, if one little mini becomes ill, a substitute is readily available. Due to the economy of the minicomputer, management would not be overly concerned if one was utilized as a "spare." When not needed in the network, the minicomputer could be assigned other tasks.

Different consultants, hired by independent companies to study their data processing problems, have supported the theory that in some cases the minicomputer network could accomplish the same results as those being obtained by a large-scale computer system. For example, one study indicated that a computer which costs about $1.4 million could be replaced by 15 minicomputers, which would cost approximately $900,000.

In a speech before the Saginaw Valley Data Processing Management Association, Captain Hopper indicated that in several cases the network of minicomputers theory is now being tested. She cited the Southern Railway's use of a minicomputer network to control railcar switching. She indicated that the system was made up of five minicomputers: two for process control functions in the yard, one for providing management information, and *two for backup.*

DECENTRALIZATION

Through the use of a corporate network of minicomputers, located at various locations throughout the country or world, the trend will once again be toward decentralization for part of the data processing functions. When more of the functions are performed at the local level, the information that is *really needed* by corporate headquarters can be transmitted to the corporation's host computer by using the minicomputer as an intelligent terminal. When a large enough minicomputer is used to handle many of the local data processing functions, the cost of transmitting the data to the corporate headquarters will decrease.

Three indications are apparent.

1. Greater emphasis on the use of minicomputer networks.
2. Decentralization of some of the data processing functions.
3. The use of the minicomputer makes it possible to combine the best of the two methods—centralization and decentralization.

LARGE-SCALE COMPUTERS

Since there is seldom one solution that solves all problem in data processing, for calculations involving very large data bases *and many users,* the large-scale computer is still considered by many to be the most efficient. Also there will continue to be radical improvements in the medium- and large-scale computers, such as the 100% fail-soft feature available (in the B 7700 system) when two I/O processors and two central processors are utilized. Due to the strong emphasis in the architecture (on the modularity concept) the B 7700 is in a sense a network of small-to-medium-size computers within one large system, since the central processors can communicate with one another; the extremely large main memory can be accessed by any of the I/O processors and is therefore also available to all of the central processors; and random access files and other peripherals can also be used by all of the I/O processors.

There will still be very definite improvements in the speed with which computers can execute commands. The cycle time of main memory is still mostly dependent upon the speed of the storage medium. As the type of computer memory moved from drum (used as early as 1948 by the University of Manchester, in England, and again in 1953 by IBM's 650) to magnetic core, and then on to semiconductor memories, the speed with which data could be transferred increased dramatically. Cycle time was first measured by the millisecond, then by the microsecond, and now by nanoseconds. Each generation was a thousand times faster than the preceding generation.

"BUBBLES" OR "OPTICAL" MEMORY?

Two basic approaches are being studied to improve the computer's memory: "magnetic bubble memory," which involves rather complex molecular theory, and "optical memory," which utilizes laser-optical technology and advanced photographic techniques. Both of the methods under study offer a possibility of providing a simplified memory, which would be more efficient but what would cost less. Either method has almost unlimited potential, since it is dependent on either electrical or light energy and *has no moving parts.*

In the "bubble" memory there really are no bubbles! Due to the materials used and the manner in which they are magnetized, however, you can see (under a microscope) bits moving. The bits, or "bubbles," can be made to spin around! Therefore, from their appearance and movements they were given the name "bubbles."

Bell Telephone Laboratories started doing research involving the use of magnetic bubbles in 1969 and have advanced the technique to the point where a prototype was demonstrated in 1973. Using the materials and techniques developed at the Bell labs, it is felt that bubble memory would have a potential density of *ten million bits of information per square inch.*

IBM has continued to work in the area developed by Bell labs. Since the crystals used in Bell's work are extremely expensive, IBM has developed techniques for manufacturing bubble memory using cheaper materials. The techniques IBM is developing may produce a density of *up to one billion bits per square inch.*

Density, however, is not the only concern in developing new memory. Access time is also a factor. When bubble memory is compared to present main memory, the results are not very favorable. Nevertheless, when contrasted to magnetic disk access times, the sub-millisecond rate achieved with bubble memory is very impressive.

Rockwell International also has experimented in the use of bubbles and claims credit for delivering the first *operational* bubble device—a 64-bit shift register—to the Air Force.

Think of the potential in terms of density for use in main memory. With main memory available in a one-inch cube and a processor on a single chip, the really "super-size" computer of the future could be less than the size of a shoebox!

The research involving the use of the optical memory using laser-optical technology and photographic techniques has established that it has the potential to be used for main memory. RCA, which has been involved in the research, reports that while it may not produce larger memories than those used today, it may be *a thousand times faster*.

Laser memory is already being used to store massive amounts of data on-line. The Social Security Administration, for example, has ordered 66 billion bits of online laser storage.

It remains to be seen how soon bubble or optical memory will actually be utilized as main memory. It is certain, however, that the large-scale computer of tomorrow will be far smaller, faster, and more powerful than any that we have now. Their random access memories will be far larger than the ones used now.

What are the implications? The potential of these huge machines will be available to everyone. They are needed because there are environmental and social problems to be solved which require massive amounts of data that the present computers, regardless of their power, cannot handle.

Just as you now enjoy cable television, if you wish to subscribe to it, you will also be able to take advantage of a computer utility. You may ask, "Why subscribe to a computer utility?"

FICTION OR FACT?

Computers in the Home

Subscribing to the computer utility service will be as common as receiving your daily newspaper—which, incidently, could become a thing of the past! Why a utility service? You know now that computers can perform any tasks they are programmed for: recording routine business transactions; controlling various manufacturing processes; or controlling the environment of your home.

You also know that the computer must have data to process! If you were to take a minicomputer home with you today, what would you do with it? Perhaps if you know its assembler language, you can use it to solve some rather simple mathematical problems. If you don't feel like working tonight, however, maybe it will just go on the shelf and be brought back tomorrow!

If you are given a time-sharing terminal to Dartmouth College, with the index of available programs, there are a great many things that you can do. You could do lessons in a number of different subject matter areas, play chess, or write some programs in BASIC. Why is this possible? You are sharing the programs and the data base that have been developed by many people over a number of years.

When you subscribe to your computer utility service, make certain that it is part of a network that shares programs and data bases. Your computer center will probably be one of the most utilized areas of your home. Your terminal's keyboard will be used for either requesting information or entering data. The cathode ray tube used to display information will do so in *color*. Voice answer back is a standard feature of the system. You have also elected to use voice input, which is an optional feature. The computer does understand about a thousand words, but still has trouble when your relatives visit—the ones with the unusual accent.

Another optional feature elected is private online disk storage. Each member of the family has his own disk used to store data for input into the "family written" programs which are stored on a separate disk. All of the household data is maintained on disk. Keeping the household inventory current and recording all expenses is a problem! Your disk pack really isn't very well organized and frequently you have to "dump" the index because you keep misplacing your listing and can't remember the key needed to retrieve the desired information.

What will you use your terminal for? You have a paper due and wish to research the life of Ernest Hemingway. After gaining access to the computer, you enter the correct codes needed to identify the topic you wish to have displayed. Since the information appears on the screen in a "page" format, it will stay there until the release key is used. Some people want a great deal of information about a topic, while others are interested only in obtaining a few basic facts. Therefore, most of the data obtained is arranged in "trees." After the first "page" of information is presented, you will be given several additional topics, pertaining to Hemingway, that you may wish to explore. In this manner you may select the types of information you are interested in and may follow any "branch" as far out as you wish.

There is one problem, however: Dad is taking a refresher course in Labor Law and wants to continue with his lesson where he left off last night. Mother would like to use the terminal to find out the recipe for a new salad she heard about and then get started on her lesson in Advanced Psychology.

Since there is so much new data requested by the users, your utility company has added more personnel to add, delete, and update the information on the data base. You also receive a weekly supplement of new programs, data, and other features that have been added to the system. The latest listing indicates that the "thought for today" feature has been dropped. "Dial-a-bill," however, which keeps you current on all of the bills in either the House of Representatives or the Senate, has been added. Dial-a-bill is a network feature, whereas thought-for-today had been a local feature.

The areas of the data base that you can access depend upon your classification. Since you have elected to take the service by the month, you can make unlimited usage of the computer. You may, of course, write your own programs and store them on disk. For your birthday you have requested a new disk in order to store additional class materials.

In addition to the computer center, microcomputers are everywhere in your home. They are often not visable, since they are used for highly specialized functions, such as the animation of the toys your younger brother received for Christmas.

Dad was thinking of getting a new microcomputer lawnmower but decided, since he works only three days a week, he would like to mow his own lawn. In the home, as in industry, there is a place for both the large computer and the micro or mini.

BUSINESS AND INDUSTRY

The new large-scale computers, which are very powerful but smaller than before, are used in much the same way as the former generation. Many more CRTs are used, however, as the data is recorded where the event takes place. A management information system has finally been developed that provides each level of management with the type of information needed. Since approximately 1.5% of the companies' gross sales are used for the support of the computer center, the manager has been held far more accountable than he was in the past.

More "standards" have been developed for use in data processing. Some of the standards were developed by the professional data processing organizations working together, while others pertain only to a given company. There still exists the problem of lack of uniform terminology within the industry.

Since top management now realizes how really valuable both the computer *and the data* are, more emphasis is placed upon security. Files are backed up more frequently. In addition, since so many employees now use terminals, a more elaborate identification code is used so that unauthorized personnel cannot gain access to online files.

IMPACT OF THE MICRO AND THE MINI

The micro and the mini were the cause of the second industrial revolution. People for a long time had been reading interesting little items, such as a "stacker-crane with no operator speeds down the aisle and deposits its load in the correct location in the warehouse." Little attention was paid to such an article. Others wrote about the vast array of jobs which would be assigned to the micro and the mini. Television programs portrayed the computer—the mini—doing fantastic things.

Prior to the second industrial revolution, people had been predicting that a four-day work week would result from the greater utilization of the minicomputer in industry. Sociologists and economists were predicting the outcome of the second industrial revolution long before it arrived.

Now that we have a three-day work week due to the second industrial revolution, which was lead by the minicomputer, are we ready for it?

CONCLUSION

Do you now understand the role of data processors and some of their strange language? People do view computers in many different ways. Dr. Hammer, when he was discussing the mind-amplifying factor of the computer, was quoted as saying, "It is the greatest challenge that ever faced mankind."

Is the challenge to use the power of the computer to help solve the problems before they are created?

GLOSSARY OF NEW AND OLD TERMS TO CHECK YOUR KNOWLEDGE

Computer Assisted Instruction.   The student interacts with the computer in a learning experience.
Fail-soft.   The ability to recover automatically from a failure.

Microcomputer. A computer that has its entire processor on a single chip.

Minicomputer. No one definition is available. Usually it costs under $20,000, has "word" memory, needs no special environmental conditions in order to operate, is rugged, and is apt to be found anywhere.

ROM. Read only memory. It is faster, cheaper, and more reliable because it cannot accidentally be overwritten.

Sensor. A device that receives and responds to a signal or stimulus.

Word. One addressable location within the CPU. It may contain, in a minicomputer, from 8 to 16 bits.

REVIEW QUESTIONS (p. 658)

12–1.   A kitchen computer.

12–2.   Your answer may differ from mine, but would the average housewife have known much about a computer in 1969? The program language used might also have been a fairly complex one.

12–3.   Manual; mechanical; punched card data processing; second-generation computers; third-generation computers with tape, disk, and DOS; third generation with multiprogramming and OS; third-generation virtual storage machine.

12–4.   The parts lists and price can be determined by using a viewer.

12–5.   The study is a two-part study: One, should they develop a time-sharing system which would centralize all of their data processing operations? Two, if more computer power is needed, should a "slave" computer be used with their present "master" or would it be better to get one very large computer?

MINI QUESTIONS (p. 664)

12–6.   One which receives and responds to a signal or stimulus.

12–7.   Twenty-thousand dollars or under in price; word memory of from 1 to 65K; rugged; doesn't require any special environmental conditions; unless a good deal of memory is available, it is programmed in assembler.

12–8.   No. IBM entered the minicomputer field much later than did many of the other computer manufacturers.

12–9.   No. There are over 50 minicomputer manufacturers.

12–10. One addressable location in the computer—in the mini it usually consists of 8 to 16 bits.

12–11. Read only memory. Microprograms are stored in the ROM and cannot accidentally be overwritten.

12–12. Until IBM's entry in the "mini" world most users were not given support and, therefore, much of the software was developed by users' groups.

MORE MINI QUESTIONS (p. 666)

12–13. Industrial—40%.

12–14. 54%

12–15. There is a very wide range of applications—from controlling a potato picker to analyzing the speech of a student who stutters.

12–16. The minicomputer is assigned to one task. Generally, it has ROM that has been programmed to do the specific task.

INDUSTRIAL APPLICATIONS (p. 674)

12–17. The computer is programmed to produce the *control* tape which is then used to instruct a machine.

12–18. The tolerance of the computer-controlled operation is far less than a manual operation, which means essentially that every part, made with the same tape, will match perfectly.

12–19. Process control makes use of a "sensor" which interprets environmental conditions, such as pressure and temperature, into numerical data which can be processed by the computer. The process is under the direct control of the computer at all times. In numerical control, the computer is used to prepare a series of instructions for a machine. The machine will do certain functions, such as drill holes in metal parts. The program tape prepared by the computer instructs the machine in performing the necessary steps in producing a given part.

12–20. Sensors

12–21. The computer's response time is far faster than an individual's. Therefore, the machine is told to react to change much sooner so the degrees of variation from the "ideal" are much smaller.

12–22. Excellent statistics were presented by IBM, which actually stated, based upon certain assumptions, that the cost of the system would be paid for if there was a 1.3% increase in productivity.

12–23. It is part of the emerging philosophy which says "take the computer to where the event of transaction is occurring." Since 40 to 60% of the cost of manufacturing occurs in the plant, why shouldn't the computer be there to record the information?

12–24. The data to be entered into the system is displayed. The individual entering the data can visually check the information and then use the "enter" key to actually cause the information to be recorded into the system.

12–25. 1. Badge reader
2. Card reader
3. Keys for entering numeric data

REVIEW QUESTIONS (p. 678)

12–26. Computer Assisted Instruction. Generally the student responds to questions asked by the computer. The action taken by the computer depends upon whether the student's answer is "true" or "false."

12–27. The cost of the hardware, until the use of the minicomputer, has been prohibitive for many school districts. Also, even today, there is not a great deal of available software.

12–28. Yes. A good deal of research regarding CAI was started in the mid-1960s.

12–29. As occupational information changes, the online files, which contain the information pertaining to job, qualifications, and availability, would need to be updated.

QUESTIONS ON MINICOMPUTERS IN BUSINESS (p. 684)

12–30. No. The same type of concern should be expressed in selecting any computer system. The basic questions of service, software, compatibility, reliability, etc., are the same, regardless of the size of the computer or of the application for which it will be used.

12–31. Fast-food industries.

12–32. The detailed information he must have to effectively manage his business.

12–33. The raw materials necessary to make the hamburger must be deducted from the inventory on hand. In dealing with mustard, relish, onion, etc., a mathematical formula could be applied to estimate the actual usage.

Based on past experience, how many people use each of the various items on their hamburger?

12–34. To retrieve data from the system.

12–35. No. Only about 10% of the businesses which have 250 employees or less have their own computer system. They may, however, use time-sharing or a service bureau.

12–36. The systems will be sold through service bureaus. The bureaus will also develop the software, provide consulting services for clients, etc.

12–37. The CPU, a limited amount of disk storage, and a typewriter-like printer.

12–38. Yes

12–39. As frontend processors

12–40. The minicomputers take care of routine functions such as polling and addressing.

12–41. If the host computer is "down," partial service is still available since messages can be transmitted from the terminal and stored on disk. The user can also continue to receive messages which had been processed and stored on disk.

B 7700 REVIEW (p. 692)

12–42. 25

12–43. The central processor can become more productive because it will not be involved in I/O interrupts. Therefore, it can process more data in a given period of time. It will be far more productive than if it were all one unit.

12–44. When an error is detected in any module, the master control program reassigns another module to the function that was being performed by the first. The error can be found, by using the maintenance diagnostic unit, and corrected while the rest of the system is operating.

12–45. When information is to be retrieved, it is the arm movement that requires the greatest access time.

12–46. 255

12–47. Over 6,000 communication lines can be connected to each I/O processor.

12–48. The location of each segment is catalogued in a "dictionary."

12–49. The scheduler determines what particular "mix" of programs will make the best use of the available resources.

12–50. No. Card input is stored either on tape or disk before it is processed.

12–51. Neither, they feel it is *user-oriented*.

12–52. It is the entire processor. If you are told that it is the entire computer remind the individual that there must also be memory. Currently the chip does not include memory.

12–53. The processor could be made much smaller.

12–54. A microcomputer has its entire processor on a single chip.

12–55. Your answer should be "yes" since the price is decreasing. For example, in quantities of 100 or more the microcomputer illustrated (without the enclosure) will sell for a little less than $500. As the price continues to decrease and the new technology is utilized to a greater extent by other manufacturers, microcomputers will be used to control many common household functions.

GLOSSARY

Access Time. Indicates the length of time needed to retrieve information from an auxiliary storage device.

Accounting Machine. Also called the tabulator or printer. It reads cards, adds, subtracts, and prints. It can compare numbers from two cards and determine if they are the same. If not, a *level break* occurs. Minor, intermediate, major, and final totals are available.

Accounts Receivable. An account showing the money owed to your firm by another firm or individual.

Action Stub. The portion of a decision table that contains the action, such as GO TO READ-CARD, EXIT FROM LOOP, or COMPUTE TAX.

Address. A location within the CPU. Each byte may be addressed individually or as part of a field or record.

Addressing. The term is used in teleprocessing when the host computer checks to see if the terminal is ready to receive a message.

ANS COBOL. COBOL standards published by the American National Standards Institute.

Application Programs. Programs written to perform particular functions, such as to print the payroll checks, compute and print the accounts receivable statements, update a master file, etc.

Arithmetic Operators. The $+, -, *, /$ and $**$ are used in programming to indicate addition, subtraction, multiplication, division, or exponentiation. The ones illustrated are used in COBOL, FORTRAN, PL/I, as well as other languages.

Array. A table established in the memory of the computer which can be used for storing data. Each element of the array can be addressed individually.

ASCII. American Standard Code for Information Interchange. A 7-bit code that is used to represent up to 128 unique numbers, symbols, and letters.

Assembler Language. A language that permits the use of symbols and mnemonics. The addresses for data and instructions are assigned when the computer compiles the program. Unless MACRO instructions are used, each command generates only one machine-language command. When used, the programmer must understand how each command is executed.

Assumed Decimal. The point in input or in the memory of the computer that a decimal point would occur. Although not actually present, the computer keeps track of the decimal's location as if it were present.

Backorder File. A file of orders that cannot be processed. Generally the delay is due to a shortage in stock of the item requested on the customer's purchase order.

BASIC. A programming language (developed at Dartmouth College) for time-sharing applications.

Batch Processing. Processing, or executing, each program in its entirety before starting the next program. Processing the entire day's sales in a "batch" at one time. After the computer completes one procedure, it proceeds to the next assigned job.

Batch Total. A total taken prior to processing the data on a specific field, such as regular hours, for a given number of transactions. This total is then checked with the computer's total taken while processing the transactions. If the two totals agree, it is another indication that the output is valid and that all of the transactions were processed.

BCDIC. A binary coded decimal code that was used in many second-generation IBM computers.

Binary. A number system used by a computer where a single bit, which may be either "on" or "off," is used to record data.

Bit. A binary digit. The smallest storage unit within the central processing unit.

Block. A group of logical records that are combined to form a physical record. A physical record is read all at one time, but each logical record is processed individually.

BPI. The density, or bytes per inch, that is used to record data on magnetic tape.

Branch. The next instruction in sequence is not executed because the program control is transferred to a location where a different command is stored, such as the program control branched to the address in memory where the command to read a card was stored.

Buffer. A temporary storage area or device. In the central processing unit it is an area reserved either for information coming into main memory or leaving main memory. The data is stored in the buffer until it can be processed or, in the case of the output buffer, until the output device is ready for the data. Buffers help to maximize throughput, since overlapping operations can occur.

Burst Mode. A method of reading or writing data that does not permit an interrupt to occur.

Byte. A location in memory made up of eight bits. Each byte may be addressed.

Calculator. The calculators, which were controlled by wiring panels, had some of the characteristics of computers since they could store a *very limited* amount of data and perform a series of mathematical operations. They were "programmed" by the operator who wired each step to be performed. One unit read the input and punched the resulting answer from processing into either the same card or a new card. A second unit performed the actual calculations.

Card Columns. A point of reference. The standard card has 80 columns.

Carriage Tape. A paper tape that controls the vertical movement of the form in either a high-speed printer or the accounting machine. Each special form usually has its own carriage tape which is used when the forms are printed upon.

Central Processing Unit. Contains the control unit, arithmetic and logic unit, input unit, output unit, and the main memory of the computer.

Channel. A physical device that transmits data from an input device to the central processing unit or from the central processing unit to an output device.

Character Set. The digits, alphabetic characters, and special characters that are recognized within a given language subset.

Check Digit. The final digit of a number that is used in a mathematical formula to determine if the number has been recorded accurately. If a wrong digit is used or if a transposition occurs, the error is detected by the computer.

Clause. A part of a COBOL statement used to describe structures or give initial values to items.

COBOL SUBSET. COBOL rules, within perhaps a much larger set of rules, that apply to a particular compiler.

CODASYL. Conference on Data Systems Languages. The committee was convened by the federal government and asked to develop a "standard" language.

Coding. After the program flowchart is constructed, the programmer codes the problem in the language to be used. Rigid adherence to the rules of the language (such as RPG, FORTRAN, or COBOL) must be followed. Each line of coding is punched in a card. The code is then translated by the computer, operating under the direction of a compiler, into actual computer commands.

Collator. A machine that can merge, match-merge, or match two decks of cards. In addition, it can sequence check the decks or do a variety of different types of selection.

COM. Computer output to microfilm. Refers to a method of producing microfilm, in a variety of forms, from computer-produced magnetic tape.

Comparing Unit. A device used on the reproducer, accounting machine, and collator to compare data from two different cards. The reproducer and the accounting machine can only detect if the cards contain the same data. The collator can determine if the data from one card is equal to, less than, or higher than the data from the second card. A unit can compare either a single card column or an entire field of data.

Compiler. A program that checks the source statements for errors, translates pseudo-commands to machine language commands, and assigns locations for instructions and data.

Compiler Language. A high-level language that permits the programmer to write programs with little or no knowledge of the way the commands will actually be executed. The languages are usually powerful since one statement may generate many machine language commands.

Computer Assisted Instruction. A teaching method used in which the student interacts with the computer. Today, slides, tapes, microfiche, and other educational media may be coordinated with the printed or displayed material.

Constant. A value that does not change during the execution of the program.

Control. Provides a means of making certain that a procedure or task is done accurately. The term is also used to refer to the management technique of contrasting the actual results with the expected results.

Control Panel. A device used in unit-record equipment in which wires are placed. Each wire represents an instruction given to direct or control the functions of unit-record equipment. Very early computers also had control panels that told the computer certain facts as where in the card the information to be processed was punched.

Control Punch. A control punch may be any digit or character which can be recognized by the equipment processing the card. It serves a variety of purposes such as enabling the equipment to tell a master card from a detail card, to add rather than subtract, or to print using locations 51–60 rather than 71–80.

Control Unit. Coordinates all computer activities including the normal execution of a program as well as the abnormal conditions that may occur.

Controller. In telecommunications the controller acts as a buffer between the very slow transmitting device and the computer. Its functions are not clearly defined at the present time. There currently is a trend to have the controller do more editing and summarizing of the data than what was done earlier.

Copy Statement. A COBOL clause used to bring the desired commands or structures into the programmer's problem from the appropriate library.

Counter. An area in the memory of the computer which is established as a numeric field. It is usually incremented each time a given event or task takes place.

Core Image Library. The core image library contains many types of programs which are self-contained and ready-to-run. The supervisor, compilers, user's application programs, etc., are stored in the core image library.

CRT. Cathode ray tube which is used to display computer output. Under certain circumstances CRTs may also be used for input.

Data. The results of a transaction or event which are still in their original state; for example, the time recorded on a time card as an employee "punches in."

Data Base. Large files of data directly accessible by the computer. The trend is to combine files, such as the payroll and personnel files, into one large data base.

Data Processing. The capturing of data and putting it in a form which can be easily utilized and retrieved.

Debug. After a program is written, it is tested. If there are logical errors in the program which produce invalid results, the errors must be eliminated. This is called debugging a program.

Decision Stub. The portion of the decision table that contains the decisions that are made. Each decision is answered by using a T or F.

Decision Table. A table of possible courses of action which can be taken depending upon the decisions that are made.

Declarative Commands. Declarative programming commands reserve space in the main memory of the computer for records, work areas, and tables. Machine language commands are not generated from declarative statements.

Detail Card or Record. One that contains primarily variable data. Its useful life is generally limited to the current fiscal period.

Detail Calculations. Calculations to be performed at other than L1–L9 or LR time. Usually the calculations occur when a given input record is read.

Detail Print Line. An output line printed using indicators other than L1–L9 or LR.

Dimension Statement. A FORTRAN statement used to establish a table in the CPU. The format is DIMENSION TNAME (100). The table is called TNAME and has 100 addressable locations.

Disk File. Contains a collection of records pertaining to a given topic, such as payroll. When the disk file is online, the records can be brought from the file into the memory of the computer for processing.

Documentation. Detailed information maintained for each procedure to enable program modifications to be made more easily. It also provides management with background information pertaining to each procedure and/or system. Included should be the statement of the problem, flowcharts, samples of input and output, and operating instructions.

Double Precision. In FORTRAN when double precision is indicated for real numbers, the significant digits allowed are usually increased from 7 to 16.

EBCDIC. Expanded Binary Coded Decimal Interchange Code. An 8-bit code which may represent up to 256 unique letters, symbols, or numbers.

Edit Mask. A print format established for numeric data that includes the use of the allowable special characters. The numeric value of the sending field moves into the field around the editing characters. Some of the special characters "float" and are printed next to the first significant digit.

Electromechanical Data Processing. Electromechanical data processing uses equipment, which is primarily mechanical in nature, to process punched cards. It is commonly referred to as unit-record, tabulating, or tab equipment.

Emulator. An optional computer feature generally rented from the manufacturer or a software company, which is a combination of both software and hardware. Its function is to permit the user to take source programs written for another computer and "run" them on the new computer. The new computer will act like the old computer in the execution of the program.

Environment Division. In COBOL the names and I/O devices to be used for each file are specified in the Environment Division. Other functions, not covered in the text, are also specified in the Environment Division.

Feasibility Study. A study that is made to determine if an existing system should be changed in order to incorporate better methods and improve performance.

Field. One or more card columns set aside for a specific purpose such as the date, a control punch, or the account number. The term can also be applied to storage of data in an auxiliary file or in the CPU.

File. A collection of records generally pertaining to one topic. In computer programming the term is also used to refer to an I/O device.

File Section. In COBOL the file section describes the input and output records in terms of field sizes and types of data contained in each field. The characteristics of the file are also given in the FD for the file.

Fixed-point. A FORTRAN term which indicates that only whole numbers are being used. The term *integer* may also be used.

Floating-point. Real numbers that may contain whole digits and decimal fractions.

Flowchart. A graphic representation of the movement of data throughout the system. Flowcharts can be used in either manual or automated data processing.

Format Statement. Provides information regarding the individual fields within a record. During the compilation of the program, provision is made for space within the CPU for each RECORD specified by a FORMAT statement.

FORTRAN. A powerful compiler language well suited to scientific and mathematical applications. It is the acronym for FOrmula TRANslation.

Function. An external function is a precoded routine that may be coded and debugged in a separate compile. The function may be stored on cards, tape, or disk and called into main programs by the use of the CALL statement.

Gangpunching. Punching constant data from one card into one or more cards which follow the master card.

Hardware. The computer and the peripheral equipment such as printers, card readers, tape drives, disk drives, and other I/O devices.

Hexadecimal. A 16-digit numbering system that contains the digits O–F.

Hierarchy. Order in which the arithmetic operations, within a formula, or statement, will be executed.

High Order. The left-most position of a field or area in storage.

Hollerith, Dr. Herman. Dr. Herman Hollerith is credited with designing both the standard punched card and the early tabulating equipment which processed the card.

Identification Division. The portion of the COBOL program that includes the program name. The other information included in the division is for program documentation.

IF. A FORTRAN statement that provides up to a three-way branch. The "logical IF" is limited to a two-way branch.

Image Mode. The image mode permits the use of a binary coded decimal system for reading or punching data in cards. When this mode is used, numeric data can be packed in the card.

Impact Printer. The most common form of printer used with a computer. Printing occurs as the result of a metal character striking against a ribbon. A common example is a typewriter.

Imperative Commands. Commands that generate machine language commands, such as to add, divide, branch to a command stored in memory, etc.

Indexes. Pointers used to identify the location of data within a computer.

Indicator. Indicators are used in RPG to tell the computer that a given situation exists. (Any number from 1 to 99 may be used as an indicator). They may be turned on by reading a given type of card, an arithmetic operation, a compare command, or a level break.

Information. The results of processing data and putting it into a more usable form.

Input. Information or data to be processed.

Interpreter. A machine that reads the punches in the card and prints what is punched in the card on the card.

Interrecord Gap. The space or gap between the physical records on the tape which permit the deacceleration and acceleration of the drive (between blocks) to occur without omitting data which should be written on or read from the tape.

Interrupt. A signal to the control unit that an event has taken place. The event could be one such as finishing reading an input record or an unscheduled occurrence such as an invalid character entering the computer.

I/O. Used to denote input/output.

IOCS. Input/Output Control System. The IOCS provides the routines for such basic functions as blocking, unblocking, error checking, reading and writing physical records, and label checking.

IPL. When the computer is IPLed the initial program loader is stored in the CPU. It requires that the data and time be entered and then proceeds to store the supervisor in the memory of the computer.

JCL. Job Control Language. JCL cards and commands are used as a means of communication with the computer. Through the JCL statements, the operator or programmer can tell the computer what options are desired for a particular task.

JOD. Journal of Development, published by the Programmer's Language Committee of CODASYL. The journal gives the recommended standards for new features added to COBOL.

Justified. Refers to how the data is to be punched or printed from a given field. Numeric data is justified to the right, whereas alphabetic data is justified to the left.

Key (file). The key is the field in the input record that is used as the address, to compute the address, or to find the address in an index of a disk file record that is to be randomly retrieved.

Keypunch. A machine similar in operation to a typewriter that is used to punch the data recorded on a source document into the card.

Last Record Indicator (LR). In RPG, the LR indicator is turned on when the end-of-file marker is found. On the file specification sheet an "E" must be coded in Column 17 if LR is to be used.

Level Break. When a change occurs in the control number, the events scheduled for "control time" will take place. Totals may be printed, counters are cleared to zero, or the form advanced in order to start printing a new page. The control number may be account number, part number, or invoice number.

Level Indicator. In RPG, the level indicators allowed are L1–L9. The indicator is specified next to a field on the input specification sheet. For example, the man number field has an L1 next to it. Each time the data stored in the man number field changes, L1 is turned on automatically and remains on for the duration of the cycle.

Library. The library (or libraries) resides either on tape or disk and contains complete programs which have been compiled, tested, and debugged. The library also contains subroutines that may be called into larger programs and source statements.

Linkage Editor. Part of the software that is stored on disk or tape. When a compile is performed, the linkage editor is loaded into the CPU and is assigned the task of link-editing the program.

Literal. Another name for a constant.

Load and Go. A common term used when a program is to be compiled, link-edited, and tested without first producing an object deck.

Logical Record. One record in a file pertaining to a single subject such as information pertaining to one student. The programmer is responsible for correctly defining the fields that make up the record.

Logical Unit Number. A number assigned to a physical device. The logical unit for the card reader could be 5, the card punch 6, tape 7, disk 8, etc. If a logical unit number is used, the programmer must determine what numbers were assigned to each I/O device.

LOOP. A series of programming steps executed one or more times.

Machine Language. The language that is used and understood by the computer without translation. Numbers are used for both the commands and the locations within the memory of the computer. It was the only way that the early first-generation computers could be programmed. Now high-level languages are used for programming which are translated, by a compiler, to machine language.

Macro Program Flowcharts. Macro flowcharts provide the major concepts of a program or procedure.

Management. The individuals responsible for planning, organizing, and controlling a function or organization.

Mark Sensing. Data, in the form of pencil marks, is put on a card with an electromagnetic pencil, which is then machine processable. The reproducer converts the marks to punches.

Master Card or Record. Contains constant, or fixed, information. It is generally used over a long period of time and for many different uses.

Mechanical Data Processing. A method of data processing which involves the use of relatively small and simple (usually nonprogrammable) mechanical machines. Some of the machines are adding machines, calculators, cash registers, billing machines, and duplicating machines. Today, however, many of the smaller "new generation" office machines are electronic and may perform a series of commands in a given sequence.

Merge. Combining the records from two or more files into one file.

Microcomputer. A microcomputer uses a single board which contains the processor and memory. Its processor is on a single chip. It functions much the same as a minicomputer.

Minicomputer. No specific definition is available for the mini, but it is *generally* considered to cost less than $20,000, has from 2 to 64K of memory, occupies no more area than a 19-inch cube, requires no special environmental conditions in order to operate, is rugged, and is likely to appear anywhere.

Mode. In FORTRAN, mode refers to the use of integer (fixed-point) or real (floating-point) numbers. In using the keypunch, mode refers to the shift—either numeric or alphabetic—that the keypunch is in.

Multi-Function Card Unit. The device that reads, punches, and interprets the small 96-column System/3 cards. The MFCU can also function as a reproducer, collator, or sorter. Other computers, such as the 360-20, also have MFCUs.

Multiprogramming. Multiprogramming provides the ability to store more than one program in the memory of the computer at one time. The programs take turns doing the actual computations that are required. When slower I/O devices are used, multiprogramming *gives the appearance* that it is executing the programs simultaneously.

Nonnumeric Literal. A constant that is either alphabetic or alphanumeric and is always enclosed in single quote marks—'This is a nonnumeric literal'.

Note. An error message generated during an RPG compile which aids the programmer in determining the error made. Only clerical type errors and violation of the basic rules are noted during compilation of the program.

Object Deck. A deck that may be punched, at the option of the operator, during the compilation of a program that contains the machine language translation of the source program.

Occurs Clause. In COBOL, the occurs clause tells the number of times a described field is to be repeated in a table being established within the CPU. Each field within the table has a unique address. The clause may also be used to specify tables in cards, tapes, or disk.

Offline. Offline refers to either the storage of data in auxiliary devices, rather than the CPU; or the processing of data by a method not directly controlled by the computer.

Offset Reproducing. A reproducing operation in which the card format of the new card differs from the format of the original card.

Online. A device, such as a card reader or printer, that is online is under the direct control of the program that the computer is executing.

Operating System. A combination of hardware and software under the control of a supervisor or monitor program that resides in the central processing unit that coordinates all the activities of the computer and its components.

Optical Character Recognition (OCR). By optical methods, typewritten, printed, or handwritten characters may be recognized and read into the CPU.

Output. The results if processing data. The output from one procedure may be input for the next procedure.

Output Stream. A continuous stream of information is established by the computer which will be written out all at one time. It is established by moves, filling in unused areas with blanks, moving literals, etc. The computer collects all the information, edits when told to, and then writes the entire stream of data at one time. The term is usually associated with the printer.

Overflow Indicator (OF). In RPG, the use of OF is indicated on the File Specification sheet, and then utilized on the output specification form to inform the computer to print headings. The OF indicator is usually turned on when the computer attempts to print a detail line past the punch in channel 12 of the carriage tape.

Page. Used in virtual storage to denote a record which may contain either data or commands that are stored on a random access storage device. The page size is usually 2 or 4K.

Page Frame. A location in the real memory of the computer that can store one page (which usually consists of either 2 or 4K) of commands or data.

Paragraph Name. In COBOL, statements or sentences make up paragraphs. Each paragraph has a user-supplied name that may be used in a branching instruction. They are also referred to as "procedure names."

Parallel Reading or Printing. An entire row is read or printed at one time.

Parity Check. A check made to determine if the correct number of bits are turned on as data is read into, or written out of, the CPU. Auxiliary devices such as intelligent terminals may also make use of a parity check.

Peripherals. Input or output devices used in electronic data processing other than the CPU.

Physical Record. A block of logical records that are read, stored, or written as a unit of information. The IOCS (Input rather than Output Control System) takes care of both the blocking and unblocking of the records.

Point-of-Sale (POS). A term used to indicate that data regarding a sale is entered directly into the computerized system without being converted to another form.

Polling. A method of inquiring if a terminal has data to be transmitted. The polling can be done by line, by terminal, or by a predetermined priority.

Procedure. A precise step-by-step method of effecting a solution to a problem. Complex systems are divided into procedures which may in turn be divided into tasks.

Program. A series of commands used to instruct the computer. Unless a "branching" command is encountered, the instructions are executed in the sequence in which they are stored in the computer's memory.

Program Card. A card used on the keypunch containing special codes which provide for automatic skipping, duplicating, and shifting. When the punched cards are verified, the same card is used on the verifier.

Random Access. The ability to access any record in a file without first processing the preceding records.

Read Check. A read check, or parity check, occurs when valid data is not read and stored correctly.

Real-time System. In a real-time system the results of processing are available in time to have an immediate effect on the transaction.

Record. A unit of information, within a file, made up of fields. For example, the data pertaining to one employee in a payroll file is a record.

Relational Operators. Symbols used to determine if one number is less than, equal to, or greater than the second number. Relational operators are used in IF statements to determine which of two commands will be executed.

Relocatable Library. In a DOS system the IOCS routines and other subroutines are stored in the relocatable library. The linkage-editor is responsible for incorporating the ones needed or specified into the user's program.

Remote Batch Processing. Data from remote locations is received into the computer center through the use of time-sharing terminals. All of the data for a particular application from a given customer is accumulated and then processed all at one time.

Reproducer. A machine, controlled by a wired panel that can be used to make new decks of cards, gangpunch, summary punch, or convert mark sensed data to punches.

Reserved Word. COBOL words that have a particular meaning in the COBOL statement. They may be used only in the manner prescribed, and may *not* be used for data names, paragraph names, or file names.

Rows. A point of reference. Each standard 80-column card has 12 rows designated from 12–9.

RPG. The abbreviation for Report Program Generator, which is a programming language used on several different manufacturers' computers.

Rule. In a decision table, the decision stub and action stub are combined to formulate rules.

Sales Invoice. A form printed by the vendor showing the merchandise shipped to the customer who placed the order.

Sales Order. An order for merchandise placed by a customer with a vendor.

Sensor. A device that receives and responds to a signal or stimulus.

Sequential Access. All records in the file must be processed in the order that they appear in the file.

Serial Reading or Printing. A single character is either read or printed. If the term is used to refer to the card reader, the data is read column-by-column.

Service Bureau. A professional organization which provides data processing service for other individuals or organizations.

Significant Digits. The digits to the left of the decimal place.

Simulator. Allows a program written for one computer to be run on another computer. The simulator is the program, or software, used to accomplish the conversion.

Single Precision. In FORTRAN, when single precision is used, the significant digits allowed in a real number are generally limited to seven.

Software. The compilers, operating system, application, and utility programs that are necessary for the computer to function.

Sorter. A machine used to sequence decks of cards. Under certain conditions, it is used for selection of cards and merging of two or more card files.

Source Data. When using the RPG, the term *source* is used to represent the sending field. The programmer need not write a move command. The data in the field will be moved prior to printing the report line since the commands generated during the compiling of the program will add the instructions necessary to achieve the desired results.

Source Data Automation. The data which is created while an event is taking place is entered directly into the system in a machine processable form.

Source Library. Structures, file descriptions, MACRO statements, etc., are stored in the source library. It is used almost exclusively by COBOL and assembler language programmers.

Source Program. A program written in a pseudocomputer language, such as FORTRAN or RPG, which must be translated to machine language prior to execution of the program.

Specification Sheet. A form used for coding RPG statements. Each column of the form has a very specific function. Coding the sheets, or keypunching from the sheets, requires the use of the exact column which is specified.

SPOOLing. Simultaneous Peripheral Operations On Line.

Standard. A uniform method of accomplishing a task, or a basis of comparison.

Standard Labels. A tape or disk label used to identify the file. It is checked before the file is processed to make certain that the right file is being used. In writing a file, the label is created.

Stored Program. A program that was written, compiled, and then loaded into the central processing unit for execution. If the program is already tested, it may be loaded directly into memory from disk, tape, or cards.

Straight Reproducing. Using the reproducer to make a new deck exactly like the original deck.

Subroutines. Prewritten routines, either provided by the manufacturer or written by the user, that may be called into large programs. They are generally stored in a library residing on disk or tape.

Subscripts. A value used to formulate a unique address for each field within a table.

System/3. A series of computers, relatively small in scale, introduced by IBM in 1969. An interesting departure was made when a 96-character card, which uses a BCD code, was introduced with the system.

System Interrupt. A break in the normal execution of a program or routine which is accomplished in such a way that the usual sequence can be resumed from that point later on.

Systems Flowcharts. Uniform symbols are used to show the input, processing, and resulting output. Detail is not provided as to how the data is processed. When all of the procedural flowcharts are combined into one systems flowchart, a graphic presentation is available showing the movement of data throughout the entire system.

Systems Manual. Contains information on the operation of a system. Sufficient detail is provided so that management can determine the data flow, forms used, reports generated, and controls exercised. Job descriptions are generally provided.

Systems Study. A comprehensive study made of an existing system, with recommendations for alternate methods of more effectively achieving the stated objective.

Symbolic Address. A number or name used which will generate an actual computer address when the program is compiled. A data-name, statement number, and format number are all symbolic addresses.

Symbolic Device. A name used to indicate an I/O file; for example, SYSRDR used to specify the card reader. The names to be used are determined when the system is generated.

Symbolic Language. A type of language that permits the use of symbols in writing computer commands rather than using only numbers. It must be translated to machine language before it is understood by the computer. It is somewhat easier to use than machine language.

Syntax. A set of rules governing a computer language that must be followed in coding a program.

Sysgen. A systems generation is done in order to add to, or delete from, the existing operating system. The user has many options to select from in determining what features are to be included in the operating system.

Tape Dropout. Loss of bits or bytes of data which make the tape data incomplete and unreliable. When this occurs, a new tape must be created from the backup tape.

Terminal. A device used to communicate with the computer. Some terminals can be used only to receive, others only to transmit, and still others to provide two-way communication.

Time-sharing. The utilization of a computer system by a number of different users. The term usually implies that the user communicates with the computer through a terminal or remote job entry station (RJE).

Time Slice. The duration of time that each user is given. A typical time slice may be .15 seconds. During this time the user's program is brought into the CPU and executed. The input may be either online file data or what is transmitted to the system by means of a terminal.

Transfer Time. Bytes per millisecond that may be transferred from tape or disk into the CPU.

Transport Light. A transport light on the card reader generally indicates that there is an internal card jam.

Unit Position. The extreme right position of a field.

Usage Clause. Used in COBOL to tell the computer how data is to be stored: binary, fixed decimal, zoned numeric, etc.

Utility Program. A program, often provided by the manufacturer, which performs a task such as a sort, sort/merge, card-to-tape conversion, disk-to-printer listing, etc.

Validity Check. A validity check occurs on the card reader when a card contains a combination of punches in a card column which are not recognizable as a valid character.

Variable. Values that change as a program is being executed. They normally are either values read as part of the input record or values computed in an arithmetic statement.

Verifier. A machine used to check the accuracy of the keypunching operation. Some keypunches may be put in a VERIFY MODE and function as a verifier.

Virtual Memory. Virtual memory is a technique for managing a limited amount of high-speed memory, and generally a much larger amount of lower-speed memory, in such a way that the distinction is largely unnoticeable to the programmer or operator.

VTOC. Volume Table Of Contents for a disk pack. It generally provides the file name, where it is located on the pack, the creation date, and the expiration date.

WATFOR. A version of FORTRAN developed at the University of Waterloo in Waterloo, Ontario. WATFIV is a revision of WATFOR.

Word. When used in describing a computer's memory, a word refers to one addressable location.

INDEX